JOHN AND EMPIRE

Initial Explorations

WARREN CARTER

t&t clark

NEW YORK • LONDON

For Lee

2008

T &T Clark International, 80 Maiden Lane, New York, NY 10038

T &T Clark International, The Tower Building, 11 York Road, London SE1 7NX

T &T Clark International is a Continuum imprint.

www.continuumbooks.com

tandtclarkblog.com

Library of Congress Cataloging-in-Publication Data

Carter, Warren, 1955–
    John and empire : initial explorations / Warren Carter.
        p. cm.
Includes bibliographical references and index.
    ISBN-13: 978-0-567-02703-0 (hardcover : alk. paper)
    ISBN-10: 0-567-02703-1 (hardcover : alk. paper)
    ISBN-13: 978-0-567-02840-2 (pbk. : alk. paper)
    ISBN-10: 0-567-02840-2 (pbk. : alk. paper)
    1. Bible. N.T. John—Criticism, interpretation, etc. I. Title.

BS2615.52.C36 2007
226.5'067—dc22

2007020989

JOHN AND EMPIRE

Contents

List of Abbreviations

AJAH	American Journal of Ancient History
ANRW	*Aufstieg und Niedergang der römischen Welt: Geschichte und Kultur Roms im Spiegel der neueren Forschung.* Edited by H. Temporini and W. Haase. Berlin, 1972–
Appian, *Bell. civ.*	*Bella civilia*
Aristotle	
Eth. Eud	*Eudemian Ethics.*
Pol.	*Politica*
Rhet.	*Rhetorica*
BZNW	Beihefte zur Zeitschrift für die neutestamentliche Wissenschaft
Cicero	
Amic.	*De amicitia*
Att.	*Epistulae ad Atticum*
Off.	*De officiis*
Resp.	*De republica*
Dionysius of Halicarnassus, *Ant. rom.*	*Antiquitates romanae*
Horace	
Carm.	*Carmen saeculare*
Ep.	*Epistulae*
JBL	*Journal of Biblical Literature*
Josephus	
Ag. Ap.	*Against Apion*
J. W.	*Jewish War*
JRS	*Journal of Roman Studies*
JSNTSup	Journal for the Study of the New Testament: Supplement Series
JTS	*Journal of Theological Studies*
Juvenal, *Sat.*	*Satirae*
Martial, *Epig.*	Epigrams
Minucius Felix, *Oct.*	*Octavius*
NovT	*Novum Testamentum*
Ovid, *Metam.*	*Metamorphoses*
Philo	
Alleg. Interp. 1, 2, 3	*Allegorical Interpretation 1, 2, 3*

Emb.	*On the Embassy to Gaius*
Mos.	*De vita Mosis* I, II
Spec. Laws 1, 2, 3, 4	*On the Special Laws*
Philostratus, *Vit. Apoll.*	*Vita Apollonii*
Pliny the Elder, *Nat.*	*Naturalis historia*
Pliny the Younger	
Ep.	*Epistulae*
?*Mor.*	
Pan.	*Panegyricus*
Plutarch, *Brut.*	*Brutus*
Polybius, *Hist.*	*Histories*
SBLRBS	Society of Biblical Literature Resources for Biblical Studies
Seneca	
Ben.	*De beneficiis*
Ep.	*Epistulae morales*
Sib. Or.	*Sibylline Oracles*
Strabo, *Geogr.*	*Geographica*
Suetonius,	
Aug.	*Divus Augustus*
Cal.	*Gaius Caligula*
Dom.	*Domitianus*
Tib.	*Tiberius*
Vesp.	*Vespasianus*
T. Zeb.	*Testament of Zebulun*
Tacitus	
Ann.	*Annales*
Hist.	*Historiae*
TDNT	*Theological Dictionary of the New Testament.* Edited by G. Kittel and G. Fiedrich. Translated by G. W. Bromiley. 10 vols. Grand Rapids, 1964–1976
Tertullian	
Apol.	*Apologeticus*
Nat.	*Ad nations*
TS	*Theological Studies*
TynBul	*Tyndale Bulletin*
Virgil, *Ecl.*	*Eclogae*
WUNT	Wissenschaftliche Untersuchungen zum Neuen Testament

Introduction and Assumptions

Throughout this study I argue that John's Gospel with its "rhetoric of distance" is a text of imperial negotiation. It seeks to make normative for Jesus-believers a distanced relationship to Roman imperial power in provincial Ephesus, resisting those who negotiate the empire with a much more accommodated societal participation. In making this argument, I assume rather than argue the following six elements. I have engaged a number of these issues in a previous book, *John: Storyteller, Interpreter, Evangelist* (Hendrickson, 2006). That discussion provides at least a starting point for further exploration of some of the related issues.

1. Location. No one knows where John's Gospel was written. Traditionally it has been linked with Ephesus. Over the centuries scholars have made arguments for and against this location and suggested other possible sites such as Alexandria or somewhere in Judea-Galilee, or for any Jesus-believers anywhere. For this study, I have adopted the traditional view that associates John's Gospel (at least in its final form; see point 3 below!) with Ephesus, the capital of the Roman province of Asia (in modern-day Turkey). As with the important study of Sjef van Tilborg, I am not trying to prove this location, nor even insisting that John was *written* here. Rather, it is sufficient to recognize that in all likelihood John was *read* in Ephesus. I am, then, interested in how John's Gospel negotiates an imperial context such as that of Ephesus, capital city of the province of Asia.[1] I think it would be interesting, for instance, to undertake a similar project of reading John in Alexandria, another important imperial center. I will return to the notion of cultural intertextuality implicit in this assumption in point 4 below.

2. Date. Similarly, no one knows when John's Gospel was written, at least in its final form (see point 3). With many scholars, I assume that it was written around the end of the first century. Hence, this is not a study of the historical Jesus but of the possible interaction between John's text and Jesus-believers in the last decade or so of the first century.

3. Author. Though there are plenty of theories, no one knows for sure who wrote the Gospel or the identity of the "John" with whom the Gospel is linked. It is not even clear whether it is appropriate to speak of one author or several since many scholars think John's Gospel developed through various editions with several writers.[2] While recognizing the possibility of multiple versions and authors, I am chiefly interested throughout only in the "final" form of the Gospel, the form that significantly resembles the text as we know it. For those who are intrigued by theories of multiple versions and a developing Johannine tradition, I have included an Appendix to argue that imperial negotiation does not occur only with the final form of the Gospel but also in the period between about 30 to the 90s CE, throughout the formation and development of the Johannine traditions. In mentioning this issue of authorship, I am not seeking the

intention of this author or authors, but investigating interactions between this text and a particular context of which it is a part.

4. Cultural intertextuality. To explore how John could have been engaged in an imperial city such as Ephesus requires setting this text in relation to other texts. Such intertextual engagement involves much more than simply listing a few Greek and Latin texts in an endnote. Nor is it to be considered under those approaches of "parallels" or "background" that have so significantly distorted attempts to understood the developing Jesus movement. The Roman Empire was the foreground, not the background, of late first-century daily life. Nor am I positing an historical context in order to identify the text's "real" meaning. Rather, influenced by "new historicism," I see John's text not merely reflecting a set of historical circumstances but contributing to and constructing a sense of cultural reality that interacts through other conceptualizations of the world and relationships with "the actual conditions of its existence."[3] As part of a "complex textualized universe," John "participates in historical processes and in the political management of reality," as do numerous other texts. Throughout I will indicate this participation and management, and the competing forces thereof, with the term "cultural intertextuality." Cultural textuality involves locating this Gospel text "within (the text of) society and history," placing this specific text "within the general text (culture) of which [it is] a part and which is in turn part of [it]," as Julia Kristeva describes it.[4]

The general cultural text comprises much more than the inscriptions of Ephesus that van Tilborg insightfully engaged, though the inscriptions certainly provide a very rich source of information, and I will draw significantly on them and on van Tilborg's fine discussion. The "texts" also include models of imperial structures, myths of Roman power, remains of buildings, coins, written documents, and ideas that either originate from imperial Ephesus or which had general currency in the larger imperial world, rituals, social practices and conventions, institutions, societal structures, personnel, and so forth. That is, for this study the texts of culture and history are centered on but not confined to imperial Ephesus. Such intertextual study is concerned with how one text (John's Gospel) participates within this larger context as it intersects with other imperial "texts." Are the intersections benign and inconsequential, essentially neutral, whereby one set of texts may imitate and at a distance parallel the other set but without interfering with its claims? Or are the intersections much more contestive in raising questions about the others' "political management of reality," perhaps invalidating or relativizing or undermining them in offering its own version of and vision for reality? At the considerable historical distance of two thousand years, determining intertextual functions with any certainty may be difficult, but pursing the question may help us understand the contours and force of the Gospel's participation more clearly.

Such an approach that takes seriously the Gospel's participation in the imperial world might be deemed reductionist if it is not correctly understood. That is, it might be tempting to think that discussion of John's engagement with the imperial world means attention only to sociopolitical realities but not, for instance, to the Gospel's rich Christology or eschatology. Such a bifurcation of the political and the theological or religious is quite false, as I will insist throughout. In the imperial world there is no such division. Jupiter sanctions and guides Rome's world. It would be quite reductionist to insist—as has been standard fare in Johannine studies—that the claim that "in the beginning" the Word that becomes flesh existed with God and was an agent in creation was only a religious or theological statement.

5. Commentaries. Any one who writes on John's Gospel has to decide how to deal with the vast and rich secondary literature on the Gospel. It is not possible to engage it all, and it is not possible to include discussion with every author on every point in one study and hope to make one's own contribution to the dialogue. Initially I summarized the views of numerous commentators on particular passages and issues as part of my discussion. Though I have retained some indications of interaction with this vast literature, limits of space have forced me to remove numerous discussions and lengthy notes in order to offer my own analysis and argument, and to include engagement with numerous other studies not often brought within the orbit of Johannine studies. I do not, though, for one moment want to suggest that I have not benefited from numerous insightful discussions even while pursuing a distinctly different analysis of John's Gospel. So I note here the leading commentaries and other Johannine studies that I have regularly engaged:

Ashton, John A. *Understanding the Fourth Gospel*. Oxford: Clarendon, 1991.
Barrett, C. K. *The Gospel according to St. John*. London: SPCK, 1955.
Beasley-Murray, George. *John*. Word Biblical Commentary 36. Waco: Word, 1986.
Brown, Raymond. *The Gospel according to John*. 2 vols. Anchor Bible 29–29A. New York: Doubleday, 1966–70. 2nd ed., 1979.
Bultmann, Rudolf. *Theology of the New Testament*. 2 vols. London: SCM, 1952–55.
――――. *The Gospel of John*. Philadelphia: Westminster Press, 1971.
Culpepper, Alan. *The Gospel and Letters of John*. Interpreting Biblical Texts. Nashville: Abingdon, 1998.
Keener, Craig. *The Gospel of John: A Commentary*. 2 vols. Peabody: Hendrickson, 1993.
Lindars, Barnabas. *The Gospel of John*. New Century Bible Commentary. Grand Rapids: Eerdmans, 1972.
Malina, Bruce, and Richard L. Rohrbaugh. *Social Science Commentary on the Gospel of John*. Minneapolis: Fortress, 1998.
Moloney, Francis. *The Gospel of John*. Sacra Pagina 4. Collegeville: Liturgical Press, 1998.
O'Day, Gail. "The Gospel of John." Pages 491–865 in vol. 9 of *The New Interpreter's Bible*. Edited by L. Keck. Nashville: Abingdon, 1995.
Schnackenburg, Rudolf. *The Gospel according to St. John*. 3 vols. New York: Seabury, 1980–82.
Sloyan, Gerard. *John*. Atlanta: John Knox, 1988.
Smith, D. Moody. *John*. Abingdon New Testament Commentaries. Nashville: Abingdon, 1999.
Talbert, Charles. H. *Reading John*. New York: Crossroad, 1992.
Witherington, Ben, III. *John's Wisdom: A Commentary on the Fourth Gospel*. Louisville: Westminster John Knox, 1995.

6. Other topics. This study is subtitled *Initial Explorations*. I do not think that this one book exhausts the exploration of John as a work of imperial negotiation. I hope that

many further studies will examine the Gospel in relation to this issue. I would like to have included chapters on other topics such as the role and presentation of Jerusalem, festivals, the use of Scripture, the roles of women, and the Gospel's conception of peace, to name only several. I would like to develop numerous aspects that receive at least some discussion here. But twelve chapters and a lengthy appendix are sufficient for one book.

Finally, I wish to thank several scholars—all of whom have vast expertise in John's Gospel and have produced fine studies of it—with whom I have been in dialogue concerning this project or who have graciously read parts of the manuscript and given me feedback: Paul Anderson, Mary Coloe, Craig Koester, Bob Kysar, Sharon Ringe, Marianne Thompson, Tom Trotter. I am very appreciative of their expertise, input, and kindness. I wish to thank David Garber for his careful editorial work, and Morgan Whitaker and Kathleen Brennan for various contributions, especially their work on the indices.

Warren Carter
May 2007

Notes

1. Sjef van Tilborg, *Reading John in Ephesus* (Leiden: E. J. Brill, 1996), 3. Paul Trebilco (*The Early Christians in Ephesus from Paul to Ignatius* [Tübingen: Mohr Siebeck, 2004], 11–52) does not include John's Gospel in his history of Christianity in Ephesus (6): "We cannot use John's Gospel as evidence for a Johannine community in the city since I have been convinced by recent arguments that the Gospels were written for all Christians and that we cannot deduce the history and life of a particular community from a Gospel." While I am not finally persuaded by Trebilco's approach (which he elaborates on 237–63, 271–73, arguing that John was in fact written in Ephesus but not specifically for Ephesus), it should be clear that my argument in this book is not made on the basis that John was shaped by and produced only for Jesus-believers in Ephesus. Rather, I am examining how John (even if it were produced for all Jesus-believers) might have been engaged in a city such as Ephesus, given traditional links between the city and this Gospel.

2. Warren Carter, *John: Storyteller, Interpreter, Evangelist* (Peabody, MA: Hendrickson, 2006), chaps. 7–8.

3. Citing Jean Howard, "The New Historicism in Renaissance Studies," in *The New Historicism and Renaissance Drama*, ed. R. Wilson and R. Dutton (London: Longman, 1992), 28, cited in an important article by Colleen Conway, "The Production of the Johannine Community: A New Historicist Perspective," *JBL* 121 (2002): 479–95, esp. 493.

4. Julia Kristeva, "The Bounded Text," in *Desire in Language: A Semiotic Approach to Literature and Art*, ed. L. Rondiez (New York: Columbia University Press, 1980), 36–63, esp. 36–37.

Part 1

1

Invisible Rome

Reading John's Gospel

Does John's Gospel have anything to do with the Roman Empire? Not according to the two dominant strategies employed in contemporary readings. These two dominant readings of John's Gospel—which I will identify as "spiritualized" and "sectarian-syna-gogal" readings—render Rome invisible. Neither term is entirely satisfactory for several reasons that will become apparent in the following discussion. And the use of two categories cannot hide the fact that the two approaches overlap with each other in some significant ways. The two terms, nevertheless, name central aspects of dominant reading strategies by which interpreters seek to make meaning of John's Gospel without any relation to Rome's empire.

The first, combining populist approaches with some scholarly support, reads the Gospel in relation to the individual believer's relationship to Jesus. It is spiritualized in that it usually focuses on salvation and eternal life in which a believer's soul goes to heaven when one dies. In the meantime, the believer lives as one of Jesus' sheep, hearing his voice and following him (10:1–21). Or to change the metaphor, one lives as a branch that draws life from Jesus the vine and produces "fruit" in daily living (15:1–17).

The sectarian-synagogal approach, quite common in scholarly circles during the last fifty years or so, is communal in focus. It sees John's Gospel emerging from an alienated community or sect of Jesus-believers who have just been painfully separated or expelled from a synagogue. The Gospel helps this sectarian community make sense of its estrangement by understanding Jesus as the stranger from heaven who is also a rejected stranger on earth, but who finds his home, as do his believers, in heaven with God.[1]

If Jorge Pixley is correct in arguing that "every biblical reading has a political dimension,"[2] both of these readings are political, even though their proponents would not use that language. They are political by the very nature of what they choose to include and exclude from the discourse. The first claims that God is revealed to and encountered by individuals rather than communities. It also claims that relationship with God is concerned primarily, and often to the exclusion of all else, with one's soul. Bodies, in so much as they are means for participating in larger "bodies" such as economic and political structures, do not matter much. Nor is there much interest in evaluating the impact

3

and beneficiaries of such structures. The second reading is also political in its choice of focus on a sectarian religious community alienated from the rest of the world. Engagement with and participation in the rest of the world are considered to be unimportant except perhaps as an object of missions, seeking to convert it.

I will argue throughout that both readings inadequately view John's Gospel as a text that reflects external realities, whether the contemporary individual or an ancient religious community. The first neglects the Gospel's communal language and material focus. The second confuses the Gospel's perspective with the actual social experience of the community of Jesus-believers. Both misread the Gospel as a religious text that is removed from and a nonparticipant in societal, political, economic, and cultural realities.

An Inadequate Spiritualized Reading:
The Individualistic Approach

Some of the problems with the first approach can be seen in one of the Gospel's concluding statements:

> Now Jesus also did many other signs in the presence of his disciples, which are not written in this book; but these things are written that you might believe that Jesus is the Christ, the son of God, and that believing you may have life in his name. (John 20:30–31)

This statement is often cited as sustaining this first way of reading John's Gospel, casting it as the "spiritual gospel," as Clement of Alexandria named it late in the second century CE. The Gospel includes stories and verses, according to this common reading, that help individuals understand Jesus properly—which means believing he is "the Christ, the Son of God" and thereby being confident of having eternal life. Individual believers, so the common reading goes, enjoy a personal relationship with Jesus now and anticipate the time when they go to heaven to be with Jesus forever, after they have died.

John is often thus read in quite individualistic terms, whereby the Gospel makes religious claims that concern an individual's relationship with God. The meaning of the Gospel's story is privatized, internalized, and spiritualized to relate to a person's—or often more accurately in popular sentiment, a soul's—eternal destiny with God. Society, let alone Roman imperial society, is not on the radar.

There is no doubt that understanding Jesus "properly" and enjoying eternal life are very important for John's Gospel. And there is no doubt that relationship with God matters a great deal. But this common, spiritualized and individualized, understanding of John's Gospel raises some questions that need attention. What exactly does "believing" entail? Is it a matter of gaining particular understandings, or does it also involve how people live their daily lives (3:18–21; 7:7)? If it does include the latter, how does the "believing" one engage or relate to the various people and structures that one encounters in daily life and in which one participates? Does "believing" not involve more than only individualistic, religious, internal, and personal matters?

And what does it mean to confess Jesus as "the Christ, the Son of God"? Often "Christ" and "Son of God" are usually understood in religious terms to denote Jesus' nature, which individuals must recognize and believe in order to ensure eternal life for themselves. Of what consequence, however, is it that the term "Christ" could be used in the first century for various figures who by various means would end Rome's world? And does it matter that the term "Son of God" was used of the Roman emperor, not to claim a transcendent nature but to identify his origin from a deified emperor and his role as an agent of the gods? With these echoes—and many others that I will show in chapter 7—is it adequate to understand Jesus in John's Gospel primarily as a religious figure interested only in the eternal destinies of individuals or their souls? Moreover, to posit that Jesus is interested only in individual souls overlooks his actions through the Gospel's plot of healing sick bodies, feeding hungry people, shaping a community of followers, and being crucified by Rome. These actions have somatic, communal, and political dimensions. What role do they play in confessing or "believing" who he is and what he is about?

Moreover, we need to press the questions about eternal life that the Gospel offers to those who believe in Jesus (20:30–31). Is "eternal" only or primarily a matter of quantity or length of time whereby life is uninterrupted by death? Does it have any quantitative dimensions, and if so, what areas of existence do these quantitative dimensions impact? Do Jesus' feeding and healing actions in any way reveal aspects of this "eternal life"? And how does this "life" compare to other forms of life, including daily life? Why does "life" matter so much? If experiencing this life takes place through accepting the Gospel's proclamation, it sounds as though there are rival conceptions and experiences of life. What are they, and why are they not commended as is the Gospel's "life?" Hence, is it adequate to John's Gospel to understand "eternal life" as only individualistic, religious, internal, and personal?

I will take up some of these matters explicitly in chapter 8 below. Immediately, though, we can make three important observations from 20:30–31 (quoted above) that suggest the importance of these questions and the inadequacy of the individualistic approach.

First, it is significant that these two verses (20:30–31) come near the end of the Gospel. This placement means that readers can understand Jesus, eternal life, and believing only after we have read and understood the whole of John's Gospel. The "signs" that the Gospel records Jesus doing, such as turning water to wine, healing the sick, feeding the hungry, and "these things written here," provide necessary information for unpacking the importance of Jesus and the experience of eternal life. Thus we cannot interpret these terms or answer the questions about their claims that I have noted above with whatever content we like. Rather, the Gospel's story of Jesus shapes and defines our understanding of Jesus, "believing," and having "eternal life." That story includes actions of somatic and physical transformation, as well as sociopolitical conflict and his death on a Roman cross at the hands of an alliance of Roman and Jerusalem ruling elites.

Second, another factor from within 20:30–31 raises questions about the adequacy of the individualized, religious, internal, and spiritualized reading of John's Gospel. The "you" that appears twice in these verses is a plural, not a singular, form. In English the pronoun "you" can refer to one person or to several people. But in Greek, the language in which the Gospel was originally written, there are different forms of "you" and different forms of second-person verbs that clearly designate one person or two or more people. In these verses, the Greek verbs are without a doubt in a second-person plural form: "These things are written that *you* [plural] might believe, . . . and that believing *you* [plural] might have eternal life." The use of the plural forms makes it clear that questions about Jesus, eternal life, and believing cannot be answered only in individual terms. Believing and having eternal life have communal dimensions. They require a community. *Together* people believe that Jesus is the Christ, the Son of God, and experience eternal life.

This communal dimension raises interesting questions. What sort of community of believers and those who share eternal life does John's Gospel shape? What sorts of community does it conflict with or contest or reject, and why? What communities do not experience eternal life? How are communities of believers to live? How are they to relate to other communities? With what sort of boundaries—with high fences or a much more flexible or permeable interaction? What sorts of communities—local and global—existed in John's world?

A third implication of the placement of these verses near the end of the Gospel's story is that our responses must take account of Jesus' crucifixion and resurrection. Crucifixion happened to individuals, but it was not an individualistic, private, internal, and spiritual event. It did not happen secretly, behind tall walls around midnight, and it did not impact only souls. It was definitely a public event. It was a societal event. And it was a quite somatic event. It was one of the ways in which the Romans, the first-century ruling power in the area, maintained their hold on power, removed those who opposed or threatened its interests, and intimidated others into submission. Crucifixion upheld a particular vision of the world enacted in social structures that favored the ruling elite at the expense of the rest, as I will outline in chapter 3. This form of the death penalty maintained societal boundaries of what was acceptable to the powerful, defined who and what was welcome, denoted who and what was considered a danger or threat, embodied a definitive rejection of those who transgressed social norms, and provided an exit strategy for removing transgressors and challengers. It was certainly societal, political, public, external, and fatal. That Jesus was crucified raises important questions about what Jesus did—according to John—that merited such reaction, and what it might mean to follow one who was crucified. That God raises Jesus from the dead (John 20–21), that the worst the empire can do was not sufficient to keep him dead, that God outpowers the ruling power—all this raises questions as to God's verdict on the way of life created, protected, and enforced by the Roman Empire and any other empire. And it raises questions about the sort of communal life that God's power and life might create for those who follow or believe in one crucified by Rome but resurrected by God. How do believers in one who was crucified by Rome but raised by God live in Rome's world?

We cannot dismiss such questions simply because we are not familiar with them. And however we answer them, our answers must take into account that in the world that shapes John's Gospel and the world to which the Gospel refers and in which it participates, religion and politics are not separate or separated entities. The interpretive practice of spiritualizing John's Gospel reflects a long development in Western civilization embracing at least the periods of the Reformation and Enlightenment, among other phenomena, whereby religion was often detached from core political and societal institutions and events, constituted as a separate sphere, and restricted to privatized and individualized experience.[3] Recent Johannine interpretation has not been immune from this cultural process, as Bultmann's hugely influential individual, spiritualized, and existentialist reading demonstrates.[4]

But it was not so in John's world. Yet describing John's world has been a challenge for Johanine scholars. There has been no shortage of effort in trying to locate the particular religious-cultural traditions—or combinations thereof—impacting this Gospel: Mandaean, Gnostic, Hermetic, Qumranic, Philonic, and rabbinic traditions have all had their champions.[5] Whatever one's preference, it cannot be overlooked that the search has inevitably been partial at best because in the Greco-Roman world, religion was not understood only or even primarily as a privatized experience of a god. As Hanson and Oakman demonstrate in their discussion of first-century Palestine,[6] and as Beard, North, and Price demonstrate in their discussion of *Religions of Rome*,[7] religion was also very much a "public" or societal phenomenon, intricately identified with political and societal institutions, communal rituals and civic events, economic and military activities, kinship and domestic structures. The Greco-Roman world's constituting of religion as an integral part of the political and societal landscape that among other things functioned to bind people together with each other and with their gods suggests that any attempt to understand John's "good news" cannot allow our contemporary restricted notions of privatized and spiritualized religion to limit and distort the inquiry. John's inclusion of signs of material transformation and of the narrative of Jesus' crucifixion by Pilate, the Roman governor, for example, attests the Gospel's participation in the material, the physical, the somatic, the societal, and the political: John does not regard these spheres as irrelevant. As I will elaborate throughout, religion, politics, economics, societal structures, and cultural contexts are interrelated. Religion in the world of John's Gospel is not a privatized, individualized, spiritualized, internal matter. It is public, societal, communal, and quite political.

An Inadequate Communal Reading:
The Sectarian-Synagogal Approach

These questions take us into and raise questions about the sectarian-synagogal approach, the second dominant approach to reading John that I noted above. This approach also renders Rome invisible by failing to consider any possible interaction between John's Gospel and imperial society. Sectarian models have been widely used both in relation to John's Gospel and in relation to the emerging Christian movement in Asia Minor.[8] Several of the issues raised above—the somatic and physical transformations that Jesus effects, the political-imperial nature of crucifixion, the interlinking of religious, political, social, and economic dimensions of imperial life—also expose some of the inadequacies of the sectarian approach.

This approach is often associated with the pioneering work of J. Louis Martyn, Wayne Meeks, and Raymond Brown[9] and takes seriously the communal dimensions of the Gospel; it often—though there are exceptions[10]—focuses attention on the expulsion and separation of John's Jesus-believers from a synagogue community. As a result a sense of alienation is understood to pervade the Gospel as the Gospel's telling of the story of Jesus, the rejected stranger from heaven, seeks to help this sectarian community of believers make sense of their experience in a rejecting and hostile context by constructing an alternative order that manifests God's purposes.

Significantly contributing to this sense of alienation are the three references in the story to tensions between followers of Jesus and the rest of a synagogue community (9:22; 12:42; 16:2). These references, central to much discussion about the Gospel in the last fifty or so years, have been interpreted to mean that the Jesus-believers addressed by the Gospel have been expelled from and by the synagogue for professing belief in Jesus as the Christ.

> His parents said this because they were afraid of the Judeans; for the Judeans had already agreed that anyone who had confessed Jesus to be the Messiah would be put out of the synagogue. (9:22 NRSV alt.)[11]

A similar claim appears in 12:42, where some of the authorities do not confess belief in Jesus because they fear expulsion from the synagogue. The third reference repeats the reference to expulsion from the synagogue, though now with the future tense (16:2). The expulsion is presented as a future reality, and there is no reference to a decision that has already been made. The three verses agree, though, in placing the responsibility for a separation on the synagogue and not on the Jesus-believers. The last of the three verses makes its own contribution, however, by increasing the level of conflict. It adds a claim that believers will also be put to death (16:2).

> They will put you out of the synagogues. Indeed, an hour is coming when those who kill you will think that by doing so they are offering worship to God. (NRSV)

There is no doubt that a strong sense of separation between Jesus-believers and the rest of the world exists *in the world created by the Gospel*. Scholars have often appealed to social-science models of sectarian groups to identify the sectarian existence that the Gospel constructs. Bryan Wilson, for instance, created a model of sectarian groups that identifies seven types of engagement or nonengagement with the larger world.[12] Of his seven types, several have been seen to be applicable to John's Gospel. Utopian and introversionist groups turn their backs on the larger societal order: rather than seek its change, they focus on themselves and their own existence as an expression of God's purposes. Thaumaturgical groups look to supernatural help to cope with their difficult situations. Conversionist groups do not try to effect structural changes in the world but convert individuals to join their group. These four types have some affinity with aspects of John's Gospel. The Gospel's pervasive dualistic language—children of God or children of the devil—expresses the alienation and commitment to God's purposes. Yet they are to do greater works than Jesus' miraculous signs (14:12), and they are also sent into the world to continue Jesus' mission (17:18; 20:21b). Nor should we overlook another type of sectarian existence, the revolutionist, which looks for the complete overthrow of the present world; compare the Gospel's focus on eschatological realities, both present and future (see chap. 8 below).

As Jaime Clark-Soles remarks, "The sectarian nature of the Johannine community has largely been granted."[13] And there is no denying that features of the sectarian typology offered by Wilson, for example, highlight aspects of the world created by John's text. But several questions need to be engaged.

One concerns the assumption that John's Gospel *reflects* external circumstances. In the three expulsion verses, does the Gospel describe or prescribe a sectarian existence, or neither? Do these references to expulsion from a synagogue and being put to death reflect actual historical actions under way at the time of the Gospel's writing or completed by then, or does the Gospel, participating in the struggle for the "political management of reality,"[14] present and/or seek to create an alternative vision and separation in an attempt to counter some current practices of more friendly or accommodated societal participation? The former option has been by far the common approach taken, though as we will see in chapter 2, when we return to a more detailed analysis of this sectarian synagogal reading, every aspect of the scenario commonly advocated for this expulsion has been questioned.

In the meantime it is sufficient to recognize that the common predilection to claim that the Gospel *reflects* a historical situation of an alienated and estranged community is not a strictly accurate claim. No matter how one defines "sectarian" and allows for ambivalency, especially around the mission texts (such as 20:21), the sectarian model ends up privileging an isolationist and society-rejecting stance. The Gospel, however, presents a much more diverse picture. In John 17:15, Jesus declares his opposition to a sectarian existence as he clarifies that he is not asking the Father to take his followers out of the world. To focus only on the experience of alienation also misses the Gospel's strong assertion of the specialness, the uniqueness, of Jesus-believers who have discerned Jesus' significance. "We have beheld his glory, glory as of the only son from the Father" (1:14).[15]

Nor should we overlook that throughout the Gospel narrative Jesus actively engages synagogues and temples. He teaches in synagogues (whether gatherings, buildings, or both are in view is not clear), and he seems to be at least tolerated if not welcomed there. In 6:59 he teaches in the synagogue at Capernaum without being thrown out and long after he has been confessed to be the Christ (1:41). And toward the end of the Gospel, in his passion narrative, Jesus declares, "I have spoken openly to the world; I have always taught in synagogues and in the temple" (18:20 NRSV). The summary statement names his frequenting of synagogues while also identifying the openness of his teaching. And as many have noticed, he is regularly in Jerusalem, around the temple and present for festivals (2:13; 5:1; 7:10; 10:22–23). Olsson concludes that "according to John, Jesus' revelation of himself . . . was not done in secret. . . . According to the witness of the Gospel, the Johannine Christians were not an isolated and dangerous sect that would lead the people of God astray."[16] Thus, Jesus does not model the sectarian existence that the Gospel supposedly describes or prescribes. One could reply by arguing that the Gospel's famous "two-level drama" enables hearers/readers to not do as Jesus did, but the Gospel does not explicitly signal any such move.

Moreover, the sectarian model is limited in focusing almost exclusively on one community, a synagogue, and on religious ideas. By isolating religious ideas from the rest of life and rarely engaging other dimensions of societal life, the model presents a one-dimensional community of minds and not bodies, and an audience that appears decidedly nonhistorical and docetic. Clark-Soles, for example, describes "the world" (κόσμος, *kosmos*) as hating Jesus and, citing Bultmann, as turning from revelation.[17] Yet, she does not ask who constitutes "the world" and how this opposition is expressed. She goes on to discuss conflict with "the government" in John, but by this she only means Jesus and Pilate since she observes that the Gospel is concerned only with "fear of the Jews" (7:13; 12:42; 19:38; 20:19) and not fear of the Romans. Though "Jesus suffers violence at the hands of Pilate," he does not experience fear. Throughout, the discussion is circumscribed by religious matters isolated from first-century societal structures in which the Jerusalem leaders were embedded as Rome's allies, and by the mistaken assumption that interaction with "the government" can only mean an antithetical and conflictual interaction expressed in violence.

In a fifty-page discussion of "Embedding John in the City Life of Ephesus,"[18] Sjef van Tilborg counters this sectarian approach. He focuses on "interferences," or as I label them, cultural intertexts, between references in the corpus of inscriptions from Ephesus[19] and John's Gospel. Van Tilborg identifies intertexts that refer to city and country, temples, work and ideas about work, freepersons and freedpersons, the working population, servants and slaves, income, possessions, expenses, professional activity, social contacts, and people in authority. From this discussion of economic activity and social order, too detailed to reproduce here, van Tilborg concludes:

> The most important effect of this research is that it shows how much the interference on this level is pulverized into an almost limitless number of small data. In fact, this means that on almost every page of John's text there are interferences to be discovered, some small and some more important. In an indirect way these data offer a commentary on all the authors who read John's text as a report about a group which is closed in upon itself and is more or less sectarian. The proven interferences show that the book knows also another movement, which points in a carefree way to the external world, to innumerable social realities which have their own interest in giving meaning to the texts.[20]

Van Tilborg's argument is not that the social and economic realities of Ephesus caused these references to be entered into the Gospel or that the Gospel *reflects* them. Rather, he is concerned with the interference, the meanings, that are created when these social realities and the world created in the Gospel narrative come into contact with each other. His observation that there are rich and numerous intertexts between the Gospel's world and this Ephesian context suggests less of a sectarian and closed community and one more open to and participative in daily Ephesian life.

Moreover, in the last decade or so there has been considerable scholarly research on Diaspora synagogues or communities in areas such as first-century Asia.[21] The studies of such scholars as Trebilco, Barclay, Rajak, Harland, and others (elaborated in chap. 2 below), have argued that synagogues were generally not introverted, withdrawn sects or enclaves of Jewish identity, satellites of a singular controlling hub to which they were accountable and which exercised control over them.[22] Rather, they were much more participationist and acculturated. Participationist behavior is shown by involvement in civic networks of benefaction, attendance at theater and gymnasium, engaging in a wide range of occupations, and belonging to trade groups or associations.[23]

Yet accompanying this participation is observance among Jewish groups of some distinctives such as circumcision, Sabbath and festival observance, and monotheism.

Like John's Jesus-believers, synagogues were involved in finding their way in their complex late first-century world dominated by Rome. They were places of imperial negotiation. Their members knew the experience of what postcolonial approaches, such as those of Homi Bhabha, identify as the hybridity or ambiguity that so often pervades the identity and way of life of those who negotiate imperial power (chap. 3 below). The reality of existence somewhere between and involving accommodation and the maintenance of (defying?) distinctives, while much discussed in the studies of synagogue communities in the Roman world, has been much neglected in the discussion about the interaction between John's community and a synagogue that has been central to much scholarship on John's Gospel in the last fifty years. The neglect of the role and challenge of imperial negotiation for synagogue communities has led to a serious distortion in reconstructing the supposed sectarian nature and separation from a synagogue of John's Jesus-believers.

These factors raise questions about the common claim that John's Gospel reflects a historical situation of expulsion and alienation for Jesus-believers. We will need to elaborate this material in chapter 2 to identify more specifically the Gospel's "political management of reality" and other depictions of reality with which it may be interacting.

A Wider Community: Reading John in the Roman Empire

Sectarian-synagogal readings with their emphasis on a separation or exclusion from a synagogue community take the Gospel's communal dimensions seriously. But they are also limited in that they circumscribe this sense of community too tightly and ahistorically. In most studies of John's believers, the Jesus-believers seem to inhabit only their own community and harbor hostile feelings toward another community. But like any society, the world in which John's Gospel was read embraced numerous forms of communities in which people participated: the Roman Empire, a city or town, multigenerational households, artisan groups, funerary societies, and ethnic-religious groups such as synagogues and worshippers of Isis and so forth. What role might participation in these communities play in engaging the Gospel?

Though scholarship on John's Gospel has almost universally neglected the matter, there is no doubt that the dominant community in John's world was the Roman Empire. The neglect of Rome's empire in Johannine studies is not surprising given the individualized and religious readings of John's Gospel that have pervaded its interpretation. Yet at its heart, the Gospel tells the story of the crucifixion of its main character, Jesus, in a distinctly Roman form of execution. The empire pervades this story. But just as other areas of New Testament study (historical Jesus, Paul, Mark, Matthew)[24] have begun to explore interaction between NT writings and the empire, it is time to investigate the issue of imperial negotiation in relation to John's Gospel if for no other reason than to understand why, according to this story, the main character is crucified by Rome. To say that Jesus "takes away the sin of the world," as John the Baptist testifies about Jesus' mission (1:29), does not necessarily mean that he must die, let alone be crucified by Rome—unless Rome has something to do with that "sin of the world."

Centered in the city of Rome, the empire extended through Europe to Britain in the north, west through Gaul and Spain, south along North Africa, and east to Judea and Syria, embracing some sixty million or so people. One of the ways the empire presented itself was as a big household presided over by the emperor, who was the "father of the fatherland." The world of the empire was, in a sense, "the Father's house," and it was very much a "house of trade" (cf. 2:16). Throughout, cities such as Carthage in North Africa, Alexandria in Egypt, Antioch in Syria, Ephesus in Asia, Corinth in Greece, Lyons in Gaul, and Colchester in Britain—to name but a few—provided important hubs of Roman presence, alliances with local ruling elites, and administration for surrounding rural areas, thus ensuring that a percentage of the resources of land and sea served the interests of Rome and its provincial elite allies.[25] Within these cities, diverse ethnic communities and trade guild associations, for example, were constituent parts of the complex urban landscape; the imperial cult was observed, and Rome's military, economic, and political presence was evident. How were Jesus-believers, perhaps still engaged with a synagogue community, to live in such cities? Or better, how were they to negotiate life on a daily basis in the cities that comprised the Roman Empire?[26]

The silence of much Johannine scholarship on negotiation of the Roman world hardly needs documenting. Some scholars have explicitly denied that there is any connection. Such denials often appear in relation to the Pilate-Jesus scene, in which Roman power is very visible, since in Stephen Moore's words "the face of Rome in John is the blurred face of the Prefect of Judea, Pontius Pilate."[27] Raymond Brown, for example, declares, "Pilate now understands that Jesus claims no political kingship,"[28] a declaration implying that to claim political kingship explicitly is the only form of political expression, and that somehow Jesus dies as one who is politically innocuous. Or Hans Kvalbein approvingly quotes Martin Hengel's argument that "Jesus . . . is no political challenge to the Roman Empire. . . . He had no intentions of undermining the Roman authorities."[29] This statement is made in relation to claims that the "message and the methods of Jesus were not at all comparable with the Zealots." The fallacious implications of this comparison and the conclusion based on it include that the Zealots define the only means of political engagement available to first-century groups, that Rome crucifies Jesus because he is friendly to the empire, and that the religious and the political are somehow separate from each other. And we will need to return to the mistaken and common claim that anything Roman is only evident in Caiaphas's words in 11:45–53 and in the Pilate scene.

In the midst of silence and erroneous claims, some scholars have taken up aspects of imperial negotiation.[30] Typically, as I will outline in chapter 3, these discussions have either posited a context of persecution or have paid particular attention to vocabulary shared between empire and Gospel, some christological titles and themes such as "Savior of the world," and "Son of God," and the Pilate scene. These previous studies have helpfully refused to accept that readers or hearers of John's Gospel were concerned with only their own spiritualized and individualized religion or with their sectarian introverted existence in a fight with a synagogue and committed only to making sense solely of their own experience. They have established that this Gospel is concerned with Roman imperial power. In frequently arguing that the Gospel contests and opposes Roman power, they provide a good basis for our further investigation. They have dared to imagine that John's Gospel and its audience encounter more than one institution (the local synagogue) in their daily lives and have recognized that they must negotiate the political, economic, and societal dimensions of everyday, material, physical life under Rome's rule.[31]

These helpful and pioneering discussions of John's Gospel and Rome's empire, though, have also created some false pictures. In chapter 3 I will take up the misleading and unsupported claim of persecution and argue that persecution did not provide the central dynamic for interaction between John's Jesus-believers and the empire. Moreover, none of these studies attempts to integrate its discussions of individual aspects of the Gospel into an analysis of the whole Gospel. The selectiveness and bitsy-ness of the discussions gives the impression that Roman imperial power is encountered only at occasional moments, as in the titles "Savior of the world" or "Son of God" or in the confrontation between Jesus with Pilate, but that it disappears the rest of the time. These selective discussions give the impression that negotiating Rome's world was a peripheral matter for Jesus-believers that was necessary only occasionally. But the pervasive empire surely did not go away in the late first century. For followers of Jesus crucified by Rome but raised by God, the question of how to negotiate Rome's world is never peripheral. The discussion in this book will assess aspects of the whole Gospel as a textual negotiation of Rome's world, even when Rome is not explicitly mentioned in the text but its empire is experienced daily as the realm in which they live their lives.

Further, in addressing John's negotiation of Rome's world, previous discussions generally take too monolithic an approach to the issue. They reject any accommodation between the empire and John's Gospel, style the interaction predominantly in terms of the Gospel's opposition to Roman power, and conceive of that opposition primarily in terms of "conceptual reframing" or "re-lexification." These terms mean that the Gospel gives believers a different way to think about their world mainly by giving language associated with the empire some different meanings. The use of an imperial title for Jesus in 4:42, "Savior of the world," for example, means that believers in Jesus are to think of him, not the emperor, as Savior. Or, in the crucifixion story, the emphasis on Jesus as king is supposed to make them understand that Jesus, not the emperor, rules.

There is no doubt that opposition and conceptual reframing are important elements in the Gospel's negotiation of, and negation of, Roman power. They will figure significantly in this discussion. But they are by no means the whole story. Can any group live an unqualified existence of opposition to the dominant society without some degrees of participation and even accommodation? Postcolonial studies of subaltern negotiation of imperial power indicate ambiguity or hybridity, both accommodation and resistance, as a key dimension of daily interaction. I will suggest throughout that consideration of John's Gospel as a work of imperial negotiation requires modifying a monolithic stance of opposition by attending to a whole span of practices and attitudes signified by the terms—"negotiation," "interaction," and "engagement"—in which the Gospel engages. The Gospel's encounter with Rome is much more multifaceted and complex than allowed by a limited and ahistorical binary construct of "us against them," of opposition to Rome. I will subsequently develop some of the complex ways with which provincials negotiated imperial power, including imitation and a mix of distance and participation, compliance and defiance, putting Rome in its place by turning to the past and appealing to "the beginning," as did other groups. I will also suggest—and this is a key element in the following analysis—that differences existed among Jesus-believers over appropriate forms of negotiation, notably between the more accommodated practices of many Jesus-believers (and Jews) in Ephesus, and the Gospel's attempt to create a much more distanced and differentiated interaction through its "rhetoric of distance." The language of negotiation recognizes that engagement with Rome's world involves not only reconceptualizations but also practices that are lived in daily life and societal interactions that involve dynamics other than opposition. The act of "thinking something" cannot be separated from its implications—or lack thereof—for how one lives.

This discussion, then, focuses on John's Gospel in relation to the Roman world. I will pursue two questions: How did the Jesus-believers addressed by John's Gospel live in a city such as Ephesus? How does the writer/s[32] of John's Gospel want them to live? The answers to these two questions, I am arguing, are quite different and at odds with each other. Hence, I am not assuming that a *reflective* relationship existed between John's Gospel and the people it addressed. I am not assuming, as has commonly been argued, that the Gospel affirms or reflects what is already happening in the community, that the community's alienation from the synagogue is confirmed and explained by its theological claims, whether the "Man from Heaven" or the dualistic "them and us" thinking of the Gospel. In fact, I will argue that among the various attempts to manage reality, John's telling of the story of Jesus does not support the overaccommodated way in which many Jesus-believers in Ephesus engage the Roman world. Throughout this book my argument is that via its rhetoric of distance John's Gospel guides believers in Jesus in this daily task of negotiating the Roman imperial world somewhere in the vast space between and involving opposition and accommodation by emphasizing distance from societal participation. By "negotiating" I do not mean formal discussion between the representatives of John's community and local Roman officials. Rather, I am interested in how John's Gospel guides its readers and hearers in engaging the task of how to live in Rome's world. The Gospel addresses Jesus-believers whose lives are, I am suggesting, at least according to the Gospel, too accommodated, too comfortable, too "at home" with the Roman world. With its rhetoric of distance and differentiation, the Gospel seeks to disturb cozy interactions and ready participation in Rome's world by emphasizing Jesus' challenge to and conflict with the Roman world, by delineating an either/or dualistic worldview, and by emphasizing the alternative world created by God's life-giving purposes manifested in Jesus. The Gospel's rhetoric of distance should not, though, mislead us into thinking that such a differentiated way of life already exists. The Gospel works so hard to create it precisely because levels of accommodation are high. In making this argument I am not assuming that the more accommodated way of life is inferior or bad or sinful while the more distanced alternative is more faithful, pristine, and blessed. While that may well be the evaluation of the writer/s of the Gospel, I am not willing to assume that the Jesus-believers fit into that box. Rather, this Gospel and other texts from Asia bear witness to struggles among the Jesus-believers over the issue of how to negotiate Roman imperial power on a daily basis, its benefits, challenges, rewards, and displeasure.

I am arguing that confessions that Jesus is the Christ, the Son of God, and the certainty of eternal life do not exist in isolation from the realities of Rome's world but are part of negotiating that world. They participate in a world along with various other confessions, including confessions about Rome's identity, relation to the gods, and mission in the world. And in guiding people to believe in Jesus the Christ, who was crucified by the Roman Empire as a dangerous threat (John 18–19), these confessions are not only intellectual or religious or internal but also communal and political. Confessions express understanding of the world and engagement with it. They are embodied, practical, lived, communal.

This study, then, views John's Gospel, in Tat-Siong Benny Liew's words, as "a struggle for community" that concerns how the Gospel "constructs community,"[33] or in Benedict Anderson's language, "imagines community."[34] And further, how are the Gospel's confessions and promises to be embodied in daily life? According to John's Gospel, how are those who believe in Jesus and have eternal life to live each day and conduct their daily affairs in Rome's world with its different confessions and promises? How does John's Gospel guide communities of believers in Jesus in this complicated task?

I thus understand the statement of the Gospel's purpose in 20:30–31 to involve not just individuals but also a community, not just religious understandings but also ways of understanding life and the world, not just correct thinking but also daily living in the city of Ephesus in Rome's empire, not just matters private and spiritual but also political and societal, not just opposition but also accommodation. I am suggesting that John's Gospel is quite concerned with negotiating Rome's world; with its rhetoric of distance, it is concerned that its audience interacts with the empire too easily, participates in it too readily, engages it on a daily basis too comfortably, and needs to be much more differentiated. Hence, the Gospel participates in the complex, diverse, and societal political management of reality.

Outline

My argument will proceed in this way. In chapters 2 and 3 I turn to the two big communities I have identified in this chapter as being crucial for the interactions of John's Jesus-believers, the synagogue (chap. 2) and the Roman Empire (chap. 3). In chapter 2, I evaluate the enormous amount of attention that recent scholarship has given to the sectarian scenario based on the expulsion or separation of the Jesus-believers from the synagogue. I argue that this scenario is unsustainable. I also argue that much Johannine scholarship has ignored the considerable body of scholarship that has engaged issues concerning Jewish negotiation of the Roman world, in which accommodation and participation are to the fore. In chapter 3 I delineate Roman presence in Ephesus and review a few brave but inadequate studies that have engaged the question of John's relationship with Roman power. In chapter 4 I consider an important form of imperial negotiation by Ephesians and residents of Asia Minor, including the synagogue community and John's Gospel. I observe the phenomenon of a "turn to the past" among Greek and Jewish Diaspora groups and within John's gospel involving Moses, Abraham, and wisdom to negotiate Roman presence politically and culturally. In chapter 5 I deal with the "turn to the past" represented also by the Gospel's choice of genre as an ancient biography and its cultural intertexuality with other examples of this genre, to make claims about Jesus. In chapter 6 I outline the Gospel's plot centering on Jesus crucified by Rome and raised by God as sustaining the Gospel's call for greater distance from Rome's daily world. Chapter 7 further explicates the Gospel's Christology by examining various titles used for Jesus. In chapter 8 I take up the Gospel's promise of eternal life, and consider the presentation of this "life of the age" in relation to the intertexts of

Jewish eschatological traditions and Roman imperial claims of an "eternal empire" and "eternal city." In chapter 9 I look at the interface between the dominant presentation of God in the Gospel as Father, and the cultural intertext of the title for the emperor as "Father of the Fatherland." Chapter 10 takes up the nature of the alternative community of Jesus-believers that the Gospel seeks to create and will consider five images that the Gospel offers in the cultural intertextuality of Ephesus. Chapter 11 engages the clash between Jesus and Pilate, Roman governor and agent of Roman imperial purposes. Chapter 12 considers Jesus' resurrection and ascension in relation to Jewish resurrection traditions and Roman traditions of the apotheosis of the emperor.

In the appendix I argue that in urging less accommodation with and more distance from Rome's empire in the late first-century Ephesian context, the Gospel does not engage a new issue in the Jesus traditions, but draws on understandings developed early in the Johannine tradition. I will pay particular attention to the claims and actions of Gaius Caligula around 40 CE as one influential focal point impacting the Johannine traditions and Gospel. I argue that Johannine traditions were engaged in imperial negotiation not only in the late first-century but also from their outset.

Notes

1. The classic statement is from Wayne Meeks, "The Man from Heaven in Johannine Sectarianism," *JBL* 91 (1972): 44–72; for a recent statement from one of Meeks's students, see Jaime Clark-Soles, *Scripture Cannot Be Broken: The Social Function of the Use of Scripture in the Fourth Gospel* (Boston: Brill Academic Publishers, 2003).

2. Jorge Pixley, "The Political Dimension of Biblical Hermeneutics," in *God's Economy: Biblical Studies from Latin America*, ed. Ross and Gloria Kinsler (Maryknoll: Orbis, 2005), 18–33, esp. 32.

3. See the discussion of "religion" and separateness in W. L. King, "Religion," in *Encyclopedia of Religion*, ed. M. Eliade (New York: MacMillan, 1987), 12:282–93; A. E. Barnes, "Church and Society," in *Encyclopedia of European Social History from 1350 to 2000*, ed. P. N. Stearns (New York: Charles Scribner's Sons, 2001), 263–73, esp. 267–72; B. McGrane, *Beyond Anthropology: Society and the Other* (New York: Columbia University Press, 1989), 55–61; I. Gradel, *Emperor Worship and Roman Religion* (Oxford: Clarendon, 2002), 1–32.

4. Rudolf Bultmann, *The Gospel of John* (Philadelphia: Westminster, 1971).

5. For example, C. H. Dodd, *The Interpretation of the Fourth Gospel,* repr. (Cambridge: Cambridge University Press, 1968), part 1.

6. K. C. Hanson and D. E. Oakman, *Palestine in the Time of Jesus: Social Structures and Social Conflicts* (Minneapolis: Fortress, 1998), 131–59.

7. Mary Beard, John North, Simon Price, *Religions of Rome,* vol. 1 (Cambridge: Cambridge University Press, 1998); also James Rives, "Religion in the Roman Empire," in *Experiencing Rome: Culture, Identity, and Power in the Roman Empire,* ed. Janet Huskinson (London: Routledge, 2000), 245–75; Bruce Malina and Richard Rohrbaugh, *Social Science Commentary on the Gospel of John* (Minneapolis: Fortress, 1998).

8. For overview and critique, see Philip Harland, "Honouring the Emperor or Assailing the Beast: Participation in Civic Life among Associations (Jewish, Christian and Other) in Asia Minor and the Apocalypse of John," *JSNT* 77 (2000): 99–121, esp. 99–107, discussing Paul, Revelation, and 1 Peter.

9. J. Louis Martyn, *History and Theology in the Fourth Gospel* (Nashville: Abingdon, 1968; 3rd ed., 2003); idem, *The Gospel of John in Christian History* (New York: Paulist Press, 1978); Meeks,

"Man from Heaven"; Raymond Brown, *The Community of the Beloved Disciple* (New York: Paulist Press, 1979).

10. For example, Judith Lieu, "Temple and Synagogue in John," *NTS* 45 (1999): 51–69; Adele Reinhartz, *Befriending the Beloved Disciple* (New York: Continuum, 2001), 37–53.

11. I will subsequently take up the question of the meaning of the term "the Jews" that appears so frequently in the Gospel. Here I substitute the term "Judeans," recognizing that it is not without its own problems.

12. Bryan R. Wilson, *Magic and the Millennium: A Sociological Study of Religious Movements of Protest among Tribal and Third-World Peoples* (New York: Harper & Row, 1973), 22–26; Clark-Soles, *Scripture*, 56–60.

13. Clark-Soles, *Scripture*, 11.

14. The language is that of Jean Howard, "The New Historicism in Renaissance Studies," *English Literary Renaissance* 16 (1986): 25, cited by Conway, "Production of the Johannine Community," 493.

15. Warren Carter, "The Prologue and John's Gospel: Function, Symbol and the Definitive Word," *JSNT* 39 (1990): 35–58.

16. Birger Olsson, "'All my Teaching Was Done in Synagogues . . .' (John 18,20)," in *Theology and Christology in the Fourth Gospel*, ed. G. van Belle, J. van der Watt, and P. Maritz, Bibliotheca ephemeridum theologicarum lovaniensium 184 (Louvain: Leuven University Press, 2005), 223. Olsson recognizes some separation from a synagogue but locates John in intra-Jewish disputes.

17. Clark-Soles, *Scripture*, 332–34.

18. Van Tilborg, *Reading John*, 59–109.

19. Hermann Wankel, ed., *Die Inschriften von Ephesos*, vols. 1A–8.2 (Bonn: Rudolf Habelt, 1979–84). I will reference inscriptions in this way: IEph 3.3123 means vol. 3, no. 3123. See G. H. R. Horsley, "The Inscriptions of Ephesos and the New Testament," *NovT* 34 (1992): 105–68; also Gilbert Wiplinger and Gudrun Wlach, *Ephesus: 100 Years of Austrian Research*, Österreichisches Archäologisches Institut (Vienna: Böhlau, 1996).

20. Van Tilborg, *Reading John*, 101.

21. It is not helpful to think of synagogues primarily as buildings. The term more readily denotes communities of people who have gathered together. Such gatherings sometimes took place in special buildings but often in people's houses or workshops. No first-century synagogue building has been found in Ephesus. That does not mean that there was no synagogue-community in Ephesus but that its gathering space was, more probably, in a household or workshop. Nor is it helpful to think of synagogue communities only as religious gatherings. Such communities did meet to pray and study Torah, but they also provided educational, hospitable, social, economic, and cultural services. Anne Fitzpatrick-McKinley, "Synagogue Communities in the Graeco-Roman cities," in *Jews in the Hellenistic and Roman Cities*, ed. John R. Bartlett (London: Routledge, 2002), 55–87, esp. 58–63.

22. Paul Trebilco, *Jewish Communities in Asia Minor*, SNTSMS 69 (Cambridge: Cambridge University Press, 1991); idem, *The Early Christians in Ephesus*, 11–52; John M. G. Barclay, *Jews in the Mediterranean Diaspora from Alexander to Trajan (323 BCE–117 CE)* (Edinburgh: T&T Clark, 1996); Tessa Rajak, *The Jewish Dialogue with Greece and Rome: Studies in Cultural and Social Interaction* (Leiden: Brill, 2001); Philip Harland, *Associations, Synagogues, and Congregations* (Minneapolis: Fortress, 2003).

23. A convenient list of examples from Harland, "Honouring the Emperor," 107–9.

24. For example, Richard Horsley, *Jesus and Empire: The Kingdom of God and the New World Disorder* (Minneapolis: Fortress, 2003); John Dominic Crossan and Jonathan Reed, *In Search of Paul: How Jesus's Apostle Opposed Rome's Empire with God's Kingdom* (HarperSanFrancisco, 2004); Richard Horsley, ed., *Paul and Politics* (Harrisburg: Trinity Press International, 2000); idem, ed., *Paul and the Roman Imperial Order* (Harrisburg: Trinity Press International/Continuum, 2004); idem, *Hearing the Whole Gospel: The Politics of Plot in Mark's Gospel* (Louisville:

Westminster John Knox Press, 2001); Warren Carter, *Matthew and the Margins: A Sociopolitical and Religious Reading* (Maryknoll: Orbis, 2000); idem, *Matthew and Empire: Initial Explorations* (Harrisburg: Trinity Press International, 2001).

25. For a good introductory discussion, see Phil Perkins and Lisa Nevett, "Urbanism and Urbanization in the Roman World," in *Experiencing Rome: Culture, Identity, and Power in the Roman Empire*, ed. Janet Huskinson (London: Routledge, 2000), 213–45, and 218–27 for Asia Minor.

26. For an overview, see Warren Carter, *The Roman Empire and the New Testament: An Essential Guide* (Nashville: Abingdon, 2006).

27. Stephen Moore, *Empire and Apocalypse: Postcolonialism and the New Testament* (Sheffield: Sheffield Phoenix Press, 2006), 82.

28. Raymond E. Brown, *The Gospel according to John*, 2 vols., AB 29–29A (New York: Doubleday, 1966–70), 2:885.

29. Hans Kvalbein, "The Kingdom of God and the Kingship of Christ in the Fourth Gospel," in *Neotestimentica et Philonica: Studies in Honor of Peder Borgen*, ed. S. Aune, T. Seland, J. H. Ulrichsen (Leiden: Brill, 2003), 228; Martin Hengel, "Reich Christi, Reich Gottes und Weltreich in Johannesevangelium," in *Königsherrschaft Gottes und himmlischer Kult im Judentum, Urchristentum und in der hellenistischen Welt,* ed. M. Hengel and A. M. Schwemer (Tübingen: Mohr Siebeck, 1991), 163–84.

30. For example, Adolf Deissmann, *Light from the Ancient East* (New York: Hodder & Stoughton, 1909); B. A. Mastin, "The Imperial Cult and the Ascription of the Title θεός to Jesus (John xx.28)," *Studia evangelica* 6 (1973): 352–65; F. Vouga, *Le cadre historique et l'intention théologique de Jean* (Paris: Beauchesne, 1977), 11, 97–111; David Rensberger, *Johannine Faith and Liberating Community* (Philadelphia: Westminster, 1988), 87–106; Craig R. Koester, "'The Savior of the World' (John 4:42)," *JBL* 109 (1990): 665–80; Richard J. Cassidy, *John's Gospel in New Perspective: Christology and the Realities of Roman Power* (Maryknoll: Orbis, 1992); van Tilborg, *Reading John*; G. van den Heever, "Finding Data in Unexpected Places (or: From Text Linguistics to Socio-rhetoric): Towards a Socio-Rhetorical Reading of John's Gospel," *Neotestamentica* 32 (1999): 343–64; Seon-Jeong Kim, "The Johannine Jesus and Its Socio-political Context," *Yonsei Review of Theology and Culture* 6 (2001): 209–21; Michael Labahn, "'Heiland der Welt,' Der gesandte Gottessohn unter der römische Kaiser—ein Thema johanneischer Christologie?" in *Zwischen den Reichen: Neues Testament und Römische Herrschaft,* ed. M. Labahn and J. Zangenberg (Tübingen: A. Franke, 2002), 147–73; Beth Sheppard, "The Rise of Rome: The Emergence of a New Mode for Exploring the Fourth Gospel," *Summary of Proceedings: Fifty-Seventh Annual Conference of ATLA* [June 26–28, 2003] (Portland, OR: ATLA, 2003), 175–87; Warren Carter, *Pontius Pilate: Portraits of a Roman Governor* (Collegeville, MN: Liturgical Press, 2003), 127–52; L. Richey, "'Truly This Is the Savior of the World': Christ and Caesar in the Gospel of John" (Ph.D. diss., Marquette University, 2004); Stephen Moore, *Empire and Apocalypse*; Bill Salier, "Jesus, the Emperor, and the Gospel according to John," in J. Lierman, *Challenging Perspectives on the Gospel of John*, WUNT 219 (Tübingen: Mohr Siebeck, 2006), 284–301.

31. See the essays in *God's Economy,* ed. R. and G. Kinsler, esp. Pixley, "Political Dimension," 18–33; and José Miguez Bonino, "The Economic Dimensions of Biblical Hermeneutics," 34–42.

32. I use this formulation to keep open the possibility of several editions of the Gospel, and its origin in a "school" or group of members (leaders and supporters?) seeking to "correct" the behavior of the rest.

33. Tat-Siong Benny Liew, "Ambiguous Admittance: Consent and Descent in John's Community of 'Upward' Mobility," in *John and Postcolonialism: Travel, Space, and Power,* ed. M. W. Dube and J. Staley (London: Continuum, 2002), 193, though Liew and I pursue our respective analyses in different ways.

34. Benedict Anderson, *Imagined Communities: Reflections on the Origin and Spread of Nationalism.* London: Verso, 1991.

2

Synagogues, Jesus-Believers, and Rome's Empire

Bridges and Boundaries

In chapter 1, I identified two communities with which the Jesus-believers engaging John's Gospel in Ephesus probably interact, a synagogue community and the macrostructure of the Roman Empire as manifested in the city. This chapter focuses on the synagogue community, first its interactions with the Jesus-believers addressed by John's Gospel, and second, its negotiation of and interactions with Roman imperial power.[1] The first area of attention—interaction with the Jesus-believers—has received much attention from Johannine scholars so it is necessary to evaluate the scenario that has been constructed. The second area—negotiation and interactions with Roman imperial power—has received some attention in recent scholarship but, strangely, Johannine scholars have paid little attention to it.

My argument is, accordingly, twofold: that the widely asserted view that a synagogue community has expelled the Jesus-believers is not sustainable, and that the synagogue community in Ephesus in which John's Jesus-believers participated was in all likelihood predominantly at home in and accommodated to Roman power even while observant of some distinctive practices. This accommodated form of imperial negotiation and cultural interaction in all likelihood shaped the accommodation level of the Jesus-believers. I recognize that our data is somewhat limited in relation to this question of degrees of societal participation, that this generalization of considerable accommodation must be understood to embrace a range of behaviors and interactions, and that levels of engagement can differ according to the activity or sphere under consideration. Borgen argues, for instance, that in relation to the pervasive and difficult question of cultic participation (to which we will return below), Jews and Jesus-believers sought to discern appropriate behaviors resulting in a spectrum of responses involving participation, degrees of interaction, and refusal to participate.[2] While recognizing such diversity, I am following recent work in arguing that within a spectrum of such diverse engagements, considerable accommodation and "at-homeness" dominates the interactions of the synagogue and Jesus-believers with the Roman world. With Erich Gruen, I am thus avoiding the unnuanced alternatives of either opposition or accommodation, resistance to assimilation or conformity to the alien environment, that have marked some previous studies of Jewish interactions.[3] Rather, I identify this diverse interaction in which accommodation is to the fore without the loss of cultural distinctives as a "boundaries and bridges" dynamic.

I am also arguing that this considerable ease with Roman power evident in Jewish communities—in which many of John's Jesus-believers participated—seems to have been problematic for some, including the writer/s of John's Gospel and their supporters. The Gospel's rhetoric of distance presents claims about Jesus that are troubling for the synagogue's accommodation, and thereby attempts not only to separate Jesus-believers from the synagogue, but also to create a more antithetical relationship between Jesus-believers and the empire. Hence, the Gospel's rhetoric seeks to create a much more oppositional and resistant stance, thereby disrupting the dominant accommodationist interactions.

Previous Discussion

In the centuries since the Enlightenment, Johannine studies have sought to free John's Gospel from ecclesially controlled readings in which the Gospel was made to serve later Trinitarian, christological, and pneumatological doctrines formulated by the church. The main means used to free the Gospel from ecclesial control has been a sustained quest to interpret John in its late first-century CE historical setting or settings prior to subsequent ecclesial doctrinal formulations.[4] Critical historiography—with its concern for historically explainable causes and effects, and recognition of the historical development of communities and confessional understandings through changing circumstances—has thus decentered the focus on ecclesial confession by investigating the Gospel's origin and claims, as well as the community from which it originated and to which it was addressed. Historical forces such as the impact of Hellenistic culture and, more recently, of relations with a synagogue community have come to the fore in the place of concerns with doctrinal orthodoxy. Much insightful and top-quality scholarship has marked this rich and energetic quest that has significantly transformed understandings of the Gospel. Since the mid-twentieth century discovery of the Dead Sea Scrolls, scholars have focused on late first-century Judaisms and, with the groundbreaking work of Martyn and Brown in the 1960s–70s, on the expulsion—or more moderately, the separation—of John's community from a synagogue.[5]

Yet, despite much insightful work, this historical quest has, ironically, produced some decidedly ahistorical results. For instance, while post-Enlightenment Johannine studies have sought to break the hold of ecclesial controls over interpretation and to locate and interpret John's Gospel in its late first-century context, one thing has not changed: the commitment to read John as a religious text. One religious context, that of ecclesial dogmatic concerns and control, has given way to another, John's fight with a late first-century CE synagogue. Predictably in this latter scenario, scholars view both John's Jesus-believers and the synagogue exclusively as "religious" groups and continue to present the issues under debate as "religious" ones: Jesus and God; Jesus, Moses, and Torah; Jesus and other figures; and Jesus' messianic identity—to note those named by James McGrath.[6]

As I mentioned in chapter 1, a fundamental anachronism marks this continued religious approach to John and to framing this conflict and its issues in religious terms. This religious approach employs the modernist notion that religion is a separate entity, independent of and able to be isolated from political, economic, and cultural contexts. But such a notion is, as a few quick examples confirm, anachronistic for the first-century world, as these examples show:

- Jerusalem priestly personnel offered daily sacrifices for but not to the Roman emperor in the Jerusalem temple as an act of imperial negotiation. (Josephus, *Jewish War* 2.197)

- Josephus identifies the Jerusalem temple-based chief priests and their allies as the rulers of Judea (*Jewish Antiquities* 20.251), an incredibly important observation for understanding their role, along with their Roman allies, in Jesus' crucifixion, as well as for understanding John's pivotal scene involving conflict in the temple, located so prominently in chapter 2 of the Gospel.

- As the general Titus—a divinely chosen and legitimated Roman and agent of Jupiter's sovereignty, will, and presence—burns Jerusalem and its temple, a "superhuman voice" is heard to cry, "The gods are departing." (Tacitus, *Hist.* 5.13; with variations, Josephus, *J.W.* 5.412)

- Josephus attributes the dominance of Rome's empire and the whole imperial act of subjugating these rebellious provincials to the will of God. (*JW* 2.360, 390–391; 5.362–368, 378)

- John's chief priests declare, "We have no king but Caesar" (John 19:15), as they and their imperial ally Pilate testily contest each other's power in crucifying Jesus, in itself a well-attested act of imperial control.

- John's Pilate crucifies Jesus as king of the Jews (John 19:19–22), using a term for Jesus (βασιλεύς) attested for Roman provincial client kings like Herod and as in 19:15 for the Roman emperor.

In the late first-century world, religion and politics did mix. Imperial politics, economics, societal structures, and religion were interwoven, each playing an interconnected part in the societal fabric and maintaining elite control. Trying to read John as a religious text concerned only with "religious" issues in conflict with another group, the synagogue, also misunderstood as an exclusively "religious" group, is ahistorical and anachronistic. This approach, shaped by our Western attempts to separate religion from the rest of life, arbitrarily selects and elevates this religious aspect of the late first-century world, while ignoring political, economic, and cultural factors and their interconnectedness.

In much Johannine scholarship, focusing on John as a religious text for a religious community involved in a religious dispute with another religious group, the synagogue, has created a one-dimensional, religiously obsessed, ultimately ahistorical audience isolated from the rest of human life and society. This misdirected focus locates John in a most unconvincing historical context and creates an audience that is decidedly ahistorical, concerned only with one institution, a synagogue, and only with narrowly defined religious issues. This chapter will expand the discussion to take account of the interconnectedness of religious, social, economic, cultural, and political forces, and to recognize the pervasive presence of imperial realities in late first-century life.

John's Jesus-Believers and the Synagogue: Evaluation

Scholars have generally made a post-70 dispute between John's community and a synagogue community central to their reading of John's Gospel. They have understood this crucial dispute within a larger history of the community of John's Jesus-believers, which sees this community beginning somewhere in Judea-Galilee, being influenced by an influx of Samaritans and later an influx of Gentiles and adoption of a Gentile mission,[7] and moving to a city such as Ephesus, where conflict with the synagogue occurs, causing the Jesus-believers to be expelled and form a separate community.[8] Significantly, these events do not impact only the geographical locations and social experience of John's Jesus-believers, but also their understandings of Jesus and telling of the stories about Jesus. Accordingly, John's Gospel is understood to develop over the first century through multiple versions that reflect the changing circumstances and understandings of John's community.[9] Various scholars, such as Richter, Martyn, Brown, and Painter,[10] have offered detailed developmental theories to explain the emergence of John's Gospel through multiple stages involving three to five versions.

It is beyond my purposes here to rehearse the developmental schemes in any detail. It is sufficient to identify their main contours; I will engage them further in the appendix below. Given the speculative nature and widespread deployment of these theories of developing understandings about Jesus and of various Gospel versions, it is not surprising that they have been widely debated. Under scrutiny have been not only the details of the reconstructions but also fundamental aspects of the whole approach. I will briefly mention five challenges to this developmental approach that underline its very tentative nature:

1. The identification of multiple versions has often depended on noticing aporias, or inconsistencies,[11] involving sequences of material,[12] content,[13] and theology[14] in the finished form of John's Gospel. These inconsistencies are interpreted as arising from and thereby indicating earlier editions or different versions of the Gospel. But this explanation is not the only possible one. Some scholars have reasonably suggested that the aporias point to a more dialectical way of thinking that is not bothered by such differences and that can hold together diverse elements.[15]

2. These approaches raise the important question of the relationship between texts and their contexts. Does John's text narrate events in a story about Jesus, or does it reflect actual events that have taken place from which a history of John's community can be constructed? Does 16:2 attest, for example, the trial and execution of Christian preachers, as Martyn, for example, claims?[16] Or does the use of the future tense and presentation of a stereotypical charge common in polemical texts indicate a hypothetical scenario?[17] The same question about polemic and historical reality has to be asked about the key verses that reference separation from a synagogue (9:22 and 12:42).

3. Likewise, how sustainable is Raymond Brown's claim that the entry of Samaritans into the Johannine community provided an important catalyst for the development of

the Gospel's christological thinking?[18] Brown argues that the account of the Samaritan woman who testifies to Jesus in John 4 reflects the historical event of the entry of a number of Samaritans into the Johannine community, Samaritans whose expectations concerning an eschatological revealer significantly stimulated the development of Johannine Christology in the presentation of Jesus as the revealer of the Father's words and actions. How, though, does Brown know that John 4 narrates not just an event in the story of Jesus, but also a key event for the history of the Johannine community? By the same logic, on the basis of John 1 should we perhaps posit that those who stood under fig trees in Galilee (1:43–51) or those who experienced rural (over)catering in Galilee (6:1–14) played an equally significant role in stimulating christological developments? Readings of John 9 as a history of the Johannine community, which we will discuss shortly, raise the same question of whether to read the Gospel as reflecting the community's history and experience. It thus is hard to avoid the conclusion that the attempt to read the history of John's community of Jesus-believers out of some but not all passages of the Gospel has been selective and therefore somewhat arbitrary.

4. John's Gospel employs very dualistic language. People either belong to God or the devil (8:42–44), to the light and not the darkness (8:12), to life and not death (3:16; 5:24), to truth and not lies or falsehood (8:4–46), to the Father or to the world (8:23; 17:9, 14, 16).[19] How does this language function? Does it reflect and reinforce the social division of John's community from the synagogue, as is commonly argued? Or does it try to create a division precisely because in the writer/s' view such a separation is lacking but is desirable?

5. These developmental models assume written sources and versions of the Gospel. But increasingly NT scholars are recognizing the predominant oral/aural nature of the first-century world, where even written texts reflect the practices and styles of oral communication. The recognition of an oral milieu leads us to think of multiple performances of John's story of Jesus more than it leads to a (misguided?) quest for written sources and versions. In a very astute contribution, Joanna Dewey has identified seven issues related to oral literature that raise significant questions about the whole developmental approach.[20] Especially significant are her arguments that in oral cultures short stories about heroes coalesce quickly into larger narratives rather than circulating independently over longer periods of time, that audiences of oral narratives tolerate inconsistencies readily, and that oral thought operates on a "both-and" basis to incorporate disparate elements.

These five factors raise significant questions about the foundations of this developmental approach and indicate that this model has some serious flaws. A key element of the developmental approach has been an emphasis on and reconstructions of what scholars often present as the central catalyst for the near-final form of the Gospel: the references in 9:22; 12:42; and 16:2 to Jesus-believers being expelled from the synagogue by synagogue authorities. All three verses refer to this expulsion with the very uncommon Greek term ἀποσυνάγωγος (*aposynagōgos*) meaning "out of the synagogue." According to the dominant theory as advocated by J. L. Martyn, a group of rabbis committed to rebuilding Judaism in the time after the 70 CE fall of Jerusalem to Rome, meeting in the town of Yavneh (Jamnia) near the Mediterranean coast, issued a "curse on the heretics" (*Birkat ha-Minim*) directed against followers of Jesus.[21] Synagogue leaders in various communities, so the argument goes, incorporated this curse into their worship to flush out believers in Jesus as the Christ, who would not participate in cursing themselves.

Foundational for Martyn's analysis is the story of the blind man whom Jesus heals in John 9. Martyn reads this chapter as a "two-level drama" or an allegory of John's community. On one level, Martyn argues, the chapter tells the story of an episode in the ministry of Jesus from around 30 CE. Yet it also narrates, according to Martyn, the growing understanding of Jesus that John's community developed through circumstances of crisis, dispute, and expulsion from the synagogue throughout the first century. In 9:11 the man whose sight has just been miraculously restored identifies Jesus as "the man called Jesus." In 9:17, under hostile questioning from the Pharisees, the man now identifies Jesus as "a prophet." In 9:22, he is "the Christ," according to the narrator, though the man does not make this confession; and in 9:35 Jesus discloses himself to be "the Son of Man," whom the man addresses as "Lord" in 9:38. The story shows the man, a personification of John's community, according to Martyn, becoming more insightful and confessional as opposition to him intensifies. For Martyn, while the chapter tells the story of a scene set in Jesus' time around 30 CE, the narrative also reflects aspects of the experience of John's community much later in the century, notably its developing "higher" understanding of Jesus in circumstances of opposition and separation of John's community from the synagogue (9:22) and from Judaism. Thereafter John's community is involved in a mission to Gentiles, and Gentiles are present in the Johannine community.

Though this theory has received much support, and though traditions about Jesus will likely reflect developing understandings and changing circumstances, the argument has considerable problems and does not seem to offer a stable basis for the sort of reconstruction that Martyn derives from it.

1. Several crucial details in Martyn's reconstruction are not supported by the chapter. For instance, the scenario in John 9 concerning the man whose sight has been restored is not set in a synagogue building, nor even in a large "gathering together" of people to which the noun "synagogue" literally refers.[22] Neither the noun "synagogue" (συναγωγή, *synagogē*) nor its cognate verb "gather together" (συνάγω, *synagō*) appears anywhere in the chapter. The scene happens in Jerusalem (8:59; 9:1, 7, 11), but no more precise information is given on the location. Moreover, when verses 34 and 35, referring to the healed blind man, say twice that they, the *Ioudaioi* (9:18) and Pharisees (9:16), "drove him out" (εξέβαλον, *exebalon*, 9:34–35), it cannot be assumed that the warning of 9:22 (that those who confess Jesus to be the Christ are put "out of the synagogue," ἀποσυνάγωγος γένηται, *aposynagōgos genētai*) has taken effect. If verses 34 and 35 were to be understood as enacting the reported action of verse 22 of exclusion from the synagogue, we would reasonably expect the man to have confessed Jesus as the Messiah by 9:34. But he does not do so until 9:38 ("Lord, I believe") *after* he has been "driven out." Moreover, his christological confession in verse 38 uses the term "Lord," not Christ. Further, in verse 34 they cast him out for his effort, as one "born in utter sin," to "teach us," not for his christological confession. Moreover, if the driving out of 9:34–35 were to be understood as enacting 9:22's driving out of the synagogue, we would expect the narrative to highlight the link by using the same language in both places, to draw the threat and its accomplishment together. But as the Greek phrases and verbs cited above show, the constructions and the vocabulary are quite different. The "driving

out" of 9:34–35 indicates, then, a scenario of the authorities dismissing the man from their presence rather than casting him out of a synagogue gathering.

2. Tobias Hägerland can find no ancient parallels for a genre comprising a two-level drama in the way that Martyn reconstructs this chapter, and he cannot identify in the Gospel any literary clues indicating that the reader should adopt an allegorical reading (or hearing) strategy.[23]

3. Adele Reinhartz has questioned the privileging of John 9 as a "two-level drama" to produce the model of forced expulsion from the synagogue.[24] The central issue concerns the basis on which Martyn knows to focus on chapter 9 as central to the community's history, rather than any other chapter. Reinhartz exposes the arbitrary and selective privileging of chapter 9 by applying Martyn's "two-level" reading strategy to John 11–12. There she finds two further possible models of relationship between Jesus-believers and nonbelievers: caring coexistence (11:19, 31, 33), and freely chosen separation (12:11). Reinhartz suggests that it is impossible to reconcile the three scenarios of hostility/expulsion (9:34–35), caring coexistence (11:19, 31, 33), and freely chosen separation (12:11) with each other, that the "two-level drama" is not able to identify the changing historical-societal circumstances that might have produced the Gospel, and that "the expulsion theory is difficult to maintain."[25]

4. Numerous studies have questioned Martyn's claim that the Birkat ha-Minim could have been the means to effect a post-70 exclusion of Jesus-believers from the synagogue. Almost every aspect of Martyn's separation scenario concerning the Birkat has been challenged, including the dating, wording, role, audience, function, Yavneh origin, and relevance of the Birkat ha-Minim.[26] Space precludes a detailed discussion of each of these aspects.

5. Martyn's reliance on the Birkat ha-Minim is also undermined by the absence from John 9 of any formal confession and expulsion prior to 9:34, as Martyn postulates.

6. Moreover, other aspects of the separation scenario that Martyn constructs are missing from chapter 9. The blind man is not cursed, there is no worship setting, and no prayer is involved. Hence, though Martyn attempts to read chapter 9 as descriptive of the experiences of the Johannine community, his reconstruction and the chapter do not match.

7. The Birkat ha-Minim curses heretics but does not specify that Jesus-believers are in view, and it does not mention physical expulsion from a synagogue.

8. It is not clear that the Birkat existed by the time of the Gospel's writing, or that its wording was directed against Jesus-believers, or that the post-70 Yavneh gathering had the authority or the means to issue decrees regulating synagogue practices.

9. Martyn's emphasis on the Birkat does not explain why believers needed to be flushed out of the synagogue by such means when on Martyn's own theory they were readily identifiable from their long-term presence in the synagogue, their involvement in disputes, their supposed possession of their own Gospel in some form, and their evangelizing activity.

10. Kimelman and others have observed that even through to John Chrysostom in the late fourth century CE, preachers found it necessary to discourage Jesus-believers from attending synagogue meetings.[27] Ignatius in the early second century, around 110, rebukes Christians for attending synagogues (*Magn.* 8:1; 10:1–3; *Phld.* 6:1), a highly unlikely situation if Martyn's imagined ban had forced Jesus-believers out of synagogue communities some ten to twenty years previously.

Two conclusions are to be drawn from this extensive discussion of the Martyn-Brown hypothesis. One is that the case for the synagogue's bitter expulsion of the Jesus-believers has not been made. Daniel Boyarin summarizes much of the scholarly discussion: "Martyn's reconstruction simply cannot stand because the historical foundations upon which it rests are so shaky that the edifice falls down. . . . There are, therefore, it seems, hardly the slightest historical grounds for accepting Martyn's elegant hypothesis."[28]

The second conclusion concerns the three references to a dispute with and separation from the synagogue (ἀποσυνάγωγος, *aposynagōgos,* 9:22; 12:42; 16:2). If they do not reflect a separation that has already occurred, how are they to be understood? Various suggestions have been made: these texts arise from the tensions and logic of the narrative and not from historical circumstances;[29] they say more about the perceptions and fears of John's group than about actions of a synagogue;[30] they function to create (or seek to create) separation and distance between two closely entangled groups;[31] they belong to the story of Jesus as a divinely ordained etiology from his time for the Gospel audience's later experience of separation.[32] Most of these explanations have some degree of plausibility, and several of them (such as the first three) could be readily combined to provide a convincing explanation for the presence and function of these verses in the Gospel's story.

My own preference—the argument that I am developing through this book—is that since there is no historically convincing and sustainable scenario for a separation of the Jesus-believers from the rest of the synagogue having already taken place, these three references to synagogue expulsion exist in the narrative as texts consequential rather than descriptive, as performative rather than reflective. That is, and the future tense of 16:2 points to this suggestion, they function as part of the Gospel's rhetoric of distance to indicate that some conflict and division between the Jesus-believers and the rest of the synagogue *ought* to exist as a consequence of allegiance to Jesus. Chapter 9 is not a descriptive text, as Martyn posits, but a performative text. The textual scenario of synagogue-separation, along with 12:42 and 16:2, is intended in this polemical text to *create* such a division. There are factors that I will now outline that suggest this attempt to create separation confronts a dominant unity within the synagogue community including Jesus-believers, a unity marked in part by generally shared accommodation with imperial society.

Jesus-Believers, Synagogues, and the Roman Empire: Boundaries and Bridges

Three limitations in previous discussions have especially hindered consideration of how John's believers participated in imperial society.

First, as I have observed above, scholars have often depicted the interaction between the synagogue and Jesus-believers narrowly as involving only religious matters, while failing to recognize that in the late first-century world, religion was interwoven with politics, economics, and social structures. Second, though positing that John's Jesus-believers were separated from the synagogue and now in mission to convert individual

Gentiles, Johannine scholars have often failed to press the question of how both Jesus-believers and synagogues engaged the Gentile world *in terms of its being the world of the Roman Empire.* And third, Johannine scholars have often treated the synagogue in their discussions as introverted and isolated, withdrawn from the surrounding society. Rarely have discussions of this Johannine context utilized the recent extensive work on synagogues in both Judea-Galilee and the Diaspora.[33] By utilizing these discussions, one can recognize, among other things, that John's Gospel is a Jewish text that participates in extensive Jewish negotiation of Rome's world, just as synagogues did.[34] Those who engaged John's Gospel in late first-century Ephesus thus were concerned not only with religious matters; they also were participants in the Gentile world and engaged with the Roman imperial world. To these discussions we now turn.[35]

In his influential work *Jews in the Mediterranean Diaspora,* John Barclay helpfully identifies at least seven areas or spheres in which different kinds and degrees of Jewish interaction with the Diaspora world might be explored.[36] Barclay identifies the following spheres: the political (relations with political authorities), social (participation and maintenance of distinctives practices), linguistic (use of Greek language), educational (acquisition of Greek *paideia,* training), ideological (commitment to cultural norms and values), religious (relation to religious language and practices), and material (participation in material culture [food, dress, etc.] and the maintenance of distinctive practices). He further distinguishes three terms, "assimilation," which concerns social integration and degrees of similarity to one's neighbors; "acculturation," which concerns the linguistic, educational, and ideological spheres; and "accommodation," the degree to which Jewish and Diaspora practices are merged or polarized. For each term, he sketches a spectrum or scale that spans high levels of integrative living through to high levels of oppositional living. *Assimilation,* or social integration, spans at its highest level abandonment of key Jewish social distinctives; at midlevel, some integration (attending the gymnasium for education, Greek athletic competitions, or the theater; employment with non-Jews); at lowest level, social life confined only to the Jewish community. *Acculturation* (language/education) spans at its highest level scholarly expertise and familiarity with Greek literary, rhetorical, philosophical, and religious traditions; at midlevel, some acquaintance with common moral values; at lowest level, no familiarity with Greek. *Accommodation* spans at its highest level submersion of Jewish cultural uniqueness; at midlevel, reinterpretation of Judaism that preserves some uniqueness; at lowest level, antagonism to Greco-Roman culture.

The scope of Barclay's project is ambitious; the limits of both the availability and types of sources for a city like Ephesus as well as the difficulty of distinguishing the descriptive (what is) and performative (what should be) functions of various texts—these all hinder its execution. Nevertheless, his categories helpfully alert us not only to what we do not know but also to areas that might be explored, the types of questions that might be pursued, and the types of responses that might be encountered. One of the significant merits of Barclay's approach is that it can recognize varying degrees of interaction and various patterns of behavior shaped by the particular sphere of interaction and the observance of traditional markers of Jewish identity.

Barclay's (and others') exploration of Jewish communities in Ephesus and the Roman province of Asia indicates on his spectra significant middle levels of assimilation, acculturation, and accommodation, along with the preservation of Jewish distinctives. Recent investigations of Jewish interaction with the larger structures of the Gentile-Roman world have thus challenged assumptions that often underlie the Johannine "synagogue-scenario" discussed above, that Diaspora synagogues were introverted and exclusive, isolated, and in retreat from Greco-Roman society as detached defenders of Jewish cultural identity.[37] This recent scholarship has established the multiple functions, various civic activities, and cultural embeddedness of synagogues. Synagogues emerge as places of political and cultural negotiation with Rome's world, as communities both actively participating in their urban contexts and maintaining their cultural distinctives. In Barclay's work, boundaries between synagogues and their surrounding society emerge as considerably but not completely porous, with degrees of bridge-building and interaction, along with maintenance of cultural distinctives and ongoing discernment about appropriate levels of participation.

Barclay begins his short discussion[38] of Jews in the province of Asia by recognizing that the data is "extremely limited." Josephus's collection of various, mainly first-century BCE, letters and decrees concerning the rights of Jewish groups in various Asian cities in *Antiquities* 14 and 16 provides "the bulk of our evidence" for some political, social, ideological, religious, and material engagement. This evidence, though, is not without its problems. One is its date in that the texts refer to situations over a century before John's Gospel. A second issue is that it is not without bias. Josephus's agenda is evident in his selective emphasis on Jewish alliances with Rome, Rome's benefactions to Jews, and tolerance of traditional Jewish practices by both Romans and Greeks (*Ant.* 16.174–178) even while, ironically, his data shows conflicts over and challenges to these traditional practices and rights. Barclay argues against those who think the letters are a universal "Charter" of Jewish rights[39] but sees them as directed to specific, first-century BCE, local, and recurring situations of conflict between Jewish groups and city administrations concerning, in particular, Jewish finances. Conflicts emerged in a changing political landscape, in the humiliating economic circumstances of the province of Asia in the first century BCE, and in a series of financial and civic disasters experienced by cities, precipitated by war, fines, and heavy taxation. In relation to Ephesus, Josephus records the letter of Dolabella, governor of Asia, dated January 43 BCE, exempting Jews from military service,[40] upholding observance of their customs concerning assembly for "sacred and holy rites," and allowing "offerings for their sacrifices" (presumably collection of the Jerusalem temple tax; *Ant.* 14.223–230, upheld by the consul Lucius Lentulus; 14.234, 237–240). Sabbath observance is also upheld (*Ant.* 262–264). Later in the first century BCE, in a decree concerning all Asia, the emperor Augustus upholds the inviolability of the Jews' "sacred monies" sent to the Jerusalem temple, as well as of synagogal sacred books and monies. He threatens penalties of confiscation of property for those who steal Jewish property (*Ant.* 16.160–165; repeated by Agrippa, 16.167–168; and by the proconsul Julius Antonius, 16.172–173).

Barclay argues that the decrees attest the reputation of Jewish communities for some prosperity, as well as civic levels of both prominence in civic affairs and also some distance from them. In times of social, political, and economic difficulties as well as wounded civic pride, Jewish noncontributions to struggling civic communities, faithful observance of traditional practices such as Sabbath observance, support of the Jerusalem temple, and frequent refusal to participate in worshipping civic gods (Josephus, *Ag. Ap.* 2.79, 258) apparently were resented and perceived to be unsupportive of the city. At times resentment resulted in attacks on and seizure of property and wealth, and challenges to Jewish rights and practices, which in turn caused Jews to appeal for imperial protection of their cultural identity and practices. Their wealth and social position (some are identified as citizens in *Ant.* 14.228) brought favorable imperial responses. Barclay notes that the issues involved—collection of the temple tax, rights of assembly, property ownership, Sabbath observance, military exemption—indicate the observance of distinctive practices that derived from Jewish ethnic and ancestral tradition (to which we will return in chapter 4), as well as sufficient levels of civic participation for these differences to be noticed and resented when circumstances were difficult. The decrees also indicate the presence of representatives of Jewish communities socially and politically powerful enough to gain protective imperial action.

These sources attest conflicts in the first century BCE, a hundred years or more before John's Gospel. Barclay reports that in the first century CE evidence for these conflicts disappears. He argues that the lack of first-century CE evidence indicates improving economic conditions in the cities of Asia and in the empire's political stability. Augustus's Pax Romana significantly benefited the province of Asia, especially its elite. Political, economic, and social pressure on Jewish communities seems to have eased in the first century CE so that "Jewish communities could practice their own customs unhindered" (thereby maintaining identity), yet the easing of pressures also "enabled the Jews' greater integration and acculturation in the cities they inhabited."[41] The exception that proves the point is the emperor Claudius's edict issued around 41–42 CE, again in circumstances of crisis, after the outbreak of violence against Jews in Alexandria during Caligula's reign (37–41 CE; Josephus, *Ant.* 19.278–291). After Caligula's death, Claudius reaffirms all Jewish rights in the city but also sends a similar edict "to the rest of the world" (*Ant.* 19.286, 291) to ensure that Jews can "observe the customs of their fathers without let or hindrance" (*Ant.* 19.289). Barclay further suggests that the presence of Gentile God-worshippers in various synagogue communities attested in Acts (13:16; 14:1; 16:14; 17:4, 12) and actions such as those of a leading Gentile woman Juilia Severa, who donated a synagogue building in Akmoneia (east of Ephesus; see further discussion below) suggest both Jewish openness as well as respectability in the eyes of some Gentiles at least.[42]

The picture that Barclay presents of Jewish negotiation of Roman imperial power in the province of Asia through a tensive interaction involving both considerable Jewish societal participation and at-homeness, along with observance of traditional Jewish practices, is consonant with the results of Paul Trebilco's study of Jewish communities in Asia Minor.[43] Trebilco similarly sees significant observance of traditional expressions of Jewish identity in the first century BCE, with conflict between Jewish groups and civic authorities. These civic relationships improved significantly in the first century CE.[44] Drawing on often fragmentary and widely scattered evidence from the first few centuries of the Common Era,[45] Trebilco offers evidence for some Jews at various times and places holding "significant offices in their cities," for civic benefactions in which Jews made financial contributions for their cities' well-being, for Jewish attendance at the theater, for active participation in the civic and cultural life, for recognition as good residents, for involvement in gymnasia (centers of social and educational life), for imitation of some civic cultural practices such as honoring prominent women who were benefactors and adopting Greek and Roman names, for having non-Jews as patrons or benefactors of synagogues, for the existence of Gentile God-fearers in synagogues who identified with the synagogue and adopted some but not all Jewish practices such as circumcision, and for exposure to situations (theater, gymnasia) in which pagan religion activities took place. Trebilco concludes his study of Jewish communities in Asia Minor by observing that "many members of the communities interacted regularly with Gentiles and were involved to a significant degree in city life. Moreover, some Jewish communities were influential and respected in their cities. . . . They were a part of the social networks of the city and shared in many of the characteristics of daily life."[46]

A third study, that of *Associations, Synagogues, and Congregations,* by Philip Harland, reaches similar conclusions. Covering much of the same ground, Harland identifies "positive interactions" between Jewish groups and their urban contexts, concluding that "there is clear evidence from Roman Asia . . . that being a member in a Jewish group did not mean the dissolution of all participation in conventions, institutions, and constituent groups of the polis."[47] Harland's discussion, though, highlights two areas of participation often overlooked in other studies. One area concerns the participation of Jews in the network of subgroups that pervaded cities, especially a wide variety of occupational guilds or associations. In Ephesus, an inscription (IEph 5.1677 = *CIJ* 745) identifies Julius as "the chief physician at Ephesus, and hence leader of the *synedrion* of physicians, but he had the Jewish group there take care of his family grave."[48] Beyond Asia, Philo identifies Jews involved in Alexandria as shippers, merchants, and artisans (*Flaccus* 57).[49]

Second, Harland points out that while these associations provided members with various benefits such as social occasions (especially for meals) and networks, they also provided opportunities in various ways to honor deities, leading local benefactors, and imperial figures.[50] Meetings of associations could include an offering of wine, food, or incense to a sponsoring deity and to imperial images. Associations also honored leading local figures with inscriptions and monuments. Jewish participation in associations meant both social interactions and honorific activity. It is not abundantly clear how Jews negotiated the latter activities especially in regard to deities and the imperial cult. Harland argues that Jews participated in noncultic, nonidolatrous honoring activity such as prayers on behalf of rulers, and dedication of inscriptions and monuments,[51] though the paucity of evidence and the ready integration of cultic honorary practices into meals, gatherings, and civic occasions may belie more complex and diverse negotiations that could include cultic participation. What is significant, however, is that Harland provides a glimpse of a significant involvement of nonelite Jews in the social, economic, political, and religious life of cities like Ephesus through participation in occupational guilds or artisan associations.

Four Examples of Jewish Participation

The discussion thus far has summarized three, recent, and detailed studies of Jewish participation in cities in Asia under Roman power; it has also established some general conclusions about positive Jewish civic interactions while maintaining traditional Jewish distinctive practices. The goal has been to establish the likely civic mode of being for those in the synagogue in Ephesus in which John's Jesus-believers participated. I will now provide four brief examples from across Asia to illustrate in greater detail this interaction marked by "boundaries and bridges," or active civic participation while maintaining cultural distinctives. I am suggesting that this dominant pattern of societal interaction provides the context for the Gospel's rhetoric of distance.

An Honorific Inscription

Josephus records a letter from Augustus to provincial officials in Asia, reaffirming Jewish rights to observe their ancient customs, to collect and control sacred monies for the Jerusalem temple, to observe Sabbath, and not to have their sacred books and monies stolen from a synagogue (*Ant.* 16.162–164). Augustus continues (*Ant.* 16.165):

> As for the resolution which was offered to me by them on account of the piety [εὐσέβεια] which I show to all people, and on behalf of Gaius Marcius Censorinus, I order that it and the present edict be set up in the most conspicuous (part of the temple) assigned to me by the federation [κοινοῦ] of Asia in Pergamum.[52]

Josephus does not identify which Jewish synagogue or synagogues was/were responsible for this resolution honoring Augustus and Gaius Marcius Censorinus. Augustus's response, though, allows us to observe not only considerable Jewish participation in the Roman order but also some of the ways in which this action promoted Jewish involvement.[53]

- Such honoring of the emperor and/or other imperial figures was a common practice among various associations and eastern provincial cities. It was a voluntary act, not coerced or required by Rome, but a crucial means whereby groups participated in civic and imperial society. This synagogue imitates a common cultural practice that constitutes patterns of civic and imperial friendship.

- Augustus is honored for εὐσέβεια (*eusebeia*) shown not toward the gods (a common usage) but toward people.[54] Here the term designates his rule as evidencing respect for societal order and upholding proper conduct within it. By implication Augustus is honored for protecting Jewish rights and practices derived from ancestral customs.

- The Jews responsible for the honorific act imitated cities' and other associations' practice of informing Augustus of their action, perhaps by sending some representatives and a copy of the resolution to him in Rome. This act of communication was a means of participating in the network of patron-client, benefactor-beneficiary relations that constituted imperial society.

- Informing the emperor maintained ties between provincial groups and the emperor, customarily drew the appreciative response outlined in Augustus's decree quoted by Josephus, secured imperial favor, and furthered the interests of the group initiating the action, in this case renewing imperial protection for Jewish rights and privileges.

- Moreover, the emperor's order to display their expression of imperial honor in stone in the temple at Pergamum conveyed important messages to other groups in their own community about the place of this synagogue or synagogues in civic and imperial society. This synagogue or synagogues was/were now seen by others to be significant participants in and contributors to the network of imperial benefaction that was so vital for the well-being of provincial cities. Their act of honoring the emperor thus contributed to their own social honoring and prestige, winning them favor in their own community for promoting its profile. But also, for groups not accorded such honor in the competition for civic honor, favor to synagogues could result in synagogues being objects of resentment. How the synagogue viewed the imperial honoring of its act of honoring by displaying it in the Pergamum temple is not indicated.

- The placement of this honorific in the temple in Pergamum provided the emperor with the opportunity to display prominently this declaration of honor, ensuring that others imbibed the appreciative message, and fostering an environment for the expression of further such sentiments of loyalty to him by other groups.

- Not only is the emperor Augustus honored, but so too is the imperial official Gaius Marcius Censorinus. He was a member of the senatorial order who had a distinguished career in the East as a legate of Augustus in 13–12 BCE and, after being consul in Rome in 8 BCE, as proconsul of Asia in 2–3 CE.[55] He is honored by several other communities with a decree and cult and games. Positive relationships with imperial officials in provinces also belong in the networks of benefaction and friendship noted above, and provided the basis for granting subsequent favors to groups and cities.

This honor for Caesar Augustus shows at least this synagogue community in Asia to be deeply embedded in societal practices. Further evidence suggests that such embeddedness was by no means unusual.

Julia Severa: Synagogue-Builder

A second example concerns an inscription from the city of Akmoneia, east of Ephesus, dating from the 80s–90s, the same time as the likely final form of John's Gospel. The inscription reads:[56]

> This building was erected by Julia Severa: P[ublius] Tyrronios Klados, the head for life of the synagogue, and Lucius, son of Lucius, head of the synagogue, and Publius Zotikos, archon, restored it with their own funds and with money which had been deposited, and they donated the [painted] murals for the walls and the ceiling, and they reinforced the windows and made all the rest of the ornamentation, and the synagogue honored them with a gilded shield on account of their virtuous disposition, goodwill, and zeal for the synagogue.

The inscription monumentalizes the renovation of a synagogue building previously built by Julia Severa perhaps in the 50s or 60s CE. The inscription is significant for several reasons, not the least of which is that it attests the earliest synagogue in Asia Minor.

Julia Severa was a member of a distinguished family in Akmoneia, descended from Galatian and Attalid royalty. She belonged to a network of leading families marked by great power, status, and wealth. She married Lucius Servenius Capito from another leading family, and her son Lucius Servenbius Cornutus. Cornutus became a senator during Nero's reign, and a legate to the proconsul of Asia around the mid 70s CE. Various other relatives had distinguished careers, holding elevated imperial positions. Julia Severa herself held several prominent and prestigious civic positions in Akmoneia, including agonothete (director of contests) and ἀρχιέρεια (*archiereia*), high priestess of the temple of the imperial cult, on three occasions during the reign of Nero (54–68 CE). Both of these positions are attested in a monument erected to her honor by the local elders' organization.

As a leading citizen, she engaged in acts of benefaction for her city and local groups. Her construction of a synagogue for the local Jewish community, attested in the beginning of the inscription cited above, is one such act.[57] We should probably understand her involvement with the synagogue to be ongoing in ensuring the material well-being of the community, rather than comprising only an isolated act. In return for her funding of the construction, she received social honor and loyalty from the group, including the reference to her beneficence in this inscription.

Of interest is that the Jewish group accepted and honored this act of benefaction from a leading, wealthy, Gentile woman who also served as high priestess of the imperial cult. Such receptivity suggests the group's considerable openness to and participation in civic networks. The group had attracted the attention of such a wealthy patroness, though how it did so and the reasons for her involvement are not clear. She is a Gentile and not a Jew, so ethnicity alone cannot explain her interest. Perhaps the group was sizeable or generally held in high social esteem, or had connections with other leading families. The suggestion has been made that "P[ublius] Tyrronios Klados, the head for life of the synagogue," was not a Jew but was connected in some way (relative? freedman? client?) with the Tyrronius family, another leading family in Akmoneia. C. Tyrronius Rapon had served as a magistrate with Julia Severa. Perhaps her involvement with the synagogue reflects competition among leading families to gain civic honor through benefactions, as well as competition among groups such as synagogues to attract prestigious and influential patrons who might protect or further their interests. It is also possible that Julia Severa was some sort of Gentile God-fearer, attracted to and sympathetic with aspects of synagogue life and practices. Whatever the motivation, the inscription attests a synagogue's attention to imperial negotiation by winning the favor of and being receptive to the beneficence of a leading citizen.

Honorary Titles

In the Julia Severa inscription, the term ἀρχισυνάγωγος (*archisynagōgos*), "head of the synagogue," appears twice. In an important discussion, Tessa Rajak and David Noy examine the scattered data on holders of the title ἀρχισυνάγωγος.[58] They reject older claims that *archisynagōgoi* functioned in synagogues to provide liturgical and practical services in a mode akin to contemporary (Christian) clergy. Rather, the term must be understood, they argue, in the context of Greco-Roman status distinctions and under-

standings of office-holding as evidenced in the many clubs and associations that prolif-
erated in urban settings. Rajak and Noy observe that synagogues and associations often
replicated city government, organization, and status systems in structuring their group
life. They locate the title ἀρχισυνάγωγος (along with other synagogal titulary except
perhaps that of γραμματεύς, *grammateus,* scribe, which may stipulate particular tasks)
in empirewide "honor-driven patterns of office distribution."

Such office-holding is marked by four fundamental features: (1) offices required little administrative expertise or time since honor, not function, was determinative for
them; (2) appointments were not based on competence but reflected demonstrated
honor and privilege and hence could be for life and continue through families; (3) there
is a close correlation between social standing and appointment to high position; and (4)
since beneficence was crucial to being selected for and executing the office, wealth was
a vital criterion. Thus to be an *archisynagōgos* required social standing, influence, family connections, and wealth, not expertise, competence, Jewish ethnicity, masculine
gender, or even adulthood. Sufficient wealth to fund various beneficent or euergetistic
acts (such as renovations to or construction of a building) qualified one for such a social
function and for the further honor that accumulated through it. Those who held this
honorary function as benefactor and patron were individuals of some or considerable
social standing and wealth, well embedded in a city's hierarchical social structure, and
could represent and mediate for the synagogue community in the larger civic setting.[59]

Such imitation of conventional office-holding and patterns of benefaction by synagogues suggests acceptance of pervasive civic values by synagogue groups and their
active participation in the wider societal structures. Holders of synagogal leadership
positions in particular (but not exclusively) benefited with enhanced social honor and
access to structures of power. Rajak and Noy's argument reinforces a sense of considerable accommodation to and imitation of imperial society among synagogue communities, particularly in relation to the patronal participation of elites.

Aphrodisias

A fourth example comes from the city of Aphrodisias, some 90 miles east of Ephesus
(to which we will return in the next chapter) and concerns a likely early third-century
CE monument or stele discovered in 1977.[60] This monument is inscribed on two surfaces with lists of names. It is clearly Jewish, both in the pervasive use of biblical names
and in designating some as proselytes (converts to Judaism) and some as *theosebeis,*
"God-worshippers" or "God-fearers." The text sets out three lists of names of those who
comprise groups within the Jewish community and were contributors to a building
project. The first list comprises about nineteen members (including three proselytes
and two God-fearers) belonging to a "decany," or subgroup of students of the law who
praise God, who had initiated and made major contributions to funding a memorial
building for relief of suffering in their community. Reynolds and Tannenbaum describe
the building as a distribution center for food for the needy, a soup kitchen.[61] The second list names about fifty-five Jews by birth who also contributed to the building. The
third lists fifty-two "God-fearers" (θεοσεβεῖς, *theosebeis*), none of whom is a Jew, who
were also contributors.

The inscription is significant in a number of ways. First, it honors the involvement of over one hundred members of this synagogue community in a charitable project for their city. The nature of and commitment to this project—relief for local suffering through distribution of food—suggests considerable interaction with their civic context, as does the existence of such a socially conventional monument and its use of Greek language.

Second, one of the members of the "decany" is a woman with the name Jael, named (perhaps) after the woman of Judges 4:17–5:31 who killed Sisera the Canaanite commander.[62] She is actually the first member of the first list (members of the decany) to be named, suggesting her premier status. She is identified as a *prostatēs* (προστάτης), a term that can mean "leader" or "patron" (cf. Phoebe in Rom. 16:2), also suggesting that she has the highest standing of those named. She has a son Iosoua, named in the next line, but no husband or father is named. She was clearly a prominent figure in the group, with leadership and patronal responsibilities not derived from a significant male.

Third, the high number of "God-worshippers" or "God-fearers" is significant. Though the exact meaning of the term is debated, it seems to cover a range of behaviors of Gentiles sympathetic to and involved in various ways in synagogue communities.[63] This involvement could span attending services, learning Torah (three God-fearers belong to the decany, which is identified as students of the law), participating in synagogal life, in this instance donating funds for this charitable memorial building, and following some ethical teachings. No fixed or standard requirements for all God-fearers, though, can be established.[64] On this inscription they are differentiated from proselytes or converts, suggesting that they have not adopted all the markers of Jewish identity such as circumcision. Their placement on the inscription as the third group also suggests their lower status in the synagogue community. Nevertheless, their participation in this Jewish community implies its considerably porous boundaries and involvement with the Gentile society of Aphrodisias, as well as some level of prominence in attracting Gentiles.

Fourth, this last observation is strengthened by the fact that nine of the God-fearers are city councillors. This office required considerable property ownership and among other duties related to the city's well-being, involved attendance at public civic sacrifices. These nine wealthy men had significant status within Aphrodisias and participated in the synagogue. Just how they, and the rest of the synagogue community, may have negotiated their cultic and imperial responsibilities is not clear, though Reynolds and Tannenbaum point out in relation to the centurion Cornelius (Acts 10:1–2) that tolerance for participation in such worship (required of Cornelius in the army) may well have fallen in the realm of what was acceptable for God-fearers.[65]

Fifth, the inscription identifies various occupations engaged in by some of those named. Up to twenty-seven have some occupational designation, ten of the Jews and seventeen of the God-fearers. Jews are identified as a rag-trader, grocer, poulterer, confectioner, shepherd, bronze-worker, tailor, and goldsmith. Among the God-fearers are an athlete, treasurer in a senator's household, missile or weapons-maker, fullers (3), sculptor or painter of pictures and images, producer of mincemeat, boot-maker, stone-cutter or carver, marble-worker, plasterer, linen-worker, ink-maker, maker of wooden tablets, purple-dyer, boxer, customs-collector, knob-turner, carpenter, money changer, bronze-smith, and armlet-maker. Those identified are clearly involved in the production of food and textiles, as well as goods from leather, stone, metal, and wood; they are also involved in construction, finance, athletic activities, and representational arts. Several occupations suggest considerable wealth (goldsmith, a Jew; purple-dyer, a Gentile) while some of the occupations of the God-fearers—the producer of mincemeats, sculptor, carver—could, theoretically, pose some problems for Jews in terms of Jewish traditions. But the presence of the names indicates that such was not the case at least in this instance. Again, considerable openness to and interaction with society are attested.

Not Enough Boundaries, Too Many Bridges: Is All Well?

The survey above of the extensive studies of Barclay, Trebilco, and Harland on first-century Jewish communities in the province of Asia, and these four more detailed examples from Josephus, Akmoneia, Rajak and Noy's study of the title *archisynagōgos*, and Reynolds and Tannenbaum's study of this inscriptional monument from Aphrodisias— all together show that Jewish groups negotiated imperial society through considerable levels of participation in and openness to Gentile society, while also maintaining some distinctive practices. Regrettably, how levels of acceptable involvement were established (the city councillors in Aphrodisias?) is often not clear. Nevertheless, on this basis we could conclude that in all likelihood the synagogue community to which John's Jesus-believers belonged, and from which they were not separated (sect. 1 above), engaged its late first-century Roman-dominated, Hellenistic, Asian city of Ephesus in the same active, interactive, participationist way, though with some ambivalence due to observance of certain identity markers.

But what about the Gospel text? Does it support similar significant levels of participation, accommodation, and openness?

As I have suggested above, the world, practices, and perspectives of the Gospel narrative may not reflect the practices and perspectives of all or most or some Jesus-believers in Ephesus. In terms of the spheres of cultural interaction that Barclay identifies, and anticipating the discussion of the following chapters, for example, it is immediately evident that the Gospel participates in the linguistic sphere with its use of Greek, indicating that its audience also employs the dominant language of Ephesus. In terms of the social sphere, van Tilborg's study of the Gospel's prosopography indicates considerable similarities between the Gospel's names and those found on Ephesian inscriptions (along with some differences).[66] And the discussion in the next chapter will show that the Gospel employs the societal structure of the empire as it was experienced in Ephesus. Materially, this societal structure, along with incidental references in the Gospel to work, societal roles, possessions, and money,[67] suggests further significant embeddedness in Ephesian civic life. In terms of cultural intertextuality, the Gospel narrative thus indicates important participation in its societal context.

But along with this involvement, three other spheres—the political, religious, and ideological—on which the Gospel focuses so much of its attention attest much more oppositional interaction. One obvious example concerns the Gospel's plot whereby Rome crucifies Jesus, whom God raises from the dead and who ascends into the heavens (see chap. 6 below). I will elaborate various other areas in the following chapters.

Anticipating that discussion, it seems that *in the Gospel* opposition exists not only alongside integration but often dominates it.

The Gospel attests the importance of some Jewish distinctives. These include valuing the Scriptures (passim),[68] honoring the Sabbath (5:1–18; 9:1–16), honoring one God (5:18; 10:33), and observing festivals such as Passover (2:13, 23; 6:4; 11:55–56; 12:1, 12, 20; 13:1, 29; 18:28, 39; 19:14), Tabernacles (7:2, 8, 10, 11, 14, 37), Dedication (10:22), and the unspecified festivals of 4:45 and 5:1.[69] In the narrative there is certainly debate with Jesus over the significance and meaning of observing these festivals, but the practices themselves are not attacked. Similarly, Jesus mentions circumcision as something "you" do but he does not question whether it should be observed (7:22–23). Purity is mentioned though it is given some explanation (2:6), suggesting that it does not receive regular observance.[70] There is no mention of collecting the temple tax.

How are we to evaluate these indicators of integration along with opposition and observance of Jewish distinctives in the text of the Gospel? Do they reflect the actual patterns of interaction which synagogue-members and Jesus-believers observe in their daily lives, or do they present interactions that the author/s think/s more desirable? In Barclay's terms, do the author/s reflect current patterns of assimilation, acculturation, and accommodation, or do they want less assimilation (less similarity), less acculturation, and less accommodation?

The absence of advocacy for the practices that mark Jewish distinctives, and scenes of debate over their proper interpretation, imply that their observance is taken for granted. Assimilation is low. The numerous textual accounts of disputes over how these distinctives are observed may suggest that there is some dispute or debate within the synagogue over the significance of these actions. The Gospel commends a more Jesu-centric observance.

How might we assess the issue of societal interaction? As numerous scholars acknowledge, our data from late first-century Ephesus on Jewish communities is partial and its predominantly epigraphical and textual nature urges caution about these claims. Because of historical factors, we have inherited sporadic public rather than private utterances, and the legacy of elites much more than the numerically majority nonelites. It is, accordingly, difficult to assess whether or how much the evidence for positive interaction needs to be qualified by acts or words of (private?) dissent (see chap. 3 below) and modified for factors of social status and gender. One might guess, for example, that elite males might generally be more societally active than women, but the example of Julia Severa warns against any stereotyping. Two male elites, Philo and Josephus, themselves attest polyvalent engagement with Roman power, thus urging great caution about claiming one pervasive and unnuanced form of interaction.[71]

For instance, how did Jews living in Ephesus respond to the news of the Jewish military revolt against Rome in 66 CE and the final defeat and destruction of Jerusalem and its temple in 70? Josephus indicates that those who revolted hoped for extensive support from Diaspora communities, which did not seem to materialize, just as Agrippa II had warned (in retrospect?) it would not (*J.W.* 1.4–5; 2.345–404). There were demands in cities such as Alexandria and Antioch in Syria to revoke Jewish rights when war broke out, and there was violence against Jews in various parts of Syria and in Alexandria (*J.W.* 2.457–498). Josephus comments that the outbreak of war was a time "when hatred of the Jews was everywhere at its height" (*J.W.* 7.46–62). Yet Vespasian and Titus refused to grant demands to remove Jewish rights, suggesting that they perceived no active support in these Diaspora cities for those who had revolted (Josephus, *Ant.* 12.119–124; *J. W.* 7.100–115). Interpreting this lack of support is challenging. Martin Goodman suggests that it reflects "overconfidence" from concluding that the risk of any danger to Jerusalem and its temple was "minimal."[72]

No such "hateful" action against Jews in Ephesus is recorded at the outbreak of the war, nor is there any indication of how Jews responded when news came of Jerusalem's defeat and the temple's destruction. It seems unlikely, though, that Jews in Ephesus responded with unambiguous joy at the news. Moreover, the circulation of Judea Capta coins, proclaiming Judea's defeat, and Vespasian's act of co-opting the temple tax and levying it on Jews as a penalty for the war, as a sign of their humiliation and defeat, and as a source of funds to rebuild the temple of Jupiter Capitolinus in Rome, the sponsoring deity that had ensured the defeat of the Jews' God—these could not have gone unnoticed or produced no impact in Ephesus (Suetonius, *Domitian* 12.2)![73] Does the silence of the historical record in Ephesus mean that there was no increase in tension because geographical distance lessened the impact, that the news was absorbed without any disruption to the status quo, that there had been little investment in the war, that no one recorded disruption, or if they did, that the record didn't survive?

Or perhaps the silence could be understood to involve at least in part a level of societal accommodation that Diaspora Jews did not want to jeopardize. Several texts indicate that levels of societal embeddedness in the province of Asia were considerable. The post-70 text of *4 Ezra* (= 2 Esdras), for instance, perhaps written in Palestine, announces judgment on oppressive, insolent, and arrogant Rome, whose empire the "Most High" and "Mighty One" is about to end ("You will surely disappear") so that "the whole earth, freed from your violence, may be refreshed and relieved" (11:39–46). Nevertheless, *4 Ezra* goes on to condemn the province of Asia (especially its elite?) for its complicity in and benefits from Roman power:

> And you, O Asia, who share in the glamour of Babylon, . . . woe to you, . . . for you have made yourself like her. (15:46–47)

The empire violently opposes and kills God's "chosen people" (indicating not peaceful interaction but opposition and destruction), for which it will be judged:

> "As you will do to my chosen people," says the Lord, "so God will do to you, and will hand you over to adversities." (15:56 NRSV)[74]

The text presents Asia as a compliant ally of Rome and unmoved by Jerusalem's fate (15:46–63). The *Fifth Sibylline Oracle,* dating from around the end of the first century, similarly presents the province of Asia as complicit with Rome and like Rome subject to God's impoverishing punishment and destruction:

> Woe to you Sardis, woe lovely Trallis,
> Woe Laodicea, beautiful city, how you will perish
> Destroyed by earthquakes and changed to dust. . . .
> The well-built shrine of Artemis of Ephesus

With cleavings and earthquakes will fall to the wondrous sea,
Headlong, as storm winds overwhelm ships.
Ephesus, supine, will wail, weeping on the shores,
seeking the temple that is no longer there.
(5:286–327, esp. 289–297; cf. 3:350–380)

How extensively, if at all, were such sentiments expressive of attitudes and practices among synagogue and Jesus-believer communities in Asia in general, and Ephesus in particular? Public masks and private responses are not always consonant, but even if such sentiments existed among the Jewish community in Ephesus, we cannot assume that they were acted on or that they impacted the involvements and interactions of daily life.

Further texts indicate that some in synagogue and Jesus-believing communities in Asia were not accepting positive engagement with Roman society. Three texts, all written about the same time as John's Gospel, and all involving address to Jesus-believers in Ephesus, indicate significant levels of societal interaction while also attesting unease with significant levels of accommodated civic participation, even if that participation was not unqualified or unilateral. There is evidence for considerable tension and disputes among Jesus-believers as to how to negotiate the Roman imperial world.

Revelation

One text, the book of Revelation addressed to seven churches in Asia Minor including Ephesus, shares the hostile perspectives of *4 Ezra* but directs its protest against (some/many) Jesus-followers, and probably against (some/many) synagogue members also. Recent scholarship on Revelation argues, from an examination of life in imperial Asia and of the letters to the seven churches in Revelation 2–3, that this text addressed not situations of persecution as previously thought, but situations of what the author regards as overaccommodation and compromise with Roman imperial society.[75] The author challenges the overaccommodated lifestyle of the majority in the churches, urging them to discern the (demonic!) nature of the empire and to distance themselves from societal participation. In the words of 18:4, they are to "come out of her, my people, so that you do not take part in her sins, and so that you do not share in her plagues" (NRSV). Revelation reveals that Rome, a "dwelling place of demons" (18:2), is already under God's judgment (Rev 6), asserts the devilish nature of Rome's empire and imperial worship (Rev 12–13), exposes its political power and economic greed (Rev 18), envisions God's supreme rule even now and in the future (Rev 4–5; 22), and anticipates Rome's imminent and final demise in the establishment of God's purposes by Jesus, the Lamb slaughtered by Rome but raised by God's power (Rev 18–22). In the meantime, the author urges the seven churches to distance themselves from imperial society.

In Revelation 2:1–7 the writer addresses the church in Ephesus. The letter begins by commending the church for not tolerating evildoers and for discerning false teachers and leaders (2:2–3). But then with the formulaic clause, "But I have this against you," the writer turns to problems in the Ephesian church, the loss of their "first love," an image that suggests a loss of zeal and lived faithfulness. Verse 6 flags a problem in the church with the Nicolaitans. Even though the writer commends the church for "hating" them, the reference to the loss of their "first love" and the demand for repentance suggest that not all have hated and that not all have hated enough.

Letters to other Asian churches elaborate the identity, teaching, and practices of the Nicolaitan Christians. In 2:15 they are also active in the church in Pergamum. The author refers to the Nicolaitans immediately after condemning those in the church who "eat food sacrificed to idols and practice fornication" (2:14), suggesting that the Nicolaitans think it permissible for Jesus-believers to participate in cultic activity. The reference to fornication is probably a metaphor, common in the prophets (Hos 1–3), for participation in idolatry. The issue appears again in the letter to the church in Thyatira (2:20–23) and involves a woman teacher symbolically named Jezebel, after the queen who, married to king Ahab, encouraged idolatry (1 Kings 18–19; 2 Kings 9). Some (many?) in the church at Thyatira participate in civic cultic activity. It also seems likely that such participation is the issue in the letter to the church in Sardis, which the writer pronounces to be "dead" though a few (ὀλίγα, *oliga*) have remained faithful (3:1–6). The majority of Jesus-believers in Sardis seems to participate in cultic activity. The church in Laodicea is denounced for being lukewarm and in need of repentance (3:14–22), again indicating considerable accommodation there.

Perhaps involvement in cultic activity is also the reason why the writer denounces some members of two synagogues—with whom the churches have close connections—as "synagogues of Satan who say they are Jews but are not," in Smyrna (2:9) and Philadelphia (3:9).[76] In Smyrna there is tension between Jesus-believers and some in a synagogue, whereby some threat of imprisonment exists for some Jesus-believers (2:10). The nature of the slander (βλασφημία, *blasphēmia*) that so bothers the writer is not clear. The term is not especially common in the tradition, but a cluster of uses appear in 1–2 Maccabees, where it refers to Antiochus Epiphanes' program (1 Macc 1:41–64), to which "many" Jews accommodated (1:11–15, 52), to replace worship of Israel's God, covenant faithfulness, and observance of Torah with idolatry (2:6; 2 Macc 8:4; 15:35). Perhaps the "slander on the part of those who say that they are Jews and are not, but are a synagogue of Satan" comprises significant levels of accommodation and societal participation by some Jews, as with some Jesus-believers, a way of life opposed by other synagogue members who see a denial of an important cultural marker. Perhaps these advocates of accommodation and significant societal participation—including eating food offered to idols in various civic contexts—plan to report or are already reporting (cf. Rev 3:10) those who choose not to honor local and/or imperial gods, thereby stirring up the sort of communal resentment evident in the first century BCE decrees recorded by Josephus.

These seven churches in Asia addressed in Revelation 2–3 lived in a society where opportunities to partake of food associated with idols pervaded their world. Meat sold in the marketplace often originated in such acts. Temples commonly included restaurants for social gatherings in which food previously offered to idols was eaten. Civic festivals and feasts as well as association and guild meetings similarly included meals part of which were offered to idols, images of imperial figures, and blessed by various deities. Participation in the civic, social, and economic interactions of everyday life often occurred in the shadow of such actions, posing a problem for how Jews and Jesus-believers with traditions affirming monotheism and prohibiting idolatry might negotiate such situations. Paul in 1 Corinthians 8:1–13 seems to think that such participation is harmless, though he recognizes different perspectives among believers and the need to respect the diverse practices. The decree in Acts 15:28–29 forbidding food offered to idols would be completely unnecessary unless this practice was widely observed. Later in the second century, Tertullian's argument against Christians participating in any activity or occupation involving idolatry also attests considerable participation (*Idol.* 17.1).

There are also examples of Jewish involvement in idolatrous observances. Peder Borgen cites an inscription from Cyrene (ca. 60 CE) in which appears the name of a Jew, Eleazar, who with others honors Hermes and Heracles. Philo (*Spec. Laws* 1.315–318) warns strongly against prophets and relatives who urge Jews to "resort to their temples, and join in their libations and sacrifices." Josephus (*J. W.* 7.50–53) describes Antiochus and others who offer sacrifices and abolish Sabbath observance.[77] From Revelation 2–3 it seems that a number in the churches and in several synagogue communities took a similar approach.

The writer of Revelation, though, is bitterly opposed to this accommodation and participation and wants it ended because, as the document's rhetoric of distance reveals throughout, Rome's empire is not benign. Hence, in 18:4 he calls them to "come out from her," meaning to adopt lifestyles of much greater social isolation, likely with economic hardship resulting from being disconnected from economic networks such as associations, and suffering resentment and retaliation from civic and social connections for undermining the well-being of the city. The writer thus urges a much more detached and antithetical existence vis-à-vis imperial society. Important for our discussion of John's Gospel is to recognize that the writer of Revelation, addressing churches in Ephesus and six other Asian cities, assumes the considerable level of societal interaction that our previous discussion has suggested; that he (and his supporters) oppose this dominant practice; and that throughout the book he advocates a costly alternative of greater societal alienation from Roman imperial society, which he regards as devilish, exploitative, and under God's judgment.

1 Peter

A second text, 1 Peter, addresses Jesus-believers in Asia (1:1). Significant for our purposes is the teaching in 2:13–17 to "accept the authority of every human institution," including emperors and governors, along with the command to "honor the emperor" (NRSV). The purpose of this socially compliant behavior is public acceptance whereby Gentiles will see their honorable deeds and glorify God (2:12). Doing the good, which comprises living socially compliant lives, provides the best defense against misrepresentations of the Jesus-believers (3:13–17). As I have demonstrated elsewhere, commonly interpreters have understood these commands to mean that Jesus-believers should honor the emperor in all ways *except* where it involves sacrifice.[78] But 1 Peter offers no exceptive clauses, and among its forty-plus Hebrew Bible citations none speaks against idolatry. Rather, doing the societally expected thing that is going to ensure civic honor would include participation in cultic, sacrificial occasions in households (for slaves and wives), associations, and civic imperial cult observances.[79]

But there is an important modification. Along with this submissive and socially compliant behavior, Jesus-believers are to "reverence Christ as Lord in your hearts" (3:15). Their external behavior is matched and sustained by inner devotion to Christ. This strategy of public compliance and participation, yet private devotion to Christ, a strategy that Origen commends in the third century (*Homilia in Exodum* 8.4), is 1 Peter's way of negotiating the demands of social, civic, and imperial life. It ensures that Jesus-believers actively participate in all aspects of daily societal life, for which they are rewarded with a good reputation, but it also offers a way of maintaining their devotion to Christ.

Interestingly, this approach advocated by 1 Peter seems to be akin to that advocated by the Nicolaitan Christians, the Balaamites, and the teacher Jezebel in Revelation 2–3. The active interaction that they advocate seems to be widely practiced in these churches in Asia addressed by 1 Peter. But the writer of Revelation opposes it strongly and wants much more public distance, whatever the cost. First Peter remarks that Jesus-believers have been "maligned as evildoers" (2:12) and that the compliant behavior that 1 Peter urges will ensure a better public reputation for them. Perhaps the reputed "evil" refers here to those who have followed the sort of teaching offered by Revelation, whereby some Christians have distanced themselves from active societal participation and provoked the ire and suspicions of civic groups. First Peter, then, seeks to confirm participation as the norm for these Jesus-believers just as it seems to have been for synagogue groups. But it does so by pointing to the groups' central commitment expressed in "reverencing Christ in your hearts." There is diversity of practice among Asian Jesus-believers over societal interaction and imperial negotiation.

Acts 19

A scene in Acts 19:21–41 concerning trouble in Ephesus over Artemis worship confirms our argument of considerable participation by synagogues and Jesus-believers, but also the presence of some dissenting voices and practices. It is not my intention here to engage in a full discussion of the numerous issues of the Acts 19 scene.[80] I want to highlight just two points from this Act's account.

First, the incident concerns action taken by Demetrius and other silversmiths to protect their livelihood as makers of silver shrines of Artemis, against Paul's influential preaching that "gods made with hands are not gods" (19:26). Such an understanding that idols are nothing may have sanctioned practices of civic involvement (attendance at the gymnasium or theater or association meetings, for instance) among members of synagogues and Jesus-believers (cf. 1 Cor 8:4). Yet on this visit[81] Paul's proclamation of this principle may, for whatever reason, have led some to reach a different conclusion, arguing that the "nothingness" of idols was a reason not for civic involvement but for nonparticipation. Demetrius certainly thinks that Paul has drawn people away from participation (Acts 19:26). Significantly, throughout, the focus remains on *Paul's* disruptive work. No initiative for challenging the honoring of Artemis seems to come from local believers before or without Paul's leadership. They seem to live peaceably in the city until Paul's visit and Demetrius's response of stirring up first his fellow workers and then the city. The fears about the dishonoring of Artemis by nonobservance are directed solely to Paul and not to local Jesus-believers. At the end of the scene the town clerk allays their fears (19:35–36), clears Paul of any wrongdoing (19:37), and holds Demetrius responsible for the civic disorder, urging him to observe the proper channels (19:38–39).

Second, Paul is not able to address the crowd gathered in the theater (19:30–31). Instead, a Jew named Alexander tries to address the crowd to "make a defense" but is shouted down (19:33–34). We are not told what Alexander might have said or who or what he was going to defend, but several options seem possible. He could have been a supporter of Paul and ready to speak in Paul's defense, though this seems unlikely given the crowd's hostility and unwillingness to let Paul speak. More likely, he belonged to a synagogue community in Ephesus and wanted to distance the synagogue from Paul (since Paul had taught there; 18:19; 19:8–10) and assure the crowd that the synagogue posed no threat to the civic order presided over by Artemis.[82] Alexander thus would have presented an accommodationist alternative to the more distancing and disruptive position vis-à-vis Artemis, which Demetrius attributed to Paul. If this conjecture is on track, the scene provides some evidence that both the Jesus-believers and the synagogue community actively participated in their city's life (to what extent is not clear) while also attesting some (new?) challenge to the status quo associated with Paul's preaching. As with Revelation, there are voices challenging, while simultaneously attesting, the dominant practice of societal participation and interaction.

John's Gospel

At this point we can return briefly to John's Gospel and the question of whether the Gospel narrative reflects or seeks to impose societal distance. My proposal is that John's rhetoric of distance seeks in part to disturb the Jesus-believers' general sense of at-homeness in late first-century Ephesus and impose greater distance. I have demonstrated this pervasive sense of at-homeness in synagogue communities to which the Jesus-believers belonged (while also recognizing some distance in the observance of traditional practices), and in the three texts of Revelation, 1 Peter, and Acts 19. I have also recognized dissenting voices that were seeking greater cultural distance, such as the writer of Revelation. Among the latter the writer or writers of John's Gospel and their supporters apparently belong in thinking that there *ought* to be more distance. They are not happy with levels of participation that do not seem to be impacted by the commitment of believers to Jesus, who was crucified by the empire.

Wherein lies this "oughtness" for more distance will concern us throughout this book, but I will mention one dimension briefly here, that of christological confession. In the first of three passages mentioning expulsion from the synagogue, the reason given is the confession that Jesus is the Christ (9:22). Neither of the two successive references (12:42; 16:2) explicitly mentions the Messiah, though 12:42 makes "believing in him" central to the exclusion. The "him" is identified in the previous verses as the Messiah and Son of Man (12:34–36), and of course the Gospel is written that "you may believe Jesus is the Christ" (20:30–31). John 16:2 assumes such belief in its address to "you," believers in Jesus. We therefore ask, What is it about confession of Jesus as Messiah (Hebrew word) or Christ (same word in Greek) that might be so disruptive and divisive? Our answer must make sense of the analysis of what we know about first-century synagogue communities outlined in this chapter. And it must make sense of clues evident in the Gospel such as the prominent role given to Moses as revealer of God's purposes. We will return to the role of Moses in chapter 4 below; here it is sufficient to recognize that loyalty to Moses (evidenced by Jesus' opponents) is set over against loyalty to Jesus in John 9. "You are his disciple, but we are disciples of Moses" (9:28 NRSV).[83]

Recent investigations of first-century Messiah traditions have established that messianic expectations among first-century Jews were neither unitary nor ubiquitous.[84] There was no unified, pervasive, monolithic expectation about the Messiah in the first century. Yet without trying to collapse these diverse expectations into one, it is fair to observe that where Messianic expectations are attested, they often overlap in presenting a Messiah as agent of God's eschatological purposes, who effects Rome's demise, judges its evil and unjust world, and establishes God's good and just purposes. This understanding is evident in some form in *Psalms of Solomon* 17, Qumran texts, *1 Enoch* 37–71, *2 Baruch* 39–40, and *4 Ezra* 7; 11–12.[85] Moreover, in John 9:35, the Messiah Jesus is further identified as "Son of Man," a term that in Daniel 7 designates one who ends the world's empires and establishes God's empire (cf. *1 En.* 46–48 for a similar role). We will return to these terms and texts in chapter 7 below.

Attention to synagogues as places of negotiation with and significant participation in the Roman world clarifies why the confession of Jesus as the Messiah mandates greater societal distance for those seeking to disrupt the more accommodated practices of Jesus-believers within a synagogue community. Confession of allegiance to a "messiah," if understood to involve an agent of God's transforming purposes and the overwhelming of Rome's empire, and if allowed to flourish in the midst of a somewhat accommodated synagogue community, would disrupt its negotiation with Rome's world and trouble or jeopardize its (elite-dominated) societal participation, status, and rewards. The position of the writer/s of the Gospel and their supporters seems to be that to confess Jesus as Christ, or Messiah, cannot involve high levels of societal participation without regard for the confession's political and societal implications. Rather, their view seems to be that to claim that as Messiah Jesus the Son of Man reveals and institutes God's eschatological and empire-ending purposes is not good news for Rome and provincial elites allied with imperial interests. It means the end of the Roman order and the comfortable participation of synagogue communities and Jesus-believers in that order. One purpose of writing the Gospel, therefore, was to elaborate the societally disruptive implications of the confession of Jesus as Messiah. The writer/s and their supporters know that pressing this claim and its implications will mean increased tension and conflict within the more-accommodated synagogue community (as well as among Jesus-believers) and could in all likelihood result in a subsequent parting of the ways as the Gospel sets forth in the story of John 9, for instance. The awareness of what is at stake in terms of societal involvement in the assertion of the implications of belief in Jesus as Messiah is evident in 12:42–43. Those of the rulers who believed did not openly confess for "they loved the glory/honor of people more than the glory of God."

Why do the writer/s and their supporters need to assert the confession and its implications? Perhaps Jesus-believers have not pressed this confession of Jesus and its implications because in their daily realities they do not share the conviction of this messianic tradition that the imperial world is evil and in need of transformation. Or perhaps they, along with other synagogue participants, are aware of how troublesome and disruptive it would be to their lives if they took these sociopolitical dimensions of the confession of messiahship seriously. Or perhaps what began as a countercultural confession in a tensive context—as I will argue in the appendix below—has gradually been tamed with the passing of some time and in different contexts marked more by accommodation than by conflict. In these circumstances, where in their view too much bridge-building has taken place, the writer/s and their supporters sense the need to reassert the disturbing implications and to draw much clearer boundaries between the community of Jesus-believers, the synagogue, and the Roman Empire.

Conclusion

In this chapter, I have taken up two issues concerning the (Ephesian) synagogue community in which the Jesus-believers addressed by John's Gospel participate: first, its interactions with the Jesus-believers; and second, its interactions with Roman imperial power. In relation to the first I have argued that the widely asserted view that John's Gospel is written after a synagogue community has expelled the Jesus-believers is not sustainable. There is little historical evidence to attest such a separation. I have instead suggested that in the view of the writer/s and their supporters, a division ought to exist, and that the Gospel was written in part to create or exacerbate a division. This claim needs to be developed, but I have pointed briefly to how important the author deems the confession of Jesus as Messiah. Second, I have argued that the synagogue community in Ephesus in which John's Jesus-believers participated was in all likelihood reasonably at home in and accommodated to Roman power. I have suggested that this ease with Roman power—on the part of many in the synagogue and among John's Jesus-believers—seems to be problematic for the Gospel writer/s (as well as for the writer of Revelation, but not for the writer of 1 Peter). The Gospel presents claims about Jesus as troubling for the synagogue's accommodation, thereby attempting not only to separate Jesus-believers from the synagogue, but also to create a more antithetical relationship between Jesus-believers and the empire.

Notes

1. Though no synagogue building has been identified in the excavations at Ephesus, Acts (if it is accurate) attests a synagogue in the city where both Paul (twice: Acts 18:19; 19:8–9) and Apollos (18:24–26) speak in the early 50s. Paul's second visit, predictably in the Lukan acceptance-rejection synagogal pattern, causes a division whereby Jesus-believers seem to leave. Of course, the building could be a house in which a Jewish group gathered, so finding a distinctive "building" would be impossible. Josephus cites a letter from Marcus Agrippa which, with its recognition that Jews exercised judicial powers over their own affairs, suggests that the Jewish community had some autonomy within the city (*Ant.* 16.168). Van Tilborg (*Reading John*, 145–49) notes some inscriptions mentioning a synagogue or Jews, but these inscriptions in all likelihood originate in the second or third centuries. Trebilco (*Early Christians*, 43–44) also cites

Josephus, *Ant.* 14.227, as suggesting a building, but while Josephus attests permission for Jews to "come together," the reference does not specify any (type of) synagogue building.

2. Peder Borgen, "'Yes,' 'No,' 'How Far?' The Participation of Jews and Christians in Pagan Cults," in P. Borgen, *Early Christianity and Hellenistic Judaism* (Edinburgh: T&T Clark, 1996), 15–43.

3. Erich Gruen, *Diaspora: Jews amidst Greeks and Romans* (Cambridge: Harvard University Press, 2002), 5–6.

4. See the relevant sections of Werner Kümmel, *The New Testament: The History of the Investigation of Its Problems* (Nashville: Abingdon, 1972); and Stephen Neill and Tom Wright, *The Interpretation of the New Testament, 1861–1986*, 2nd ed. (New York: Oxford University Press, 1988). For more recent scholarship, see Robert Kysar, *The Fourth Evangelist and His Gospel: An Examination of Contemporary Scholarship* (Minneapolis: Augsburg, 1975), 83–172. For an example, see James D. G. Dunn, "Let John Be John: A Gospel for Its Time," in Peter Stuhlmacher, ed., *The Gospel and the Gospels* (Grand Rapids: Eerdmans, 1991), 293–322.

5. Martyn, *History and Theology*; idem, "Source Criticism and Religionsgeschichte in the Fourth Gospel," in *The Interpretation of John*, ed. John Ashton (Philadelphia: Fortress, 1968), 99–121; idem, "Glimpses into the History of the Johannine Community," in *The Gospel of John in Christian History* (New York: Paulist, 1979), 90–121; Brown, *John*, 1: xxiv–xl; idem, *Community*.

6. James F. McGrath, *John's Apologetic Christology: Legitimation and Development in Johannine Christology* (Cambridge: Cambridge University Press, 2001).

7. Martyn ("Glimpses," 120–21) recognizes a Gentile mission, while Brown (*Community*, 55–58, 63–66) and John Painter (*The Quest for the Messiah* [Nashville: Abingdon, 1993], 78–79) claim Gentile presence (prepared for by the previous inclusion of Samaritans), Gentile resistance (a key element of the term "world"), and a geographical move to Ephesus late in phase one, just before the Gospel's first version, and into phase two.

8. Richey ("'Truly This Is the Savior,'" chap. 1) surveys the development theories and argues that three "secure conclusions" emerge: (1) the move to Asia Minor; (2) an influx of Gentile converts; (3) excommunication and continuing hostility from a synagogue. These "conclusions" establish a situation in which the Christian community is exposed to "harassment and persecution by the Roman authorities" (44). As my subsequent discussion will show, I am not convinced by several aspects of this formulation: (1) It posits no negotiation of Rome's world until these three factors occur late in the tradition's development. As I will argue below, synagogue communities were also loci of imperial negotiation (as was Judea around 30 CE!), and so "John's" negotiation of Rome's world occurred throughout the tradition's development (assuming the development model). (2) Its reliance on the persecution scenario is far too restrictive, as I have suggested. As I will later demonstrate, postcolonial studies and investigations of peasant resistance indicate that imperial negotiation is much more diverse.

9. For an introductory survey, see Carter, *John: Storyteller*, 155–74.

10. Georg Richter, "Präsentische und futurische Eschatologie im 4. Evangelium," in *Studien zum Johannesevangelium*, ed. J. Hainz, Biblische Untersuchungen 13 (Regensburg: Pustet, 1977), 346–82; for discussion, see A. J. Mattill, "Johannine Communities behind the Fourth Gospel: Georg Richter's Analysis," *TS* 38 (1977): 294–315; Martyn, *History and Theology*; idem, "Source Criticism"; idem, "Glimpses;" Brown, *Community*; Painter, *Quest*, 61–135.

11. For discussion, see Carter, *John: Storyteller*, 107–54.

12. In John 5 Jesus is in Jerusalem, but 6:1 locates him on "the other side of the Sea of Galilee." In 11:2 Mary is identified as anointing Jesus, but this action is not narrated until chapter 12. In 14:31 Jesus seems to end his chapter-long sermon, but then he talks for two more chapters (15–16). In 20:30–31, the Gospel seems to end, but then chapter 21 follows.

13. In 3:22 Jesus baptizes but 4:2 says he does not baptize. In 7:8 Jesus says he is not going to Jerusalem, but in 7:10 he goes.

14. Do signs lead to faith (2:11), or is faith without signs preferable (20:29)? In 4:23 and 5:25 Jesus declares that his "hour is coming, and is now here." In 5:22 he says the Father has given all judgment to the Son, but in 12:47 he says he does not judge anyone. Does the Gospel emphasize (6:51–58) or demote sacraments (no institution of the Lord's Supper scene)? Are God's eschatological, end-time purposes known fully in the present (5:24), or is there a future dimension (5:28–29)?

15. C. K. Barrett, *The Gospel according to St. John* (London: SPCK, 1955), 18–21; Paul Anderson, *The Christology of the Fourth Gospel: Its Unity and Disunity in the Light of John 6* (Valley Forge, PA: Trinity Press International, 1996).

16. Martyn, *History and Theology*, 72–83; Brown, *Community*, 41–43.

17. Luke T. Johnson, "The New Testament's Anti-Jewish Slander and the Conventions of Ancient Polemic," *JBL* 108 (1989): 419–41.

18. Brown, *Community*, 36–54.

19. Carter, *John: Storyteller*, 107–28.

20. Joanna Dewey, "The Gospel of John in Its Oral-Written Media World," in *Jesus in Johannine Tradition,* ed. Robert Fortna and Tom Thatcher (Louisville: Westminster John Knox, 2001), 239–52, esp. 248–51. For discussion, see Carter, *John: Storyteller*, 131–96.

21. Martyn, *History and Theology*.

22. Olsson, "'All My Teaching,'" 203–24, esp. 219.

23. Tobias Hägerland, "John's Gospel: A Two-Level Drama?" *JSNT* 25 (2003): 309–22. Hägerland's suggestion that somehow his argument might support the recent claim that the Gospels do not originate in specific communities (e.g., Richard Bauckham et al.) is much less convincing.

24. Reinhartz, *Befriending*, 37–53.

25. Ibid., 51.

26. Peter Schäfer, "Die sogenannte Synode von Jabne: Zur Trennung von Juden und Christen im ersten/zweiten Jahrhundert n. Chr.," *Judaica* 31 (1975): 54–64, 116–24; Lawrence Schiffman, "At the Crossroads: Tannaitic Perspectives on the Jewish-Christian Schism," in *Jewish and Christian Self-Definition,* ed. E. P. Sanders, A. I. Baumgarten, and A. Mendelson (Philadelphia: Fortress, 1981), 2:115–56; Reuven Kimelman, "Birkat Ha-Minim and the Lack of Evidence for an Anti-Christian Jewish Prayer in Late Antiquity," in *Jewish and Christian Self-Definition,* 2:226–44; Stephen Katz, "Issues in the Separation of Judaism and Christianity after 70 C.E.: A Reconsideration," *JBL* 103 (1984): 43–76; P. Alexander, "'The Parting of the Ways' from the Perspective of Rabbinic Judaism," in *Jews and Christians: The Parting of the Ways A.D. 70 to 135,* ed. J. D. G. Dunn, WUNT 66 (Tübingen: Mohr-Siebeck, 1992), 1–26; P. Van der Horst, "The Birkat Ha-Minim in Recent Research," *Expository Times* 105 (1994): 363–68; Daniel Boyarin, "The *Ioudaioi* in John and the Prehistory of 'Judaism,'" in *Pauline Conversations in Context: Essays in Honor of Calvin J. Roetzel,* ed. J. C. Anderson, P. Sellew, C. Setzer, JSNTSup 221 (London: Sheffield Academic, 2002), 216–39; R. Kysar, "The Expulsion from the Synagogue: The Tale of a Theory," in R. Kysar, *Voyages with John: Charting the Fourth Gospel* (Waco: Baylor University Press, 2005), 237–45; A. J. Köstenberger, "The Destruction of the Second Temple and the Composition of the Fourth Gospel," in *Challenging Perspectives on the Gospel of John,* ed. J. Lierman, WUNT 2.219 (Tübingen: Mohr Siebeck, 2006), 69–108, esp. 69–76.

27. J.-P. Migne, *Patrologiae graeca* 48.845, 847, 849, 850, 851, 859, 860–61, 881, 933–35, 940). For discussion, Robert Wilken, *John Chrysostom and the Jews: Rhetoric and Reality in the Late Fourth Century* (Berkeley: University of California Press, 1983), passim, esp. 73–94.

28. Boyarin, "The *Ioudaioi*," 218, 220.

29. Margaret Davies, *Rhetoric and Reference in the Fourth Gospel,* JSNTSSup 69 (Sheffield: JSOT Press, 1992), 299, 301.

30. W. McCready, "Johannine Self-Understanding and the Synagogue Episode in John 9," in *Self-Definition and Self-Discovery in Early Christianity: A Study in Changing Horizons,* ed. D. Hawkin and T. Robinson (Lewiston: Edwin Mellen, 1990), 149–66.

31. Kimelman, "Birkat Ha-Minim," 234–35.

32. Reinhartz, *Befriending*, 50.

33. As one example, see the absence of any such consideration from D. Moody Smith, "John," in *Early Christian Thought in Its Jewish Context*, ed. John Barclay and J. Sweet (Cambridge: Cambridge University Press, 1996), 96–111.

34. In discussing Palestinian synagogues, Lee Levine ("The Nature and Origin of the Palestinian Synagogue Reconsidered," *JBL* 115 [1996]: 425–48) and Donald Binder (*Into the Temple Courts: The Place of the Synagogues in the Second Temple Period*, SBLDS 169 [Atlanta: SBL, 1999], 155–226, 389–450) agree that synagogues were "community centers." Using language that Binder rightly contests as creating an artificial distinction (*Temple Courts*, 212–15), Levine emphasizes "non-religious" functions of synagogues as "community centers" (441) including "political meetings, social gatherings, courts, schools, hostels, charity activities, slave manumission, meals (sacred or otherwise) and, of course, religious-liturgical functions" (Levine, "Nature and Origin," 430). Josephus, for example, attests the key role of meetings in the synagogue in Tiberias in negotiating the Roman threat in the 66–70 war (*Life* 276–282; see also *Ant.* 14.235, 260).

35. For an introduction, see Margaret Williams, "Jews and Jewish Communities in the Roman Empire," in *Experiencing Rome: Culture, Identity, and Power in the Roman Empire*, ed. J. Huskinson (London: Routledge, 2000), 305–33.

36. Barclay, *Jews*, 88–98.

37. Victor Tcherikover, *Hellenistic Civilization and the Jews* (Philadelphia: Jewish Publication Society of America, 1961), 296; E. Mary Smallwood, *The Jews under Roman Rule from Pompey to Diocletian* (Leiden: Brill, 1981), 123.

38. Barclay, *Jews*, 259–81, some 22 pages in a book of some 500 pages. Gruen, *Diaspora*, 84–103, insightfully covers much of the same material and reaches similar conclusions.

39. Barclay, *Jews*, 278, contra, for example, Smallwood, *Jews*, 128–38.

40. Sabbath observance prevents them bearing arms and marching on the Sabbath, and they cannot procure their customary foods; *Ant.* 14.226.

41. Barclay, *Jews*, 281.

42. Ibid., 279; Trebilco, *Jewish Communities*, 145–66.

43. Trebilco, *Jewish Communities*; idem, *Early Christians*, 11–52, esp. 37–51.

44. Trebilco, *Jewish Communities*, 34–36; Gruen, *Diaspora*, 105–32.

45. Trebilco, *Jewish Communities*, 173–185.

46. Ibid., 186.

47. Harland, *Associations*, 177–237, esp. 201. Harland (201–10, 219–28) observes evidence for Jewish participation in central sociocultural institutions of the polis such as the theater and gymnasium; civic networks of benefaction; various social, business and cultural relationships and guilds or occupational associations; and in the noncultic honoring of the emperor. Borgen ("'Yes,' 'No,' 'How Far?'" 15–43) identifies Jews and Christians who participated in cultic observances. See also Warren Carter, "Going All the Way? Honoring the Emperor and Sacrificing Wives and Slaves in 1 Peter 2:13–3:6," in *A Feminist Companion to the Catholic Epistles and Hebrews*, ed. A.-J. Levine and M. M. Robbins (London: T&T Clark, 2004), 14–33.

48. Harland, *Associations*, 206.

49. T. Seland, "Philo and the Clubs and Associations of Alexandria," in *Voluntary Associations in the Graeco-Roman World*, ed. John S. Kloppenborg and Stephen G. Wilson (London: Routledge, 1996), 110–27; on Philo, Alexandria, and associations, see Fitzpatrick-McKinley, "Synagogue Communities," 77–86.

50. Harland, *Associations*, 55–173.

51. Josephus, *Ag. Ap.* 2.68–78; *J.W.* 2.195–98, 409–16; Philo, *Embassy* 132–40; *Flaccus* 49–52; Harland, *Associations*, 213–28, 239–43.

52. There is a dispute as to whether this reference should be read as Ancyra (modern Ankara in Galatia) or Pergamum.

53. Harland, *Associations*, 219–24.

54. W. Foerster, "εὐσεβής, εὐσέβεια, εὐσεβέω," *TDNT* 7 (1971): 175–85.

55. For details see Harland, *Associations*, 224.

56. I am citing the translation from Trebilco, *Jewish Communities*, 58–59; for discussion, 58–60; Harland, *Associations*, 140–43, 227–28; A. R. R. Shepherd, "Jews, Christians, and Heretics in Acmonia and Eumeneia," *Anatolian Studies* 29 (1979): 169–80.

57. For a somewhat similar act in which a centurion funds the construction of a synagogue in Capernaum in the Galilee, see Luke 7:5.

58. Tessa Rajak and David Noy, "*Archisynagōgoi*: Office, Title, and Social Status in the Greco-Jewish Synagogue," in *The Jewish Dialogue with Greece and Rome: Studies in Cultural and Social Interaction*, ed. T. Rajak (Leiden: Brill, 2001), 393–429. Lee Levine ("Synagogue Leadership: The Case of the *Archisynagōgoi*," in *Jews in a Graeco-Roman World*, ed. Martin Goodman [Oxford: Clarendon, 1998], 195–213) thinks Rajak and Noy present the role in a too restrictive way and sees it as being more encompassing "as leader and representative of his community." In a series of articles written through the 1980s and 1990s, Tessa Rajak has considered Diaspora synagogal practices and boundaries, civic involvements, Jewish "epigraphical habits," benefactions, leadership titles, and structures that mimic civic patterns and show considerable synagogal cultural engagement. See Rajak, ed., *Jewish Dialogue*, esp. 335–429, 463–78.

59. The use of the term *archisynagōgos* in Luke 13:14 and Acts 13:15 suggests some actual leadership function in the gathering. In Corinth, synagogue leaders led by Sosthenes take Paul to the proconsul Gallio, suggesting considerable involvement in the city and access to imperial power (Acts 18:12–17). Yet Gallio's quick rejection of the matter and indifference to Sosthenes' beating suggests some distance in standing.

60. Joyce Reynolds and Robert Tannenbaum, *Jews and God-Fearers at Aphrodisias,* Proceedings of the Cambridge Philological Society 12 (Cambridge, UK: CPS, 1987).

61. Ibid., 26–27.

62. For discussion, Trebilco, *Jewish Communities,* 107–10, contra Reynolds and Tannenbaum, *Jews,* 41, 101.

63. For discussion, Bernd Wander, *Gottesfürchtige und Sympathisanten: Studien zum heidnischen Umfeld von Diasporasynagogen,* WUNT 104 (Tübingen: Mohr [Siebeck], 1998); Gary Gilbert, "Pagans in a Jewish World: Pagan Involvement in Jewish Religious and Social Life in the First Four Centuries CE" (PhD Diss., Columbia University, 1992); and the helpful review by Robert Mowery, in *CBQ* 61 (1999): 607–9. Also Irina Levinskaya, *The Book of Acts in Its Diaspora Setting* (Grand Rapids: Eerdmans, 1996), 1–126.

64. Reynolds and Tannenbaum, *Jews,* 48–66.

65. Ibid., 58–66.

66. Van Tilborg, *Reading John,* 1–23.

67. Ibid., 59–109.

68. For a brief overview, Carter, *John: Storyteller,* 131–40, and references.

69. For Jesus-believers, John seems to interpret these feasts in relation to Jesus (e.g., 6:35; 7:37–39).

70. The term καθαρός, *katharos,* appears only four times, all in the farewell discourse (chaps. 13–17). Three uses are associated with the footwashing (13:10 [2x], 11), and the fourth appears in 15:3 in reference to Jesus-believers being cleansed by Jesus' word. The Gospel does not use the verb καθαρίζω, *katharizō,* but ἁγνίζω, *hagnizō,* meaning "purify oneself," appears in 11:55.

71. On Philo, see E. R. Goodenough, *Politics of Philo Judaeus: Practice and Theory* (Hildesheim: G. Olms, 1967); Robert A. Kraft, "Philo and the Sabbath Crisis: Alexandrian Jew-

ish Politics and the Dating of Philo's Works," in *The Future of Christianity: Essays in Honor of Helmut Koester*, ed. B. Pearson (Minneapolis: Fortress, 1991), 131–41; Peder Borgen, "Emperor Worship and Persecution in Philo's *In Flaccum* and *De Legatione ad Gaium* and the Revelation of John," in *Geschichte—Tradition—Reflexion*, ed. H. Cancik, H. Lichtenberger, P. Schäfer (Tübingen: Mohr Siebeck, 1996), 3:493–509. On Josephus, see Menachem Stern, "Josephus and the Roman Empire as Reflected in *The Jewish War*," in *Josephus, Judaism, and Christianity*, ed. Louis Feldman and G. Hata (Detroit: Wayne State University Press, 1987), 71–81; James McLaren ("A Reluctant Provincial: Josephus and the Roman Empire in *Jewish War*," in *The Gospel of Matthew in Its Roman Imperial Context*, ed. John Riches and David Sim, JSNTSup 276 [London: T&T Clark, 2005], 34–48) identifies three analyses of Josephus as happily accommodated, pragmatically accepting, or anticipating Rome's divinely ordained demise. The formulation of three quite different stances, whichever is preferred, nevertheless suggests a provincial's complex negotiation of Roman presence. Also see T. Rajak, "Benefactors," in *Jewish Dialogue*, 373–91.

72. Martin Goodman, "Diaspora Reactions to the Destruction of the Temple," in *Jews and Christians: The Parting of the Ways, A.D. 70 to 135* (Grand Rapids: Eerdmans, 1999), 27.

73. See Warren Carter, "Paying the Tax to Rome as Subversive Praxis: Matthew 17:24–27," in *Matthew and Empire*, 130–44.

74. For similar perspectives in the *Sibylline Oracles*, see 3.350–57; 4.145–50; 5.155–78.

75. Leonard Thompson, *The Book of Revelation* (New York: Oxford University Press, 1990); Wilfrid Harrington, *Revelation*, SP 16 (Collegeville: Liturgical Press, 1993).

76. For some discussion and bibliography, see Friedrich Wilhelm Horn, "Zwischen der Synagogue des Satans und dem neuen Jerusalem: Die christlich-jüdische Standortbestimmung in der Apokalypse des Johannes," ZRGG 46 (1994):143–62; Philip Mayo, *"Those Who Call Themselves Jews": The Church and Judaism in the Apocalypse of John*, Princeton Theological Monograph Series 60 (Oregon: Pickwick Publications, 2006), 51–76, who favors a theological rather than praxis explanation.

77. Peder Borgen, "'Yes,' 'No,' 'How Far?'" 18–24; also Carter, "Going All the Way."

78. Carter, "Going All the Way," 14–33.

79. The condemnation of "lawless idolatries" in 1 Peter 4:3 is consistent with the concern for civic honor. It appears at the end of a list condemning *immoderate behaviors* that are socially dishonorable. Sex and wine are not prohibited *per se*, but only in excess. See Carter, "Going All the Way," 28–29.

80. Larry Kreitzer, "A Numismatic Clue to Acts 19:23–41: The Ephesian Cistophori of Claudius and Agrippina," *JSNT* 30 (1987): 59–70; Robert Stoop, "Riot and Assembly: The Social Context of Acts 19:23–41," *JBL* 108 (1989): 73–91; Trebilco, *Early Christians*, 155–70.

81. It is not his first visit to Ephesus. There have been references to previous visits there in 18:19–21 and 19:1–20, where he remained for over two years (19:8–10).

82. Trebilco (*Early Christians*, 160) claims, "Most scholars argue that Alexander was put forward by the Jews in order to dissociate the Jewish community from Paul and the accused Christians."

83. Martyn (*History and Theology*, 90–151) and Brown (*Community*, 26–27, 43–45), albeit in different ways, see this confession that Jesus is God's anointed agent as crucial in the developing traditions. Yet while they explore the confession in relation to Samaritan and Jewish eschatological traditions (especially involving Moses and eschatological prophetic figures), they are silent concerning the implications of this confession for Rome's empire and for a synagogue community, especially its elite leadership, in negotiating Rome's world. Martyn (*History and Theology*, 106–28), for instance, emphasizes traditions associated with a "prophet-messiah-like-Moses" (Deut 18:15–18), but most of the texts he cites do not use the term "Messiah." That is not to deny an expectation about an eschatological prophetic figure like Moses (1:45; 3:14; 6:14, 30–31; 7:40,

52), but it is to observe that the Gospel refers to this figure more often as the prophet than as Messiah. One exception is 7:31, where the people, not the elite, use the term. Yet the Gospel does not hesitate to use the term "Messiah" for Jesus (1:17; 20:30–31).

84. Marinus de Jonge ("Messiah," *ABD* 4:777–88, esp. 777) argues that "in the OT the term 'anointed' is never used of a future savior/redeemer, and that in later Jewish writings of the period between 200 B.C. and A.D. 100 the term is used only infrequently in connection with agents of divine deliverance expected in the future." See also Richard Horsley, "Messianic Movements in Judaism," *ABD* 4:791–97; see also George W. E. Nickelsburg, "Agents of God's Activity," in *Ancient Judaism and Christian Origins* (Minneapolis: Fortress, 2003), 89–117. The major texts present diverse figures including *Pss. of Sol.* 17–18 (kingly); 1 *En.* 37–71 (heavenly judge); Qumran (e.g., 1QS 9.11; CD 7.18–21; priestly and prophetic); *4 Ezra* 12 (kingly); *2 Bar.* 29:3; 30:1; 39:7; 40:1–4 (ruler-judge); Josephus refers to popular messianic figures in prophetic and kingly traditions.

85. *Psalms of Solomon* celebrates God's kingship "over the nations in judgment" (17:1–3), catalogs the arrogant actions of the "lawless one" and "criminal king" (17:5–20), and anticipates the Davidic king and Lord Messiah, who will dismiss the Romans, gather the people, and establish God's just purposes over the nations (17:21–46). In the Qumran texts, the Messiah/s is/are part of a pervasive eschatological expectation that awaits the establishment of God's righteous purposes, a new creation, resurrection from the dead, and standing in the presence of the holy ones" involved in worship (Nickelsburg, *Ancient Judaism*, 128). *First Enoch* 37–71 anticipates a heavenly figure, the Messiah and Son of Man (46:3; 48:10), who judges the world, defeating the oppressive kings of the earth, the landowners, and mighty ones, thereby preparing for God's just reign (46–48). In *2 Bar.* 39–40, the Messiah is a kingly figure who destroys God's enemies and the leader of the fourth harsh and evil empire, and sets up the eternal paradisaic kingdom of God's purposes (29:2–30). In *4 Ezra* 7:26–29 the Messiah discloses God's purposes for four hundred years, then dies, and after seven days of silence, judgment and a new incorruptible creation follow. In the vision of *4 Ezra* 11–12, the Davidic Messiah destroys Rome's empire and delivers God's people. See Philip Esler, "Rome in Apocalyptic and Rabbinic Literature," in *The Gospel of Matthew in Its Roman Imperial Context*, ed. J. Riches and D. C. Sim (London: T&T Clark International, 2005), 9–33, esp. 20–28.

3

Expressions of Roman Power
in Ephesus

In chapter 2 I discussed the synagogue community, the first of two communities in
which Jesus' believers who engage John's Gospel in Ephesus participated. I argued that
the scenario claiming that the Jesus-believers were expelled from this community is not
sustainable. Second, I argued that Asian synagogue communities, including the Jesus-
believers, generally actively participated in Roman imperial society, while maintaining
some distinctive practices. And third, I argued that some Jesus-believers, including the
writer/s of John's Gospel and their supporters, were troubled by these levels of accommodation. Their telling of the story of Jesus seeks to renew commitment to Jesus the
Christ, crucified by Rome (20:30), to create distance from the rest of the synagogue, and
to set Jesus-believers in a relationship much more distanced from and antithetical to
the Roman world.

This chapter focuses on the second of the two communities in which the Jesus-believers participated in Ephesus: the Roman Empire. To inquire into "how John's text was
read or could have been read in first-century Ephesus,"[1] to borrow van Tilborg's phrase,
means not just pursuing the "marvelous mixture" of Jewish and Hellenistic influences on
the Gospel,[2] as van Tilborg frames his study. His own data reveals what his terminology
conceals. An Ephesian context positions the Gospel and its audience in the Roman
imperial world, a world much bigger than a solitary synagogue, in the era of the Flavian
emperor Domitian (81–96 CE) and in the capital of the Roman province of Asia.

We will begin with a brief general overview of the empire's structure and ways of
exercising its power. Then we will focus on some specificities of Roman power as it was
expressed in Ephesus.[3] This discussion will reject the unsustainable scenario offered by
some scholars that Roman power was expressed in Ephesus by persecuting John's Jesus-
believers. Finally we will identify some approaches that alert us to common dynamics
of engaging imperial power.

The Roman Empire: Models of Empire

Scholarly disciplines such as archaeology and classical studies provide important information about Rome's empire and its local manifestations in a city such as Ephesus.

Teams have recovered much material from Ephesus through extensive and continuing excavations. But various factors limit our understanding. Two thousand years of history distance us from this first-century world, and a full record has not survived. Sources that have survived commonly originate with elites, who dominated the hierarchical Roman world. Such sources privilege elite rather than nonelite experience. Accordingly, surviving sources give us an uneven, patchy, and limited understanding. And there is the constant challenge of knowing how to connect the various pieces of knowledge that we do have. These factors pose problems for our efforts to examine the pervasive presence of Roman power in Ephesus and ways in which it was negotiated.

The use of models of the structures of empire provides one way of joining the dots and filling in the gaps. These models, constructed by social scientists from the study of various empires, provide a (more) heuristic or systemic overview of the Roman imperial system.[4] Models map an overarching context in which we can locate particular aspects of Rome's system, and observe the interconnectedness of the parts. But while models facilitate understanding, they also have limits. By their very nature they focus on generalities more than particularities. Their levels of abstraction can oversimplify and obscure important local variables, details, exemptions, and circumstances.[5] Even as they reveal the larger system, they can conceal nuances. Hence I will employ here a modified form of the models of agrarian-aristocratic-commericialized empires developed by G. Lenski and J. Kautsky.[6] With broad brush strokes I will identify some of the main features of the Roman imperial system and then look at data from Ephesus to understand the presence and power of Rome as it was expressed and experienced in this particular locale in the late first century CE.

The Lenski-Kautsky model of agrarian-aristocratic empires focuses on the exercise of power as a central dynamic of empires. This model poses and answers the question, "Who gets what and why?" In an agrarian empire like Rome's, a small group of about 1–3 percent of the population (comprising senatorial, equestrian, and decurion orders) controlled much of the power, wealth, and status. The remaining 97 percent or so experienced varying but significant degrees of powerlessness and poverty. Elite-controlled land and labor (slaves) were the basis of wealth, though trade was also lucrative. Elites, often residing in urban centers, controlled production and consumption whereby by some estimates 2–3 percent of the population consumed over 50 percent of agrarian production. Rent and taxes, commonly paid in kind, literally transferred goods from nonelite producers to elite consumers (Pliny, *Ep.* 10.8.5).[7] Cities like Ephesus were "consumer" cities that siphoned off the productivity of surrounding territory. Elites also controlled much urban production, intercity trade and commerce, and urban-rural interactions involving trade, investment, and banking. Elite households gained necessary cash flow from land, loan interest and repayment, trade, inheritances, and rents from houses, warehouses, apartments, and shops.[8]

The empire was very hierarchical, with a huge gap between the wealthy, powerful elite and the rest of the population. Kautsky observes that elites, especially but not exclusively elite males, conventionally occupied roles such as warrior, ruler, judge, administrator, patron, and priest in imperial and civic cults (funding buildings, celebrations, meals, sacrifices). Inscriptions attest these elite activities in Ephesus.[9] Elite values and practices involved euergetism (acts of civic benefaction and patronage), the quest for public honor, contempt for manual labor, the superiority of their own social status and race, and the conspicuous consumption and display of wealth through education, housing, clothing food, and acts of patronage.

This governing elite exercised its rule through a retainer class. Usually based in cities, retainers comprised scribes, personal assistants, officials, administrators, professional soldiers, religious functionaries, and household slaves (including freed slaves who often remained obligated to perform various services for former owners). As agents of the elite, they represented the aristocracy's power, enacting its decisions and will, and ensuring its hold over people, land, and production. In return, retainers shared in some of the benefits of rule such as wealth, power, and status by association.

There was no middle class and minimal opportunity for social advancement, though some gained a higher living standard through trade, skilled business or artisan service for a wealthy patron or former owner, or inheritance or legacy. For the elite, life was comfortable; for most of the rest, it involved a daily struggle that cycled through periods above, around, and under subsistence levels. Not surprisingly, numerous tensions marked this stratified society: rich and poor (and poorer), Roman and provincial, propertied and nonpropertied, male and female, rural and urban.

A huge socioeconomic gap separated the wealthy and powerful from skilled and unskilled urban workers, rural peasants working small landholdings, day laborers, and slaves.[10] Inscriptions attest the presence of all of these nonelites in Ephesus.[11] For most, survival—finding work, gaining adequate wages, providing basic necessities of food and shelter, paying taxes, paying rents, surviving disasters and disease, asserting dignity in a dehumanizing system—was always the name of the game. Peter Garnsey comments that "for most people, life was a perpetual struggle for survival."[12] Macro thinks that little elite wealth "filtered down to the urban masses."[13] In terms of allegiance to the empire, Peter Brunt concludes that "we can never know how deeply that loyalty penetrated the masses,"[14] though clearly they were not immune from the continual visual and systemic displays of Roman power.

C. R. Whittaker observes that the "term 'poor' in Roman status terms usually meant anyone not of the ruling orders."[15] While most were poor, there were gradations of poverty. Estimates of preindustrial cities identify 4–8 percent as incapable of earning a living, 20 percent in permanent crisis, and 30–40 percent (artisans, shopkeepers, officials) who temporarily fall below subsistence levels for at least short periods. Falling below subsistence levels, whether permanently or temporarily, depended on availability of work, harvest yields, disease, weather, prices, profiteering, supply, wages, and so forth. At the lowest end were those who could not find work or housing and lived as beggars (Martial, *Epig.* 10.5). In a recent discussion, Steven Friesen estimates, while conceding the provisional nature of the numbers, that 28 percent lived below subsistence level, 40 percent at subsistence, 22 percent stable near subsistence, 7 percent with moderate surplus, and elites constituted the remaining 3 percent.[16]

Is this a likely description of Ephesus? Rarely has this kind of data entered discussion of John's Gospel, but it is important for considering the Gospel as a text that negotiates this sort of imperial world. More common in scholarly discussions are references to David Magie's chapter on Flavian Asia Minor, which highlights "Centralization and Prosperity."[17] Magie writes that the post-Augustan century "had introduced an era of prosperity such as the country had never known even under its native kings."[18] As support, he goes on to cite building activity in Ephesus and other cities funded by "members of the various communities who gave liberally of their wealth for the benefit of their fellow-citizens. . . . Of the cities which thus profited from the prosperity of the time, the most conspicuous example was Ephesus."[19] Later in this chapter I will survey building activity in Ephesus, and there is no doubt that it transformed the city and gave it a significant Roman appearance. But to generalize the displays of wealth of a small ruling elite to include all residents of the whole city (and province) is a major error. Magie's claim fails to take account of social strata and the hierarchical nature of Ephesian society; he shows no awareness of the vast discrepancies in wealth between those at the top and the bottom of the social pile.

Since Ephesus was a typical ancient city, and there is no reason to think that it was not on the basis of the studies summarized above, a significant number of its inhabitants lived in cramped conditions marked by noise, filth, squalor, garbage, human excrement, animals, disease, fire risk, crime, social and ethnic conflicts, malnutrition, natural disasters (a major earthquake occurred in 23 CE), and unstable dwellings (Seneca, *Ep.* 56; Martial, *Epig.* 12.57).[20] Fear and despair were pervasive. The life span for nonelites was low: for men 25–40 years, and less for women. Infant mortality was high: about 28 percent born alive in Rome died within a year; 50 per cent did not survive a decade.[21] Though precision is impossible, on the basis of such demographics, hearers of John's Gospel included many (most? all?) who were poor. Later we will need to consider how to explore the interactions of these nonelite with the Gospel and with the pervasive yet multifaceted imperial power that they negotiated on a daily basis.

The empire's elite, based in and/or allied with Rome, exercised political, economic, social, military, and religious power. The broad brush-strokes of the Lenski-Kautsky model of the Roman Empire identify at least nine means of control exercised by the empire's elite.[22]

Small Bureaucracy

A small bureaucracy of officials enacted Roman power and oversaw administration. The two primary tasks comprised maintaining law and order and collecting taxes. The chief official in the province of Asia was the governor or proconsul.[23] His small staff comprised legates or assistants, and a quaestor, or financial officer, responsible for collection of tax revenues. The governor, or proconsul, was selected from the ranks of senators since Octavian had in 27 BCE designated Asia a province of the Roman people (rather than an imperial province directly under the emperor's control). It is likely that the governor or proconsul had a house and headquarters in Ephesus, but no such buildings have been identified. Provincials could protest the actions of corrupt and harsh governors by appealing to the emperor and senate in Rome. In reality such appeals could face numerous obstacles,[24] though the province of Asia successfully took action against several corrupt governors. In about 12 CE the emperor Augustus indicted one proconsul, Volesus Messala, for misgoverning. Around 20–21 CE, another proconsul, C. Iunius Silanus, was successfully accused of extortion before Tiberius and the senate by "the most fluent advocates of all Asia," and by his legate and his quaestor.[25] And the next year, the procurator Lucilius Capito was indicted and condemned for inappropriate use of military force, in gratitude for which the province built a temple for Tiberius in Smyrna.[26]

Alliances with Local Elites

Rome avoided the expense of a large administrative civil service by making alliances with local elites. Power was shared with and exercised by provincial, often urban-based, elites and client-kings. These local elites benefited from the spoils of empire such as taxation, office, and status in return for their loyalty to Rome and the maintenance of the status quo. We will see (below) some examples of the prominent role of elites in Ephesus. To be recognized, though, is the often ambiguous nature of the relationships between Rome's representatives and local elites. Both parties needed each other to maintain the status quo, from which they both benefited. Yet because the rewards of power were so great, struggles for power and honor often meant tensive interactions, as the prosecutions of several proconsuls indicate.

Economic Control

Economic control was exercised through ownership of resources, notably land and labor (slaves, day laborers, tenant farmers, et al.), property, and trade. Kautsky argues that Rome's empire exhibits some commercialization in that elites not only took peasant production through taxation, as traditional agrarian empires do, but also controlled the land itself.[27] Slaves supplied labor and sometimes skills, for agriculture, manufacture, mining, education, households, management, and so forth.

Taxes and Tribute

Taxes and tributes, usually collected in kind, transferred wealth from peasant farmers, fishermen, local artisans and workers to local landowners, regional officials, and the emperor. Detailed information on taxes in most parts of the empire, including Ephesus, is scarce.[28] Refusal to pay taxes, though, was considered an act of rebellion.[29]

Roman Military Power

Roman military power, both actual and legendary, ensured compliance with and the maintenance of Roman honor.[30] According to Livy, Romulus, "Father of this City," who has ascended post-death to the gods in heaven, declares "to the Romans the will of Heaven that my Rome shall be capital of the world: so let them cherish the art of war, and let them know and teach their children that no human strength can resist Roman arms" (Livy 1.16.7). Valerius Maximus, writing during Tiberius's emperorship (d. 37 CE), presents Rome's military discipline as "the chief glory and mainstay of the Roman empire," which ensures that the empire is "preserved intact and safe" and guarantees "our serene and tranquil state of blessed peace" (*Memorable Doings and Sayings* 2.7 pref.).

In Ephesus, by the first century CE, stability and integration dominated relations with Rome, so there was minimal military presence in the city. As Sjef van Tilborg comments, "Ephesus is not a garrison city. Soldiers are mentioned only exceptionally" in the inscriptions.[31] One sign of this minimal presence is a burial chest now in the British Museum. It dates from between 50–100 CE and was excavated from beside the road leading from Ephesus to the sanctuary of Artemis.[32] The chest honors Titus Valerius Secundus from Liguria, a soldier in the Seventh Praetorian Cohort who died at age 26 after eight years' military service. He commanded an outpost (a *stationarius*) of soldiers in Ephesus.

A second example comes from the temple of the Sebastoi dedicated in 88/89 CE in Ephesus for observances of the imperial cult. The front of the altar comprises a sculptured marble relief, added probably in the second century. It depicts various pieces of military armor and weaponry, graphically demonstrating the interconnectedness of religion, political power, and military might.[33]

Patron-Client Relations

Pervasive patronage operated throughout the empire. From the emperor down, a network of favors and loyalty, privilege and dependency, operated throughout the empire (e.g., Seneca, *De beneficiis*).[34] Elites valued calculated and self-benefiting displays of wealth, power, and civic euergetism, or good works. They enriched civic life by sponsoring a festival, constructing or repairing a building, presiding over and supplying group meetings of various associations, providing a statue, funding a handout, and so forth. In Ephesus, for instance, inscriptions attest that a very wealthy elite leader, Ti. Fl. Montanus, restored the harbor, paid for gladiatorial games, funded a banquet, renovated the theater, and served as high priest of the imperial cult.[35] Displayed in the British Museum is a marble relief dated from the first or second century CE and excavated from near the Magnesium Gate at Ephesus. It depicts gladiators and oxen dragging carts of grain and honors a benefactor who supplied grain and funded games.[36] Such acts enhanced social and political standing for the individual, displayed influence and wealth, secured loyalty through gratefulness and indebtedness, and benefited the city, thereby maintaining the status quo.

Imperial Theology

Imperial theology promoted the claims that the gods, especially Jupiter, had chosen Rome and its emperor to rule the world and manifest the gods' will and blessings among the nations.[37] These messages were asserted through civic celebrations of victories and rulers, as well as by image-bearing coins, statues, buildings, imperial personnel, festivals, poets, writers, and so forth. The imperial cult, frequently promoted by local elites, provided a way of understanding the world and Roman presence as reflecting the will and pleasure of the gods. It offered residents of a city like Ephesus a mostly voluntary means of marking their participation in that world by expressing loyalty and gratitude through sacrifices to images in temples, and at games, street parties, artisan guild meals, and so on.

Rhetoric

Rhetoric was the art of persuasive speech, and it was learned in elite (male) education (Cicero, *On the Orator* 1.60.257; cf. Aristotle, *Rhetoric* 1.1). It played a prominent part in civic life, especially at civic occasions. Ephesus's magnificent theater, facing westward to the harbor, provided a gathering place for civic ceremonies, debates, imperial festivities, and even spontaneous meetings of concerned residents (Acts 19:21–41). All these occasions required speechmaking. Whereas military force and judicial punishment played on fear to effect coerced compliance, according to Cicero, spoken and written rhetoric sought consent by persuasion, seeking to secure social control, cooperation, and cohesion (e.g., Cicero, *De republica* 5.6). Speeches appropriate to various civic occasions articulated the power relations of domination that maintained the civic order and privileged role of the elite.[38]

Justice

Roman "justice" sought to ensure civic order, which of course meant the protection of the elite-dominated status quo. The province of Asia was divided into thirteen areas called assizes, or conventus districts based on a central city.[39] Ephesus was the center of one such conventus, where the governor or proconsul held court days and heard petitions. As Peter Garnsey has demonstrated, justice often reflected and reinforced the societal status quo with punishments fitting not so much the crime as the offender's social status.[40]

These nine areas attest various ways in which the Roman elite and its provincial allies exercised power and control. While models provide helpful heuristic frameworks for understanding these structures, they can oversimplify and obscure important variables, details, exemptions, and local circumstances. Hence these models need to be qualified and elaborated by understandings of the particular experience of empire in Ephesus and of its representation in John's Gospel. It is to those areas we now turn.

Roman Presence in Ephesus

In his wonderful study of "the sacred identity of Ephesus," to which we will also return in the next chapter, Guy Rogers concludes that Roman citizens—including imperial agents from Rome, Latin-speaking immigrants, Greeks who were Roman citizens from other cities, and Ephesians—had by the end of the first century CE,

> transformed the upper city architecturally and spatially, changed the calendar of the city, [taken] control over the celebration of major festivals, and celebrated the cult of the new god—the emperor. In short it is extremely difficult to find even one area of Ephesian institutional or social life documented in the huge epigraphical corpus of the city in which Roman presence . . . was not pervasive or persistent by the end of the first century AD.[41]

Rogers's point is that in late first-century CE Ephesus, capital of the Roman province of Asia since 29 BCE, both elite and nonelite encountered Roman power and presence everywhere. Roman and Rome-related personnel were active in the city.[42] The city's physical space, material objects, societal structures, and networks of power exhibited Roman presence intertwining political, economic, civic, judicial, and religious spheres. By the time of John's Gospel in the late first century CE, urban Asian elites clearly had long recognized Rome's unassailable power. They also experienced the benefits and rewards of status, power, and wealth that loyalty and assimilation into these political, societal, and economic networks produced. They evidenced the practices and behaviors of Romanization that marked elites elsewhere in the empire.[43] They actively participated in civic patronage, euergetism, trade, political leadership, rhetoric, and priesthoods. They owned land and considerable wealth. They promoted Ephesus's identity, seeking to outdo other Asian cities in exhibiting imperial allegiance. Displays of imperial edicts, documents (such as, perhaps, Augustus's *Res gestae*[44]), and imperial images,[45] as well as participation in imperial cult observances including civic festivals, processions, and games,[46] involvement in Roman judicial processes, payment of various direct and indirect taxes on persons, land, traded and transported goods—all these things embedded the city's population in the Roman world.

Roman power had first been established in Ephesus in the late 130s BCE, when the Roman province of Asia came into existence.[47] Attalos III, the last king of Pergamum, died in 134 BCE without an heir. To Rome he bequeathed his personal fortune, as well as royal land and subject cities. A slow Roman response as well as military revolt meant that it was not until around 126 that the province was organized into conventus, or assize, districts for judicial administrative purposes, with Ephesus the urban center of one such district. The following century was often marked by unrest and hardship. There were frequent disputes involving aggressive tax collectors (called *publicani*). Ephesian delegations appealed to Rome for protection especially when governors did not provide it.[48] Not surprisingly, Ephesus warmly supported the military campaign of Mithridates VI of Pontus in the 80s BCE to liberate the city from Roman rule. Considerable anti-Roman feeling resulted in a massacre of Romans and Italians in Asia (Appian, *Mithridatic Wars*). Roman reprisal under the general Sulla was swift, with Ephesus losing its freedom and being subjected to a hefty fine of 20,000 talents, which along with renewed activity from the publicani and disruption of trade by pirates, left the city significantly impoverished.

Rome's civil strife of the 40s and 30s BCE impacted Ephesus positively at first. The city hailed the victorious Caesar as "a god made manifest and the common savior of human life" (IEph 2.251).[49] He lowered taxes in 48 BCE, removed the publicani, and made taxes payable to the province's quaestor. But things deteriorated in 41 BCE when the victorious Antony punished Ephesus for supporting Brutus and Cassius. Antony demanded that nine years' taxes be paid in two years. In 31 Octavian defeated Antony at Actium and punished the cities of Asia with further fines for having supported Antony.

Octavian's victory, though, resulted in some significant improvements. He promoted economic growth by issuing gold and silver coins at Ephesus. He made the province a senatorial province to be governed by proconsuls.[50] He empowered and protected the *Kourētes,* a college of priests for Artemis's temple. He protected the rights of the Jewish community, as mentioned in chapter 2 (above). He also permitted the observance of the imperial cult in Ephesus dedicated to Rome and to the emperor under the supervision of the *koinon*. This provincial assembly increasingly became a place of negotiation with Rome on behalf of the province and a means by which elites in Ephesus and Asia were integrated into the imperial structure.

Appreciation for the increasing stability and prosperity (at least for elites) in the province in part motivated the *koinon* to celebrate the rule of Octavian, known now as Augustus. In 9 BCE they set about reordering the calendar so that the year should begin on Augustus's birthday.

> When the providence which divinely ordered our lives created with zeal and munificence the most perfect good for our lives by producing Augustus and filling him with virtue for the benefaction of humankind, sending us and those after us a savior who put an end to war and established all things; and whereas [Augustus] Caesar when he appeared exceeded the hopes of all who had anticipated good things, not only surpassing the benefactors born before him, but not leaving those to come any hope of surpassing him; and whereas the birthday of the god marked for the world the beginning of good tidings through his coming . . . [Concerning Augustus's birthday] . . . we could justly hold it to be equivalent to the beginning of all things. . . . Therefore people would be right to consider this to be the beginning of the breath of life for them. . . . And since no one could receive more auspicious beginnings for the common and individual good from any other day than this day which has been fortunate for all, . . . therefore it seems proper to me that the birthday of the most divine Caesar shall serve as the same New Year's Day for all citizens.[51]

Building Programs

With the reign of Augustus, much of the instability and public strife of the first century BCE gave way throughout the first century CE to much greater stability and considerable integration of Ephesus into Rome's world. While the record no doubt remains incomplete, considerable building took place in Ephesus.[52] Buildings were material and tangible signs of Roman power and presence. They were often dedicated to the emperor, often constructed by prominent Roman citizens, and often used for administration or the imperial cult. Construction provided employment for nonelites and opportunities for elites to parade their wealth and loyalty and to gain civic honor. Monuments, buildings, statues, and the accompanying inscriptions rendered empire and emperor visible to the residents of Ephesus. They constituted the very environment of the daily world of Ephesus's citizens. The reigns of the emperors Augustus (d. 14 CE) and Domitian (81–96 CE) especially, but not exclusively, effected material transformation of the public face of Ephesus.

Under Augustus, "the small plateau between [the slopes of] Bülbüldag and Panayirdag was chosen as the new center of the Roman city." This new center was dominated by the construction of the two largest buildings, the temple for Divus Julius and the Sebasteion (for Augustus), both of which focused attention on Rome.[53] Buildings constructed under Augustus in this new center included:[54]

- Temples for Divus Julius and Dea Roma (29 BCE; Dio Cassius 51.20.6).

- The Prytaneion, the location of the city's sacred hearth (the cult of Hestia), and the place of welcome for city guests and ambassadors.

- The Bouleterion, the center of the city's administration, and meeting place for the *boulē*, or city council, comprising some two hundred men.

- A three-sided peristyle in which were celebrated the cults of the city goddess Artemis and the emperor Augustus. This combination linked Ephesus and Rome, goddess and god, old and new. It located Ephesus in the Roman order and Rome in Ephesian antiquity.[55]

- A three-aisled Basilika Stoa dedicated between 4 and 14 CE to Artemis, Augustus, Tiberius, and the city of Ephesos (IEph 2.404). It was built by a leading member of Ephesus's civically active and illustrious elite, G. Sextilius Pollio; his wife, Ofillia Bassa; and their children. At the eastern end of the stoa were large statues of the emperor Augustus and his wife, Livia, as well as other members of the imperial family such as Germanicus. There were also statues of the donors Sextilius Pollio and Ofillia Bassa. Sextilius Pollio was subsequently buried on the western side of the State Agora. His tomb, dedicated by his son Proculus, was visible to Curetes Street, honoring him and demonstrating to passers-by the honor of civic investment.

- To the west, where the sacred way intersected with the processional way to the sacred site of Ortygia, two imperial freedmen Mazaeus and Mithridates, dedicated monumental or triumphal gates between 4–2 BCE.[56] The complex included statues of Augustus, and his designated heirs Gaius and Lucius Caesar. It is also possible that it was the burial site of both freedmen. Another group of statues includes Augustus with his designated heirs Lucius and Gaius, as well as another son of Augustus's brother-in-law, Agrippa. (IEph 2.253)

In addition, aqueducts were built by Augustus (IEph 2.401) and by Sextilius Pollio along with a fountain at the temple for Divus Julius (IEph 2.402). Augustus's name is also associated with road-building (IEph 2.459). The buildings set Roman power and presence in stone, and the imperial temples provided Ephesians with a way of understanding, participating in, being loyal to, and honoring the creators of the new Roman world in which they now participated.

During the reign of the emperor Tiberius (14–37 CE), an earthquake in 23 CE destroyed buildings or houses on the lower slopes of Bülbüldag. The quake cleared space for further buildings in the Embolos west of the new center on Curetes Street. The other significant building was the square and two-storied Tetragonos Agora, or marketplace on Marble Street, which replaced its Hellenistic predecessor, and for which the gate of Mazzaeus and Mithridates became the south gate. Subsequent additions to the agora included an equestrian statue of Claudius dedicated by Roman citizens in 43 CE, and a hall forming the eastern upper story dedicated to Artemis, the god Claudius, Nero, Agrippina, and the people of Ephesus (IEph 7.3003).

During the reign of the emperor Nero (54–68 CE), the theater was enlarged and the stadium reconstructed. A tollhouse of the fishermen and fishmongers was dedicated to Nero; his mother, Agrippina; his wife, Octavia; and the people of the Romans and the

Ephesians (IEph 1.20).[57] Also related to the harbor and the promotion of the city's economic well-being were its dredging by the proconsul Barea Soranus to relieve the silt-
ing from the Kaystros River, and the reorganization of the customs of Asia (Tacitus,
Annals 16.23).

Under the Flavian emperors Vespasian, Titus, and Domitian in particular (69–96
CE), Roman visibility through the construction and renovation of various buildings,
especially in the upper agora area, received new attention.

- Most prominent was the temple of the Flavian Sebastoi. It is also called the temple of Domitian since it was dedicated originally to Domitian in 89–90 and contained a huge, seven-meter tall statue of Domitian. The plural term Sebastoi,
  though, indicates that the temple venerated various members of the imperial family (the Sebastoi), including emperors Titus (79–81) and Vespasian (69–79).[58]
  After Domitian's death in 96 and the condemnation of his memory, the temple was
  rededicated to Vespasian. Although the temple honored the emperors, its presence in Ephesus also brought honor to the city. The temple honored Ephesus as a
  neokorate city, a term that recurs repeatedly in the inscriptions, signifying the
  privilege given to Ephesus as "warden" or "keeper" of the imperial temple.[59] Yet
  inscriptions also indicate that other Asian cities saw themselves as the benefactors
  of Ephesus. They claim that it was by their grace (*charity*, χάριτι) that Ephesus was
  permitted the temple.[60] It was funded by the wealthy Ephesian citizen T. Claudius
  Aristion, who served as the first high priest. He along with his wife, Julia Lydia Lat-
  erane, "were the most important couple in the city at the end of the first century
  and the beginning of the second."[61]
- A hydrekdochion with columns and statues was built by the proconsul C. Laecanius Bassus (IEph 3.695) in 80–81.
- The monument to Sextillius Pollio had been expanded by the proconsul Calvisius
  Ruso in 92–93 to include a fountain dedicated to Domitian (IEph 2.413, 419).
- The Embelos, the road connecting the upper agora and the Tetragonos Agora,
  lined with statues of various significant Ephesians, was paved and beautified in
  94–95. M. Tigellios honors Domitian for doing so (IEph 7.3008).
- A gymnasium was finished near the harbor in 92–93 CE.[62]
- Baths were also completed near the harbor before Calvisius Ruso was proconsul
  in 92–93 CE.[63] These complexes near the harbor area were inaugurated by T.
  Claudius Aristion (and friends), who in addition to being imperial high priest also
  occupied the prestigious civic offices of prytany[64] in 92 CE and scribe of the demos
  or assembly in 93.[65]

These building projects have several implications. First is that these buildings, numerous statues,[66] and copious inscriptions render the emperor and empire everywhere
present. Imperial power is constantly displayed. The emperor's name is everywhere, as
is his image, along with those of members of his family.[67] Statues, some venerated, are
located in temples, the theater, fountains, near the harbor, in houses, in gymnasia, in
the market. Everywhere the emperor is watching out for and/or over Ephesus. Everywhere there are opportunities for veneration. As with the constant building and reno-

vating activity, the statues communicate that Rome is attentive. Rome has a face. It seeks and provides for personal engagement.

Second, evident are links between Rome, emperors, and various gods. The brief summary above mentions Dea Roma, Divus Julius, Artemis, Augustus, and the Flavian Sebastoi. The association communicates that Rome and the emperors enjoy the favor of the gods as does Ephesus, and that Rome manifests the presence, will, and blessing of these gods in Ephesus. Thanksgiving, loyalty, veneration, and submissive participation are appropriate responses to both gods and emperors to ensure continued blessing. Politics and religion mix in this imperial world.

Third, the mix of Ephesian and Roman is very evident. Most obviously, Ephesus and Rome are interconnected in the Augustan three-sided peristyle in which both the cults of Artemis and Augustus are celebrated, and in the dedications to the people of Rome and of Ephesus. Van Tilborg also cites numerous instances of inscriptions dedicated to emperors Augustus, Tiberius, Claudius, Nero, Domitian, and the Sebastoi, in combination with the Ephesian goddess Artemis. He reports few examples of emperors linked to other deities, heightening the special association with Artemis.[68] An association between foreign ruling powers and Artemis was centuries old in Ephesus. A statue of Philip II of Macedonia (d. 336) was set up in the temple of Artemis after expelling the Persians, and his son Alexander was honored as a god in the temple also. Rome was the latest power to employ the strategy.[69] Alliance and inclusion, not competition and supersession, marked the public construction of the relationship between Ephesus and Rome, between the traditional and the new, Artemis and the emperor. They coexist in shaping the first-century CE Ephesian world even though there is no doubt as to which is greater.

Fourth, while emperors are on public display, so too are members of their families. Evident in the inscriptions and statues are imperial wives, mothers, brothers-in-law and their family members, and children. The inclusion of relatives magnifies imperial presence and increases its influence. This magnification of imperial presence is seen in the interest in women members of the imperial household such as Nero's mother, Agrippina, who is mentioned before his wife, Octavia, in the fishery tollhouse inscription (IEph 1.20). Agrippina, Nero's mother, is included in the dedication of the hall on the eastern side of the Tetragonos agora even though Nero's wife is not mentioned (IEph 7.3003). Other inscriptions honor Domitia, Domitian's wife, identifying her as Sebasta, whereby she shares in his status.[70]

The references to children reflect a valuing of stable succession (after the instability of the first century BCE). Several inscriptions on buildings and monuments identified above identify the coprincipate of Augustus and his designated heir Tiberius. The linking of the two reflects the same valuing of a stable succession. The emphasis on succession also asserts the permanence and endurance of the (reputedly eternal) empire.[71]

Fifth, predictably, imperial power is constructed as benign and beneficial, as well as far-reaching, in its impact. Because of emperors, the city has important civic buildings for its administration (Prytaneion, Bouleterion). Because of Rome's presence, it has amenities such as water supply, paved roads, harbor access, baths, gymnasia, temples, markets. The empire's presence is good for Ephesus. Honoring Rome with inscriptions, veneration, and sacrifices ensures the continuation of such blessings. The unspoken price, certainly, is compliance, but when the benefits are so tangible and positive (in the modern phrase), what is not to like?

Sixth, local elites are prominently presented as active in this transformation of Ephesus. On one hand, they fund buildings, gaining honor for themselves and displaying their power, wealth, and status. In Augustus's reign, Sextilius Pollio and his wife, Ofillia Bassa, are prominent in constructing the Basilika Stoa. Imperial freedmen Mazaeus and Mithridates dedicated a gate. In Flavian Ephesus, T. Claudius Aristion funds the neokorate temple and has significant leadership in relation to the harbor baths, the harbor gymnasium, and as high priest of the imperial cult. Proconsuls C. Laecanius Bassus and Calvisius Ruso build fountains. There are copious more examples. In turn, local elites are honored with monuments (such as that of Sextilius Pollio) and inscriptions. The promotion of and representation of Rome's presence and power thus is not exclusively or even predominantly the work of Rome and its emperor. Both imperial agents and the local Ephesian elite find in these honorific practices ample opportunity for self-benefit and civic reward. Such actions suggest considerable embeddedness in Rome's world. The result is an elite culture of competition for honor through euergetism, wherein wealth and power are displayed for civic benefit and personal gain. Patronage and networks provide crucial means for functioning in the city.

Coins

Coins provide a further example of pervasive Roman power and presence.[72] Coins were the empire's handheld, personal, billboards, whose carefully chosen images performed similar functions for residents as did buildings, statues, and inscriptions. Coins displayed the emperor's image. They depicted imperial presence as a household and thereby expanded the sense of imperial presence. They evoked divine sanction by linking emperors and deities. They integrated Roman power with Ephesian institutions.

We can make at least six observations from surviving coins. First, coins were issued during the emperorships of Augustus (d. 14 CE), Tiberius (14–37), Claudius (41–54), Nero (54–68), Vespasian (69–79), and Domitian (81–96). They played a constant role in promoting the presence of imperial power in the city throughout the first century. Second, the dominant presentation of emperors features a bust of an emperor and some representation of Artemis, either temple, cult statue, or the stag, the sacred animal of Artemis.[73] This link with Artemis allied the emperor with a central Ephesian institution. It integrated the new imperial power with the city's traditional goddess. It expressed their mutual sanction, Roman and Ephesian, for Rome's presence and power in the city. Third, coins also frequently present the emperor with another imperial figure or show another imperial figure (wife, son) on her or his own.[74] Artemis also figures prominently on these coins. The use of family members expands the sense of imperial presence. Fourth, coins present the emperor (or a relation) with gods or goddesses other than Artemis, such as Roma, Zeus, and Nike, thereby reinforcing the impression of Rome's power as divinely sanctioned.[75] Fifth, while the coins commonly depict an emperor or imperial person with a god or goddess, emperors occasionally appear with buildings, especially temples.[76] This association further reinforces the claim of divine sanction for the Roman imperial order. Sixth, Ephesus was in the 70s–90s CE the second largest producer of coins in Asia.[77] Coins thus played a prominent role in presenting Rome's power and presence in Ephesus.

Roman Presence in the Narrative World of John's Gospel

If space permitted, we could identify other areas in which Roman power and presence were experienced in Ephesus, such as entertainments, access to food, style of housing, and clothing, to name several. Instead I will turn to the Gospel of John itself to show that the Gospel's narrative world is deeply embedded in Rome's hierarchical structures. Without claiming comprehensiveness, the following table indicates some of the points of contact between the Lenski-Kautsky model of the empire's hierarchical structures and characters that people the Gospel narrative.[78]

I.	RULING ELITE	
1.	**Emperor**	
	Caesar	19:12, 13, 15
	Friend of Caesar	19:12
2.	**Provincial Figures**	
	Governor Pilate	18:29, 31, 35, 37, 38; 19:1, 4, 6, 8, 10, 12, 13, 15, 19, 21, 22, 31, 38
	Jesus as King	1:49; 6:15; 12:13, 15 (Zech 9:9); 18:33, 37, 39; 19:3, 14, 15, 19, 21
	Rival king	19:12
	The Romans	11:48
3.	**Allied Local Elites**	
	Chief priests	7:32, 45; 11:47, 49, 51, 57; 12:10; 18:3, 13, 15, 16, 19, 24, 35; 19:6, 15, 21; **Caiaphas** 11:49; 18:13, 14, 24, 28
	Rulers/authorities	3:1 (**Nicodemus**, 3:4, 9; 7:50; 19:39); 7:26, 48; 12:42 (ruler of the world, 12:31; 14:30; 16:11)
	Pharisees	1:24; 3:1; 4:1; 7:32, 45, 47, 48; 8:13; 9:13, 15, 16, 40; 11:46, 47, 57; 12:19, 42; 18:3 (often linked with chief priests, 7:32, 45; 11:47, 57; 3:1; 7:48; 12:42; with *Ioudaioi*, 1:19, 24)18:3; with authorities/rulers,
	The *Ioudaioi* (recognizing the term's diverse use, Jerusalem-based, alliances with other elites and with local supporters)	1:19; 2:18, 20 (temple authorities); 3:1 (one of Pharisees); 5:10, 15, 16, 18; 6:41, 52; 7:1, 11, 13, 15, 35; 8:22, 31, 48, 52, 57; 9:18 (with Pharisees, 9:15, 16), 22; 10:19, 24, 31; 11:8, 45; 13:33; 18:12, 14, 33, 35, 36, 38, 39; 19:7, 12, 14, 19, 20, 21, 31, 38; 20:19
	Royal Official	4:46, 49

4.	**Retainers (do the bidding of/agents of ruling elites)**	
	Chiliarch/officer in command of 1000 soldiers	18:12
	Soldiers	19:2, 23, 24, 32, 34
	Band of soldiers	18:3, 12
	Servant/slave of high priest	18:10 (Malchus), 26
	Priests	1:19
	Levites	1:19
	Officers	7:32, 45, 46 (from and to the chief priests and Pharisees); 18:3 (from chief priests), 6, 12, 18, 22, 36 (of Jesus); 19:6
	Temple money changers	2:14
	Sellers in temple	2:14, 16

II.	**NONELITE**	
5.	**Artisans**	
	Fishermen	21:3
	Teacher	**Jesus**, 1:38; 3:2; 11:28; 13:13, 14; 20:16; **Nicodemus**, ruler) 3:10.
6.	**Rural Peasants and Urban Poor**	
	Crowds	5:13; 6:2, 5, 22, 24; 7:12, 20, 31, 32, 40, 43, 49; 11:42; 12:9, 12, 17, 18, 29, 34
	City/village dwellers	4:8, 28, 39; 7:25; 9:8; 11:1, 18
	Laborers	4:38
	Sowers	4:36, 37
	Reapers	4:36, 37, 38
	Poor	12:5, 6, 8; 13:29
	Door-/gatekeeper	10:3; 18:16–17 (woman)
	Hired worker	10:12, 13
	Shepherd	10:2, 11, 12, 14, 16
	Tenant-farmer	15:1
	Gardener	20:15

7.	**Slaves**	
	Slaves	δοῦλος, *doulos*, 4:51; 8:34, 35; 13:16; 15:15, 20; 18:10, 18, 26; **Malchus** 18:10
	Head servant at wedding feast	2:8, 9
	Servants	διάκονος, *diakonos*, 2:5, 9; 12:26
8.	**Expendables**	
	Diseased	4:46; 5:3, 5, 7; 6:2; 11:1, 2, 3, 6
	Blind	5:3; 9:1, 2, 13, 17, 18, 19, 20, 24, 25, 32, 39, 40, 41; 10:21; 11:37
	Lame	5:3
	Paralyzed	5:3
	Mad	10:20
	Demon-possessed	**Jesus** 7:20; 8:48–49, 52; 10:20–21
	Bandits	10:1, 8; **Barabbas** 18:40
	Thieves	10:1, 8, 10; 12:6

This table indicates that the narrative world of John's Gospel is deeply embedded in and reflective of Rome's hierarchical structures. Categories 1–3 comprise the ruling elite centered on the emperor in Rome and personified in his provincial representatives, such as the governor Pilate. I have included the references to Jesus the king in category 2 to highlight his contesting and challenging of Roman power, but perhaps these references belong more accurately, at least from a Roman perspective, in category 8 (with bandits). Category 3 comprises local provincial elites and allies of Rome's rule dominated by the chief priests and Pharisees (18:3). It may be surprising to see chief priests and Pharisees in this category since we usually think of them as "religious leaders." But as I have demonstrated, such labeling is anachronistic for the first century since politics, religion, and societal structure are much intertwined. Josephus describes the chief priests as the rulers of Judea (*Ant.* 20.251). Tony Saldarini concludes his discussion of Pharisees in John by saying that "John's view of the Pharisees fits much of what we know about societies embedded in the Roman Empire. Religion is part of the political and social structure. The leaders of society are traditional, in this case the chief priests. . . . John pictures the Pharisees as the most successful and influential group."[79] Also prominent are the *Ioudaioi*, a term used interchangeably with Pharisees (9:15, 16, 18) and chief priests (18:13–14, 19, 28, 38). This much-debated term is difficult to translate and understand in one consistent way throughout the Gospel. In category 3 I have listed those references that show the *Ioudaioi* to be members of the local ruling elite, as allies of Rome. I will return to the term in chapter 6 below.

Category 4 presents retainers or agents of this ruling elite. Their primary purpose is to accomplish the elite's will and purposes. Though not matching the elite's wealth, power, and status, they nevertheless have some wealth, power, and status from association with the elite. Prominent in John's presentation and consistent with the Lenski-Kautsky model are military representatives and temple officials (priests, Levites, officers, temple money changers, sellers of temple supplies). In John's plot, the Jerusalem temple is the power base for the Jerusalem elite. Like the temple of Artemis and the imperial temples in Ephesus, the Jerusalem temple played a quite prominent and diverse role in Judean society, exercising vast economic, political, and societal power along with its religious functions.

The remaining categories concern nonelites, some 97 percent of the population. Missing from John's Gospel but present in the Lenski-Kautsky model are traders and merchants, who often accumulated some wealth. (I have included the temple traders in the retainers' category). Likewise, the Gospel identifies only a couple of artisans. Much more pervasive are the urban poor and rural peasants that are often referred to as "crowds" or people from a particular city, village, or area. These groups probably include merchants and artisans, but their presence is not emphasized. Slaves (category 7) are crucial to the workings of Roman society. The expendables (category 8) comprised, according to Lenski's estimate, between 5–15 percent of the population.[80] They typically included the physically damaged who could not support themselves, and those who tried to survive through crime and attacks on imperial society (thieves and bandits).

The diagram clarifies that the central conflict between Jesus on one hand and the Jerusalem and temple-based elite leadership allied with Rome (2:13–21) on the other hand is not primarily a religious conflict but concerns fundamental issues of societal power, order, and vision. It also highlights Jesus' interventions with the urban and rural poor and the expendables as actions that seek to transform the damage that the imperial structure causes. Overall it shows that John's narrative world participates in the hierarchical societal structures of the Roman Empire.

Evaluating the Interaction between John's Jesus-Believers and Roman Imperial Power in Ephesus: Persecution and Resistance?

Thus far in discussing synagogue communities (chap. 2) and Roman presence and power in Ephesus (chap. 3), I have suggested that for Jesus-believers, members of synagogue communities in Ephesus, there seems to be considerable participation and interaction with the urban context. Such an emphasis runs contrary to oft-repeated and popular scenarios in which Jesus-believers experience Roman persecution and the empire is understood to be in constant ferment, on the brink of violent revolt. To conclude this chapter, I will take up two questions: (1) Did Jesus-believers in Ephesus have to negotiate Roman power expressed in persecution? (2) Was violent revolt against Roman power a viable option for Jesus-believers?

Did Rome Persecute Jesus-Believers in Ephesus?

Some scholars have argued that Jesus-believers in Ephesus suffered official imperial persecution. This approach has suggested three possible scenarios: (1) persecution after separation from a synagogue when Jesus-believers were vulnerable with the loss of the protection of so-called Jewish *religio licita* status, (2) persecution by the emperor Domitian, and (3) persecution such as that attested in the correspondence between the provincial governor Pliny and the emperor Trajan. Aspects of the three scenarios are often intertwined; the first option often appears as the basis for the other two. I will describe each in turn and suggest that none of these three claims can be sustained.

1. As I indicated in chapter 2, some scholars have erroneously claimed that Judaism enjoyed a protected status of *religio licita,* whereby Rome guaranteed its religious liberty with charters of rights.[81] The separation of John's Jesus-group from a synagogue community (9:22; 12:42; 16:2), so the argument runs, left the group without the protection of these charters and persecuted by Rome for failure to participate in the imperial cult.[82] Yet this scenario fails, for several reasons:

- The scenario of the separation or expulsion of Jesus-believers from a synagogue is not sustainable, as I argued in chapter 2 above.

- There is no evidence for an official category of *religio licita* in the first century. The term originates with the Christian writer Tertullian (*Apol.* 21.1) late in the second century CE, a hundred years later than John's Gospel. No evidence attests that Rome approved certain religions like Judaism and protected them with a universal charter of rights. The notion of protection through charters is medieval in conception.[83] As I argued in chapter 2, following Rajak, Barclay, Trebilco, and others, the decrees that Josephus records in *Antiquities* 14 and 16 point to specific and atypical situations of tension between Jewish groups and local city elites. In crises, Jewish groups appealed to Rome for protection of their traditional practices. Josephus's data show that Rome occasionally intervened by imperial decree in some urban centers, including Ephesus in the first century BCE, to protect Jewish practices when requested. The basis for the protection did not lie in an appeal to a charter but to usual practice and civic order. In the normal scheme of things, synagogue communities negotiated their civic and imperial contexts with a mixture of participation and observance of traditional practices, as we saw in chapter 2. To leave a synagogue community (even if that scenario could be established for Jesus-believers) would not expose a group to a situation unprotected by a legal charter (there was none) and to persecution (there is no evidence). Rather, the group would have to negotiate its own place in the civic and imperial context.

- The argument presupposes that Jewish groups were uniquely alien and socially introverted, needing special legal protection in the hostile world. But as I argued in the last chapter, such a view is quite false. Contrary, for instance to Richey's claim, separation from a synagogue (if it occurred) need not mean separation from Judaism, and it by no means follows that John's Jesus-believers would no longer pay the tax imposed on Jews after the defeat of 70 CE.[84]

- Nor is there any evidence for Roman persecution of Jesus-believers in Ephesus in the last decades of the first century, as I will discuss below. Often cited in support, John 16:2, with its future tense and framing of "killing" as "offering worship/service," suggests a future scenario. The significance of the future tense seems to be that persecution will arise if the radical implications of the confession of Jesus as Messiah are pressed in daily living, thus comprising much greater detachment from Ephesian society.

2. A second scenario asserts that Domitian (81–96 CE) persecuted John's Jesus-believers.[85] This scenario raises two interrelated issues, one concerning the nature of Domitian's reign, and the other concerning evidence for claims of persecution. The two issues are connected: for some, the madder and more tyrannical one can present Domitian to be, the more likely his persecution of Jesus-believers! I will start with the more general picture and then take up the specific claims of persecution of Jesus-believers.

The nature of Domitian's rule has been much debated. The older view saw him as a mad and unrelentingly evil tyrant, who with vanity aggressively and uncompromisingly promoted the imperial cult and worship of himself. His "reign of terror" meant persecution of senators and Christians who did not pay him sufficient homage. In recent times this view has been challenged. It has been argued that the portrait of "Domitian the very bad tyrant" reflects not accurate historical analysis but the negative agenda of his detractors. After his death, a circle—including Pliny, Tacitus, Suetonius, who had successful careers under Domitian; and a century later, Dio Cassius—created and secured this image.[86] They malign Domitian as savage and cruel, scheming and lacking genuine motivation, mad and tyrannical, unbridled in passions and power hungry, alienated from his father, Vespasian (emperor, 69–79), and plotting against his older brother Titus (emperor, 79–81). They mock his military accomplishments in Germany as emperor, style his reign as one of disorder and slaughter, highlight his economic greed and incompetence, and claim that he is out of favor with the gods.[87]

Several factors suggest that this portrait owes more to the agenda of the writers than to historical reality. As Magie argues, "In these provinces there is little evidence of cruelty on the part of Domitian or even of exaggerated pretensions to grandeur.... In fact in his administration of the provinces Domitian seems to have shown both vigor and intelligence."[88] The negative accounts are also undermined by contradictions within their own works, by other sources including literary, epigraphic and numismatic evidence, and by references to the careers of various senators.[89] The negative presentations seem to reflect strained relationships between Domitian and the senate over senatorial power and over Domitian exiling and executing senators charged with conspiring against him.

Another major factor influencing this portrait includes the conventional practice of denigrating a predecessor as a foil for offering support to the new emperor, Trajan. Pliny, for instance, composed his *Panegyricus* warmly hailing the new emperor, Trajan, and contrasting him with the denigrated Domitian. Also at work seem to be the self-interested efforts of this group to establish loyalty to the new ruler, and to demonstrate support for his agenda of establishing a new age of liberty and senatorial power.[90] Yet more recently some have voiced reactions against this revisionist view and a renewed advocacy of the view of Domitian as a particularly ruthless and efficient oppressor.[91]

Assessing Domitian's rule is difficult because every emperor presided over a system created, as we have seen, to further the interests and well-being of the elite at the expense of the nonelite. Such a system breeds considerable struggle for power and its rewards among elites. Domitian was not innocent of participating in an oppressive system, but it seems dubious that he was significantly worse than other emperors. The accounts of his rule from Pliny, Tacitus, and Suetonius probably include some truth as well as exaggeration in support of the new emperor, Trajan, and in furtherance of their own careers. Either way, it does not increase the likelihood of his persecuting Jesus-believers.

The second issue involves the "evidence" for the claim that Domitian persecuted Jesus-believers. The "evidence" comes from the fourth-century Christian writer and bishop Eusebius. He identifies Irenaeus and Hegesippus, who wrote a century after Domitian, as sources for claims of persecution in Asia Minor, and he cites Melito, bishop of Sardis (late second century), for claiming that Domitian falsely accused Christians (*Hist. eccl.* 3.17–20; 4.26.9). There are several issues with dating Eusebius's information that render it dubious. The first is that Eusebius writes over two centuries after the time of Domitian. The second is that while we do not have the writings of Hegesippus and Melito independently of Eusebius, we do have Irenaeus's writings, so we can test Eusebius's appeal to Irenaeus. Writing a century after Domitian, Irenaeus mentions him only in relation to the date of the book of Revelation (written "almost in my own lifetime, at the end of Domitian's reign"; *Against Heresies* 5.30). Yet Irenaeus does not say anything about persecution. The failure of Irenaeus to confirm what Eusebius attributes to him suggests that Eusebius's claims about Hegesippus and Melito may not be accurate either. Eusebius's unreliability, the gap of about a century between Domitian's time and the time of these sources, and the silence of other writers—these all cast considerable doubts on claims of persecution.[92]

The situation for this supposed persecution is usually identified as Domitian's aggressive promotion of the imperial cult and worship of himself. It is usually claimed that his self-aggrandizing demand to be addressed as *dominus et deus* (Lord and God), the same phrase with which Thomas addresses the risen Jesus in John 20:28, exemplifies his aggressive and unyielding promotion of imperial cult observance that forced a confrontation with Christians.[93] But this claim is not convincing. Imperial cult observance had been well established in Ephesus for a century before the writing of John's Gospel, as we saw earlier in this chapter. And as the data cited above shows, local Ephesian elites actively participated in it. Moreover, Jesus-believers had in various ways negotiated the imperial cult for decades without reference to persecution. Participation in it was voluntary. It was not mandatory or decreed, though some social pressure was doubtless exerted in associations and civic observances. An emperor's active enforcement of observance and persecution of nonparticipants was neither necessary nor customary nor evidenced. The claim that Domitian demanded heightened devotion is also undercut by Ephesus's dedication of the imperial temple in 89/90 not to the one emperor Domitian alone, but to a collective imperial entity, the Sebastoi. Moreover, interface between the dedication of this temple with John 20:28 may be dubious since the dedications do not address Domitian as "Lord and God" but as emperor

(Αὐτοκράτορι, *Autokratori*).[94] This would be crassly insulting, and quickly remedied, if the claims about Domitian's demand to be so addressed were reliable. And when the Greek writers Dio Chrysostom (*Defense* [*Or. 45*] 1) and Dio Cassius (67.13.4) refer to Domitian as "Lord and God," they employ the Greek terms δεσπότης καὶ θεός (*despotēs kai theos*) not as in John 20:28, κύριος μου καὶ ὁ θεός μου (*kyrios mou kai ho theos mou*).

Richard Cassidy has offered a third persecution scenario.[95] He argues that John's Gospel addresses Christians in persecutory situations akin to that attested by the famed exchange of correspondence between Pliny, governor of the province of Pontus-Bithynia northwest of Asia, and the emperor Trajan around 112 CE (*Ep.* 10.96–97). Governor Pliny writes to the emperor because he does not know what to do with negative reports about Christians. Pliny does not describe persecution of Jesus-believers initiated by Rome or by imperial officials. Rather, the initiative comes from local people. Locals make sporadic reports against Christians to Pliny, though Pliny does not specify what their concern was. Pliny requires the reported to invoke the gods, and offer wine and incense to the emperor's image and images of the gods. This action suggests that the issue, at least in Pliny's mind, involves honoring the gods *with sacrifices* as much as the emperor. His concern with declining attendance at local temples supports this idea. It may also suggest that the complainants made their living in ways associated with temples, akin to the silversmiths of Artemis in Ephesus in Acts 19. The reports, though, do not concern Pliny enough to search out believers.

The localized nature of this activity warns against universalizing the scenario to the rest of Pliny's administrative area, the province of Bithynia-Pontus. Likewise, there is no evidence for Cassidy's claim that this scenario somehow illuminates what was happening in Ephesus, over which Pliny had no jurisdiction. No evidence links John and Pliny. And no evidence suggests that Christians in Ephesus encountered situations of persecution in the 90s akin to that described by Pliny some ten to twenty years later. In addition to these factors of geography (Bithynia-Pontus is not Asia) and chronology (some twenty years later), Pliny makes clear that part of his uncertainty in knowing how to respond, and a major reason for his writing to the emperor, is that there are no precedents to guide his response.[96]

Though persecution has often figured prominently in popular stereotypical scenarios of the early Christian movement, no evidence sustains these three scenarios. Persecution is not one of the means by which Rome asserted its power in late first-century Ephesus, and it does not comprise the central dynamic for the Gospel's complex interaction with the empire.

Did Anyone Revolt or Rebel against Roman Rule in Ephesus?

Often the Roman Empire is imagined, at least in popular circles aided by homiletically shaped Christian imagination, to be a seething mass of revolting malcontents. But the discussion above of Roman power and presence in late first-century CE Ephesus has not mentioned revolt or rebellion: it has presented a picture of considerable compliance. Is this picture accurate, or does it need modifying? Was everyone indeed happy with Roman rule, including all of John's Jesus-believers?[97]

In a discussion of opponents of Rome, Martin Goodman reports that ancient sources include few references to outbreaks of violent revolt:

> In those regions where no unrest is attested over long periods, any one of three explanations of such non-attestation can be assumed. Either trouble occurred but was not reported, or the provincials concerned were essentially happy with their lot, or they were unhappy but did not dare to revolt. According to the standard accounts of the Roman Empire, the middle explanation, that of contentment, is usually attributed to those subjects of Rome in provinces such as Asia.[98]

Clifford Ando offers an example of this middle explanation, the "everyone-happily-submitted-to-Rome" approach. In seeking to account for the empire's stability and the supposed quietude and obedience of loyal provincials, Ando posits "a slowly realized consensus regarding Rome's right to maintain social order and to reestablish a normative political culture."[99] He observes that there were relatively few violent or military revolts against Rome's rule in the provinces of the empire. The Jewish revolt of 66–70 CE, which resulted in the destruction of Jerusalem and its temple and reassertion of Roman control by various means (including the tax on Jews, which I discussed in chap. 2), provides a reasonably rare outbreak of violent protest. This absence of revolts, in Ando's view, evidences the essential happiness of compliant provincials: "The scarcity of revolts among those residents provides the best measure of that compliance. . . . Residents demonstrated their faith in the system when they played by its rules and attempted to exploit them."[100] Throughout his interesting and informative study, Ando outlines various ways by which Rome promoted its ideology and practice of beneficent rule and by which provincials willingly acquiesced to a "culture of loyalism."

Although a full discussion of Ando's work is not possible here, there are good reasons for not accepting his unnuanced claim that provincials negotiated Roman power by happily embracing it, without at least recognizing that such a claim is not the whole picture. One fundamental problem concerns his lack of attention to questions of status or social location and to gender.[101] Much of Ando's data originates from or concerns the behaviors of provincial elites (males?), yet he readily generalizes it to nonelites in describing "the faith of fifty million people."[102] The focus on sources originating from the elites is understandable given the weighting of the historical dice. And I have suggested above that provincial elites in urban centers like Ephesus had good reason to cooperate with Rome, and Rome had good reasons to encourage and reward cooperation. As allies they had vested interests in, as well as better chances of, maintaining a hierarchical societal structure from which both Roman and provincial/Ephesian elites benefited greatly at the expense of the rest of society.

But while Ando may have given us a helpful study of *elite* "provincial loyalty," his readiness to generalize it to all provincials is questionable. Elites had the most to gain from, as well as the opportunity and means for, ready cooperation with and participation in Rome's rule. Nonelites, as Ramsay MacMullen underlines, often focused on survival.[103] It is not adequate to assume, even if one can cite occasional evidence,[104] that the ruling minority speaks for the ruled majority.

Moreover, Ando's framing of the interaction between Rome and the provinces is too limited. He naively sets up an antithesis of compliance or (rare and local) violent revolt.

Finding little evidence for the latter, he concludes for compliance, asking, "In short, what induced quietude rather than rebellion?"[105] But the question is inadequately posed because it leaves unconsidered the possibility that nonelites (and elites for that matter) might negotiate Roman power in numerous other ways.[106] Anticipating the following discussions of postcolonial approaches (e.g., Homi Bhabha) and the work on peasant societies by James Scott below, absent is consideration of various forms of nonviolent dissent, mimicry, flattery, calculated acts of (self-protective) resistance, hybridity, and fantasies of revenge, not to mention the recognition that such negotiations might be simultaneous occurrences. I will (below) return to these options, which do not fit into Ando's limited alternatives. Ando tries to secure his false antithesis of violence or compliance by dismissing other possibilities such as the "arrogance" of patronizing "subject populations with deterministic ideologies of rebellion" (67), or as regrettable and anachronistic "cynicism" that does not take elite Roman claims at face value.[107] It is neither arrogance nor cynicism to employ a hermeneutic of suspicion in considering the claims and practices of a self-benefiting ruling elite—what we would call "spin"—and in attending to the experience of the majority subjugated. Nor is it arrogant or cynical or patronizing to fill in some of the huge gaps in our sources, tentatively, with insights from other studies of the various and simultaneous ways in which powerless groups negotiate the powerful.

These inadequacies in Ando's approach, nevertheless, emphasize that though elites had much to gain from actively cooperating with Rome's power, there is also evidence that some elites did a lot more than simply happily comply. We have previously observed that the Jews Philo and Josephus provide good examples of complex elite negotiation with Roman power. So too do the actions of the leading citizens of Ephesus who in the 20s CE protested over the heads of the proconsuls Gaius Silanus and Lucilius Capito to the senate and emperor in Rome and used judicial means to have them removed from office. Ando's work requires that we attend to the question of how we might gain some access to elite and nonelite provincial negotiations of Roman power, including the more contestive negotiation evident in John's rhetoric of distance, beyond the "official" or public record we have described above. Three theoretical frameworks from sociolinguistics, peasant studies, and postcolonial studies will help us.

M. A. K. Halliday and Antilanguage

The sociolinguist M. A. K. Halliday has used the concepts of antilanguage and antisociety to discuss the distinctive language and communal experience of alternative and countercommunitarian groups alienated from and alternative to the rest of society.[108] He describes an antisociety as "a society set up within another society as a conscious alternative to it. It is a mode of resistance."[109] It has its own system of values, behaviors, sanctions, rewards, and punishments that differ significantly from the dominant society. An antisociety generates its own way of talking that Halliday calls an antilanguage. This antilanguage reflects a "form of closed community." It functions to secure "inner solidarity under pressure" and is both a reflection of and source of an "alternative identity." The distinctive antilanguage is a "reality-generating system" that socializes community members into a different way of experiencing and understanding the world as members of a community in opposition to and tension with the rest of society.[110] The antisociety's antilanguage functions to "express, symbolize, and maintain [its] social order."[111]

Readers of John's Gospel have long observed its distinctive and dualistic way of speaking. Halliday's approach suggests that John's Gospel is an example of this sort of antilanguage, which I have identified throughout as John's rhetoric of distance.[112] The Gospel's distinctive, dualistic, stark either-or language is usually understood to reflect and maintain an alternative identity and understanding of the world, an antisociety in some tension with and counter to dominant values. The Gospel's language has thus been interpreted as reflecting, reinforcing, and explaining the societal alienation experienced by John's community in being expelled from the synagogue.

But our analyses above of this expulsion theory and of Jewish and Christian engagement in late first-century Asian society suggest that with evidence for considerable levels of social participation, the societal experience of alienation may be much less likely than previously thought. Rather, the experience of alienation seems to be more entexted in John's antilanguage than comprise societal interaction, which seems to be marked by considerable accommodation. If this context is correct, the force and starkness of John's antilanguage would function not to reinforce and explain the alienation of an existing antisociety but to create an antisociety. The antilanguage counters levels of accommodation that are considered to be too great. The rhetoric of distance creates societal boundaries, establishes clarity of identity, and urges distance among those who the writer or writers think lack boundaries, clarity, and distance. In terms of this approach, the Gospel's rhetoric of distance or antilanguage provides a rhetorical strategy for negotiating Rome's world by challenging the current practices of Jesus-believers and creating greater societal distance.

James C. Scott: Domination and the Arts of Resistance

When power is asserted, resistance is inevitable.[113] If this sociological maxim is true, we would expect some forms of resistance to play some role in provincial negotiation of imperial power. Thus Ando's simple binary of peaceful acquiescence or violent rebellion does not exhaust all options for negotiating the empire and does not sufficiently recognize the complexities and nuances of multiple forms of negotiation. The work of cultural anthropologist and political scientist James Scott elaborates the diversity of forms—violent and nonviolent, open and hidden, direct and masked, onstage and offstage, public and private—that resistance can take among dominated groups.[114] Scott argues that the absence of violence should not be mistakenly equated with the absence of resistance.

Scott uses the term "public transcripts" to denote the "open interaction between subordinates and those who dominate." From the perspective of the dominant, this interaction is designed to convey the sense of a stable, "natural," and immutable societal and cosmic order, to awe, impress, and cower the subordinated, and to bolster those who dominate.[115] Scott identifies three spheres of domination by elites, all of which are evident in our (above) discussion of the manifestations of Rome's power in Ephesus. Elites exercise *material domination* that exacts agricultural production through taxation, services, and labor. The hard manual work of nonelites and the coerced extractions of production sustain the elite's extravagant and elegant elite way of life. Second is *status domination* that deeply impacts and damages the personal well-being of the subjugated.[116] Social and economic practices, rituals, interactions, and punishments ensure humiliation, indignities, insults, assaults on dignity, and forced deference. Status domination deprives people of dignity. It degrades and humiliates. It exacts not only agricultural production but an enormous personal toll of anger, resentment, and learned inferiority. Third, elites employ *ideological domination* by utilizing a set of convictions and/or narrative that justifies and expresses their domination, privilege, self-benefiting rule, and societal inequality. Frequently they assert that the elite's political, economic, societal, and cultural order and practices are the will of the gods. Ideological domination or imperial theology seeks to persuade the subordinated that social hierarchy and exploitation are both what the god/s intend and simply the unchangeable way things are. This ideological domination comprises the "Great Tradition," the official version of reality.

To negotiate this context in which direct and open confrontations with power prove very dangerous, nonelites ensure survival by wearing masks of obedience and playing the roles that the public transcript assigns to them. Yet, Scott argues, apparently compliant behavior is ambiguous. Apparently compliant behavior can mask and conceal resistance. Off-stage, where there exists both a "social space insulated from control, surveillance, and repression" along with effective human agents who spread the discourse of dissent,[117] a "hidden transcript of indignation" develops that embraces both discourse and practices.[118] This hidden transcript reveals that the public transcript is not the whole story.[119] While material domination might be met with *public* actions of demonstrations, boycotts, or strikes, the hidden transcript comprises disguised, calculated, self-protective acts of resistance such as grumbling, foot-dragging, poaching, pilfering, sabotage, arson, evasion, anonymous threats. While status domination might be met with *public* actions that assert through speech, gesture, or dress the worth of the subordinated and attack the status symbols of the elite, the hidden transcript comprises gossip and rumor, slander, insider gestures of defiance, coded talk, jokes, tales of revenge, rituals of aggression, and the protection of autonomous social space, where dignity is asserted. While ideological domination might be met with *public* defiance or confrontations, the hidden transcript negates the ruling ideology by developing a dissident subculture with millennialist visions, myths of social banditry and class heroes, "world-upside-down" imagery, alternative egalitarian patterns of social interaction, and myths of good rulers or times before the current ruler. Over against the Great Tradition develops a Little Tradition, or counterideology, that narrates an alternative way of societal being.

Scott sums up something of this sort of protest with a proverb whose origin he attributes to Ethiopia: "when the great lord passes [or the general or the emperor or the landowner or the governor or the master], the wise peasant bows deeply and silently farts."[120] The public act of bowing seems to express appropriate deference. But apparent compliance is qualified by the offensive and dishonoring act of passing gas. This nonviolent act, though, is hidden, disguised, anonymous, shielding the identity of the one who dissents. If other peasants are present, the communal context further protects the protestor. The action certainly is not going to change the system in which the nonelites have no access to power, but it does express dissent and anger. It affirms the peasant's dignity as one who refuses to be completely subjected. It attests the "hidden transcript," the much larger web of resistance to and dissent from the elite's societal order and version of reality, which is disguised by acts of apparent compliance, the bowing. It points to a vision of human dignity and interaction that is an alternative to the elite's "public transcript," or official version of how society is to be run.

In this matrix of interaction between the powerful and the subordinated, I am suggesting that John's Gospel comprises part of a "hidden transcript of indignation" that originates from some among the group of Jesus-believers in Ephesus. It is not a public writing addressed to the elite or to the public in general. It is written from and for communities of believers in Jesus, who was crucified by the empire. It challenges, I am arguing, a different way of negotiating Roman power: active participation in it. Such participation seems to be regarded as overaccommodation to and excessive at-home-ness in Rome's world. The Gospel text emphasizes the conflict that inevitably occurs between on one hand the Roman Empire, committed to preserving the status quo, and on the other hand Jesus the Messiah, revealer of God's life-giving purposes, and his believers; the text does so by telling the story of Jesus, who conflicted significantly with the Jerusalem-centered and Rome-allied elite and was crucified by the Roman governor Pilate. It frames this story with an eschatological dualism contrasting God and the devil, truth and falseness, life and death. The Gospel story's antilanguage seeks to guide Jesus-believers in negotiating Rome's world by challenging what it regards as overaccommodation, by distancing them from it, and by creating an antisociety that reflects a different cosmic order.

Postcolonial Studies

Scott's approach can be linked to the diverse field of postcolonial studies.[121] Nearly everything about this approach is contested, including its name and its applicability to Johannine studies; a comprehensive discussion is not possible here.[122] It is sufficient to recognize that the term "postcolonial," influenced by the contemporary experience of the continuing legacy of European imperialism, denotes the examination of the imperializing experience, its means, dynamics, impact, and legacy. It thus provides the broad framework for our discussion of John's Gospel as a text of imperial negotiation. More specifically, Sugirtharajah describes postcolonialism as "an interventionist instrument which refuses to take the dominant reading as an uncomplicated representation of the past and introduces an alternative reading."[123] In chapter 1 I argued that dominant readings of John's Gospel as nonpolitical, religious, and concerned with only one social entity (a synagogue) are far too uncomplicated and inadequate representations of the past. Moreover, I am arguing that dominant readings of Roman power such as Ando's, that residents of Asia and Ephesus found Roman rule quite acceptable, are also too uncomplicated. One of the alternative readings troubling this scenario is John's Gospel. Said has emphasized a "contrapuntal reading" of imperial sources that engages both the official discourse as well as resistant discourse and the interactions between the two.[124] John's Gospel is resistant discourse. This study provides a contrapuntal reading of John's Gospel in two senses. First, it reads John as a largely resistant discourse (marked of course also by some accommodation as well as imitation) that contests the dominant view of Rome's empire as benign and beneficial. Second, this contrapuntal reading sees John as a work that seeks to disrupt significant levels of accommodation to the empire evident among many (some?) Jesus-believers.

Accordingly, postcolonial studies especially focus on the experiences of the subjugated's engagement with or negotiation of the massive power differential between the dominating imperial power and the subjugated locals. Involved are factors of race, class, gender, culture, and political, economic, societal, religious, and cultural dimensions. Postcolonial perspectives have unmasked the various means by which imperial powers often mask their imposition of far-reaching control, disguise the tyrannical nature of power relations, and silence local and dissenting voices. At the heart of postcolonial discussion is consideration of the experience, strategies, and effects of power—political, economic, societal, cultural, religious, military—over minds, bodies, resources, societal interactions, cultural expressions, institutions, media, the past and the future, and so forth. This analysis of the means by which power is exerted, control disguised, wealth extracted, and "normality" defined unveils the exploitation and oppression that comprise the long-lasting cost and destructive human face of subjugation.

Accordingly, postcolonial work sets the imperialized's cultural history, experience, voices, and texts at the center. A significant element of this task involves identifying the inevitable, various, complex evaluations formulated by local populations as they negotiate imperial power and its representatives. Such a context is volatile as traditions and cultures interact in complex ways that are simultaneously creative, contentious, compromised, and contested. While resistance usually accompanies the exertion of power, we cannot assume it to be pervasive and/or monolithic or even, as Ando mistakenly posits, violent in expression. Local evaluations of imperial power, as we have already seen above, include self-benefiting accommodation, cooperation and/or co-optation, self-protective compliance, and mimicry, as well as calculated and disguised forms of resistance, fantasies of revenge and destruction, and open protest (nonviolent and violent) that directly confronts the ruling power. This "catalog" is not to suggest that provincials chose one means of interaction, but rather illustrates a complex range of simultaneous interactions and negotiations among elite and nonelite.

Such diverse negotiations of imperial power disqualify overly simple binaries of domination and subjugation, exploitation and deprivation, power and resistance, oppression and injustice, good and bad—as apt as they often seem to be or as appealing as we might want them to be. Such simplicity is deficient not only because imperial control is experienced in different ways by groups of differing societal status and interests (and not always as something to be resisted, as we have seen), but also because imperial control is effected not only through force, intimidation, and spin, but also through complex and disguised means such as alliances, client kings, interdependence, patronage, calculated benefits, and self-beneficial euergetism. These strategies often benefited the subordinated in some ways, thereby mixing gift with obligation, benefits with exploitation, appreciation with resentment, complicity with coercion, enablement with dependency, accommodation with dissent.

Fanon illustrates, for example, the interaction of envy and mimicry in the pervasive ambivalency or "permanent tension" of the oppressed. "The settler's world is a hostile world, which spurns the native, but at the same time is a world of which he is envious."[125] Envy translates into desire for the power and benefits of the oppressor's world. Mimicry seeks to gain that which is hated and despised. Mimicry means the quest for countermastery in various forms.[126] This hybridity of ambivalent and ambiguous interactions between oppressor and oppressed interweaves subjection with opportunity, damage with benefits, opposition with accommodation, resistance with co-option, submission with critique, participation with alternative visions.[127]

John's Gospel, I am suggesting, emerges from, is a textual expression of, and is a product of such interactions between subjugated and dominant power. Often its dualistic framing suggests the simple binary of opposition to coercive power, which postcolonial studies rightly resists. The negotiations of empire highlighted by postcolonial studies, though, provide a more complex framework for considering the particular negotiations in which the Gospel narrative engages in its imperial context among elites and nonelites.

For Example: Mission

John's text, narrating the story of a crucified provincial, expresses the voice of a dominated provincial who "writes back" while surrounded by empire. A brief example from John's Gospel illustrates the hybridity highlighted by postcolonial studies and the interaction between hidden and public transcripts discussed by Scott. Rome's public transcript presented itself as a city with a divinely originating and sanctioned mission. Cicero described Rome as "light to the whole world" (*Cat.* 4.11), in which provincials such as Jews and Syrians were born for servitude (*Prov. cons.* 10). Livy (1.16) recalls Proculus Julius's announcement that Romulus "the father of the Roman city" descended from heaven and commanded, "Go and declare to the Romans the will of Heaven that my Rome shall be the capital of the world, so let them cherish the art of war, and let them know and teach their children that no human strength can resist Roman arms."

Virgil exhibits the same themes of divine sanction for Rome's worldwide mission carried out with military might and marked by the imposition of "peace" and "justice." Venus reminds Jupiter, "Surely it was your promise that from them some time, as the years rolled on, the Romans were to arise; from them, even from Teucer's restored line, should come rulers to hold the sea and all lands beneath their sway." Jupiter responds that Romulus "shall call the people Romans, set no bounds in space and time, but give [them] empire without end." Juno will "with me cherish the Romans, lords of the world, and nation of the toga." Augustus Caesar will emerge and be welcomed "to heaven laden with Eastern spoils. . . . Then wars shall cease and savage ages soften; hoary Faith and Vesta . . . will give laws. The gates of war . . . shall be closed" (*Aeneid* 1.234–237, 274–282, 289–294). Subsequently Jupiter sends Mercury with a message that Italy will "bring all the world beneath his laws" (4.231). In the underworld Anchises, after previewing subsequent Roman history including the ever-expanding empire of Augustus Caesar (6.791–797) commissions his son Aeneas, "You Roman, be sure to rule the world (be these your arts), to crown peace with justice, to spare the vanquished and to crush the proud" (6.851–853).

In the first century CE, Seneca has the emperor Nero contemplate his divinely given role as Rome's ruler, "Have I of all mortals found favor with heaven and been chosen to serve on earth as vicar of the gods? I am the arbiter of life and death for the nations; it rests in my power what each man's [*sic*] lot and state shall be." (*On Mercy*, 1.1; Josephus endorses Rome's worldwide dominance as God's will (*J.W.* 4.370; 5.60–61, 362–368, 376–378). In his second-century *Roman Oration* 103, the orator Aristides from Asia Minor celebrates Rome's accomplishment in ensuring that "universal order entered as a brilliant light over the private and public affairs of humans, laws appeared, and the altars of gods received faith (πίστιν, *pistin*).[128]

These are but a few literary examples of Rome's claim to a divinely given mission to employ military might to conquer the world and to order it according to its laws. As we have seen, this mission is also proclaimed throughout the empire by Roman personnel, coins, buildings, inscriptions, and so forth. This is Scott's "great tradition," the official view of reality, the dominant discourse of the Roman world and very evident, it seems, in Ephesus. The existing evidence suggests that members of synagogues in Ephesus, including Jesus-believers, participate in this world and have substantially accommodated to it.

Not surprisingly, given the pervasiveness of mimicry in contexts of domination, John's Gospel is also quite concerned with divinely given mission. The mission presented in John's Gospel can be seen as an alternative that contests Roman claims to sovereignty because it asserts God's life. This mission is part of a little tradition, hidden discourse, an alternative reading, antilanguage, a contestive view of reality. Yet while it is a contestive mission, the fact that an alternative mission is asserted attests the mimicry and the desire for countermastery that pervades imperial contexts. This is the ambiguity, the hybridity, of simultaneously living in and against empire.

John's mission centers on Jesus, whom God has charged to reveal God and God's purposes (1:18). God is presented as the creator of the world and thus its sovereign (1:1–3). Jesus is light for the world (1:8–9; 3:19–21; 8:12; 9:5). His mission is possible because he was with God in the beginning before creation (1:1–3). God has revealed Godself to Jesus (1:18; 5:20; 8:38, 40; 12:50; 14:8–9) and commissioned Jesus to reveal God. God's revealing activity in Jesus is expressed fundamentally by two key verbs: "send" and "give." The narrative uses the verb "send"[129] over forty times to describe God as the sender of Jesus. This sending is expressed in God's sealing (6:27) and consecrating (10:36) of Jesus. God initiates, authorizes, and guarantees the revelation of God and God's life-giving purposes in Jesus' ministry. God "gives" or entrusts to Jesus "all things" (3:35; 13:3; 17:7), including judgment (5:22, 26–27), life (4:10, 14; 5:26; 6:27, 33; 10:28; 17:2), actions/works (5:36; 17:4; cf. 14:10), words (12:49; 17:8), God's name (17:11–12), and the cup of Jesus' suffering (18:11). God gives Jesus as an expression of God's love for "the world" (3:16). The divine purposes that Jesus reveals can be summed up in the term "life," as we saw in chapter 1 (above) in the Gospel's statement of purpose in 20:30–31 (cf. 3:16; 10:10).

In subsequent chapters I will elaborate the relationship between God and Jesus, as well as Jesus' mission of revealing God's life. In that discussion I will argue that Jesus' actions of providing abundant nutrition (2:1–11; 6:1–14) and healing and wholeness for the sick and suffering (4:46–54; 5:1–9; chaps. 9; 11) manifest God's life-giving purposes. Inadequate nutrition and diseases of deficiency and contagion result from the inequities of the imperial system that I have described in this chapter. Jesus' actions roll back and repair this imperial damage as he asserts God's purposes for humanity. Jesus' actions and the Gospel narratives mimic elite abundance.

Nor does Jesus' mission end with him. He commissions his disciples, "As the Father has sent me, so I send you" (John 20:21). Jesus' sending of the disciples is modeled on and continues God's sending of Jesus. Thus the antisociety of Jesus-believers that the Gospel's story seeks to shape is to continue Jesus' mission of manifesting God's life-giving purposes in the midst of Rome's empire. This link between God sending Jesus and Jesus sending disciples and between Jesus' mission and the disciples' mission confirms Jesus' earlier promise: "The one who believes in me will also do the works that I do and will do greater works than these" (14:12). Antilanguage creates an antisociety. The Gospel's rhetoric of distance urges less accommodation to imperial society.

There is much here that could be developed. Important for this discussion is to notice the interplay of similarity and difference, imitation and opposition, mimicry and resistance in the interaction between Rome's mission and Jesus' mission. Both Rome and Jesus have divinely sanctioned missions (18:36–37). Both have missions of light that extend to the whole world (3:16). Both seek to shape the world in certain ways. Both assert sovereignty. But Jesus' mission seems significantly different in means and goals. There is no reference to military power: Jesus actually renounces it (18:36–37). There is no forcible imposition of one's will. Jesus' mission community is not restricted to one ethnicity. Its goal is not subjugation but is presented as wholeness and abundant life. The mission of Jesus and his disciples collides with, contests, and repairs Rome's mission.

Yet mimicry lurks. John's rhetoric mimics Rome's mission in announcing dire penalties for resisting Jesus' mission and failing to participate in it. Those who fail to commit to it are condemned (3:18), exposed as evil (3:20), judged (5:22), revealed to be liars and murderers (8:44–47), and consigned to death (3:16; 5:24). Even in forming an antisociety to negotiate Roman power with an alternative existence, imperial society is pervasive.

Conclusion

In this chapter I have with broad brush strokes outlined the structure of the Roman Empire and identified some quite specific ways in which it was encountered in Ephesus, especially among elites. I have also used the work of M. A. K. Halliday, James Scott, and some aspects of postcolonial criticism to complexify Ando's picture of all provincials happily participating in Roman rule, suggesting that the interaction between the Ephesians and Roman power, both elites and nonelites, was much more multifaceted, spanning participation, compliance, and some covert and calculated (nonviolent) resistance.

Included in this depiction are the Jesus-believers. I am suggesting that given a picture of significant, though by no means one-dimensional positive interaction in the empire, their lives are marked by significant accommodation. Halliday's work on antilanguage and antisocieties, Scott's study of "peasant" negotiations of power, and postcolonial criticism warn us, though, that their interaction is likely to be more complex. These discussions also help us to locate John's Gospel in the complex matrix of negotiations that constitute interactions between imperial power and subjugated provincials. They direct our attention to contestive voices in imperial contexts, and to those who present an alternative reality, even one that is significantly shaped by imperial realities. I am suggesting that John's Gospel is a "hidden transcript," part of a debate among Jesus-believers over imperial negotiation, yet contestive of imperial power, whose rhetoric of distance tries to create lines between the empire and faithful followers of Jesus, urging Jesus-believers to a less-accommodated and to a more-distinctive way of life as an antisociety or alternative community.

In the next chapter we will consider one way in which the Gospel draws this line. I will identify a significant means of negotiating Roman power that I have not yet discussed. Evidence indicates that to assert their power and presence in Rome's world, elite Greeks and faithful Jews made a "turn to the past," recalling sacred traditions, making present the past. I will argue that John's rhetoric of distance also employs and imitates this "turn to the past," thereby evidencing its significant societal participation even while it resists such accommodation among Jesus-believers.

Notes

1. Van Tilborg, *Reading John*, 3.

2. Ibid., 3.

3. For discussion, see Anthony D. Macro, "The Cities of Asia Minor under the Roman Imperium," *ANRW* II.7.2 (1980): 658–97; Guy M. Rogers, *The Sacred Identity of Ephesos* (London: Routledge, 1991); P. Scherrer, "The City of Ephesos: From the Roman Period to Late Antiquity" (with map), and L. Michael White, "Urban Development and Social Change in Imperial Ephesos," in *Ephesos: Metropolis of Asia,* ed. Helmut Koester (Valley Forge, PA: Trinity Press International, 1995), 1–79; Paul Trebilco, "Asia," in *The Book of Acts in Its First Century Setting,* ed. David Gill and Conrad Gempf (Grand Rapids: Eerdmans, 1994), 2:291–362; on Ephesos, 302–57 with a focus on Artemis; Sjef van Tilborg, *Reading John*, passim.

4. For a good overview of several models, see Dennis Duling, "Empire: Theories, Methods, Models," in *Gospel of Matthew in Its Roman Imperial Context*, ed. J. Riches and D. C. Sim (London: T&T Clark International, 2005), 49–74.

5. John H. Elliott, "Social-Scientific Criticism of the New Testament: More on Methods and Models," in *Social-Scientific Criticism of the New Testament and Its Social World,* ed. J. H. Elliott, Semeia 35 (Decatur, GA: Scholars Press, 1986), 1–33.

6. John Kautsky, *The Politics of Aristocratic Empires* (Chapel Hill: University of North Carolina Press, 1982); Gerhard Lenski, *Power and Privilege: A Theory of Social Stratification* (Chapel Hill: University of North Carolina Press, 1984).

7. Philo (*Spec. Laws* 3.159–163) narrates an account of excessively cruel tax collection.

8. C. R. Whittaker, *Land, City and Trade in the Roman Empire,* Collected Studies 408 (Aldershot: Variorum, 1993); Helen Parkins, ed., *Roman Urbanism: Beyond the Consumer City* (London: Routledge, 1997), esp. H. Parkins, "The Consumer City Domesticated? The Roman City in Elite Economic Strategies," 83–111.

9. Van Tilborg, *Reading John*, 100–109; royal officials, high priests and priestesses, patrons, council members, rulers/proconsuls.

10. One elite figure, Cato the Younger, by one estimate enjoyed revenues of 550–600 sesterces a day from property valued at 4 million sesterces, while an unskilled laborer earned 1–3 sesterces (Matt 20:2).

11. For references to slaves (domestic, temple) and the freed (by private citizens and the emperor), van Tilborg, *Reading John*, 86–90; for workers, including various kinds of sellers (of

food, clothing, wool), porters and gardeners, construction workers, fishermen, grain producers, viticulturists, soldiers, and teachers, see ibid., 90–100. Van Tilborg connects these occupations to references in John's Gospel; see the table below.

12. Peter Garnsey, *Food and Society in Classical Antiquity* (Cambridge: Cambridge University Press, 1999), xi.

13. Macro, "Cities," 690.

14. Peter Brunt, "The Romanization of the Local Ruling Classes in the Roman Empire," in *Roman Imperial Themes* (Oxford: Clarendon, 1990), 277.

15. C. R. Whittaker, "The Poor," in *The Romans*, ed. Andrea Giardina (Chicago: University of Chicago Press, 1993), 272–99; Peter Garnsey, *Cities, Peasants and Food in Classical Antiquity* (Cambridge: Cambridge University Press, 1988), 28–44, 91–106, 134–50; Ramsay MacMullen, *Roman Social Relations* (New Haven: Yale University Press, 1974). For wealthy elite disdaining the poor, see Cicero, *De officiis* 1.150; 2.52–56; *Ad Atticum* 1.16; Juvenal, *Sat.* 3.147–53; Tacitus, *Hist.* 1.4.

16. Steven Friesen, "Poverty in Pauline Studies: Beyond the So-called New Consensus," *JSNT* 26 (2004): 323–61, esp. 347; with responses from John Barclay, "Poverty in Pauline Studies: A Response to Steven Friesen," 363–66, and Peter Oakes, "Constructing Poverty Scales for Graeco-Roman Studies: A Response to Steven Friesen's 'Poverty in Pauline Studies,'" 367–71.

17. David Magie, "Centralization and Prosperity under the Flavians," in *Roman Rule in Asia Minor to the End of the Third Century after Christ* (Princeton: Princeton University Press, 1950), 1:566–92.

18. Ibid., 582.

19. Ibid., 582–84; repeated, for instance, in Paul Trebilco, *Early Christians*, 15–16.

20. Quite helpful is Rodney Stark, "Urban Chaos and Crisis: The Case of Antioch," in *The Rise of Christianity: A Sociologist Reconsiders History* (Princeton: Princeton University Press, 1996), 147–62.

21. A. Scobie, "Slums, Sanitation, and Mortality in the Roman World," *Klio* 68 (1986): 399–433; Whittaker, "Poor," 288.

22. For some discussion, see Peter A. Brunt, "Laus Imperii," in *Paul and Empire: Religion and Power in Roman Imperial Society*, ed. R. A. Horsley (Harrisburg, PA: Trinity Press International, 1997), 25–35.

23. Magie, "Centralization," 567–70.

24. A famous example involves the obstacles encountered by Philo and his Alexandrian delegation in seeking redress against the governor Flaccus. See Philo, *Against Flaccus*.

25. Tacitus, *Annals* 3.66–69. He was allowed voluntary exile on the island of Cythnus.

26. Tacitus, *Annals* 4.15.

27. Kautsky, *Politics*, 159–82.

28. For discussion, Magie, "Centralization," 567; Brent Shaw, "Roman Taxation," in *Civilization of the Ancient Mediterranean*, ed. M. Grant and R. Kitzinger (New York: Charles Scribner's Sons, 1988), 2.809–27; Macro, "Cities," 667–68, 677–80; Stephen Mitchell's discussion of taxation in relation to the ancient economy, city and country relations, grain and transport, supplies for troops, and coinage in Anatolia often references Asia: *Anatolia: Land, Men, and Gods in Asia Minor* (Oxford: Clarendon, 1993), 1:241–57.

29. Stephen Dyson, "Native Revolts in the Roman Empire," *Historia* 20 (1971): 239–74.

30. Cf. the speech given to Agrippa II, arguing against revolt because, in part, Rome's military was too powerful; Josephus, *J.W.* 2.356–57, 361–64.

31. Van Tilborg, *Reading John*, 98–99. He notes four inscriptions (IEph 6.2069; 6.2274C; 7.1.3291A; 7.2.4112) and a dedication of a statue erected by eight soldiers (IEph 3.680).

32. Displayed in the Ephesus collection in the British Museum, June 2006.

33. For an image, Helmut Koester, ed., *Cities of Paul: Images and Interpretations from the Harvard New Testament Archaeology Project* (Minneapolis: Fortress, 2005), under "Ephesos."

34. Richard Saller, *Personal Patronage under the Early Empire* (Cambridge: Cambridge University Press, 1982); Andrew Wallace-Hadrill, ed., *Patronage in Ancient Society* (London: Routledge, 1989).

35. IEph 6.2037, 2061–2063.

36. Displayed in the Ephesus collection in the British Museum, June 2006.

37. Simon Price, *Rituals and Power: The Roman Imperial Cult in Asia Minor* (Cambridge: Cambridge University Press, 1984); Carter, *Matthew and Empire*, 9–34.

38. V. Nutton, "The Beneficial Ideology," in *Imperialism in the Ancient World*, ed. Peter Garnsey and C. R. Whittaker (Cambridge: Cambridge University Press, 1978), 209–21, esp. 210–12. Of course, rhetoric could also be critical of governing powers and tyrants, especially by employing "figured speech"; see F. Ahl, "The Art of Safe Criticism in Greece and Rome," *American Journal of Philology* 105 (1984): 174–208. Ahl omits discussion of Philo; see Goodenough, *Politics of Philo*.

39. See C. Habicht, "New Evidence on the Province of Asia," *JRS* 65 (1975): 64–91; G. P. Burton, "Proconsuls, Assizes, and the Administration of Justice under the Empire," *JRS* 65 (1975): 92–106; Macro, "Cities," 670–72. A conventus could also function as an administrative area for tax collection, army recruitment, and the composition of the provincial assembly. Assize tours also provided opportunities for proconsuls to intervene in civic financial and administrative matters.

40. Peter Garnsey, *Social Status and Legal Privilege in the Roman Empire* (Oxford: Clarendon, 1970).

41. Rogers, *Sacred Identity*, 141.

42. Analyzing inscriptions from Ephesus, van Tilborg (*Reading John*) distinguishes "the names of the Romans (from Rome or more generally from the West) from the people from Ephesus" (14–16), notes the presence and influence of imperial freedmen (89–90, 100), the presence of Roman noblemen with military careers (17, 98–99), and interactions between the proconsul (appointed for a year) and the city (107–9).

43. Brunt, "Romanization," 267–81; Macro, "Cities," 660–63, 678–89 (civic administration and magistracies), 682–84 (intercity rivalry), 684–85 (elite wealth and civic euergetism), 692–93 (rhetoric); Ramsay MacMullen, "Notes on Romanization," in *Changes in the Roman Empire: Essays on the Ordinary* (Princeton: Princeton University Press, 1990), 56–66.

44. The *koinon* of Asia authorized the setting up of Augustus's *Res gestae* ([list of] things done) on monumental inscriptions in several major cities of Asia in the second decade of the first century CE. White, "Urban Development," 30, n5.

45. Clifford Ando, *Imperial Ideology and Provincial Loyalty in the Roman Empire* (Berkeley: University of California Press, 2000), 73–273; on imperial images in Ephesus, 232–33; van Tilborg, *Reading John*, 192–96; Paul Zanker, *The Power of Images in the Age of Augustus* (Ann Arbor: University of Michigan Press, 1988).

46. Steven Friesen, *Twice Neokoros: Ephesus, Asia, and the Cult of the Flavian Imperial Family* (Leiden: Brill, 1993); idem, *Imperial Cults and the Apocalypse of John: Reading Revelation in the Ruins* (Oxford: Oxford University Press, 2001), 23–131, esp. 43–52 on the temple of the Sebastoi established in Ephesus in the late first century, and 95–101 on an Augusteion in the upper agora at Ephesus (repaired during the reign of Titus as a prayer for the emperor's health and support for Roman rule); van Tilborg, *Reading John*, 101–7; 188–212; Trebilco, *Early Christians*, 30–37; for 17 images of the temple of the Sebastoi, see H. Koester, ed., *Cities of Paul*; also Kenneth Scott, *The Imperial Cult under the Flavians* (Stuttgart: W. Kohlhammer, 1936); Price, *Rituals and Power*.

47. I am selectively following Rogers, *Sacred Identity*, 2–16.

48. For example Strabo, *Geogr.* 13.4.12.

49. On references to inscriptions of Ephesus, see chap. 1, note 19 (above).

50. Strabo, *Geogr.* 17.3.25.

51. Text cited from Price, *Rituals and Power*, 54–55.

52. Rogers (*Sacred Identity*, 127–35) lists 60 constructions, location, date, and inscriptional references.

53. Scherrer, "Ephesos," 4; Rogers, *Sacred Identity*, 91; Friesen, *Imperial Cults*, 99–101.

54. I am largely following Scherrer, "Ephesos," 4–7; see also Rogers, *Sacred Identity*, 128–35; van Tilborg, *Reading John*, 174–212.

55. An inscription (IEph 3.859) records that a wealthy freedman, G. Julios Nikephorous, funded sacrifices to Rome, Augustus, and Artemis.

56. IEph 7.3006–3007.

57. For text and discussion, G. R. Horsley, "A Fishing Cartel in First-Century Ephesos," in *New Documents Illustrating Early Christianity,* vol. 5, *Linguistic Essays* (North Ryde, N.S.W.: Ancient History Documentary Research Centre, Macquarrie University, 1989), 95–114. The inscription names nearly 100 donors, listing them by the size of their contributions, from most to least. About 50 percent are Roman citizens, some 41–46 percent Greeks and/or Ephesians, and 3 percent slaves.

58. Friesen, *Imperial Cults*, 43–52. Friesen notes that the term θεός (*theos*) is not used to describe Domitian.

59. Van Tilborg, *Reading John*, 199–200, n57.

60. Friesen, *Imperial Cults*, 44–50.

61. Van Tilborg, *Reading John*, 102–3.

62. IEph 3.621, 633, 661.

63. IEph 2.508; 4.1104.

64. Friesen (*Imperial Cults*, 97–98) explains that the prytanis had four functions in Ephesus: (1) to maintain the cult of Hestia and the city's eternal flame; (2) to welcome official city guests including hosting dinners at the prytaneion; (3) with the Kouretes to exercise oversight of the mysteries of Artemis; and (4) to have oversight of an official cycle of 365 sacrifices for various deities in the city.

65. IEph 2.427, 461, 508.

66. Van Tilborg, *Reading John*, 192–96.

67. Price, *Rituals and Power*, 136.

68. Van Tilborg, *Reading John*, 188–92; Trebilco, *Early Christians*, 19–30.

69. E. Badian, "Alexander the Great between Two Thrones and Heaven: Variations on an Old Theme," in *Subject and Ruler: The Cult of the Ruling Power in Classical Antiquity*, ed. A. Small, Journal of Roman Archaeology: Supplementary Series 17 (Ann Arbor, MI: JRA, 1996), 11–26, esp. 13, 24–25.

70. IEph 2.263C; 2.241; Van Tilborg, *Reading John*, 181–88.

71. IEph 2.402, 404; 7.3092; Van Tilborg, *Reading John*, 182.

72. C. V. Sutherland, "The Intelligibility of Roman Imperial Coin Types," *JRS* 49 (1959): 46–55. On coinage originating from Ephesus, see A. Burnett, M. Amandry, and P. P. Ripollès, *Roman Provincial Coinage,* vol. 1, parts 1–2, *From the Death of Caesar to the Death of Vitellius* (London: British Museum Press, 1992), 363–81, 431–38, plates 112–14; A. Burnett, M. Amandry, and I. Carradice, *Roman Provincial Coinage,* vol. 2, parts 1–2, *From Vespasian to Domitian* (London: British Museum Press, 1999), 117–26, 165–69, plates 47–49.

73. For Augustus, see Burnett et al., *Roman Provincial Coinage,* vol. 1, nos. 2575, 2777–79, 2581, 2586, 2588, 2590–96, 2599–2606, 2607–12; for Tiberius, nos. 2613–18; for Claudius, ibid., nos. 2620–25; for Nero, nos. 2630, 2632; for Vespasian, Burnett et al., *Roman Provincial Coinage,* vol. 2, nos. 1066–67, 1070–72, 1077–79, 1081–87, 1089.

74. For example, Livia, Augustus's wife, by herself (ibid., vol. 1, nos. 2576, 2580) or with Augustus (nos. 2582, 2587, 2589, 2593–96, 2599–2606, 2608–12); Agrippina II, Claudius's wife

and mother of Nero, with Claudius (nos. 2620–24); Nero, Claudius's adopted son by himself (no. 2625); Poppaea, Nero's wife in 62 CE, who died in 65, with Nero (nos. 2629–30); Statilia Messalina, whom Nero married in 66 CE, with Nero (no. 2631) and without (no. 2632). Also Vespasian's sons Titus (ibid., vol. 2, no. 1068) and Domitian (no. 1069); Domitian's wife, Domitia, by herself (nos. 1072, 1083, 1084, 1091–93) and with Domitian (no. 1076).

75. For example, Nero, Poppaea, and Roma (ibid., vol. 1, no. 2629). Also Domitian and Zeus (ibid., vol. 2, no. 1073); Domitian and the two river gods Marnas and Claseas since an aqueduct whose construction was dedicated by the proconsul of Asia in 92–93 was fed by these two streams (nos. 1074–75; see pp. 166–67); Domitian, Domitia, and Nike (no. 1076, though which specific victory is not clear).

76. For example, Nero and a temple (ibid., vol. 1, nos. 2626–28; no. 2626 includes the term *neokoron*. Conventionally, this temple is identified as the temple of Artemis, though ibid., p. 433, suggests that it might be an imperial temple; Vespasian and the temple and cult statue of Artemis (ibid., vol. 2, no. 1067).

77. Ibid. vol. 2, p. 17.

78. For an analysis of Matthew, see Duling, "Empire," 64–66. Duling has eleven categories compared with my eight. I have collapsed his misleading divisions of priestly and lay aristocracy (because it suggests a false distinction of religious and secular power), omitted merchants, and included herders with peasants.

79. Anthony J. Saldarini, *Pharisees, Scribes, and Sadducees* (Wilmington: Michael Glazier, 1988), 187–98, esp. 197.

80. Lenski, *Power and Privilege*, 283.

81. Mary Smallwood, *The Jews under Roman Rule from Pompey to Diocletian* (Leiden: Brill, 1976; 2nd ed., Boston: Brill, 2001), 135–36; 344–45.

82. Vouga, *Le cadre historique*, 11; Richey, "'Truly This Is the Savior,'" 95–105. Less strongly, Brown, *Community*, 42–43.

83. Tessa Rajak, "Was There a Roman Charter for the Jews?" in *The Jewish Dialogue with Greece and Rome: Studies in Cultural and Social Interaction* (Leiden: Brill, 2001), 300–333, esp. 300–301; Trebilco, *Jewish Communities*, 8–12.

84. Richey, "'Truly This Is the Savior,'" 99; for negotiation of this tax in Matthew 17:24–27, see Carter, *Matthew and Empire*, 130–44.

85. Dominique Cuss, *Imperial Cult and Honorary Terms in the New Testament* (Fribourg: University Press, 1974), 39, 148, 152–54; B. A. Mastin, "Imperial Cult," 352–65; idem, "A Neglected Feature of the Christology of the Fourth Gospel," *NTS* 22 (1975–76): 32–51, esp. 46; Vouga, *Le cadre historique*, 11; Richey, "'Truly This Is the Savior,'" 197. Rightly rejected by Harland, "Honouring the Emperor," 99–121, esp. 102–4.

86. E.g., Pliny the Younger, *Pan.* 33.3–4; 48.3–49:1; 52.6; 53:1–2; 76.3–5; *Ep.* 4.11.5–16; Tacitus, *Agricola* 39–45; *Hist.* 4.48; Suetonius, *Domitian* 10–11; 14–15; 22; Dio Cassius 67. T. A. Dorey ("Agricola and Domitian," *Greece and Rome* 7 [1960]: 66–71) argues, for example, that Tacitus creates the negative presentation of Domitian in *Agricola* for rhetorical effect and that it does not reflect historical realities.

87. Summary in L. Thompson, *Revelation*, 96–101.

88. Magie, "Centralization," 577.

89. For discussion, see H. W. Pleket, "Domitian, the Senate, and the Provinces," *Mnemosyne* 14 (1961): 298–315; K. Waters, "The Character of Domitian," *Phoenix* 18 (1964): 49–77; Brian W. Jones, "Domitian's Attitude to the Senate," *American Journal of Philology* 94 (1973): 79–91; idem, *The Emperor Domitian* (London: Routledge, 1992); P. Southern, *Domitian: Tragic Tyrant* (London: Routledge, 1997); L. Thompson, *Revelation*, 95–115.

90. E.g., Pliny, *Pan.* 94; Edwin Ramage, "Denigration of Predecessor under Claudius, Galba, and Vespasian," *Historia* 32 (1983): 201–14, who comments that this denigration tradition

reaches "a kind of culmination in Pliny's *Panegyric*" (210n3); idem, "Juvenal and the Establishment: Denigration of Predecessor in the Satires," *ANRW* II.33.1 (1989): 640–707; L. Thompson, *Revelation*, 109–15.

91. Timothy Peter Wiseman, "Domitian and the Dynamics of Terror in Classical Rome," *History Today* 46 (1996): 19–24; Marcus Wilson, "After the Silence: Tacitus, Suetonius, Juvenal," in *Flavian Rome: Culture, Image, Text*, ed. A. J. Boyle and W. Dominik (Leiden: Brill, 2003), 523–42.

92. The Domitian-persecution scenario is critiqued by the data of T. D. Barnes, "Legislation against the Christians," *Journal of Roman Studies* 58 (1968): 32–50; J. C. Wilson, "The Problem of the Domitianic Date of Revelation," *NTS* 39 (1993): 587–605. The Roman letter of *1 Clement* has a vague reference to "misfortunes and calamities" (1:1), but the letter is more interested in strife internal to the Christian communities than in external persecution (cf. 3:1–3; also Eusebius, *Hist. eccl.* 3.16E).

93. So Suetonius, *Domitian* 13.2; Philostratus, *Life of Apollonius* 8.4; Dio Cassius 67.4.7; 67.13.4; cf. Pliny, *Pan.* 33.4; 52.6; contra, for example, Mastin, "Imperial Cult," 357; following L. Thompson, *Revelation*, 104–7.

94. Text in Friesen, *Imperial Cults*, 44.

95. So Cassidy, *John's Gospel*, ix, 17–26.

96. In sketching out his understanding of the history of the Johannine community, Paul Anderson (*The Fourth Gospel and the Quest for Jesus: Modern Foundations Reconsidered*, Library of New Testament Studies, 321 (New York: T&T Clark, 2006], 33–34, 63–66, 198) includes the experience of persecution after expulsion from the synagogue. He combines Cassidy's scenario with persecution by Domitian to assert six key points: Domitian requires emperor worship; he was to be addressed by officials as "Lord and God"; Jews had been given a dispensation; Gentiles saw little wrong with emperor laud; synagogue separation meant vulnerability; Christians were to confess Caesar or die. Our discussion above indicates that every part of this scenario is unsustainable.

97. For a discussion of five major armed revolts, see Dyson, "Native Revolts," 239–74; for a survey of different forms of resistance, see Warren Carter, "Vulnerable Power: The Roman Empire Challenged by the Early Christians," in *Handbook of Early Christianity*, ed. A. J. Blasi, J. Duhaime, and P.-A. Turcotte (Walnut Creek: AltaMira, 2002), 453–488, esp. 466–71.

98. Martin Goodman, "Opponents of Rome: Jews and Others," in *Images of Empire*, ed. L. Alexander, JSOTSSup 122 (Sheffield: JSOT Press, 1991), 222–38, esp. 231. Goodman goes on to argue that the third option, that of fear and intimidation, played a large role. See also Steven Dyson, "Native Revolts" and "Native Revolt Patterns in the Roman Empire," *ANRW* II.2.3 (1975): 138–75, emphasizing protests against the existing order more than attempting to replace it; also Richard Horsley, *Jesus and the Spiral of Violence: Popular Jewish Resistance in Roman Palestine* (San Francisco: Harper & Row, 1987), chaps. 1–5; Ramsey MacMullen, "How to Revolt in the Roman Empire," in *Changes in the Roman Empire: Essays in the Ordinary* (Princeton: Princeton University Press, 1990), 198–203, emphasizes the roles of elite figures.

99. Ando, *Imperial Ideology*, xi.

100. Ibid., 374.

101. Ramsay MacMullen, "Notes on Romanization," 56–66, esp. 63.

102. Ando, *Imperial Ideology*, 373–85.

103. MacMullen, "Notes on Romanization," 65–66, in discussing the roles of coercion, capacity for cultural change, and choice.

104. Ando, *Imperial Ideology*, 71–80.

105. Ibid., 5, also 1.

106. Ando's interest in quietude is reflected in entries in his index on "obedience," "legitimacy," and "victory," and the lack of entries on revolt or violent rebellion.

107. Ibid., 6, 67, 74, 120, 409.

108. For "antilanguage" and "antisociety," see M. A. K. Halliday, "Antilanguages," *American Anthropologist* 78 (1976): 570–84.

109. Ibid., 570.

110. Ibid., 572–76.

111. Ibid., 580.

112. Bruce Malina and Richard Rohrbaugh, *Social Science Commentary on the Gospel of John* (Minneapolis: Fortress Press, 1998); N. R. Petersen, *The Gospel of John and the Sociology of Light: Language and Characterization in the Fourth Gospel* (Valley Forge, PA: Trinity Press, 1993), 87–89; for a similar understanding, see Rensberger, *Johannine Faith*, passim; and J. H. Neyrey, *An Ideology of Revolt: John's Christology in Social-Science Perspective* (Philadelphia: Fortress, 1988), 106.

113. J. M. Barbalet, "Power and Resistance," *British Journal of Sociology* 36 (1985): 521–48.

114. James C. Scott, *Weapons of the Weak: Everyday Forms of Peasant Resistance* (New Haven: Yale University Press, 1985); idem, *Domination and the Arts of Resistance* (New Haven: Yale University Press, 1990). For use of Scott in NT studies, see Richard Horsley, ed., *Hidden Transcripts and the Arts of Resistance: Applying the Work of James C. Scott to Jesus and Paul,* Semeia Studies 48 (Atlanta: SBL, 2004).

115. Scott, *Domination*, 2.

116. Ibid., 111; see 198 for summary chart.

117. Ibid., 118–24.

118. Ibid., 7.

119. Ibid., 3.

120. Ibid., v.

121. The bibliography is immense. For example, F. Fanon, *The Wretched of the Earth* (New York: Grove, 1968); Edward Said, *Culture and Imperialism* (New York: Alfred Knopf, 1993); Homi Bhabha, *The Location of Culture* (London: Routledge, 1994); P. Williams and L. Chrisman, eds., *Colonial Discourse and Post-Colonial Theory* (New York: Columbia University Press, 1994); B. Ashcroft, G. Griffiths, H. Tiffin, eds., *The Post-colonial Studies Reader* (New York: Routledge, 1995); P. Mongia, ed., *Contemporary Postcolonial Theory: A Reader* (London: Arnold, 1996); B. Moore-Gilbert, *Postcolonial Theory: Contexts, Practices, Politics* (London: Verso, 1997); H. Schwarz and S. Ray, ed., *A Companion to Postcolonial Studies* (Oxford: Blackwell, 2000); G. Castle, ed., *Postcolonial Discourses: An Anthology* (Oxford: Blackwell, 2001); N. Harrison, *Postcolonial Criticism: History, Theory and the Work of Fiction* (Oxford: Polity/Blackwell, 2003). For biblical studies, Laura Donaldson, ed., *Postcolonialism and Scriptural Reading,* Semeia 75 (Atlanta: Scholars Press, 1996); Fernando F. Segovia, *Decolonizing Biblical Studies: A View from the Margins* (Maryknoll, NY: Orbis, 2000); R. S. Sugirtharajah, *The Postcolonial Bible* (Sheffield: Sheffield Academic Press, 1998); idem, *Postcolonial Criticism and Biblical Interpretation* (Oxford: Oxford University Press, 2002); idem, *The Bible as Empire: Postcolonial Explorations* (Cambridge University Press, 2005). For Roman studies, see J. Webster and N. J. Cooper, eds., *Roman Imperialism: Post-Colonial Perspectives,* Leicester Archaeology Monographs 3 (Leicester: University of Leicester, School of Archaeological Studies, 1996); D. J. Mattingly, ed., *Dialogues in Roman Imperialism: Power, Discourse, and Discrepant Experience in the Roman Empire,* Journal of Roman Archaeology: Supplementary Series 23 (Portsmouth, RI: JRA, 1997). For John, see Musa W. Dube and Jeffrey Staley, eds., *John and Postcolonialism: Travel, Space, and Power* (London: Continuum, 2002).

122. For instance, late first-century Ephesus is not a *post*colonial situation; Roman power is a present, not past, reality for John's Gospel. Nor is Ephesus a *colonia*, in the sense of being founded as a settlement of veterans. Nor is Rome's empire, so the argument goes, comparable to recent capitalist empires (what Lenin called "the highest stage of capitalism"). But to the contrary, empires have taken different forms and motivations; yet common to them is the key reality of

imperialism, "the practice, the theory, and the attitudes of a dominating metropolitan center ruling a distant territory" (Edward Said, *Culture and Imperialism*, 9). Though Rome was not a nineteenth-century capitalist empire, its elite certainly knew numerous ways of being a "dominating metropolitan center" and of exercising the power discrepancy between the powerful center (Rome) and the rest of the empire and cities such as Ephesus.

123. Sugirtharajah, *Bible as Empire*, 3.

124. Said, *Culture and Imperialism*, xxv. See (above) Scott's concern with public transcripts and hidden transcripts.

125. Fanon, *Wretched*, 52.

126. Bhabha, "Of Mimicry and Man: The Ambivalence of Colonial Discourse," in *Location of Culture*, 85–92.

127. For example, Reg, the fictional leader of the People's Front of Judea and a staunch opponent of Roman control in the movie *Life of Brian*, expresses the ambiguity of complicity in oppositional practices by conceding (in a list that also reflects his creator's socialization) that the Romans have provided "better sanitation, medicine, education, irrigation, public health, roads, freshwater systems, baths, and public order." Contemporary studies have noted the ambiguous roles of African mission schools, which were both a means of imperial control (imposing Western language/culture and silencing local languages, for example), while simultaneously productive of power in providing educated leaders who articulated dissent, organized protest, and subsequently led independent states.

128. Text and translation in James H. Oliver, *The Ruling Power: A Study of the Roman Empire in the Second Century after Christ through the Roman Oration of Aelius Aristides,* Transactions of the American Philosophical Society: New Series 43.4 (Philadelphia: APS, 1953).

129. Two verbs meaning "send" are used: *pempō* (πέμπω), 1:33; 4:34; 5:23, 24, 30, 37; 6:38, 39, 44; 7:16, 18, 28, 33; 8:16, 18, 26, 29; 9:4; 12:44, 45, 49; 13:16, 20; 14:24; 15:21; 16:5; and *apostellō* (ἀποστέλλω), 3:17, 34; 5:36, 38; 6:29, 57; 7:29; 8:42; 10:36; 11:42; 17:3, 8, 18, 21, 23, 25; 20:21.

Part 2

4

Negotiating the Imperial Present by Turning to the Past

Artemis, Abraham, Moses, and Jesus Wisdom

"In the beginning was the Word" (John 1:1). Scholars have readily and correctly identified various intertexts for the Gospel's well-known opening verse in Genesis 1:1 and in wisdom traditions (Prov 8:22–36; Sir 24:1–23). Not noticed in most discussions, though, is the fact that with this opening verse the Gospel's rhetoric of distance employs a common strategy also utilized by other Jews and Greeks to negotiate Roman power. This strategy, a turn to the past, will be the focus of this chapter.

In chapters 2 and 3 I have discussed two significant communities in which John's Jesus-believers participate, a synagogue community and the Roman Empire. I have argued that synagogue communities to which John's Jesus-believers belonged generally participated actively in the Roman world though maintaining some distinctive practices. I have elaborated a number of ways in which Roman power was expressed and experienced in Ephesus in the late first century and suggested that Ephesian synagogue members also generally engaged this society actively, combining accommodation with maintenance of cultural distinction. The conclusion from both of these discussions is that in all likelihood many/some of John's Jesus-believers were among these active participants.

Yet toward the end of chapter 3, I identified three approaches that warn against a monolithic understanding of interactions in imperial contexts. These approaches argue that interactions are multivalent and include both compliance and various and often covert expressions of calculated resistance and dissent. Along with active participation in Rome's world, then, simultaneously we can expect to find in Ephesus, including among Jesus-believers, some distance from Rome's world and some expressions of dissent. I have also argued that the writer/s of John's Gospel and their supporters are concerned about levels of societal participation that they consider to be too great. The Gospel functions as a "hidden transcript," a contestive voice whose rhetoric of distance offers an alternative reality, urging Jesus-believers to a less-accommodated and more-distinctive existence as an alternative community even while the Gospel's rhetoric participates in and mimics imperial ways.

In this chapter, by focusing on aspects of the presentation of Jesus in John's Gospel,

I discuss one of the ways in which the writer/s of John's Gospel do their contestive though imitative work. I begin by describing a turn to the past as one way that (elite) Greeks and faithful Jews negotiated contemporary Roman power. Erich Gruen, for example, discusses ways in which both Romans and Greeks claimed the Trojan Aeneas as an ancestor so as to derive honor from him and to link Rome to the Hellenistic world.[1] Accordingly, discussions of social memory emphasize that any act of remembering cultural and sacred traditions anew is always selective: it involves constructing the past in life-giving ways convenient to a particular group. This reconstructive process, as Susan Alcock describes it, comprises "a form of vital self-presentation and prideful self-assertion" vis-à-vis other groups and powers with other interests who could and did contest various fresh rememberings to construct a different past and shape a different present.[2] The past, remembered in certain ways, offered not an escape into nostalgia but a basis for defining and empowering Jewish and Hellenistic groups to participate in the imperial present.

I will then argue that this "turn to the past" is an important strategy in John's Gospel for negotiating Roman power. The attention given to Abraham and Moses provides examples of this negotiation. Rememberings of Abraham and Moses are disputed in the Gospel by Jesus and his opponents, suggesting in all likelihood contested forms of imperial negotiation among Jesus' believers. I will argue that some remember Abraham and Moses in order to sanction active societal participation, while others remember these figures to urge greater societal distance. Moreover, on the basis of Jesus' greater antiquity, the presentation of Jesus as being "in the beginning with God" (1:1) outweighs any turn to Abraham and Moses, thus providing greater authority for the crucified yet risen and ascended Jesus to shape present engagement with Roman power. Antiquity thus remembered has authority and is a means of power, a source of identity and sanction for a particular way of life. The Gospel's "turn to the past," to the very beginning with God, reasserts the origin and task of the one to whom Jesus-believers are committed as the basis for a distinctive rather than accommodationist identity and lifestyle in Roman Ephesus. This turn to the past comprises a further aspect of the Gospel's rhetoric of distance.

Thus in response to Peter Burke's question about the function of social memory, "Who wants whom to remember what and why?"[3] I am arguing that John's Gospel participates in attempts to urge Jesus-believers, more happily accommodated than not in Ephesus's Roman world, to remember that they are committed to one who was in the beginning with God, who definitively revealed God's life-giving purposes in the Roman world, and who was rejected and crucified by that world. This remembering as a form of self-presentation and purposeful self-assertion defines Jesus-believers and is to empower the living of God's purposes that are at odds with and resisted by Rome's world.

Before moving to John, we begin with four examples of Greeks and Jews turning to the past.

The Presence of the Past in the Present

In the Beginning Was Artemis

I begin with a significant act of elite imperial negotiation in Ephesus from about the same time as the writing of the final form of John's Gospel. In 103–104 CE, a wealthy, landowning Roman of the equestrian order, C. Vibius Salutaris, made a large donation to the city council (the *boulē*) and the citizens (wealthy elites) of Ephesus.[4] His bequest was approved by the authorities of the temple of Artemis, ratified by the citizens of Ephesus, and endorsed by the Roman proconsuls, thus ensuring that the gift had considerable civic "ownership." This ownership is also attested by its being recorded in an inscription (IEph 1A.27) of some 568 lines in length, displayed prominently at the southern entrance to the theater in Ephesus as well as in the Artemision.

Salutaris's bequest made generous financial provision for two sacred, public, civic events. One event involved lotteries through which cash donations were made to carefully selected recipients numbering some twenty-seven hundred people.[5] A few recipients were to spend their donations on caring for statues or providing sacrifices. The other recipients, from important Ephesian civic groups, kept the donation for themselves. Benefiting from the donation were functionaries of both the imperial cult and the Artemision, and about 300 members of youth organizations. Also among the recipients were 1,500 citizens from Ephesus's tribes, which originated with the city's founding by the Ionian[6] Androklos. According to the founding story, Androklos and other settlers from Athens followed Apollo's oracle and founded the city on a spot to which a wild boar led them.[7] The final recipients of Salutaris's benefactions were elite members of powerful civic institutions in Ephesus's hierarchy, such as the *boulē* (city council, 450 members) and *gerousia* (a hereditary and influential body of elders, 314 members). The distribution occurred at the temple of Artemis on the occasion of celebrating Artemis's birth. According to Strabo (*Geogr.* 14.1.20), Leto gave birth to Artemis in the sacred grove, attended by her nurse Ortygia. The birth was endangered by Hera, who jealously spied on Leto. The Kouretes, though, protected Artemis by frightening Hera away and concealing Artemis's birth.

The "turn to the past" and "the presence of the past in the present" are quite evident in this first event of Salutaris's bequest. Most obvious is the location and occasion of the distribution. Center stage are the temple of Artemis, the celebration of the goddess's birth, and the mythical founding of the city. Salutaris's bequest assembles a large cast for the celebration, but more so, assembles carefully chosen recipients. The recipients reflect Ephesus's hierarchical society, with pride of place going to citizens, and members of the *boulē* and *gerousia*. These recipients are also linked to the past, notably to the Ionian founding of the city by Androklos (the tribes). The inclusion of imperial cult officials along with those from the Artemis temple integrates both Roman power and Artemis into this civic festival. The event also included 300 youths, the future of the city, who participated along with members of Ephesus's civic hierarchy. According to Guy Rogers, the event taught these young men

> to look to the institutional structure of their city for a social sense of rightness about the roles they would play in Ephesian public life, to the Ionian foundation of the city for a historical sense of where those roles came from . . . , and finally to the birth of the goddess Artemis at Ephesos, for a theological sense of how Ephesian social and historical identity was grounded in a "sacred" reality, which was impervious to all human challenges.[8]

The second event funded by Salutaris was a procession through Ephesus every two weeks. Taking perhaps about ninety minutes, it followed a circular route that began at the temple of Artemis, wound through the main city streets, and returned to the temple of Artemis.[9] The procession, comprising mainly youths of the city, bore some thirty-one images. Nine images represented Artemis, with others representing various Roman personnel (Augustus, the Roman emperor, and his wife; the Roman senate; the Roman people). Fifteen represented aspects of Ephesus. Others depicted Androklos, who was responsible for the founding of the city, and Lysimachos, a Hellenistic king responsible for the city's refounding in the 280s BCE.

After leaving the temple of Artemis, the procession entered Ephesus at the Magnesium gates and proceeded west, traversing

- The Roman Road. Heading west, it passed the upper or civic agora with its display of predominantly Roman ruling power, with some Ephesian representation also (see discussion in chap. 3 above). Here were temples for Divus Julius and Dea Roma, Augustus and Artemis, and the Sebastoi. Also prominent were large statues of imperial figures like Augustus and Domitian. The Bouleuterion (council building) and Prytaneion signified elite Ephesian power. Eight of the twelve major buildings on this section of the route had been built since Augustus's reign.

- The Elite Embelos. The procession moved along the Embelos or Curetes Street, passing statues of emperors, proconsuls, and local Ephesian elites. This select area of the city attested Ephesian elite accomplishments. It resonated with the image of the Hellenistic king Lysimachos carried in the procession. Lysimachos had been responsible in the 280s BCE for relocating, repopulating, renaming, and enclosing the city with a wall. He had also reformed the celebration of Artemis's birth.

- Marble and Stadium Streets. The procession turned north, past the Tetragonos Agora, with the harbor and warehouses to the west. This was the center of the city's economic and commercial activity. The procession stopped to place images in the theater.

- The Koressian Gate. At the end of Stadium Street the procession turned east to exit the city through the Koressian Gate, in the sight of the temple of Apollo. This gate, along with the temple of Apollo, recalled the city's Greek foundation legend in which Androklos and other settlers from Athens followed Apollo's oracle and founded the city on a spot to which a wild boar led them. An image of Androklos was carried in the procession. Ephesians celebrated a special day in his honor each year (IEph 3.644). Five of the city's six tribes were associated with this founding.

- Temple of Artemis. The procession returned to the temple of Artemis.

Rogers argues that the procession's route was not haphazardly chosen but served to dramatize the historical identity of Ephesus. It created and expressed a civic ideology, presenting a "privileged mental map" of the city. The procession route recalled the city's foundation legends in reverse historical order: Rome, Lysimachos, Androklos, and Artemis. Rome's recent building activity and Lysimachos's Hellenistic refounding were confirmed and integrated into the city's history and identity. The heart of it, though, centered on Androklos and finally on Artemis, who provided the ultimate civic identity of Ephesus as a sacred community. The city, like the procession, began and ended in the past with Artemis. Roman presence was not denied or invalidated, but it was shown not to be ultimate. The claim in the edict of the provincial assembly of Asia that Augustus's birthday was "the beginning of all things," for example, was shown to be hyperbole in the extreme.[10] Rogers argues that the procession entered the city in the upper agora, where Roman construction was quite evident, not because Roman presence was "the most memorable; it was only the most recent."[11] The route ensured that Rome's power was set in a grander and more-ancient scheme of things centered on Androklos and Artemis, who provided the city's sacred identity. Androklos's founding of the city "provided a tradition against which new founders might be measured first, and then cut down to size."[12] The procession's beginning and ending points in the temple of Artemis underlined the city's identity as the defenders of Artemis. The procession's main members, youths of the city, were thus acculturated into this reconstruction of the past as the basis for their present and future participation.

Both of Salutaris's provisions—the lottery donations and the procession—involved a profound turn not just to the past but also to the beginning, ensuring the presence of Ephesus's Hellenistic, Ionian, and ultimately sacred past in the Roman present. The past did not provide escape or nostalgic pleasure. Rather, argues Rogers, the past

> was a present source, and framework of power, used, first, to give order, point, and direction to the lives of the young men of Ephesos, and second, to justify the positions of authority held by the fathers of the city. . . . The Ephesians did not merely reflect upon the past or resort to it as an alternative to a politically unsatisfactory present; rather this past [as articulated through Salutaris's donation] was a source of power wielded by the men of Ephesos over the young, over new founders, and, at last, over new gods.[13]

The past justified their present social hierarchy in Rome's present and provided meaning for their lives as defenders of Artemis. Rogers argues that this reassertion of Ephesus's identity as a sacred community occurs in a context of pervasive Roman presence and power in the city. "New citizens, new founders, and new gods" were negotiated by fitting them into Ephesus's sacred and ancient framework of reference. Rogers rightly argues that this framework "left social room for foreigners, historical room for founders, and theological room for new gods."[14] But it is also true that "leaving room" was not a disinterested act. It meant putting new gods and new foreign powers in their place in relation to the city's ancient sacred identity grounded in its patron goddess: Artemis. Antiquity is authority.[15]

In the Beginning Were Ancient Greeks

Simon Swain provides a second example of turning to the past as a strategy of imperial negotiation. He examines the empowering and identity-constituting impact of the turn to the past among Greek elite writers in the years 50–250 CE, a period known as the second sophistic.[16] Swain sees the turn to the past by writers of the second sophistic as a means of securing "the identity of the Greeks of this time with respect to their ancestors, the 'ancient Greeks,' who were the source of their moral and political authority."[17] The second sophistic was obsessed with a particular past, imitating the archaic language, style, and themes (the glory of ancient Athens, Sparta, and Alexander the Great) of fifth and fourth century BCE Attic prose writers.[18] Swain argues that this turn to the past was motivated not by escape, nostalgia, or leisurely interest. Rather, it secured the identity and power of elites in Hellenistic cities within the Roman Empire in the present. The Greek male elite's respect for and closeness to "the traditions and history" of cities, the Greek world, and the leaders of classical Greece "furthered their own claims to rule in the present."[19] Despite Roman presence and power in Greek cities, this obsession with classical Greeks "reflects the special confidence of the Greek elite at this time. This confidence was due to their perceived closeness to the classical Greeks."[20]

How did such an identity enable elite Greeks, prominent as leaders in civic affairs of cities like Ephesus, to negotiate Roman power? The cultural-political identity created by such an obsession and closeness was "avowedly Greek," Swain argues, yet "at the same time many of these and other members of the elite accepted a Roman political identity. The past assisted the local Greek elites [in Hellenistic cities] to secure their power by allowing them to claim a connection with the recognized leaders of the great days of their countries."[21] Thus, while the formation of this Greek identity was in part a reaction to Roman rule, and a recognition of the reality of elite dependence on and submission to Roman power,[22] there was no general hostility to Rome, and the identity allowed them to exercise power in Rome's world. Greek cultural identity, not Roman presence, ultimately defined these men:

> But with regard to the feelings of such Greeks themselves, we cannot assume more than a political identification with the ruling power for particular reasons. Greeks identified with Rome politically because Rome encouraged them and needed them . . . , because there were solid benefits to be gained from Roman citizenship, and because they appreciated the benevolent regime. . . . But cognitively and spiritually none of this means that Greeks did not remain Greeks.[23]

Hence, the formation of an elite Greek identity associated with great Greeks of the past secured an ideological-cultural identity that empowered the civic leadership of elites to rule within Rome's empire.

But Swain warns, echoing James Scott's cautions about monolithic interactions in imperial situations, "In the case of the Greeks we must never confuse the absence of direct political action against Rome with genuine political integration and harmony."[24] He goes on to warn that similarly public expressions of apparent pro-Roman sentiments do not tell the whole story precisely because they are public expressions. Swain discusses the writings of ten elite Greek males (Plutarch, Dio of Prusa, Arrian, Appian, Aristides, Lucian, Pausanias, Galen, Philostratus, and Cassius Dio) to ascertain "how these figures saw Rome." Predictably there are different perspectives. Plutarch is cool toward Rome; Dio is closest to hostile; the remainder mostly seem positive, exhibiting political allegiance without genuine loyalty, while some like Galen show little interest in Rome. Swain concludes that "the identity the Greek elite constructed for itself involved a certain distance from Roman rule." He recognizes that "Roman influences penetrated the Greek world deeply," including among elites (such as games, imperial cult, baths, etc.), and that accommodation and compromise were necessary. Yet he does not think that Roman influences "impinged greatly on people's cultural identity . . . [or on] the elites' ideological conception of themselves as heirs of the classics."[25]

Swain's study shows elite Greek males negotiated Roman power and presence by turning to the past and constructing an identity for themselves, sustained by ancient great Greeks that empowered them in civic leadership and put Rome in its place in the grand cultural scheme of things. Rome was not one of the barbarians lacking Greek culture and speech, but nor were they Greeks. They formed a "tertium quid, an unstable position that was neither one nor the other."[26] Rome's political power was undoubted, but Greek elites knew their own power in cities within the empire, a power based in their cultural heritage and association with great Greeks of the past. Swain's study of this contestive but not hostile interface between Roman political power and Greek cultural power certainly raises questions, as Pamela Gordon observes, about that "problematic hyphenization, 'Graeco-Roman,'" much beloved in New Testament studies.[27]

In the Beginning Was Greek Mythology: Aphrodisias

Aphrodisias, a city to the east of Ephesus, provides a third example of how a turn to the past provided a means for people in Asia to negotiate Roman power.[28] The city had a Sebasteion, a temple dedicated to Aphrodite (or Venus, the goddess of love) and to the divine emperors, Augustus and his successors, notably Tiberius (14–37), Claudius (41–54), and Nero (54–68). The temple was probably dedicated during Tiberius's rule but not completed until the reign of Nero.

Significant is the design of the physical approach to this imperial temple. Worshippers approached the Aphrodisias temple, set on a platform, at the end of a large paved area or processional way, eighty meters long (about 250–300 feet) and fourteen meters wide (about 45 feet). This large paved or processional way was flanked on both its north and south sides by porticoes or three-storey-high walls, about forty feet high. In each portico, a series of columns was connected on the second and third stories by large carved panels, about five feet by five, inserted between the columns. By one estimate there were ninety spaces for panels on each side, making a total of one hundred and eighty spaces. Worshippers were thus funneled toward the temple through this walled and paved area. They were enclosed in and dwarfed by the physically imposing architecture of forty-foot-high walls. They were not just reminded of, but were enabled to experience, the divinely sanctioned and overwhelming power of Rome. Members of two very wealthy Aphrodisian families were responsible for funding these impressive structures. Two brothers Menander and Eusebes funded the northern wall, and another two brothers Diogenes and Attalus funded the southern wall. The porticoes were not required by Rome but were voluntary actions by two rich Aphrodisian families intent on honoring Rome as well as displaying and enhancing their own wealth, power, and prestige.

But along with honoring Roman power, the walls also manage to subvert it. The 180 spaces that comprised these columned, multistoried walls were filled with carved panels, which worshippers passed as they approached the temple. These carved panels were carefully designed to convey messages, some predictable and some surprising. Among the predictable, for example, were those of the second tier of the north portico. The second tier comprised panels and inscribed bases for statues consisting of personified peoples and provinces. These statues, presented as female figures, depicted peoples who had been conquered by Augustus, including Cretans, Cypriots, Sicilians, Egyptians, Judeans, Arabs, Bosporans, Bessi, Dacians, Dardanians, Iapodes, Andizeti, Pirousti, Rhaeti, Trumpilini, and Callaeci. This storey thus presented a review of Roman power, an empire gained by military conquest.

But while this turn to the past to celebrate Roman military might and rule over the present empire is predictable in the approaches to a temple celebrating Roman power, the top storey suggests something a little unpredictable. Though not fully preserved, its surviving panels comprise personifications of Day and Ocean, suggesting that there were other personifications concerning at least time and place, such as Night and Land. This storey likely consisted of a series of allegorical cosmic figures, drawn from a quite different past, that of Greek myth. Thus, Roman imperial and military history, depicted in the second storey as a story of victory and conquest, is placed under a storey of Greek mythological depictions of cosmic foundations. Roman power is fitted into this more ancient cosmic mythology. Though Rome now dominates this time and space, these entities were "in the beginning," long before Rome. The paneled wall honors Rome's vast temporal and geographical power, but it does so by sketching a much-larger, temporal and locational, canvas. Antiquity has authority.

A similar turn to the past to honor and subvert Roman power exists on the better-preserved southern portico. The third storey celebrates Roman conquest by depicting its agents (emperors) and divine sanction (gods). Four panels include the goddess of victory, the winged Nike, whose divine will was expressed through Roman emperors victorious over local people. Included among the imperial figures are Augustus (several times); a sacrificing woman who is probably Livia, the wife of Augustus and mother of Tiberius; Claudius and his wife, Agrippina; Germanicus; Tiberius with a captive; and Nero being crowned by his mother, Agrippina. Several scenes depict violence. In one panel, Claudius with a spear stands over and holds down a defeated female figure Britannia, who raises her right hand either in defense or to beg for mercy. The scene personifies Claudius's invasion and annexation of Britain (43–47 CE). A similar panel presents Nero subduing a slumping female figure, who represents Armenia. But missing from the presentations are any scenes depicting the defeat of Greeks. R. R. Smith explains this selective "remembering" in terms of local identity and claims of the place of Greeks in the Roman world. He observes that the scenes depict "victories over Barbarians of various kinds: Britons, Armenians, and the like. The conquest of Greeks is long forgotten. That was before the emperors. The Greeks were now partners, not subjugated recalcitrants."[29]

Further, while the third storey depicts history, the second storey comprises mythology. Predictably various scenes reference Rome, especially its origins and founders, such as the flight of Aeneas from Troy toward Rome, and Romulus and Remus. But most of the scenes comprise standard Greek myths well known to many in the first-century.[30] Smith concludes that the southern portico evokes

the world of Greek culture and religion into which the Roman emperors are to be incorporated in the upper story. . . . Augustus, the Julio-Claudians, and the

Roman Empire were the natural outcome or continuation of *Greek* myth-history.
. . . The emperors are gods ruling over, and accommodated smoothly into, the
conceptual structure of the Greek world. . . . The relief panels as a whole present
a detailed and broadly expressed vision of the fortunate position of the Greek
world under Roman imperial rule.[31]

But while Smith emphasizes that these porticos depict the integration of the Greek
world into the Roman world, it is also true that they depict the integration of the
Roman world into the Greek world. In the very existence of the walls themselves and in
the details of the reliefs, the structure expresses much appreciation for the benefits of
Roman rule. Missing is any hostility toward Rome. There is no doubt about Rome's
mastery of the world. Yet the panels of this walkway leading to the imperial temple are
not only about Rome. In the beginning was not Rome, but the Greek mythological
world. Rome is set in its cosmic and historical place. Antiquity is authority.

Jewish Turning to the Past

This turn to the past as a means of negotiating Hellenistic culture and Roman power
through maintaining distinctives, ensuring integration, and at times expressing opposition[32] is also very evident in Jewish literature. Erich Gruen identifies two broad
expressions of this turn:

> Jews engaged actively with the traditions of Hellas, adapting genres and trans-
> forming legends to articulate their own legacy in modes congenial to a Hellenis-
> tic setting. At the same time they re-created their past, retold stories in different
> shapes, and amplified the scriptural corpus itself through the medium of the
> Greek language and Greek literary forms.[33]

The Gospel of John attests both the importance of the turn to the past to establish
identity as well as numerous conflicts over key figures and texts as the past is contested
to sustain particular identities and practices.[34] Moreover, given the above discussion of
the pervasiveness of this strategy for negotiating the first-century imperial world, it is
also likely that the conflicts in the Gospel narrative over "remembering" the past attest
not only Jewish religious conflicts (the common claim[35]) but also various strategies
employed in negotiating Roman power. Gail O'Day, for example, cites C. H. Dodd's verdict that the passage in which conflict centers on Abraham, 8:31–59, is "the *locus clas-
sicus* of Johannine theology" that identifies "the fundamental lines of debate and
disagreement between Judaism and Christianity."[36] But such a claim is problematic. Not
only is the language of "Judaism" and "Christianity" inappropriate, because it mistakenly and anachronistically assumes a clear-cut separation of two clearly defined entities
that simply did not exist by the end of the first century CE, it also draws the horizons
of the text too narrowly to focus only on "religious" matters and to exclude the well-
attested use of the past to negotiate Roman power. The discussion below will elaborate
this negotiation as it concerns initially two prominent and contested figures, Abraham
and Moses.

Prominent Jewish Figures

Abraham in John's Gospel

In John 8:31–59, Jesus conflicts with "the Jews who had believed in him" (8:30–31) over Abraham, mentioned eleven times[37] in the passage.[38] While the identification of this group of "Jews who had believed in him" is difficult to determine with certainty, in light of what happens throughout the passage it seems best to see them as a group committed to Jesus but whose commitment is exposed throughout this exchange as inadequate as far as the Gospel narrative is concerned, so that by 8:48 they are simply "the Jews."[39] The passage divides into two units. In verses 31–47 the focus falls on the relationship between Abraham and those "who had believed in" Jesus, highlighting claims of freedom, slavery, and descent from Abraham and from God. Verses 48–59, addressed perhaps to a different group or at least to the original group now redefined,[40] focus on the relationship between Abraham and Jesus. Throughout, the issues concern the significance and nature of descent from Abraham for the lives of those "believing in Jesus" as his disciples (8:31).[41]

The exchange in verses 31–47 concerning the relationship between these Jesus-believers and Abraham begins with Jesus instructing the Jesus-believers about their ongoing discipleship (8:31–32). Basic to discipleship, says Jesus, is "continuing in," or literally, "abiding in my word." The same verb appears eleven times in 15:1–17. *If* believers "abide in my word"—the construction is conditional—there are three consequences: truly being Jesus' disciple, knowing truth, and being set free (8:31–32). It is the last claim about freedom that these "Jesus-believers" take up in responding to Jesus.

In their response, they assert two things: "We are descendents of Abraham" and "have never been slaves to anyone" (8:33).[42] For them, some sort of relationship exists between the first two assertions, being descendents of Abraham and never being slaves, though the two claims are joined only by an "and." While the relationship between "Abraham" and "freedom" is not elaborated, it is nevertheless clearly asserted.

What is striking, and often given little attention by commentators, is the apparent falseness of their blanket assertion in 8:33 that as descendants of Abraham we "have never been slaves to anyone." The claim flatly contradicts another understanding of Jewish history, where there have been a continual series of conquering masters over many centuries, Egyptian, Assyrian, Babylonian, Persian, and Hellenistic. And to that list must be added Rome, their present master. Their claim of perpetual freedom completely ignores this past, marked by captivity. In its place they construct a past marked only by freedom, and they link this past comprising freedom to Abraham. The impact of this construction is to assert a surprising identity of freedom in the imperial present. Whatever its particulars, clearly demonstrated in their claim of never being slaves are the selective and constructive dimensions of turning to the past. They already have freedom and don't need what Jesus offers. What is it about being descendents of Abraham that allows them to "forget" the history of captivity and to assert their history of freedom and free identity in the present? What does their freedom look like?

Their construction of this past participates in a network of first-century Jewish reconstructions of the ancient figure of Abraham that negotiate the present. The

Genesis 12:1–3 scene depicts God calling the Gentile Abraham from "Ur of the Chaldeans" and "Haran" (11:31) and promising him that he will father a great nation, that his name will be great, and that in Abraham everyone will be blessed:

> I will make of you a great nation, and I will bless you, and make your name great, so that you will be a blessing. . . . And in you all the families of the earth shall be blessed. (Gen 12:2–3 NRSV)

The tradition adds further pieces to this promise, but by the first century "the turn to the Abrahamic past" had taken two main directions. One stream spanning texts such as Sirach, *Jubilees*, and the *Apocalypse of Abraham* emphasized connections between contemporary Judaism and Abraham, who had modeled trust in God, obedience to Torah and its particular requirements (e.g., circumcision), and affirmation of Israel's covenant identity and separation from the nations.[43] So Sirach, while affirming that "Abraham was the great father of a multitude of nations," locates Abraham especially in relation to the Torah, covenant, and circumcision:

> He kept the law of the Most High,
> and entered into a covenant with him;
> he certified the covenant in his flesh,
> and when he was tested he proved faithful. (Sir 44:19–21 NRSV)

Sirach chooses to emphasize Abraham's observance of the law and his covenant with God long before the time of Moses and the giving of the law! This strand emphasized Abraham's embracing of Jewish distinctives (Torah, circumcision) and separation from the nations.

In the post-70 CE *Apocalypse of Abraham*, for example, Abraham rejects idolatry, a feature of Gentiles (*Apoc. Ab.* 1–8), to embrace the one God known without idols, to whom he offers sacrifice (9). He encounters a vision and revelation from God of creation, human evil, and lawlessness (18–32). Israel's faithlessness to the covenant God has made with Israel is revealed to result in the destruction of Jerusalem in 70 CE. Monotheism, the rejection of idolatry, covenant, and the law (which Israel fails to obey) express Israel's special identity, distinctiveness, and separateness or distance from the nations.

The other stream, evident for instance in the second-century BCE Jewish writer Artapanus and the first century CE writers Philo and Josephus, constructed a very different Abraham.[44] Abraham is presented with universal appeal as a means of integration with Hellenistic culture and Roman power. For Artapanus, Abraham taught the Egyptians to study the stars.[45] For Philo, Abraham is a foreigner who leaves astrology and polytheism to seek truth and the one cause and God of all, reconciling reason[46] (including study of all academic disciplines[47]) and revelation (*On the Virtues* 211–219; *On Abraham* 66–88). He also reconciles nature and Torah as a "religious mystic" who lives not just in relation to Moses' teaching but also in accord with the "higher" or "more basic" or "antecedent" law of nature—of which the law of Moses is "at best a copy" or "secondary" (*On Abraham* 3–6, 275)—whereby his soul rises "above the obstacles of the body" and finds "communion with God" (88, 119–132).[48] His faith in

God is not equated with but supersedes all other factors of identity and human situation (262–276).

For Josephus, Abraham the philosopher engages in natural theology to be a monotheist (*Ant.* 1.155–156). For Josephus, according to Feldman, he is an "ideal statesman, . . . a philosopher-king."[49] He exports culture to other peoples and embodies all virtue. For instance, he teaches the Egyptians arithmetic and astronomy and shows himself to be intelligent, virtuous, sagacious, and persuasive (1.166–168). He opposes the Sodomites because they, unlike Abraham, hate foreigners (1.194). Abraham is welcoming to strangers (1.200).

The post-70 Mishnah tractate '*Abot* 5:19, dating from around 200 CE, also affirms openness to and enjoyment of the world. Being a disciple of Abraham is defined as having "a good eye, a humble spirit, and a lowly soul," in contrast to those who as disciples of Balaam have "an evil eye, a haughty spirit, and a proud soul." The text then asks, "How do the disciples of Abraham our father differ from the disciples of Balaam the wicked? The disciples of Abraham our father enjoy the world and inherit the world to come." Being a disciple of Abraham means not retreating from the world or heightening Israel's distinctive identity, but conducting oneself in the world with integrity so as to enjoy the world.

Whereas the first stream emphasized the distinctiveness of Abraham for Judaism, the second presented Abraham as a universal and world-affirming figure, a bridge linking Jews and non-Jews.

What sort of identity as "descendents of Abraham" are Jesus' listeners claiming in turning to the past to associate freedom with Abraham? In part, they claim ethnic solidarity as "seed" of Abraham. They are physically descended from Abraham (8:33). But to which Abraham do they appeal? Do they associate themselves with Abraham as the father of the Jewish nation and responsible for the covenant and distinctive Jewish customs like circumcision, which separated Jews from Gentile (the first stream above)? To emphasize the specialness or distinctiveness of this ethnic identity—the first stream above—would take them into a particular history marked by Jewish alienation and enslavement, beginning with slavery in Egypt, and experienced subsequently under Assyria, Babylon, Persia, Hellenistic rulers, and now Rome. But that is precisely what they do not claim. They do not acknowledge any enslavement by Gentiles, and nor do they appeal to any distinctive practices as does Sirach in remembering Abraham as one who kept the law, was in the covenant, and obediently was circumcised (Sir 44:19–21). Instead they claim freedom as Abraham's children.

They appear to "forget" this particularist history and link themselves to the second rendition of the past that emphasizes freedom. Their "free" Abraham is much more akin to the second stream that remembers Abraham in terms of openness to and participation in Gentile culture. This tradition emphasized Abraham the Gentile, who leaves the Chaldeans and ventures into the world. He does not hide away but is at home in and protected by God in Egypt (Gen 12:10–20; cf. Josephus, *Ant* 1.161–165), a player in international affairs (Gen 14:13–24), hospitable to outsiders (Gen 18), and one who learns that defensiveness and fear in foreign lands are not necessary since God is active there in enriching Abraham and healing others (Gerar, in Gen 20, esp. 20:11–18; cf. Josephus, *Ant.* 1.207–209). If this identification is correct, their remembered history of a "free" Abraham comprises and sanctions what Susan Alcock calls their "vital self-presentation and prideful self-assertion." Their identity as "Jesus-believers" finds in this tradition of "free" Abraham a means of bridging Jewish and non-Jewish worlds that empowers their engagement with and significant accommodation to the imperial present. That is, they are descendents of Abraham, who was open to and an active participant in the Gentile world. They construct Abraham in their own image. Though under Roman rule, they are essentially free in most ways from Roman restraints but able to observe Jewish distinctives without interfering with significant degrees of societal interaction. Evoking this Abraham facilitates the sort of imperial negotiation evident among Diaspora Jewish groups noted in chapters 2 and 3 above.

The response of John's Jesus, though, suggests little tolerance for this construct and the identity and societal interaction it creates and validates for these "Jesus-believers." Jesus immediately recasts their claim of freedom as enslavement to sin (8:34–35). In the context of his teaching in 8:31–32 and their appeal to a "free" Abraham (8:33), their sinfulness resides, according to Jesus, not only in the accommodationist or "free" way of life that they claim Abraham sanctions, but also in their rejection of Jesus' teaching. As slaves of this sinful way of life, they do not continue in his word, they are not his disciples, they do not know the truth, and they are not free (8:31–32).

Whose perspective on Abraham is more definitive? The continuing exchange makes clear the greater authority attributed to Jesus' words. His teaching is authoritative because it originates in "what I have seen in the Father's presence" (8:38a NRSV). The origin of his teaching means that these Jesus-believers "should do what you have heard from the Father" (8:38b NRSV). So as well as condemning their current "free" way of life as contrary to the Father's will, Jesus demands that they change it. His revelation, his "word," as "Son" of the Father and close to the Father's heart (cf. 1:18), can free them from their sinful practices (8:36). Presumably their new life in loyalty to him as descendents of Abraham would exhibit greater societal distance, higher boundaries, and much less toleration for accommodation. Jesus also indicates, though, that he expects no such change from them. In their sinfulness, they are determined to maintain the status quo. They are looking, Jesus claims twice, for an opportunity to kill him (8:37, 40), an action that shows "there is no place in you for my word" that comes from the Father (8:37 NRSV). Chapter 7 identified a number of such plans (7:1, 25, 30, 44–45; 8:20). In trying to kill Jesus, these "Jews who had believed in him" are shown to be not genuine believers in him, as 8:31 describes them to be, but allies with the Jerusalem elite and Pilate in putting Jesus to death (18:12, 28). Appropriately, they are identified in 8:48 simply as "the Jews."

Jesus does not dispute their physical descent from Abraham (8:37) but sets about defining what this means (8:39–47). Jesus shares their understanding that claims of descent identify a group that should live out the commitments or "works" of the ancestor. Like Father, like son. Jesus redefines what is central to Abraham, thereby contesting and rejecting their reconstruction of Abraham and their claim that Abraham sanctions their freedom. That is, the two parties struggle over reconstructing Abraham, to remember Abraham in ways that sanction their own practices and present identity.

Jesus sharply differentiates these Jesus-believers from Abraham (8:39–40). Abraham did not do what they want to do. Abraham did not try to kill one "who speaks the truth (to you), which I have heard from God" (8:39–40). Abraham embraced, not rejected, God's word. What exactly John's Jesus alludes to in the story of Abraham is not clear, though there are numerous possibilities. Abraham was receptive to the initial call to leave Ur of the Chaldees (Gen 12). He was obediently circumcised, a significant marker of cultural distance (Gen 17). He was hospitable to divine messengers (Gen 18). He was willing to sacrifice Isaac (Gen 22).[50] Because they don't emulate Abraham in receptivity and obedience to God's word revealed by Jesus, they are Abraham's genetic descendents (8:37) but not his children (8:39).[51] This distinction between "descendent" (*sperma*) and "children" (*tekna*) is crucial for the exchange.

Jesus presses the point. Because they do not emulate Abraham in receptivity and obedience to God's word now manifested by Jesus, they forfeit being God's children. Jesus disqualifies their assertion to be God's children (8:41) because they do not "love" him even though he comes from God who sent him (8:42). They do not accept his teaching, which also comes from God (8:43, 47). Being Abraham's children and being God's children are linked not by ethnicity but by the key qualities of receptivity and obedience to God's word. Genetic descent counts for nothing. Emulation of Abraham in receiving God's word is, though, archetypal. For John, that word of course is now Jesus: "To those who received him, who believed in his name, he gave power to become children of God" (1:12). Their nonreception of Jesus' word and their desire to kill Jesus reveals their sin, that they are not God's children, but they are the devil's children (8:44–47). Jesus has depicted their commitment to and accommodationist societal lifestyle based on "free" Abraham as not only sinful (8:34–35), enslaving (8:34–35), murderous (8:37, 40), and contrary to God's will and word (8:38, 43, 47), but now also as of the devil (8:44).

Verses 48–59 pick up a further issue, the relationship between Abraham and Jesus. This link provides another reason to reject their appeal to freedom sanctioned by Abraham. Their appeal to Abraham is further dismissed because Jesus has greater authority based in his antiquity. Abraham is set in his lesser place in the history of Jesus.

Jesus' disqualification of their claim to be children of God based in physical descent from Abraham brings a swift response in the form of name-calling (8:48). "The Jews who had believed in him" now become "the Jews," either a new group or a renaming of the Jesus-believers stripped of this identity because of their inadequate responses concerning Abraham and Jesus. They ironically accuse Jesus of not belonging to the covenant (Samaritan) and, turning the tables of 8:42–47, of belonging to the devil (being demonic; cf. 8:44). Jesus denies the latter and does not address the former (8:49).

A further claim about Jesus' word moves the exchange forward (8:51). Whoever keeps or observes his word (cf. 8:31) "will never see death," a reference to participating in "life of the age" (20:30–31; see chap. 8 below). His opponents counter by observing that this ridiculous claim confirms Jesus' demonic identity. The deaths of Abraham and the prophets show his absurdity. They provocatively ask a question about Jesus' identity: "Are you greater than our father Abraham, who died?" (8:53 NRSV). The question, introduced by *mē* (μή), expects a negative answer even as it ironically names the key issue in this section. In response, Jesus asserts his relationship to God ("know him") in contrast to their false claims (liars, 8:55), and affirms his "keeping" of God's word, like Abraham, and unlike them (8:55). In this regard Jesus is like Abraham. He has allied himself with Abraham.

Then Jesus asserts that he is greater than Abraham. "Your ancestor Abraham rejoiced that he would see my day; he saw it and was glad" (8:56 NRSV). Whereas they had claimed Abraham's authority to legitimate and empower their identity and way of life (8:33, 39, 53), now Jesus claims Abraham as a witness to himself and against them.

Jesus' claim that Abraham had "seen his day" evokes another remembering of Abraham in apocalyptic traditions that present Abraham as gaining special knowledge of God's purposes. In the *Testament of Abraham* 10–15, written around the same time as John's Gospel, the archangel Michael takes Abraham on a chariot ride over the earth and ascends to the heavens to see righteous judgment and merciful purposes.[52] In *4 Ezra* (= 2 Esd) 3:13–14, also written around the same time as John, God makes special revelation to Abraham: "You loved him and to him only you revealed the end of the times, secretly by night."[53] In *2 Baruch* 4:2–4, from the same time period, God creates the new Jerusalem: "It is that which will be revealed, with me, that was already prepared from the moment that I decided to create Paradise. . . . After these things I showed it to my servant Abraham in the night."[54] In the *Apocalypse of Abraham*, God orders Abraham to sacrifice and says, "In this sacrifice I will place the ages. I will announce to you guarded things and you will see great things which you have not seen" (9:6–7). Later Abraham ascends into the heavens (chap. 15), encounters God, tours the heavens, and glimpses the future (chaps. 18–30).[55] John's Jesus claims that the content of these mystical revelations and experiences associated with Abraham concerns himself. By these means Abraham previewed Jesus' ministry and rejoiced in it, showing his commitment to Jesus, not a desire to kill him.

This claim leads to a further credulous question about Jesus seeing Abraham: "You are not yet fifty years old, and have you seen Abraham?" (8:57). The ridiculed assumption is that somehow Jesus knew Abraham in his lifetime. Jesus' counterclaim is startling: "Before Abraham was, I am" (8:58). Jesus asserts temporal priority over Abraham. Jesus has greater antiquity. The answer to verse 53's question about being greater than Abraham, to which they expect Jesus to say "No," turns out to be "Yes." Jesus is not set in relation to Abraham, as they think, but Abraham is set in his place in the context of Jesus' existence "in the beginning" with God (1:1). Abraham, like John the Baptist (1:19–27) and (as we will see) like Moses (5:39), bears witness to Jesus, so any appeal to Abraham to sanction any identity, "free" way of life, or practice in the present needs to be consistent with Jesus, not at odds with him. The two different tenses of 8:58, Abraham's "was" (γενέσθαι, *genesthai*) and Jesus' "am" (ἐγὼ εἰμί, *egō eimi*), links one who is confined by time with one who was "in the beginning" (1:1). The former is diminished, the latter elevated. The former witnesses to the latter. Jesus has greater authority. His superiority rests partly in his temporal priority to Abraham, and significantly in his relationship with God. Throughout the exchange he has asserted his origin from and unity with God as the basis for his authoritative word (8:38, 42, 55). The "I am" that Jesus announces expresses both (cf. 1:1). Antiquity is authority. Such claims provoke stone-throwing violence in confirmation of Jesus' accusations (8:37, 40, 44).

The exchange reflects, I am suggesting, a struggle for the past as a means of defining identity and lifestyle in the imperial present. This struggle is not only or even primarily intramural between Judaism and Christianity, as is commonly claimed, but concerns ways in which Jesus-believers (and other synagogue members?) negotiated the imperial world. One group finds empowerment for its identity as children of God and for its "free" or societally interactive and accommodationist way of life by appealing to kinship with Abraham, who in one remembering of Abraham embraced the Gentile world.

Abraham justifies their imperial negotiation marked by significant accommodation and maintenance of distinctives. Jesus declares such a way of life not to be free but to be enslavement to sin. He denies their identity because they do not emulate Abraham in the key quality of receptive obedience to God's word, which in John's dualistic schema should set them at odds with the nonbelieving world. The verdict on their present accommodation is that it is enslaving sin, not freedom. Jesus makes these assertions, disqualifying their identity and lifestyle, and asserting an alternative identity and lifestyle shaped by his word, on the basis of his unity with God and his temporal priority to Abraham. He was in the beginning with God. Abraham witnesses to him and against them. Antiquity is authority.

Moses in John's Gospel

Another turn to the past concerns the figure of Moses.[56] Moses is explicitly mentioned twelve times in this Gospel, though engagement with this towering figure from the past extends well beyond the specific references.[57] In conventional readings, there is wide scholarly agreement that references to Moses reflect "church-synagogue" conflicts, with Jesus presented as a (greater) "prophet like Moses" or Mosaic king. Following Martyn's claim of a two-level drama, this conflict is evident in 9:28–29, for instance, as Jesus' opponents declare themselves to be "disciples of Moses" and to confess that they know "God has spoken to Moses." They identify the former blind man as "his [Jesus'] disciple" and declare that they "do not know where [Jesus] comes from." Issues of allegiance, revelation of God's purposes, and origin, so the argument goes, seem to be especially to the fore in this church-synagogue conflict.

Three modifications are needed to this view. If the separation scenario is not convincing and if synagogues are locations of imperial negotiation, as I have argued in chapters 2 and 3 and as the above brief discussion of Abraham further demonstrates, the intensity of the conflicts over Moses needs to be dialed back from separation/expulsion to that of dialogue, their intramural nature among Jesus-believers and synagogue members emphasized, and their hitherto neglected role in the synagogue's negotiations of the Roman imperial world investigated. How do the various and conflicted rememberings of Moses participate in imperial negotiation? Do the disputes over Moses run along the same "distinctives versus accommodation/world citizen" axis evident in the Abraham conflict, or is the presentation somewhat different?

The remembering of Moses took various forms in Jewish traditions. One form emphasized the rooting of various practices that were widely understood to express Jewish identity as well as mark its distinctiveness—rejection of cultic worship, circumcision, Sabbath observance, separatism at meals—in Moses' teaching, the Torah.[58] Circumcision marked covenant loyalty (Gen 17). Concerning worship of other gods, Moses warns the people, "Take care that you are not snared into imitating them. . . . Do not inquire concerning their gods" (Deut 12:30–31 NRSV). He likewise warns against using images in worship (Exod 20:4–6; Deut 5:8–10). Moses also commands Sabbath observance (Exod 20:8–11) and separatism at meals (Lev 11; Deut 14). The making present of the past certainly required interpretation of the past, and not surprisingly different understandings and observances emerged in the present. But the past, notably the teaching of Moses, provided, for some Jews, clear instruction about maintaining distinctive identity in the (Roman) present.

In this tradition, *Jubilees* 22:16 commanded, "Separate yourselves from the nations and eat not with them." In the *Letter of Aristeas* (139, 142), Moses "the legislator . . . surrounded us with unbroken palisades and iron walls to prevent our mixing with any of the other peoples in any matter. . . . So to prevent our being perverted by contact with others by mixing with bad influences, he hedged us in on all sides with strict observances connected with meat and drink and touch and hearing and sight, after the manner of the law." It is this tradition of separateness that Roman authors especially seem to associate with Moses. Quintilian, for instance, in referring to the unnamed Moses and refusing to call him a lawgiver, laments how troublesome it is for cities when some one has "brought together a people which is bent on the destruction of others, as for example the creator of the Jewish superstition" (*Inst.* 3.7.21). Tacitus condemns Moses as one who "introduced new practices which are opposed to all other men." After attacking Jewish worship of animals, abstention from pork, unleavened bread (commemorating "grains which they stole"), and observance of the Sabbath as a form of laziness, Tacitus concedes that "these practices . . . are supported by their antiquity," though their institutions "are foul and perverse and have survived only by their depravity" (*Hist.* 5.4–5). Tacitus is no admirer of the novel and the distinctive, though he seems to recognize Moses' significant though misguided contribution. Juvenal aligns Jewish "disdain [for] Roman customs" alongside Jewish reverence for "everything that Moses handed down" and Jewish general antipathy to those who do not share "the same rites" (*Sat.* 14.100–104). Thus the Jewish turn to the Mosaic past in this rendering highlights distinctive Jewish identity and practices. It defines Jewish identity by, in Susan Alcock's words, a "vital self-presentation and prideful self-assertion" of Jewish distinctiveness over against a dominant culture, whether Hellenistic or Roman.

Yet as much as the turn to the past to Moses' teaching was a source of Jewish distinctiveness, it also functioned as a source of pride and "reaffirmation of their own lustrous legacy" to enable participation in Hellenistic-Roman political and cultural power. Such pride engendered by a turn to the Mosaic past was expressed not in separateness but in considerable association and engagement with Gentile cultures, playing down distinctives to varying extents and finding sanction for participation. In a chapter appropriately entitled "Pride and Precedence," Gruen continues:

> The pride of Jews in the precedence of their character, creed, and accomplishments sustained them through this era. . . . Jews recast biblical tales and rewrote history in order both to embellish antique traditions and to elevate their places within the recent past. . . . Their inventiveness found a still greater variety of means whereby to broadcast associations with Hellenic culture and society while underscoring superiority.[59]

Moses especially functions as a source for such associations with Hellenic culture and society. John Gager observes that Moses was "by far the best-known figure of Jewish history in the pagan world."[60] While negative views of Moses existed, Moses is also located among the greats of various cultures and writers attribute to him a key role in shaping certain cultures. Hecataeus of Abdera (writing early fourth century–late third century BCE) praises Moses as "highly distinguished in practical wisdom," courageous, a founder of cities, and as legislating and regulating political affairs, though he comments that Moses "introduced a way of life which was somewhat unsocial and hostile to foreigners."[61] Poseidonius of Apamea (first century BCE) emphasizes Moses' monotheism and rejection of images along with his accomplishment of setting up an "excellent government."[62] According to Artapanus, a second-century BCE Jewish figure probably from Egypt, Moses is known to the Greeks as Musaeus, who, Artapanus claims, taught Orpheus, the founder of Greek culture. He also "bestowed many useful benefits on humankind for he invented boats and devices for stone construction and the Egyptian arms and the implements for drawing water and for warfare and for philosophy." He does not oppose Egyptian gods and makes no effort to convert anyone to the Jewish God.[63]

The second-century BCE Alexandrian Jewish biblical interpreter Aristobulus presents Moses as the teacher of the Torah, with widespread cultural impact. It is from Torah that Plato "imitated our legislation" and Pythagoras "integrated [many of our doctrines] into his own system of beliefs."[64] Pythagoras, Socrates, and Plato "copy [Moses] when they say that they hear the voice of God, when they contemplate the arrangement of the universe." Aristobulus also finds in Orpheus an understanding of monotheism and God's power over all, and presents Homer and Hesiod as supporting the Sabbath, making it an ancient practice valued by the poets and not a strange practice for which Jews could be maligned. Greek thought and Moses' teaching are in harmony with each other, but the latter has greater antiquity and therefore superiority.[65]

For the first-century CE Jewish writer Josephus, "our legislator," Moses, "is the most ancient of all legislators in the records of the whole world," more so than Lycurgus, Solon, or Zaleucus. This antiquity matters, say Josephus, because it shows that the Jewish nation, "far from imitating others, . . . has been the one to set its neighbors an example of orderly life under law" (*Ag. Ap.* 2.151–156). But Moses provides more than example. Josephus goes on to argue that in relation to understandings of God, "the wisest of the Greeks learned to adopt these conceptions of God from principles with which Moses supplied them." Josephus points to Pythagoras, Anaxagoras, Plato, and the Stoics as examples (2.168). And Moses' "Law has found its way among all humankind" (2.284). Throughout, Josephus presents Moses as a Stoic sage.[66] This strand of Mosaic tradition, while not denying Jewish distinctives, presents Moses as significantly engaged with and influential in Gentile cultures, the basis for "vital self-presentation and prideful self-assertion" by Jews as participants in these cultures.

Where are the various re-presentations of Moses in John's Gospel to be located in relation to these diverse depictions? The first of the twelve explicit references to Moses in John's Gospel appears in the Gospel's opening Prologue. The turn to the Mosaic past introduces Moses in relation to Jesus and recognizes Moses as Israel's lawgiver: "For the law was given through Moses; grace and truth came through Jesus Christ" (1:17).[67] The relationship between the two clauses and the two figures is difficult. The double "through" draws them together as mediators of God's gifts,[68] but if the giver is the same, are the gifts of equal value and the mediators of equal status? Is Jesus a prophet like Moses or, as numerous scholars have suggested, greater than and even somewhat antithetical to Moses?[69] Has the second gift replaced or supplemented or added to the first?

The question is difficult to answer with regard to 1:17, and there is not much help from the previous verse, where the same issue essentially surfaces. Verse 16 picks up the claim of verse 14 that the "word became flesh" and was "full of grace and truth." From this "fullness," Jesus-believers ("we") have received "grace *in place of*" or "grace *upon* grace" (1:16). While the continuity of grace is maintained, the preposition ἀντί (*anti*) is ambiguous in indicating replacement or accumulation, as many observe. Verse 17b repeats the claim of verse 14 but now in the context of Moses, named in verse 17a. The use of the divine passive to refer to God giving the law to Israel through Moses establishes that the law was a gracious gift from God, but it does not clarify whether the second clause and its reference to Jesus replaces or adds to this gift. Many have seen the double phrase "grace and truth" translating the Hebrew covenant terms *ḥesed* and *ĕmet*. This pair appears, for instance, in Exodus 34:6 to refer to God's loving-kindness or covenant love (*ḥesed*) for Israel and to God's faithfulness (*ĕmet*) to Israel, though Greek translations of the first term often use a different, albeit appropriate, word (*eleos*, mercy) rather than the term *charis* (grace) used here. If the link is sustainable, it foregrounds the importance of Israel's distinctive covenant and its teaching, while establishing the presence of mercy/grace and faithfulness/truth in the law as part of God's covenantal relationship with Israel. It does not, though, clarify the relationship of the gifts of Moses and of Jesus.

One could posit that the placement of Moses before Jesus in 1:17 suggests that Moses has temporal priority over Jesus, and since antiquity is authority, that Moses has greater authority. But the context of the Prologue disqualifies this argument, while providing a clue to the relationship between Moses and Jesus. Jesus is the word become flesh in 1:14. Verse 1 locates the word "in the beginning . . . with God" (1:1). Jesus has temporal priority over Moses. Antiquity is authority. God gives the law to Moses in the context of the word's being with God "in the beginning." Moses, it seems, is put in his place in the scheme of things. Jesus precedes and follows God's gift through Moses.

But does Jesus supersede it? The only definitive way for establishing the relationship between the two is to read on through the Gospel. Subsequently, it appears that Jesus does not replace or abolish the law. Jesus, for instance, refers to Moses giving the law and the practice of circumcision without denigrating or abolishing either (7:19–23). Likewise, while there are conflicts over the Sabbath in John 5 and 9, Jesus does not advocate its abolition or denigrate it. Jesus seems to uphold these distinctives or particularities established through Moses' teaching.

Yet the questions of the role of the law, along with the value of loyalty to Moses, are frequently to the fore. In various conflicts with Jesus, his opponents claim loyalty to Moses while Jesus shows such loyalty to be inadequate or a misunderstanding of Moses' role.

The conflicts over the Sabbath in 5:1–18 and chapter 9 provide good examples. Both chapters share two issues. One concerns the appropriate *observance* of the Sabbath (5:18, lit., "he was loosening the Sabbath"), not its abolition. In both scenes, the question about observance concerns the legitimacy of healing on the Sabbath: "making whole" in 5:14 and restoring sight in 9:14–21. The second issue concerns who has the authority to determine adequate observance. It is no accident, as has often been observed, that the disputes in both chapters move from the issue of Sabbath praxis to that of Jesus' authority to interpret Sabbath traditions in terms of God's will (5:18; 9:28–

29). In both chapters, appeals to Moses' authority are set against Jesus' authority. In John 5, Jesus, not his opponents, raises the question of his relationship to Moses. Their failure to accept Jesus' authority and entrust themselves to Jesus means, says Jesus, their condemnation by Moses. "Do not think that I will accuse you before the Father; your accuser is Moses, on whom you have set your hope" (5:45 NRSV). He goes on to question their commitment to and understanding of Moses: "If you believed Moses, you would believe me, for he wrote about me" (5:46 NRSV). Jesus co-opts Moses, the giver of the law, as one who has an ongoing role of bearing witness to Jesus. Whereas Philip has recognized this and become a disciple of Jesus, these opponents have not (1:45). Jesus upholds the observance of Jewish distinctives derived from Moses as well as emphasizing that Moses must be understood correctly as bearing witness to Jesus. Moses joins Abraham as subject to and as a witness to Jesus, who was "in the beginning . . . with God." Antiquity is authority.

The narrative of John 9 draws Moses and Jesus together in recognizing that both are revealers of God (9:28–33) but relativizes the value of the respective revelations. The *Ioudaioi* or Pharisees (9:13, 15, 16, 18) declare their loyalty to Moses; in response to the healed man's taunt, they identify themselves: "We are disciples of Moses" (9:28). The healing occurred on the Sabbath (9:14), causing some to conclude that Jesus "does not observe the Sabbath" and so cannot be from God (9:16). Others reject this conclusion (9:16b), and the investigation into the healing continues with the questions about Jesus' identity and origin to the fore, rather than matters concerning the Sabbath (9:24–34). As disciples of Moses, they affirm the common pentateuchal theme that God has spoken to Moses (Exod 33:11; 34:29–35; Num 12:2, 8), but they do not know Jesus' origin (9:28–29). The healed man is quite sure that Jesus' origin is from God (9:33).

The relative merits of Moses' and Jesus' revelation is a recurring issue. The exclusivity of the claim of 1:18 that "No one has ever seen God" except Jesus the Son reinforces the greater authority of Jesus, albeit by selectively neglecting the claim of Deuteronomy 34:10 (cf. Num 12:8) that Moses was a prophet "whom the Lord knew face to face." John's claim underlines Jesus' greater authority and undermines Moses' by evoking the Prologue's opening verse and Jesus' exclusive (!) access to and face-to-face relationship with God "in the beginning with/toward [πρός, *pros*] God."

A similar move happens in 3:13–14, where a reference to Moses is contrasted with another declaration of Jesus' exclusive access to, and superior revelation of, God.

> No one has ascended into heaven but he who descended from heaven, the Son of Man. And as Moses lifted up the serpent in the wilderness, so must the Son of man be lifted up. (3:13–14)

While claims of Moses' encounter with God or traditions of Moses' ascent into the heavens (see below) are denied, Moses' role of bearing witness to Jesus is again affirmed. His lifting up the serpent (Num 21:8–9) anticipates and points to Jesus' lifting up. And similarly in 6:25–34, Moses' giving of manna anticipates the gift of Jesus, the bread of life. Both incidents recall the narrative of Moses' role in God's covenant with Israel, and the revelation of Torah and its distinctive requirements for Israel.

But while there is some continuity in that Moses bears witness to Jesus and in that both recognize particular Jewish customs though interpreting their observance somewhat differently, both John 6 and 3:13–14 emphasize the limits of Moses' acts and gifts. The long "bread of life" conversation in 6:25–71 follows the miracle of feeding the five thousand (6:1–14).[70] The crowds seek a sign from Jesus to justify belief in him (6:30), thereby confirming Jesus' verdict in 6:26 that they do not recognize the significance of the signs he has just performed as revelations of God's life-giving and reigning power (6:1–21). The crowd evokes their ancestors' experience whereby Moses provided manna for them in the wilderness (6:31). Jesus immediately rejects the ascription of the gift to Moses. God "my Father" provided it; Moses is the mediator (6:32). And Jesus changes the tenses, from "gave" (ἔδωκεν, δέδωκεν, *edōken, dedōken*; 6:31–32) to "gives" (δίδωσιν *didōsin*), thus refocusing attention on his own continuing present activity. And he contrasts that bread with the "true bread," himself now present among them (6:32). The changes elevate Jesus, who is the gift available in the present. Moses' power is trimmed (God did the miracle) and not operative in the present. Likewise in 3:13–14, it is the limits of Moses' access to and revelation of God that especially stand out. Only Jesus, the descending-ascending Son of Man, ascends into heaven.

To what does John's Jesus refer in 3:13–14? Numerous Jewish sources remember Moses as ascending not only Sinai but also ascending into or experiencing visions of heaven to meet with God, who gave him both special knowledge and the power to rule the world.[71] Ezekiel the Tragedian, for instance, has Moses exercise rule over the world in God's place. In a dream Moses mounts the heavenly throne and later says, God "gave to me the crown" (*Exagōgē* [*Leading Out*] 68–69, 75). Jethro interprets these actions to mean that "you yourself [Moses] shall rule and govern men" (86). Discussions of Philo's understandings of Moses have emphasized that Moses in his roles as lawgiver, prophet, and priest is the ideal Hellenistic king and is enthroned in heaven at the time of the Sinai revelation. Philo says that Moses "was named god and king of the whole nation" (*Moses* 1.158, 334). God rewarded Moses by giving him "the wealth of the whole earth and sea and rivers and of all the other elements and the combinations which they form. . . . He gave into his hands the whole world as a portion well fitted for his heir." Moses is a "world citizen, and therefore not on the roll of any city of human habitation, rightly so because he has received no mere piece of land but the whole world as his portion" (*Moses* 1.155–157). As ruler of the world, Moses is a cosmopolitan figure consonant with the various Jewish traditions noted above that find in Moses a significant openness to and engagement with Gentile cultures, whereby Moses greatly impacts Greek and other cultures by imparting knowledge of laws, government, and monotheism while also respecting and not deriding even the gods of other peoples (so Josephus, *Ag. Ap.* 2.237).

Are such claims in view in the claims of Jesus' revelation and relationship with God in 1:18, 3:13–14, and 9:29, "We know God has spoken to Moses"? Does John's Jesus counter the claims of Moses' cosmic rule and engagement with Gentile culture by adding spatial authority to Jesus' temporal authority over Moses by antiquity, thus claiming that heaven is accessible to Jesus alone?

A complete denial of God speaking to Moses would preserve the exclusive access Jesus has to God, but it would be quite problematic in being at odds with the tradition (Exod 33–34) as well as being at odds with Jesus' honoring of Torah-sanctioned practices like circumcision and Sabbath observance. Moreover, Jesus has claimed that Moses "wrote of" Jesus and witnesses to him (5:45–46), claims that are strengthened by upholding the tradition of God talking to Moses. Further, we have seen that John's Jesus understands traditions about Abraham's heavenly ascent in terms of his seeing Jesus' day in the heavens (8:56–58). It could well be that claims of Moses bearing witness to Jesus (1:45; 5:45–46) reinterpret Moses' heavenly ascent traditions in terms of glimpsing Jesus, and bearing witness to him (as does Isaiah also: John 12:41). Moses did not see God but saw Jesus (1:18).

What, then, of the claim of 3:13 that "no one has ascended into heaven"? The explanation resides in the order of the verbs that "no one has ascended" except the one who "descended," the term "Son of Man," and the verb "lifted up," which point in directions other than Moses' heavenly visits. As many have observed, the verb "lift up" carries a double meaning, referring to both Jesus' kingly lifting up on the cross, and his lifting up/exaltation[72] through resurrection and ascension to God (also 8:28; 12:32–34). John 3:13 refers, then, to the exclusivity of Jesus' final exaltation to God, which Moses cannot equal. Only Jesus, who first descended, has ascended to God through crucifixion and resurrection. Moses has not ascended into heaven by these means. And Jesus returns to his origin, to where he was "in the beginning," something Moses cannot do.

The existence of polemic in 3:13 against "disciples of Moses" (9:28) has been frequently recognized.[73] But the nature of the polemic is clarified somewhat by the use of the term "Son of Man," along with the reference to crucifixion and ascension whereby the verb "lifted up" (ὑψόω, *hypsoō*) is used for exaltation to kingship, as in Ps 89:19 (88:20 LXX). The introduction of the term "Son of Man" into the discourse at this point—it has been absent from the first twelve verses—and its repetition in both verses 13 and 14 frame Jesus' ascension in a particular light. The term draws on Daniel 7:13, where the Son of Man is a heavenly figure. To him God gives

> dominion and glory and kingship, that all peoples, nations, and languages should serve him. His dominion is an everlasting dominion that shall not pass away, and his kingship is one that shall never be destroyed. (Dan 7:14 NRSV)

To identify Jesus as Son of Man is to assign him the role of exercising God's dominion over all peoples. The reference in John 3:14 to Moses raises the possibility that this identity is asserted in part because of and against the claims described above about Moses, that he represented God's rule over the world. Jesus is much greater than Moses.

If, then, 3:13–14 is polemical, perhaps we find in it a clue that suggests, among some in the synagogue community including among Jesus-believers, not only loyalty to Moses and to his authority for Jewish distinctives (like Sabbath and circumcision, which Jesus does not challenge), but also an appeal to his identity as a king and world citizen who participates in God's rule and is understood therefore to sanction active engagement with and considerable participation in daily life in imperial Ephesus. Moses' influence as ruler and citizen of the world would appear to reach beyond Jewish distinctives to validate active societal interaction and participation.

The claim that the risen Jesus as the descended Son of Man is the only one to have ascended into heaven (postcrucifixion) and has been given dominion over all peoples elevates him over Moses, and it disputes claims about Moses' ascension into heaven to participate in God's ruling purposes. Further, this claim about Jesus disputes the appeals to Moses to sanction ready engagement with the imperial world. "No one has ascended into heaven except. . . ." The claim that Jesus as Son of Man has ascended is not good news for accommodated synagogue members and Jesus-believers in Ephesus, nor for the Roman Empire. At first glance it might seem that there is not much here with which to trouble an empire that seems so comfortably in place and so readily at home in Ephesus and the province of Asia. The troubling dimension, though, appears first in clarifying the process of his ascension. He is exalted through crucifixion and resurrection. His crucifixion seems to be the empire's victory, an assertion of its power, a means of ensuring and protecting the status quo against one who would trouble it. Assertions of the empire's power in the act of crucifying Jesus require and expose a fundamentally antithetical relationship between Jesus and the empire. The act of crucifixion reveals a context of challenge, collision, and contest, only apparently won by Rome. That Jesus-believers follow one whom the empire crucified undercuts any lifestyle of ready accommodation and any appeal to Moses as world ruler but as one who was not crucified. An accommodated way of life allies with an empire that is shown in Jesus' crucifixion to be fundamentally at odds with God's purposes and agent. That way of life cannot continue.

Moreover, resurrection and exaltation expose Rome's victory as hollow, the empire's power as limited, and its rule as temporary. It is hollow because it cannot keep Jesus dead. Its power is limited because it cannot order the world against the agent of God's power and purposes. The implications for Jesus-believers are profound. The fundamental antipathy between God and Rome revealed in Jesus' resurrection means that any ready alliance with Rome is not the way ahead for Jesus-believers. A lifestyle marked predominantly by accommodation with Rome is not consistent with either Jesus' crucifixion or his exaltation. These events mandate more distance than accommodation, more suspicion than participation.

And finally, that Jesus is identified as Son of Man underlines the temporary and inferior nature of Rome's rule because dominion over all creation is given to the risen and exalted Jesus. To him is given "everlasting dominion, glory, and kingship" over all people (Dan 7:14). For the gospel, the ascended Jesus, Son of Man, not Rome and not Moses, enacts God's purposes for all people. Rome does not have the last word. Jesus is the word who was "in the beginning with God," before Moses, before Rome. As Son of Man exalted into heaven to God, where he was "in the beginning," he enacts God's purposes over all people. Antiquity is authority.

Jesus as Wisdom

Behind and beyond these disputes over the ancient figures of Abraham and Moses is the Gospel's locating of Jesus "in the beginning . . . with God" (1:1). In this claim, scholars have rightly seen the evoking of the creation story in Genesis 1, as well as of wisdom traditions in which Wisdom dwells with God "before the beginning of the earth" (Prov 8:23 NRSV). The identification of Jesus as Wisdom, which pervades the Gospel, locates Jesus "in the beginning," before all else.[74] This turn to the past as a turn to the beginning comprises the ultimate antiquity and ensures ultimate authority for Jesus.

Sharon Ringe traces the development of wisdom traditions within the Hebrew Bible, arguing that they develop "from principle to presence."[75] Initially in writings such as Psalm 104 and Job 28, wisdom concerns the order in creation and human society that shapes human lives and is understood to conform to and thus reveal God's ways. This quest for the order of creation and society developed into a realization of God's active presence in creation and social interaction (Prov 1–9). Wisdom was with God before and during creation (Prov 8:22–36; Sir 24:9). Writers personified this presence as a woman, Lady Wisdom, who reveals God's purposes and mediates between the divine and human.[76] She has a counterpart, Lady Folly, who resists God's ways.

In these traditions, Wisdom is an ambiguous figure. She personifies divine power, presence, and purposes, yet protects monotheism. She is immanent in creation, yet distinct from it. She is a heavenly figure enjoying intimate relationship with God, yet she is active on earth (Prov 8:22–36). She pervades creation, yet is especially identified with God's people, Israel (Sir 24:8–12), guiding Moses and leading the people in the exodus (Wis 10–11). She is a revealer who seeks out people (Sir 24:19–22), yet many people do not welcome her, and she goes away and hides (*1 En.* 42:1–3). She frequently ignores traditions about the covenant and exodus, and yet she is identified with Torah (Sir 24:23; Bar 4:1). At heart, wisdom mysteriously manifests God and God's presence and purposes.

John reinterprets this wisdom paradigm in relation to Jesus, identifying Jesus as Wisdom. The Gospel's opening eighteen verses, the Prologue, present Jesus in terms of at least twelve qualities that he shares with wisdom.[77] Both Jesus and Wisdom exist in the beginning before creation (John 1:1; Prov 8:22–30; Sir 1:4; 24:9; Wis 9:9), are "with God" (John 1:1; Prov 8:30; Wis 9:4), share divine life (John 1:1; Wis 7:25–26), are instruments of creation (John 1:3; Prov 3:19; 8:30; Wis 7:22; 9:1–2), are sources of light and life (John 1:4; Prov 8:35; Bar 4:1b–2; Wis 7:26), cannot be overcome by darkness/evil (John 1:5; Wis 7:29–30), are sent or descend from heaven and come into the world to reveal and manifest God's presence (John 1:9; Prov 8; Wis 6:13, 16; 7:27; Sir 24:6–7; Bar 3; *1 En.* 42), are rejected by humans (John 1:10b, 11b; *1 En.* 42:2; Bar 3:20–21), enable receptive humans to relate to God (John 1:12–13; Wis 7:27; 9:18), lived among humans (John 1:14; Bar 3:37; Sir 24:8, 11–12), possess unique glory (John 1:14, 18; Wis 7:22, 25), know God and make God known (John 1:18; Wis 8:4; 9:9–10).

The wisdom motifs in the Prologue's presentation of Jesus continue through the Gospel.[78] For instance, in all but one of the complements of the famous "I am" sayings (ἐγὼ εἰμί, *egō eimi*), Jesus reveals that God's presence and gifts are associated with wisdom and with God, whom Wisdom manifests.[79] John interprets Jesus as Wisdom, the manifestation or revelation of God.

1. As Wisdom, Jesus mediates God's presence and gifts, especially life. Jesus' words and deeds convey what he saw/learned with God in the beginning (John 3:11–15; 5:19–46; 6:46). Thus to see or know Jesus is to see or know God (14:7–14). Jesus manifests God's presence or light (8:12–20; 9:5; 11:9–10; 12:35–36, 46). He mediates "eternal life" or "life of the age," which transforms physical suffering (4:46–54), overcomes death (Lazarus, John 11), and establishes intimate, everlasting friendship with God (6:35–40, 47–51; 8:51; 10:10, 28; 14:1–4). Conversely, to reject Jesus is to reject God (15:18–25). Jesus is God (1:1) in the sense that he makes God visible (12:45; 14:9), audible (14:10, 24), and knowable (14:7).

2. Some people accept and others reject the revelation of God made by Jesus/Wisdom. Those who accept become children of God (1:12–13), having been born "from above" (3:1–10). They "abide/remain" with Jesus and form a new community of love for

one another (15:1–17). Others, frequently identified as "the world," reject Jesus (1:10–11) and his followers (15:18–24; 16:1–4). As Wisdom, Jesus causes divisions, dividing believers from nonbelievers, cosmically and socially.

3. As Wisdom Jesus reveals God's glory. He displays the presence and power of God ("glory") among humans, in his life and death (7:18, 39; 8:50, 54; 11:4; 12:23, 27–29; 13:31–32; 14:13).

4. As Wisdom, Jesus manifests God's saving presence among people. Like Wisdom Jesus encounters people in public places (Prov 1:20–33; 8:1–36). John 1–11 presents a series of public encounters as Jesus reveals God's purposes at the wedding of Cana (2:1–11), in the Jerusalem temple (2:13–21), at a well in Samaria (John 4), to the official at Capernaum (4:46–53), to the sick at the pool with five porticoes at the Sheep Gate (John 5), on a mountain (6:1–14), and by the sea (6:25–71). As a teacher/rabbi (1:38; 3:2; 8:4; 13:12–14; 20:16), Jesus teaches or reveals God's just, loving (13:34; 14:15–17, 21; 15:10, 12–17), and life-giving ways (6:59; 7:14–24; 8:2, 20, 28; 18:20). The Paraclete (παρά-κλητος, *paraclētos*) continues this task in Jesus' absence (14:26; 16:4–15). Just as Wisdom invites people to feasts as expressions of God's good presence, life, and blessing (e.g., Prov 9:5), so also Jesus provides wine (2:1–11), gives "water of life" to the Samaritan woman (chap. 4), feeds the multitude (6:1–14) and describes himself as "bread of life" (6:25–65). He hosts a meal in John 13. He describes the Spirit as abundant living water (7:37–39). Jesus like Wisdom supplies necessities, mediates life, and protects from danger.

The basis and authority for Jesus' revealing God's saving presence is his origin "in the beginning . . . with God" (1:1). He is "from God," and his destiny is to return to God (3:11–21; 7:32–36; 8:21–30; 13:1–3; 14:1–17, 28–31; 16:7). He descends from heaven (6:35–50) but must be "lifted up" to return through crucifixion, resurrection, and ascension (3:14–15; 8:28; 12:34). He is sent from God (5:38; 7:18, 28–29; 12:44; 13:20) to "save the world" or mediate God's redemptive presence (3:16–17; 5:34; 10:9; 12:47). As Wisdom he gives life (3:16–17). His return to heaven means absence from his followers, so he reassures them (John 14–16) of his abiding presence through the Spirit (14:26; 16:13–14) until they join Jesus in the place he has prepared (14:1–7).

This presentation of Jesus as Wisdom shapes the Gospel. His origin "in the beginning . . . with God" and his identity as God in that he is the revelation of God (1:1) provide the basis for his authoritative revelation. There is no rival to his antiquity "in the beginning" and hence no rival to his authority. Abraham and Moses bear witness to him. That is not to deny that there is wisdom in Torah (Sir 24). But its subsidiary role comprises its witness to Jesus (John 1:45; 5:45–47) and its incompleteness in relation to Jesus' revelation, which has "fullness" (1:14, 16).

Conclusion

For John's Gospel, this "turn to the past," to the beginning and to Jesus as Wisdom, exceeds all others. Such a claim has implications for understanding Jesus, but it also has implications for the identity and way of life of Jesus-believers and those in the synagogue community who claim to be "descendents of Abraham" (8:33) and "disciples of Moses" (9:28). Through this chapter I have argued that on the basis of what we know about imperial Ephesus, synagogue communities, and traditions about Abraham and Moses, it is likely that some/many appealed to Abraham and Moses to sanction an identity marked by a significantly free or cosmopolitan or accommodated way of life (without surrendering Jewish distinctives such as Sabbath and circumcision). Some/many Jesus-believers in the synagogue emulate this way of life. This Gospel's rhetoric of distance resists it. Rooted in Jesus' unmatched antiquity "in the beginning . . . with God," John's rhetoric of distance establishes Jesus as the authoritative revealer of God's purposes, not Abraham and Moses, who are subservient to him. Jesus' crucifixion, resurrection, and ascension reveal fundamental antipathies between him and the empire. Jesus-believers are to emulate a more contestive and alternative, less-accommodated and less-imitative, way of life.

Notes

1. Eric Gruen, *Culture and National Identity in Republican Rome* (Ithaca, NY: Cornell University Press, 1992), 6–51.
2. Susan E. Alcock, "The Reconfiguration of Memory in the Eastern Roman Empire," in *Empires: Perspectives from Archaeology and History*, ed. Susan Alcock et al. (Cambridge: Cambridge University Press, 2001), 323–50, esp. 330.
3. Peter Burke, "History as Social Memory," in *Memory: History, Culture, and the Mind*, ed. Thomas Butler (Oxford: Blackwell, 1989), 97–113, esp. 107; cited by Alcock, "Reconfiguration," 330.
4. I am following the wonderful study of Rogers, *Sacred Identity*; for the inscription, 153–185.
5. Ibid., 39–79.
6. Ionia was the name for the western coastal region of Asia Minor.
7. Athenaeus, *Deipnosophistae* 8.361; cited by Rogers, *Sacred Identity*, 106.
8. Rogers, *Sacred Identity*, 69. Rogers observes the absence of representatives of trade guilds, so central to the economy of the city and well-being of the elite. Salutaris's event was about encouraging participation in the elite's political, civic ideal, not economic activity of this sort (72).
9. Ibid., 80–135.
10. Price, *Rituals and Power*, 54–55.
11. Rogers, *Sacred Identity*, 138.
12. Ibid., 138.
13. Ibid., 140.
14. Ibid., 148.
15. Space limits prevent an investigation of Ephesus in Greek novels of Xenophon and Achilles Tatius. For some discussion, see Simon Swain, *Hellenism and Empire: Language, Classicism, and Power in the Greek World AD 50–250* (Oxford: Clarendon, 1996), 101–31. Christine Thomas, "At Home in the City of Artemis: Religion in Ephesos in the Literary Imagination of the Roman Period," in *Ephesos Metropolis of Asia: An Interdisciplinary Approach to Its Archaeology, Religion, and Culture*, ed. H. Koester (Valley Forge, PA: Trinity Press International, 1995), 81–117. On 112, she comments, "The novels respond to Roman presence by failing to place it at center stage," a conclusion with which Swain, *Hellenism and Empire*, 130, seems to agree. Also Tomas Hägg, *The Novel in Antiquity* (Berkeley: University of California Press, 1983), 18–32 on Xenophon, and 41–54 on Achilles Tatius.
16. Swain, *Hellenism and Empire*. For a description of various ways in which this "obsession" was expressed, see Ewen L. Bowie, "Greeks and Their Past in the Second Sophistic," in *Studies in*

Ancient Society, ed. M. Finley (London: Routledge & Kegan Paul, 1974), 166–209. Bowie's thesis, though, that Greek preoccupation with the past reflects "dissatisfaction with the political situation of the present" (167) and that "the political greatness of the past" provided an alternative to or escape from or favorable point of comparison with "the tedious present" of Roman power is not so convincing (208–9).

17. Swain, *Hellenism and Empire*, 1.

18. Bowie, "Greeks and Their Past."

19. Swain, *Hellenism and Empire*, 65. Swain goes on to discuss this empowering identity vis-à-vis Rome, but throughout he emphasizes that elites were also defining themselves over against the noncultured, noneducated, nonelites (e.g., 21, 68, 411).

20. Ibid., 6. While the focus is on elites, Swain observes that the permeation of the past also extended through "ordinary" people (e.g., 65, 72).

21. Ibid., 70–72.

22. Bowie, "Greeks and Their Past," 183, cites Plutarch's advice to local urban elites to prevent Roman intervention (*Precepts of Statecraft* 813D–E): "You who rule are a subject, ruling a State controlled by proconsuls, the agents of Caesar. . . . You should arrange your cloak more carefully and from the office of the generals keep your eyes upon the orator's platform and not have great pride or confidence in your crown since you see the boots of Roman soldiers just above your head." Plutarch goes on in 814D–E to underline the importance of friendships with the Romans.

23. Swain, *Hellenism and Empire*, 88, 412.

24. Ibid., 412.

25. Ibid., 418–20.

26. Ibid., 68.

27. Pamela Gordon, "Review," in *Bryn Mawr Classical Review* 8 (1997): 482–86.

28. I am following Kenan Erim, *Aphrodisias: City of Venus Aphrodite* (New York: Facts on File, 1986), esp. 106–23; R. R. Smith, "The Imperial Reliefs from the Sebasteion at Aphrodisias," *Journal of Roman Studies* 77 (1987): 88–138; idem, "*Sacra Gentium*: The *Ethnē* from the Sebasteion at Aphrodisias," *Journal of Roman Studies* 78 (1988): 50–77.

29. Smith, "Imperial Reliefs," 98.

30. These include (ibid., 97) "Leda and the Swan, Semeter and Triptolemus, Bellerophon and Pegasus, Orestes at Delphi, Meleager and the Boor, Centaurs and Lapiths, Achilles and Thetis, Achilles and Pehthesilea, Ajax and Cassandra." Apollo appears three times, Dionysus five times, Heracles six times.

31. Ibid., 97, 135–38.

32. For example, Jews especially in Egypt but also in Syria and Asia Minor take over a form in which statements about the world are attributed to the Sibyl and identified as her oracles. In the *Sibylline Oracles*, book 3, probably from Egypt, the Sibyl prophesies the demise of Rome (3.46–62) and the revenge of Asia over Rome (3.350–380). Book 5, also from Egypt and after the destruction of Jerusalem (5.160–61, 397–413), bitterly denounces Rome and anticipates its eternal desolation by God because of its arrogant claims: "I alone am, and no one will ravage me" (5.162–78). The Sibyl also repetitively employs the Nero-redivivus myth, anticipating his return and his destruction by a king sent from God (5.93–110). She also announces woes on various cities in Asia including Sardis, Trallis, Laodicea, and Ephesus and the temple of Artemis (5.286–327) for allying themselves too much with Rome.

33. Erich S. Gruen, *Heritage and Hellenism: The Reinvention of Jewish Tradition* (Berkeley: University of California Press, 1998), xv; idem, *Diaspora*; John M. Barclay, *Jews in the Mediterranean*; J. J. Collins, *Between Athens and Jerusalem: Jewish Identity in the Hellenistic Diaspora* (New York: Crossroad, 1986).

34. Space prevents discussion of other areas in which John's Gospel employs this turn to the past, notably through festivals and the use of Scripture.

35. Gail R. O'Day, for example, says ("'The Gospel of John,'" in *The New Interpreter's Bible*, ed. L. E. Keck [Nashville: Abingdon, 1995], 647, n260) that "Jewish Christian status under Roman rule had an effect on Jewish-Christian relations in the late first-century, . . . but for the Fourth Gospel, intra-Jewish concerns are pivotal." As I have argued in chapters 2 and 3 above, such a division is artificial and the claim unconvincing.

36. O'Day, "John," 636.

37. John 8:33, 37, 39 (3x), 40, 52, 53, 56, 57, 58.

38. For details and different perspectives, see the commentaries. Also Samuel Sandmel, *Philo's Place in Judaism: A Study of Conceptions of Abraham in Jewish Literature* (New York: Ktav, 1971); Jeffery S. Siker, *Disinheriting the Jews: Abraham in Early Christian Controversies* (Louisville: Westminster John Knox, 1991), 128–43; K.-J. Kuschel, *Abraham: Sign of Hope for Jews, Christians, and Muslims* (New York: Continuum, 1995), 29–49, 110–16.

39. By 8:37 Jesus accuses them of wanting to kill him; in 8:38 they do not want to accept Jesus' teaching, which comes from God; in 8:44 they belong to their father the devil. Francis J. Moloney (*The Gospel of John*, ed. D. J. Harrington, SP 4 [Collegeville, MN: Liturgical Press, 1998], 275–77, with reference to various discussions) sees the verb with the dative as another indication that, in the Gospel's perspective, they exhibit partial or inadequate faith.

40. Most interpreters note the difficulty. The modifying perfect participle "who had believed in him" (8:31) has in 8:48 been dropped from *Ioudaioi*. Is this because another group enters the discussion, or is it because 8:31–47 shows them not to be believers at all?

41. See Malina and Rohrbaugh, *Social-Science Commentary*, 159–67, for discussion of the importance of kinship and lineage for group identity.

42. Jesus' reference to freedom may recall the Exodus story though this verb is not generally used in relation to that event. Perhaps they hear it as reference to a fundamental division in the first-century world, the social-legal status of being free or being a slave. The cognate adjective refers to slaves and freedom in Exod 21:2, 5; Deut 15:12, 18. If so, they claim the elevated status of being among the free in contrast to the lower status of the freed (former slaves) and even lower status of slaves.

43. Kuschel, *Abraham*, 29–40. Kuschel discusses Josh 24; Ps 105; Sir 44:19–21; *Jub.* 12–23; *Apocalypse of Abraham*.

44. Kuschel, *Abraham*, 40–49.

45. J. Collins, *Between Athens*, 33. For text, see *Old Testament Pseudepigrapha* (*OTP*), ed. J. H. Charlesworth, 2 vols. (Garden City, NY: Doubleday, 1983–85), 2:897, fragment 1.

46. Sandmel, *Philo's Place*, 160–67.

47. See Philo's *De congressu eruditionis gratia* 11, where Philo has Abraham study grammar, geometry, astronomy, rhetoric, music, "and all the other branches of intellectual study."

48. Sandmel, *Philo's Place*, 103, 168–85, 197, with these emphases repeatedly emphasized (e.g., 107–9, 191, 202).

49. Louis H. Feldman, "Hellenizations in Josephus' *Jewish Antiquities*: The Portrait of Abraham," in *Josephus, Judaism, and Christianity*, ed. Louis H. Feldman and G. Hata (Detroit: Wayne State University Press, 1987), 133–53, esp. 138.

50. Siker, *Disinheriting*, 141.

51. On the grammatical construction of verse 39, see ibid., 136–37.

52. For introduction and text, Edward P. Sanders, "Testament of Abraham," in *OTP* 1:874–95.

53. Bruce M. Metzger, "Fourth Ezra," in *OTP* 1:528.

54. A. F. J. Klijn, "2 (Syriac Apocalypse of) Baruch," in *OTP* 1:622.

55. R. Rubinkiewicz, "Apocalypse of Abraham," in *OTP* 1:693. O'Day, "John," 646, mentions later "midrashic traditions that the future was revealed to Abraham by God," and cites *Gen. Rab.* 44:25.

56. In addition to the commentaries, T. Francis Glasson, *Moses in the Fourth Gospel* (Naperville, IL: Allenson, 1963); Wayne Meeks, *The Prophet-King: Moses Traditions and the Johannine Christology* (Leiden: Brill, 1967); Marie-Émile Boismard, *Moses or Jesus: An Essay in Johannine Christology* (Minneapolis: Fortress, 1993); Barclay, *Jews*, 424–28; John Lierman, "'The Mosaic Pattern of John's Christology," in *Challenging Perspectives on the Gospel of John*, ed. J. Lierman, WUNT 2.219 (Tübingen: Mohr Siebeck, 2006), 210–34. Also of note is Scott J. Hafemann, "Moses in the Apocrypha and Pseudepigrapha: A Survey," *JSP* 7 (1990): 79–104.

57. John 1:17, 45; 3:14; 5:45–46; 6:32; 7:19, 22 [2x], 23; 9:28, 29. John 6 provides a good example of extensive influence, though Moses is named only once (6:32).

58. Barclay, *Jews*, 424–44.

59. Gruen, *Heritage*, 246.

60. John G. Gager, *Moses in Greco-Roman Paganism* (Nashville: Abingdon, 1972), 18; wise lawgiver, 25–79; deficient, 80–112.

61. Ibid., 26–37.

62. Ibid., 38–43.

63. For text, see *OTP* 1:898–99; Barclay, *Jews*, 127; J. Collins, *Between Athens*, 32–38.

64. For text, see *OTP* 1:839–42.

65. Gruen, *Heritage*, 246–253.

66. Louis H. Feldman, "Josephus' Portrait of Moses: Part Three," *JQR* 83 (1993): 301–30, esp. 320–22.

67. Moses is explicitly named in John 1:17, but similarities of theme and vocabulary between 1:14–18 and Exod 33–34 evoke the Sinai revelation. See Anthony T. Hanson, "John 1:14–18 and Exodus 34," in *The New Testament Interpretation of Scripture* (London: SPCK, 1980), 97–109, who focuses on the debate as to whether "full of grace and truth" (John 1:14) evokes Exod 34:6 as the basis for exploring links between John 1:14–18 and Exod 33–34. Henry Mowvley ("John 1:14–18 in the Light of Exod. 33.7–34:35," *ExpTim* 95 [1983–84]: 135–37) identifies links comprising God's word, the tent of meeting (Exod 33:7; John 1:14), glory (Exod 33:18–19; 34:29; John 1:14), full of grace and truth (Exod 33:16; 34:6; John 1:14), grace on/instead of (Moses') grace (Exod 33:12–13, 17; John 1:17), giving the law (Exod 34; John 1:17), no one has seen (Exod 33:20; John 1:18).

68. Also drawing them together is the experience of being rejected: 5:45–47; 7:19–24.

69. Boismard, *Moses*, chap. 1; 59–68, "new Moses"; 98, "superior to Moses." Meeks, *Prophet-King*, 318–19, concludes that Jesus is not a "new Moses"; instead, "Jesus is greater than Moses," and Moses is a witness to Jesus.

70. Peder Borgen, *Bread from Heaven: An Exegetical Study of the Concept of Manna in the Gospel of John and the Writings of Philo* (Leiden: Brill, 1965); R. Alan Culpepper, ed., *Critical Readings of John 6* (Leiden: Brill, 1997).

71. Ezekiel the Tragedian, *Exagōgē* 68–89, where Moses mounts the heavenly throne and rules; Philo, *Moses* 1.158; *Questions on Exodus* 2.29, 40, 46; Josephus, *Ant.* 3.96–97; 4.43; *2 Bar.* 4:5; 59:3–12; *4 Ezra* 14:4–6; cf. *L.A.B.* (Ps.-Philo) 19:10.

72. For references to exaltation, see Ps 68:18 (67:19 LXX), quoted in Eph 4:8; Ps 89:19 (88:20 LXX), David.

73. E.g., Meeks, *Prophet-King*, 296–301; idem, "Man from Heaven," 44–72; Godfrey Nicholson, *Death as Departure: The Johannine Descent-Ascent Schema* (Chico, CA: Scholars Press, 1983).

74. Here I summarize Sharon H. Ringe, *Wisdom's Friends: Community and Christology in the Fourth Gospel* (Louisville: Westminster John Knox, 1999). Also Martin Scott, *Sophia and the Johannine Jesus*, JSNTSup 71 (Sheffield: JSOT Press, 1992).

75. Ringe, *Wisdom's Friends*, 31.

76. Key passages: Ps 104 and Job 28 (principle of creation); other texts (Prov 8–9; Sir 24; Bar 3:9–4:4; Wis 7–10; *1 En.* 42:1–2; and Philo) present Lady Wisdom.

77. Charles H. Talbert, *Reading John* (New York: Crossroad, 1992), 68–70.

78. I follow Ringe, *Wisdom's Friends*, 54–63. For John 6, see Marianne Meye Thompson, "Thinking about God: Wisdom and Theology in John 6," in Culpepper, *Critical Readings*, 221–46.

79. Bread (Sir 24:21), vine (Sir 24:17, 19), way (Prov 3:17; 8:32; Sir 6:26), light (Wis 7:26; 18:34), truth (Prov 8:7; Wis 6:22), life (Prov 3:18; 8:35), gate/door (Prov 8:34–35). The one exception is "good shepherd," which is used for God (Ps 23:1), but not for wisdom. On this term, see chap. 7 below.

5

Genre as Imperial Negotiation

Ancient Biography and John's Gospel

In chapters 1–4 I have been suggesting that John's Gospel is involved in the multifaceted task of negotiating the Roman Empire. Addressing Jesus-believers whom it regards as overaccommodated, the Gospel's rhetoric of distance urges greater differentiation and less societal participation. In this chapter I will argue that the Gospel's genre is part of this negotiation.

Two related issues concerning the Gospel's genre will be to the fore. One concerns the choice of "ancient biography" as the Gospel's genre. This choice of an old and well-established literary form continues the turn to the past as a means of imperial negotiation noted in chapter 4 (above). The second issue concerns the conventional content of ancient biographies. In the Greek and Roman worlds, biographical literature typically celebrated important elite figures such as statesmen, military commanders, and philosophers, and thereby upheld and celebrated dominant elite cultural values and imperial claims. But though the Gospel employs a genre typically associated with upholding elite and imperial values, it undermines these claims in presenting the story, actions, and teaching of a low-status provincial, Jesus, crucified by Rome but raised by God.[1] This choice of genre, I am suggesting, continues the Gospel's task of urging less accommodation with, more suspicion of, and greater distance from imperial Ephesian culture for Jesus-believers. Our contrapuntal reading, to use Edward Said's phrase,[2] attends to the interplay between a genre typically associated with elite discourse intent on maintaining the societal status quo on one hand, and its use in John's Gospel for resistant discourse that seeks to create a distinctive and alternative community on the other hand (Halliday's "antisociety"). This interplay is part of what James Scott calls the "hidden transcript" or "little tradition" that contests the dominant view of reality while also self-protectively ensuring the survival of John's community.[3] That is, the Gospel's genre simultaneously exhibits both participation in the imperial world as well as critique of its elite commitments while urging an alternative communal identity and existence.

Genre

John's Gospel explicitly identifies itself in very general terms as a "book" (20:30). That term, located near the end of the document, can refer to all sorts of writings, so it is not a very helpful indicator of what we are reading. Rather, we will need to look for other clues in the document to identify what sort of book this is.

As readers, we determine a communication's genre—whether written or oral—from the various literary conventions or traits that a speaker or author employs in creating the work's form and content.[4] We observe these conventions or features from the beginning of a work (for a written work, its cover, title, a contents page if it has one, chapter headings, layout, etc.) and confirm or modify our recognition of its genre from subsequent features like the settings for events, the type of events, the characters, conflicts, style, word choice, and so forth. These literary conventions or clusters of features form part of the larger communication codes and conventions with which members of that society are familiar. From the cluster of features, and from our experience of other literature in our society, we as readers or hearers decide what sort of work we are encountering, what we can reasonably expect from it, how it might function for us, and what sort of "work" or roles we might have to perform as readers.

Accurately identifying the genre of a piece of literature accurately ensures that we notice its features as clues on how to read it appropriately. Getting the genre wrong will inevitably mean a "literary malfunction," in which we have little chance of making satisfactory sense of what we're reading. Identifying genre can be difficult because various generic features (e.g., characters, setting, plot, etc.) belong to different genres, and authors can and do combine features from various genres. Such combinations enrich the reading experience with uncertainty, complexity, humor, creativity, surprise, intrigue, tension, delight, and so forth. Determining a work's genre or genres, then, involves recognizing the various literary conventions and traits that are employed so that the work can function appropriately for us as readers or listeners. Identifying the work's traits or conventions guides us in our efforts to make appropriate sense of what we are reading.

The Genre of John's Gospel

What, then, is the genre or genres of John's Gospel?[5] The question might seem unnecessary since we have been referring to the work as a "Gospel." But that simply takes us in a circle back to the starting point: What is a Gospel?

The term "gospel" has two meanings in relation to the early Christian writings. Sometimes, "gospel" refers to certain beliefs and experiences about God's saving work encountered in Jesus (Rom 1:16–17; Gal 1:6–7; Eph 1:13; 2 Tim 2:8–9). In Romans 1:16–17, for example, Paul refers to the gospel as the experience of "the power of God for salvation" and as the revelation of the righteousness or faithfulness of God. Paul does not have a written work in mind but refers to the experience of God's saving and faithful power. Second, the term "Gospel" refers to written texts. Mark's Gospel begins, "'The beginning of the gospel of Jesus Christ" (Mark 1:1), where the term could refer to both the experience of God (the first meaning) as well as to the whole written story about Jesus. By one count, thirty-four of these "gospel" writings exist from the early centuries of the Christian movement even though only four of them are included in the Christian New Testament, the Gospels according to Matthew, according to Mark, according to Luke, according to John.[6] Interestingly, with the possible exception of

Mark 1:1, none of these four NT documents calls itself a "Gospel."[7] Later Christian readers applied the term to them because they saw the four documents doing a similar thing: telling the story of Jesus from the perspective of faith, to strengthen the discipleship of an audience (or congregation) of believers. According to one definition, "a Gospel is a narrative of the public career of Jesus, his passion and death, told in order to affirm or confirm the faith of Christian believers in the Risen Lord."[8]

Although most scholars do not dispute that the Gospel employs some historical information, most recognize that the Gospel is not primarily concerned with conventional historical tasks like providing accurate and verifiable historical information, and analyzing the causes and effects of historical events.[9] John's Gospel is much more concerned to present this information in relation to and as part of its much larger agenda, to proclaim the significance of Jesus as the one who makes available "life" to those who entrust themselves to him (20:30–31). The Gospel is not passing on information about Jesus for its own sake, or trying to understand the person of Jesus in a disinterested way. Rather, it is deeply invested in the importance of Jesus. It seeks to elicit and sustain the believing response of its audience because it thinks nothing is more important in the whole world, this one and the next! In doing so, the Gospel is as much concerned with the present (and future) as with the past, and as much concerned with the response of the reader as with the material it presents. This is more like preaching than historiography.

If later readers designate the genre of John as a "Gospel," what genre might its first readers late in the first century assign to it to guide their engagement with it? What sorts of literature did it resemble? Scholars have made several suggestions. I will identify three approaches to this issue and discuss one genre, ancient biography, that seems to be most persuasive.

A Unique Genre?

A long tradition of scholarship has claimed that the Gospels form their own genre. Some have argued that the Gospels are without parallel in other contemporary literature, thus "of their own kind" (sui generis).[10] Primarily this argument appeals to the unique content of the Gospels and their proclamation about the identity of Jesus as the risen Christ and Lord, in whom people are to believe in order to know life. This proclamation about Jesus in story form utilizes traditions about Jesus that are theologically and pastorally interpreted. The Gospels comprise "tradition remembered and interpreted in the light of faith."[11] Ultimately, so the argument goes, the Gospels' content makes them unique.

Such a description helpfully identifies the interconnection between traditions about Jesus and interpretations of his significance evident in the Gospels. But such content and technique cannot be the basis for determining their genre or for deciding that they are like no other written document. Lots of different kinds of writings present material about a historical figure with a particular spin to it. Paul's Letters do this in part, and we recognize them as Letters, not Gospels. And numerous types of writing want to either persuade readers to their point of view or confirm and strengthen the commitments that readers already have. It is evident in historical studies, biographies, newspaper articles, political propaganda, and sermons, to name but five.

Moreover, from a literary and cultural point of view, the claim that the Gospels form their own genre and are unlike any other makes little sense. If they were unique, no writer could create them and no audience would understand them. Every writer is constrained and shaped by the conventions and genres of their literary culture. A writer can, as many great artists have done, creatively extend and stretch existing genres. But inventing a new genre is culturally doubtful. Moreover, even if a writer did somehow manage to invent a unique genre, no reader would comprehend it because, as we have seen, genres depend on the ability of readers to recognize the cluster of features that comprise it and to be guided by those features in engaging the work.[12]

A Combination of Various Genres?

I observed above that genres are not rigidly fixed categories and can combine features of various genres. Using Northrop Frye's notion of archetypal patterns of storytelling, Mark Stibbe thinks John's Gospel evidences "generic depths" that account for its "abiding appeal."[13] Frye argues that in world literature there are four basic modes of storytelling: romance, tragedy, antiromance (satire and irony), and comedy. Stibbe argues that John is none of these genres in total, but elements of all four modes are evident at key points, creatively rendering a compelling and appealing story.

Frye argues that at the heart of what he identifies as romance is a successful quest in three stages: a journey and some initial minor adventures, a struggle in which the hero and/or his opponent die, and the exaltation of the hero.[14] According to Stibbe, the same three elements of conflict, death, and recognition are present in John. Jesus, sent from God, is not recognized by most people despite his signs and teaching. He comes into conflict with the authorities. The conflict leads to his death, though it is not the opponents' victory since Jesus gives himself to die. Recognition comes from his disciples and in his vindication by his Father God through his resurrection and ascension to God.

But features of tragedy are also present. For Frye, the tragic hero is central to tragedy.[15] The hero appears divine but is very human and behaves in ways that provoke revenge. The carrying out of this revenge produces sacrificial suffering. Likewise in John, Jesus, who existed "in the beginning" and comes from God, reveals God's purposes for human life in a way that challenges the power and societal vision of the Jerusalem-based, Rome-allied elite. They repel his challenge by putting him to death, a sacrificial death on the cross.[16]

Moreover, features of satire and irony (antiromance) are present.[17] Both are important for the Gospel.[18] In places the Gospel satirizes Jesus' opponents. John 3 mocks the elite leader Nicodemus, who does not understand Jesus, by having him ask a silly question: "Can one enter a second time into the mother's womb and be born?" (3:4 NRSV). The question is based on a misinterpretation of the ambiguous term ἄνωθεν (*anōthen*), which for John's Jesus denotes origin ("from above"), not time ("a second time"). In John 9, Jesus' opponents object to Jesus' giving sight (both physical and spiritual) to a blind man while they themselves remain (unknowingly) blind to his identity (9:40–41)! Basic to irony is an inequity of knowledge or recognition. From the outset of the Gospel, readers know answers to the crucial questions about Jesus: his origin, identity, and mission. But through the Gospel, especially the first twelve chapters, the readers watch (and learn more) as characters in the story fail to recognize these crucial dimensions about Jesus.

Stibbe also finds Frye's concept of comedy to be important for John's story of Jesus.[19] Comedy is not primarily about laughter and triviality. Rather, it denotes action that descends through numerous obstacles until it rises to a successful resolution. John's Jesus descends from heaven and confronts numerous obstacles from those who do not accept his revelation or believe his claims to be God's commissioned agent, the Christ or Son of God. Even those who say they believe, the disciples, prove unreliable (6:60–66; 18:15–18, 25–27). Yet at the end after his crucifixion, Jesus is raised in resurrection and ascension, recognized by his disciples, and returns to God. But absent from this comedic-like ending is any reconciliation or successful resolution with the opponents.

As Stibbe points out, none of Frye's four genres adequately fits the whole of the Gospel. Rather, the Gospel creatively employs aspects of these genres at particular points as it presents the story of Jesus. The question remains, though: What genre of literature is produced when the Gospel draws these various elements together?

Revelatory Literature?

The notion of revelation or disclosure is central to John's Gospel.[20] The Gospel claims that God sends Jesus to reveal God's life-giving purposes (1:18; 14:7–10; 20:30–31). These purposes involve saving people from the current sinful and unjust world so that they might know a different sort of life in relationship to God and each other, untouched by sin and death (1:29).

John's concern with revealing God's purposes is not unique. A long tradition of Jewish revelatory or apocalyptic literature exists. The adjective "apocalyptic" and its related noun "apocalypse" come from a Greek word that means "revelation" or "unveiling." This revelatory literature was written prior to, contemporary with, and after the Gospel of John. One of the earliest examples, dating from the second century BCE, is Daniel 7–12. Another notable example, *1 Enoch*, comprises five sections and collects material from about the same time period through to around the time of Jesus and Paul in the first century CE. Two other works, *4 Ezra* (= *2 Esdras*) and *2 Baruch*, probably originated at the same time as John, late in the first century CE, and wrestled with the Rome-dominated post-70 world, after the defeat of Jerusalem and destruction of its temple. The most well-known example of such literature for Christian readers is the New Testament book called (significantly) Revelation, or Apocalypse, also written late in the first century, and very concerned to reveal the destructive and demonic nature of Roman power in opposition to God's purposes.

It is difficult to understand apocalypses or revelatory literature, often replete with strange symbols, animal-like creatures, and mystifying numbers. So, too, is defining this literature. One definition helpfully understands apocalyptic literature as

a genre of revelatory literature with a narrative framework, in which the revelation is mediated by an otherworldly being to a human recipient, disclosing a transcendental reality which is both temporal, insofar as it envisages eschatological salvation, and spatial insofar as it involves another supernatural world.[21]

There are some limitations to this definition. It does not, for example, include circumstances of perceived unrest or crisis (political, social, religious) and powerlessness in the face of great injustices that often produce this literature. Nevertheless it helpfully draws attention to important features of revelatory literature.

At first glance it would seem to strain all credulity to link John's Gospel with such strange writings as Daniel 7–12 and Revelation, and often scholars have not done so. Certainly John's Gospel is not an "apocalypse" like Daniel 7–12 and Revelation. But John does share some literary and thematic features of apocalyptic literature. Apocalyptic literature typically employs (some variation on) a "two-age" scheme to denote the present time as unjust, oppressive, and contrary to God's will, and the new age of justice and salvation that God will bring about. John employs such a scheme in anticipating a new age marked by resurrection (6:40) and the return of Jesus (14:1–3) as God's life-giving purposes are established in full over Rome's control. But John also modifies the scheme to emphasize that this life is manifested already now through Jesus (5:24; 17:3).

John Ashton points out further connections between John and features at home in apocalyptic literature.[22] The most obvious connection, apart from that of narrative, is the notion of revelation. John presents the story of Jesus as an account of one who comes from heaven to reveal God's purposes concerning life (10:10). The parallels are not exact since Jesus, being the revelation himself, combines the features of both the otherworldly agent (often an angel in apocalyptic literature) and the human recipient that apocalyptic literature usually employs (see Rev 1). And somewhat unusually, John's Gospel emphasizes that God's life is experienced in the present as well as in the future (5:24; 6:40). But despite these differences, the Gospel's concern with revelation is very clear. It appears at the outset.

> No one has ever seen God; the only Son, who is in the bosom of the Father, he has made him known. (1:18 RSV)

It is also continually reiterated through references to Jesus' origin as being from God and his purpose to reveal God's purposes in his words and works (5:36; 14:7–10). For Ashton, this focus on revelation is an essential feature of apocalyptic traditions, as expressed often in the term "mystery" to denote "a secret once hidden and now revealed."[23] Disclosure of God's purposes follows a time of concealment. John presents Jesus as the one who makes the revelation.

But John employs a further apocalyptic feature. In some apocalyptic texts such as Daniel (9:23; 10:21; 11:2), the revealer's revelation is obscure and needs further interpretation and elucidation by another figure. Jesus' revelation is certainly obscure for many in John's Gospel, both his opponents and at times his disciples. John employs this motif of the need for subsequent elaboration of the revealer's revelation in presenting the role of the Spirit, also called the Spirit of Truth or the Counselor (Paraclete). In Jesus' absence the Spirit comes to disciples to

> guide you into all truth; for he will not speak on his own authority, but whatever he hears he will speak, and he will declare [explain] to you the things that are to come. (16:13 RSV)

Long after Jesus has returned to heaven, Jesus' revelation continues to be elaborated by the Spirit for the disciples' ongoing existence.

Yet while some understand the revelation, others do not (1:10–12). One of the perplexing features of John's story of Jesus is that Jesus' revelation, paradoxically, often remains a riddle. As is typical of much revelatory literature, insiders or believers or disciples understand his "riddling discourse" (at least to some extent), but outsiders do not understand. The more Jesus speaks, the more his words seem to confuse rather than enlighten his hearers even though Jesus claims that he has spoken plainly (18:20; cf. 10:24–25), something only disciples can perceive (16:29). Often these outsiders are ridiculed for stupidly not understanding. In 3:4, for example, Nicodemus is made to ask how a grown person can enter into their mother's womb to be born again![24] Commonly in apocalyptic literature, the "wise," often a minority, receive the revelation while the "fools," the majority, cannot understand.

John's presentation of Jesus' revelation employs a further common apocalyptic feature, that of "correspondence" or similarity between heaven and earth. Jesus reveals on earth the oneness that he and the Father enjoyed "from the beginning." He reenacts and displays the heavenly reality of God's will on earth among people. This reality, this knowing God, is the plan and life that Jesus offers to people.

One further dimension that Ashton does not pursue should be recognized. It concerns the content of John's revelation. Apocalyptic literature often reveals a new world that is free of injustice and oppression and marked by fertility, wholeness, and justice as God's purposes are established in the place of exploitative empires. The revelation of "life" made by John's Jesus incorporates the same features, as I will argue in chapter 8 below. Jesus' signs or miracles that point to God's saving purposes include healings (4:46–54; 5:1–9; John 9), feedings (John 6), and the raising of Lazarus bodily from death (John 11). These signs, like Jesus' corporeal existence, indicate God's faithfulness to God's material creation and its redemption from Rome's oppressive rule. The Gospel reveals or identifies this tyranny as part of what it calls sin and death (including sickness and want), that which is contrary to God's purposes. Jesus' signs anticipate the reestablishment of an Edenic existence marked by justice, abundance, and wholeness. Life in relation to God involves right relationships and structures among people so that all have access to the resources they need to sustain life.

The Overarching Genre: Ancient Biography

While the Gospel may include aspects of various genres such as comedy, tragedy, and revelatory literature, the challenge to identify its overarching or dominant genre remains. I am arguing here that in reading John's Gospel, we encounter a text that belongs to the genre of ancient biography, or *bios*. This genre was complex and diverse, generally originating from elite literary figures and centered on an elite person's life, often an eminent political, military, philosophical, hagiographical, or artistic figure.[25] By the late first century, it was an old and well-established genre. The earliest Greek biographical writings originated in the fifth century BCE and became more common in the fourth century. Roman biographical interest developed around the end of the republic in the first century BCE.[26] Biographies could be organized on chronological lines, or around the particular virtues that a character exhibited, or a combination of both.

The adjective "ancient" has a key role in describing this genre. *Ancient* biographies differ from modern biographies and contemporary kiss-and-tell books in some important ways. One crucial difference is that, pre-Freud, ancient biographies did not focus on a person's internal processes, and on the growth and development of their particular personality.[27] Rather, ancient biographies understood external actions to reveal a person's character or virtue (and vices), which was understood to be somewhat fixed. That did not rule out any concern with development, but it did shift the focus significantly from internal development to external actions as expressions of a person's relatively unchanging and usually virtuous character. Moreover, and especially important for our purposes, is the recognition that eminent figures are presented as representatives of (elite) group values, as largely "static personalities who function as paradigms of traditional virtues,"[28] rather than as unusual or special individuals. Hence biographies usually choose as their subjects eminent, public, elite males, and are often marked by an idealistic quality in presenting the figure's virtues as representative of elite commitments.

In describing the features of ancient biographies, Richard Burridge observes that it is impossible to isolate this genre from other types of literature.[29] Features of one genre are mixed with features from another. A genre exists in relationship to and in some overlap with neighboring genres. There is, for example, some overlap between ancient biographies and moral philosophy, religious teaching, encomium, stories and novels, political beliefs, and history.

Burridge discusses ten ancient biographies, or more precisely, ten collections of biographies.[30] One of his selections, Suetonius' *Lives of the Caesars*, for example, includes eight chapters covering the lives of twelve emperors.

Author	Dates	Title of biography	Subject's roles
Isocrates	436–338 BCE	*Evagoras*	King of Cyprus; ideal king
Xenophon	428–ca. 354 BCE	*Agesilaus*	King of Sparta; king, warrior
Satyrus	ca. 4th–3rd cents. BCE	*Euripides*	Poet; other studies involve orators, philosophers, kings.
Nepos	ca. 99–24 BCE	*Atticus*	Patron; literary figure
Philo	ca. 30 BCE–45 CE	*Moses*	King, lawgiver, priest, prophet
Tacitus	ca. 56 CE–ca. 117	*Agricola*	Provincial governor
Plutarch	ca. 45/46 CE–ca. 120s	*Parallel Lives: Cato Minor*	Politician; philosopher
Suetonius	ca. 69 CE–ca. 120s	*Lives of the Caesars*	12 emperors
Lucian	ca. 120 CE–ca. 180s	*Demonax*	Philosopher
Philostratus	ca. 170 CE–ca.250	*Apollonius of Tyana*	Philosopher

Burridge identifies the cluster of features that readers would expect to find in works of this genre, organizing these features under four divisions: opening features, subject, external features, and internal features. He analyzes the four canonical Gospels, finds these features present, and concludes that John's Gospel, like the other three Gospels, belongs to the genre of ancient biography.[31]

An examination of these four divisions in relation to John's Gospel sustains the claim that it belongs to this genre of ancient biography. Under *Opening Features*, Burridge identifies two conventional features of biographies:

- Title: there is no original title for John's Gospel, but the title, "According to John," added probably in the second century, resembles the titles added to the other Gospels. The addition of the same sort of title suggests John is understood as the same literary genre.

- Opening formulae/prologue: as do other biographies, John begins with a Prologue, a poetic or hymnic celebration in 1:1–18 of God's revelation through the "Word." As in other biographies, the name of the main character, Jesus, is included at the end of the Prologue (1:17), identifying him as the subject of the Prologue. It also appears at the beginning of the subsequent narrative (1:20, 29–34, 35–37).

Under *Subject*, Burridge identifies two further features typical of ancient biography:

- Analysis of the verbs' subjects: Biographies typically focus on the actions and words of their central character. In John, Jesus is the subject for over 30 percent of the verbs, and over half of the verbs in the Gospel concern his deeds or words. Jesus, in both his deeds and his teaching, is the central focus of the narrative.

- Allocation of space: More specifically, a number of biographies focus significant attention (approximately a quarter to a third of the narrative) on events surrounding the end of the subject's life. This is true for John's Gospel, in which the last week of Jesus' life occupies about one-third of the narrative.

Under *External Features*, Burridge discusses seven features typical of biographies:

- Mode of representation: Like other biographies, John is a continuous prose narrative that includes dialogues and extended discourses.

- Size: John comprises 15,416 words, in the medium range of length for biographies.

- Structure: Like many biographies, John employs a basic chronological order to tell the story of Jesus, with discourse and dialogue material inserted into it.

- Scale: Also like many biographies, John employs a narrow scale with attention focused on the main subject, Jesus.

- Literary units: Biographies, especially those concerning philosophers and teachers, typically employ three kinds of units, stories, dialogues, and speeches or discourses. John follows this pattern.

- Use of sources: While the question of sources–oral and/or written–and of multiple versions of the Gospels is difficult (as I have pointed out in chaps. 1–2 above, with further consideration in the appendix), it is sufficient to observe here that John's Gospel has, as is typical of ancient biographies, probably employed some oral and/or written sources in making its presentation of Jesus.

- Methods of characterization: Like many biographies, John's Gospel presents Jesus' character through the narration of his words and actions. Occasionally it offers some insight into his inner thought world (e.g., 6:15).

Under *Internal Features*, Burridge identifies seven conventional features of ancient biographies:

- Setting: The Gospel's focus on its central character, Jesus, typical of biographies, determines where things happen. Burridge observes that Jesus is absent from only 9 percent of the Gospel's verses, and in most of these he is the subject of the conversation (e.g., 1:19–28; 7:45–52; 11:45–53, 55–57; 20:24–25).

- Topics: Biographies conventionally discuss five topics related to the central character: ancestry, birth and upbringing, great deeds, virtues, death and consequences. John covers the same range of topics, though with minimal attention to the second, Jesus' birth and upbringing (cf. 1:46; 7:40–42, 52). Concerning his ancestry, the opening Prologue traces it back to "the beginning . . . with God" (1:1–3). As I mentioned in the last chapter, the Gospel narrates at least seven or eight "great deeds" or signs: changing water to wine (2:1–11), healing the official's son (4:46–54) and paralyzed man (5:2–15), feeding the crowd (6:1–14), walking on water (6:16–21), giving sight to the blind man (John 9), raising Lazarus (John 11), miraculously catching many fish (21:1–14). Jesus' extensive teaching is a further notable act (John 3; 5; 6; 13–17). Jesus' virtues emerge through his actions and words. And as we have observed, about one-third of the narrative concerns Jesus' death and resurrection, along with his teaching in chapters 13–17 to the disciples on how they should live, with the Spirit's help, once he has ascended to heaven.

- Style: Burridge recognizes that John's style, like that of other biographies, is not literarily elevated. It is straightforward, often joining sentences with "and" (parataxis) or supplying no connection (asyndeton). The vocabulary is limited, with certain key words (like "life") frequently repeated.[32]

- Atmosphere: Like other biographies, John employs a serious, steady, and reverent atmosphere.

- Quality of characterization: Biographies frequently combine the stereotypical with the real in presenting characters. Likewise John mixes both elements. Jesus appears very much in control and almost superhuman as he unwaveringly does God's will, yet he is capable of very human responses: tired and thirsty (4:6–7), disappointment with the disciples (6:67), grief and anger at the death of his friend Lazarus (11:33, 35, 38), and troubled at the close of his ministry and in the face of death (12:27).

- Social setting and occasion: Like other biographies, John engages the issues of its time by telling the story of Jesus in such a way as to address these issues and the community of his followers. Scholars have conventionally argued, as we observed in chapters 1–2 (above), that a dispute with/in a synagogue provides this context. I am arguing that this context is far too restricted because it ignores the fact that synagogues are places of negotiation with Rome's world, that politics and religion are tightly intertwined, and that the Gospel's narrative focuses on its main character, who was crucified by Rome.

- Authorial intention and purpose: Biographies have diverse purposes: to praise their central character, to provide examples for readers to follow, to offer information, to entertain, to preserve the memory of the central character, to teach, to engage in debate by defending or correcting opinions about the character (an apologetic purpose) and/or by attacking opponents (a polemic purpose). Several of these purposes are clearly applicable to John's Gospel. As we have seen from 20:31, the focus is on Jesus and on sustaining believers in the way of life. So the Gospel informs and teaches. But also, the extensive attention through the story to Jesus' opponents suggests an apologetic and polemic purpose, an engagement in debates about the significance of Jesus, thereby securing the identity of its readers as a distinctive community and guiding its way of life. This way of life often embodies commitments and practices at odds with those of elite Roman society.

John: An Ancient Biography That Contests Imperial Practices

Burridge's helpful work, summarized above, indicates the Gospel's extensive use of features consistent with the genre of ancient biography. In employing the genre of "ancient biography," the writer/s again turn to the past; to negotiate imperial power in the present, they utilize a well-established literary form with a significant history. But Burridge does not explore an implication of his work: while John's Gospel participates in and employs generic features of this elite genre, its focus on a non-elite hero is very unusual. This focus on Jesus opens the way to distinctive content. Although it often incorporates as well as imitates aspects of the imperial world, it does not endorse but contests the elite values and commitments that ancient biographies usually commend to their readers. To highlight this contrast in values and commitments, I will compare John with another biography, *Agricola*, written by Tacitus at the same time as John's Gospel, one of the ten biographies included in Burridge's analysis. Because my interest here is on the biography's content and values, I will discuss only three topics that Burridge lists under his fourth category of "Internal Features": origin; great deeds; and death.[33]

To be clear, in comparing John's Gospel with this elite biography, I am not suggesting that John's Jesus-believers are necessarily familiar with Tacitus's biography of Agricola and make a conscious, point-by-point comparison between it and the Gospel. Burridge suggests that Tacitus's work was "possibly intended to be read at a dinner party or similar gathering" of educated upper classes.[34] Since Tacitus became governor of Asia in 112 CE, it is likely that the work was read in such circles in Ephesus. But it is most unlikely that any of John's Jesus-believers moved in such circles. Rather, what I am suggesting is that *Agricola* exemplifies elite roles, values, and practices conventionally associated with an elite literary genre but contested or at least reframed by John's Gospel. Moreover, these roles, values, and practices are well familiar to the Gospel's audience from its involvement in elite-controlled daily life in Ephesus, where these roles, values, and practices are constantly displayed in interactions, festivals, statues, buildings, inscriptions, speeches, and so forth. And further, these roles, values, and practices are, in terms of the postcolonial thinking of Fanon and Bhabha, the likely objects of nonelite resentment and envy, as well as imitation. John's Gospel resists them by urging alternative practices derived from commitment to Jesus, crucified by Rome, even while it also imitates some imperial elite practices.

Tacitus's Biography of Agricola

Tacitus's biography of his father-in-law, Agricola, was written shortly after Agricola's death in 93 CE at the age of 53 and published about 98–99, as the reign of the emperor Trajan was beginning (98–117). In chronological order the biography narrates Agricola's senatorial career through various political offices and military appointments (sections 1–9), his governorship in Britain from 77–84 (10–39), his return to Rome in 84, his death in 93, and the emperor Domitian's failure to give him due honor (41–46). It does not present a disinterested account of Agricola's life but is an encomium, or *laudatio,* that celebrates his life (3.3), especially his governorship of Britain. Tacitus turns to the past to locate and justify his biography: "To hand down to posterity the works and ways of famous men was a custom of the past" (1.1). He declares that he is "about to write a life (*naturo . . . vitam*) of a man who was already dead" (1.4) because this offers an example of "some great and noble virtue" (1:1).

Agricola was written around the same time as John's Gospel. Like John, this ancient biography was also concerned with imperial negotiation, although in a quite different way and from a quite different social location. Tacitus's work, in contrast to John, is not primarily concerned with how nonelite provincials might negotiate the empire, even though some dimensions of this negotiation emerge through his account of Agricola's governorship of Britain. Tacitus gives the British chief Calgacus, for example, a powerful speech articulating why the provincials violently resist Roman power (30–32), while the accounts of Agricola's military successes show the futility of resisting Roman military power. The "authenticity" of Calgacus's speech and its content is very dubious. Rather, Tacitus writes, as Paula James notes, as "a representative and beneficiary of Roman *imperium*," as one who champions "the Roman right to conquest and occupation" while simultaneously complaining about the threat to elite or senatorial freedom and Rome's destiny to rule as posed by the emperor Domitian. The noble Agricola provides an example of astute negotiation of Domitian's threat.[35]

Accordingly, Tacitus is quite concerned with the negotiation of power between the senate and the emperor Domitian. He shows how Agricola as a noble member of the elite negotiates the challenges and dangers of the imperial system, as Domitian, according to Tacitus, enslaves and deprives the Roman senate and people of liberty (2–3).[36] The work exemplifies Agricola's "virtue" that "has overcome and surmounted the vice (of) ignorance of what is right and jealousy" (1.1), a reference to Domitian's oppressive rule and to his jealous failure, according to Tacitus, to appreciate Agricola's accomplishments in subduing Britain (39). Tacitus emphasizes the difficult political times in which his father-in-law lived by locating his writing of the biography at a time when "at last heart is coming back to us," after Domitian's death in 96 CE. He engages in the conventional practice of denigrating the previous emperor Domitian to uplift the current one, Trajan. He applauds the now-deceased emperor Nerva (96–98), who had "united things long incompatible, the principate and liberty; [and] Trajan is increasing daily the happiness of the times" (3.1). Agricola's life of apparent cooperation, submission, competency, humility, and virtuous behavior during Domitian's reign shows that "great men can live even under bad rulers; and that submission and moderation, if animation and energy go with them, reach the same pinnacle of fame" (42.4). This anti-Domitian polemic, especially to the fore in the opening (3) and final sections (39–46), combines with the fostering of admiration for Agricola's life and instruction on important elite values and practices; both serve a larger purpose made explicit at the end of the work. Tacitus closes with an exhortation to contemplate Agricola's virtues, not only with reverence and thankfulness, but also with imitation: "Let imitation even . . . be our tribute" (46.2). He suggests that his literary tribute is more fitting than a statue (though he does not rule that out entirely) because it enables people to "ponder each word and deed" (46.3) and to live accordingly.

Agricola's virtue was exhibited, according to Tacitus, in his faithful public service as a member of the ruling elite under an oppressive emperor (1–3; 39–46). This service comprised his role as an agent of Rome's power, notably as military commander and administrator "who first thoroughly subdued" Britain (10) and spread Roman "culture" among the British by constructing temples, marketplaces, and houses; by educating sons of chieftains; and by advocating the use of Latin and wearing the toga (21).[37] His greatest accomplishment was the military victory over the united British tribes in 84 CE. One-quarter of the work (sections 29–39) is concerned with this year, especially the daylong battle of Mount Graupius, where Agricola's defeat of the British ensures a "peaceful and safe" province (40.3). The elite virtues celebrated in this work, and thereby held up for admiration and imitation, are akin to those identified in the discussion of chapters 2–3 (above). Agricola appears as warrior (18; 22–25, 35–38), ruler and administrator (19), judge (19; 21.1), and priest (9). He collects taxes and tributes (13; 19), and throughout he imposes and upholds Roman order. There certainly is some idealizing and stereotyping in Tacitus's presentation of Agricola. Ogilvie comments, "A coherent picture of a devoted public servant emerges which is contrasted with the jealous despotism of Domitian. Qualities are attributed to Agricola which are as much conventional hallmarks of the good soldier and the good administrator as particular characteristics of the man himself."[38] This stereotyping serves the purpose of celebrating as well as providing instruction in and models of elite roles, values, and practices for imitation.

A comparison between three aspects of John's Gospel and Tacitus's biography of Agricola illustrates the Gospel's use of the genre of ancient biography, at times to imitate and at times to contest the elite imperial values advocated by Tacitus as worthy of imitation and in contrast to Domitian's practices.

Origin

Burridge notes that "most *bioi* (βίοι, ancient biographies) begin with mention of the subject's ancestry and heritage, his family, or his land or city."[39] Several writers trace their subjects' ancestry back to gods—Evagoras to Zeus and Agesilaus to Heracles—but by far the dominant emphasis is on noble and distinguished human ancestors. Tacitus is typical in identifying Agrippa's place of origin (the "illustrious Roman colony of Forum Julii") and the elite accomplishments of Agrippa's ancestors. "Each of his grandfathers was 'Procurator of Caesar,' a noble equestrian office. His father, Julius Graccinus, reached the rank of senator" and was put to death under the emperor Gaius Caligula for his virtue. Agrippa's "mother was Julia Procilla, a woman of rare virtue" (*Agrippa* 4). Elite social status and political office mark Agrippa's origins.

John's Gospel is very concerned with Jesus' origin. It establishes his origin in three unequal ways, the juxtapositions among which are crucial for the Gospel's frequent ironies (e.g., 7:25–31). First, of paramount importance is his origin with God. As we have seen, the opening Prologue employs a wisdom paradigm to turn to the past and locate the Word "in the beginning . . . with God" (1:1) and declares that this "Word became flesh" (1:14).[40] Subsequently Jesus is said to come "from God" (3:2; 8:42), "from heaven" (3:13; 6:32), "from above" (3:31; 8:23), and is "sent" from God (5:24), often described as "he/him who sent me" (6:38–39, 44). His origin in antiquity, "in the beginning . . . with God," is the foundation for Jesus' identity and role as the agent and revealer of God's life-giving purposes. Discerning this origin, identity, and function presents a challenge for those who encounter Jesus (7:15–18, 25–31). Of much lesser significance are two other sets of claims about his origins. One concerns his human parents. Jesus is identified as the son of Joseph (1:45; 6:42) and his mother, Mary, is named (19:25–27). The other concerns his place of origin, identified as Nazareth in Galilee (1:45–46; 18:5, 7; 19:19).

The origin of a famous figure from divine action and intervention is not unusual in ancient biographies, as I have noted. And in this regard John imitates other ancient biographies. But what is significant about John's presentation of Jesus' origin in relation to the conventions of ancient biographies is the *absence* of any association with elite ancestors. Jesus' father and mother are named, and Joseph is identified as known to some of the (nonelite) crowds from Galilee (6:42). But no prestigious political office or notable accomplishments are mentioned in relation to Joseph and Mary, nor are any elevated ancestors identified. Nor is Jesus' place of origin, Nazareth, presented as an "illustrious" (so Tacitus) place. In fact, the Gospel uses one of the disciples, Nathanael, to disparage it: "Can anything good come from Nazareth?" (1:46). Other characters cast doubts that the Christ is to come from Galilee and evoke a connection with king David's line by suggesting Bethlehem in Judea. The Gospel does not support such a connection (7:40–43, 52).

In contrast to the elite values of prestigious ancestors and sociopolitical power, wealth, and status evident in Tacitus's biography, "the Word became flesh" in a place of no significance and of nonelite parents. The Gospel locates God's action not in a significant center of power but in a nowhere place that has no expectations or associations of importance. The "Word became flesh" not of elite, wealthy, powerful, and prestigious ancestors in the imperial service but of unaccomplished, nonprestigious, nonelite, provincial parents. This divine preference for the nonelite—both persons and places—rejects the elite valuing of centers of power and ancestral lines of prestige as well as the conventions and emphases of the genre of ancient biographies. The Gospel does not value what the cultural elite value, another element in the Gospel's rhetoric of distance that resists ready accommodation with Rome's world in Ephesus.

Great Deeds

Burridge comments that great deeds

> form the bulk of the narrative but vary according to subject. Thus, for a statesman like Evagoras, great deeds include government in peace (40–50) and direction of war (51–64). . . . Xenophon recounts the deeds of Agesilaus on campaign in I.7–II.31. . . . Philo depicts Moses' great deeds as a king, . . . but also his greatness as lawgiver, priest and prophet. . . . Suetonius arranges his account of the emperors' deeds under his various headings. As with most philosophers, Demonax' greatness is expressed more in mighty words.[41]

Tacitus's presentation of Agricola emphasizes his accomplishments in military leadership and governance of the province of Britain. He takes over an unstable province (*Agricola* 14–17) and immediately sets about restoring military control with an initially effective campaign, which established his reputation "as a brilliant and a great man," displayed his virtuous qualities of "hard work and peril," and exhibited his self-deprecating style and commitment to fair treatment of subjugated provincials (18–19). The subsequent narrative emphasizes his skills in military strategy (20; 22), his attempts to "Romanize" the locals (21), his annual military campaigns over six years to subdue the provincials (22–28), and a final successful battle against "the flower of all their tribes" led by Calgacus (29–38). Agricola's victory is as decisive as it is bloody: "everywhere were weapons, corpses, lopped limbs, and blood upon the ground; . . . the enemy's slain amounted to ten thousand men" (37). Also featured are Agricola's rhetorical skills in a speech that rallies his troops for this final battle (33–34). In emphasizing these achievements of military skill and establishing provincial control, the narrative presents Agricola as a representative member of the elite, who functions as an effective agent of Roman power. He exhibits conventional elite values of "virtue, courage, and piety" and a concern for "moderation and public good" (42) despite a bad emperor.[42] It ends with an exhortation to imitate Agricola's actions, thereby ensuring the continuation of imperial ways among elites (46.2).

The Gospel's presentation of Jesus' "great deeds" centers on his words or teachings, mostly monologues with small dialogical features (3:1–21; 4; 5:19–47; 6:25–59; 8:12–59), and his eight deeds of power: Jesus changes water into wine (2:1–11), heals the royal official's son (4:46–54), heals the crippled man (5:1–18), feeds the large crowd (6:1–14), walks on water (6:16–21), heals the man born blind (9:1–7), raises Lazarus from death (11:1–46), and at the command of the risen Jesus, the disciples catch 153 fish (21:1–14).

The Gospel does not identify these actions as "miracles" or "works of power." In fact, the word *dynamis* (δύναμις), used in the Synoptic Gospels for Jesus' miracles, does not appear in John. Rather, the Gospel signals their significance by labeling them as "signs" (*sēmeia*, σημεῖα).[43] Thus, rather than emphasizing these actions as displays of power, the term "signs" indicates that these powerful actions point beyond themselves to a greater significance. They are signs in that they provide those who experience these miraculous actions an opportunity to discern Jesus' identity as the definitive revealer of God's purposes, to understand what God's purposes involve, and to commit themselves to Jesus and to the divine purposes he reveals.

Most of these miraculous signs concern the giving and sustaining of life. This emphasis contrasts remarkably with Tacitus's celebration of Agricola's sustained efforts to impose Roman military control by inflicting death, suffering, and subjugation. Jesus' "great deeds" especially involve acts of transformation: healing and nourishment. Both wholeness and nourishment were in short supply in Rome's imperial world, where the elite-dominated structures removed food supply and resources from much of the population through taxes and rents.[44] The resultant inadequate diets, variable food supply, anxiety, and overwork caused poor health and short life spans for many.[45] These realities are reflected in the crowds' demand of John 6:34, "Give us this bread always" (RSV). Physical brokenness and deficient resources were typical of empires like Rome; prophetic (Isa 25:6–10; 35:5–6) and apocalyptic traditions (*2 Bar.* 72–74) expected God to end such injustice and transform the world, with the establishment of God's purposes expressed in abundant food, fertility, and physical wholeness. Jesus' actions of healing and supplying nourishment draw on these visions of life free from injustice and as God intends it to be. They are signs that God's purposes for human life comprise wholeness, fertility, and abundance, not deprivation and brokenness. The Jerusalem-based, Rome-allied leadership with whom Jesus conflicts (see chap. 6 below, on the Gospel's plot) are not able to accomplish these purposes because they structure a hierarchical society for their own benefit.

In presenting Jesus' "great deeds," John's biography of Jesus again employs conventions of the elite genre of biography while it contests the genre's commitments to celebrate elite values of military prowess and political domination. Tacitus celebrates Agricola's display of justice to the pacified provincials in Britain by ensuring that "injustices" (*iniuriae*) do not follow conquest. Agricola eliminates personal favors, spreads grain, and makes tribute demands less burdensome "by equalizing burdens" (*aequalitate munerum*), and makes their collection less corrupt (19). But he does not seem to contemplate that the *removal* of Roman presence or tribute might be an act of justice, as the British chief Calgacus does in declaring: "To plunder, butcher, steal, these things they misname empire; they make a desolation and they call it peace" (30). John's Gospel, though, offers an alternative agenda, a revelation of God's life-giving purposes that, in healing and supplying nutrition, interrupt and roll back the damage that imperial control causes for nonelites. While Agricola takes life in imposing Roman power, Jesus provides life in manifesting God's purposes.

Moreover, John's Jesus calls Jesus-believers to the same sorts of actions. In his farewell instructions to his followers, given to shape their lives in his absence after the crucifixion, Jesus declares, "Truly, truly I say to you, the ones who believe in me will also do the works that I do; and greater works than these will they do, because I go to the Father" (14:12 RSV alt.). These transforming actions seem to comprise, at least in part, the mission to which Jesus-believers are called (17:18; 20:21). According to the writer/s of the Gospel, the community of Jesus-believers is to continue Jesus' transforming actions in Ephesus from a protected location of considerable though not complete societal distance (17:15).

Death

Burridge notes that all the biographies "conclude with the subject's death. Agricola's death is carefully described, together with the emperor's interest in it," and occupies about 10 percent of the work (43–46).[46] Tacitus narrates Agricola's illness, frequent visits from "the chief freedmen and the confidential physicians of the Palace with a regularity unusual in a prince who visits by deputy, whether this was interest or espionage" (43). The last comment refers to rumors that Agricola was poisoned, a motif that plays up the negative presentation of Domitian, though Tacitus recognizes that there was not "any firm evidence." Yet while Agricola's death brought "mourning" to his family, "melancholy" to his friends, and even "anxiety" to those who did not know him, Domitian was unmoved except to receive joyfully the news that Agricola's will named him coheir (43.3–4). Tacitus's verdict on Agricola's life is to admire his accomplishment as an elite agent of Roman military and provincial domination. Agricola "lived to a ripe old age measured by renown. . . . What more could fortune have added to one who had been consul and had won the decorations of triumph?" (44.3). And he was blessed to escape the last years of Domitian's excessive tyranny when he "poured forth the life-blood of the state" (44–45).

As with other biographies, John's narrative ends with an account of Jesus' death (and resurrection) in narrative sequence in John 18–21. Consistent with other biographies, this topic forms about 15 percent of the Gospel.[47] But again, while the Gospel employs features of the elite genre of biography, it subverts them to present a quite different sort of death.

Jesus' death is not the completion of a life committed to upholding elite imperial ways and mourned by all (except Domitian), as with Agricola. Rather, it is the ignominious death of a provincial who has resisted and challenged imperial practices, a death brought about by an alliance of elite leaders committed to defending the imperial societal status quo against such a challenge.[48] Jesus dies by crucifixion (19:16–23), a shameful and painful way to die, which Josephus describes as the "most pitiable of deaths" (*J.W.* 7.203). It was rarely used for Roman citizens (except for those guilty of treason, Cicero, *Pro Rabirio Perduellionis Reo*, 9–17) but was reserved for rebellious foreigners (Josephus, *J.W.* 2.306, 308; 5.449–53; Philo, *Flaccus* 72, 84), violent criminals and robbers or bandits (Martial, *On the Spectacles* 9), and uncooperative slaves (Cicero, *In Verrem* 2.5.162; Juvenal, *Sat.* 6.219–224; Tacitus, *Ann.* 13.32.1), who threatened elite control and way of life. It was carried out in public to deter noncompliance and to elicit cooperation (Josephus, *J.W.* 5.550). In the next chapter, we will need to examine how Jesus' death comes about. At this point, it is sufficient to recognize that he dies the sort of death that identifies Jesus as a threat and challenger to, not an upholder of, elite societal control. The Jerusalem-based, Rome-allied leadership, the Pharisees and chief priests, describe Jesus in precisely these terms: "If we let him go on thus, everyone will believe in him and the Romans will come and destroy both our holy place and our nation" (11:48 RSV). His death reveals a fundamental antipathy between Jesus and the empire, an antipathy that should shape the identity and lives of John's Jesus-believers.

Second, this apparent victory is modified by several indications that Jesus' death is, ultimately, under God's and Jesus' control. Throughout its first half, the Gospel indicates that Jesus' "hour" has not yet come, and so no one is able to arrest him (2:4; 7:30; 8:20). But in 12:23, 27 and 13:1, in the context of references to Jesus' death, his "hour" is declared to have come. His death takes place in God's timing. And Jesus declares in 10:11–18 that he actively and voluntarily lays down his life for his followers. "No one takes it from me, but I lay it down of my own accord. I have the power to lay it down, and I have the power to take it up again" (10:18 RSV). Jesus' death, as the arrest scene in 18:1–11 indicates, does not take him by surprise. It is not the victory of the imperial forces. He lays down his life.

Third, in contrast with the other biographies in which the death of the subject ends the story, John's Gospel narrates the resurrection of the crucified provincial Jesus. The last two chapters (20–21) detail appearances of Jesus restored to life. Thus, the worst that the elite allies and agents of the empire can do is put him to death; yet that death does not effectively remove, control, or subdue him. Their rejection of God's commissioned agent is not the final word on the Word who comes from God. Or to restate, God's life-giving power, at work in and through Jesus, is shown to be greater than Rome's death-dealing power. Jesus' resurrection is not good news for Rome since it displays God's superior power and anticipates what would seem to be Rome's inevitable subjugation to God's life-giving purposes. This revelation of God's greater power is not surprising since, as we have just observed, the Gospel has presented Jesus' death not as a defeat, not as the victory of the elite powers, but as a working out of God's purposes (10:17–18) and as an enthronement of Jesus as king or agent of God's rule (18:33–37; 19:15).[49] In chapter 8 below, I will examine what the Gospel means by this life or eternal life that Jesus reveals.[50]

Conclusion

In this chapter, I have considered the genre of John's Gospel. I have argued that previous attempts to classify it as unique are not convincing. Recognition of its "generic depth" and of its affinities to aspects of revelatory literature is helpful but does not adequately identify an overarching genre. Using Richard Burridge's work, I have argued that the Gospel's dominant genre is best classified as an ancient biography. I have also gone beyond Burridge in claiming that the Gospel's genre is involved in the multifaceted task of negotiating the Roman Empire. The Gospel's dominant genre, ancient biography, is a form of literature with a lengthy history. Its adoption represents another turn to the past. But it is a genre that typically celebrates important elite figures such as statesmen, military commanders, and philosophers, and upholds and celebrates central elite cultural values and claims. While the Gospel employs this genre, it also undermines these claims in presenting the story, actions, and teaching of a provincial, Jesus, crucified by Rome but raised by God. Discussion of matters of origin, great deeds, and death in Tacitus's biography *Agricola* and in John's Gospel has highlighted that the Gospel's dominant genre exhibits both participation in the imperial world as well as critique of its central commitments. The genre contributes to the Gospel's efforts to distance Jesus-believers from the empire and to shape their alternative identity and existence.

Notes

1. Interestingly, contemporary Johannine scholarship has not devoted much attention to John's genre. There is no discussion in the groundbreaking study of R. Alan Culpepper, *Anatomy of the Fourth Gospel: A Study in Literary Design* (Philadelphia: Fortress, 1987), nor in several recent collections of essays on the Gospel such as R. Alan Culpepper and C. Clifton Black, eds., *Exploring the Gospel of John: In Honor of D. Moody Smith* (Louisville: Westminster John Knox, 1996); Robert T. Fortna and Tom Thatcher, eds., *Jesus in Johannine Tradition* (Louisville: Westminster John Knox, 2001).

2. See chap. 2 above; Said, *Culture and Imperialism*, xxv.

3. See chap. 2 above.

4. See the fine discussion by Richard A. Burridge, *What Are the Gospels? A Comparison with Graeco-Roman Biography* (Cambridge: Cambridge University Press, 1992), 26–54; David E. Aune, "Gospels, Literary Genre of," in *The Westminster Dictionary of New Testament and Early Christian Literature and Rhetoric* (Louisville: Westminster John Knox, 2003), 204–6.

5. Burridge (*What Are the Gospels?* 3–25) outlines a history of scholarship. Harold W. Attridge ("Genre Bending in the Fourth Gospel," *JBL* 121 [2002]: 3–21) focuses on diverse genres within the Gospel but pays little attention to the Gospel genre itself (though see 8).

6. Charles Hedrick, "The Four/Thirty-Four Gospels: Diversity and Division among the Earliest Christians," *Bible Review* 18 (2002): 20–31, 46–47.

7. Some would say that Mark 1:1 raises a question about this claim. Does the term "gospel" refer to the document or its message and claims, or both?

8. John A. Ashton, *Understanding the Fourth Gospel* (Oxford: Clarendon, 1991), 409.

9. I discuss historical information about Jesus in John, and a claim that the Gospel belongs to the genre of Jewish theodicy narratives in Carter, *John: Storyteller*, chap. 1, with bibliography.

10. Rudolf Bultmann, "The Gospels (Form)," in *Twentieth Century Theology in the Making*, ed. J. Pelikan (London: Collins/Fontana, 1969), 1.86–92; see the survey in Burridge, *What Are the Gospels?* 7–13.

11. Ashton, *Understanding*, 433.

12. Davies (*Rhetoric and Reference*, 67–109) argues that "the genre of the Fourth Gospel, therefore, like that of scriptural narratives, is a theodicy, a vindication of divine providence in view of the existence of evil" (89). While this approach helpfully highlights connections with the Jewish Scriptures, theodicy is a theme or philosophical issue, not a genre. The Scriptures she cites comprise numerous genres, not one.

13. Mark W. G. Stibbe, *John's Gospel* (New York: Routledge, 1994), 62–72; Northrop Frye, *Anatomy of Criticism: Four Essays* (Princeton: Princeton University Press, 1971), 131–239.

14. Frye, *Anatomy*, 187.

15. Ibid., 206–23, esp. 206–8.

16. Bruce Grigsby, "The Cross as an Expiatory Sacrifice in the Fourth Gospel," *JSNT* 15 [1982]: 51–80) sees three emphases (the casting of Jesus as the paschal victim [1:29; 19:14, 29, 36], Christ as the Isaac figure [1:29; 3:16; 19:17], Christ the cleansing fountain [19:34]) that elaborate the sacrificial dimension of Jesus' death.

17. Frye, *Anatomy*, 223–39.

18. See Carter, *John: Storyteller*, 107–28.

19. Frye, *Anatomy*, 163–86; also Craig R. Koester, "Comedy, Humor, and the Gospel of John," in *Word, Theology, and Community in John*, ed. J. Painter, R. A. Culpepper, and F. F. Segovia (St. Louis: Chalice, 2002), 123–41.

20. E.g., Gail R. O'Day, *Revelation in the Fourth Gospel: Narrative Mode and Theological Claim* (Philadelphia: Fortress, 1986); Ashton, *Understanding*, 383–406; also Painter, *Quest*, 249–50.

21. John J. Collins, *The Apocalyptic Imagination: An Introduction to the Jewish Matrix of Christianity* (New York: Crossroad, 1984), 4. Ashton (*Understanding*, 383–87) expresses some reservations and offers his own revised definition.

22. Ashton, *Understanding*, 383–406; also Painter, *Quest*, 249–50.

23. Ashton, *Understanding*, 387.

24. For riddles in John, see Carter, *John: Storyteller*, 116–18; Tom Thatcher, *The Riddles of Jesus in John: A Study in Tradition and Folklore*, SBLMS 53 (Atlanta: SBL, 2000).

25. David E. Aune, "Biography," in *Westminster Dictionary*, 78–81.

26. Burridge, *What Are the Gospels?* 70–81.

27. Christopher Pelling, ed., *Characterization and Individuality in Greek Literature* (New York: Oxford University Press, 1990), esp. the article by Christopher Gill, "Character-Personality Distinction," 1–31.

28. Aune, "Biography," 80.

29. Burridge, *What Are the Gospels?* 55–69; also David E. Aune, *The New Testament in Its Literary Environment* (Philadelphia: Westminster, 1987), 17–76.

30. Burridge, *What Are the Gospels?* 128–90.

31. Ibid., 109–239. I am summarizing Burridge's excellent work.

32. Carter, *John: Storyteller*, 86–128.

33. Burridge's discussion of all the generic features of *Agricola* appears throughout *What Are the Gospels?* 160–90.

34. Burridge, *What Are the Gospels?* 185.

35. Paula James, "Essay Ten: The Language of Dissent," in *Experiencing Rome: Culture, Identity, and Power in the Roman Empire*, ed. Janet Huskinson (London: Routledge, 2000), 277–303, esp. 278. Following Ogilvie and Richmond, James argues that Calgacus's speech includes numerous critiques of elite Roman characteristics such as Rome's worldwide power, the cosmopolitan organization of the army, greed and ambition, slavery and freedom. Calgacus shows precisely the courage to resist that cowardly senators had not shown (282–85).

36. For some discussion, see Burridge, *What Are the Gospels?* 155–56, 160–90; T. A. Dorey ("Agricola and Domitian," 66–71) thinks that Tacitus exaggerates or manufactures the negative presentation of Domitian as part of a rhetorical strategy to persuade readers that Agricola did not enjoy Domitian's favor; also idem, "Agricola," in *Tacitus* (New York: Basic Books, 1969), 1–11; C. Tacitus, *De vita Agricolae*, ed. R. M. Ogilvie and Ian Richmond (Oxford: Oxford University Press, 1967); F. R. Goodyear, *Tacitus* (Oxford: Clarendon, 1970), 3–8.

37. Tacitus's commentary (*Agricola* 21.2) is biting: "Little by little the Britons went astray into alluring vices: to the promenade, the bath, the well-appointed dinner table. The simple natives gave the name of 'culture' to this factor of their slavery." See James, "Language of Dissent," 285–89. For a similar tactic carried out by Sertorius, the governor of Spain, see Plutarch, *Sertorius*, 13–14. According to Tacitus, *Hist.* 4.64.3, Civilis, a Batavian military commander, warns his people against Roman culture: "Away with those pleasures which give the Romans more power over their subjects than their arms bestow."

38. Ogilvie and Richmond, *De vita Agricolae*, 20.

39. Burridge, *What Are the Gospels?* 146, 178.

40. Or perhaps better, "the Word was born flesh," following the argument of Adele Reinhartz ("'And the Word Was Begotten': Divine Epigenesis in the Gospel of John," in *Semeia* 85 [1999]: 83–103, esp. 92), which attends to the notion of divine epigenesis in John and gives weight to the meaning of γίνομαι as "to be born or to become." J. C. O'Neil, "The Word Did Not 'Become' Flesh," *ZNTW* 82 (1991): 125–27.

41. Burridge, *What Are the Gospels?* 146, 179.

42. Ibid., 181.

43. *Sēmeia* appears in John 2:11, 18, 23; 3:2; 4:48, 54; 6:2, 14, 26, 30; 7:31; 9:16; 10:41; 11:47; 12:18, 37; 20:30. Just once, at 4:48, it also calls them "wonders" (*terata*, τέρατα); the phrase "signs and wonders" appears in Exod 7:3–4 and Deut 29:3; 34:11 in reference to the liberation from Egyptian oppression; also Wis 10:16.

44. Garnsey, *Food and Society*.

45. See the description of levels of poverty in chap. 3 above.

46. Burridge, *What Are the Gospels?* 164, 179, also 146–47.

47. Ibid., 224, 232.

48. See chap. 6 below for elaboration of the Gospel's plot and chap. 13 for a discussion of Jesus and Pilate.

49. For further dimensions of Jesus' death, see Carter, *John: Storyteller*, chap. 3. For Jesus' death as of little salvific consequence, see E. Käsemann, *The Testament of Jesus* (Philadelphia: Fortress, 1966), 7; as glorification, Bultmann, *Gospel of John*, 632–33; as revelation, idem, *Theology of the New Testament*, 2 vols. (London: SCM, 1952–55), 2:53; T. Forestell, *The Word of the Cross: Salvation as Revelation in the Fourth Gospel* (Rome: Pontifical Biblical Institute, 1974), 191–93; as sacrifice, Grigsby, "Cross as an Expiatory Sacrifice," 51–80; G. Carey, "The Lamb of God and Atonement Theories," *TynBul* 32 (1981): 97–122; as ascension, Nicholson, *Death as Departure*; as cosmic victory over Satan, J. Kovacs, "'Now Shall the Ruler of This World Be Driven Out': Jesus' Death as Cosmic Battle in John 12:20–36," *JBL* 114 (1995): 227–47; as noble death, J. Neyrey, "The 'Noble Shepherd' in John 10: Cultural and Rhetorical Background," *JBL* 120 (2001): 267–91.

50. For other implications of John as an ancient biography, see Carter, *John: Storyteller*, 3–20.

6

The Plot of John's Gospel

In identifying the genre of John's Gospel in chapter 5, I observed that ancient biographies conventionally organize their accounts of the significant elite person in a chronological sequence covering ancestry, birth and upbringing, virtues, greet deeds, death, and consequences. John's Gospel includes most of these elements in its account of the life of the nonelite provincial, Jesus, though it pays little attention to Jesus' birth and upbringing.[1] I also showed that matters of genre are closely related to questions about types of plot (comedy, tragedy, and so forth). This chapter pursues the issue of plot. How does the Gospel construct its account of Jesus' life to form the Gospel's plot? And how does the plot serve the purposes of the Gospel's author/s in guiding Jesus-believers in their imperial negotiation?

I will begin by examining what constitutes a plot, and then outline the plot of John's Gospel. I will argue that John's plot comprises a further dimension of the Gospel's rhetoric of distance. With its focus on Jesus crucified by Rome, the plot plays a significant part in the writer/s' strategy to distance Jesus-believers from too great an accommodation to Rome's Empire. The Gospel's plot is, in James Scott's terms, part of a "hidden transcript" that contests and dissents from the public transcript or official version of the empire's self-presentation and the roles ascribed to nonelites within its societal order. The story of a crucified provincial whom Rome is unable to keep dead denies ultimate power to Rome, exposes its death-bringing commitments, and celebrates God's greater life-giving power manifested through Jesus' words, works, and resurrection. It is these transformative and not accommodationist words and works that are to mark the identity and societal existence of Jesus-believers. The Gospel tells a story that guides Jesus-believers in interpreting the present and living accordingly.

I will also draw some attention to the Gospel's use of intertexts. John frequently evokes texts from the Hebrew Bible, sometimes quoting directly, sometimes using Hebrew Bible images, sometimes employing Hebrew Bible paradigms such as wisdom, and sometimes setting events in relation to festivals. Often the references are, in John's Foley's word, metonymic, whereby, as typical of literature derived from oral societies, a brief reference evokes a much larger narrative or tradition of God's activity.[2] The Gospel does not spell out these texts, but as common in oral cultures it assumes that hearers (readers) share this cultural repertoire and can elaborate the reference. The interface between the Gospel's story and the evoked text functions to provide commentary on Jesus' actions and words, supplying a larger context in which to interpret his ministry.

Significantly, John often evokes scenarios that involve the establishment of God's life-giving purposes, judgment on nations, God's victory over them, and God's reign. All of this comprises a negative verdict on Rome's world and its Jerusalem allies. It functions to reveal the empire's evil to Jesus-believers (3:19–20; 7:7), thereby warning them against accommodation with a world at odds with God's purposes and under judgment. Because they evoke traditions and narratives known only to insiders, the intertexts often function self-protectively to disguise this judgment from outsiders.

What Is a Plot?

Discussions of John's plot have not been numerous.[3] Typically interpreters have preferred to outline the "structure" of John's Gospel, taking a "sectional" approach to the Gospel. A standard but minimalist analysis of the Gospel's "structure" sees it as consisting of two sections, each marked by some thematic unity and with a major break between chapters 12 and 13:[4]

> Chapters 1–12, The Book of Signs
> Chapters 13–21, The Book of Glory

More detailed approaches identify a greater number of sections and discern some unity for each section's content, either by concentrating on events or, more often, themes. For example, Gail O'Day identifies eight sections:[5]

> 1:1–51, The Prelude to Jesus' Ministry
> 2:1–5:47, The "Greater Things": Jesus' Words and Works
> 6:1–10:42, Jesus' Words and Works: Conflict and Opposition Grow
> 11:1–12:50, The Prelude to Jesus' Hour
> 3:1–17:26, The Farewell Meal and Discourse
> 8:1–19:42, "The Hour Has Come": Jesus' Arrest, Trial, and Death
> 20:1–31, The First Resurrection Appearances
> 21:1–25, Jesus' Resurrection Appearances at the Sea of Tiberias

Fernando Segovia helpfully proposes an outline based on a biographical sequence (the three major sections) with the second section subdivided in terms of journeys to Jerusalem:[6]

> 1:1–18, Narrative of Origins
> 1:19–17:26, Narrative of the Public Life or Career
> 1:19–3:36, First Galilee/Jerusalem Cycle
> 4:1–5:47, Second Galilee/Jerusalem Cycle
> 6:1–10:42, Third Galilee/Jerusalem Cycle
> 11:1–17:26, Fourth and Final Journey to Jerusalem
> 18:1–21:25, Narrative of Death and Lasting Significance

Such analyses of the Gospel's structure are helpful in identifying main sections of the Gospel.[7] And they reflect a well-justified sense that often the "action" and characters of this Gospel are subordinated to its dominating theological ideas. But while there is some truth to the notion that the Gospel often seems theologically programmatic in its presentation, structure is not the same as a plot. Structure emphasizes "blocks" and divisions; plots are concerned with sequences of and connections among events that comprise a unity of action. Events or individual incidents occur in sequences and in various relationships to other events. Conflicts occur among characters. Elements of causation, consequence, surprise, and discovery (the effect of the plot) are operative.

The leading literary theorist in the ancient world, Aristotle, discusses plot in his work *On the Art of Poetry* (chaps. 6–17).[8] Among Aristotle's emphases are these:

- A plot comprises not just a series of events but an ordered combination of incidents.

- This combination of incidents forms a unity of action, not just by focusing on one man but from the representation of the action.

- The action has a beginning, middle, and end; it comprises events that are probable and/or necessary.

- The sequence of events must be necessary and/or usual; causation and consequence guide the sequence. The end is a "necessary or usual consequence" of what goes before it.

- The plot needs amplitude or reasonable length, long enough to be taken notice of, short enough to be held in the memory.

- Reversals (change from one state to another) and/or recognitions (from ignorance to recognition/discovery that causes love or hate) are especially important in the plot's overall shape.

- Plots have an effect on audiences, moving them, especially awakening fear and pity.

Recent literary critics, often focusing on contemporary novels, short stories, movies, and TV shows, have developed aspects of Aristotle's insights. Some emphasize the importance of causality in linking events.[9] Others highlight the unity of the action determined by the work's end.[10] Others focus on the plot's impact on the audience.[11] Seymour Chatman explores the relationship among events, emphasizing "the logic of hierarchy" whereby key events called *kernels* provide major branching points that advance the plot, that are consequent on previous actions, and that raise questions leading to subsequent events.[12] These major events provide a plot's unity and causality, while minor events, called *satellites*, elaborate aspects of the kernels.[13]

These discussions identify some important issues to consider in formulating John's plot. What elements does the story of Jesus include? How does it sequence these elements? How does it connect them? Where does it begin? What happens in the middle? How does the action progress? What causes things to happen? How are episodes linked? What characters are involved? How does it end? And what effect does organizing the story in this way have on the Gospel's readers or hearers?

What Are Some Typical Plots?

Some literary critics such as Northrop Frye,[14] A. J. Greimas,[15] and Seymour Chatman[16] have ventured in another direction. They have considered the type of action in which the main character is involved and have attempted to describe general or even universal types of plots that a narrative might employ. Biblical scholars have sought to use some of these models to elucidate the plots of the Gospels, sometimes with good success (see Stibbe's use of Frye in chap. 5 above), sometimes unsuccessfully because these ancient biographies are not (contemporary) novels.

Mark Stibbe, for instance, has tried to employ A. J. Greimas's model of a universal "deep structure" for storytelling to elucidate John's plot.[17] For Greimas, plots comprise three axes and four character-types (called actants). The first axis (called communication) concerns a commission or task that a Sender gives to a Receiver. The second axis (volition) concerns the Receiver carrying out the commission. The third axis (power) centers on the opposition the Receiver experiences from Opponents. Because of this opposition, the Receiver gets assistance from a Helper. That is, the three axes of communication, volition, and power involve four characters or actants: Sender, Receiver, Opponent, Helper.

Stibbe sees John's plot in these terms. God is the sender, who gives Jesus (the receiver) a commission to manifest God's life among humans (3:16; 20:31).[18] Jesus carries out this work of doing God's will (cf. 4:34) but is opposed by the devil and its agent,[19] the Jerusalem leadership (whom the Gospel names the *Ioudaioi*). Jesus has no helper, but he does extend his work by becoming a sender in commissioning the disciples to continue his work (20:21b; 14:12). They have a helper (the Paraclete or Holy Spirit, 14:15–17, 26; 16:7–15) and opponents (15:18–20; 16:2). The Gospel also has a counterplot. The devil is the sender, who gives the Jerusalem leadership a commission to oppose and kill Jesus (8:34–45). Their principal helper is Judas; directed by Satan (13:2, 27), he betrays Jesus.

Greimas's scheme enables Stibbe to identify an overarching unity of the plot, important lines of action, features of characterization, and theological motifs. The fit, though, is not perfect. Stibbe's effort is not convincing in trying to reframe the absence of a helper for Jesus by highlighting Jesus' resolute and solitary commitment to God's will. And while the scheme clarifies aspects of John at a somewhat generalized or abstract level, it does little to show how the plot is formulated on a chapter-by-chapter basis. It gives little attention to specific episodes, connections, conflicts, and characters in the Gospel. And it does not attend to the intermingling and interweaving of the various plot lines in which repetition, contrast, and cumulative effect play significant roles.

Moreover, Stibbe does not express well the element of recognition that Culpepper, borrowing from Aristotle, highlights as being central to John's plot.[20] Culpepper rightly argues that the plot does not develop around the unfolding or development of Jesus' character, because Jesus is a static character, defined in terms of his identity as God's agent, commissioned to reveal God. Rather, the plot develops in terms of the struggle of characters to recognize Jesus' identity. Repeatedly in his signs (2:1–12; 4:46–53), discourses (John 5–6; 8; 10), conversations with individual characters such as Nicodemus in chapter 3 and the unnamed Samaritan woman in chapter 4, and his use of various symbols and images (light, door, vine, good shepherd, way, life, and others), Jesus discloses his identity. Each scene or individual episode encapsulates the same challenge as to whether the characters will recognize Jesus.

Culpepper's emphasis on recognizing Jesus' identity is well placed, but his focus is too limited. John's story is not just about people recognizing or not recognizing Jesus' identity. This emphasis, indebted to Bultmann, presents the Gospel as a religious text in which individuals are placed in a "crisis of decision" (to use Bultmann's phrase) in response to Jesus. Lacking is an adequate explanation of Jesus' death by crucifixion: one can fail to recognize his identity without killing him. Also lacking, more importantly, is an adequate formulation of the content and context of Jesus' revelation. Crucifixion is a sociopolitical event. This is one clue that Jesus' crucifixion is related not just to claims about his identity but also to the content of his revelation of God's life-giving purposes. Both elements are needed to account for Jesus' crucifixion in the Gospel's plot. The Gospel is not just about knowing that Jesus is the Christ, the Son of God, but about experiencing life as shaped by and expressive of God's just purposes (20:31) that Jesus, the Christ, is commissioned to reveal (as Chapter 8, below, will demonstrate). Thus the focus on recognition/nonrecognition of Jesus' identity does not adequately address Aristotle's concern with a unity of action that accounts for the end of the story as the necessary consequence of what proceeds it. The question that must be addressed in a discussion of John's plot concerns what happens through the Gospel to bring about Jesus' death by crucifixion. This political event and weapon of Roman imperial control directs our attention to Jesus' actions and words, and to the story's conflicts, especially between Jesus and the Rome-allied Jerusalem elite. Attention to the contribution of individual scenes and specific episodes indicates that a key aspect of this struggle involves understandings of God's purposes that are at odds with Rome's purposes and structures. Jesus' revelation is, I will argue, fatally in conflict with imperial societal vision and practices that uphold elite power and privileges.

John's Plot: A Proposal

I suggest that rather than the theme of recognition, Aristotle's emphasis on the end of the plot as the "necessary or usual consequence" of the preceding action directs our attention to the conflict that pervades John's Gospel. This conflict centers on the interaction between the Rome-allied, temple-based, ruling Jerusalem elite and God's commissioned agent, Jesus. In general terms, I propose that John's story of Jesus enacts Jesus' claim to be God's chosen agent, authorized by God to make a definitive revelation of God's life-giving purposes and to take away the sin of the Roman-ruled world. In living out this claim in his words and works, Jesus conflicts with the Rome-allied Jerusalem elite and their Roman ally, the provincial governor Pilate, confronting and challenging their power over, and vision of, an unjust societal order, which is contrary to God's life-giving purposes. The Jerusalem elite reject Jesus' claim and revelation of God's purposes of life, preferring to defend the status quo by putting him to death. But surprisingly his death is not the end. God raises him, thereby revealing the limit of their power and the error of their societal order. Meanwhile some people discern Jesus' origin, identity, and mission; commit themselves to his revelation; and form a countercommunity or antisociety that, assisted by the Holy Spirit, continues Jesus' life-giving mission.

How does this plot function for John's Jesus-believers in imperial Ephesus? My argument is that this telling of the story of Jesus is part of the author/s' strategy to create more distance between Jesus-believers and the empire. This rhetoric of distance emphasizes Jesus' antipathy to the Roman order and its Jerusalem-based allies, along with their opposition to Jesus. The plot depicts the conflict between and the incompatibility of these two entities, even placing it in a dualistic cosmic framework comprising Satan's struggle against God (8:39–47; 13:2, 27). And this telling of the story works hard, evident for instance in its lengthy "farewell discourse" (John 13–17), to form an "antisociety," a community of disciples committed to a different identity and way of life.[21] This hard formational work to create an antisociety is necessary not because there has been so much chaos and pain from a putative separation/expulsion from a synagogue, as has often been argued, but precisely because in the author's/authors' perspective, there is too much accommodation to and participation in daily imperial life, and not enough societal distance.

John's Plot

Throughout, I will take cues from Aristotle's emphasis on the plot's end as the "necessary and/or usual" consequence of the previous events. The question then becomes, How does Jesus' death by crucifixion (and resurrection/ascension), the end of the plot, come about? What does Jesus do and/or say that causes the Jerusalem-based, Rome-allied leadership and their ally, the Roman governor, to crucify him? Conflict is crucial. Recognition and, in the end, reversal play important roles in producing John's ending. And what are the events that lead to the Gospel's surprising conclusion in Jesus' resurrection and ascension?

Beginning: The Prologue (1:1–18) and 1:19–4:54

The Gospel has a double beginning. The plot itself, comprising the ordered combination of events that leads through challenge and conflict to Jesus' death, resurrection, and ascension, begins at 1:19. The first eighteen verses (the Prologue) offer a big-picture narrative, a thematic preview of and perspective on the Gospel plot's general movement. They also begin the Gospel's negotiation of Roman Ephesus, shaping the more societally distanced identity of Jesus-believers by contesting central imperial claims concerning legitimate sovereignty and agency of the gods' will and blessing. They evoke and contrast the Gospel audience's cultural knowledge of common imperial realities.

The Prologue thus does not only engage significant matters pertaining to first-century Judaisms, as much scholarship claims by focusing only on intrasynagogal religious matters, but it also interacts with matters central to Roman power, the great tradition, in Scott's terms.[22] The question of how the Prologue's emphases function in the Roman imperial context does not deny the presence of the wisdom and/or apocalyptic revealer traditions identified in much recent scholarship. Rather, it is to ask how the claims of

such traditions connected to Jesus the Word function in negotiating the Roman imperial world. The question is one of cultural intertextuality, the study of the Gospel
"within (the text of) society and history," as Julia Kristeva has emphasized.[23]

One other issue needs brief attention. Given the absence of explicit imperial references from the Prologue and most discussions of it, the exploration of how this unit
might be heard in an imperial provincial capital such as Ephesus might be considered
illegitimate, or unfounded, or a strange import. The Prologue's silence on Rome,
though, is complex and not easily dismissed.

On one hand, Rome explicitly surfaces in the Gospel in chapters 11 and 18–19,
where the main character of the plot is crucified, a distinctively Roman form of execution. These texts indicate that Rome is on the Gospel's radar. Yet it would be false to conclude that Rome is only in view in sections where it is explicitly named, just as it would
be false to conclude that synagogue debates are in view only and exclusively in 9:22;
12:42; and 16:2. Many scholars have rightly connected the Prologue to the tension
within a synagogue on the basis of the Gospel's context. So too for Rome. The empire
does not go away when it is not mentioned. As I have demonstrated in chapters 1–5
above, it pervades the world and daily experience of the Gospel's audience, who make
it present in their hearing of the Gospel. The Prologue, like the rest of the Gospel,
evokes, imitates, and contrasts the Gospel audience's cultural knowledge of common
societal realities, not only Jewish but also imperial—divine legitimation, revelation,
agency, response—while it frames and reflects on the story of Jesus crucified by Rome.[24]
My concern is to explicate the identity that the Gospel and Prologue create in relation
to the Roman Empire and to the modes of negotiating it deployed by some/many Jesus-
believers in Ephesus, modes the Gospel's writer/s is/are not supportive of.

Further, the work of James Scott on forms of resistance among powerless groups
indicates that an expectation of explicit naming is unlikely in a text that originates with
those subjected to imperial power and yet are concerned, in part, to contest it.[25] The
powerless rarely engage in direct and open confrontation but employ self-protective,
calculated, disguised arts of resistance along with continual acts of accommodation.
They rely on coded references and on assumed and insider knowledge that thrives in
safe spaces, away from public gaze. We would expect the Prologue to be consistent with
these approaches.

Third, the discussion of Simon Swain's study in chapter 4 above indicates that in the
writings of some Greek elites a somewhat parallel phenomenon exists. While there is
little overt hostility to Rome in these writers, there is also generally little explicit interest in Roman culture. Swain argues that while some Greeks took a "sympathetic and
active interest in Rome, Romans, and Roman history, . . . the majority of Greeks whose
testimony we can call on had no deep interest in Rome's past or culture."[26] Greek novels such as the *Ephesian Story*, by Xenophon of Ephesus, frequently create "a Greek
world independent, indeed oblivious of Rome."[27] Plutarch's work *Should Old Men Take
Part in Politics?* like his *Political Advice*, deals with local Greek politics and is interested
in maintaining "the status quo in a world of local Greek politics without Rome."[28] Galen
shows "no warm admiration for Roman achievements," and most of his work displays
"his insulation from the Roman world."[29] Swain's concern is, having observed a pervasive focus on Greek culture, to explore "what implications an identity of this sort had
for the Greeks vis-à-vis Rome." He suggests that the result of this bifurcated elite iden-

tity of participation in the Roman political world yet commitment to Greek culture meant that "however close individuals got to Rome, overall we notice a certain distance, a resistance to integration."[30] It seems that John's Gospel takes a somewhat similar approach. Some participation in Rome's world is inevitable for Jesus-believers and synagogue members in Ephesus—including for the Gospel writers, as the use of the ancient biography genre documents, for instance (Chapter 5, above)—but the Gospel's writer/s and supporters think levels of accommodation or integration are too high. The telling of the story of Jesus reinforces an identity of allegiance to Jesus that creates some distance, resists integration, and fosters an alternative community. This is the sort of hybridity needed to negotiate Rome's world.

The Prologue's opening five verses present Jesus' origin in relation to God and as participant in creation. These opening verses locate the Word, identified by subsequent verses as Jesus (1:14, 17), "in the beginning . . . with God" (1:1–2), as cocreator, in whom is light and life (1:3–5). This cosmological recalling of God's creative, life-giving sovereignty in Genesis 1 and of wisdom traditions from Proverbs 8 and Wisdom 7–9 (see the discussion in chap. 4 above) strongly asserts God's life-giving power and sovereignty over all creation, and locates the origin of Jesus, God's agent and wisdom, "in the beginning" with God. These claims, shaped by creation and wisdom traditions, have often been seen correctly as contestive of other—unnamed in the Prologue—Jewish revealer figures.[31]

Yet it would be entirely arbitrary not to recognize that claims of sovereignty and agency pervaded the audience's imperial world and that John's Prologue participates in the competition for sovereignty over the earth.[32] The media of Roman imperial theology—imperial poets, coins, provincial inscriptions, speeches before battles, imperial cult rituals and civic festivals, temples, taxes and tributes—for example, commonly declared Rome and its emperors as agents of the gods, as rightly exercising divinely sanctioned sovereignty over the earth, and as manifesting the will and blessing of the gods in a new golden age on earth and brought about by Rome and its rulers' military might (e.g., Virgil, *Aeneid* 6.792–793).[33] For example, Jupiter "Father of men and gods" bestows on Rome "empire without end" (*imperium sine fine*) and promises to "cherish" Rome as "lords of the world" (*Aeneid* 1.279, 281–282). Anchises, Aeneas's father, elaborates its political, military, and judicial dimensions: "You, Roman, be sure to rule the world, . . . to crown peace with justice, to spare the vanquished, and to crush the proud" (*Aeneid* 6.847–853).[34] Numerous texts and images present the victorious Augustus in the guise of Jupiter, as instigator of the new golden age, as agent of the gods, and revealer of their blessings, abundance, and will (e.g., Horace, *Ode* 1.41–52; idem, *Carmen saeculare*).[35]

These emphases were continued by subsequent emperors. Gaius Caligula identifies himself as Jupiter/Zeus Latiaris (Suetonius, *Cal.* 22; Dio Cassius 59.28.5). His attempts to rename the Jerusalem temple after himself as "Gaius the New Zeus/Jupiter Epiphanes" (Philo, *Emb.* 346) signal his understanding of his role as agent and revealer of Jupiter's presence and purposes. Domitian rules the world at Jupiter's command (Silius Italicus, *Punica* 3.625–626; Statius, *Silvae* 4.3.128–129, 139–140); he "holds the reins of earth, he who nearer than Jupiter directs the doings of humankind" (Statius, *Silvae* 5:1.37–39).

Moreover, Chestnut shows that Roman political philosophical traditions—especially Neopythagorean, Middle Platonic, and Stoic traditions—also understood the emperor as the earthly agent of and the one who embodies the logos principle or cosmic order.[36] The emperor's task "was to be in his own life the ensoulment of cosmic order, and thereby bring it down to earth, so that the earthly state might mirror the cosmic harmony." Chestnut traces this line of thinking through Neopythagorean philosophers such as Diotogenes, Sthenidas, and Ecphantus. In the first and second centuries CE, the middle-Platonic philosopher Plutarch regards the emperor as the one in whom heavenly Logos or Nomos "was enshrined, . . . who ruled the earthly state with godly wisdom and virtue" (*To an Uneducated Ruler* 780b–781a).[37] Likewise, the Stoic Seneca saw the emperor Nero, at least initially, as "the spirit or reason [deriving from the divine logos] which guided and organized the enormous multitude of Roman subjects," ruling for their benefit (*On Mercy* 1.1.2; 1.3.5–1.4.1). He was "the good ruler [who] was the embodiment of the divine Reason or Logos."[38]

The Prologue's opening claims about God's creative and life-giving sovereignty and the preexistent origin of the (revelatory) Word express similar, though alternative, imperial claims of divine sanction, sovereignty, agency, and revelation. While they contradict Jewish revealer traditions such as those associated with Abraham and Moses, as I argued in chapter 4 above, they also contest Roman claims even as they seem to imitate them. In the context of pervasive imperial cultural intertexts, these opening verses of the Prologue assert that it is God's world, not Rome's, by virtue of God's life-giving and creative power. They trump imperial claims for the emperor as the chosen agent of the gods by turning to the past to locate the origin of Jesus' agency in his preexistence with God, a claim that imperial poets generally do not make for emperors.[39] The origin and nature of Jesus' agency, preexistent with God "in the beginning," is greater than any emperor's.

Moreover, the Prologue's claim that Jesus, not Rome, brings life and inextinguishable "light for people" (1:4b–5) also imitates and contests common Roman claims to bless the world. The image of light frequently appears to symbolize Roman rule and beneficence. Cicero (*In Catalinam* 4.11), for instance, describes Rome as "light to the whole world." Both Gaius Caligula and Nero claimed affinity with Apollo the sun god and presented themselves as emanating the sun's rays.[40] Seneca (*Polyb.* 13.1) prays for the new emperor Claudius after Gaius Caligula's death: "May this sun, which has shed its light upon a world that had plunged into the abyss and was sunk in darkness, ever shine!" Statius (*Silvae* 1.1.77) describes Domitian's "immortal brightness"; Domitian is "more brilliant than [the heavenly constellations] and outshines the early morning stars" (4.1.1–5). Martial (*Epig.* 8.21) greets Domitian's return to Rome as the restoring of light to the darkness, and describes Domitian as "coeternal with sun and star" (*Epig.* 9.1.7). Aristides celebrates Rome's rule and establishment of "universal order" as a "brilliant light over the public and private affairs of humans." The "all-seeing Helius, moreover, casting his light, saw no violence or injustice in your case and marked the absence of woes such as were frequent in former times" (*Roman Oration* 103–104).[41] Such common prayers and attributions are false, in the Prologue's perspective. They constitute the falseness and darkness (1:5) that mark the rejecting world even in the face of the revelation of God's life-giving power and light manifested in Jesus and narrated throughout the Gospel's plot. The Gospel constantly repeats Jesus' origin and relationship with God as a major point of conflict between Jesus and his opponents because it is foundational for his identity as God's Son or agent. No other—whether Abraham,

Moses, or the emperor—can match his credentials for such an identity. Jesus' origin "in the beginning with God" guarantees the reliability or truth of his revelation of God and God's life-giving purposes (20:30–31), invalidating any other claims about divine sanction and purposes, whether Jewish revealer figure or Roman emperor, governor, senator, or general.

The Prologue's second emphasis concerns John's witness to or legitimation of Jesus (1:6–8, 15). Some scholars have suggested that the references to John function as polemic against followers of John who claim greater importance for John than for Jesus.[42] Perhaps so. But prophetic legitimation is not confined to Jewish traditions. Audiences in the imperial world know the role of prophecy in legitimating and magnifying imperial figures.[43] The Augustan poets locate Rome and Augustus in predictions and overviews of world history to provide divine sanction for their accomplishments on behalf of Rome's empire (e.g., Virgil, *Aeneid* 6.752–892; Propertius, *Elegies* 4.49–50; Horace, *Carmen saeculare* 1–8).[44] Immediately prior to the near-final form of John, the new Flavian line, established with Vespasian's accession in 69 CE after the civil war of 68–69 and embracing his sons Titus (79–81) and Domitian (81–96), found legitimation in "a quantity of divine oracles, omens, and portents which indicated his rise to imperial dignity" as part of a divinely sanctioned historical sequence (Tacitus, *Hist.* 1.10; 2.78; 4.82; Josephus, *J.W.* 1.23; 3.399–408; 4.623; Suetonius, *Vespasian* 5; Silius Italicus, *Punica* 3.593–621, on the Flavians).[45] John the Baptist's role belongs with such legitimating practices (also 1:19–36; 3:25–36) while intertextually employing Jewish prophetic traditions, ironically from a previous experience of liberation from Babylonian imperial aggression (John 1:23; Isa 40:3), to attest Jesus' legitimate role in God's purposes. The claims present Jesus as a prophetically sanctioned figure and as the legitimate agent of God's life-giving purposes in the midst of imperial assertions; they invalidate any other claims to sanctioned agency, whether of the baptizer's followers or of the emperor.

A third emphasis concerns responses to Jesus. John 1:9–16 sums up what happens when "the Word becomes flesh" to reveal God's beneficent purposes (1:14). Some receive Jesus, are empowered to become God's children (1:12–13), behold Jesus' glory (1:14), while others reject him (1:10–11). Verses 10–13 function as a plot summary that will be elaborated through the Gospel's accounts of his acceptance and rejection. The rejection motif, expressed particularly by the alliance of the Jerusalem elite and the Roman governor Pilate, leads to his crucifixion. But their most powerful and destructive action cannot prevent Jesus from returning to God in his resurrection and ascension.

These verses, 1:9–16, locate Jesus' ministry in "the world" that "did not know him" (1:9–10). A detailed examination of the multivalent meanings of the term "world" is not possible here.[46] Yet discussions frequently overlook the "world's" social-political-economic dimensions that embrace the Roman Empire.[47] It is Pilate, the Roman governor and representative of Roman interests in alliance with the Jerusalem elite, who by crucifying Jesus enacts the ultimate rejection of Jesus, God's agent, and thus of God's life-giving purposes for the world.[48] Throughout the Gospel, Jesus brings light to the world's darkness (8:12; 9:5), exposes the evil of its works (3:19–20; 7:7), and experiences its hostility and hatred (7:7; 15:18–25).

The clash concerns sovereignty. To evoke the affirmation of Psalm 24, "The earth was the emperor's and the fullness thereof," claimed and enjoyed, for example, through taxes, tribute, rent, and trade. Ovid declares that "Jupiter controls the heights of heaven, . . . but the earth is under Augustus's sway. Each is sire and ruler" (*Metamorphoses* 15.859–861). Seneca celebrates Nero's power over all people, "Have I of all mortals found favor with Heaven and been chosen to serve on earth as vicar of the gods? I am the arbiter of death and life for the nations" (*On Mercy* 1.1.1–2). Statius calls Domitian "lord of the earth (*Silvae* 3.4.20), "Great Father of the World" (4.1.17), and "ruler of the nations" (4.2.14–15). Philostratus (*Life of Apollonius* 7.3) identifies him as "master of sea and land." Such understandings were commonplace and did not require intimate knowledge of elite writers. Constant taxation, as John Kautsky observes, enacted this proprietary understanding of the world as Rome's empire, under the emperor's owner-ship.[49] So too did the confiscation of property that Suetonius attributes to Domitian (*Domitian* 12.1–2). Refusal to pay taxes and tribute signified revolt against such asser-tions of sovereignty.[50] It is precisely because the imperial "great tradition" claimed own-ership—enacted through Rome's agents and allies such as the provincial elite based in Jerusalem—that Jesus' mission to manifest God's life-giving sovereignty and purposes, and to take away the sin of the world, is necessary. It is precisely because of such misdi-rected power to structure the status quo and defend it against any challenges that Jesus is crucified. Those who receive him constitute an alternative community of "children of God" (1:12–13), while those who reject him defend and uphold the societal status quo.

A fourth emphasis emerges in the Prologue's final verses: Jesus' relation to Moses. We have already considered this relationship in chapter 4 (above). As noted there, John 1:17 is difficult, seeming to both distinguish and yet link Jesus and Moses. Both seem to reveal God's purposes, yet Jesus' revelation takes precedence. Both are kings (Philo, *Mos.* 1.158; John 18:33–37; 19:19–22). While Moses entered heaven according to Philo (*Questions on Exodus* 2.40; *Mos.* 1.158) and displayed in his life what he saw,[51] Jesus began there "in the beginning," in intimate relation to God, to whom he returns (1:1). Antiquity is authority. As verse 18 indicates with its selective claim that "no one has ever seen God" except Jesus, central is the matter of determining who makes the definitive revelation of God's purposes, how people encounter this revelation, and what com-prises the divine purposes. These matters will be debated through the Gospel as vari-ous characters interact with Jesus. Opponents, for example, identified as Pharisees and *Ioudaioi* who are synagogue leaders (9:13, 22), claim to be "disciples of Moses" and con-fess that "we know God has spoken to Moses" (9:28–29). Yet in the Gospel's presenta-tion, Moses bears witness to Jesus, and the refusal to listen to Jesus means, according to the Gospel, that they are not Moses' disciples (John 5:45–47). Jesus' origin with and return to God guarantees the reliability of his revelation as well as the inability of his opponents to destroy or thwart it (1:18).

But claims about and against Moses are not the only ones in view. As we have already observed, Roman imperial theology claims Rome as the revelation of the gods' will and purposes. Thus, the exercise of Roman power and the sort of world created by it are divinely sanctioned. Rome is agent of the gods and benefactor of (submissive) people. Moreover, in being "full of grace" (1:14), bestowing "from his fullness . . . grace upon grace" (1:16–17), Jesus is, as Richey declares,[52] a benefactor and patron with cos-mic reach, just like the emperor. Around the year 9 BCE, the provincial council of Asia considered the cosmic gifts or "benefactions" of Augustus in giving "a new appearance to the whole world" to resemble a new creation (compare the Word's role in 1:3, "all things were made through him"). Augustus's benefactions have constituted so great a "beginning of life and of existence" that the cities of Asia reorganized the calendar so that his birthday was the beginning of the new year.[53] Philo indicates that Gaius Caligula was first received as "the Savior and benefactor . . . (to) pour fresh streams of blessings on Asia and Europe" (*Emb.* 4.1). Seneca's Nero is the agent of whatever gift Fortune "would bestow on each human being" (*On Mercy* 1.2). The Gospel reserves such roles for Jesus, the benefactor of life and light, the revealer of God's purposes among humans.

More specifically, some vocabulary common to both the Prologue and some inscriptions from Ephesus create a significant intertextuality, especially since the Gospel and the inscriptions date from the same time. One term is "grace" (χάρις, *charis*), used in John 1:14–17 to designate God's gift through Jesus. When the temple of the Sebastoi was dedicated in Ephesus in 89/90 CE, cities in the province of Asia erected and dedicated statues to Domitian in the temple precincts.[54] In their dedications, they use the word "grace" (χάρις, *charis*) to designate the emperor's gift or benefaction of political status to them. The word *charis* (grace) is commonly used in association with benefactions. The cities present themselves as "being free and autonomous from the beginning by the grace of the Sebastoi." In addition to recognizing the emperor's grace in granting their free status, they emphasize that this is not a new occurrence but that it has been the way of things "from the beginning" (ἀρχῇ, *archē*). This is another term shared with the Prologue; the "Word" was "in the beginning . . . with God" in 1:1. With the inclusion of the term "beginning," the cities' inscriptions recognize continuity of Roman practice toward them and are able literally to set this status in stone in the inscription. Because of the power of the word "beginning" (*archē*) "to indicate priority in time and priority of authority,"[55] the cities make a bold move in negotiating imperial power, submitting to and honoring it in the statue, describing its "gracious" action, and reminding Rome of their own long-standing status.

The larger questions relating to the intertextuality between these inscriptions and the Prologue concerns not only the nature and impact of the benefaction of Roman rule, but also its authority. The use of "beginning" both in these statue inscriptions and in the inscription from a century earlier declaring the emperor Augustus's birthday as the new year, since his "benefactions" had constituted so great a "beginning of life and of existence"—these inscriptions recognize Rome's supreme authority. But the imperial language of "grace" and "beginning," and the cultural dynamics of benefaction in these inscriptions, collides with the Prologue's similar claims. The Prologue's scope is not individualistic, internal, private, religious. It is cosmic: "All things were made through him; . . . in him was life" (1:3–4). Resembling but contesting the claim that Rome has created the world, the Prologue asserts that "in the beginning" God has created through the Word, Jesus (1:1–5). Resembling but contesting the claim that Rome reveals the gods' purposes, the Prologue asserts the revelatory role of "the Word become flesh" (1:10–14). Resembling but contesting claims that the empire is gracious, the Prologue asserts "the fullness of grace" demonstrated in Jesus (1:16–18). Antithesis impacted by imitation is very evident.

How shall we adjudicate these competing claims? Since we are dealing with polemic on both sides, there is no objective measure. As far as the empire and its provincial elite allies are concerned, all is benevolent. As far as the Gospel is concerned, nothing matches God's superior giving of Jesus to reveal God's purposes. After all, he was "in the beginning" with God (1:1). And antiquity is authority.

The Gospel's opening Prologue alerts the Gospel's audience to important emphases in the story and frame all that follows. It signals the Gospel's initial negotiation of Rome's world: it contests Rome by mimicking and disqualifying its claims to ultimate sovereignty and agency, by summoning prophetic legitimation for Jesus, and by asserting divine sanction for Jesus "in the beginning . . . with God." It also divides the world neatly into two groups on the basis of relation to Jesus, the divinely commissioned agent. Its rhetoric of distance defines Rome and its imperial system and allies as "the world," opponents of God's purposes (the in-house audience knows Rome's crucifixion of Jesus as the ultimate rejection). It constitutes an alternative community comprising "those who received him, . . . children of God" (1:12; "us . . . we," 1:14, 16) brought into being by God's action. And, according to James Scott, it has done so self-protectively by disguising all such claims in a poetic discourse intended for in-house and not public consumption.[56]

But while the eighteen verses orient the Gospel's audience to important emphases in the story and frame all that follows, they also raise questions that require answers, make affirmations that require elaboration, and conceal what will require revelation. These eighteen verses name the main character only in verse 17. How does he do his revealing work? What does he reveal? What difference does it make and to whom? Why do some reject him? What interaction do these rejecting people have with Jesus? How do they express their rejection? How do "children of God" live? What happens to Jesus after he has made God known? These questions render the rest of the plot "necessary" as it works out the consequences of these declarations and shapes the action that leads to his death—and resurrection/ascension. The only way of answering these questions is to read the Gospel's story.

John Bears Witness

The plot commences in 1:19–34 by developing the legitimating role of John the Baptist, first introduced in 1:6–8, 15. In his first scene, John testifies that he, John, is not the light (cf. 1:8a) but prepares the way for Jesus the light (1:19–28). In the second scene (1:29–34), John testifies to Jesus (1:8b) as the Lamb[57] who takes away the sin of the world (1:29), a mission that presents the world under Roman rule as contrary to God's purposes and in need of having its sin taken away. He also witnesses to Jesus as one who bears the Spirit as God's agent or Son (1:32–34). We will have to read on to find out how Jesus carries out the tasks to which John bears witness.

Ioudaioi

Equally important is the context in which John makes this testimony. The scene introduces a group of characters who will play a prominent role as opponents of Jesus. "The Jews sent priests and Levites from Jerusalem to ask him, 'Who are you?'" (1:19 NRSV).

This group called "the Jews" (*Ioudaioi*) figures prominently in the Gospel, over seventy times, and mostly as opponents of Jesus, though some believe in Jesus (8:31; 11:45; 12:9–11), others warmly support Mary and Martha at Lazarus' death (11:19, 31, 33, 36, 45), and one of their leaders, Nicodemus, comes to show some sympathy for Jesus' mission (3:1; 7:50–52; 19:38–42). Since the term *Ioudaioi* is so common and its use complex, it is worth pausing to clarify the identity of this group.

There has been much debate about the identity of the *Ioudaioi* and about the related issue of how to translate the term. In 1:19–34 the term does not designate all Jews but seems to identify a subgroup, since John and Jesus are also Jews but are differentiated from the *Ioudaioi*. There are, though, some exceptions to this subgroup identification. In 18:35 the term is a synonym for "your own nation," and in 19:19 Pilate labels Jesus "King of the Jews," presumably referring to both those within the land and in the Diaspora. But much more often than not, a subgroup is in view.[58]

A second view interprets them as "Judeans" or residents of Judea in opposition to Galileans and Samaritans.[59] This approach breaks down, though, because in chapter 6, set in Galilee beside the Sea of Galilee/Tiberias (6:1), *Ioudaioi* who must be Galileans engage Jesus (6:41, 52). And this geographical identification fails to explain why they conflict with Jesus.

A third view sees them as Judean leaders. Several aspects of this scene with John (1:19–34) support this identification. Verse 19 asserts their base in Jerusalem. They have power over temple-related personnel, Levites and priests, whom they send to John, thereby indicating their connection to the temple. These factors suggest an elite leadership group sanctioned by religious observance and marked by great privilege, wealth, status, and power for the small elite (perhaps 2–3 percent) at the expense of the rest.[60] Their inquiries into John's identity are consistent with a leadership role of societal control. Their lack of interest in joining John's movement suggests that their inquiries are surveillance; they exhibit at least suspicion if not antagonism toward figures that they have not authorized. In 1:24 their identity is further clarified by identifying them with the Pharisees, a group that Josephus counts as allies of Jerusalem's power elite, the chief priests (*J.W.* 2.411; *Life* 189–198), as does John (18:3). Josephus identifies the chief priests as the rulers of the nation (*Ant.* 20.251).

That the term *Ioudaioi* designates the Jerusalem leadership group seems to be confirmed by 2:18, 20, where this group demands an explanation from Jesus about his actions in the Jerusalem temple. In 3:1, moreover, Nicodemus, a Pharisee (cf. 1:24), is identified as a leader of the *Ioudaioi*, suggesting further links with the elite. But other references in chapters 2–3 also complexify an identification only in terms of leaders. In 2:6 the term designates the purity rites of the *Ioudaioi*, and in 2:13 it links the festival of Passover to the *Ioudaioi*.[61] In 3:25 John's disciples and one of the *Ioudaioi* discuss purification. Moreover, in 3:22 and 4:3 the term has a geographical reference, identifying Judea in distinction from Galilee. And as we have observed in 6:41 and 52, there are Galilean *Ioudaioi*.

These data are best understood as elaborating or nuancing, rather than undermining, the identification of their societal leadership role.[62] The *Ioudaioi* comprise a subgroup of Israel in Judea consisting in part of Jerusalem and temple-based leaders. They exercise leadership over Judea and advocate a piety of purity and observances of festivals such as Passover and Booths, in association with the temple. But they are not only leaders; they also have supporters and followers, including in Galilee (6:41, 52; 11:19, 31, 33, 36, 45, 54). This subgroup, especially its leaders, exercises considerable societal power. The Gospel presents this group's leaders as subordinates of and yet allies with Rome (11:45–53). Its leaders and members include Pharisees and chief priests, who are major power players and allied with the governor Pilate (18:3, 12; 18:28–19:25, esp. 19:14–15). This leadership role, along with their supporters, explains in part the use of the term *Ioudaioi* for the whole nation (18:35; 19:19). Not surprisingly, some Israelites fear them and do not readily support them (7:11–13, 40–43, 9:22).[63] Jesus will conflict with them throughout.

Jesus and His Disciples

As John bears witness to Jesus (1:35–36), Jesus appears. There is no account of his birth or upbringing. The Prologue has emphasized his origin with God and his commission to bring light and life into the world, while John has announced his task to take away the world's sin (1:29). The plot narrates this mission's impact beginning with positive response to his ministry (cf. 1:10). Through a series of "quest stories,"[64] Jesus begins to call followers in both Judea (Andrew, Simon Peter, 1:35–42) and Galilee (Philip, Nathanael, 1:43–51). In both instances, the first disciple bears witness to the second one. Jesus greets Nathanael as an "Israelite," indicating that he is not a follower of the *Ioudaioi* (1:47). Two features of the scene—the description of Nathanael as being "without deceit" (1:47) and the reference to the place of their encounter as "under the fig tree"—recall prophetic announcements of God's salvation over the nations. In Zephaniah 3, after announcing judgment on Jerusalem (3:1–5) and on the nations (3:6–8), God announces salvation for the remnant of Israel and for Jerusalem, in whom there will be no "deceitful tongue" (3:13). In Zechariah 3:8–10 God removes "the guilt of the land" and establishes peace and security as "people invite each other to come under your vine and fig tree" (3:10 NRSV).[65] Jesus' calling of followers enacts his mission to take away sin (John 1:29), but the evoking of the prophets points to a salvation that is not inward and "soulish" but involves Israel and the nations, judgment and conversion, and creates a world of peaceful and unthreatened societal interaction. With a series of titles that also point to the establishing of God's purposes over all human existence and have important echoes of and implications for imperial titulature (Messiah, 1:41; Son of God, 1:49; king of Israel, 1:49; discussed in chap. 7 below), they recognize Jesus as one whom God has commissioned to reveal and accomplish God's life-giving and transforming purposes that challenge and transform the societal and imperial status quo.

Through two incidents in chapter 2, Jesus reveals God's disruptive and life-giving purposes and displays contrasting ways of negotiating the Roman world. At the wedding in Cana in Galilee, the wine runs out (2:1–12). Jesus performs his first sign, changing water into abundant and high-quality wine.[66] The working of a miraculous sign not only mimics a standard means of legitimating and enhancing the identity of prestigious imperial figures, such as the various signs legitimating Vespasian's emperorship;[67] it also reveals God's purposes, which are at odds with and reverse the impact of imperial rule. Both weddings and wine figure prominently in Israel's traditions about the future establishment of God's good and just purposes. In such scenarios, God blesses all people with abundant fertility, including abundant wine (Isa 25:6–10; Amos 9:13–15; *2 Bar.* 29:5), healing (Isa 35:5–6; *2 Bar.* 29:4–8; 73:1–7; the second sign in Cana of Galilee, John 4:46–54), and security from enemies, whether by destruction (Zech 14:3, 16) or conversion to Israel's God (Isa 2:2–4; Mic 4:1–4). The scene thus reveals God's life-giving purposes, manifested in Jesus, that contrast with and reverse the present exploitative imperial world, where many lack resources to sustain life.[68] The scene delivers the verdict that, in contrast to Jesus' actions, Rome's world does not manifest God's life-giving purposes. Jesus' action takes away the sin of the Roman world (1:29). The disciples discern God's power and presence with Jesus (his "glory," 2:11) and commit themselves to him ("believe in" him, 2:11).

Conflict with the Elite

The next scene in chapter 2 continues to contrast the Roman-dominated, Jerusalem-allied status quo with God's purposes. It occurs at the center of power in Jerusalem, at the temple, around the time of Passover (2:13–23).[69] Jesus' action against the temple resembles prophetic sign actions such as that of Jeremiah, who smashes a pot in the temple to signify judgment (Jer 19:10–14). The action draws a challenge to Jesus' authority from the temple elite (John 2:18, *Ioudaioi*). The account does not spell out why Jesus attacks the temple commerce in cattle, sheep, and doves needed for sacrifice and the money changers, who made available Tyrian half-shekels instead of Roman denarii and Attic drachmas.[70] The best clue perhaps comes in 2:16, when he orders them to stop making his Father's house a "marketplace," a command that echoes the eschatological victory yet imperially imitative scene of Zech 14:21. Zechariah 14 speaks of Jerusalem under foreign control (14:1–2). God will defeat these nations (14:3–6, 12–15), transform the city into a place of light and life (14:7–8), become king (14:9), make Jerusalem secure (14:10–11), draw Jew and Gentile to Jerusalem to worship in purity, with no traders in God's house (14:16–21). This transformation is not good news for Roman power and its allies.

In the light of this eschatological intertext, the scene that John's Jesus evokes points to the defeat and the conversion of Roman power and a time when all people, Jew and Gentile, worship God. The defeat of Roman power also means a loss of power, status, and wealth for the Jerusalem elite, who were Rome's allies and representatives. The Jerusalem elite—the *Ioudaioi*, 2:18, 20—held power in alliance with Rome but under Rome's supervision. They offered daily sacrifices in the temple for but not to the emperor (Josephus, *J.W.* 2.197, 410–411). The Roman governor appointed the chief priest (Josephus, *Ant.* 18.33–35, 95). Romans controlled the chief priestly garments by keeping them in the Antonia fortress next to the temple (*Ant.* 15.403–408; 18.90–95; 20.6–14). Jesus' action against the temple threatens the world that this alliance oversees for its own benefit.

We can recognize that John's Jesus-believers in Ephesus were well familiar with Rome's integration with the temple of Artemis. As the discussion in chapter 3 above established, the temple of Artemis contained imperial images; Salutaris's procession included imperial images with those of Artemis; and Ephesian coins depict Artemis with emperors. The likelihood exists that Jesus-believers participated in civic celebrations of Artemis as part of their accommodated societal interactions (chap. 2–3 above). If so, John's Jesus signifies the end of such observance, pointing to a time when the new temple community is constituted by his resurrection or victory over Roman power (2:19–22).

The significant Passover context for this scene, the first of several such festival occasions (2:13–25; 5:1–30; 6:4; 7:1–10; 10:22; 12:1, 12, 20; chaps. 13–17), supports the above analysis. Passover celebrated a coming out from Egypt and a liberation from slavery as God's act of saving the people from the tyrannical Pharaoh (Exod 11–15). This victory included the exodus journey to the promised land, during which God supplied the people with manna and water (Exod 16–17), revealed God's will in giving the torah (teaching), including the Ten Commandments (Exod 19–24; Deut 8:2–3; Neh 9:13–15, 20), and made a covenant with the people (Exod 24). The Passover setting thus supplies an intertext of distancing from Roman power, of liberation from it and of national identity in conflict with its presence. Josephus attests Jewish awareness that festival celebrations provided incentive and opportunity for revolt (*J.W.* 1.88) as well as Roman measures such as the increased presence of Roman troops in Jerusalem during festivals "to repress any insurrectionary movements" (*J.W.* 5.244; also 2.224; *Ant.* 20.106). The Passover context reinforces the significance of Jesus' action as one of liberation and the establishment of God's saving purposes in a national context.

The citation of Psalm 69:9 in verse 17 ("Zeal for your house will consume me" [NRSV]) and Jesus' comments about his own resurrection and the "temple of his body" point to the inevitable outcome of Jesus' challenge. The reference anticipates Jesus' death, links the temple leaders to it, and sets up the intensification of the conflict that will develop through subsequent exchanges frequently in the context of temple-based festivals (unspecified, 5:1–18; Tabernacles, John 7–8; Dedication, 10:22). It also raises the question of how this death will come about while signaling that their attempts to remove him will not, finally, be successful, being thwarted by God's resurrecting power. Moreover, the text points to the end of the temple—accomplished through Roman power in 70 CE—and establishes the risen Jesus as the locus of God's presence. As James Scott recognizes, direct confrontations between nonelites and the powerful elite can mean both the destruction and success of the former.[71] Jesus' challenge will turn out to be fatal; he will die at their hands. But they will not have the last word.

This temple scene is thus of great importance for the plot.[72] It introduces the conflict between Jesus and the Jerusalem, temple-based, Rome-allied authorities, which will intensify through the Gospel in Jesus' repeated trips to Jerusalem and the temple.[73] With its reference to resurrection, it anticipates the end of the story: it signals the limits of the elite's power, the vindication of Jesus, the special relationship between Jesus and God, and the inevitable triumph of God's life-giving purposes. The scene introduces and anticipates these developments.

Jesus' relationship with these Jerusalem elites deteriorates in 3:1–21 as Jesus exposes the limits of one of their leaders, Nicodemus. The narrative mocks Nicodemus, whose question in 3:4 about "entering into the mother's womb again" embarrassingly reveals his literal approach to Jesus' metaphorical speech.[74] He is unable to understand Jesus' explanation of how God works to bring people into God's kingdom or empire (3:1–10; *basileia*, 3:3, 5).[75] The use of "kingdom" or "empire" language is quite unusual in John and is a synonym for the Gospel's preferred term, "life of the age" (3:15, 16). Nicodemus is like others in Jerusalem whom Jesus does not trust; with apparent superhuman powers Jesus is able to see through them (2:23–25). Jesus' explanation of God's work centers on his own role as the revealer of God who descended "from above" to bring life (3:3, 7; "from heaven," 1:18, 51) and dies (3:13–14), the second reference to Jesus' death (2:19–22). Jesus also emphasizes God's love (3:16a), participation in eternal life as the benefit of receiving him by believing or entrusting oneself to him and his revelation of God's purposes (3:16b–17), judgment for those who do not believe (3:18), and the importance of how one lives (3:19–20). Two short scenes follow, restating John's significance as subordinate to Jesus but a legitimating witness to him (3:22–30), and Jesus' significance as sent from God to reveal God's purposes (3:31–35).

A Samaritan Woman and Village (4:1–42)

The subsequent scene contrasts the negative response of the male Nicodemus, one of the power elite in Jerusalem, with a positive response from a nonelite Samaritan woman from an apparently insignificant area. Nicodemus is named; she is not. He is a man; she is a woman. He lives in the powerful city of Jerusalem; she lives in the small and powerless city or village of Sychar (4:5, 29–30, 39–42; perhaps Shechem[76]). He is a Judean; she is a despised Samaritan with a long history of antagonism toward Judeans like Jesus (4:9). Nicodemus is wealthy, powerful, and of high societal status (3:1); she is poor, powerless, and of low societal status (4:7). He is reputed to be a teacher of Israelites (3:10), yet he is unable to understand Jesus' theological talk (3:3–10). She persistently questions Jesus and gains understanding from him (4:11–12, 15). He recognizes Jesus as "a teacher who has come from God" (3:2), though he cannot learn from Jesus. She recognizes Jesus as a prophet (4:19, 29, 39). In response to her confession of waiting for a revealer-messiah (4:25), Jesus identifies himself as such a figure (4:26), a possibility to which she seems open (4:29, 39). In John 3 Nicodemus appears not to believe; the woman believes and, like a good disciple and missionary, bears witness to others who commit themselves to Jesus' revelation (4:39–42). They declare him, and not the emperor, to be "the Savior of the world."[77] Not surprisingly, God's purposes are seen to take root not among the powerful elite but among the nonelite, the "rest" of society, the 97 percent who are marginal to the center of power in Jerusalem for reasons of low status (cf. 7:49), pervasive poverty (12:8), disabling disease (9:34), geographical and ethnic prejudice (John 4), and gender (John 4). They bear the cost of the exploitative, elite-dominated social structure.[78]

Jesus returns to Galilee where, unlike his conflictual sojourn in Jerusalem (2:13–3:21), he is welcomed (4:43–45). Another positive interaction occurs. In the village of Cana, where he had turned water into wine (cf. 2:1–11), Jesus heals the son of a royal official, probably a retainer (and perhaps a Gentile) in the service of Herod Antipas (4:46–54).[79] This second sign enacts God's purposes for wholeness. Disease was rife in the world ruled by imperial Rome, often the result of poor food supply and nutrition, and impacted by payment of taxes and rents in kind, overwork, anxiety, and medical ignorance. Diseases caused by deficiency and by contagion were rife.[80] Jesus' action repairs its damage. Health and wholeness demonstrate the establishment of God's will and reign (Isa 35:5–6).

In these opening four chapters the plot has begun with Jesus carrying out his task of revealing God's purposes in gathering disciples, through his words, and by his actions of supplying wine and healing. Some have received or entrusted themselves to his revelation and thereby encountered God's purposes. But the plot has also put into play another response. Suspicion from the ruling elite attends John's task of bearing witness to Jesus (1:19–24). Jesus has directly challenged their center of power and their societal structure in his attack on the Jerusalem temple (2:13–22). Jesus has shown one of their leaders to be incapable of understanding God's purposes at work in him (3:1–15). References to Jesus' death indicate the high stakes involved in this negative response (2:19–22).

The Middle (5:1–12:50; 13:1–17:26)

The negative, as well as positive, responses continue to develop in the middle part of the story until Jesus' public ministry ends at the close of John 12. Jesus' challenge to the elite necessarily intensifies through a series of actions and disputes toward his death at the hands of the Jerusalem-based elite (John 5–12). Chapters 13–17 address the consequences for those who have responded positively to Jesus' mission, delineating their identity and way of life as an alternative community or "antisociety" in the midst of Rome's empire for the time of his absence after he goes back to heaven.

Jesus' challenge to the power group in John 2–3 inevitably leads to further conflict. In chapter 5, he is in Jerusalem again for an unidentified festival (5:1). His journey to Jerusalem suggests that it could be one of the pilgrimage festivals of Passover, Pentecost, and Tabernacles, or Booths. Following 4:46–54, Jesus performs another healing, this time of a paralyzed man. Important for the scene is the timing of the action on the Sabbath (5:9). The Sabbath features regularly through this middle section (5:1–47; 7:14–24; 9:1–41). The Sabbath celebrated God's deliverance of the people from Egypt (Deut 5:12–15), God's covenant with Israel (Exod 31:16), and God's creative work and rest from it (Gen 1:31–2:3). These events were extended in Israel's traditions to observance of Sabbath and Jubilee years, which emphasized God's justice in renewing the land, supplying the poor with food, canceling debt, returning land, and liberating slaves (Exod 23:10–11; Lev 25; Deut 15:1–18). In John 5 and 9, Jesus' healings are consistent with such emphases on transforming injustice into justice. The conflicts arise not over the question of whether to observe the Sabbath or not, but over *how* the Sabbath is to be honored.

Jesus continues to manifest God's purposes for wholeness and health by enabling a man paralyzed for thirty-eight years to walk again (5:1–15). But this action provokes a hostile response from the Jerusalem elite because it violates their (scriptural) understanding of Sabbath as a day of rest (5:10, 12, 16), and because Jesus claims, in the face of their opposition, God's sanction for his transformative actions, thereby making himself equal with God in knowing and doing God's will (5:16–18). They decide that such a claim is an affront to God (Num 15:30–31), in a word, blasphemy, and that he should die (Lev 24:13–16; John 5:18). It is, of course, also an affront to their authority. Over against their interpretations that focus on rest and maintaining the status quo, Jesus interprets the Sabbath traditions to permit life-giving actions that repair and transform the world over which they preside as allies of Rome. Such transformational purposes subvert the status quo and enliven the nonelite. And he claims to be God's agent in declaring and powerfully enacting such purposes. They do not think that he has any such right or role outside their control.

Jesus elaborates these claims about his identity and authority in the long monologue that follows (5:19–47).[81] His authority is based in his loving yet dependent relationship as Son with God his Father. Jesus carries out God's cosmic purposes in giving life (5:21–22) and passing judgment (5:26–27), two activities that express God's ultimate sovereignty over human affairs, roles often associated with imperial power. But Jesus' relationship with God and his doing of these activities reveal not only his identity but also that of his hearers, either as those who by committing themselves to Jesus share in God's life (5:24–25, 28–29), or by rejecting him miss out on that life (5:29). In 5:31–47 he provides five witnesses to these claims: John the Baptist (5:32–35), Jesus' works (5:36), God (5:37–38), the Scriptures (5:39–44), and Moses (5:45–47).

That Jesus does so much talking throughout his public ministry is not surprising, given the Prologue's claim that he is "the Word" (1:1) and that the "Word became flesh" (1:14). Jesus' words manifest what the Word saw and heard from God (3:10–11, 31–34; 8:38a, 40). Jesus presents his words or teaching as originating with God, who sent Jesus (7:16; 8:25–26; 14:10, 24). In speaking, he attests God's authority and follows God's instruction (4:34; 12:49). His words carry out God's purposes to reveal the world's evil (3:19–20; 7:7; 15:22), to reveal life (6:63), to save from sin and death (5:34; 8:51), to draw disciples into ongoing and obedient relation with Jesus (10:27) and loving relations with each other (13:34–35). Response to Jesus' words shows who are disciples and who are opponents of God's purposes revealed in Jesus (3:1–11, 18; 4:39–42; 5:47).

Jesus' discourse in John 5 has emphasized his authority and relationship to God, his role as agent of God's purposes in giving life and judging, and the consequences of belief and unbelief. Chapters 6–10 develop these same themes by employing in several of the chapters a pattern similar to John 5. Jesus performs a sign, conflictual dialogue follows, from which Jesus develops a monologue. Throughout, a few believe, while the interaction between Jesus and the Jerusalem leadership intensifies. Their intentions to put Jesus to death figure prominently.

In John 6, Jesus is back in Galilee, the location of several of his previous signs of healing power (mentioned in 6:2), which manifest God's purposes as well as his identity as God's agent (2:1–11; 4:46–54). The Passover festival is again the setting (2:13). But instead of making a pilgrimage to Jerusalem, Galileans gather with Jesus for what Allen Callahan calls "a counter-Passover: without money, without sacral slaughter and without the Jerusalem priesthood that oversees the exchange of the one for the other."[82] Jesus further demonstrates his God-given authority and threat to the status quo by performing two signs that evoke the exodus story, in which God delivers the people through the sea from oppressive Egyptian power and feeds them in the wilderness. Demonstrating God's purposes for abundant fertility (cf. 2:1–11), Jesus feeds five thousand people with so much food that there are twelve baskets of extras (6:1–14). The people are so impressed that they want to make him king, an act that would directly and openly challenge Roman authority, but Jesus "withdrew" (6:15). Manifesting God's authority over all creation, including the sea (Gen 1:6–13; Ps 107:23–32; Isa 43:2, 16), and revealing his own identity as God's agent, Jesus walks on water so as to ensure that the disciples reach the shore safely (6:16–21). Both scenes employ Hebrew Bible themes to manifest God's life-giving purposes, presence, and power over the nations and creation. Evoking stories of deliverance from tyrannical nations is certainly not good news for Rome. The following dialogue/monologue centers on the feeding story as a display of God's life-giving purposes (6:25–34). Jesus asserts his identity as "the true bread from heaven" (6:32) and claims that as the bread of life, he has "come down from heaven" or been sent from God into the world to reveal these purposes (6:35–59). But the leaders find these claims difficult to understand (6:52–59), as do some disciples (6:60–71).

In John 7, Jesus initially avoids Jerusalem, the center of elite power, because of increasing danger from attempts to kill him (7:1). Motifs of fear of the *Ioudaioi* (7:13) and their wanting to arrest and kill him proliferate in chapter 7 (7:19–20, 25, 30, 32, 44, 45, the temple police), though Nicodemus's reluctance indicates some break in the ranks of the *Ioudaioi* (7:50–51). They will make further attempts to eliminate him in the following chapters (8:20, 37, 40, 44; 10:31, 39; 11:50, 57; 12:9–11). Jesus explains that these attempts originate with the "world's" hatred of him because "I testify against it that its works are evil," a stunning indictment of the society administered by Rome and its Jerusalem allies (7:7). Also prominent throughout are debates and divisions over Jesus' identity and origin. Several inadequate verdicts are offered: he is "a good man" (7:12), a deceiver (7:12), perhaps the Messiah (7:26, 31, 41), the prophet (7:40), perhaps from Galilee or from Bethlehem (7:42, 52).

After initially dissembling in declaring he would not go to Jerusalem (7:8), Jesus then elusively returns to the city for another festival, that of Tabernacles, or Booths (7:2, 10, Sukkoth). This was an eight-day festival in fall, originally celebrating the olive and the grape harvest (Deut 16:13). It became a celebration of God's provision for the people during their sojourn in the wilderness after escaping from Egyptian domination (Lev 23:34–43; Passover, John 6). In the postexilic period, as in Zechariah 14 (quoted by Jesus in the temple, John 2:16), Booths also came to anticipate the eschatological time of the "Day of the Lord" (Zech 14:3), when God would assert God's purposes over all nations (14:3), night would give way to constant light (14:7), "living waters" would flow from Jerusalem (14:8), God would be "king over all the earth" (14:10), God would defeat the nations (14:12–15), and all survivors would journey to Jerusalem to celebrate Booths and honor Israel's God (14:16–21). Again the intertext of Zechariah 14 provides crucial content for the scene. In the subsequent discourse Jesus declares that God's purposes for the nations (Zech 14:3) are being manifested in him (John 7:16–18, 28–29), that he is the living water (7:37–39, referring to the Spirit), and "the light of the world" (8:12). The intertext portrays Rome and its allies as under judgment, offering an implicit warning to Jesus-believers in Ephesus not to identify closely with a condemned empire.

The locating of this and other scenes in the context of festivals creates intertexts with Israel's traditions that provide an ever-present framework for and commentary on Jesus' activity. He is defined in relation to the festivals—Passover, Tabernacles, and to the Sabbath—even as he redefines them. These intertexts contribute to the Gospel narrative of Jesus' activity as a hidden transcript that evokes God's redemptive work among resistant nations, first Egypt (in the exodus) and then all nations. This evoking of these intertexts announcing judgment and anticipating the establishment of God's purposes is not good news for Rome and its Jerusalem allies. The hidden transcript contests the public transcript of Roman control by asserting, for those with ears to hear, its condemnation, the imminent end of its world, and establishment of God's sovereignty and purposes. Jesus continues to assert his origin from God (7:28–29) along with the life-giving benefit of accepting/believing and obeying his revelation. The leaders' threat to Jesus' life manifests their opposition not only to him but also to God's activity.

John 8 continues the Tabernacles setting. The same themes are to the fore as Jesus dominates a series of increasingly bitter dialogues with the *Ioudaioi*, especially the temple-based elite (8:22, 31, 48). Prominent are his claims to come from God, whose will he does and who sanctions his words and works (8:14–17, 23, 26–29; etc.). While some believe him, others do not. Jesus speaks of the unacceptable identity of and destructive consequences for those who reject his claims and revelation (8:12–30). He and the leaders debate what it means to be a descendent of Abraham and child of God (8:31–59; see the discussion in chap. 4 above). Their failure to accept the truth of Jesus' revelation of God (8:32, 40–43, 45–47) discloses their origin from and commitment to the devil (8:44–46). They charge him with being a despised Samaritan and controlled by a demon (8:45–55), misunderstand his claims that Abraham witnesses to him (8:53–58), and try to stone him to death (8:59).

After several chapters of conflictual verbal exchanges, John 9 continues Jesus' life-giving mission with another healing, a sign that repairs imperial damage and reveals God's purposes for human existence marked by wholeness (Isa 35:5–6). Again on a Sabbath (John 9:14; also 5:9), Jesus restores sight to a man born blind (9:1–7). The rest of the chapter concerns the investigation of the incident by the Pharisees (9:13–14), who are *Ioudaioi* (9:18). The chapter outlines responses to the healing from the man's neighbors (9:8–10), parents (9:18–23), the Jerusalem leaders (9:13–41), and the man himself. The leaders continue their opposition and disparage Jesus as not sent from God (9:16), a sinner (9:24), and one whose origin is not known and to whom God has not spoken (9:29). They also confess their allegiance to Moses (9:28). But their hostile interrogations of the man who has gained his sight do not deter the man. In fact, they seem, ironically, to assist him in gaining insight into Jesus' identity. He identifies Jesus first as the man Jesus (9:11), then as a prophet (9:17), then as one from God (9:33), and finally as Son of Man and Lord (9:35–38). As their hostility toward him increases, his confessional insight develops regardless of the consequences of being "driven out" from them (and probably not from the synagogue, 9:34–35).[83]

The tension increases in John 10 as the dialogue of chapter 9 continues to unfold without a break. In a monologue, Jesus condemns the leaders not only as blind (9:40) but also as false shepherds, in contrast to himself as the true shepherd. The image of a shepherd depicts God's care for the people (Ps 23). The same metaphor is used for Israel's leaders, kings, and priests, as false representatives of God's purposes (Ezek 34). Evoking such intertexts, Jesus evaluates a good or bad shepherd in terms of being a leader or ruler who does or does not represent God's just rule and life-giving purposes in protecting, feeding, and caring for the sheep/people. The image of a shepherd is commonly used for imperial officials. Suetonius has the emperor Tiberius reject a provincial governor's requests for increased taxes by saying, "It was the part of a good shepherd to shear his flock, not skin it" (*Tib.* 32).[84] Jesus claims a close and caring relationship with the sheep/people, so much so that he is willing to lay down his life for them in order that they live (John 10:10b, 11, 15, 17). By contrast, Jesus attacks the Jerusalem elite as destructive "thieves and bandits," who through the temple structures of tithes and offerings steal resources from the people and threaten their well-being (10:8, 10a). Again his words cause a division (10:20–21).

Another festival, Dedication, or Hanukkah, provides the setting for the last part of the chapter. This winter festival evokes another liberation of Israel from foreign control, through the Maccabean-led resistance to and victory over the Seleucid tyrant Antiochus IV Epiphanes in the 160s BCE. In 164 BCE, the Jerusalem temple had been rededicated after its violation by Antiochus (1 Macc 4:36–59). Antiochus had aggressively pursued his program of spreading Hellenistic culture, proclaiming that "all should be one people, and that all should give up their particular customs" (1:41–42 NRSV). For Israel this meant abandoning worship of God in the Jerusalem temple and ignoring Torah commandments concerning distinctives such as circumcision and food purity (1:44–61). According to 1 Maccabees, "many even from Israel gladly adopted his religion; they sacrificed to idols and profaned the sabbath" (1:43 NRSV). The end of temple sacrificial practices and installation of a statue of Zeus in the temple indicate that among those who accommodated were (many of) the Jerusalem priesthood and elite. The festival of Dedication (Hanukkah) thus evokes a situation of significant cultural accommodation and apostasy being reversed by those who were faithful to God's commandments.

In this context Jesus' renewed use of the sheep image identifies the *Ioudaioi* as bad shepherds who have committed apostasy by accommodating to Rome and rejecting God's word, which Jesus reveals (10:24–26). Jesus further claims to be God's agent and one with God in doing God's will of providing life. These claims sound like blasphemy to the leaders (10:22–38; cf. 5:16–18). They attempt to stone him and arrest him, but Jesus withdraws, and many entrust themselves to him (10:25–30). The plot continues to advocate distance from such a society.

After the escalating animosity of John 5–10, with Jesus' intensifying challenge to the integrity, identity, legitimacy, authority, and societal vision of the Jerusalem elite and their supporters, and his repeated claims to be the definitive revealer of God's purposes, only one outcome seems possible. Jesus' challenge cannot go unanswered. Jesus will die at their hands. Chapters 11–12 play out these consequences and provide the final provocation for putting him to death.

Jesus' raising of Lazarus from death provokes this action (11:1–44). The scene is marked variously by love (11:5), misunderstanding (11:7–15), fear (11:16), neighborly kindness and consolation from the *Ioudaioi* (11:19, 31), the grief of Mary and Martha (11:19, 33–35), their rebukes to Jesus (11:21, 32), Martha's confidence and belief (11:22–27), concern for propriety (11:39), and above all, God's life-giving power (11:41–44). But ironically Jesus' act of giving life becomes the catalyst for the leaders' act of killing him. Fearing Jesus' popularity (11:45, 48), perhaps as the king who will deliver Israel (12:12–19), their own loss of power since many "were believing in Jesus" (12:11) presumably as the deliverer-King (12:12–19),[85] and retaliation from their Roman patrons and allies, the elite plot to arrest and kill Jesus (11:45–57). The death theme increases as Mary, Lazarus's sister, lovingly anoints Jesus for burial (12:1–8), and it is continued by death threats against Lazarus (12:9–11), Jesus' enthusiastic welcome from Jerusalem (12:12–19), and from Gentiles (12:12–22). His entry into

Jerusalem with people waving palm branches in 12:13 as symbols of national victory (1 Macc 13:51; 2 Macc 10:7); the shouts of "Hosanna" or "Save us, O King"; the use of the title "King of Israel" from Zephaniah 3:15–16 to denote the establishment of God's rule; the quote in John 12:13 from the royal Psalm 118, which gives thanks for victory over enemies; and the citing in John 12:15 of Zech 9:9, which anticipates God's victorious entry into Jerusalem as king of the nations—these features resemble street theater in proclaiming God's triumph and Rome's defeat. It is an antitriumphal entry into Jerusalem, evoking and mocking Roman displays of greatness and conquest while proclaiming God's victory, which is taking place in Jesus even now. Such a subversive scene continues the plot's momentum toward Jesus' death. Jesus theologically confirms this momentum by declaring his death in accord with God's purposes. Jesus speaks of the arrival of his "hour,"[86] the time of his death and ascent to the Father (12:23, 28; 13:1; 17:1), and rehearses his claims of God-given authority, his role as agent of God's purposes in giving life and judging, and the consequences of belief and unbelief (12:23–50).

While the movement to Jesus' inevitable death stops in John 13–17, the reality of his death pervades these chapters.[87] Facing imminent death, Jesus gathers his disciples to prepare them for life in his absence. During a farewell meal, in an act of loving service as the host and a slave, Jesus washes their feet (John 13). He invites them to share in his intimate relationship with God (13:5–11) and challenges them to lives marked by love and seeking the best for the other, practices that contest imperial values of domination and elite self-interest (13:12–20, 31–35). In contrast to such love, he predicts that Judas and Peter will betray him as his own death approaches (13:21–30, 36–38). He then instructs them at length about their discipleship in his absence (John 14–16). Prominent in his teaching are repeated assurances of his continuing presence with them after his death, the necessity of his return to the Father so that he can send the Spirit to assist them until Jesus returns to earth, exhortations to continue in love, and the expectation of continuing opposition as they faithfully live out God's purposes in a rejecting, imperial-controlled world. The Spirit, the Paraclete, is charged with the task of reminding disciples of Jesus' words when Jesus returns to God (14:26). By recalling Jesus' words, the Paraclete continues the work of revealing God's life-giving purposes. Jesus closes the instruction session with a lengthy prayer for God to display God's purposes in Jesus' death (17:1–8), in the community of disciples (17:9–19), and in the ongoing life of their successors (17:20–26).

The End (John 18–21)

Chapters 18–19 narrate the "necessary and/or usual" consequences of what has happened in the beginning (John 1–4) and middle (John 5–17) sections of the plot. Chapter 18 takes up the momentum of John 11–12, in which the raising of Lazarus has sealed Jesus' fate (11:45–57). Chapters 18–19 narrate how his death comes about through betrayal by Judas, denial by Peter, and arrest by Roman soldiers and police from the Jerusalem temple-based elite (18:1–18, 25–27). Jesus appears before the high priest (18:12–14, 19–24) and Pilate, who condemns him to be crucified as a kingly pretender (18:28–19:16a). He is crucified for the treasonous claim of being "King of the Jews"

(19:16b–30). Since Judea and Galilee are under Roman control, only Rome appoints a "King of the Jews." During the revolt in Jerusalem against Rome in 66–70, for example, Menehem armed himself from an armory at Masada and "returned like a veritable king to Jerusalem," to take command for a short time until he was killed (Josephus, *J.W.* 2.433–434, 444–448). Another leader, Simon, attracted followers "subservient to his command as to a king," and he was ceremonially beheaded as part of the triumph celebration in Rome in 71 (*J.W.* 4.510; 7.153–155).[88] Jesus' death is confirmed (19:31–37), and Joseph and Nicodemus bury Jesus (19:38–42).

We will consider the exchanges between Pilate, Jesus, and the *Ioudaioi* in more detail in chapter 11 below. Suffice it to note here that Pilate exhibits conventional Roman elite prejudice and scorn for the lowly provincial Jesus, not to mention authorizing torture by scourging and personal abuse (19:1–3) before handing him over for crucifixion (19:16). In derision Pilate also taunts his upper-status allies in Jerusalem, from whom he elicits an incredible confession of loyalty to Rome and renunciation of their covenant status: "We have no king but Caesar" (18:28–19:16, esp. 19:15 RSV).[89] Jesus' claims acknowledge God's rule and defy Rome's claims and power (18:36; 19:8–11). But by the end of John 19, the story has finished as far as the Jerusalem and Roman elite are concerned. Jesus is crucified and dead, mocked as a kingly pretender even while Pilate's trilingual death notice proclaims his kingly identity to all people, suggesting overtones of coronation (19:17–22) and echoing Jesus' words of universal appeal in 12:32. They have, though, it seems, silenced his critique, claims, and challenge to their societal order. They have defended their hierarchical societal system and preserved their place in it. The elite seem to have prevailed, reducing his claims to naught.

But to use Aristotle's terms, a surprising reversal takes place in the last two chapters. Early on the morning of the third day, Jesus appears alive to Mary Magdalene (20:1–18). That evening, he passes through locked doors and appears to the disciples (20:19–23). A week later, he appears to Thomas and the disciples (20:24–29). Sometime thereafter, at the Sea of Tiberias—the name evokes the emperor Tiberius as a reminder that Rome's claims to sovereignty, even over bodies of water, are limited by God's life-giving power (cf. 6:16–21)—Jesus appears again to the disciples (21:1–14). At the resulting breakfast (21:15–24), Jesus speaks to two of the disciples, Peter in 21:15–19 and the beloved disciple in 21:20–24, about their future roles as part of the community that continues Jesus' work. Peter faces persecution and martyrdom; the beloved disciple is entrusted with mission work.

Jesus' crucifixion thus revealed the extent of the elite's opposition to God's life-giving purposes and commissioned agent. It revealed the lengths to which the elite were willing to go to protect their hierarchical, self-benefiting, unjust system. But Jesus' resurrection reveals the limits and nature of their power. The empire is unable to keep Jesus dead. Jesus' resurrection reveals not only their opposition to God's purposes but also that God does not sanction their societal order and power. And that order is unable to resist God's transforming power, which reverses the injustice and damage that the elite's power has effected. Rome's empire does not have the final word. The Gospel mimics Roman power in presenting the triumph of God's power over it. Through his words, actions, death, and resurrection, Jesus takes away the sin of the world (1:29).

This event of resurrection builds on a tradition in which God vindicates those who have suffered injustice and yet have remained faithful to God's purposes. The notion of resurrection especially takes root in the crisis with Antiochus IV Epiphanes in the 160s BCE, as mentioned above in relation to the festival of Dedication in John 10:22. Antiochus had put to death those who resisted his imperial ways, but according to Daniel 12:2–3, this was not to be their end. Daniel is promised that after a "time of anguish, . . . your people shall be delivered, everyone who is found written in the book. Many of those who sleep in the dust of the earth [a metaphor for death] shall awake, some to everlasting life, and some to everlasting contempt" (12:1–2 NRSV). Thus, God's life-giving power for justice overcomes the worst that imperial violence can do. The same conviction is evident in 2 Maccabees 7, in a story of seven brothers who refuse to obey Antiochus's order to violate food purity and eat "unlawful swine's flesh" (7:1). Each brother, watched by their mother, resists until tortured to death. Several of them taunt Antiochus with the certainty of resurrection "to an everlasting renewal of life" (7:9, 23), where their tortured bodies—cut-out tongue, cut-off hands—will be restored (7:11), and they will be reunited with each other (7:29). By contrast, Antiochus will find no resurrection to life (7:14) but will know God's punishment (7:19, 34–35). This tradition underlines that Jesus' resurrection participates in God's life-giving purposes and justice: it signifies inevitable judgment for Rome.[90]

The plot ends in John 21; there is no chapter 22. But what happens to Jesus? Several earlier references indicate that he returns to God his Father (13:1; 3:14), though the Gospel does not narrate how this happens. I will explore the intertextuality between Jesus' return and the apotheosis of Roman emperors in chapter 12 below. The end of the Gospel and the departure of Jesus, though, do not mean the end of Jesus' mission. The final commissioning scene involving the two disciples elaborates Jesus' previous sending of the disciples (20:21b) to continue his task of manifesting God's life-giving purposes. This mission continues in the midst of and contrary to Rome's commitment to *imperium sine fine*, "empire without end," and its mission "to impose the habit of peace, to spare the conquered, and to put down the proud" (Virgil, *Aen.* 1.279; 6.847–853). And the writing of the Gospel also ensures a continuing witness to Jesus' revelation of God's life-giving purposes.

Conclusion

I have shown that John's plot is best understood by attending to the sequence of events, the interrelationships among them, and the conflicts that produce its final events as the "necessary or usual consequence" of the preceding action. I have argued that John's story of Jesus is part of the Gospel's rhetoric of distance: it centers on explaining how Jesus' death comes about at the hands of the elite alliance comprising Jerusalem and Roman elites. His claim to be God's chosen agent, authorized by God to make a definitive revelation of God's life-giving purposes and to take away the sin of the Roman-ruled world threatens the status quo. In living out this claim in his words (monologues and dialogues) and works (signs), Jesus conflicts with the Rome-allied Jerusalem elite and their Roman ally, the provincial governor Pilate. Jesus confronts and challenges their power over, and vision of, an unjust societal order, which is contrary to God's life-giving purposes. The Jerusalem elite reject Jesus' claim and revelation of God's purposes of life, preferring to defend the status quo by putting him to death.

But surprisingly his death is not the end. In an act of justice and life-giving power, God raises him, thereby revealing the limit of elite power, the error of their societal order, their death-bringing power, and the greater power of God's life-giving purposes. Meanwhile some people discern Jesus' origin, identity, and mission; commit themselves to his revelation; and form a countercommunity that, assisted by the Holy Spirit, continues Jesus' mission in and to this imperial world. The Gospel's plot is a significant part of John's community's hidden transcript, a web of self-protective protest against and dissent from the elite's societal order and version of reality, and a means of securing an alternative "anti-society."

Notes

1. This chapter bears some similarity to my discussion of the Gospel's plot in Carter, *John: Storyteller,* chap. 2.

2. For this approach to intertextuality and "metonymic referentiality," see John M. Foley, *Immanent Art: From Structure to Meaning in Traditional Oral Epic* (Bloomington: Indiana University Press, 1991).

3. Culpepper's discussion (*Anatomy,* 77–98) is groundbreaking.

4. E.g., R. E. Brown, *John,* 2 vols.; idem, *An Introduction to the Gospel of John,* ed. F. J. Moloney (New York: Doubleday, 2003), 298–316; Moloney, *Gospel of John.*

5. O'Day, "Outline of John," in "Gospel of John," in *NIB* 9:512–14.

6. Fernando F. Segovia, "Journey(s) of the Word of God: A Reading of the Plot of the Fourth Gospel," in *The Fourth Gospel from a Literary Perspective,* ed. R. A. Culpepper and F. F. Segovia, *Semeia* 53 (Atlanta: Scholars Press, 1991), 23–54.

7. For my fourfold structure, see Carter, *Pontius Pilate,* 130.

8. "Aristotle: *On the Art of Poetry,*" in *Classical Literary Criticism,* trans. T. S. Dorsch, Penguin Classics L155 (Harmondsworth: Penguin Books, 1965), 29–75.

9. E. M. Foster, *Aspects of the Novel* (New York: Penguin Books, 1962), 87.

10. Ronald S. Crane, "The Concept of Plot and the Plot of Tom Jones," in *Approaches to the Novel: Materials for a Poetics,* ed. R. Scholes, rev. ed. (San Francisco: Chandler, 1966), 241.

11. M. H. Abrams, *A Glossary of Literary Terms,* 7th ed. (Boston: Heinle & Heinle, 1999), 127. Also Kieran Egan, "What is a Plot?" *New Literary History* 9 (1978): 455–73, esp. 470.

12. Seymour B. Chatman, *Story and Discourse: Narrative Structure in Fiction and Film* (Ithaca, NY: Cornell University Press, 1978), 53–56.

13. This approach is appropriate for Matthew's plot. See Carter, *Matthew: Storyteller,* 149–75. But there are difficulties in applying it to John. While we could identify some of John's key scenes or kernels such as calling disciples (1:35–51), Jesus' protest in the temple (2:13–22), and the raising of Lazarus (chap. 11), John's Gospel is very repetitive, with a number of parallel scenes that emphasize important thematic dimensions but do not particularly advance the plot. Moreover, Chatman's formulation focuses attention on actions rather than words (dialogues/monologues), which contribute so much to John's plot. Key themes or strands woven throughout the Gospel play an important role.

14. Frye, *Anatomy,* 33–67, 162, 163–71; 186–203.

15. Algirdas Julien Greimas, *Sémantique structurale: Recherche de méthode,* rev. ed. (Paris: Larousse, 1976).

16. Chatman, *Story and Discourse,* 85.

17. Stibbe, *John's Gospel,* 38–53.

18. "Life" involves the experience of God's love (3:16), salvation (3:17–18), and judgment (3:16; 5:26–27; 10:10). See the discussion in chap. 8 below.

19. 1:32–34 could be construed as indicating that the Spirit helps Jesus in his activities, but the Gospel does not identify such a role explicitly.

20. R. Alan Culpepper, *Anatomy*, 77–98, esp. 84, 88–89; also idem, *The Gospel and Letters of John*, Institute for Bible Translation (Nashville: Abingdon, 1988), 67–86.

21. For discussion of various constituent parts of the plot, see Carter, *John: Storyteller*, chap. 2.

22. I set aside discussions of structure and origin. For John as the author, see Barrett, *Gospel according to St. John*, 126; O'Day, "Gospel of John," in *NIB* 9:518; for their origin in Gnostic-Mandaean-Baptist circles, Rudolf Bultmann, "The History of Religions Background of the Prologue to the Gospel of John," in *The Interpretation of John*, ed. J. A. Ashton (Philadelphia: Fortress, 1986), 18–35; for a hymn from Jewish wisdom traditions, C. H. Dodd, *The Interpretation of the Fourth Gospel* (Cambridge: Cambridge University Press, 1953), 272–85; T. H. Tobin, "The Prologue of John and the Hellenistic Jewish Speculation," *CBQ* 52 (1990): 253–69; M. Scott, *Sophia and the Johannine Jesus*; Ringe, *Wisdom's Friends*, 29–63; for a hymn from John's own community, see Brown, *John*, 1:20–23; Robert Kysar, *John* (Minneapolis: Augsburg, 1986), 28; for the Prologue as an integral part of the Gospel, see Carter, "Prologue and John's Gospel," 35–58; Moloney, *Gospel of John*, 33–48; Fernando F. Segovia, "John 1:1–18 as Entrée into Johannine Reality: Representation and Ramifications," in *Word, Theology, and Community in John*, ed. J. Painter et al. (St. Louis: Chalice, 2002), 33–64.

23. Kristeva, "The Bounded Text," 36–63, esp. 36–37.

24. Richey, "'Truly This Is the Savior,'" chap. 4, sees the Prologue as challenging cosmological (1:1–5), prophetic (1:6–8), political (1:9–13), and doxological (1:14–18) elements of Augustan ideology "by contrasting the unique and superior character of Jesus' person and activity with that of the Emperor" (recall Suetonius, *Dom.* 13.4, Domitian as "our Lord and God") and thereby constituting a counterideology that distinguished Christ and Caesar for John's community. I will utilize selected aspects of this analysis here. As I have shown in chap. 3 above, an exclusive focus on Domitian and the presentation of Domitian as an especially wicked emperor are not convincing. Moreover, the emphasis on superiority misses the significant element of imitation.

25. J. Scott, *Domination*, passim, esp. 1–16, 136–82.

26. Swain, *Hellenism and Empire*, 88.

27. Ibid., 110, 112–13; 129–31.

28. Ibid., 184–86.

29. Ibid., 365, 377.

30. Ibid., 89.

31. See, for example, Carter, "Prologue"; Dunn, "Let John be John," 293–322.

32. Musa W. Dube, "Savior of the World, but Not of This World: A Postcolonial Reading of Spatial Construction in John," in *The Postcolonial Bible*, ed. R. S. Sugirtharajah (Sheffield: Sheffield Academic Press, 1998), 122–24; Moore, *Empire*, 45–46.

33. For Ephesus, see Price, *Rituals and Power*, passim; van Tilborg, *Reading John*, 165–219.

34. See Carter, *Matthew and Empire*, 20–34, 57–74 (selections) for elaboration of these claims.

35. Zanker, *Power of Images*, 167–238; also chap. 8 below.

36. G. F. Chestnut, "The Ruler and the Logos in Neopythagorean, Middle Platonic, and Late Stoic Political Philosophy," in *ANRW* II.16.2 (1978): 1312.

37. Ibid., 1324.

38. Ibid., 1325–26. Chestnut outlines similar views in Philo's discussions of Moses and Joseph, though not of Gaius Caligula, indicating how pervasive were such understandings, at least among elites (1326–29).

39. Richey, "'Truly This Is the Savior,'" 170–79, helpfully discusses the issue of preexistence, as well as of agency, though I am not persuaded by all of Richey's discussion.

40. Philo (*Emb.* 95) attacks Gaius Caligula for assuming divine honors like Apollo, "his head

encircled with garlands of sunrays." Nero especially identifies with the sun: see O. Neverov, "Nero-Helios," in *Pagan Gods and Shrines of the Roman Empire*, ed. M. Henig and A. King, Oxford University Committee for Archaeology Monograph 8 (Oxford: OUCA, 1986), 189–94, esp. 190, including photographs; Suetonius, *Nero* 14, 25, 31 (the Domus Aurea, "a palace of the sun, the dwelling place of cosmic divinity"), 53.

41. Text and translation in Oliver, *Ruling Power*.

42. Brown, *John*, 1:lxvii–lxx, 27–28.

43. Richey, " 'Truly This Is the Savior,' " chap. 4, 179–87, helpfully elaborates the role of prophetic legitimation.

44. On the *Sibylline Oracles*, see D. S. Potter, *Prophecy and History in the Crisis of the Roman Empire: A Historical Commentary on the Thirteenth Sibylline Oracle* (Oxford: Clarendon, 1990).

45. Kenneth Scott, *The Imperial Cult under the Flavians* (Stuttgart: Kohlhammer, 1936), 2; for discussion, 1–19.

46. Brown, "*Kosmos* = 'World,' " in *John*, 1:508–10; S. Morrow, "Κόσμος in John," *CBQ* 64 (2002): 90–102.

47. Adele Reinhartz, "Colonizer as Colonized: Intertextual Dialogue between the Gospel of John and Canadian Identity," in *John and Postcolonialism: Travel, Space and Power*, ed. M. W. Dube and J. L. Staley (London: Continuum, 2002), 179–80, interestingly calls the question "elusive," finds a "slim basis" for the claim, but concedes very cautiously that "it is certainly possible that she [Rome] is included."

48. Also Allen D. Callahan, *A Love Supreme: A History of Johannine Tradition* (Minneapolis: Fortress, 2005), 81–82, who correctly identifies "the ruler of the world" who will be driven out (12:31), who has no power over Jesus (14:30), and who has been condemned (16:11), not as the devil but as Pilate, the representative of Roman power. Contra Kovacs, " 'Now Shall the Ruler," 227–47; on the interaction between Pilate, the Jerusalem elite, and Jesus, see Carter, *Pontius Pilate*, 127–52, and chap. 11 below.

49. Note Kautsky's axiom (*Politics*, 150): "To rule in aristocratic empires is, above all, to tax."

50. Dyson, "Native Revolts."

51. Wayne Meeks, "The Divine Agent and His Counterfeit in Philo and the Fourth Gospel," in *Aspects of Religious Propaganda in Judaism and Early Christianity*, ed. E. S. Fiorenza (Notre Dame: University of Notre Dame, 1976), 43–67.

52. Richey, " 'Truly This Is the Savior,' " chap. 4, 204–6.

53. Text in Friesen, *Imperial Cults*, 32–33.

54. For discussion, photos, and the text of one of the 13 discovered inscriptions (from the city of Aphrodisias), see ibid., 44–45.

55. Swain, *Hellenism and Empire*, 89.

56. J. Scott, *Domination*.

57. Commentators suggest that this image may evoke (1) the Passover lamb, which symbolizes Israel's deliverance from Egyptian captivity (Exod 12:1–13); and/or (2) the Servant in Isa 53:7, who absorbs imperial violence and delivers God's people; and/or (3) an apocalyptic figure who destroys all sin (cf. Rev 17:14).

58. Also John 4:9, 22; Reinhartz (*Befriending*, 72–75) overstates the force of these exceptions in claiming that the term designates a "national but not geographically limited religious, political, and cultural identity."

59. Martin Lowe, "Who Were the *Ioudaioi*?" *NovT* 18 (1976): 102–7.

60. In addition to chap. 3 above, see Lenski, *Power and Privilege*, 189–296; MacMullen, *Roman Social Relations*; on the temple economy, Hanson and Oakman, *Palestine*, 99–159; for John's presentation of the Pharisees and chief priests (John does not mention scribes, Sadducees, or elders), Saldarini, *Pharisees*, 35–49, 187–98.

61. John 5:1, unspecified festival; 6:4, Passover; 7:2, festival of Booths/Tabernacles; 11:55, Passover; 19:42, day of preparation for Passover.

62. The recognition of a group with supporters nuances my emphasis only on leaders in my discussion of *Ioudaioi* in Carter, *John: Storyteller*, 65–71.

63. Attempts to depict the *Ioudaioi* as an explicitly and exclusively religious group are unconvincing. I have in mind the helpful argument of Boyarin, "*Ioudaioi* in John," 216–39. Rejecting identifications with Judeans, leaders of the Jews, or the fanatically religious (221–22), Boyarin argues that the term specifies a subset of Israel (221), originating with the group of sixth-century BCE elites exiled to Babylon who returned to Judea and established separation from outsider groups such as "the people of the land" and Samaritans; they had a Jerusalem-based, temple-centered identity marked by the reestablishment of certain pietistic practices and festivals, to which some outside of Judea gave some adherence (222, 227, 237). The leaders of the *Ioudaioi* are Pharisees, Sadducees, priestly authorities (236); John originates from Israelites who are not *Ioudaioi* (234). Boyarin's framework insightfully accounts for the identification of "Jews" as leadership authorities (John 1:19, 24, in relation to Pharisees, priests, and Levites), explains the use of "the Jews" in relation to purification rites (2:6), festivals (Passover in 2:13; 6:4), salvation (4:22), Galilean adherents (not leaders in 6:41, 52), and a division within the people and fear of the Jews in 7:11–12, 40–43. While Boyarin's emphases on historical origins, geography, and religious practices/piety are very helpful, his analysis is restricted by two factors: (1) Operative throughout is the false assumption that religion is a self-contained entity separate from politics. Boyarin describes the *Ioudaioi* as a religious group (222, 227) marked geographically and religiously (229). Though he recognizes that the exile group comprised elites (224), only their confessional development and pietistic practices figure in the following discussion while elite identity and power fall out of consideration (224–30). Similarly, while Boyarin regularly asserts their link with the temple in control of the temple-state and reintroduction of religious observances (224–25, 226, 229, 234–35, 237), there is no consideration of the temple's participation in the political negotiation of Roman power (e.g., the offering of daily sacrifices for but not to the emperor, as in Josephus, *J.W.* 2.197, 410–411; the appointment of the chief priest by the Roman governor, as in Josephus, *Ant.* 18.33–35, 95; Roman control of the chief-priestly garments, as in Josephus, *Ant.* 15.403–408; 18.90–95; 20.6–14). Nor is there any recognition that festivals (with their celebration of deliverance from political oppression in Egypt, for instance) involve a political and in fact a politically dangerous dimension whatever the accommodationist preferences of the temple leadership. Josephus, for instance, emphasizes both that "it is on these festive occasions that sedition is most apt to break out" (*J.W.* 1.88) and reports the increased presence of Roman troops in Jerusalem during festivals "to watch the people and repress any insurrectionary movements" (*J.W.* 5.244; also 2.224; *Ant.* 20.106). Nor does he take account of the Gospel's presentation of this group as subordinates of and yet allies with Rome (John 11:45–53), the linking of Pharisees and this Jerusalem group with the governor Pilate (18:3, 12; 18:28–19:25), and the priests' confession of 19:15. Religion and politics are intertwined. (2) Models of the stratification of empires such as that offered by Gerhard Lenski (see chaps. 2–3 above) as well as various classical studies emphasize the role of alliances between the central governing power (Rome) and provincial elites in exercising rule (Josephus describes the Jerusalem, temple-based priests as the rulers of Judea; *Ant.* 20. 251). The *Ioudaioi*, following Boyarin's own description of them as a Jerusalem temple-based group, are not a separated or exclusive religious group, but exercise vast political, economic, cultural, and religious power in alliance with Rome. While Boyarin is correct to point out that the term *Ioudaioi* is not adequately interpreted universally as "leaders of the Jews" (6:41, 52; 11:19, 31, 33, 36, 45, 54), he is not correct to minimize this leadership/elite role and to suggest that it is altogether alternative to his proposal (e.g., 221–22, 237). Festivals "of the Jews" (11:55) indicate the Jerusalem elite's societal control, as well as name a means of that elite control. In sum,

Boyarin's contribution is very helpful in identifying a subgroup within the larger entity of "Israel," but it is limited by his separation of religious from politics and neglect of societal status.

64. Painter, *Quest for the Messiah*.

65. Note also Mic 4:4, where the nations come to Zion to worship God, beat their swords into ploughshares, and all sit under their fig trees without fear. Callahan, *Love Supreme*, 58–59.

66. Other signs: John 4:46–54; 5:1–18; 6:1–14, 16–21; 9:1–7; 11:1–47; 21:1–14.

67. K. Scott, *Imperial Cult*, 1–19.

68. Garnsey, *Food and Society*.

69. For a good description of the temple's involvement in exploitative economic activity through landed estates, requisitioning supplies for its rituals and personnel (tithes), and collection of the temple tax, see Hanson and Oakman, *Palestine*, 131–59.

70. For theories concerning the end of sacrifice in the light of his own death, inclusion of Gentiles, judgment, and economic exploitation, as well as debates over whether the action was a judgment or a purification, see the discussion in the commentaries.

71. J. Scott, *Domination*, 202–27.

72. Mark Matson, "The Temple Incident," in *Jesus in Johannine Tradition*, ed. R. T. Fortna and T. Thatcher (Louisville: Westminster John Knox, 2001), 145–53.

73. In 2:13 Jesus travels from Galilee to Jerusalem to celebrate Passover (also 2:23; 4:45). In 5:1 Jesus again travels from Galilee to Jerusalem. In 7:1 Jesus is in Galilee. In 7:10, after saying he is not going to Jerusalem for a festival (7:8–9), he goes there "in private" and teaches (7:14). In 10:22–23, Jesus is still in Jerusalem. In 12:12, Jesus reenters Jerusalem after leaving Judea (10:40) and being in the vicinity of Bethany (cf. 11:1, 18; 12:1), where he raised Lazarus (the Bethany of 1:28 is "across the Jordan"). Jerusalem is the location for the rest of the story, which centers on Jesus' crucifixion and resurrection.

74. For John's ambiguous, riddling, and ironic style, see Carter, *John: Storyteller*, 107–28 and references.

75. The noun *basileia* refers to Babylonian, Median, Persian, and Hellenistic (Alexander's) empires in Dan 2:37–45 (LXX); to the empires of Alexander in 1 Macc 1:6 and Antiochus Epiphanes and the Seleucids in 1 Macc 1:16, 41, 51; and to Rome's empire in Josephus, *J.W.* 5.409.

76. So Brown, *John*, 1:169; Rudolf Schnackenburg (*The Gospel According to St. John*, 3 vols. [New York: Seabury, 1980–82], 1:422–23) disagrees, claiming no good reason for Sychar to displace Shechem, favoring the site of Askar. If Shechem is in view, it was a small village in the first century but had a distinguished history. In Josh 24 it was the scene for a covenant ceremony, celebrating God's deliverance of the people from Egypt and gift of the land, and requiring the people to serve God faithfully. The Samaritan woman and many from her city are now included in that covenant.

77. C. Koester, "'Savior,'" 665–80. Further discussion of this title follows in chap. 7 below. This ascription might be linked with the statement in 4:22, usually translated, "for salvation is of/from the Jews" (KJV/NRSV) and understood to affirm the crucial place of Jews in salvation history. Callahan (*Love Supreme*, 65), emphasizing a long history of antagonism and violence between Jerusalem-oriented Judeans and Samaritans, suggests that a preferable translation should read, "It is salvation from the Judeans," the Jerusalem-based, Rome-allied *Ioudaioi*, who in opposing Jesus also oppose God.

78. Robert J. Karris, *Jesus and the Marginalized in John's Gospel* (Collegeville, MN: Liturgical Press, 1990); Whittaker, "The Poor," 272–99.

79. A. H. Mead, "The *Basilikos* in John 4:46–54," *JSNT* 23 (1985): 69–72.

80. Garnsey, *Food and Society*, 43–61; R. Garland, *The Eye of the Beholder: Deformity and Disability in the Graeco-Roman World* (Ithaca, NY: Cornell University Press, 1995); Helen King, ed., *Health in Antiquity* (London: Routledge, 2005).

81. On the monologues whose content contributes significantly to the unfolding conflict (chaps. 3; 5; 6; 8; 10), Gail R. O'Day, "'I have said these things to you . . .': The Unsettled Place of Jesus' Discourses in Literary Approaches to the Fourth Gospel," in *Word, Theology, and Community in John*, ed. J. Painter, R. A. Culpepper, and F. F. Segovia (St. Louis: Chalice Press, 2002), 143–54.

82. Callahan, *Love Supreme*, 61–62.

83. It is commonly claimed that they expel him from the synagogue, but as I have indicated in chaps. 2–3 above, this is not sustainable: (1) The synagogue has not been the setting for the scene. In 9:13 the man is brought to the Pharisees, but no location is given for them in Jerusalem. (2) The verb used in verses 34 and 35 for "driven out" (ἐκβάλλω, *ekballō*) is quite different from the construction of 9:22 (ἀποσυνάγωγος γένηται, *aposynagōgos genētai*), thereby providing no indication that the two should be linked. (3) The only synagogue mentioned previously appears in 6:59 in Capernaum. The scene of John 9 is set in Jerusalem (7:10; 8:59). (4) Previously *Ioudaioi* have been linked predominantly with the temple and Jerusalem (2:18), as are Pharisees (1:19, 24; 3:1; 7:32, 45).

84. Dio Chrysostom in *Kingship 4* (43–44) reminds Trajan that the emperor is a "shepherd of peoples" and is to "protect flocks, not . . . to slaughter, butcher, and skin them." See chap. 7 below.

85. So too Moore, *Empire and Apocalypse*, 66.

86. See, for example, Brown, *John*, 1:517–18.

87. Fernando F. Segovia, *The Farewell of the Word: The Johannine Call to Abide* (Minneapolis: Fortress, 1991); John Christopher Thomas, *Footwashing in John 13 and the Johannine Community*, JSNTSup 61 (Sheffield: JSOT Press, 1991).

88. Previously, kingly pretenders such as Judas, Simon, and Anthronges had gathered followers, attacked elites and their buildings, and claimed the title against Herod, Rome's appointed "king of the Jews"; they were defeated and executed (Josephus, *Ant.* 17.271–272, 273–276, 278–285). Death often resulted for other peasant-prophet figures who gathered followers and evoked and tried to reenact Hebrew Bible narratives of liberation. For example, between 46–48 CE, Theudas anticipated an exodus reenactment with the parting of the Jordan River, only to be attacked by Roman troops and beheaded (*Ant.* 20.97–98). Others awaited reenactments of the fall of Jericho (20.169–171) or in vain awaited liberation in the wilderness (20.188).

89. MacMullen, *Roman Social Relations*; Karris, *Jesus*, 33–41; Carter, *Pontius Pilate*, 127–52.

90. It is the failure to consider the implications of traditions such as resurrection or the use of various Hebrew Bible intertexts that makes Stephen Moore's claim (*Empire*, 73) that "no end to Caesar's reign is prophesied or threatened" unconvincing.

7

Images and Titles for Jesus in
the Roman Imperial Context

In chapters 5 and 6, I have argued that both the Gospel's genre and plot are acts of imperial negotiation that constitute part of the Gospel's rhetoric of distance. Both present
Jesus as the agent of God's purposes that contest and conflict with, even while they at
times participate in and mimic, imperial structures and values. As part of the Gospel's
rhetoric of distance, the plot functions, I have argued, to provide understanding to
Jesus-believers about the conflict that developed between Jesus, God's agent, and representatives of the evil empire (John 7:7) that rejected and crucified him. As a consequence, they are to live lives as members of an alternative community, or antisociety,
which are much less accommodated to the empire. In this chapter, I take up a further
aspect of the Gospel's imperial negotiation performed by its rhetoric of distance,
namely, its multifaceted depiction of Jesus. The Gospel employs at least eight "titles"
and images for Jesus that both imitate and contest imperial claims. The Gospel attributes to Jesus six titles used of the Roman emperor, and employs at least two more evoking Jewish traditions that contest imperial claims.

Three factors justify attention to titles attributed to Jesus in John's Gospel. Titles used
for Jesus have figured in previous infrequent discussions of the Gospel's encounter with
the Roman Empire. But invariably the discussions have been quite restricted in focus
by treating the titles in isolation from a discussion of the Gospel as a whole, as though
the occasional use of a title is the only point of contact between the Gospel and the
empire. Hence a reconsideration of the role of titles is necessary in the context of the
previous chapters' discussion of the Gospel's genre and plot, and as part of a larger
coherent consideration of the Gospel's imperial negotiation.

Second, some caution is needed in considering the role of titles. In recent decades
narrative studies of the Gospels are ample testimony that titles cannot, in isolation from
either the narrative or each other, carry the christological weight that former studies
placed on them. As Leander Keck recognized some time ago, the narrative context in
which titles appear clearly frames them and supplies important content.[1] Conversely,
passages where no titles are used contribute significantly to a character's presentation.
Nor can a particular title be claimed to denote content completely unrelated to either
the unfolding plot or to other titles. This being said, however, it is also true that within
a complex of various means of characterization (actions, words, conflicts, sequences of
contrasting or parallel material, and so forth), titles also contribute by evoking tradi-

tions and intertexts, and by being ciphers for larger complexes of understanding. I will focus on eight titles and images, but it is important not to isolate them from the Gospel's plot. This chapter, then, should be seen as both a continuation of and a subset of the previous chapter.

Third, by frequently evoking Israel's traditions along with titles used for the emperor, titles and images for Jesus provide further instances of a turn to the past in order to negotiate the present. Titles such as "Christ" and "Son of Man" evoke traditions that have often originated and evolved in contexts of imperial power. These traditions have frequently negotiated imperial assertion with a counterassertion of judgment, God's sovereignty and purposes for the world, and vindication for the afflicted. John's intertextual evoking of these traditions makes the past present in order to put the current ruling power, Rome, in its place.

So, in the context of and as a continuation of the previous chapter's discussion of the Gospel's plot, and informed by these recognitions of both the limits and contribution of titles, I will consider the roles of eight titles and images used for Jesus. My argument is that, as part of the Gospel's rhetoric of distance, these titles and images contribute to the task of imperial negotiation for Jesus-believers in Ephesus. They bear central emphases in the presentation of Jesus, notably his identity as revealer and agent of God's life-giving purposes. I employ a somewhat arbitrary but convenient distinction, discussing first two titles not used for the emperor, Messiah/Christ and Son of Man, and then six titles and images used for the emperor as agent of the gods and as powerful ruler: Shepherd, King, Savior, Son of God, God, Lord. These titles and images applied to Jesus also often evoke disruptive Jewish traditions that contest Roman power and present Jesus as one who is an alternative and superior to the emperor. To be clear, I am not arguing that imperial usage provides the source for John's titles and images. Rather, I am exploring the role of titles and images as the intersection of various intertexts (Hebrew Bible, imperial theology, John's Gospel) and the contribution of this intertextuality to the identity and societal posture that the Gospel urges on Ephesian Jesus-believers. Within the limits of space, it is not possible to discuss every aspect of these titles and images. The focus will be on this relexification of Jesus and its role in imperial negotiation.

Titles Not Used for the Emperor That Evoke Jewish Traditions Challenging Imperial Claims

Messiah/Christ

The Gospel's nineteen references to the Messiah fall into three groups: John's denials that he is the Messiah (1:20, 25; 3:28); debates about whether Jesus' role, origin, revelation, and duration indicate that he is the Messiah;[2] and six texts that confess Jesus to be the Messiah.[3] If this threefold division alone is taken into account, two-thirds of the usages of Messiah/Christ indicate that the title is one of speculation or denial. One could conclude from this that the title is peripheral or of dubious value.[4] But in addition to heightening the motif of the quest for Jesus,[5] the remaining confessional uses qualify this conclusion significantly. The title "Messiah," or "Christ," appears at key points in the narrative, in the opening Prologue (1:17), in the middle near the end of Jesus' ministry (11:27), and in the concluding summary at 20:31. Moreover, the title Messiah/Christ is used in association with other important titles: in 1:17 with Word (1:14) and Son (1:18), in 1:41 with Son of God (1:41) and king (1:49), in 9:22 with prophet (9:17) and Son of Man (9:35), in 11:27 with Son of God, in 17:3 with Son (17:1), and in 20:31 with Son of God. Thus, in its six clearly confessional instances (1:17, 41; 9:22; 11:27; 17:3; 20:31), Messiah/Christ is intertwined with and an integral part of the Gospel's multifaceted Christology.

In relation to these six confessional uses, the key question concerns the content of the confession. As the use of Messiah/Christ in 20:31 indicates, the Gospel's plot provides this definition. As Messiah/Christ, Jesus is God's agent and Son, sent by God and authorized to reveal God and God's life-giving purposes in the midst of the claims, practices, ruling personnel, and structures of the Roman imperial world, leading to Jesus' crucifixion and resurrection/exaltation. Within this plot, however, I suggest that Messiah/Christ makes a particular contribution to the Gospel's rhetoric of distance by evoking first-century messianic expectations that present the Roman world to be contrary to God's purposes, reveal it to be under God's judgment, and depict the Messiah/Christ as the anointed agent of God's sovereignty, powerful judgment, and transformational new life.

The pervasiveness of first-century messianic expectations is debated. While it is often assumed that messianic expectation was widespread, the existing texts do not evidence extensive uses of the Hebrew term "Messiah" or its Greek equivalent "Christ."[6] On the basis of the use of these terms, expectations were neither universal nor univocal but multiple and minority.

The Hebrew term "messiah" literally means "anointed" and is rendered in Greek as "Christ."[7] Anointing symbolizes that God has commissioned a person to a task or service on God's behalf. Accordingly, kings in the Davidic line were anointed or commissioned to rule God's people on God's behalf.[8] Priests were anointed for temple service (Lev 4:3, 5, 16; 2 Macc 1:10), and prophets were anointed to speak the word of the Lord (1 Kings 19:16; Sir 48:8). God anointed or commissioned the Gentile, Persian king Cyrus to set the exiles free from Babylon in 539 BCE (Isa 44:28–45:4).

By the late first century CE, the time of John's Gospel, the term comes to designate special figures who would accomplish God's purposes in various circumstances. There are at least five main texts.[9]

- The *Psalms of Solomon* were written about the middle of the first century BCE, after Roman control was established in 63 BCE (*Pss. Sol.* 2; 8). They originate from a group in Judea strongly committed to God's law, who resist faithless or compromised priests and look for God's intervention. In *Psalms of Solomon* 17–18 they anticipate an "anointed one," the "Lord Messiah" (17:32: 18:5, 7), a Davidic king who will reveal God's purposes in his actions. He will rule the people (17:21) and deliver them from the Romans (17:22). This deliverance will not be by military means (17:33) but will be "by the words of his mouth. At his warning the nations will flee from his presence" (17:24–25). Those dispersed among the nations will return to the land, the nations will come to a purified Jerusalem to worship, and there "will be no unrighteousness among them" (17:32).

- The Qumran community, east of Jerusalem, was probably destroyed just before 70 CE by Rome. Its library, including its own writings, attest expectations of several different types of messiahs, notably a priestly and a kingly figure (1QS 9.11; 1QSa 2.14, 20; 1QSb 5.20–29). Of the two, the priestly figure dominates, though their roles receive little elaboration.[10]

- In *1 Enoch* 37–71, probably dating to the mid-first century CE, an anointed one or Messiah (48:10; 52:4) is a heavenly figure also identified as "Son of Man" (46:1–3).[11] This figure is primarily a heavenly judge who executes judgment on God's behalf. He condemns the unrighteous rulers and powerful who have oppressed the poor and "denied the Lord of the Spirits [God] and his Messiah" (48:10). In the first-century context, Rome is in view. The Messiah also vindicates the oppressed. "This Son of Man whom you have seen is the One who would remove the kings and the mighty ones from their comfortable seats and the strong ones from their thrones. . . . They manifest all their deeds in oppression. . . . Their power (depends) upon their wealth. And their devotion is to the gods whom they have fashioned with their own hands" (46:2–7).

- *Second Baruch* originates after the fall of Jerusalem to Rome in 70 CE and is contemporary with John's Gospel. A kingly Messiah will be revealed from heaven (29:3; 39:7), will reign eternally on earth, and will bring about the resurrection (30:1; 40:2–4). He will destroy the ruling power that is "harsher and more evil than those which were before it" (39:5; 40:1–4). After wars and distress, he will establish peace and security in the land, but judge and destroy the nations who have subjected Israel. Then there will be eternal peace, abundant fertility, and harmony among people and animals (70:9–74:4).

- *Fourth Ezra* originates from the same time and circumstances. It offers several images of messiahs. In the first (7:26–30), the Messiah will appear for four hundred years and die. After seven days of silence, a new age of judgment (carried out by God), resurrection, and incorruptibility begins. In the second, the interpretation of a vision involving an eagle and a lion identifies the coming of a Messiah from the line of David who will reveal God's verdict on Rome, denounce the Roman Empire and emperors, destroy them, and establish an age of joy (12:32–34).

These five texts cannot be understood to be the sum total of messianic expectations, since a chapter such as John 7 indicates various points of popular speculation concerning a Messiah: his origin is not known (7:27), he does many signs (7:31), he does or does not come from Galilee or the line of David (7:41–42). Yet two things are to be observed in this brief survey of these five main texts. First, the number of references to a Messiah figure in texts from around the first century is quite limited. Second, the presentations of these anointed figures are diverse. Priestly, heavenly, Davidic, earthly, and judicial figures with differing tasks (purify the land, announce judgment, rule), life spans (unending, unspecified, 400 years), and origins (heavenly, Davidic, Aaron) comprise the varied expectations. With this diversity, there is no widely agreed checklist of common identifying markers for the Messiah in the first century.

Yet it is perhaps possible to identify several common elements in the diversity. One involves the almost pervasive link to the line of David. More dominant is that these messiah figures are agents of intervention and transformation. As God's agents, they confront, judge, and overcome Roman power, albeit in quite different ways, setting up an age in which God's purposes of justice, peace, security, and fertility are enacted. Richard Bauckham concludes his survey of uses of the term "Messiah" in Jewish literature by acknowledging debate about whether Davidic messianism was continuous in the postexilic period. Yet he argues, "It is undisputed, however, that it was in the early Roman period that the hope for a new David who would liberate the people from Roman domination became especially popular."[12] Thus, there is no justification for counting these traditions as spiritualizing the Messiah and his tasks in terms of inward, personal significance only. The diverse traditions affirm the powerful, political, international, justice-bringing roles of Messiah figures that mean the end of Rome's world. How this end comes about is quite diverse, ranging from the Messiah's dismissive word (*Psalms of Solomon*), to heavenly judgment (*1 Enoch*), and to earthly judgment (*2 Baruch*; *4 Ezra* = 2 Esdras).

There is no need to repeat the analysis of the Gospel's plot from the previous chapter, in which Jesus' words and actions challenge Roman power and point to an alternative existence. To identify Jesus as Messiah/Christ in this context highlights Jesus' intervening and transformative role. Jesus is anointed, commissioned or "christed" to enact God's life-giving purposes, which surely conflict with the imperial ways of Rome and its Jerusalem allies and supporters. In this regard the use of "Christ" in the Gospel's summative declaration of purpose is significant in that the term enfolds all the Gospel's content. "These things [the Gospel's plot] are written that you may believe that Jesus is the Christ, the Son of God, and that believing you may have life in his name" (20:31 RSV).

Yet we need to observe an important difference. The Gospel does not seem to present Jesus' intervention in and transformation of the imperial world as Messiah/Christ as having the same cosmic reach—at least in the present—that often marks the scenarios of these other diverse texts. If Jesus is the Messiah, it would appear from ongoing imperial existence that the imperial and at times cosmic transformation has not taken place. Rome still rules. The structures and practices of its hierarchical and oppressive rule continue apparently unaffected. To maintain both the affirmation of the coming of Jesus as Messiah/Christ, and to explain the current apparent nontransformation, the Gospel employs at least a threefold strategy, combining the dualistic, the eschatological, and the social.

Conceptually, the narrative constructs a dualistic world. As is well known, people belong either to the light or to the darkness (8:12), to life or to death (3:16; 5:24), to truth or to lies and falseness (8:44–46), to sight or to blindness (8:12; 9:39–41), to believing or to disobedience (3:18, 36), to God or to the devil (8:42–44).[13] While this dualistic framework creates a division, each element of the pairings is not equal. The first element signifying allegiance to God manifested in Jesus is valued and superior. The second element signifying rejection of Jesus/God and alliance with the Rome-allied, Jerusalem-based power group depicts judgment. This division, created by the Gospel narrative, is certainly not self-evident in everyday life. There were no placards or inscriptions in Ephesus proclaiming it to the city. The Gospel constructs it as part of its rhetoric of distance, providing this grid as a way for Jesus-believers to understand daily life, revealing the reality beneath the facade of imperial business as usual. The Gospel makes this revelation so that Jesus-believers will understand that daily societal life is not what it seems to be.

Second, while the Gospel evokes these messianic scenarios, it reframes them eschatologically. In general terms, the messianic scenarios understand the present to be dominated by wickedness and sin because of the actions of evil empires and elites. But in the future, the Messiah in some way will judge "the kings of the earth and the mighty landowners" (so *1 En.* 48:8), and vindicate the righteous in a new age marked by peace and security, justice, fertility, and the worship of God. John employs a critical change. Instead of a future moment or event of cosmic intervention and transformation as the messianic traditions tend to depict, the Gospel employs John's oft-recognized shift of focus to the present or to a much more realized eschatology. Instead of an event, it presents a process. Instead of only anticipating the future, it focuses on the present because the Christ/Messiah has already come (1:17). The Gospel reveals that the eschatological process of transformation is already underway. That which is understood to take place in the future as a cosmic and definitive transformation accomplished by the Messiah has already started in Jesus. So in the Gospel, the Messiah is already present (1:17; 4:25–26; 20:31). Jesus, sent from God and commissioned or "christed" as God's agent to do the will of God (4:34), declares the present world to be evil (3:19–20; 7:7). He exposes and condemns the evil that pervades the structures and practices of Rome's world, which explains its hatred for and rejection of Jesus (3:20–21; 7:7). In that rejection, judgment is taking place in the present in Jesus since God has given to him the role of judge (3:19; 5:22–23, 27, 30). Those who refuse to receive Jesus are already condemned (3:18). Conversely, the giving of life or the vindication or resurrection of the righteous is under way in Jesus because God has also given this role to him (5:21, 25). Those who do receive him have already passed from death to eternal life or, to translate it more literally, to "life of the age" (3:14–17; 5:24).[14] In chapter 8 (below), I will elaborate the claims of "eternal life" in relation to the imperial claims of "eternal Rome," explicating the importance of both the present and future dimensions of John's eschatology. But here we see that the Gospel reveals this eschatological process of judgment and vindication to be underway in daily life. No inscriptions or statue announced it to the Ephesians as they went about their daily lives in this capital of the Roman province of Asia. The Gospel reveals it. It is insider knowledge. It provides a framework for understanding the Roman Empire as being under God's judgment, which is already taking place. It attests the identity of Jesus-believers as those who have already been judged and vindicated. They already know "life of the age," or eternal life. And this eschatological framework provides the basis for determining levels of accommodation and participation in imperial Ephesus. There can be no easy alliance for Jesus-believers with Rome's world, which is already experiencing God's judgment.

Yet having said this, we recognize that the Gospel does not completely recast the messianic eschatological scenarios. While declaring that the messianic intervention is underway now in Jesus in an ongoing process of judgment and vindication, the Gospel is also clear that this process will not last forever. There will also be a cosmic intervention and transformation. So the Gospel speaks in the future tense of a coming judgment

(5:28–29; 12:48). There will be a future resurrection. Jesus will raise the dead in the resurrection at the last day, some to life and some to condemnation (5:29; 6:40). Jesus talks of overcoming the "ruler of the world," who will be driven out (12:31), has no power over Jesus (14:30), and has been condemned (16:11).

Though often interpreted as the devil, it seems much more convincing to identify "the ruler of the world" as Pilate, agent of Roman power.[15] The Gospel does not refer to Satan as a ruler, and the world that rejects Jesus (1:10–11) is shown by the Gospel's crucifixion narrative to comprise Rome's empire, represented by the governor Pilate and his Jerusalem allies. The Gospel uses the language of "ruler" to refer to members of this ruling alliance (3:1; 7:26) and not to supernatural beings. Van Tilborg points out a significant interface with the Ephesian inscriptions where the term "ruler" (ἄρχων, *archōn*) similarly designates elites with leadership roles in the city.[16] Moreover, Jesus declares to Pilate that Pilate has no power over him (19:11), echoing Jesus' statement of 14:30 that "the ruler of this world . . . has no power over me" (NRSV). Jesus' overcoming of Pilate takes place in his resurrection, in which Roman power is exposed to be no match for God's life-giving power. Jesus' resurrection signifies and anticipates the final demise of Rome's empire at the coming judgment, when "those who have done evil [will come out] to the resurrection of condemnation" (5:29 NRSV).[17]

My concern is not, as so often in Johannine studies, to reconcile or more accurately to account for these varying eschatological assertions about the present and the future by resorting to theories of redactors and developing versions of the Gospel (however possible they may be). It is, rather, to recognize the function of both affirmations existing side by side in the final form of the Gospel and in relation to the messianic traditions evoked by the title Messiah/Christ and in relation to the daily reality of the Roman Empire. The affirmations disclose that in relation to judgment, there is no escape. The present world under Rome's rule, evaluated as evil (7:7), is already condemned (3:18–19) and will be condemned (5:29; 12:48). It is already judged in its refusal to listen to Jesus' revelation of God's will, and it will be judged. The representative of its power has been declared in words (14:30; 19:11) and shown in resurrecting action (John 20–21) to have no power over Jesus in anticipation of God's rule over all things.

Such a presentation, such rhetoric of distance, also has a social function. It provides Jesus-believers in Ephesus with an analysis of the empire that has crucified him and of the ruling power that in alliance with local elites shapes their everyday world. It is evil, it has rejected God's agent, it is devoid of life (dead), it is judged already, it is powerless. These messages are certainly not those proclaimed each day in vibrant, busy, Ephesus, where there are considerable levels of power and status, participation and accommodation, honor and benefit. The Gospel's dualistic and eschatological claims indicate that social interaction with and accommodation to such a world under God's judgment imposes considerable difficulties for Jesus-believers. Their "life" resides now in the community of those who believe Jesus is the Christ, agent of God's purposes and greater than Rome's emperor. Such an approach does not seem to mean complete withdrawal (17:15; cf. the cry of Rev 18:4, "Come out from her"), but it does suggest considerable differentiation, distance, and commitment to a social alternative or antisociety.

Son of Man

The thirteen[18] uses of this title in the Gospel have been subject to much debate, and the issues are multiple.[19] Again my focus will be its role in the Gospel's neglected imperial negotiation, notably on the interaction among the various biblical, imperial, and Gospel intertexts that the title evokes and the particular emphases that emerge in the Gospel's use of it.[20]

While the term is used of and by (with one exception, 12:34) the human figure Jesus, the emphasis does not fall on his humanity per se.[21] Rather, it falls on his heavenly origin, his mediatory or revelatory role, involving the eschatological realities of life and judgment, his descent from and ascent to heaven, and his exaltation to heaven through crucifixion. The first reference in 1:51 culminates the opening chapter's christological declarations—Word (1:1, 14), Son (1:18), Lamb of God (1:29, 36), rabbi/teacher (1:38), Messiah/Christ (1:17, 41), one of whom Moses and the prophets wrote (1:45), Son of God, King of Israel (1:49)—so any attempt to isolate meaning that is associated only with Son of Man is dubious.[22] With its echoes of the ladder of Jacob's dream (Gen 28:10–22) and image of heavenly messengers or agents of divine purposes ascending and descending on the Son of Man, John 1:51 presents a mediatory or revelatory role for Jesus as the Son of Man. He is the connection between heaven and earth, the locus of communication between the two, the place of revelation, the one sanctioned by God (also 3:13; 6:62). The descent of the Son of Man *from heaven* guarantees the reliability of his revelation (3:13). The refusal to recognize that any other figure has descended from and reentered heaven (3:13a) not only underlines this authoritative revelation, but is, as I argued in chapter 4 above, also polemic against claims about Moses (mentioned in 3:14a).[23]

The use of Son of Man in this context (echoing Dan 7, as I will argue below) indicates, though, a further element in the polemic. The polemic seems to be not only against Moses the revealer[24] but also against claims that God gave Moses rule over the world (Ezekiel the Tragedian, *Exagōgē* 75, 86; Philo, *Mos.* 1.155–157). By identifying Jesus as Son of Man, the verse establishes Jesus' participation in God's rule. Evoking Daniel's Son of Man figure (see below), Jesus is entrusted with an "everlasting dominion" and kingship (Dan 7:13–14). Moreover, his coronation comes about because God has "lifted up" Jesus as Son of Man into heaven to share God's rule. The verb "lifted up" (ὑψόω, *hypsoō*) is used in three of the Son of Man sayings (3:14; 8:28; 12:32–34), probably with a double meaning of "lifting up" on the cross and "exalting" to be with God (cf. Ps 89:19 [88:20 LXX], where it refers to exalting the Davidic king). Jesus is exalted or glorified (13:1, 31) in returning to the Father, from whence he came, through his lifting upon the cross. The cross, instrument of Roman control and social shame, is reframed as an enthronement, a glorification, the revelation of God's presence and life-giving power in the resurrection and exaltation/ascension of Jesus.

Son of Man is used in relation to two further eschatological realities that Jesus reveals. God "has given him authority to execute judgment, because he is the Son of Man" (5:27 NRSV; 9:35–39). This judgment is effected in the present, ironically: those who "lift up" or crucify the Son of Man judge themselves by rejecting the one who bears the divine name, "I am" (3:18; 8:28). The reverse of judgment is eternal life or "life of the age," which Jesus as Son of Man also reveals (6:27, 53, 62–63; also 3:14–15). As Son of Man he does God's will and speaks God's words (8:28b).

This focus on the relationship between Jesus and God along with the shared language of "Son of Man" indicates that the term evokes the eschatological heavenly figure, "one like a son of man," of Daniel 7:13–14 (RSV) and *1 Enoch* 37–71.[25] The use of the common apocalyptic phrase in "You will see heaven opened" in the first use of the title in John 1:51,[26] and the linguistic echo of Daniel 7:14 in John 5:27, where God gives (everlasting) "authority" or "dominion" (ἐξουσίαν, *exousian*) to the Son of Man, confirms this connection. Daniel 7:13–14 completes Daniel's vision of four beasts or world empires, Babylon (lion), the Medes (bear), Persia (leopard), and the Greeks (dragon), including Antiochus IV Epiphanes (7:1–8). Then follows a vision of the heavenly throne room in which God enacts judgment over the last beast, thus revealing the quest for world domination to be an action against God. God removes dominion from the beast and gives it to

> one like a son of man coming with the clouds of heaven. And he came to the Ancient One and was presented before him. To him was given dominion and glory and kingship, that all peoples, and nations, and languages should serve him. His dominion/authority is an everlasting dominion/authority, which shall not pass away; and his kingship is one that shall never be destroyed. (7:13–14 RSV/NRSV)

The "one like a son of man" is entrusted with God's everlasting reign over all the nations. He ends all human empires (Rome) and establishes God's kingdom. Though not identified explicitly as a king, the figure functions in this way to represent or reveal God's reign. He is the locus of God's sovereignty forever.[27] While the heavenly origins, divine agent, and revelatory role of the figure correspond to John's presentation of Jesus, one important feature, that of judgment, is absent. In Daniel's scene, God exercises the judgment, not the Son of Man, and God executes judgment before handing over authority to the Son of Man.

However, this link between the Son of Man and judgment (as well as with the title Messiah) is made in the first-century text *1 Enoch* 37–71. Here the Son of Man rules (69:27–29) and is a heavenly judge (concealed with God before creation; 48:6). And as we saw in the previous section, the Son of Man is also the Messiah (48:10; 52:4). He exercises judgment over "the kings of the earth and the mighty landowners" (48:8), "the kings, the governors, the high officials, and landlords" (*1 En.* 62–63) as well as "the holy ones in heaven" (61:8). In this judgment, in being victorious over these evil elites (46:3–6; 62:7–12), he enacts God's purposes on earth.

The use of a title for Jesus that evokes these eschatological traditions and attributes important aspects of them to Jesus (revelation, the locus of divine activity, judgment) provides an important intertext for Jesus' identity and functions to instruct Jesus-believers about God's verdict on Rome's empire. As Son of Man, Jesus enacts God's purposes, which mean the end of the empire. His interactions with the empire show it to be under judgment: its days are numbered, its rulers condemned. In turn, Jesus reveals God's rule and purposes through his words, actions, death, and resurrection. His exaltation is a victory over Roman power and the means of his return to God, from whom he originated. These revelations about both Jesus and the empire norm, shape, and sustain an appropriately distanced way of life from Jesus-believers in Ephesus.

Titles and Images Shared between Jesus and Roman Emperors

Shepherd

The term "good shepherd" is not used of Jesus by others, but he explicitly identifies himself with it (10:11, 14), and on four further occasions he is the term's referent (10:2, 11, 12, 16). The "shepherd and sheep" image pervades 10:1–21 and makes a brief return in the next scene in 10:26–28. Throughout, the passage contrasts the good shepherd and his care for the sheep with "a thief and bandit/brigand" (10:1, 8, 10), the stranger (10:5), and the hired hand (10:12), whose voice the sheep do not know and from whom they flee (10:5). The contrast creates an antithesis between a good or model shepherd and false or bad shepherds. Key elements of the antithesis emerge in the passage. The good or noble shepherd cares so much for the sheep that he is willing to give even his life for them (10:11, 15, 17–18);[28] a "bad" shepherd is interested only in his own safety (10:12–13). The good shepherd is concerned for the "abundant life" of the sheep; a bad shepherd "steals and kills and destroys" (10:10).

With Jesus identifying himself as the good shepherd, who are the bad shepherds? In the context of chapter 9—and no break is signaled in the narrative between 9:41 and 10:1—they are those opposed to Jesus, the Pharisees (9:13, 15, 16) and the *Ioudaioi* (9:18, 22), the leaders of the nation allied with Rome and their supporters.[29] In 9:40 members of this elite governing alliance are identified as "blind" and unable to "see" themselves accurately as sinners. Wherein lies their sin? Jesus' statements about the thieves, robbers/brigands, and hirelings not caring for and destroying the sheep are strong criticisms of the leaders and the sinful imperial society that they oversee, and from which they benefit (10:8, 10, 12–13).

As many have recognized, this discourse in which Jesus employs the divine name "I am" in 10:11, 14 (cf. Exod 3:14, God's revelation to another shepherd, Moses) to identify himself as the good shepherd draws the shepherd/sheep image from Israel's traditions about the relationship of the people with God.[30] Psalms,[31] prophets,[32] and later writers[33] use the image "shepherd" to depict God's care for the people, frequently in relation to liberation from Egyptian and Babylonian rule. Especially relevant for its use in John 10 in the context of chapter 9 is the common practice of identifying Israel's leaders as shepherds.[34] These identifications can be positive,[35] but often they are negative, denoting failed leadership.[36]

The classic intertext is Ezekiel 34, where God condemns the shepherds of Israel, the elite leadership, because the societal structure, over which they preside and which they maintain, benefits themselves but harms the people. The shepherds feed and clothe themselves but not the sheep (34:2–3, 8). They have neglected the people and so have not "strengthened the weak, healed the sick, bound up the injured, brought back the strayed, sought the lost, but with force and harshness you have ruled them" (34:4 NRSV alt.). But not only is their rule self-benefiting; it also is at the expense of most of the people. Not only have they neglected the people; the elite rulers also are in the process of destroying them: "I will rescue my sheep from their mouths, so that they may not be food for them" (34:10 NRSV). God will intervene to save the people by gathering them together, feeding them, healing the sick, and protecting them (34:11–22). God will "feed them with justice" (34:16). God will be king, but God's agent will be "one shepherd, my servant David" (34:23–24). An eschatological age of peace or wholeness comprising security, abundant fertility, and God's presence will follow (34:25–30).

Jesus' self-identification with the divine name "I am" and the title "good shepherd" (John 10:11, 14) allies him with the vision set out in Ezekiel 34. He reveals God's presence and purposes in his ministry (John 4:34). His signs of turning water into abundant wine (2:1–11), providing much bread (6:1–14), and healing the sick (5:2–15; chap. 9), and his judgment of an evil world (3:19–20; 5:22; 7:7) show him to be the divinely commissioned shepherd of the people, enacting God's life-giving and just purposes. In turn, the false or bad shepherds, the hirelings, thieves and robbers are Israel's Rome-allied leaders in conflict with Jesus. As in Ezekiel 34, they destroy the sheep (10:10) while they pursue only their own well-being at the expense of the sheep (10:12–13). The intertext of Ezekiel 34 exposes the nature of their rule as self-serving, self-enriching, and destructive. It also declares God's verdict on it. God is against these shepherds (Ezek 34:10) and will destroy "the fat and strong" (34:16).

Several further aspects intensify the scene's condemnation of the leaders. First, not only are the Jerusalem leaders and their followers condemned as the immediate participants in the exchange, but so too by association are their Roman allies. As I have indicated, Roman provincial administration typically formed alliances with local elites. The Jerusalem leadership holds power as allies of Rome in maintaining the current societal structure. Jesus' attack on the Jerusalem leaders is an attack on the whole imperial system, which they represent and enforce.

Further, rulers and leaders were imaged as shepherds not only in Israel's traditions such as Ezekiel 34 but also among Greeks[37] and Romans as part of a longer tradition of the emperor or king ruling for the benefit of the flock. Suetonius has the emperor Tiberius reject a provincial governor's requests for increased taxes by saying, "It is the part of a good shepherd to shear his flock, not skin it" (*Tib.* 32). Not only does the passage reflect the same self-enriching practice condemned in the Ezekiel 34 passage, but it also adds a level of measured calculation to the practice. Philo describes the role of the tutor and adviser Macro in urging the "quarrelsome and contentious" emperor Gaius Caligula to improved and more appropriate public behavior. Philo has Macro refer to Gaius as the "sovereign of earth and sea" and "a shepherd and master of the flock" (*Embassy* 44, 52). In his discourse *Kingship 1*, Dio Chrysostom says that kings should care for people as shepherds care for sheep (15–16). He admonishes that the king should be "a shepherd of his people, not . . . a caterer and banqueter at their expense" (13). In *Kingship 4* he quotes Homer and speaks against the excessive use of power in reminding the emperor Trajan that the emperor is a "shepherd of peoples," who is to "protect flocks, not . . . to slaughter, butcher, and skin them" (43–44).[38] These texts, part of a tradition that depicts the benevolent shepherd-king/emperor who is concerned for the well-being of his flock/subjects, are also intertexts for John 10:1–21, though, not surprisingly, they have been given little attention by scholars pursuing more isolated "religious" readings.[39] The presentation of Jesus as the good shepherd raises questions about the identification of the emperor as a "good" shepherd and about the common depiction of the imperial system as benevolent and a channel for divine blessing. For many in Ephesus living around the subsistence level (as described in chap. 3 above), life in the empire did not seem especially blessed nor the empire especially benevolent. The intertexts of Ezekiel 34 and traditions of benevolent imperial rule inform and contrast with Jesus' claim to be the good shepherd who enacts God's purposes for security and fertility, and who is even willing to give his life for the life of the sheep.

Moreover, the condemnation of the imperial rulers and their Jerusalem allies is intensified by the description of the "bad" shepherds as "thieves and robbers/brigands" (10:1, 8, 10). The first term, *kleptēs* (κλέπτης), refers to those who steal property that belongs to others and to kidnappers (e.g., Philo, *Spec. Laws* 4.7–19). Jesus' use of the term identifies the ruling elite as administering a system that enables them to steal from the people. Taxes, tributes, and rents were common means of doing so. Under attack here is the proprietary understanding of rule operative in the Roman Empire, which saw rulers as, in Philo's words, "masters of all properties throughout the land including those over which private citizens have apparent control." Whatever is "kept in the treasuries of subjects belongs to rulers rather than to those who have them" (Philo, *Planting* 56–57). The argument is not the modern notion of sacred individual property as much as it is an issue of who exercises control or sovereignty. "The earth is the Lord's, and the fullness thereof" (Ps 24:1 KJV).[40] The just (righteous) use, as Ezekiel 34 makes clear, means not the hoarding of most of the resources by a few, the typical imperial practice, but ensuring adequate provision for the life of all. The elite's rule is divinely condemned.

In addition to being thieves, the ruling elite is condemned as "robbers/brigands" (λῃστής, *lēstēs*). This term refers to disaffected, often peasant, groups with a charismatic leader, groups that appear in agrarian empires like Rome's and are in difficult political-economic circumstances.[41] They express their disaffection through attacks on elite property and personnel. While brigands were often supported by peasant populations, the ruling elite definitely regard them as threats to the socioeconomic and political order and seek to exterminate them. No fan of such figures, Josephus records numerous outbreaks of banditry in first-century Palestine, sometimes naming leaders[42] and sometimes using general summary statements to suggest a recurring problem.[43]

In a daring move in this passage, John's Jesus uses the term "bandits" to refer to the Jerusalem elite, allies of Rome. In so defining their societal role, he reverses the status quo, locating these rulers now "on the other side of the tracks." He labels them and their rule as threats to general well-being and social order. Society should be defended *against them*! He unmasks their rule as illegitimate and violent, whereby they grab as much power and wealth for themselves as possible, regardless of the harm to the rest of the population (so Ezek 34). This analysis seems to be confirmed: in the tense interactions over power between the Jerusalem leaders and Rome's representative Pilate before Jesus' crucifixion, they make alliance with a *lēstēs* (λῃστής) Barabbas, one who employs violence against the imperial elite. They choose to release one of their own (John 18:40)! They crucify Jesus.

The Gospel context and the cultural intertexts show that Jesus' use of the good shepherd image contests the leadership of those who administer the imperial system. The image is not to be spiritualized, as Kanagaraj does in claiming that the bad shepherds "steal people away from the path of obedience to Christ possibly by offering wrong teaching and theology."[44] It is not primarily a matter of teaching and theology but rather societal injustice and exploitative leadership practices. These leaders cannot be good shepherds because they rule to benefit themselves materially and harm the people materially. No matter what they claim, they do not provide life and are not willing to give their lives for the life of society. They steal food, shelter, clothing, health, and safety from the people. They are illegitimate and violent rulers. Jesus-believers in Ephesus, urges the Gospel, cannot follow such violent "strangers." Violence is forbidden to Jesus' followers (18:36). They must "flee from" them and follow the good shepherd, whose voice they know (10:4–5). Happy accommodation with a thieving, illegitimate, violent, destructive, and life-threatening imperial system is not possible. They are called to an alternative allegiance in an antisociety, with a different set of practices. The title "good shepherd" as a descriptor of Jesus in contrast to imperial and allied leaders forms part of the Gospel's rhetoric of distance.

Savior of the World

Jesus' mission is that "the world might be saved through him" (3:17 NRSV; 5:34; 10:9; 12:47). While the verb "saved" appears six times, five of which refer to Jesus' mission, the cognate noun "savior" appears only once in the Gospel. Samaritans from the city of Sychar (4:5), having heard the testimony of the unnamed woman (4:39) as well as Jesus' own "word" (4:41), believe and identify Jesus as "truly the Savior of the world" (4:42 NRSV, σωτὴρ τοῦ κόσμου, *sōtēr tou kosmou*).[45] What is the force of their declaration?

   The title "savior" was widely used in the ancient world. In the Hellenistic age, this title, along with several others, "came to be almost fixed epithets of royalty," with savior indicating that "the king represented military protection and security to his subjects . . . and the salvation of society" since deity was manifested in him.[46] The term also identifies Israel's God as the one who saves the people from Babylonian exile (Isa 43:3, 11; 45:15, 21–22), who sustains life (Philo, *Spec. Laws* 2.198), and who is a benefactor of the whole world (Philo, *Sobriety* 55). It is also used for gods such as Zeus (Plutarch, *Mor.* 830B). An Ephesian inscription links Zeus Soter with the emperor Hadrian (IEph 4.1243). In Ephesus the feminine form identifies Artemis as a savior in acknowledging the goddess's beneficial intervention in people's lives (4.1255, 1265). The latter inscription (4.1265) typically links her with the Sebastoi, or emperors. The term "savior" also honors high-status officials and those who benefit human affairs.[47] Its use for emperors is widespread throughout the empire.[48] An Ephesian inscription identifies Julius Caesar as "savior of human life" (IEph 2.251). The assembly of the province of Asia acknowledges that "providence" has blessed the province "by producing Augustus and filling him with virtue for the benefaction of humankind, sending us and those after us a savior who put an end to war and established all things."[49] As savior, Augustus ended the civil war and blessed the world with many benefactions.[50] Philo identifies Gaius Caligula as being "recently regarded as a savior and benefactor, who would pour new streams of blessing on Asia" (*Emb.* 22). A number of Ephesian inscriptions identify Hadrian as *sōtēr*.[51]

With such diverse uses it is impossible to claim an exclusive interface between "Savior of the world" in John 4:42 and the Roman emperor. But in addition to the fact that the passage attributes to Jesus a title used of the emperor, five further factors suggest that an interface with the emperor intertexts is at least one dimension of this multivalent scene between the Samaritan believers and Jesus.

First, the political and, more specifically, anti-imperial, associations of "savior" are to be recognized. These political-imperial associations contrast with much contemporary individualistic and spiritualized usage for the term "Savior." When the title is used for God in the Hebrew Scriptures, it frequently appears in communal-political contexts to denote God's interactions with Israel and the nations. So in Isaiah 45:15, 21 God is Savior in freeing the exiles from Babylonian hegemony. Similarly, in Psalm 79:9 the psalmist seeks the help of "God our Savior" (so 78:9 LXX) after the Babylonians have violated Jerusalem and the temple. In Psalm 65:5 the people's deliverance by "God our Savior, the hope of all the ends of the earth" (so 64:6 LXX), and God's care for the whole of creation are in view. Judas Maccabeus, successfully battling the armies of the imperialist Antiochus IV Epiphanes, seeks help from God, "Savior of Israel," by recalling God's help for David in defeating the Philistines (1 Macc 4:30). The title "Savior" evokes God's intervention to save the people from imperial interventions. It recalls the fundamental affirmation that God is sovereign of the world, including the nations, and that all are subject to God's purposes. Accordingly, it resists the empire even while it imitates it.

Second, as Craig Koester points out in relation to John 4:39–42, "by going out of Sychar to meet Jesus, inviting him into their town, and calling him "Savior," the Samaritans give Jesus a welcome similar to those granted to visiting rulers."[52] Koester cites examples from Josephus concerning rituals whereby cities welcome Vespasian (*J.W.* 3.459; 7.70–71) and Titus (*J.W.* 4.112–113; 7.100–103, 119). Thus, with the appearance of Jesus, the procession into the city, the welcoming crowds, hymnic acclamation, and speeches (but no cultic act!), the scene (like Jesus' later entry into Jerusalem, John 12:12–19) employs features commonly associated with Jewish, Greek, and Roman entrance processions for ruling figures.[53]

Third, Jesus seeks to reconcile Judeans and Samaritans, people who have been at odds with each other over religious-political differences. "Judeans have no dealings with Samaritans" (4:9b). Both Jesus and the woman function in the scene not just as individual figures but also, by frequently using plural language and speaking on behalf of their people, they function as representatives of these two peoples.[54] The representative dimensions of the woman and Jesus emerge as they discuss worship, an issue of national identity and power (4:19–22). The woman, speaking on behalf of Samaritan people, points out that "*our* ancestors worshipped on this mountain," referring to the sacred Mt. Gerizim (Josephus, *Ant.* 18.85). She continues by using an emphatic second-person plural pronoun (ὑμεῖς, *hymeis*) to refer to Jesus along with all Judeans, "but yous/you people[55] say that the place where people must worship is in Jerusalem" (John 4:20). She references a long history of dispute between Jerusalem and Samaria and Gerizim over the legitimate place for a temple in which to worship Israel's God. In 128 BCE, the ultimate statement of the "worship only in Jerusalem" position was made by the Judean John Hyrcanus, who destroyed the temple on Gerizim (Josephus, *J.W.* 1.63–66; *Ant.* 13.255–256, Cutheans are Samaritans).

The animosity had not subsided by the first century CE and had been regularly renewed.[56] During the Roman governorship of Coponius (6–9 CE), some Samaritans defiled the Jerusalem temple during Passover by scattering human bones through it (Josephus, *Ant.* 18.29–30). Several decades later, in 52, Samaritans attacked and killed Galilean pilgrims, thus sparking several rounds of violent retaliation and Roman military and administrative intervention (*Ant.* 20.118–136). The Judean Josephus, writing at the end of the century, expresses his hostility by referring to Samaritans as Cutheans, a negative term highlighting Samaritan descent from foreign colonists from Cuthah (*Ant.* 9.288).

Jesus' response in John 4:21 and unflattering contrastive comment in verse 22a continues the representative language ("you [plural] worship; . . . we worship"). In verse 21 he attempts to move past the "Gerizim-versus-Jerusalem" hostility by pointing to a new time. "The hour is coming when neither on this mountain nor in Jerusalem will yous/you people worship the Father." Again the second-person pronoun "you" is plural, referring to the Samaritan people. His statement recognizes that Judeans will not prevail over Samaritans but that both Samaritan and Judean will be involved together in a new temple where worship is in spirit and in truth. Post 70, his statement recognizes the leveling of the playing field with the demise of the Jerusalem temple by Roman action, the overcoming of national disputes, and the existence of an inclusive and international community of worshippers. In this context, Jesus' claim in 4:22b about salvation seems to have a double meaning. "Salvation is from the Judeans" in that Jesus' ministry is set in continuity with the history of Jewish experience with God (e.g., Moses, 5:45–47). But for Samaritans, the creation of an inclusive international worshipping community also means salvation or rescue or deliverance from centuries of Judean scorn and harassment. Literally, their salvation is "from the Judeans" in that such an internationally inclusive community delivers them from Judean power.[57] In ending dominance and effecting such reconciliation rather than reinforcing hostility, Jesus is "the Savior of the world."

Fourth, the scene evokes a further aspect of the Samaritan colonial past. In verse 16 Jesus instructs the woman to call her husband and in verse 18 discloses that she has had five husbands as well as her present "man," who is not her husband. Commentators have sought to explain this rather strange reference in various ways, whether as levirate marriage or divorce or death or her "sexual promiscuity,"[58] while others protest that the text (unlike generations of especially male interpreters) makes no mention of immorality.[59] Whatever her *personal* circumstances, the fact that the woman is a representative figure points to a significant aspect of Samaritan historical experience. Craig Koester argues that the language is a "double entendre" referring to Samaria's colonial history.[60] Second Kings 17:24 identifies five peoples that colonized Samaria. Josephus similarly identifies five colonizing powers (*Ant.* 9.288). And, like the woman's husbands, there is a sixth and present colonial master, Rome, allied with the hated Judean elite. Herod, king of the Jews by Rome's will (*Ant.* 16.311), promotes Roman presence in Samaria by rebuilding the city of Samaria and renaming it Sebaste (a Greek form of "Augustus"), with a temple dedicated to the emperor (Josephus, *J. W.* 403). He also settled a number of foreigners there (Josephus, *Ant.* 15.296–298). Conflict with Rome continued through the first century. In the 30s CE, the Roman governor Pilate slaughtered a large number of Samaritans who had followed a charismatic prophet to Mt. Gerizim to locate sacred vessels supposedly buried there by Moses (*Ant.* 18.85–87). In the 60s CE, Samaritans revolted against Rome. They gathered on Mt. Gerizim, and when they refused to surrender, 11,600 were killed (Josephus, *J.W.* 3.307–315). The Samaritan use of the imperial title "Savior of the world" for Jesus recognizes him as one who reveals a greater sovereignty than that of Rome's. The presence of the adverb translated "truly" or "indeed" in 4:42 (ἀληθῶς, *alēthōs*) suggests a recognition of legitimacy or actuality in contrast to one who is falsely or illegitimately identified as Savior. Jesus is more truly Savior than the emperor. The force of the adverb suggests their withdrawal of ultimate allegiance from Rome in the hope of indeed, truly, finding deliverance by some means through Jesus from their current master.

Fifth, briefly, we can examine the contribution of the term "world." I have argued above in chapter 6 that this term denotes opposition to God's purposes in all its forms (1:10). This includes the opposition of Rome and its Judean allies. The Roman governor Pilate, representative of Roman power, is identified as "the ruler of this world," but he has no power over Jesus (14:30; 19:11). Applied to Jesus, the term "Savior of the world" recognizes him as the one who manifests God's ultimate and saving sovereignty over the nations. He is the Savior from "the ruler of this world." The Samaritan welcome enacts a variant vision of the conversion of the nations who turn to acknowledge Israel's God and worship at Jerusalem (e.g., Isa 2:2–4; 25:6–10; Mic 4:1–4). But in the international version advocated by John's Jesus, instead of coming to Jerusalem, they form local communities as places of worship (see chap. 10 below).

For Jesus-believers in Ephesus, the use of this common imperial term for Jesus suggests more than just a borrowing of common language to articulate his significance. It suggests a contesting of the emperor's right to this title. It ascribes sovereignty of the earth to the God manifested by Jesus. It claims that the world that Rome has supposedly "saved" and for which it is given honor in numerous inscriptions and texts is a world that in fact needs saving from Rome. The confession of the Samaritans provides an example for Jesus-believers in Ephesus to follow in "truly" recognizing Jesus as the only Savior of the world. That means, as Koester argues (following Rensberger), "a revolution of consciousness," a revelation of the evil and oppressive nature of the current Roman world, and a rejection of violence and accommodation as means of engagement.[61] Local communities of Jesus-believers are to live and worship God as inclusive communities and at some cultural distance from imperial society. This distance would include nonparticipation in any acts of worship directed to or related to imperial power and personnel in Ephesus.

King of the Jews

The title "king," "king of Israel," or "king of the Jews" is used sixteen times for Jesus in the Gospel. Twelve of these appear in scenes involving Pilate and Jesus, and at Jesus' crucifixion, in 18:33–39 and 19:3–21, which present Jesus' death as his enthronement.[62] Since I have touched on some matters pertaining to kingship in sections above, and since the Pilate-Jesus scene will be the focus of chapter 11 below, this discussion of the identification of Jesus as king will be brief. The following five points can be identified for attending to the intertexts of competing traditions.

First to be observed is the lengthy and central tradition in the Hebrew Scriptures of God as King of Israel (Ps 24:1–10) and of the world (Ps 47:1–9). The title signifies God's saving and judging role of establishing rule over all nations, effective in the present but to be established fully and transformatively in the future (Isa 24:21–23; Zech 9:9–10, quoted in Jesus' entry into Jerusalem in John 12:15; Zech 14, esp. 14:9). The image of God the king asserts God's sovereignty over the earth and nations. When the Jerusalem leaders declare in 19:15 that "we have no king but Caesar," they disavow this tradition.

Second, God makes an eternal covenant with David (2 Sam 7:11–17) that his descendents will be Israel's kings as representatives of God's just and life-giving purposes. Royal Psalms such as Psalm 89 celebrate this covenant, whereas Psalm 72 elaborates the duties of the king as representative of God's reign in ruling justly, protecting the weak and poor, overcoming enemies, and ensuring fertility. The Deuteronomic history of Israel and Judah assesses kings as "good" or "bad" according to their faithfulness to these sorts of tasks (1–2 Kings). A tradition of popular kingship sought unsuccessfully to claim a place in this tradition. Nathanael's ascription of the title "King of Israel" to Jesus (John 1:49) evokes this sort of kingship, as does the people's welcome to Jesus as he enters Jerusalem (John 12:15). Kingship is God-given (and Rome-given) and cannot be enacted by the people (6:15).

Third, the term for "king," βασιλεύς (*basileus*), was used for various Gentile kings, including the Roman king or emperor. Josephus refers to the emperors in general with this noun (*J.W.* 3.351; 5.563), to the Flavian line of Vespasian and his sons (*J.W.* 4.596), and to Titus "under God's care" (*J.W.* 5.58–60), as do various New Testament texts (1 Tim 2:2; 1 Pet 2:13, 17; Rev 17:12). Dio Chrysostom in *Kingship 1*, referring to the emperor Trajan, declares the king is to be a father to the people (22). It is to the emperor that the chief priests, part of the *Ioudaioi* (John 19:12), declare their exclusive loyalty, renouncing their covenant identity and allegiance to God (19:15): "We have no king [*basilea*, βασιλέα] but Caesar" (RSV). Rome ruled through alliances with local elites, so Rome appointed or recognized local kings who were loyal to Rome. Herod is one such king, identified as "King of the Jews" (Josephus, *Ant.* 15.373–379; 16:311; Matt 2:1–3).[63] Rome regarded as sedition any other claims to kingship. They attacked and executed those in Judea and Galilee who set themselves up as kings in a tradition of popular kingship.[64] The attempt to make Jesus king in John 6:15 poses this danger both for Rome and for Jesus and his followers as do Nathanael's ascriptions of the title "King of Israel" to Jesus (John 1:49) and the people's welcome to Jesus as he enters Jerusalem (12:15). The *Ioudaioi* show themselves to be allies of the emperor in charging Jesus with setting himself up as a king, and they raise the question of Pilate's loyalty to the Roman emperor/king if he releases Jesus: "If you release this man, you are not Caesar's friend; every one who makes himself a king sets himself against Caesar" (John 19:12 RSV).

Fourth, when Pilate asks Jesus if he is "King of the Jews," he makes a charge of sedition and insurrection (18:33). Jesus' answer first concerns the source of Pilate's information, thereby again exposing the alliance between the Jerusalem leaders and Pilate the Roman governor (18:34–35). Then he establishes the origin of his kingship (18:36): "My kingdom/kingship/empire[65] is not from this world." This statement does not mean that Jesus is nonpolitical or apolitical, as commonly asserted.[66] To the contrary. He does not deny having a kingdom/empire or being a king. His point, repeated three times in 18:36 for emphasis, is one of origin. His kingship comes from God, not from Rome. It does not derive from the world, which resists God's purposes (1:10–11). Rather, he enacts God's good and just and life-giving reign. This reign materially benefits all people, not just the elite, no matter what their propaganda. And it thereby threatens elite self-benefiting rule. This reign is also marked by nonviolence: "If my kingship/kingdom/empire were from this world, my followers would be fighting to keep me from being handed over" (18:36 NRSV alt.). The contrast is with Rome's legendary prowess in military violence. The term for "followers" is the same one used in 18:3 and 12 to denote the "temple police," who with the governor's soldiers arrest Jesus. Military violence is evoked in order to be contrasted with nonviolence. And Jesus' reign expresses his God-given mission: "For this I have come into the world [cf. 3:17–19], to bear witness to the truth" (18:37 RSV). The term "truth," a key Johannine word, expresses the Hebrew Scriptures' sense of God's faithfulness to God's commitments to redeem or save Israel (Exod 34:6; Pss 25:10; 40:10–11; 108:4; 146:7). For John, God is the "true God" (17:3) acting faithfully in Jesus to manifest God's purposes and reign. To "know the truth" and be set free (8:32) is to participate faithfully as Jesus' disciples (8:31) in God's faithful purposes, manifested by Jesus to save people from all that resists God's purposes. Jesus' kingship means bearing witness to the faithful kingship of God, which stands over against Rome's rule in the work of transforming Rome's world (19:12). Of course, Pilate cannot hear or understand talk about truth (18:37b–38a), but the fact that he crucifies Jesus suggests that he understands the danger of kings not sanctioned by Rome to the world that Rome creates and sanctions. Yet he ironically ensures Jesus' coronation by crucifying him and stubbornly proclaiming his identity as king in three languages, Hebrew, Latin, and Greek (19:19–22).

For Jesus-believers, this exchange between Pilate and Jesus clearly sets Jesus' kingship at odds with that of Rome. Again, Rome's rule is shown to be contrary to God's purposes and ways. Again, the implication is that Jesus-believers cannot make a ready peace with such an empire. Jesus' kingship, given by God and marked by different practices, requires their allegiance in an alternative community.

Fifth, van Tilborg points out that the title "king" appears in texts and inscriptions found in Ephesus for a number of kings from Ephesus's political history.[67] Two of these kings figured in the discussion of the Salutaris inscription in chapter 4 above. Salutaris's procession carried an image of King Androklos, the founder of the city, and left the city through the Koression Gate, which commemorated Androklos's founding the city following Apollo's oracle. Strabo notes that Androklos's descendents who resided in Ephesus in the first century were known as kings and were accorded honors such as front seats at the games, wearing purple robes, and presiding over sacrifices for Eleusinian Demeter (Strabo, *Geogr.* 14.1.3). Second-century Ephesian inscriptions increasingly reference King Androklos, reflecting a reassertion of the city's "sacred identity." Another king, Lysimachos, the second founder of the city, whose image was also carried in Salutaris's procession, is also named in inscriptions, though the noun "king" is often missing. These references are important because they evoke Ephesus's "sacred identity" associated with these figures of antiquity. In this Ephesian context exists another community with a "sacred identity," the Jesus-believers (see chap. 10 below), whose founder is also a king but with a greater antiquity ("in the beginning," John 1:1), and who are called to a distinctive and alternative way of life.

Son of God

As many have observed, given the use of "Father" some 120 times in the Gospel, it is somewhat surprising that "Son of God" appears only nine times (while "Son" is used some 27 times, or 29, depending on the manuscript traditions of 1:18 and 9:35). The emphasis on the Father more than on the "Son of God" is not inconsequential since it maintains the focus on God as the one from whom Jesus originates. "Origin determines one's status."[68] In addition to origin, "Son of God" is associated with confession, revealing eschatological realities, opposition to Jesus, and Jesus' relationship to God.

Four times the title appears in important confessions: John the Baptist (1:34), Nathanael (1:49), Martha (11:27), and the concluding general confessional summary of 20:31. In all of these it is associated with other titles either in apposition or in context: Lamb of God (1:29), King of Israel (1:49), and the Christ (11:27; 20:31). Its confessional use, its association with other titles, and its summative location in 20:31 suggest that the title's significance extends far beyond the nine uses and content that might be specifically associated with the term. This last point is important for not overplaying the distinction between "Son" and "Son of God"[69] since, for instance, in 3:17–18 and 5:25–26 "Son" and "Son of God" are synonyms.[70]

In addition to confessions, the title "Son of God" is associated with Jesus' God-given roles in revealing the eschatological realities of vindication or judgment (3:18) and life (5:25; 11:4; 20:31). Not surprisingly, it is also associated with opposition. In the context of the threat of being stoned (10:31–37), Jesus declares himself to be Son of God. In 19:7 before Pilate, the *Ioudaioi* declare that Jesus "ought to die because he has claimed to be Son of God." Throughout this title also denotes Jesus' relationship with God. Twice it is used with "Father" (5:25; 10:36), once with God who sends (3:17–18), and once for Jesus glorifying God (11:4). Hence the title brings together important aspects of Jesus' identity and mission: origin, relationship with God, agency, and eschatological revelation.

Various Jewish traditions identify "sons of God" as those who in relation to God are agents of God's purposes: kings (Ps 2:7); God's people (Hos 11:1); heavenly beings (Ps 89:6 [88:7 LXX, lit., "sons of God"]); the righteous, wise, persecuted but vindicated person (Wis 2:18); the Messiah (*4 Ezra* [= 2 Esd] 7:28–29). Similar identifications appear in the Greek and Roman worlds.[71] Significant for this discussion is the use of the term for Roman emperors.

A number of the inscriptions from Ephesus attest the use of the title "Son of God" for Roman emperors through the first century[72] (Greek: *theou huios*, θεοῦ υἱός; Latin: *divi filius*[73]). Augustus is "son of God."[74] Nero is "son of God Claudius and descendant of God Caesar Augustus."[75] Titus is "son of God Vespasian."[76] Domitian is also "son of God Vespasian."[77] Trajan is "son of God" and "son of God Nerva."[78] The title denotes origin as well as divine legitimation or sanction for the exercise of ruling power. As van Tilborg argues, the intertextual relationship—or the interference, as he calls it—between John's Gospel and inscriptions employing this imperial title is "mainly oppositional" since in the inscriptions this title is reserved for the emperors and the Gospel ascribes it to Jesus.[79]

This claim of opposition is correct but it does not go far enough. As van Tilborg observes, in imperial practice, the "son of God" title claims origin from a divine figure since "origin determines one's status." The title ascribes status as "the texts . . . accentuate more the fact that the emperor-*father* is God than the fact that the present emperor is son of God."[80] John's Gospel accomplishes the same emphasis by using "Father" for God much more often than it uses "Son of God" for Jesus (see chap. 9 below). This Father sanctions or "consecrates" Jesus, Son of God (10:36). But it is precisely in the type of fathers that the oppositional dynamic of the term is most forceful. They are not equally competing powers. The Father God from whom Jesus originates, derives status, gains legitimacy, and acquires his mission is not a deified emperor. This Father God was "in the beginning" (Gen 1:1; John 1:1). Antiquity is authority.[81]

A further dimension is to be recognized. In 19:7 the *Ioudaioi* accuse Jesus of claiming "to be the Son of God" and assert that this violation of the (unspecified) law merits death.[82] Whatever law is in view, and given that these leaders are allies with Rome and addressing the Roman governor, a claim of violating the law of treason seems as likely as the more commonly alleged claim of blasphemy: they accuse Jesus of designating himself an emperor by usurping the title and place of Rome's ruler. In relation to the term *basileus,* or "king/emperor," I observed (above) that it was sedition to claim to be a king without Rome's blessing. The same charge is made in 19:7 with the language of "Son of God." Jesus' offensive identification of himself as "Son of God," understood as a challenge to imperial power, explains the "we" of 19:7 as the alliance of Pilate with the Jewish leaders, Pilate's fear in verse 8 in understanding Jesus' imperial pretensions, his question about Jesus' origin in verse 9: "Where are you from?," his assertion of greater power over Jesus in verse 10, Jesus' counterclaim in verse 11, and the repeat of the accusation by the *Ioudaioi* in verse 12: "Everyone who makes himself a king [a synonym for son of God] sets himself against Caesar" (RSV).

The "Son of God" title embraces central affirmations about Jesus: his origin from God, intimate relationship with God, mission, authority, agency, revelation, sonship, and opposition to Jesus. This term used for the emperor in first-century Ephesus sets Jesus and the emperor in opposition in terms of who manifests divinely sanctioned purposes, power, and rule. But in the Gospel's worldview, the sanctioning deities are not equal since there is only one "true God" (17:3). Thus the title drives a wedge between the two Sons of God and elevates Jesus. Again the antithetical relationship between Jesus and empire emerges for Jesus-believers in Ephesus to comprehend and imitate in more distanced lifestyles.

Lord and God

I will discuss these two designations together because they appear together in the Gospel as Thomas confesses the risen Jesus to be "my Lord and my God" (20:28, ὁ κύριός μου καὶ ὁ θεός μου, *ho kyrios mou kai ho theos mou*). The pairing is somewhat conventional. Using exactly the same language as Thomas, the Psalmist addresses God as "my God and my Lord" (ὁ θεός μου καὶ ὁ κύριός μου; *ho theos mou kai ho kyrios mou*, Ps 34:23) and Philo identifies the God of Shem as "the Lord and God (κύριον καὶ θεόν, *kyrion kai theon*) of all the world and all that is therein" and as "master and benefactor of all the world" (*Sobriety* 53–55).

As I discussed in chapter 3 above, the phrase "Lord and God" has played a prominent part in imagined scenarios of persecution, being seen (erroneously) to echo the emperor Domitian's supposed insistence on being addressed as "Lord and our God" (Suetonius, *Dom.* 13.1–2; Martial, *Epig.* 5.8.1; 7.34.8; 8.2.6). Various issues, which I outlined in chapter 3 and will not repeat here, render the posited scenario of Domitian's increased advocacy of the imperial cult unconvincing and attendant persecution of Jesus-believers unsustainable. It simply cannot be overlooked that when the Greek writers Dio Chrysostom (*Defense* [*Or. 45*] 1) and Dio Cassius (67.13.4) refer to Domitian as "Lord and God," they employ the Greek terms δεσπότης καὶ θεός (*despotēs kai theos*), not as in John 20:28, ὁ κύριός μου καὶ ὁ θεός μου (*kyrios mou kai ho theos mou*).

Nevertheless, even if 20:28 does not echo Domitian's alleged practice, it does comprise one of three instances in the Gospel in which Jesus is probably identified as God, the others being 1:1 and 1:18.[83] If this is accurate, the title is given prominence by its location at the beginning and end of the Gospel, by its function in forming two inclusios (1:1 and 1:18 for the Prologue; 1:1 and 20:28 for the Gospel), and by its association with Jesus "in the beginning" and in his resurrection/ascension.[84] This identification as God is functional and not ontological, as posed in later christological formulations. Appropriate to John's pervasive wisdom paradigm and Jesus' revelatory role as the agent sent by God, Jesus is God in God's knowability (14:7), visibility (14:9), and audibility (14:10, 24), in manifesting God's power and beneficence.[85]

It is this understanding of Jesus being the emissary and revealer of God that seems to inform the response to the accusation by the *Ioudaioi* that Jesus makes himself equal to God (5:18) and makes himself God (10:31–33). Commonly these charges have been understood to reflect debates with the synagogue. The point has been made so often that it does not need elaborating here except to revise "with" to "within the synagogue." An intrasynagogue debate about the locus of God's revelation and presence after the temple and Jerusalem's destruction in 70 CE seems likely. But the issue is not simply a two-sided and internal question. Absent from the discussions is any consideration of the implications of this claim vis-à-vis the larger imperial context in which emperors are routinely made to be gods, in local practice as well as by Roman senatorial action, a world that synagogues had to negotiate also, as I argued in chapters 2 and 3 above. That dimension is my focus here.

The Ephesian inscriptions provide numerous examples of the language of "God" being used for emperors (Latin: *deus*; Greek: *theos*).[86] Almost all these ascriptions identify emperors as "God" only after their death and deification.[87] Some emperors are not identified as God at all (Tiberius, Caligula, Nero, Domitian). The title *kyrios* (Lord, κύριος)[88] is much less common in the first-century Ephesian inscriptions.[89] It occurs, for instance, in the Salutaris inscription (see chap. 4 above), where it designates both Trajan (IEph 1A.27 lines 16, 25–26) and, within the same line (116), both Trajan and Artemis. Plenty of evidence from throughout the empire attests its use for emperors in the second half of the first century.[90] Frenschkowski concludes that the title does not designate one a god, but its use "for the emperor is part of personal piety—it is a way of expressing a personal relation to the far away *basileus* [emperor, ruler, king] who is seen as savior, Lord, supreme judge, and guardian of public prosperity."[91] Also to be noted are a number of instances of the uses of feminine forms of "God" and "Lord" in the Ephesian inscriptions to express devotion to Artemis.[92] This is not surprising since emperors closely identified with Artemis, creating a mutual exchange of honor.[93]

The Gospel's references to Jesus as God with language commonly used for the emperor function in several ways. While numerous entities could be identified as a θεός in the Greek world, Jewish traditions, such as the Decalogue (Deut 5:6–10) and the Shema (6:4–9), almost always recognized only one legitimate usage.[94] Again this intertextuality suggests an oppositional interaction between John's ascription of the title to Jesus and imperial usage.[95] The use of the term for Jesus imitates yet contests imperial usage and suggests the illegitimacy of such claims by or for any emperor or goddess such as Artemis. Rather, the designation belongs to the one who "in the beginning" created all things, with whom Jesus is associated and whom Jesus reveals (John 1:1, 18; Gen 1:1).

Moreover, as with the "Son of God" language, the force of the term "God" is not equal in the evoked cultural intertexts. Price argues that the ascription of the term θεός (*theos*, god) to a human emperor does not in Greek thinking make the emperor equal to the gods. "The Greek gods are powers, not persons." The emperor was like a god in that he exercised power. "What is a god? The exercise of power. What is a king/emperor? God-like."[96] The use of the term "placed the emperor within the traditional religious system. He was located in an ambivalent position, higher than mortals but not fully the equal of the gods."[97] For John's Gospel, God has the ultimate power and authority "in the beginning" (Gen 1:1). Jesus shares in and manifests God's power to create (John 1:1–3), to give life (5:21), to judge (5:22).

For Jesus-believers, the societal implications of this act of relexification, the rhetoric of distance, are significant. Again compromise is not an option. There is no room for explicit or implied recognition of the emperor or of Artemis, Ephesus's civic goddess, as a god. There is one God (5:44; 17:3). This prohibition eliminates any cultic and societal participation in imperial piety. Such recognition belongs only to Jesus as the revealer of God. The drumbeat calling Jesus-believers to greater cultural distance is relentless.

Yet as van Tilborg points out, along with opposition there is also imitation. He flags the general reservation in the inscriptions to identify a living emperor as god.[98] The Gospel shares this reluctance, using the title very sparingly for Jesus, and setting it in the context of the wisdom paradigm that pervades the Gospel.

Conclusion

The eight designations for Jesus discussed in this chapter continue the Gospel's rhetoric of distance, driving a wedge between Jesus and the emperor, between Jesus-believers and daily imperial society. Musa Dube's assertion that "the Johannine Jesus now emerges fully clothed in the emperor's titles" is largely correct, though it understates John's continual presentation of the superiority of Jesus as "greater than" the emperor because Jesus is the agent of God, with God "in the beginning": and sent from God.[99] The antithetical relationships created by the interactions among the scriptural, imperial, and Gospel intertexts call into question accommodation as the way of negotiating the empire. These designations for Jesus, part of the Gospel's rhetoric of distance, seek to create greater cultural distance from the empire, a distance secured by devotion to Jesus alone.

Notes

1. Leander E. Keck, "Toward the Renewal of New Testament Christology," *NTS* 32 (1986): 362–77.

2. John's Gospel attests much questing to know and debates about Jesus' identity as the Messiah/Christ (e.g., 10:24). Issues of role, origin, revelation, and duration, all evident in the expectations above, are to the fore. In 7:25–44 the term is used six times as "people of Jerusalem" contemplate whether he is the Messiah. They consider several factors: whether the rulers know but for whatever reason keep it secret (7:26); Jesus' origin, which they ironically declare to know, whereas no one will know the Messiah's origin (7:27); the signs or works that the Messiah will do (7:31), his Galilean origin and lack of Davidic origin in Bethlehem (7:41–42). The Samaritan woman uses two criteria for wondering if Jesus is the Christ: his proclamation ("When [the Messiah] comes, he will proclaim all things to us," 4:25) and his revelations ("Come and see a man who told me all I have done," 4:29). When Jesus speaks of being lifted up, the crowd, probably understanding the image as a reference to Jesus' death, observes that the Messiah is supposed to "remain forever" (12:34). Painter, *Quest for the Messiah*, passim.

3. John 1:17, 41; 9:22; 11:27; 17:3; 20:31. Most of these six references have been considered already. As I argued in the last two chapters, 1:17 belongs to claims about divine patronage that collide with the patronage of the empire; while recognizing continuity, it exceeds claims about Moses' revelation. In 1:41 Andrew confesses to Simon Peter that he has found the Messiah. On what basis? John 1:40 refers to John's testimony, but John has not called Jesus "Christ." The content of Andrew's confession in 1:41 is unspecified, but on the basis of the rest of the Gospel, we can posit central emphases such as Jesus' agency as one sent from the Father, in intimate but submissive relationship to God, authorized to reveal in his words and actions "eternal life." Such elaborated emphases would be consistent with John's testimony in 1:29 that Jesus "takes away the sin of the world," perhaps evoking the Servant of Isa 53, who absorbs imperial violence in order to bring life to others (53:4) or the Passover lamb associated with the Israelites' deliverance from Egypt as well as his testimony in 1:30–34. In John 9:22, confession of Jesus as Messiah means to be put out of the synagogue. In 11:27, Martha's confession responds to Jesus' revelation of his eschatological role in exercising power over life and death, including the resurrection, one of the cluster of events associated with the new age (11:25–26). John 17:3 links "Christ" to the name Jesus (as in 1:17) and gives the key phrase "whom you have sent," a reference to God's action and Jesus' origin, identity, authority, and mission. The final reference in 20:31 draws together the Gospel's christological material, in association with "Son of God" (see below).

4. Or if one accepts some of the evolutionary models, a "relic" of earlier christological thinking now supplanted by the later, higher Christology. This approach, though, does not explain its ongoing presence in and contribution to the narrative, its association with other terms, or its contribution by evoking particular traditions.

5. Painter, *Quest*.

6. To restrict discussion of "messianic" expectation to passages where the term "Messiah" or "Christ" is used, rather than include any and every agent of the divine purposes and deliverance, is the helpful approach of Marinus de Jonge in his very useful survey, "Messiah," *ABD* 4:777–88. De Jonge notes that the Hebrew Scriptures do not use the noun to refer to a coming agent of God's purposes. On various "Agents of God's Activity," see Nickelsburg, *Ancient Judaism*, 89–117.

7. John 1:41 is translated in the RSV, "'We have found the Messiah' (which means Christ)," while in the NRSV, it reads, "'We have found the Messiah' (which is translated Anointed)."

8. So in Royal Psalms: 2:2–9; 18:50; 89:20, 38, 51.

9. For John's Gospel as a possible witness to messianic "views held by Palestinian Jews in the time of Jesus," see Richard Bauckham, "Messianism according to the Gospel of John," in *Chal-*

lenging Perspectives on the Gospel of John, ed. J. Lierman, WUNT 2.219 (Tübingen: Mohr Siebeck, 2006), 34–68, esp. 35.

10. See also CD 7.18–21; 19.10–11; 20.1; 1QS 9.11–12; 1QSa 2.14, 20; 1QSb 5:20–29; 4Q161 (Pesher Isa); 4QFlorilegium; Lawrence Schiffman, "Messianic Figures and Ideas in the Qumran Scrolls," in *The Messiah: Developments in Earliest Judaism and Christianity,* ed. J. H. Charlesworth (Minneapolis: Fortress, 1992).

11. Also "the Elect One" (*1 En.* 39:6; 40:5) and "the Righteous One" (38:2).

12. Bauckham, "Messianism," 57.

13. Carter, *John: Storyteller,* 86–106.

14. The language of the kingdom/empire (*basileia*) of God largely recedes and is replaced by notions of "life of the age."

15. Callahan, *Love Supreme,* 81–82; contra, for example, Kovacs, "'Now Shall the Ruler,'" 227–47. It is possible, though, that the term has a double referent for both the human figure Pilate and the powers at work through him. In destroying Jesus, Satan is active in the *Ioudaioi* (8:44), who are Rome's allies, and in Judas (13:2, 27), Rome's collaborator.

16. Van Tilborg, *Reading John,* 19–20.

17. Again Moore's claim (*Empire,* 73–74) that the Gospel indicates no end to the empire is unsustainable.

18. John 1:51; 3:13, 14; 5:27; 6:27, 53, 62; 8:28; 9:35; 12:23, 34 (2x); 13:31.

19. Meeks, "Man from Heaven," 44–72; F. J. Moloney, *The Johannine Son of Man* (Rome: Libreria Ateneo Salesiano, 1978); Delbert Burkett, *The Son of Man in the Gospel of John* (Sheffield: JSOT Press, 1991); Robert Rhea, *The Johannine Son of Man,* ATANT 76 (Zurich: Theologischer Verlag, 1990); John Ashton, *Understanding,*, 337–73.

20. I follow Schnackenburg, *John,* 1:532, in treating the sayings as a coherent entity.

21. E.g., as in the emphasis of Moloney, *Johannine Son of Man,* 213, on the "human figure of Jesus" and the incarnation.

22. Word (1:1, 14), Christ (1:17), Son (1:18), Lamb of God (1:29, 36), Rabbi/Teacher (1:38), Christ/Messiah (1:41), Son of God, King of Israel (1:49).

23. In chap. 12 I will consider the interface between Jesus' ascension and apotheosis traditions concerning Roman emperors.

24. Contra Ashton, *Understanding,* 353–54.

25. The term appears frequently in Ezekiel. God addresses Ezekiel by this term over ninety times, contrasting his human status before God and/or indicating his privileged role as the chosen spokesperson for God. For the importance of apocalyptic traditions in relation to John's use of the Son of Man figure, see Kovacs, "'Now Shall the Ruler,'" 227–47, esp. 240–46.

26. Used in both Jewish (Ezek 1:1; 3 Macc 6:18; *2 Bar.* 22:1) and Roman literature (Virgil, *Aeneid* 9.20).

27. The identity of this figure is much debated. One view sees a reference to faithful Jews but the figure is a heavenly one "like" a son of man, so it could depict an angel such as Michael (Dan 12:1). John interprets it as Jesus.

28. Neyrey in "'Noble Shepherd,'" 267–91, helpfully elucidates the shepherd giving his life for the sheep, but the focus is too constricted. In concentrating on 10:11–18, he ignores the shepherd image in 10:1–10 and overlooks the fact that the shepherd image is much more extensive than only his death.

29. See the discussion in chap. 6 above.

30. Johannes Beutler, "Der alttestamentlich-jüdische Hintergrund der Hirtenrede in Johannes 10," in *The Shepherd Discourse of John 10 and Its Context,* ed. J. Beutler and R. Fortna (Cambridge: Cambridge University Press, 1991), 18–32; John D. Turner, "The History of Religions Background of John 10," in Beutler and Fortna, *Shepherd Discourse,* 33–52. Some have

argued for Mandaean and/or Gnostic origins: Eduard Schweizer, *Ego eimi: Die religions-geschichtliche Herkunft und theologische Bedeutung der johanneischen Bildreden, zugleich ein Beitrag zur Quellenfrage des vierten Evangeliums*, FRLANT 38 (Göttingen: Vandenhoeck & Ruprecht, 1939), 64–66; Bultmann, *John*, 367–38; for discussion, Meeks, *Prophet-King*, 307–9; Turner, "History of Religions," 41–48.

31. For example, Pss 74:1 (anger against sheep/people); 77:20 (people led in the exodus and wilderness); 78:52 (led, guided, victorious over Egyptians); 79:13 (deliverance; give thanks); 80:1 (listen, lead); 100:3 (sheep of his pasture).

32. Isa 40:11 (feed, gather lambs in his arms, lead, liberate from Babylon); 49:9–10 (feed, protect, lead, guide in return from Babylonian exile); Jer 13:17 (taken captive); 31:10 (gather, keep); Ezek 34:11–22; Zech 9:16 (save).

33. Sir 18:13 (rebukes, trains, teaches, turns them back); *1 En.* 89:14–90:42 (Israel's history with the "Lord of the sheep," including exodus, exile, and Antiochus Epiphanes).

34. The shepherd-sheep metaphor has a long tradition outside Hebrew Bible texts for both human leaders and for various gods, especially Hermes and Apollo; see Turner, "History of Religions Background," 35–39.

35. For example, Joseph (Philo, *Joseph* 2–3); Moses (Exod 3:1; Num 27:15–23, with Joshua; Isa 63:11; Philo, *Moses* 1.60, shepherd as kingship); David the shepherd king (2 Sam 5:2; 1 Chron 11:2; Ezek 34:23); prophets like (second) Zechariah (Zech 11:4–14; 13:7–9, a shepherd that dies). *Ps. Sol.* 17:40 uses the image for the king who is the "Lord Messiah."

36. Isa 56:11 (no understanding; pursue own gain); Jer 22:22 (kings who have not listened to or obeyed God; wickedness); 23:1–4 (scattered the sheep, not attended to them); 25:34–38 (faithless kings); 50:6–7 (lead astray; forgotten the sheep; not protected them).

37. Homer, *Iliad* 2.84–86, 243, 254 (Agamemnon); *Odyssey* 3.156 (Agamemnon); 4.24; Xenophon, *Cyropaedia* 1.1.2–5 (Cyrus); Plato, *Republic* 1.343–345 (ruler as shepherd concerned with justice for the flock); 3.415E (wolf against the fold), 416A (dogs like wolves attacking and harming the sheep). Erwin R. Goodenough, "The Political Philosophy of Hellenistic Kingship," in *Yale Classical Review*, vol. 1, ed. A. Harmon (New Haven: Yale University Press, 1928), 55–102. Goodenough (84) especially notes the "good ruler as shepherd" image in Archytas of Tarentum (ca. 400–350 BCE) and his contemporary Ecphantus (60).

38. Dio Chrysostom in *Kingship 2* claims that Zeus, "King of Kings," deposes violent and unjust kings and admires the caring king (77). John Moles, "The Date and Purpose of the Fourth Kingship Oration of Dio Chrysostom," *Classical Antiquity* 2 (1983): 251–78.

39. Cf. the lack of discussion of these traditions in Beutler and Fortna, *Shepherd Discourse*.

40. Also to be recognized are descriptions of the ancient economy as a "limited-goods" society. Unlike contemporary understandings of an ever-expanding economy, it was understood that there was a fixed amount of material available for all. If a few had too much and the rest not enough, the powerful rich had stolen what belonged to the rest. Bruce Malina, "Wealth and Property in the New Testament and Its World," *Interpretation* 41 (1987): 354–67.

41. Brent Shaw, "Bandits in the Roman Empire," *Past and Present* 102 (1984): 3–52; idem, "Tyrants, Bandits, and Kings: Personal Power in Josephus," *JJS* 44 (1993): 176–204; Richard A. Horsley and John S. Hanson, *Bandits, Prophets, and Messiahs: Popular Movements at the Time of Jesus* (San Francisco: Harper & Row, 1985), 48–87; K. Hanson and D. Oakman, *Palestine*, 86–91.

42. In ca. 4 BCE, Judah ben Hezekiah, Josephus, *J.W.* 2.56; *Ant.* 17.271–72. In ca. 35–55, Eleazar ben Danai and Alexander, *J.W.* 2.235; *Ant.* 20.121. In ca. 44–46 CE, Tholomaeus, *Ant.* 20.5.

43. 48 CE: Josephus, *J.W.* 2.235, *Ant.* 20.121; 62–64 CE: *Ant.* 20.215; 64–66 CE: *Ant.* 20.255; 66 CE: *J.W.* 2.595–598; *Life* 126–131; 66 CE: *J.W.* 2.581–282; *Life* 77–79; 67–70 CE: *J.W.* 4.135–39, 160–161.

44. Jey J. Kanagaraj, "The Implied Ethics of the Fourth Gospel: A Reinterpretation of the Decalogue," *TynBul* 52 (2001): 33–60, esp. 54.

45. C. Koester, "'Savior,'" 665–80; Labahn, "'Heiland der Welt,'" 147–73; Callahan, *Love Supreme*, 64–65.

46. Goodenough, "Political Philosophy," 98.

47. Josephus reports that Galileans greeted him as "benefactor and savior" during the 66–70 CE war against Rome (*Life* 259)!

48. Many examples could be given: Augustus, in Philo, *Flaccus* 74; Vespasian, in Josephus, *J.W.* 7.70–71. Martial (*Epig.* 2.91) addresses the emperor as "the world's sure salvation." Labahn, "'Heiland der Welt,'" 151. On salvation, see Jason Moralee, *"For Salvation's Sake": Provincial Loyalty, Personal Religion, and Epigraphic Production in the Roman and Late Antique Near East* (London: Routledge, 2004).

49. Text from Price, *Rituals and Power*, 54–55.

50. As Augustus himself pointed out in his *Res gestae*. For the text, see Werner Eck, *The Age of Augustus*, trans. D. L. Schneider (German, 1998; Malden, MA: Blackwell, 2003), 134–52.

51. IEph 2.271F, 272, 274; 5.1501; 7.1.3271, 3410. Van Tilborg (*Reading John*, 47, 56) reports that the title is not used for emperors in the first century in the Ephesian inscriptions.

52. C. Koester, "'Savior,'" 666.

53. Brent Kinman, *Jesus' Entry to Jerusalem* (Leiden: Brill, 1995), 25–65; Carter, *Matthew and the Margins*, 413–18.

54. In John 1:43–51 Nathanael represents true Israelites; in the previous chapter, Nicodemus functions as representative of the *Ioudaioi* (3:1).

55. C. Koester's translation in "'Savior,'" 672.

56. Sirach, from the second century BCE, refuses to recognize Samaritans as a proper people and calls them "the foolish people that live in Shechem" (50:26). *T. Levi* 7:2–3 (second-century BCE) scoffs at Shechem as "the city of the senseless."

57. Callahan, *Love Supreme*, 65.

58. The phrase used by Howard Clark Kee, *The Beginnings of Christianity: An Introduction to the New Testament* (New York: T&T Clark, 2005), 171.

59. Gail O'Day, "John," in *Women Bible Commentary*, ed. C. A. Newsom and S. H. Ringe, expanded ed. (Louisville: Westminster John Knox, 1998), 381–93, esp. 384.

60. C. Koester, "'Savior,'" 674–80; Callahan, *Love Supreme*, 65.

61. C. Koester, "'Savior,'" 678–80; Rensberger, *Johannine Faith*, 117.

62. The other references in John are 1:49; 6:15; 12:13, 15.

63. For Octavian's restoring Herod's crown after Herod supported the defeated Antony, see Josephus, *Ant.* 15.187–201, esp. 195.

64. During the revolt in Jerusalem against Rome in 66–70 CE, for example, Menahem, having armed himself from an armory at Masada "returned like a veritable king to Jerusalem" to take command for a short time, until he was killed (Josephus, *J.W.* 2.433–434, 444–448). Another leader, Simon, attracted followers "subservient to his command as to a king" and was ceremonially beheaded as part of the triumph celebration in Rome in 71 CE (Josephus, *J.W.* 4.510; 7.153–155). Previously kingly pretenders such as Judas, Simon, and Anthronges had gathered followers, attacked elites and their buildings, and claimed the title against Herod, Rome's appointed "king of the Jews"; they were defeated and executed (Josephus, *Ant.* 17.271–272, 273–276, 278–285). On popular kingship, R. Horsley and Hanson, *Bandits*, 88–134.

65. The noun is βασιλεία (*basileia*), a cognate of the noun "king," and can be translated "kingship," "kingdom," or "empire."

66. E.g., Reinhartz, "Colonizer," 176–77.

67. Van Tilborg, *Reading John*, 33–38.

68. Ibid., 54; Leander Keck, "Derivation as Destiny: 'Of-ness' in Johannine Christology, Anthropology, and Soteriology," in *Exploring the Gospel of John: In Honor of D. Moody Smith*, ed. R. A. Culpepper and C. C. Black (Louisville: Westminster John Knox, 1996), 274–88.

69. This is not to suggest that there are no differences. For instance, "Son of God" is used explicitly with "Father" only twice (5:25–26; 10:36); most of the 18 instances of "Son" are associated with "Father" (3:35; 5:19 [2x], 20, 21, 22, 23 [2x], 26; 6:40; 14:13; 17:1).

70. As van Tilborg (*Reading John*, 27) points out, this observation warns against pushing too hard Ashton's attempt (*Understanding*, 317–28) to distinguish different traditions informing "Son" ("son of the house," commissioned by Father to represent household) and "Son of God" (messianic). Note also 10:36 NRSV, where "Son of God" is the confession of the "one whom the Father sanctified and sent into the world," the quality most associated with "Son."

71. For gods and heavenly beings, significant individuals, rulers, and all humans, see P. W. von Martitz, "υἱός," *TDNT* 8 (1972): 335–40.

72. Van Tilborg, *Reading John*, 39. I am also indebted to the careful research on inscriptions dealing with imperial titles in Asia graciously provided to me by Dr. Robert Mowery.

73. The two terms are not conceptually equivalent. In the East, a living emperor could be θεός (*theos*, God) or θεοῦ υἱός (*theou huios,* son of God); in Rome a living emperor was not a *deus* (god), and only a dead emperor could be designated a *divus*. To be a *divi filius* indicated descent from an emperor that had been deified. Simon Price ("Gods and Emperors: The Greek Language of the Roman Imperial Cult," *JHS* 104 [1984]: 79–95) argues that the greater fluidity of Greek usage in part reflects the elusiveness of the term θεός as well as the absence of any formal process for granting divine status and honors, unlike the formal process in Rome involving a decision from the Senate (83). Accordingly, he claims that "the creation of a *divus* made little difference in the Greek world" (85).

74. Greek: IEph 2.252, 253; 5.1523, 1524; Latin: 5.1522; 7.1.3006, 3409.

75. IEph 5.1834.

76. Bilingual, IEph 2.262.

77. Bilingual, IEph 2.263B.

78. Greek: IEph 2.265, 470; Latin: 5.1500; 3.660C.

79. Van Tilborg, *Reading John*, 53.

80. Ibid., 54.

81. See chap. 9 below for discussion of "father" language.

82. Commentators commonly claim a violation of the law against blasphemy and appeal to Lev 24:13–16. But the penalty for blasphemy is stoning, not crucifixion. The opponents have unsuccessfully tried to stone him twice (8:59; 10:31); the second time Jesus talked them out of it.

83. The possibility exists that the statement is not a confession of Jesus' identity but an ascription of praise to God. Thomas does not prefix his statement with "you are" as in "You are my Lord and my God." Hence, Thomas's belief may be in God's life-giving power, which he sees demonstrated in the resurrection of Jesus. This reading would be consistent with Jesus' role as revealer of God's purposes. For discussion of 1:18, see Mastin, "Neglected Feature," 32–51, esp. 37–41; and Bruce M. Metzger, *A Textual Commentary on the Greek New Testament* (London: United Bible Societies, 1971), 198.

84. Mastin, "Neglected Feature," 42–43.

85. Contra ibid., 48–51.

86. Van Tilborg, *Reading John*, 41–43. Augustus (in chronological order): IEph 2.252; 4.1393; 5.1523; 7.2.3801; 1.17, lines 41, 57–58; 1.18D, line 14; 7.1.3042; Claudius: 7.1.3042; 7.1.3003; 3.715; 3.683; Vespasian: 2.232, 233, 235, 237, 238, 240, 241, 242; 5.1498; 6.2048; 7.2.5102, 5103; 7.1.3038; 3.710C, lines 12–13; Titus: 3.852; 7.2.5102, 5103; Nerva: 2.420; 3.684A; 3.852; 3.660C; Hadrian: 2.428; 3.921.

87. There may be an exception, referring to Claudius as θεός in 44 CE, IEph 1.17, line 67. Price ("Gods and Emperors," 81) would see nothing unusual in this Greek usage.

88. The term κύριος commonly designates God in the Septuagint. It is also used for gods and goddesses, and commonly in relationships such as ruler and subjects, master and slave, husband

and wife. See Marco Frenschkowski, "Kyrios in Context: Q 6:46, the Emperor as 'Lord,' and the Political Implications of Christology in Q," in *Zwischen den Reichen: Neues Testament und römische Herrschaft*, ed. M. Labahn and J. Zangenberg (Tübingen: Francke, 2002), 95–118, esp. 96–102; Werner Foerster and Gottfried Quell, "κύριος," *TDNT* 3 (1963): 1039–98. Van Tilborg (*Reading John*, 30–32) sorts the term's 51 uses in John's Gospel into four groups: as a mode of address (32 times, mostly for Jesus), for authority figures (13:16, master and slave), for God (1:23; 12:13, 38), for Jesus (two times before resurrection, 6:23; 11:2; nine times afterward: 20:2, 13, 18, 20, 25, 28; 21:7, 12).

89. Titus, IEph 2.412; Trajan, 1.27, line 16. Uses increase significantly in the second century, according to van Tilborg (*Reading John*, 46–47), who also reports that papyri show it to be prevalent in the empire in the first century (47, 56).

90. For Egypt, see Paul Bureth, *Les titulatures imperiales dans les papyrus, les ostraca, et les inscriptions d'Égypte (30 a.C.–284 p.C.* (Brussels: Fondation égyptologique Reine Élisabeth, 1964), 33–45. Bureth's data indicate significant prominence from Nero onward, including Galba, Vitellius, Vespasian, Titus, Domitian, and Nerva.

91. Frenschkowski, "Kyrios in Context," 95–118, esp. 99–100. Frenschkowski is hesitant to call it a title since it is not formally bestowed (99).

92. Van Tilborg, *Reading John*, 48–51.

93. For examples, see the section on coins in chap. 3 above.

94. See also Isa 14:12–14; Ezek 28:7; 2 Macc 9:8, yet also Ps 82 and Deut 32:39–43.

95. Ibid., 53–56.

96. Price, "Gods and Emperors," 95.

97. Ibid., 94.

98. Van Tilborg, *Reading John*, 54–55.

99. Musa W. Dube, "Reading for Decolonization (John 4:1–42)," in *John and Postcolonialism: Travel, Space, and Power*, ed. M. W. Dube and J. Staley (London: Continuum, 2002), 66.

8

Eternal Rome and Eternal Life

By the end of the first century CE, the approximate time of the finished form of John's Gospel, most people in Ephesus, as well as throughout the empire, knew that Rome was here to stay. Sanctioned by the gods; allied with provincial elites; efficient in gathering taxes and tribute; secured by the threat of military force; visible through coins, inscriptions, monuments, and statues; made present through festivals as the channel for divine blessing; made personal through imperial personnel; and made tangible through colonies and cities, roads and ports, aqueducts and baths—the empire constituted daily reality for some sixty million or so people. In Ephesus, Roman presence had been a reality for over a century and had become more visible through the first century CE, with increased personnel and buildings, as I outlined in chapter 3 above.

The empire had presented itself throughout this time as the golden age dawned large. About 150 years previously, Virgil had had the dead Anchises, father of Aeneas, prophesy concerning Octavian (or Augustus, as the senate retitled him), the adopted son of the slain Julius Caesar:

> Here is Caesar, and all the seed of Iulus destined to pass under heaven's spacious sphere. And this in truth is whom you so often hear promised to you, Augustus Caesar, son of a god, who shall again establish a golden age (*aurea saecula*). (*Aen.* 6.788–793).[1]

During the century or so since Augustus had exercised power, Rome had presented itself as the agent of the gods and savior in bringing about a new or golden age.[2] Augustus had brought peace after the civil war, defeating Antony at Actium in 31 BCE. He set about restoring the republic (in name at least) by empowering the senate, though he exercised considerable power himself through the dependency of patron-client relations. He maintained a standing army and rewarded veterans. Veneration for a ruler chosen by the gods—Augustus—replaced factional commitments to power-grasping generals. He expanded the empire, adding territory, for example, in Spain, Germania around the Danube and Rhine, Egypt, and Asia Minor. Throughout the provinces he consolidated political and military control with extensive road construction, and he appointed officials for tax collection. He rebuilt "downtown" Rome, including the Senate House and Forum, locating numerous statues of himself in the city. He redressed Rome's infrastructure and social problems such as water supply (12 BCE), food supply

(8 CE), and social order (permanent fire brigade [6 CE]) and police force). He revived piety and religious rituals, restoring eighty-two temples including the temple of Mars Ultor (the Avenger), and building fourteen others. Roman piety meant divine blessing, which was expressed in military victory and resulted in a greater empire and power. He also attempted, quite unsuccessfully, to revive personal morality, especially in relation to traditional values and gender roles, marriage, and family life, especially among elites. He passed legislation supporting marriage as well as providing incentives like tax breaks for both marriage and for numerous children. He made adultery a prosecutable crime, to the detriment of his own daughter Julia. He provided a successor to prevent civil strife and to maintain his legacy of power by adopting his stepson Tiberius, who assumed power on Augustus's death in 14 CE (see *Acts of Augustus [Res gestae]*).

Augustus's victories presented Augustus as the divinely sanctioned guarantor of Rome's hierarchical and elite-dominated order and imperial power. Celebrations of his victory at Actium and of his later military successes—prayers, sacrifices, holidays, shrines, temples, a triumph, loyalty oaths—not only identified him as the bringer of peace and unity, but also defined him as the one chosen by the gods. The senate built the Ara Pacis Augustae, the Altar of Augustan Peace, to honor his victories in Spain and Gaul (13–9 BCE). Pax Augusta, Augustan Peace, was certainly based on military power, conquest, submission, territorial domination, and a dependent senate. Public festivals, including religious observances, and buildings secured Roman identity and prestige, as well as Augustus's power. Various poets and writers, including Suetonius a century or so later, celebrated the divine sanctioning and agency of Augustus. Suetonius, for example, details numerous signs and omens that signaled such agency from before, during, and after his birth (*Aug.* 94).

Augustus's golden age was clearly not a future pie-in-the-sky vision: it was already here. It was a realized eschatology.[3] The "golden age" constituted, at least in terms of the public transcript, the present structure of the empire as experienced now in everyday life. Nor did it promise a utopia where everyone would enjoy equal blessing and treatment free of exploitation or domination. Elite privilege and unjust structures that benefited the elite at the expense of nonelites were the ways of empire. Nor was it an age of perpetual fun, leisure, and the freedom to do whatever one liked while awaiting for abundance and fertility to materialize magically. Rather, Augustus's golden age required moral responsibility, hard work, military action, family values, piety toward the gods, and submission to and support for the imperial status quo. Augustus's golden age comprised and sanctioned the very stratified structure of the empire, ensuring that the elite, including in the provinces, were rewarded with (dependent) power, material wealth, and status (described in chap. 3 above), often at the expense of the poor.

Yet the golden age did not feel golden to many. As so often happens, the vast majority of the empire's population did not share much in these rewards. Philo has some people, caught up in the struggle with Flaccus in Alexandria, protest, "We are poor people scarcely able to provide the daily wage needed to purchase absolute necessities" (*Flaccus* 143). Augustus and his successors had efficiently secured Roman elite interests, exacted taxation, seized land, and ensured the subordination of millions. Michael Mann observes that one of the shortcomings of the empire over successive centuries was its creation of unresolvable tensions and failure to match its rhetoric of divinely blessed material life with an appropriate social experience or sense of community.[4]

Augustus, though, was not deterred. In 17 BCE he instituted the Saeculum games to celebrate the beginning of this golden age defined by his accomplishments. The games further identified Augustus with Rome's destiny and underlined his indispensable role for the empire's well-being. The word "Saeculum" means a change in "era," the ending and beginning of a cycle, the passing of one "age" and arrival of a new one. The Augustan golden age had arrived. The celebrations comprised three days and nights of religious celebrations, theatrical performances, and a week of celebrations.

Augustus commissioned the poet Horace to write a *Carmen saeculare*, a hymn for the occasion performed by twenty-seven boys and girls, the very personification of the domestic fertility and civic order that was to mark this age. His hymn celebrated features of the Augustan golden age already present and seeks their increase.

- Morality: "Rear up our youth, O goddess, and bless the Fathers' edicts concerning wedlock and the marriage-law, destined, we pray, to be prolific in new offspring" (17–20).

- Fertility: "Bountiful in crops and cattle, may Mother Earth deck Ceres [goddess of agriculture, corn, and harvest] with a crown of corn; and may Jove's wholesome rains and breezes give increase to the harvest" (29–32).

- Social conformity and harmony: "O gods, make teachable our youth and grant them virtuous ways; to the aged give tranquil peace" (45–46).

- Blessing on Rome: "If Rome be your handiwork, . . . [give] to the race of Romulus, riches and offspring and every glory" (47–48).

- Military victory and alliances with the submissive: "And what [Augustus] . . . entreats of you, that may he obtain, triumphant o'er the warring foe, but generous to the fallen!" (49–52).

- Renewed social morality: "Now Faith and Peace and Honor and old-time Modesty and neglected Virtue have courage to come back, and blessed Plenty with her full horn is seen" (57–60).

- Eternal empire: May Apollo "prolong the Roman power and Latium's prosperity to cycles ever new and ages ever better" (66–68).

The last line sees the empire, this golden age or era that began with Augustus, lasting forever. It is to be an eternal golden age, the continuation of the status quo forever. This golden age thus involved dimensions both quantitative (forever) and qualitative (the Roman-ruled, elite-dominated, status quo of morality, fertility, submission, and Roman supremacy).

The Ara Pacis Augustae, the Altar of Augustan Peace, dedicated in 9 BCE on the Campus Martius in Rome, exhibited these qualities of the Augustan realized eschatology that would last forever. The altar measured about twenty by twenty-four feet, was about ten feet tall, and was set within an enclosed space. It was a working altar on which oxen and sheep were sacrificed to the goddess Peace, who had blessed Rome with victory over Rome's opponents. Peace resulted from piety, military victory, and submission. In addition to this celebration of Roman superiority in piety and military strength, the sides of the altar displayed key Augustan values in their frieze. Presented were members of Augustus's family, including modestly attired women and children as well as senators and aristocrats in a religious procession with priests (perhaps the consecration occasion?). The nearly life-size figures exhibited piety, family values, male leadership, public duty, religion, fertility, and order, the mainstays of the empire's realized eschatology. The decorative carving also underlined blessing on the natural world, with depictions of abundance and fertility.[5]

In addition to Horace, Augustan poets took up the theme of Rome's eternity. Virgil has Jupiter tell Venus that he has appointed Romulus to found a city and people "after his own name. For these I set no bounds in time or space; but have given empire without end [*imperium sine fine*]" whereby Romans will be "lords of the world, and the nation of the toga" (*Aeneid* 1.278–282). Livy describes Rome as a city founded to last "for eternity" (*in aeternum*; Livy, 4.4.4; 28.28.11; cf. 6.23.7). Tibullus names it the eternal city (*aeternae urbis*, 2.5.23) as does Ovid (*Fasti* 3.72). Ovid also especially associates Augustus with the goddess of the hearth, Vesta, whose cult symbolized and guaranteed Rome's eternal existence (*Fasti* 3.419–422; 4.949–954).[6]

Ovid's association of Augustus, the goddess Vesta, and Rome's eternal existence is part of a process that Martin Charlesworth traces out from inscriptions, texts, and coins involving the related notions of *providentia* and *aeternitas*.[7] *Providentia* refers not only to the care of the gods in providing Augustus, but also becomes associated with the reign of Augustus and following emperors. Augustus's reign exhibits *providentia* especially in his fatherly[8] foresight, by which the emperor cares for the life of the state notably in three ways: ensuring the welfare of the people, providing a stable succession (Augustus adopts Tiberius), and warding off conspiracies.[9] These acts of *providentia* or foresight ensure the eternal existence (*aeternitas*) of the empire. "The *providentia* of the emperor provides for the *aeternitas* of Rome."[10] The emperor as the embodiment of *providentia* and *aeternitas* both "safeguards and symbolizes the permanence of the Roman state."[11]

As Charlesworth demonstrates, successive emperors continued the same themes, modeling themselves on or identifying themselves with Augustus, claiming to continue his agenda.[12] Over fifty years after Augustus's death, Vespasian, emperor from 69–79 CE, for example, did so with his coins, which proclaimed a continuation of Augustan blessings. Vespasian especially associated himself, as did Augustus, with Jupiter and Vesta as "symbols of the lasting power of Rome."[13] Vespasian declared his sons to be his successors, thereby ensuring continuity. Vespasian's son and successor, Titus, followed suit in linking himself with Augustus.[14] Likewise, Domitian (81–96 CE) celebrated the Saeculum games again in 88 CE (Suetonius, *Dom.* 4.3), restored the temple of Jupiter, and harshly punished the Vestal Virgin Cornelia by burying her alive for violating her vows (*Dom.* 8). These actions involving Jupiter and Vesta suggest Domitian's concern to counter any "danger to the *aeternitas* of Rome."[15] Thus a century later, at the time when John's Gospel reached its final form, the Augustan age received from Domitian a makeover and reinforcement as the eternal, Domitianic, golden age.

Such sentiments were not restricted to Rome or to elite classes but were well known in Asia and Ephesus. The council of Asia in 29 BCE recognized the providential action associated with Augustus in bringing about the realized eschatology of the golden age. In an inscription found at Priene, it acknowledged that "whereas the providence which divinely ordered our lives created with zeal and munificence the most perfect good for our lives by producing Augustus," who as a benefactor exceeded all who preceded and might follow him, it was appropriate to celebrate his day of birth as the start of the new year.[16] And some seventy or more years later, a governor of Asia during Claudius's reign (41–54 CE) assured "the citizens of Ephesus that the emperor 'has taken the whole human race under his protection.'"[17] Shortly after John's Gospel was written, Pliny, governor of Pontus-Bithynia in the north of Asia, indicated that provincials appeal to the emperor's *Salus* (prosperity) and *Aeternitas* (eternal existence) in making petitions (Pliny the Younger, *Ep.* 10.59, 83). The emperor ensured that Rome was here to stay.

John's Eternal Age

While Rome was celebrating its power and societal structure as "eternal" and "without end" and celebrating a golden age of Rome-ruled life (*aurea saecula*) that would last forever, John's rhetoric of distance was proclaiming "eternal" or "everlasting life," life without end, to its hearers and readers in Ephesus:

> For God so loved the world that he gave his only Son, that whoever believes in him should not perish but have eternal [everlasting] life. (3:16 RSV)

The adjective form rendered "eternal" or "everlasting" (*aiōnion*, αἰώνιον) in English is difficult to translate. Significantly, the Greek adjective is a cognate of the Greek word for "age" or "era." This word commonly translated "eternal" could be translated "agely" or "of the age" or "of the era." John's "eternal" or "everlasting" life refers to life "of the age" or "age-ly" life.

Eternal empire. Eternal life. Golden age. Life of the age. Of what significance is it that John proclaims "eternal or age-ly life" in the midst of the eternal empire? What is the age to which John refers, and what does the life of this age look like in the midst of the eternal Roman Empire, whose golden age is (supposedly) encountered daily in Ephesus? How does John's "life of the age" interface with the structures, practices, and values of the eternal empire? What kind of life does John's Gospel seek to create for overaccommodated Jesus-believers? In the rest of this chapter I will explore the issues created in the cultural intertextuality of these claims. Again I emphasize that I am not arguing for the origin or source of one term in relation to the other. Rather, I am interested in the interaction, the cultural intertextuality, of these claims that carry such similar lexification and at times even similar features. What is John's understanding of "life of the age"?

John's "Life of the Age"

John's concern with "life of the age" is part of a larger emphasis on "life" in the Gospel.[18] The Gospel's opening verses describe the Word as the source of life: "In him was life" (1:4). The Gospel concludes:

These things are written that you may believe that Jesus is the Christ, the Son of God, and that believing you may have life in his name. (John 20:31 RSV)

Throughout the story, the Johannine Jesus declares his mission to be life-giving:

I came that they may have life, and have it abundantly. (10:10 RSV)

Jesus reveals "life"; he is "life."

I am the resurrection and the life. (11:25 RSV)
I am the way, and the truth, and the life. (14:6 RSV)

This emphasis on life and "life of the age" is distinctive to John's Gospel. Whereas the Synoptic Gospels center on the *basileia*, the kingdom or empire of God or the heavens, John prefers to speak of life. The noun "life" appears thirty-six times,[19] the verb "to live" seventeen times,[20] the verb "to give life" three times.[21]

Just why the Gospel chooses this language is not clear. Craig Keener may well be partly right but mostly wrong when he suggests that the preference for "life" reflects the fact that the language of "'kingdom' (John 3:3, 5) had political ramifications . . . that would be particularly unhelpful for Christians in Roman Asia in the mid-nineties, given the demands of the state, not the least of which was imperial religion."[22] Keener may be right if he means that "life" is a less explicitly and publicly obvious political term than "kingdom" or "empire." James Scott points out that powerless groups conduct themselves self-protectively in relation to power, contesting the "great tradition" with a little tradition that avoids direct confrontation and disguises its subversive content from outsiders.[23] But Keener is wrong in his depiction of late first-century imperial religion, where (as discussed in chap. 3 above) honoring the emperor was not mandated by Domitian and punitive state measures were not taken against those who did not comply. He is also wrong to imply that somehow "kingdom" language (or "empire," as it should be translated!) is politically innocuous in the Gospels of Matthew, Mark, and Luke.[24] Those Gospels were also heard by followers of Jesus in the Roman Empire and were also acts of imperial negotiation, as has been well demonstrated. And he is wrong to suggest that "life" might not have political implications because he overlooks both the content of the Gospel's vision of life and the dangerous intertextuality that takes place between Jesus' announcement of "eternal life" and the claims of "eternal Rome." "Eternal/age-ly life" is, as I will argue, a very political and imperially contestive entity, which is part of the Gospel's rhetoric of distance. Its danger is immediately evident in that Jesus' restoring of "life" to Lazarus (11:25–26, 43–44) is the final catalyst for the Jerusalem-based, Rome-allied, Judean elite to decide to kill Jesus (11:45–57).

So what is "life of the age"? Six times the Gospel uses the noun "the age" in the phrase "into the age,"[25] often unhelpfully translated in English as "forever." Seventeen times, the adjective *aiōnion* (αἰώνιον), meaning "agely" or "eternal" or "everlasting," modifies the noun "life."[26] This language does not refer simply to having a life or being alive (John 10:11; 12:25; ψυχή, *psychē*). Rather, it refers to what can be called eschatological life or "life of the age." In general terms, and there are important nuances and diversity, Jewish eschatologies understood there to be several "ages" or periods of time.[27] The current age is usually understood quite negatively. It is dominated by various forms of sin and evil, whether political injustice or social oppression or economic exploitation. The other age is the "new age" or "the age to come," a future age that results from God's intervention, sometimes with a Messiah or agent and sometimes not. God's intervention ends all evil and sinfulness and effects judgment. It establishes God's good, just, and life-giving purposes often involving either a new or a transformed heaven and earth. The life of this new age is quantitatively and qualitatively different from current life in that it lasts forever and is not contained by sin and death.

At the heart of this "life of the age" is encounter with God or sharing in the very life of God. In John 17:3, Jesus reminds God that "life of the age" or eternal or everlasting life comprises knowing or encountering God:

> And this is eternal life, that they know you, the only true God, and Jesus Christ whom you have sent. (John 17:3 NRSV)

It is lovingly gifted by God at God's initiative (3:16). It comprises a "share in the life of God."[28]

John modifies some aspects of the expectations surrounding this new age. Instead of it being an expected future age, John presents it as already being present, at least to a significant degree. Jesus is the revealer of this life in the present. "Life of the age" or "eternal" or "everlasting" life is available now, in the present, to believers in Jesus. Notice the tenses of the verbs as well as the requirement to be loyal to or have faith in Jesus in the following verses:

> The one who believes in the Son *has* eternal life. (John 3:36)

> Very truly, I tell you, anyone who hears my word and believes him who sent me *has* eternal life, and does not come under judgment, but *has passed* from death to life. (5:24 RSV, emphasis added)

On this basis, life of the age or eternal life compromises for Jesus-believers intimate, eschatological existence with God made possible in the present through Jesus, and is uninterrupted by sin and death.

Having What Sort of Life?

What does "life of the age" connote? Rudolf Schnackenburg offers one analysis of "the Johannine idea of life":

> It is set in the context of the individual human being, as is indicated sufficiently by the predominance of expressions in the singular. The Johannine idea of life has no direct connection with life in society or the future of the human race. Nevertheless the danger of a narrow preoccupation with individual salvation is avoided because the individual striving for "eternal life" is directed towards the commu-

nity of the brethren and the practice of brotherly love as a necessary condition for reaching the goal.[29]

Schnackenburg's description of John's "life of the age," though, is not accurate in numerous ways. For starters, Schnackenburg omits any reference to human bodies. Since "life of the age" is experienced in the present, it would reasonably need to involve life in the human body, both material and politic. "Life of the age" thus somehow embraces and impacts everyday imperial society for Ephesian Jesus-believers since the material body is the means of interacting with others and participating in society, the body politic. If "the Johannine idea of life" has nothing to do with "life in society," as Schnackenburg claims, we would expect to find in the Gospel some notion that "life of the age" is experienced only in some modes of human existence like visions or trances or ecstatic states, but not in other modes of existence such as walking down the street or carrying out one's trade or making love. But no such exceptions exist in the Gospel.

Moreover, Schnackenburg's emphasis on the "context of the individual human being" and numerous uses of singular forms is somewhat confusing in the light of his comments later in the paragraph, where he talks about what we might identify as the "context of believing community." But it seems dubious to emphasize, as he does in the first part, "individual human beings" (as characteristic of numerous discussions[30]) and qualify it a little subsequently in terms of community, since the Gospel seems to work the other way around. For instance, the statement of purpose in John 20:31 is cast in grammatical terms that are plural: "that you [*plural*] might believe and that you [*plural*] might have life." In numerous other instances "life of the age" is associated with plural verbs and pronouns (e.g., 5:39; 6:27; 10:28; 17:2, 3), with contexts addressed to crowds (as in 6:47, 54; 12:25, 50), and with substantive participles (verbals) that use the Greek word for "all" or "everyone" (3:15, 16; 6:40). From the outset of the Gospel, plural or communal terms abound. The Prologue speaks about "all who received him," identifying them with the plural verb "believe," the plural noun "children of God" (1:12), and the plural pronoun "we" who "have seen his glory" (1:14). Jesus' public ministry begins with the calling of disciples into a community, several at a time (1:35–51), and with a revelatory sign by which "the disciples (plural!) believed [ἐπίστευσαν, *episteusan*] in him" (2:11). Eternal life, as Schnackenburg goes on to admit, seems to be communal, in which these eternally alive bodies and persons relate to each other.

But what relationships exist between this communal existence constituted by "eternal life" and other societal relations and interactions: economic? societal? political? ethnic? religious? Is Schnackenburg correct to say that John's "eternal life" has nothing to do with life in society, life in Roman imperial society? I suggest not. It is surely of some societal consequence that "eternal life" is encountered in loyalty to the Jesus crucified by Rome. And of what significance is it that the community of Jesus-believers that experiences eternal life in Ephesus is exhorted to practices of love (13:34–35), servanthood (13:13–17), and "greater works" than those done by Jesus (14:12)?[31] If people live by such practices in an imperial and hierarchical society whose sociopolitical structure under Roman rule is marked by domination and by the self-interested, honor-producing rule of a tiny elite, they are at significant odds with and distanced from that society. Love, servanthood, feeding the hungry, and healing the sick constitute a significantly alternative way of life, an alternative "anti-society." Contrary to Schnackenburg's claim, the rest of "life in society" is not far away, at least by antithesis. Eternal life or "life of the age" in a context of "eternal Rome" seems not only to have some political implications but also to shape an alternative, more distanced way of life.

Nor is "the future of the human race" far away, contrary to Schnackenburg's claim. The pervasive recognition of "eternal life" as an eschatological concept and of John's emphasis on realized eschatology (focused on the present) cannot ignore the presence of future eschatological claims in the Gospel. C. K. Barrett has observed that "the theme of futurist eschatologist runs deeper into Johannine thought than is often supposed."[32] Eschatological traditions are very concerned with human destiny. The Gospel reminds its audience of a future time of accountability, "when all who are in the tombs will hear his voice and come forth, those who have done good to the resurrection of life, and those who have done evil to the resurrection of judgment" (5:28–29 RSV). John's Jesus speaks here of a future resurrection of bodies for vindication or judgment (as also in *2 Bar.* 51:1–2[33]). This somatic resurrection or "raising up" will happen "on that last day," as Jesus says four times in chapter 6 (6:39, 40, 44, 54). The phrase "on the last day" evokes the coming time of salvation and judgment announced by various prophets.[34] In 6:40 and 6:54, both "eternal life and being "raised up on the last day" occur together. Also linked to this future time are eternal life (12:25), judgment (12:48), and Jesus' return (14:3, 18, 28). These *future* events in the Gospel concerning "life of the age" bear surely on the "future of the human race." I will return to these below.

Further, one cannot help but notice that in the standard discussions of "life" in John's Gospel such as Schnackenburg's discussion summarized above, interpreters regularly refer to a common canon of Johannine texts, notably sayings about or of Jesus, to support an individualized and spiritualized construction. But rarely do these discussions include Jesus' actions or signs in which he physically and materially transforms brokenness into wholeness, scarcity into abundance, death into life—and does not accommodate to the status quo. Life is central, for example, in the final "sign" of the raising of Lazarus where in 11:25–26 John's Jesus uses both the verb (ζάω, *zaō*) and noun (ζωή, *zōē*). The words that almost conclude the Gospel—"These things are written so that you may . . . have life" (20:31)—suggest that the whole Gospel account should shape the understanding of "life of the age." There is nothing in 20:30–31 to indicate that "these things are written" refers only to Jesus' words and excludes the narratives of Jesus' actions of material transformation. In fact, the all-inclusive concluding "these things" along with the reference to Jesus doing "many other signs" in 20:30 indicate that Jesus' sayings and actions should contribute to an understanding of the Johannine construct of eternal life.

Moreover, despite great focus on John as the "spiritual" Gospel, significant parts of the Gospel, including Jesus' signs, attest God's creation of (1:3, 10) and valuing of the physical, material world. As obvious as it sounds, the word's becoming flesh (1:14) is a central affirmation about the importance of the material and physical, including the human body. Corell explains:

> ζωή (*zōē*) in the Fourth Gospel is not opposed to physical life; it is life in its perfection including physical life. For there is only one "life"—life given in creation. . . . God's creation, spoilt through sin and death, becomes God's possession. St. John 1:4 and indeed the whole Prologue stresses the continuity between created life and redeemed life: the latter is the fulfillment of the former.[35]

The Gospel's rhetoric of distance does not mean disinterested escape from the physical into some sort of religious, privatized "life" where "spiritual, eternal life" ignores or devalues "physical life." Rather, "life of the age" denotes entry into life that partakes of God's purposes, wherein all of God's creation is transformed from sin and death to life according to God's purposes. Jesus exhibits (and anticipates) such transformation of God's world, as I will argue below, through his healings of the physically damaged and his feeding of those who do not have adequate resources.[36] John does not use language of a "new heaven and new earth" but its affirmation of somatic resurrection (chaps. 20–21) shows concern with the re-creation of the physical world. Likewise, the command to Jesus-believers to perform even "greater works" than Jesus (14:12) points to God's cosmic (re-)creativity and to eschatology that is also protology.

Such factors suggest that John's "life of the age" may be much more than Schnackenburg's individual spiritual communion with God through faith in Jesus and unrelated to society or the future of the human race. John's "eternal" or "age-ly" life embraces somatic, societal, communal/ecclesial, sociopolitical, future, and material/physical dimensions. What happens when such "life of the age" interacts with Rome's claims of being the "eternal city," of being "empire without end," of having instituted the golden age, of celebrating it in the "age-ly" (Saeculum) games?

Again I emphasize that my concern is with cultural intertexts and not with locating the origin of or the major cultural influences on John's notion of "life of the age" or "eternal life."[37] I am not primarily attempting to "locate" John's understandings within the diverse notions of the afterlife that existed among Jewish people[38] nor among various Hellenistic and Roman populations,[39] as interesting and/or as challenging as this task might be.[40] Rather, I am putting John's "eternal life" into conversation with Rome's claims of "eternal empire" encountered as daily life in imperial Ephesus. My primary concern is with the cultural intertextuality of Johannine eternal life[41] and eternal Rome.

John's Eschatological Cluster

The discussion above has identified some motifs in the Gospel that comprise dimensions of John's notion of eternal life. At this point my intent is to elaborate this cluster of eschatological emphases, both present and future, that express God's life-giving purposes. I will do so with reference to both the Gospel and some appropriate elements of diverse Jewish eschatological traditions evoked by the Johannine cluster of features, to fill out the picture. The discussion will evoke some imperial claims and structures to explore the intertextuality between eternal Rome and eternal life.

John's eschatological cluster includes a present (5:22, 27) and future judgment (5:29; 12:48). The Gospel thus places all human life, including the empire, in accountability to God, to be measured according to God's purposes to bless all people with life (Gen 12:1–3; John 1:3–5). This judgment, already operative in the present in Jesus' ministry (5:22, 24, 27), asserts God's claim on and sovereignty over all human society, including Rome's supposedly unending imperial golden age.

Also included in John's eschatological cluster is a somatic resurrection either to life for Jesus-believers or to condemnation. In 5:28–29, "The hour is coming when all who are in their tombs will hear his voice and will come out, ... to the resurrection of life ...

or to the resurrection of condemnation" (RSV). And in 6:39, 40, 44, 54, Jesus declares that those who believe "have eternal life, and I will raise them up on the last day" (NRSV). Resurrection and eternal life are linked together. In 11:24 Martha confesses that brother Lazarus "will rise again in the resurrection on the last day," to which Jesus responds, "I am the resurrection and the life" (11:25 NRSV). Jesus' revelation does not contradict her expectation of future resurrection. Rather, he affirms his own integral role in that resurrection while going on to declare that resurrection is the victory of God's life over death since "those who believe in me, even though they die, will live" (11:25b NRSV). The point is demonstrated in the somatic restoration of Lazarus to life and in Jesus' own somatic resurrection, as Alan Segal stresses (20:1–18; editorial asides in 2:22; 7:39; 20:9).[42] It has been suggested that physical death may not have been a problem at Qumran,[43] but whatever the accuracy of that claim—and the Qumran scrolls include references to resurrection[44]—it does seem to have been an issue for John's community, as this Lazarus episode suggests and as Jesus' declaration in 21:23 ("Jesus did not say to him that he would not die" [NRSV]) confirms. John's assertion is, as Marianne Thompson argues, at least that physical death does not destroy the partic-ipation in the very life of God that believers currently enjoy as a somatic existence.[45] Beyond this, death is put in the context of God's resurrecting power.

This concern with death and future life also involves martyrdom. In 16:2, "The hour is coming when whoever kills you will think they are offering service to God." The phrase "the hour is coming" (ἔρχεται ὥρα, *erchetai hōra*) echoes the imminent, escha-tological, coming "day of the Lord" from the resurrection references in 6:39, 40, 44, and 54. The "day of the Lord" anticipates various events including judgment on the nations, punishment on Israel and Judah, the overthrow of the powers of evil, and the victori-ous restoration of the people (Isa 5:26–30; Amos 5:18–20; 9:11; Zech 14:4, 6, 8, 9–19). The "day" is about the establishment of justice, including against those who mistreat the Jesus-believers. The phrase "the hour is coming" recalls the affirmation of 5:28–29 about the future, somatic resurrection of the dead to either life or judgment. It also evokes Jesus' "hour" of his death and departure to the Father, in which disciples partic-ipate (12:23, 28; 13:1–3). The farewell discourse locates both this warning about mar-tyrdom and the promise of future resurrection life in the context of "tribulations" that will precede the yet-future establishment of God's just purposes in Jesus' parousia (15:18–19; 16:20–22). The reference to martyrdom emphasizes conflict between Jesus-believers and those with power to take life away, while also evoking the context of the triumph of God's just purposes.

John 14:3 ("And if I go and prepare a place for you, I will come again and will take you to myself" [NRSV]), repeated in 14:28 ("I am going away, and I am coming to you" [NRSV]), evokes Jesus' return.[46] There is much debate about whether 14:18–19 refers to Jesus' return: "I am coming to you. . . . You will see me; because I live, you also will live. On that day you will know that I am in my Father, and you in me, and I in you" (NRSV). These verses have been interpreted variously in relation to the postmortem ascent of the believer's soul, to Jesus' resurrection, the Paraclete, the parousia, and to various combinations thereof.[47] While a multilayered reading is probable, a (partial?) reference to the parousia is at least sustainable on the basis of John's embrace of future eschatol-ogy, as noted above, of the language of "coming again," and of the eschatological time "on that day." If a reference to Jesus' resurrection appearances is granted, a link between his resurrection and that of disciples is clear from 14:19c ("Because I live, you also will live"). The Gospel provides no descriptive scenario for the parousia. The tradition, though, suggests a forcible imposition of God's purposes, imitative of imperial power.

How are these references to martyrdom, future judgment, resurrection life, and parousia to be read as part of the Johannine narrative and worldview and in the context of assertions of Rome's "forever" golden age? How do we join the eschatological dots to fill out the picture? One approach, epitomized by Bultmann, is to resort to theories of sources and redactions that dismiss these future references.[48] He counts them as later additions, clashing with John's emphasis on the present, added by the ecclesiastical redactor to render the Gospel acceptable. Or conversely, some have argued that they are traditional affirmations maintained in the Gospel out of respect for the tradition, but after decades of nonfulfillment they are no longer important because the evangelist's focus is now on present realities.[49] But however deep the hold of such theories in Johannine studies, they have to be set alongside insights from recent narrative or literary work on the Gospels that have emphasized engagement with the Gospel's finished form. Pesky "contradictions," especially those in a written text that originates in an oral culture,[50] need to be engaged and interpreted, rather than relegated and dismissed. How do we join the Johannine dots?

When these future dimensions are engaged, they affirm that eternal life, which Jesus-believers already experience in the present, participates in the very life of God, which is not bound by death (resurrection) or condemnation (judgment) but is somatic, justice-bringing, communal, societal, and material. Beyond this, Thompson rightly emphasizes that this eschatological material cannot be separated from the "convictions regarding God's creation and sovereignty, which are expressed through the Father-Son relationship."[51] But Thompson unfortunately does not pursue her own insight to elaborate how "God's creation and sovereignty" might define eternal life. These eschatological realities seem to provide crucial insight into John's eternal life both now and in the future. The eschatological nature of John's "life of the age" directs attention to the assertion of God's ultimate purposes for the world now and in the future, in imperial style. As Ernst Käsemann has argued, at the heart of eschatological thinking is the question, "To whom does the sovereignty of the earth belong?"[52] By all appearances, the answer from late first-century daily life in imperial Ephesus is obvious. Rome's sovereignty is supreme and eternal. John's rhetoric, however, contests that assessment, revealing Rome's sovereignty to be limited and temporary, contextualized by the imperial purposes of God that are being worked out through Jesus and yet to be completed. The most obvious implication for Jesus-believers is distance from imperial society, which is under imminent condemnation, and commitment to God's purposes alone.

Eternal Life Is Somatic

Eternal life for John is certainly somatic in the present since Jesus-believers have eternal life now. But it is also somatic in the future since John affirms a somatic resurrection both for Jesus (chaps. 20–21) and for believers (5:28–29; 6:39–40, 54; 11:44). Participation in God's future eschatological purposes means bodily participation, though the Gospel does not engage the question of the kind of body even if scenes like

20:11–18, 19–20, and 26–29 suggest continuity and transformation (cf. 1 Cor 15). Significantly, though, in affirming the future somatic resurrection of those "in the tombs" (5:28–29), "on the last day" (6:39–40, 44, 54), and in his warning about martyrdom (16:2), John evokes a Jewish tradition especially evident in 2 Maccabees 6–7 that affirms God's eschatological purposes to embrace the created, the material, and physical in a cosmic display of God's justice at work. Gregory Riley has shown that Greek and Roman thought on the afterlife has no expectation of a resurrected body.[53]

It is significant, as I have noted previously, that understandings of resurrection emerge from Jewish negotiations of imperial power. Perhaps the earliest explicit reference to resurrection in the biblical writings is found in Daniel 12:1–3. This text originates, at least in its final form, from the struggle of the 160s BCE against Antiochus IV Epiphanes, the Seleucid king of Syria who desecrated the Jerusalem temple; ordered the end of temple worship and of the observance of Torah, including circumcision, Sabbath, and festivals; and commanded the establishment of images in the temple (1 Macc 1). Jewish responses comprised both accommodation and various forms of resistance, including military action led by Judas Maccabeus, reliance on God to act, and martyrdom resulting from the refusal to comply. Resurrection was understood to accompany the final defeat of the Seleucid and the establishment of God's purposes. It expressed God's faithfulness to those killed for being loyal to Torah and to the covenant in the face of Antiochus's demands. Resurrection was an act of justice whereby God's faithful power extended beyond death to redress Antiochus's acts of injustice. It set right his acts of death by ending his rule and restoring somatic life. Resurrection was the means of participating in the establishment of God's good, just, and life-giving purposes. Resurrection is not good news for imperial powers like Antiochus Epiphanes and Rome. It ends their sovereignty by reasserting and establishing God's claim on creation.

In Daniel 12, the martyred righteous will be raised (ἐξεγερθήσονται, *exegerthēsontai*) from the dust. The reference may involve bodily resurrection, though the picture is complicated by their destiny: they will "shine . . . like the stars forever and ever" (NRSV). The image of shining might suggest a glorious transformed existence or an astral existence whereby they "join the angelic host."[54] Either way, whatever the exact details, this resurrection participates in Daniel's vision of the establishment of God's reign in "one like a human being/son of man"[55] to whom is given "everlasting dominion," and "glory and kingship" over "all peoples, nations, and languages" who will "serve him" (Dan 7:13–14; see chap. 7 above). Being raised to life participates in God's triumphant and just purposes, overcoming the fatal worst that the imperial power can do.

Some fifty to a hundred years later, eternal life through somatic resurrection is evident in 2 Maccabees. Again the setting for the narrative is resistance to Antiochus Epiphanes, though the emphasis is more on God's intervention than on the military prowess of Judas Maccabeus. God defends and rewards those who are loyal to the covenant, even to death. Resurrection is victory over Antiochus Epiphanes. Chapter 7 narrates the martyrdoms of seven brothers, watched by their mother. They represent faithfulness even to death because they refuse Antiochus' command to eat "unlawful swine's flesh" (2 Macc 7:1). Antiochus tortures them one by one to force them to comply. They remain loyal, alternately declaring their confidence in God's resurrecting power and taunting Antiochus with threats of his judgment by God. The second brother declares to Antiochus, "You accursed wretch, you dismiss us from this present life, but the King of the universe will raise us up into an everlasting [eternal] renewal of life [εἰς αἰώνιον ἀναβίωσιν ζωῆς, *eis aiōnion anabiōsin zōēs*], because we have died for his laws" (7:9 NRSV here and below). It is a matter of sovereignty and justice. The life-giving faithfulness of the "King of the universe" means participation in God's purposes for the oppressed along with the demise of Antiochus. The third brother declares his confidence in the resurrecting power and justice of God over somatic mutilation as he puts out his tongue and holds out his hands to be cut off: "I got these from Heaven, and because of his laws I disdain them, and from him I hope to get them back" (7:11). The fourth brother announces his own resurrection and Antiochus's destruction. He chooses "to cherish the hope God gives of being raised again by him. But for you [Antiochus] there will be no resurrection to life!" (7:14). The sixth brother warns Antiochus not to think "that you will go unpunished for having tried to fight against God!" (7:19). The mother exhorts her sons to expect a somatic resurrection as they die. "The Creator . . . will in his mercy give life and breath back to you" (7:23). And she expects this somatic resurrection life to be communal. She exhorts the last son to die so that "I may get you back again along with your brothers" (7:29). Resurrection is somatic, communal, imperially contestive, justice-working, and theological in its assertion of God's mercy and life-restoring justice for the faithful and punishment for the one who resists God's sovereignty. Subsequent references in 2 Maccabees 12:43–45 and 14:46 confirm the importance of this somatic resurrection.

Shortly after Roman power was established over Judea-Galilee by Pompey in 63 BCE, the *Psalms of Solomon* assert resurrection as part of the triumph of God's life-giving sovereignty. Now the imperial power has changed from Syrian aggression to Rome's activity, but God's victory over it and establishment of justice through resurrecting power continues to be asserted. Bodily resurrection seems to be in view as 2:31 ("raising me up to glory") and 3:12 ("Those who fear the Lord rise up to eternal life") link resurrection and eternal life as the mode of existence for a life that "goes on forever" (13:11) on earth. This life follows the nonmilitary king-Messiah's intervention and assertion of God's reign over Israel and the sinful Gentiles/Romans (chap. 17).[56] The sinners are destroyed (2:31, 34; 15:12) while only the righteous are raised to life. The dispersed return to Israel (17:26–31; 11; 8:28): to redistributed land (17:28), a rededicated temple and Jerusalem (17:30–31), and a life of justice without war and taxes (17:33); to be part of a wise, joyful, and just people under God's rule (17:34–46). This rule means "faithfully and righteously shepherding the Lord's flock" (17:40). In chapter 7 above I discussed the image of a "shepherd" as a common image for political rule that, like John 10, evokes Israel's faithless rulers/shepherds in Ezekiel 34, whose unjust rule "with force and harshness" does not provide food, clothing, shelter, healing, strength or restoration" for the population. Eternal life, the manifestation of God's sovereignty through just rule, differs greatly from Roman rule, replacing and triumphing over it. Eternal life is a different societal vision, one that enacts God's life-giving and just purposes, not Rome's death-bringing practices. The affirmation of earthly, somatic, resurrected eternal life that awaits the righteous in *Psalms of Solomon* contests and contextualizes Roman imperial aggression by anticipating its end and defeat.

In *1 Enoch* 37–71, probably written in the mid-first century CE and thus several decades before John's Gospel, resurrection is part of a transformation of life on earth that involves judgment accomplished by the Son of man and a significant change in sociopolitical structures. The main problem with the present age comes from the ruling elite, the "kings," "mighty ones," and "the strong" who are sinners (46:4–5). They do not acknowledge or obey the source of their rule, the "Lord of the Spirits," the text's leading name for God (46:5b). Their ways on earth are marked by oppression, power, and wealth (46:7; 62:11). Judgment is effected on these oppressive "wicked kings of the earth and the mighty landowners," on "the kings, the governors, the high officials, and the landlords" (62:3, 9), who have apparently denied access to land and its produce as resources to sustain life (48:8). There is no mercy or resurrection for them (46:6), only annihilation (38:6), worms (46:6), and flames of judgment (54:6; 63:10). On the other hand, the righteous will experience a bodily resurrection (51:1–5) to a joyful and transformed life on earth (45:5; 61:5; 62:15–16; cf. 38:4; 48:7), "without the oppression of sinners" (53:7) and without "the sinners and the oppressors" (62:13). This transformed "eternal life" (37:4; 48:7) depends on repentance (40:9), is never ending (58:3), and is lived in the "garden of life" (61:12), reminiscent of the Garden of Eden.[57] The end is a return to the beginning. Justice and life are the hallmarks of this resurrected somatic existence.

John's insistence on somatic resurrection and judgment as part of "life of the age" evokes these sorts of Jewish eschatological traditions. Somatic resurrection emerges in contexts of imperial power. It is an instrument of God's restorative justice, a reassertion of God's life-giving sovereignty in setting right God's creation. Such actions involve the removal of imperial powers that claim such sovereignty and resist God's ways.

There are several implications of this future somatic resurrection for Jesus-believers in Ephesus, who already experience "age-ly life" in the present. One implication is that since God will raise the body, somatic existence, the means by which one participates in daily life in the present, is very important. It cannot be overlooked through a spiritualized reading of the Gospel. A second is that Rome's imperial order evident in Ephesus, Rome's golden age, is under certain judgment. The "eternal empire," the "empire without end," is presented as being subject to God's "eternal life" manifested by Jesus.[58] A third implication is that the Gospel reveals how much "at home" it is in this imperial world, ironically imitating it even as it depicts its downfall. Putting these factors together suggests that "eternal life" is part of the Gospel's rhetoric of distance. Jesus-believers must truly be discerning about their daily participation in Rome's world in the present. God's purposes embrace somatic existence. Daily life matters. The empire is under judgment. These factors norm more distanced participation in daily societal life.

Eternal Life Is Material, Political, and Societal

A further dimension of eternal or "age-ly" life emerges in these evoked traditions. As strange as it might sound, given the proclivity to label John the "spiritual Gospel," eternal life has emerged in the previous discussion as not only political, somatic, and societal, but also as material and physical. Support for this latter dimension is evident in the texts discussed above, as well as in John's Gospel itself with the eternal empire's crucifixion of the one who offers "eternal life." Here I want to develop it specifically in relation to Jesus' "signs."[59] The concluding verses of John 20:30–31 include Jesus' signs in the "these things [that] are written . . . that you might have life."

Signs have, among other things, a legitimating function in both revealing and confirming divine presence and purposes. Josephus, for example, refers to the many "omens" or "signs" (*semeia*, σημεῖα, Josephus *J.W.* 4.623) whereby Vespasian "was led to think that divine providence had assisted him to grasp the empire."[60] Dio Cassius comments that "Heaven was thus magnifying him" (65.8.1). Interestingly, these signs recorded by Tacitus (*Hist.* 4.81), Suetonius (*Vesp.* 7), and Dio Cassius (65.8.1) include several healings, that of a blind man (cf. John 9), a lame man (cf. John 5), and a man with a withered hand. In similar vein, the *Ioudaioi* ask Jesus about his "sign" that would legitimate his temple actions (2:18; cf. 6:30). In addition to legitimating Jesus' origin and identity as one from God, Jesus' signs are also revelatory in eliciting (ambiguous) believing responses (2:11; 2:23–25; 4:48; though see 20:29). The question to be explored here concerns what contribution Jesus' supplying of abundant wine (2:1–11) and food (6:1–14; 21:1–11), healings (4:46–54; 5:1–18; 6:2; 9:1–7), and raising of Lazarus (11:38–44) might contribute to the revelation of John's "life of the age" in relation to eternal Rome.

Commonly these stories are read as symbolic or spiritualized narrative and without material content,[61] concerned with the identity of Jesus, and the revelation of the "glory," the power and purposes, of God.[62] John 6 provides a classic example of this "symbolic" reading. Verse 27, in which Jesus urges his listeners not to labor for "perishable food" but for "food that endures to eternal life," is seen as a rejection of anything material and an elevation of the symbolic and spiritual.[63] The repeated claim that Jesus is the "bread of/for the world" (6:35, 41, 51) is interpreted in terms of "spiritual" and individual relationship with Jesus, while Jesus' miraculous act that evokes the liberation of the people from Egyptian hegemony (as well as wisdom's presence among humans) disappears into the background, a remnant of earlier layers and time in the Johannine telling, now superseded by more sophisticated spiritual reflection.[64] According to Fortna, in the Gospel's final form, "in the miracle of the loaves it matters not that a great crowd is fed."[65]

I am not suggesting that christological revelation and the challenge to discern God's power and presence and Jesus' identity as God's agent are unimportant or not part of the presentation of John's signs. But I am insisting on pressing the significance of retaining these stories in the final form of the Gospel, and on engaging questions about what God's power and presence might accomplish among humans other than content-less "life." As agent of God's purposes, what does Jesus reveal and effect? Why leave these stories in the Gospel and include them in "these things" narrated so that readers and hearers might have life?

Responses to these questions cannot miss the major role that physical transformation and abundance play in the (final Gospel) accounts of these actions. From water, Jesus supplies some 120 to 180 gallons of wine (2:6–10). Five loaves and two fish (6:9) become twelve surplus baskets after five thousand have eaten (6:10, 13). The sick child "at the point of death" lives (4:47). The man paralyzed for thirty-eight years walks (5:5–9). A blind man sees again (9:1–7), and a dead man lives (11:38–44). An "empty net" after a night's fishing (21:3) becomes so heavy with 153 fish (21:11) that it is a challenge to pull it ashore (21:6). Whatever the figure of "153" might mean (21:11)—and that there have been at least that many explanations—it certainly denotes a large catch of fish. Physical abundance pervades these scenes. It is not sufficient to say, as Fortna does, that some "profounder sense" has replaced the significance of "the physical healing of a dying boy," or that "it matters not that a great crowd is fed." John's Gospel does not offer a hierarchy of understandings of "life" or "salvation" that relegates the physical out of the picture: the one who does the revealing is the one who takes "flesh" (1:14). Of what significance is this prominent spiritual and material transformation? Why do these stories emphasize abundance and wholeness? And what do they have to do with the "glory," the power and purposes of God that Jesus reveals? What are the purposes of God? And what does any of this have to do with the "life of the age" the Gospel story reveals (20:30–31)?

Two contexts may help us to join the Johannine dots. First, as I have argued above, Jewish texts such as Daniel 12 and 2 Maccabees 7, linking somatic resurrection and eternal life, do so in the context of political crises involving imperial powers: they affirm the victory of God's justice and life over the worst that imperial tyrants can do. Two other texts contemporary with John also share some of John's conceptual framework.[66] Both 4 Ezra (= 2 Esdras) and 2 Baruch, written after the assertion of Roman power in 70 CE in the destruction of Jerusalem and its temple, and seeking to negotiate a way ahead, also know resurrection life in the age-to-come. This life forms part of the definitive establishment of God's life-giving and sovereign purposes through a Messiah, triumphing over the present age dominated by Roman imperial power. Under the literary fiction of Babylon's destruction of Jerusalem in 587 BCE, both 4 Ezra and 2 Baruch envision a two-age scenario of remarkable contrast and transformation. In 4 Ezra, after numerous tribulations, a Messiah reigns for four hundred years, resurrection and judgment follow, and a new world is established (7:26–44; chaps. 11–13; 14:35). Rome is condemned and God's purposes for a just and life-giving paradise are established (cf. 8:52–55). In 2 Baruch, a messianic kingdom, resurrection, judgment, and a new world appear (chaps. 26–30; 49–52; 72–73).

Important for our purposes is the recognition that in both texts, as in Psalms of Solomon and 1 Enoch 37–71, under God's sovereignty the life of the age-to-come blatantly and profoundly contrasts with, overcomes, and transforms material life in the present age under Roman rule. Somatic resurrection and life of the age participate in a material transformation of the world. In Ezra's new world, Paradise, "the tree of life is planted, the age to come is prepared, plenty is provided, a city is built, rest is appointed, goodness is established and wisdom perfected beforehand." There is no more sinful excess (7:112–115), no more evil, illness, death, hell, corruption, and sorrow (8:52–54). Material transformation is enacted. Second Baruch's new world is similarly marked by nourishment, abundant fertility, the end of hunger, and the dew of health (29:5–8). "The earth will also yield fruits ten thousandfold. And on one vine will be a thousand branches, and one branch will produce a thousand grapes, and one grape will produce a cor of wine" (29:5). Moreover, there will also be the end of imperial rule (72:5–6) and the establishment of peace, joy, rest, health, and harmony between people and animals, along with the absence of social contentions and evil (2 Bar. 73).[67] Both texts envision the end of Rome's world and establishment of a transformed material world marked by God's sovereignty, justice, and life.

A second important context comprises the socioeconomic structure of daily life in Rome's empire (see chap. 3 above). In his analysis of agrarian empires, Gerhard Lenski argues that control of resources and production lies in the hands of the small ruling elite, the 2–3 percent of the population who through such means as taxation and trib-ute, land ownership, debt and military intimidation, transfer resources (not just the limited surplus but also what should sustain life for many) from the bulk of the peasant population to itself.[68] Whittaker observes that the "term 'poor,' in Roman status terms, usually meant anyone not of the ruling orders,"[69] and thus disdained by elites (Cicero, *De officiis* 1.150; 2.52–56; *Ad Atticum* 1.16; Juvenal, *Sat.* 3.147–153; Tacitus, *Hist.* 1.4). Vast extremes of wealth separated elite and nonelite. An unskilled laborer could earn a daily wage of one to three sesterces (Matt 20:2) while Cato the Younger, according to Whittaker, earned 550–600 sesterces a day from property valued at 4 million sesterces, a daily income about two hundred times greater than many nonelites. Stratification also existed within urban and rural nonelites, though not to the same extent. Whittaker claims that estimates of preindustrial cities identify 4–8 percent as incapable of earning a living; 20 percent in permanent crisis due to price fluctuations and low wages, and 30–40 percent (artisans, shopkeepers, officials) who temporarily fall below subsistence levels. The permanent or temporary descents below subsistence levels depended on available work, harvests, crop failure, disease, weather, high prices, profiteering, short supply, wages, and so forth. Some notably "successful" freedmen such as Petronius's ridiculed Trimalchio gained moderate income, some reserves, and a higher living stan-dard through trade, skilled business, or artisan service valued by a wealthy patron or former owner, or by inheritance or legacy. At the lowest end, others could not, by work, provide housing or food and lived as beggars (e.g., Martial, *Epig.* 10.5). Urban living conditions for most were overcrowded, with noise, squalor, garbage, human excrement, animals, disease, fire risk, crime, conflicts, and unstable dwellings (Seneca, *Ep.* 56; Mar-tial, *Epig.* 12.57). Life span for nonelites was low: for men, 25–40 years, and less for women.[70] Infant mortality was high, about 28 percent born alive in Rome died within a year; 50 percent did not survive a decade.[71]

Food supply and quality of health so often reflect levels of wealth and access to power. Peter Garnsey remarks that in the Roman Empire, "for most people, life was a perpetual struggle for survival."[72] Food production, distribution, and consumption were shaped by and expressed the elite-controlled, hierarchical, exploitative political-economic system. Food involved power and hierarchy. The imperial system meant abundance for a few and deprivation for many, with most knowing at least some peri-ods of time each year under subsistence level. Lack of food was injustice. In the limited space here, I will summarize (and supplement) some emphases in Garnsey's work con-cerning food availability, diet quality, and (mal)nutrition levels.

- *Famine* was rare because both the elite and peasants employed strategies to pre-vent it. But *food shortages* were frequent (caused by bad harvests, unfavorable weather, distribution difficulties, speculation by traders (cf. Philostratus, *Life of Apollonius* 1.8), wars, taxes, and so forth).[73] Supplying the city of Rome had first claim on provincial food production, as an inscription reminds the city of Eph-esus: "bearing in mind the necessity that first the imperial city should have a boun-teous supply of wheat procured and assembled for its market" (IEph 2.215).[74] Shortages meant *endemic undernourishment or chronic malnutrition*, especially for nonelites, women, and children.

- Food is divisive. Distribution and either abundant or minimal consumption reflect societal hierarchies and lines of power.

- The "Mediterranean diet" is theoretically healthful. Staples of cereals (perhaps 70–75 percent of the diet,[75] of various types and qualities), olives, vine products (wine), and legumes (beans) supply energy, protein, vitamins B and E, calcium, and iron.

- Numerous factors reduced the diet's *actual* healthfulness: lack of availability due to harvests and distribution control; seasonal variations; affordability; storage limitations;[76] limited range of foods resulting in deficiencies in vitamins A, B2, C, and D; varying qualities of wine and cereals; geographical location; social status.

- Peasants produced some surplus for trade, to store against crop failures, and to pay rents and taxes.[77] Numerous references attest subsistence, poor quality, and limited quantities. City dwellers (about 10 percent of the empire) largely depended on the production of the surrounding *chōra*, or *territorium*. Most urbanites had minimal resources to buy food; their diets were limited by high prices, low supply, and limited range of goods.[78]

- Malnutrition was widespread, especially among nonelites.[79] Malnutrition was evident in deficiency diseases such as painful bladder stones (caused by deficiency of animal products), eye diseases (from vitamin A deficiency, diets low in animal-derived products and green vegetables), and rickets (limb deformity; deficiency in vitamin D; high levels of phytate-rich cereals hinder absorption of nutrients like calcium and iron). Skeletal remains give evidence of considerable malnutrition.

- In addition to diseases from these deficiencies were diseases from contagion. Malnutrition renders people vulnerable to infectious diseases: malaria, diarrhea, dysentery, cholera, typhus, and the plague bacillus meningitis.[80] High population densities in cities, inadequate sewage and garbage disposal, limited sanitation with restricted water supply, inadequate water distribution and unhygienic storage, public baths, animal feces, flies, mosquitoes and other insects, and other conditions ensured widespread infection. Swollen eyes, skin rashes, lost limbs, measles, mumps, scarlet fever, and smallpox affected many.

- Child-raising practices contributed to high infant mortality rates, unhealthy development, or selective malnutrition.[81] There is some evidence for denying protein-rich, infection-fighting colostrum to newborns, for early weaning onto nutritionally inadequate foods, for deprivation of sunlight, and for swaddling that contributed to limb deformation.

- Poor nutrition diminishes capacity for work, challenging earning and manual labor capacity.

Given these daily imperial realities, it is not surprising that eschatological scenarios of life in the age-to-come should envisage a transformed life that reverses much of this hardship. In *2 Baruch* and *4 Ezra*, the future world under God's sovereignty is free of oppression and marked by abundant fertility and health. Prophetic traditions announcing the establishment of God's reign frequently depict it in similar terms of abundant food, wine, and feasting as well as health and wholeness (Isa 25:6–10; 35:1–10; Joel 3:16–18; Amos 9:13–15).

But it would be a mistake to think that only Jewish traditions envisaged such a future world. Before Augustus came to power, Virgil saw it already dawning in the decade of the 30s BCE, after Antony had married Octavian/Augustus's sister Octavia. When their male child is born, this "glorious age" begins; he rules a peaceful world and fertility abounds: "The earth untilled will pour forth its first pretty gifts. . . . Unbidden, the goats will bring home their udders swollen with milk. . . . Every land will bear all fruits." He will be victorious at war, trade will not be necessary, land will not need cultivating, and wool will not need dye (Virgil, *Ecl.* 4.12–45). It did not quite work out that way: nine years later Octavian/Augustus defeated Antony at Actium (31 BCE), and Antony committed suicide. But Horace took up a similar vision in his hymn for Augustus's games in 17 BCE. Augustus's golden age, already present, is also marked by abundant fertility: "Bountiful in crops and cattle, may Mother Earth deck Ceres [goddess of agriculture, corn, and harvest] with a crown of corn; and may Jove's wholesome rains and breezes give increase to the harvest" (*Carmen Saeculare* 29–32). Elsewhere Horace sings, "For when [Augustus] is here, the ox in safety roams the pastures; Ceres and benign Prosperity make rich the crops; safe are the seas o'er which our sailors course" (*Odes* 4.5.17–19). And again, "Thy age, O Caesar [Augustus], has restored to farms their plenteous crops, . . . has put a check on license, . . . has banished crime and called back home the ancient ways whereby . . . the fame and majesty of our dominion/empire were spread" (*Odes* 4.15.4–16). Tibullus sees an age when war is absent, in which peace tends the fields and makes the vines grow (1.10.45–53). Philo paints the beginning of Gaius Caligula's reign in similar terms: "so great was the prosperity and well-being, the freedom from grief and fear, the joy which pervaded households and people" (*Emb.* 13). Philo also attributes to Augustus the accomplishment of not only bringing peace ("calmed the torrential storms on every side") but also of "healing the diseases (νόσους, *nosous*) common to Greeks and Barbarians" (*Emb.* 145). While *Testament of Zebulon* 9:7 attributes sickness and oppression to Gentiles, Aristides (*Roman Oration* 97) sees Rome bringing the previously "sick" world to "a state of health." Late in the first century, Statius celebrates the new age in Domitian's reign: "Hail, great Father of the world who with me [Janus] prepares to begin the ages anew. . . . With me shall you found a second age [*saeculum*]." Thus Domitian will celebrate the Saeculum games just as Augustus had done (Statius, *Silvae* 4.1.17–37).

These contemporary traditions, both Jewish and Roman, raise questions about the means by which these ages are established (violence or justice?), who benefits (the elite or everybody?), whose world it is (Rome's or God's?); and in claiming the golden age and "age-ly life" to be present already, how do the realities of daily, material, somatic, and societal life match the visionary rhetoric?

Clearly a golden age did not encompass the daily experience of most folks in Rome's empire.[82] Misery, sickness, and a lack of adequate resources was more the norm for most, as the work of Peter Garnsey and others has established. Precise information is not available for Ephesus, but there is some evidence for severe food shortages in Achaia and Asia, for instance, during the 40s through 60s CE.[83] It would be quite misleading to imagine that these were the only decades of such challenges. There just happens to be some evidence for it perhaps in part because it was worse than usual and began to impact elite writers. John's emphasis on "eternal" or "age-ly" life and accounts of Jesus' "signs" are intertexts with this context of daily realities, imperial claims of the already-present "golden age," and with Jewish traditions of transformation.

In this context, Jesus' turning of water into wine (John 2:1–11), supplying of abundant food (6:1–14) and fish (21:1–11) are not contentless revelations of the "glory," the power and purposes, of God with a restricted agenda of christological revelation (revealing Jesus the revealer) and human discernment ("for or against the Revealer"[84]). Nor is the narrative to be interpreted as a symbolic or spiritualized narrative without material content. The setting of the water-into-wine narrative at a wedding and involving abundant wine evokes common eschatological imagery depicting the establishment of God's justice and fertile existence.[85] The story emphasizes the provision of much literal wine (some 120–180 gallons; 2:6–8) of good quality (2:10). Such abundance and fertility is typical of prophetic and apocalyptic visions of eternal life, life of the age to come, as we have seen. It is also typical of imperial claims and in contrast to imperial practices in which the few enjoy abundant luxury at the expense of the rest. The Gospel's contestive verdict on such claims seems to be that the God of Jesus will supply all people with abundant food and fertility as part of the "eternal life" present now in part among Jesus-believers, something Rome cannot do. The disciples believed Jesus (2:11) because they saw a display of God's power and presence reversing the damage of Rome's "golden age" and an anticipation of God's just and life-giving purposes.

There is a further interaction between the "water-to-wine" scene and the prominent place of Dionysus, god of wine, in Ephesus.[86] The inscriptions attest a yearly festival, extensive veneration of Dionysus, a possible association comprising players and musicians protected by Dionysus and the emperor, many statues, and a cult association dedicated to Dionysus. There are also traditions associating Dionysus with turning water into wine in Teos, close to Ephesus (Pliny the Elder, *Nat.* 2.231; Diodorus Siculus 3.66). The nature of the intertextual interaction between the scene and these Dionysian traditions is more difficult to determine. Does Jesus outdo or supersede Dionysus? Does the interaction instruct them that Jesus and not Dionysus supplies their abundance and fertility? Does the scene again urge Jesus-believers to distance themselves from and not participate in such veneration of Dionysus, but remain loyal to Jesus? The interaction could well be multifaceted.

Similar issues are to the fore in the feeding scenes in 6:1–14 and 21:1–11, in which Jesus does a very Godlike thing and enacts God's will to feed hungry people (Isa 58:6–8; Ezek 18:5–9; 34:2–3). The location on a mountain (John 6:3; cf. Zion in Isa 25:6–10), the limited resources (five loaves and two fish in 6:9), the repeated apparent futility of trying to do anything (6:5, 7, 9), the vast numbers (6:2, 5, a large crowd; 6:9, so many; 5,000 in 6:10), the language of "as much as they wanted" and "when they were satisfied" (6:11–12), the twelve baskets of leftovers (6:12–13), and the fertile location (6:10, "there was a great deal of green grass") emphasize the life-giving fertility and material abundance of "life of the age" effected by Jesus. The scene evokes not only the wilderness feeding of the people to ensure their survival after fleeing Egyptian power (Num 11:4–35), but also prophetic eschatological depictions such as Isa 25, where a "feast for all peoples" overflows with rich food, "well-aged wines," and "rich food filled with marrow," and disgrace and death are ended in God's salvation (25:6–10).

John 6:2 links this act of providing abundant food with the healing of the sick, demonstrated more fully in 4:46–54, 5:1–18, 9:1–7, and 11:38–44. Health or physical wholeness, like abundant food, is a standard motif in the prophetic and eschatological traditions, just as we have seen its presence in imperial claims. Isaiah anticipates that God's saving of the people from oppressive ruling powers means a transformed fertile creation and the healing of the blind, the deaf, the lame, and the dumb (Isa 35:1–7). *Fourth Ezra* anticipates no more evil, illness, death, corruption, and sorrow (8:52–54). *Second Baruch*'s world is similarly marked not only by nourishment, abundant fertility, and the end of hunger, but also by the dew of health (29:5–8). The same motifs appear in John 9–10, where the healing of the blind man leads directly into Jesus' condemnation of the ruling Jerusalem-based, Rome-allied elite, the shepherds, the "thieves and bandits" who have "destroyed" the sheep (10:8–10; see chap. 7 above). The shepherd image evokes Ezekiel 34, with its condemnation of shepherds who have fed themselves: "You eat the fat, . . . but you do not feed the sheep. You have not strengthened the weak, you have not healed the sick, you have not bound up the injured" (34:3–4 NRSV; also 34:8–10). They have ruled "with force and harshness" (34:4), not in the sense of military suppression but in terms of harmful societal structures and self-serving practices that fail to ensure adequate resources for all. God, though, will ensure adequate food and healing for the sheep (34:10–14).

Jesus' actions reveal the limitations of the status quo of Rome's "golden age" in being unable to feed people and heal the sick despite the imperial spin. The "golden age" has not dawned through Rome's actions. Much to the contrary. Imperial power endangers people's health because it deprives them of adequate resources. Moreover, Jesus' actions indicate that a sociopolitical and religioeconomic system that causes such hunger and disease is contrary to God's purposes. Jesus, agent of God and greater than the emperor, brings the wholeness and health that repairs the damage done by the current imperial order. His subsequent death and resurrection, resulting from his threat to the status quo and precipitated by his giving of life to Lazarus (11:45–53; 18:33–40), demonstrate that the alliance of the ruling elite—the Jerusalem leaders and the Roman governor—does not have the final word on who exercises sovereignty over the world and how it is to be structured.[87] Somatic, political, and societal eternal life is available now in anticipation of a world in which God's just and life-giving purposes are established, where abundance and wholeness, food and healing are the norm for all people. Jesus-believers cannot live lives accommodated to such a sick order.

In addition to exposing the destructive nature of Rome's supposed "golden age," there are several other likely intertextualities associated with John's scene of abundant food distribution. Van Tilborg, for example, notes the honoring of Demeter (the Latin goddess Ceres) in Ephesus, the goddess literally of "growth" but commonly associated with fertility, especially agriculture and the cultivation of "cereals" such as wheat, oats, barley, rye, and millets.[88] In the Ephesian inscriptions, Demeter or Ceres is honored as the "fruit bearer" (καρποφόρος, *karpophoros*; IEph 1.10; 2.213; 4.1210; 7.2.4337). There is a "priest of the fruitful earth" (3.902) and an association of "the demetriasts before the gate." Demeter is integrated into imperial life and allied with the emperor. The association starts a priesthood for Livia, the wife of Augustus (7.2.4337), and they ask the Roman proconsul in 88–89 CE for financial assistance to fund the annual *mysteria* and sacrifices (2.213). Van Tilborg declares there to be no interference between this veneration of Demeter and John's Gospel. But that conclusion seems unlikely. The veneration of Demeter in Ephesus, as in numerous locations through the empire, attributes to her the fertility of the earth and the food supply, and in associating her with the Sebastoi, establishes the emperor and imperial family as guarantors of fertility and food. In her study of Ceres/Demeter, Barbette Spaeth demonstrates that Ceres gained a "new political meaning" in the time of Augustus, as evident in ritual, texts, coins, and artwork: "She is attached to the figure of the princeps and to his family. Through his association with the goddess, the princeps receives the benefits of her benevolence which he then transmits to the people of the empire. . . . [This association] signals his guarantee . . . of the agricultural fertility of the Empire."[89] This identification continues with subsequent emperors. In my view, John's feeding scene in 6:1–14 may well contest such understandings associated with Demeter/Ceres and the emperor by attributing the supply of food and the abundant fertility to God's power manifested in Jesus (6:11). Traditions such as Psalm 24:1, "The earth is the Lord's, and the fullness thereof," and the wilderness feeding in the exodus inform the action and counterclaim.

Beyond Demeter, there is a further cultural intertext that is part of the network of patron-client relationships. Throughout the empire, both the emperor and local elites engaged in euergetistic *liberalitas*, or "generosity," that comprised distributions of money and food such as grains to nonelites.[90] Coins from Nero and subsequent emperors depicting both the emperor and a personified *Liberalitas* picture distribution scenes. The symbol of the cornucopia, representing wealth and fertility, often appears on these coins to celebrate wealth and fertility. The letters AVG, an abbreviation for Augustus, link the current emperor with the blessings attributed to Augustus and evoke the continuing golden age. The Salutaris inscription from Ephesus discussed in chapter 4 above establishes an annual distribution of money at the temple of Artemis on the occasion of her birthday. John's scenes of the bread and the fish (6:1–14; 21:1–11) present distributions effected by Jesus, agent of God with whom and through whom all things were made (1:1–3). The evoking of Dionysus and Demeter/Ceres, as well as the *liberalitas* of the emperor and local officials and elites, suggests that imitation forms a significant part of John's scene. Anything they can do, Jesus (and God) can do—but better. The abundance in these feeding scenes suggests, in part, an outdoing of these powers. The display of God's power encourages Jesus-believers to rely on God as the source of their "daily bread" and "daily fish," which in 21:9 Jesus provides apart from the effort of the disciples and without reference to any imperial intervention.[91] Whether this means a recognition of God at work through the imperial system and the source of all things despite imperial claims (cf. John 1:1–4), or independently of it (as the isolated locations may suggest, 6:1–5; 21:4) is not entirely clear. Either way, the Gospel's emphasis on independence and distance from entanglement with and reliance on imperial society continues.

Conclusion: Eternal Empire, Eternal life

The material transformation evident in John's narratives of Jesus' actions or "signs" has often been demoted in importance, viewed as the dispensable and disposable shell that falls away to reveal the inner, deeper insight (e.g., the identity of Jesus). Johannine scholars have frequently claimed that Jesus' ministry is a revelation, but exactly what John's Jesus reveals has been more elusive. Either consistent with or in reaction to Bultmann's claim that Jesus is a revealer without a revelation,[92] scholars have commonly argued for a revelation of Jesus' identity as the agent or revealer of God, and much less frequently, for a revelation of God.[93] But without attention to God's life-giving purposes revealed through both John's narrative and through the eschatological traditions that inform the Gospel's narratives, such claims are relatively empty also. Discerning Jesus' identity as God's agent matters enormously, but so too do the means by which that revelation is made, and the content of the revelation of God's purposes that Jesus is commissioned to make.

Seen in the context of the eschatological traditions detailed above, the material transformations are not irrelevant to but an integral part of the life-giving and just purposes of God that John's Jesus, the one sent from God, reveals and embodies in his actions. The revealer of God's purposes enacts those purposes of life-giving wholeness, justice, abundance, and sovereignty in his transforming actions. The literal physical and material abundance and wholeness that Jesus' actions accomplish do not just point to his identity but also express God's purposes now. John elaborates his notion of eternal life throughout his story of Jesus by evoking eschatological traditions that expose and conflict with the norms and claims of elite imperial practices and propaganda, that envision the redressing of the injustice of the Roman imperial world, that urge Jesus-believers to more distanced interaction with Rome's severely tarnished "golden age" in the meantime, and that anticipate the day when God's life-giving sovereign purposes to restore all creation are accomplished. In these contexts, so ironically imitative of imperial ways, John's eternal or "age-ly life" appears to be much more somatic and societal, much more political and subversive, than has been recognized.

But John's presentation also faces a challenge. By moving the emphasis for the experience of this somatic, communal, material, and imperially contestive "life of the age" from the future to the present, the Gospel runs the risk of repeating Rome's mistake of claiming too much. To proclaim that greater blessing—whether golden age or "age-ly life"—is present than is actually experienced in daily life results in undermining the credibility of the source, the agent, and the narrative of such claims.

Notes

1. Harold Mattingly, "Virgil's Golden Age: Sixth Aeneid and Fourth Eclogue," *Classical Review* 48 (1934): 161–65.

2. For much of what follows on Augustus, see Eck, *Age of Augustus*; Crossan and Reed, *In Search of Paul*, 75–104, 125–52; Augustus, *Acts of Augustus* (*Res gestae*).

3. This description of Augustus's age derives from Helmut Koester, "Jesus the Victim," *JBL* 111 (1992): 3–15, esp. 10–13.

4. Michael Mann, *The Sources of Social Power*, vol. 1, *A History of Power from the Beginning to A.D. 1760* (Cambridge: Cambridge University Press, 1986), 301–40, esp. 306–10, 323–28.

5. H. P. L'Orange, "The Floral Zone of the Ara Pacis," in *Art Forms and Civic Life*, ed. H. P. L'Orange (New York: Rizzoli, 1985), 211–30; Zanker, *Power of Images*, 117–25, 158–62, 172–83; D. Castriota, *The Ara Pacis and the Imagery of Abundance in Later Greek and Early Imperial Art* (Princeton: Princeton University Press, 1995).

6. Andrew Wallace-Hadrill, "The Golden Age and Sin in Augustan Ideology," *Past and Present* 95 (1982): 19–36; T. Woodman and D. West, *Poetry and Politics in the Age of Augustus* (Cambridge: Cambridge University Press, 1984); Dieter Georgi, "Who Is the True Prophet?" in

Christians among Jews and Gentiles: Essays in Honor of Krister Stendahl, ed. G. MacRae, G. Nickelsburg, and A. Sundberg (Philadelphia: Fortress, 1986), 100–126; Karl Garlinsky, *Augustan Culture: An Interpretive Introduction* (Princeton: Princeton University Press, 1996).

7. Martin Charlesworth, "Providentia and Aeternitas," *HTR* 29 (1936): 107–32.

8. I will elaborate the image of the emperor as father in the next chapter.

9. Ibid., 110.

10. Ibid., 110, 113.

11. Ibid., 125.

12. Ibid., passim. For example, Philo evokes the Saturnalia in celebrating the first seven months of Gaius Caligula's reign as emperor. This golden or Saturnian age was marked by the absence of social hierarchies and legal inequalities, and by the presence of "prosperity and well-being, freedom from grief and fear, [and] joy" (*Emb.* 13).

13. M. Charlesworth, "Providentia," 125.

14. K. Scott, *Imperial Cult*. Vespasian, for example, follows Augustus by minting coins claiming that various divine personifications of abstract qualities were manifested through him. Like Augustus he restores peace (*Pax*) and Victory (*Victoria, Nike*) after the civil war of 68–69, as well as "other personifications . . . much like those introduced under Augustus," such as *Salus* (safety), *Securitas* (security), and *Fides* (loyalty). He also rivaled Augustus in restoring and building temples of the gods (ibid., 25–32, coins; 32, temples). For Titus, ibid., 51; Domitian and the Saeculum games celebrated in 88 CE, ibid., 96.

15. M. Charlesworth, "Providentia," 127.

16. Price, *Imperial Cult*, 54–55.

17. M. Charlesworth, "Providentia," 113.

18. Gerhard von Rad, G. Bertram, Rudolf Bultmann, "ζάω, ζωή," *TDNT* 2:832–72, esp. 870–72; H. Sasse, "αἰών, αἰώνιος," *TDNT* 1:197–209; Alf Corell, *Consummatum Est: Eschatology and Church in the Gospel of St. John* (London: SPCK, 1958), 139–52; David Hill, *Greek Words and Hebrew Meanings: Studies in the Semantics of Soteriological Terms* (Cambridge: Cambridge University Press, 1967), 163–201, esp. 192–201; Brown, *John*, 1:505–8; Dodd, *Interpretation*, 144–51; George E. Ladd, *A Theology of the New Testament* (Grand Rapids: Eerdmans, 1974), 254–63; Schnackenburg, *John*, 2:352–61; Sandra Schneiders, "Death in the Community of Eternal Life: History, Theology, and Spirituality in John 11," *Interpretation* 41 (1987): 44–56, emphasizing address to the community's problem with physical death in relation to claims of realized eschatology; Marianne M. Thompson, "Eternal Life in the Gospel of John," *Ex auditu* 5 (1989): 35–55; Ashton, *Understanding*, 214–20; D. Moody Smith, *The Theology of the Gospel of John* (Cambridge: Cambridge University Press, 1995), 149–51; Andrew T. Lincoln, "'I Am the Resurrection and the Life': The Resurrection Message of the Fourth Gospel," in *Life in the Face of Death: The Resurrection Message of the New Testament*, ed. Richard N. Longenecker (Grand Rapids: Eerdmans, 1998), 122–44; Marianne M. Thompson, *The God of the Gospel of John* (Grand Rapids: Eerdmans, 2001), 80–87.

19. ζωή (*zōē*), the basis for English words like "zoology": 1:4 (2x); 3:15, 16, 36 (2x); 4:14, 36; 5:24 (2x), 26 (2x), 29, 39, 40; 6:27, 33, 35, 40, 47, 48, 51, 53, 54, 63, 68; 8:12; 10:10, 28; 11:25; 12:25, 50; 14:6; 17:2, 3; 20:31.

20. ζάω (*zaō*): 4:10, 11, 50, 51, 53; 5:25; 6:51 (2x), 57 (3x), 58; 7:38; 11:25, 26; 14:19 (2x).

21. ζωοποιέω (*zōopoieō*): 5:21 (2x); 6:63.

22. Craig Keener, *The Gospel of John: A Commentary*, 2 vols. (Peabody: Hendrickson, 2003), 1:328.

23. J. Scott, *Domination*, passim.

24. See, for instance, Carter, *Matthew and the Margins*; idem, *Matthew and Empire*.

25. John 6:51 and 58 (live into the age); 8:51, 52; 10:28; 11:26.

26. αἰώνιον (*aiōnion*): 3:15, 16, 36; 4:14, 36; 5:24, 39; 6:27, 40, 47, 54, 68; 10:28; 12:25, 50; 17:2, 3.

27. For an overview, see George W. E. Nickelsburg, "Eschatology (Early Jewish)," *ABD* 2:579–94; idem, *Ancient Judaism*, 120–46.

28. This phrase recurs; see, for example, Brown, *John*, 1:507; Schnackenburg, *John*, 2:355; D. M. Smith, *Theology*, 149; M. Thompson, *God of the Gospel*, 87.

29. Schnackenburg, *John*, 2:361.

30. Bultmann (*Theology*, 2:62) speaks of the individual hearer's "life-and-death decision." Brown (*John*, 1:507) maintains the individual focus by saying that "the eternal life of the Christian has come through the action of the Son of God," and Ashton (*Understanding*, 217) similarly talks in the singular of the "believer's participation in the life of faith."

31. I will discuss these practices further in chapter 10 below.

32. C. K. Barrett, "Christocentric or Theocentric? Observations on the Theological Method of the Fourth Gospel," in *Essays on John*, ed. C. K. Barrett (Philadelphia: Westminster, 1982), 1–18, esp. 5.

33. Other traditions seem to expect the destruction of the wicked before the resurrection of the righteous (*Ps. Sol.* 3:9–12) and without participation in a "resurrection to life" (2 Macc 7:14).

34. "On that day": Isa 10:20; Hos 1:5; 2:21; Joel 2:1; Amos 9:11; Zech 14:4, 6, 8, 9, 13, 20; also *1 En.* 45:3.

35. Corell, *Consummatum Est*, 140. Regrettably Corell does not develop the implications of this observation.

36. John 2:1–11, turning water into wine; 4:46–54, healing the sick child; 5:1–18, curing the paralyzed man; 6:1–14, feeding the crowd; 6:16–21, walking on the sea; 9:1–41, giving sight to the blind man; 11:1–44, raising the dead Lazarus.

37. Discussions of Jewish texts include Robert. H. Charles, *Eschatology: The Doctrine of a Future Life in Israel, Judaism and Christianity: A Critical History* (1899; New York: Schocken Books, 1963); R. Martin-Achard, *From Death to Life* (Edinburgh: Oliver & Boyd, 1960); George W. E. Nickelsburg, *Resurrection, Immortality, and Eternal Life in Intertestamental Judaism*, HTS 26 (Cambridge: Harvard University Press, 1972); Hans C. C. Cavallin, *Life After Death*, part 1, *An Inquiry into the Jewish Background* (Lund: Gleerup, 1974); John J. Collins, "Apocalyptic Eschatology as the Transcendence of Death," *CBQ* 36 (1974): 21–43; Martin Hengel, *Judaism and Hellenism* (Philadelphia: Fortress, 1974), 196–202; J. J. Collins, *Apocalyptic Imagination*; Gregory J. Riley, *Resurrection Reconsidered* (Minneapolis: Fortress, 1995), 10–23; Richard Bauckham, "Life, Death, and the Afterlife in Second Temple Judaism," in Longenecker, *Life in the Face of Death*, 80–95; Joseph Sievers, "Josephus and the Afterlife," in *Understanding Josephus: Seven Perspectives*, JSPSup32 (Sheffield: Sheffield Academic Press, 1998), 20–34: Josephus does not use "eternal life" but speaks commonly of the soul's liberation from the body (21, 27–31); Alan Segal, *Life After Death: A History of the Afterlife in Western Religion* (New York: Doubleday, 2004), 248–396; James H. Charlesworth et al., *Resurrection: The Origin and Future of a Biblical Doctrine* (New York: T&T Clark, 2006); George W. E. Nickelsburg, "Early Judaism and Resurrection," *ABD* 5:684–91; idem, "Eschatology," *ABD* 2:579–94. Pseudepigraphical texts and introductions are found in J. H. Charlesworth, *Old Testament Pseudepigrapha* (*OTP*), 2 vols.

38. As the studies of Cavallin (*Life After Death*) and Nickelsburg (*Resurrection*), among others, have demonstrated, there was no standard or uniform Jewish conception of the afterlife. From his investigation of Diaspora and other texts, Cavallin (for summary, see *Life After Death*, 197–99) distinguishes 19 different expectations involving various forms of postdeath transformation, including resurrection of the body, immortality of the soul, intermediate states, heavenly and astral blessedness, and punishment, not to mention the apparent Sadducean denial of any form of afterlife (Josephus, *J.W.* 2.165; *Ant.* 18.16; Mark 12:18; Acts 4:1–2; 23:8). This variety indicates that investigating the Gospel's presentation of eternal life requires much more than simply listing references to "eternal life."

39. Riley, *Resurrection*, 23–58; for Plato's notion of the soul (its divine origin, journey to the world of the senses, longing for the true reality, and return home from exile after purification by

philosophy), see Werner Jaeger, "The Greek Ideas of Immortality," in *Immortality and Resurrection*, ed. Krister Stendahl (New York: MacMillan, 1965), 97–114; also Franz Cumont, *After Life in Roman Paganism* (New Haven: Yale University Press, 1922); Peter G. Bolt, "Life, Death, and the Afterlife in the Greco-Roman World," in Longenecker, *Life in the Face of Death*, 51–79; Segal, *Life After Death*, 204–47.

40. The challenges are at least threefold. The first involves adjudicating the variety of cultural options on offer. The second concerns identifying an analogous worldview appropriate for John's Gospel. But over a century of Johannine studies has demonstrated the difficulty of such identification. For example, one of the current favorites is Qumran, especially for the "presentness" of John's eternal life. Thus Nickelsburg, "Resurrection," *ABD* 5:690, identifies Qumran (in the *Hodayot*, 1QH 3 and 11) as well as Wisdom of Solomon. Yet the future dimensions of John's eschatology present a problem: Nickelsburg (*ABD* 2:690) notes Johannine references to "future resurrection and universal judgment" but accounts for (dismisses?) these "tensions" on the basis of "hypotheses of sources, redaction, and recension." More helpful attention to future dimensions is found in M. Thompson, *God of the Gospel*, 80–87. For a questioning of Qumran's influence on John, see Richard Bauckham, "Qumran and the Fourth Gospel: Is There a Connection?" in *The Scrolls and the Scriptures: Qumran Fifty Years After*, ed. Stanley Porter and Craig Evans, JSPSup 26 (Sheffield: Sheffield Academic Press, 1997), 267–79. The third challenge is to account adequately for the particular shape that eternal life takes in John's different literary context and in relation to other historical forces at work on the Gospel.

41. In Jewish texts, "eternal life" appears in various contexts to refer to various forms of afterlife:

1. In Joseph's prayer that Aseneth "live in your eternal life for ever and ever" (*Jos. Asen.* 8:11), it is not clear to some interpreters that it is even a postdeath reference (Cavallin, *Life After Death*, 155–58). C. Burchard (*OTP* 2:194) declares that in *Joseph and Aseneth* there is "individual afterlife in heaven (8:9; 15:7–8; 22:13)," possibly an angelic existence, but with "a body (cf. 16:16; 18:9)."

2. Similarly, while the Qumran *Damascus Document* (CD) promises eternal life to the righteous (3.20), it is not clear that it refers to a postdeath existence. It at least describes the present existence of the community as a participation in the community of angels, and it may denote existence after the final judgment (1QS 4.7–8). Cavallin (*Life After Death*, 60–68) emphasizes realized eschatology, as do Nickelsburg, *Resurrection*, 144–51, and J. Collins, "Apocalyptic Eschatology," 35–37; contrary to J. Collins, J. Charlesworth ("The Dead Sea Scrolls and the Gospel according to John," in *Exploring the Gospel of John*, ed. R. A. Culpepper and C. C. Black [Louisville: Westminster John Knox, 1996], 65–97, esp. 73) reads 1QS 4:7–8 as a reference to "final judgment at the messianic end time." For discussion of future dimensions in Qumran eschatologies, see Nickelsburg, "Eschatology," *ABD* 2:586–88. The classic contribution is H.-W. Kuhn, *Enderwartung und gegenwärtiges Heil*, SUNT 4 (Göttingen: Vandenhoeck & Ruprecht, 1966). For critique, see Ashton, *Understanding*, 217n25.

3. In *T. Ash.* 5:2, eternal life "wards off death," but it is not clear what sort of existence it is. Elsewhere in the *Testaments of the Twelve Patriarchs*, resurrection seems to be affirmed (*T. Sim.* 6:7; *T. Jud.* 25:1, 4; *T. Zeb.* 10:2), though with few details. Cavallin, *Life After Death*, 53–57.

4. In *1 En.* 15:4, 6, eternal life is the immortal existence in heaven of the heavenly watchers.

5. Other texts clearly link eternal life with some form of immortality of the soul. In *T. Ab.* 20:10–14, Abraham's body is buried under the oak tree, while the angels escort his soul into heaven and endless life (cf. *Jub.* 23:27–31). *First Enoch* 22 attests an intermediate state and places for souls until the final judgment. In Wis 3:2–4; 8:13; cf. 9:15; 4 Macc 15:3; cf. 10:15; 16:13, 25; 18:23; and Philo's solitary use of "eternal life" (*Flight* 78), the soul lives forever

with God. Cavallin (*Life After Death*, 135) notes that Philo's concept of the immortality of the soul differs from Wisdom of Solomon and 4 Maccabees because of Philo's anthropology. For Philo, humans possess this immortality before death by virtue of their creation with a share in the Divine. Immortality is an inherent quality of the soul or mind. Josephus (Cavallin, *Life After Death*, 141–47) emphasizes the immortality of the soul (e.g., *J.W.* 7.344–347), though his own predilection as a Pharisee (*Life* 12) may be to resurrection of (a new) body (*J.W.* 2.163). In *Ag. Ap.* 218–219, Josephus claims that most expect an afterlife. Cavallin (*Life After Death*, 145–46) claims that the language is weighted toward resurrection and re-creation of the universe, but concedes some uncertainty due to the vagueness of the language. Sievers, "Josephus and the Afterlife."

42. Segal, *Life After Death*, 456–57.

43. J. Collins, "Apocalyptic Eschatology," 35.

44. J. Charlesworth, "Where Does the Concept of Resurrection Appear and How Do We Know That?" and "Resurrection: The Dead Sea Scrolls and the New Testament," in J. Charlesworth et al., *Resurrection*, 1–21, 138–86; C. D. Elledge, "Resurrection of the Dead: Exploring Our Earliest Evidence Today," in ibid., 22–52, esp. 32–35.

45. M. Thompson, *God of the Gospel*, 84–85; Corell, *Consummatum Est*, 148.

46. O'Day, "John," 740–41, 751.

47. M. Thompson, *God of the Gospel*, 85n52; Bultmann, *John*, 601–2, 629; idem, *Theology*, 2:57.

48. E.g., Bultmann, *John*, 219–20.

49. See the summary of Robert Kysar, *John: The Maverick Gospel*, rev. ed. (Louisville: Westminster/John Knox Press, 1993), 99–106.

50. See the Appendix.

51. M. Thompson, *God of the Gospel*, 82.

52. Ernst Käsemann, "On the Subject of Primitive Christian Apocalyptic," in *New Testament Questions of Today* (Philadelphia: Fortress, 1969), 108–37, esp. 135.

53. Riley, *Resurrection*, 23–68.

54. J. Collins, "Apocalyptic Eschatology," 34; Cavallin, *Life After Death*, 26–30.

55. See the discussion in chap. 7 above.

56. I am following R. B. Wright, "*Psalms of Solomon*: Theological Importance," in *OTP* 2:643–46. Cavallin (*Life After Death*, 57–60) recognizes resurrection in *Ps. Sol.* 3:10–12 but is reticent about claiming a bodily resurrection, and *Ps. Sol.* 17 plays no part in his analysis.

57. Cavallin (*Life After Death*, 40–53) argues for a reference to resurrection in *1 En.* 90:33, in the earliest section of the document. The Enoch tradition combines resurrection with other conceptions of the afterlife. *First Enoch* 91–104 and esp. 91:10 and 92:3–4 attest a resurrection, but whether of the soul or body is not clear. In 102:4–5 and 103:3–7 souls enjoy a joyful eternity. Nickelsburg (*Resurrection*, 112–30) sets the references in 102–4 in the context of political and socioeconomic oppression by the wealthy and powerful.

58. Contra Moore, *Empire and Apocalypse*, 73–74.

59. John 2:11, 23; 3:2; 4:48, 54; 6:2, 14, 26; 7:31; 9:16; 11:47; 12:18, 37; 20:30.

60. K. Scott, *Imperial Cult*, 1–19.

61. Bultmann, *John*, 218; cf. Ashton, *Understanding*, 219. Both Dorothy A. Lee (*The Symbolic Narratives of the Fourth Gospel*, JSNTSup 95 [Sheffield: Sheffield Academic Press, 1994]) and Craig R. Koester (*Symbolism in the Fourth Gospel* [Minneapolis: Fortress, 1995]) make material transformation itself relatively immaterial and subservient to the greater purpose of christological and anthropological revelation. Even in his signs source, Robert Fortna (*The Fourth Gospel and Its Predecessor* [Philadelphia: Fortress, 1988], 251) maintains that the signs only legitimate Jesus' messianic status: "Even the healings are Christological not soteriological."

62. For example, Fortna, *Fourth Gospel,* 223–50.

63. Ibid., 259.

64. Ibid., 223–314. Among the changes that the Fourth Gospel makes to the signs source is recasting Jesus' messiahship so that "it is not to be understood in a political or earthly sense" (229), the wonder-working stories "are now only the starting point for extended discourses by Jesus" (231), a sign is not "something in itself" but conveys Jesus' "divine sonship" (237–38) and elicits faith (239–50), the Gospel gives them a "symbolic meaning" such as "the bread of life" (6:27–51; p. 241), salvation comprises life in "the profounder sense" and not simply the physical healing of a dying boy" (259).

65. Fortna, *Fourth Gospel,* 261–62.

66. Cavallin, *Life After Death,* 80–94; J. Collins, *Apocalyptic Imagination,* 155–80. Also to be noted is *Sib. Or.* 4.176–191, with its similarities to the resurrection claims of *4 Ezra* 7.

67. In the vision of the very fertile "Garden of Eden and its fruits" in *Apoc. Ab.* 21, "I saw men doing justice in it, their food and their rest." The scene offers a quite material vision of the afterlife but does not explicitly indicate whether it involves resurrection of the body or immortality of the soul.

68. Lenski, *Power and Privilege,* 189–296.

69. Whittaker, "The Poor," 272–99; Garnsey, "Peasants in Ancient Roman Society," in *Cities, Peasants,* 91–106, and "Non-Slave Labour in the Roman World," in ibid., 134–50; Géza Alföldy, *The Social History of Rome* (Totowa, NJ: Barnes & Noble Books, 1985), 133–46; MacMullen, *Roman Social Relations*; Garnsey, "Independent Freedmen and the Economy of Roman Italy under the Principate," in *Cities, Peasants,* 28–44.

70. Sherry C. Fox ("Health in Hellenistic and Roman Times: The Case Studies of Paphos, Cyprus, and Corinth, Greece," in *Health in Antiquity,* ed. Helen King [London: Routledge, 2005], 59–82) concludes that at Corinth the average age (of the skeletal remains) was 42.3 years for males and 39.5 years for females, and at Paphos, 34.4 years for males and 34.5 years for females.

71. Stark, "Urban Chaos," 189–210; Scobie, "Slums," 399–433; Whittaker, "The Poor," 288; Bruce W. Frier, "Roman Demography," in *Life, Death, and Entertainment in the Roman Empire,* ed. D. S. Potter and D. J. Mattingly (Ann Arbor: University of Michigan Press, 1999), 85–109; Scobie, "Slums," 25 years, 399; Garnsey, "Child Rearing," in *Cities, Peasants,* 256.

72. Peter Garnsey, *Food and Society,* xi, 1–4, 31, 34–36; idem, *Famine and Food Supply in the Graeco-Roman World* (Cambridge: Cambridge University Press, 1988), 3–39; idem, "Mass Diet and Nutrition in the City of Rome," in *Cities, Peasants,* 226–52; idem, "Responses to Food Crisis in the Ancient Mediterranean World," in *Hunger in History: Food Shortage, Poverty and Deprivation,* ed. L. F. Newman (Oxford: Blackwell, 1990), 126–46. For Rome, see Greg S. Aldrete and David J. Mattingly, "Feeding the City: The Organization, Operation, and Scale of the Supply System for Rome," in Potter and Mattingly, *Life, Death, and Entertainment,* 171–204; D. V. Sippel, "Some Observations on the Means and Cost of the Transport of Bulk Commodities in the Late Republic and Early Empire," *Ancient World* 16 (1987): 35–45; Peter Garnsey and Richard Saller, *The Roman Empire: Economy, Society, and Culture* (Berkeley: University of California Press, 1987), 83–103; Peter Garnsey, "Grain for Rome," in *Trade in the Ancient Economy,* ed. P. Garnsey, K. Hopkins, and C. R. Whittaker (London: Hogarth, 1983), 118–30; G. Rickman, *The Corn Supply of Ancient Rome* (Oxford: Clarendon, 1980).

73. For example, Garnsey, *Famine and Food Supply,* 218–27, reports crises in Rome in the years 5 CE, 6, 7, 8, 9, 32, 41, 51, 62, 64, 69, 70, with undated incidents in the reign of Domitian.

74. Ibid., 231–32, 255–57.

75. L. Foxhall and H. Forbes, "*Sitometreia:* The Role of Grain as a Staple Food in Classical Antiquity," *Chiron* 12 (1982): 41–90, esp. 74; David J. Mattingly, "First Fruit? The Olive in the Roman World," in *Human Landscapes in Classical Antiquity: Environment and Culture,* ed. G. Shipley and J. Salmon (New York: Routledge, 1996), 213–53; N. Purcell, "Wine and Wealth in

Ancient Italy," *JRS* 75 (1985): 1–19; Garnsey, "The Bean: Substance and Symbol," in Garnsey, *Cities, Peasants*, 214–25. Meat and fish were more commonly elite food: Garnsey, "Mass Diet," 243; Mireille Corbier, "The Ambiguous Status of Meat in Ancient Rome," *Food and Foodways* 3 (1989): 223–64.

76. For storage, see John K. Evans, "Plebs Rustica: The Peasantry of Classical Italy," *AJAH* 5 (1980): 144–47; K. D. White, *Greek and Roman Technology* (London: Thames & Hudson, 1984), 62–63; for wheat, see Garnsey, "Mass Diet and Nutrition," 229–39; elites favored white bread made from the best-quality and most-refined wheat, leaving heavier, less-processed, less-digestible cereals and bread for the poor (Horace, *Ep.* 2.1.123; Seneca, *Ep.* 18.7; 119.3; Martial, *Epig.* 11.56.8). L. A. Moritz, *Grain-Mills and Flour in Classical Antiquity* (Oxford: Clarendon, 1958).

77. L. de Ligt, "Demand, Supply, Distribution: The Roman Peasantry between Town and Countryside; Rural Monetization and Peasant Demand," *Münstersche Beiträge zur antiken Handelsgeschichte* 9 (1990): 24–56; Galen, *On the Properties of Foodstuffs* 38–39; V. Nutton, "Galen and the Traveler's Fare," in *Food in Antiquity*, ed. J. Wilkins, D. Harvey, and M. Dobson (Exeter, UK: University of Exeter Press, 1995), 359–70.

78. Neville Morley, "The Salubriousness of the Roman City," in King, *Health in Antiquity*, 192–204; for attempts to gather information from specific cities, including from limited skeletal remains, see Fox, "Health," in ibid., 59–82; and Ray Laurence, "Health and Life Course at Herculaneum and Pompeii," in ibid., 83–96.

79. For the following, see Garnsey, *Food and Society*, 34–61; D. V. Sippel, "Dietary Deficiency among the Lower Classes of Late Republican and Early Imperial Rome," *Ancient World* 16 (1987): 47–54; Garland, *Eye of the Beholder*, 11–27; Garnsey, "Mass Diet," 245–49; D. and P. Brothwell, *Food in Antiquity* (New York: Praeger, 1969), 175–92.

80. Garland, *Eye of Beholder*, 18–44; Scobie, "Slums," 421–24, 425–27; John Stambaugh, *The Ancient Roman City* (Baltimore: Johns Hopkins University Press, 1988), 135–37; Whittaker, "The Poor," 282–87; Rodney Stark, "Antioch as the Social Situation for Matthew's Community," in *Social History of the Matthean Community*, ed. D. Balch (Minneapolis: Fortress, 1991), 189–210; K. White, *Greek and Roman Technology*, 165–68. G. Downey ("The Water Supply of Antioch on the Orontes in Antiquity," *Annales archéolgiques de Syrie* 2 [1951]: 171–87) is limited. For elite struggle with, control of, and dependence on water, see N. Purcell, "Rome and the Management of Water: Environment, Culture, and Power," in Shipley and Salmon, *Human Landscapes*, 180–212.

81. Garnsey, *Food and Society*, 52–54, 106–8; idem, "Child Rearing in Ancient Italy," in *Cities, Peasants*, 253–71, esp. 261–70. D. Engels ("The Problem of Female Infanticide in the Greco-Roman World," *Classical Philology* 75 [1980]: 112–20) warns against overstating the practice of exposing infants.

82. K. D. White, "Food Requirements and Food Supplies in Classical Times in Relation to the Diet of the Various Classes," *Progress in Food and Nutrition Science* 2 (1976): 143–91.

83. Pliny the Elder, *Nat. Hist.* 5.58; 18.1168, reporting severe flooding along the Nile; papyri (P.Mich. 594) record high numbers of tax-defaulters; Josephus (*Ant.* 3.320–321; 20.51–53, 101) mentions famine in Judea during Claudius's reign; cf. Acts 11:28; the actions of Tiberius Claudius Dinippus, three times during this period appointed as *curator annonae* to oversee grain distribution in Corinth; Suetonius, *Claud.* 18; Tacitus, *Ann.* 6:13; 12.43; Bruce W. Winter, "Acts and Food Shortages," in *The Book of Acts in Its Graeco-Roman Setting*, ed. David W. Gill and Conrad Gempf (Grand Rapids: Eerdmans, 1994), 59–78, esp. 62–65; Kenneth S. Gapp, "The Universal Famine under Claudius," *HTR* 28 (1935): 258–65. For some elite observations, see Seneca, *On the Brevity of Life* 18.5; Dio Chrysostom, *Tumult.* (*Or. 46*) 10–12; Lucan, *Pharsalia* (*Civil War*) 3.55–58; Philostratus, *Life of Apollonius* 1.15.

84. Bultmann, *John*, 119–21, 213–14.

85. Eschatological banquet: Isa 25:6–10. Marriage metaphor: 54:4–8; 62:4–5. Feast, wine, grain: Isa 25:6–10; Jer 31:12 (cf. John 6:1–14). Abundant wine and God's new age: Hos 14:7; Joel 3:18; Amos 9:13–14.

86. Bultmann, *Gospel*, 119n1; van Tilborg, *Reading John*, 95–98.

87. Carter, *Pontius Pilate*, chaps. 1–2, 7.

88. Van Tilborg, *Reading John*, 94–95.

89. Barbette Spaeth, *The Roman Goddess Ceres* (Austin: University of Texas Press, 1996), 23, 24–30.

90. Per Gustaf Hamberg, *Studies in Roman Imperial Art* (Uppsala: Almqvist & Wiksell, 1945), 32–40.

91. For the entanglement of the fishing industry in the imperial economy, see Hanson and Oakman, *Palestine*, 106–10; for a fishing inscription and tollhouse at Ephesus dedicated to Nero, see IEph 1a.20; G. Horsley, "Fishing Cartel," 95–114.

92. Bultmann, *Theology*, 2:66.

93. Paul W. Meyer, "'The Father': The Presentation of God in the Fourth Gospel," in Culpepper and Black, *Exploring the Gospel of John*, 255–73; M. Thompson, *God of the Gospel*.

9

John's Father and the Emperor as
Father of the Fatherland

The identification of God as Father is one of the distinctive features of John's Gospel. John's Gospel designates God as "Father" about 120 times compared with Matthew's 44 times,[1] Mark's four times,[2] and Luke's 17 times.[3] Scholars have explored John's use of "Father" language in several ways. Its possible origins have been one area of focus, whether the Hebrew Bible, the historical Jesus, or the influence of Greco-Roman patriarchal household structures (*patria potestas*).[4] Feminist scholars have especially examined the implications of such a gendered image of God for contemporary readers of John.[5] Other scholars have sought to tease out the rich and distinctive contours of John's presentation of God as Father, emphasizing the intimacy yet subordination of the Father-Son relationship,[6] and identifying the central activity of the Father as giving life,[7] or as sending the Son.[8]

In this chapter, my approach continues to center on John's rhetoric of distance and to be framed by intertextual concerns. My focus is on a dimension of the Father language that has been largely ignored in Johannine scholarship, not attuned to the imperial realities of the world in which John's Gospel was first engaged.[9] I want to put this distinctive Johannine language for God into conversation with the language of "Father" commonly used for the Roman emperor. More specifically, from the first century BCE onward, numerous authors, inscriptions, and coins identify the emperor as *pater patriae*, "Father of the Fatherland," or "Father of the Country."[10] What did this title designate, and what happens when John's favorite designation for God is heard in relation to it?

Putting one set of texts (John's use of Father) in relation to another set (the use of *pater patriae* to designate the emperor) continues the emphasis on cultural intertextuality whereby specific texts are located within (the text of) "society and history . . . within the general text (culture) of which they are a part and which is in turn part of them."[11] What relationships are created, for instance, when John's repeated affirmation of God as Father is heard in a context that affirms the emperor to be father? At the considerable historical distance of two thousand years, determining intertextual functions with any certainty may be difficult, as the previous discussion attests, but pursuing the question, commonly ignored in previous studies of "Father" language in John, may help us understand further the contours and force of the Gospel among Jesus-believers in Ephesus as a work of imperial negotiation.

I will suggest that exploring John's use of Father language in relation to the imperial phrase *pater patriae* provides an example of what Edward Said calls "contrapuntal reading,"[12] the interplay between a term associated with elite imperial discourse and a term used in the resistant though imitative discourse of the Gospel. This interplay expresses the "hidden transcript" or "little tradition" of John's community that contests the dominant imperial elite's construction of reality (the great tradition or public transcript) while also self-protectively ensuring the survival of John's community.[13]

To be clear, my concern is with the language's function and not with its origin. I am not arguing that imperial usage is the origin for John's Father language. As previous studies have shown, Father was an appellation for God in the Hebrew Bible and Jewish traditions, as it was for Zeus and Jupiter.[14] I am also setting aside the issue of the possible origins of father language from the historical Jesus and from Greco-Roman household structures. My focus concerns the intersection of John's language for God as "Father" with the common designation of the Roman emperor as "Father of the Country," or "Father of the Fatherland" (*pater patriae*, sometimes *parens patriae*).

The Emperor as Father of the Fatherland

John's late first-century audience was very familiar with the phrase *pater patriae* as a key imperial claim describing the emperor's identity and diverse roles in relation to his subjects. The title appears in both Latin and Greek inscriptions from Ephesus: for example, it identifies the emperor Claudius around 48 CE (*pater patriae*, πατὴρ πατρίδος), and later in the century, when John's Gospel was written, it refers to the emperors Titus, and Domitian (IEph 2.259A, 259B, 262, 263B). Coins minted at Ephesus or elsewhere in Asia also identify emperors as *pater patriae*, notably Vespasian and Domitian, associating them with peace, fertility, social harmony, Jupiter, victory, and war.[15] By the late first century CE, the designation was widely used throughout the empire to define the idealized relationship between ruler and ruled, capturing the duties and obligations of the benign and beneficent patron-emperor and his client-subjects, the emperor's children. Yet at another level, the metaphor functioned to mask the brutalities of a massively unbalanced power relationship marked by tyranny, exploitation, and subjugation. In this imperial context, how might John's frequent designation of God as Father be heard?

"Father" gained prominence as a political title in the republic in the first century BCE in two interrelated contexts. First, it was used of Romulus as founder of the city Rome.[16] Ennius (*Ann.* 113V) hails Romulus as "*o pater, o genitor*," father and founder of the community, the source and origin of its existence. Cicero (*Div.* 1.3) similarly identifies Romulus as the "father [*parens*] of this city." To this recognition of his role as the origin of the city's life, Livy (1.16.3) adds the role of ordering and ruling it. He identifies "Romulus as a god and a god's son, the king and Father [*regem parentumque*] of the Roman city."

Further, in the republic it was also used as a title of honor for those who saved the city from internal and external enemies (conspirators and invaders) and who preserved and/or renewed its life.[17] Weinstock demonstrates that such benefactors and saviors were regarded as refounding the city, doing again what Romulus had previously done in giving life to the city.[18] So Camillus (d. ca. 365 BCE) overcame the Gauls who had occupied Rome, and according to Livy (5.49.7), "having recovered his country from her enemies" was hailed "as a Romulus and Father of his Country [*parens patriae*] and a second Founder of the City." Cicero describes Gaius Marius (d. 86 BCE) as "father of his country" after he had saved Rome from invading German armies and had been a great legislator: "Shall Gaius Marius whom we may in very truth entitle the father of his country, the parent [*patrem patriae, parentem*], I say, of your liberties and of our state, be condemned by us?" (*In Defense of Rabirius* 27). Plutarch (*Mar.* 27.9) later identifies Marius as "the third founder of Rome." Cicero's own opposition to the Catilinarian conspiracy merits his being addressed as "the savior and founder of his country" and by Cato and the people as "father of his country" (πατέρα πατρίδος; Plutarch, *Cic.* 22.5; 23.6), though Cicero claims Quintus Catulus gave him the title in the senate (*In Pisonem* 6; *Pro Sestio* 121). Not surprisingly, the designation is also used for Julius Caesar as a savior and refounder of Rome. It appears in literary texts (Appian, *Civil Wars* 2.16.106, πατὴρ πατρίδος, *patēr patridos*; 2.20.144, "the father of his country [πατέρα πατρίδος, *patera patridos*], the benefactor, the peerless protector"; Suetonius, *Deified Julius* 76.1, *patris patriae*; Dio Cassius 44.4.4, πατέρα πατρίδος, *patera patridos*), on coins from 44 BCE,[19] and on inscriptions.[20]

Weinstock argues, though, that its use for Caesar goes beyond its use for Cicero, Camillus, and Marcius, as those who saved the city from enemies and preserved and/or renewed its life. While these others were honored for significant actions, Caesar was honored not just for particular acts but also for a permanent position as Rome's leader and ruler. Consequently, in being used for Caesar, the term was more than an ascription of glory; it redefined the relationship between ruler and ruled. It presented his "unlimited political power" not in terms of tyranny but in terms of *patria potestas*, binding his fellow citizens to him like sons to a father in *pietas*, the loyalty or allegiance of appropriate duties and obligations. And in turn it defined Caesar's relationship to them as that of "the patron to his clients (rather than that of an autocrat)."[21] It presented an ideal relationship while masking the disparities of the power arrangement.

In describing his consulship, Cicero had used the well-established contrast between "a cruel tyrant" and a "tender parent" (*mitissimum parentem*, in *De domo suo* 94) to express his commitment to use his power in the latter style.[22] More than a century later, Pliny the Younger continues the distinction, contrasting the tyrant Domitian with Trajan. The latter is a "fellow-citizen, not a tyrant, one who is our father, not our overlord" (*Pan.* 2.3). And later again, Dio Cassius has Caesar use the same image in a speech set in 46 BCE to the senate, when Caesar returns to Rome victorious. Dio says that Caesar perceived "that the people were afraid of his power and suspicious of his proud bearing and consequently expected to suffer many terrible evils" (43.15.1) because of the actions of previous conquerors such as Marcius, Cinna, and Sulla. Caesar sought to reassure them by renouncing the role of tyrant (43.17.2) and by appealing for them to make a "beginning to love each other without suspicion." Accordingly he instructs them: "You will conduct yourselves toward me as toward a father (πρὸς πατέρα, *pros patera*), enjoying the forethought and solicitude which I shall give you, . . . and I will take thought for you as for my children" (43.17.5–6). His fatherly role, marked by non-suspicious love, means praying for them to accomplish "noblest deeds," enduring the limits of human nature, exalting the good, and "correcting the rest" (43.17.6). They are exhorted to suspend their suspicions and accept the perspective (practice the self-deception?) that their ruler has their best interests in view rather than his own. The title thus presents a complex and idealized relationship between ruler and ruled in which the latter is expected to render obedience and duty, while the ruler is expected to lovingly seek their well-being, reward their efforts, recognize his power to punish the noncompliant, and inherit the task of preserving, whether by government or military action, the life of the city and its empire.

This language of "Father of the Fatherland" that defined and idealized the relationship between the ruler and the ruled is secured with Augustus.[23] In 2 BCE Augustus officially accepted the title after lengthy resistance to it, perhaps because it named too explicitly the dominating power relationship that he often sought to disguise (*Res gestae,* or *Acts of Augustus* 35). From a century or so later, Suetonius's account of the offering of the title emphasizes several important dimensions (*Aug.* 58). Augustus does not take the title for himself. It is offered to him three times, thereby eliciting from the ones who offer it—people and senate—an escalating expression of their acceptance of, submission to, and gratefulness for his rule.[24] The offering, according to Suetonius's account, expresses the *consensus* that exists between ruler and ruled. Suetonius locates its origin in an act of the "whole body of citizens with a unanimous impulse." Augustus, after humbly refusing it three times, accepts it tearfully, wishing that "I may retain this same unanimous approval of yours to the very end of my life." The people's consent—whatever the reality, and no one was taking a poll of the nonelite—is thus seen in Suetonius's account as a crucial element in defining his rule not as tyranny but as paternal care. But the title is offered not only as a recognition of their compliance and his eminence; it is also offered as a reminder to him to fulfill faithfully his role of ensuring the empire's security and eternity, and maintaining elite well-being.[25] In hailing Augustus as "Father of thy Country," the senator Valerius Messala declares, "We feel that we are praying for lasting prosperity [*felicitatem,* blessedness] for our country and happiness for our city" (Suetonius, *Aug.* 58). Offering the title expresses the expectation that Augustus will carry out the father's task of preserving and prospering the life of city and empire. The ruled depend on the ruler. Duties and obligations, not tyranny and submission, shape the relationship.

What the term denotes in terms of defining the relationship of ruler and ruled is elaborated by Augustus's work, *Res gestae.* Augustus wrote this account of his "accomplishments" in his seventy-sixth year (13 CE), a year before his death (*Res gestae* 35). After his death, copies of it were displayed at various urban locations in the empire, including in Asia.[26] What is striking is that Augustus ends his account with the "senate and the equestrian order as well as the whole of the Roman people" naming him "Father of the Country," an event that happened in 2 BCE (*Res gestae* 35).[27] The narrative effect of ending the work with the bestowal of this honor and title is that the designation "Father of the Country" functions in terms of the ruler-ruled relationship to summarize all his accomplishments and roles as creator, benefactor, and preserver of Rome's world.

These accomplishments and roles can be categorized in six overlapping areas:

Savior and Benefactor of Life

Augustus begins his first-person account by presenting himself in the *pater patriae* tradition of saving the empire from external and internal enemies. He "made the entire world subject to the power of the Roman people," and he "freed the republic oppressed by the tyranny of a faction" (*Res gestae* 1). Subsequently, he gave life to the freed republic through a series of benefactions: supplying grain by which "I liberated the whole city [Rome] from immediate fear and present danger" (5, 15, 18), making financial gifts on numerous occasions to the plebs in Rome (at least "250,000 men") and to soldiers who were colonists (15), buying land for veterans as colonists in Italy and the provinces (16), donating his money to the treasury (17), building the senate house, numerous temples, and various other public works including aqueducts to ensure water supply (18–21), paying for entertainments and games including a naval battle (22–23), and restoring temples in Asia damaged by Mark Antony (24).

Such actions present Augustus as the supreme patron or benefactor of the empire, whose euergetism comprises benefactions for his subjects and redefines them as clients. Accordingly they respond with deference, appreciation, gratitude, and loyalty. "As victor [over internal and external foes], I spared all citizens who asked for forgiveness" (3). They honored him in triumphs and in offering political office (4–6, 10); in making vows, offerings, and altars (9, 11, 12); in sending embassies and ambassadors (31–32); and in bestowing the name "Augustus" in 27 BCE and the title "Father of the Country/Fatherland" (34–25).

Ruler of the World

Augustus ensured Rome's security and extended "the power of the Roman people" over "the entire world" (*Res gestae* 1). He did so by filling political offices at the behest of the senate (1, 7); waging many battles "throughout the whole world" and extending mercy where appropriate (3); subduing and administering Spain and Gaul (12); "securing peace on land and on sea . . . by victories throughout the whole empire of the Roman people" (13); taking "control of the sea from pirates"; returning rebellious slaves to their owners; securing with oaths of loyalty the allegiance of "all of Italy" and "the provinces of Gaul, Spain, Africa, Sicily, and Sardinia" (25); enlarging "the territory of all provinces of the Roman people"; pacifying Gaul, Spain, Germany, the Alps, and Arabia and Ethiopia, where "great forces of both peoples were cut down in battle and many towns captured" (26); adding Egypt, subduing Armenia, and recovering the provinces from the Adriatic to the east (27); recovering military standards lost in battle in Spain, Gaul, Dalmatia, and Parthia (29); extending the "authority of the Roman people" over Pannonia, Illyricum, and Dacia (30); and making friendships and alliances with various eastern (client) kings (31–33).[28] As ruler of the world, he extended the empire "where the ocean encloses it" (26). His benefaction was the rare situation of peace, effected through submission to Roman will and rule. "The doorway of [the temple of] Janus Quirinus" (with gates of war) had been shut—to signify "peace on land and on sea"—only twice "from the time of the city's foundation until before my birth," but during Augustus's time "the senate ordered it shut three times" (13).

Judge and Lawgiver

Augustus presents himself as committed to justice. He avenges the murders of his father, Julius Caesar, through exile, war, and "through legal proceedings" (*Res gestae* 2). He accepts the task bestowed by "the senate and the Roman people" of being "the guardian of laws and morals with supreme power" (6). He passes laws to revive "many exemplary ancestors of our ancestors," thereby passing on "many models of conduct to be imitated" (8). He fulfills his father's will (15). Constantly he claims to attain offices and power only from and for the benefit of the Roman people and at the behest of the senate, in accord with "the customs of our ancestors" (e.g., 5, 6, 34). His commitment to justice is celebrated in the golden shield "given to me by the senate and the Roman people" (34).

Creator of a People; Shaper of a Community

Augustus introduces his accomplishments as being "for the republic and for the Roman people." He claims to have created a freed people who had formerly been "oppressed by the tyranny of a faction" (*Res gestae* 1). He set about establishing law and order (6), increasing the number of patricians, and taking a census of the people followed by a *lustrum*, or purification ritual, that "symbolized the newly constituted citizenry"[29] (8). He provides this people with "peace on land and on sea secured by victories" (13). His military victories and alliances forcibly expanded the empire's membership as a community subjugated to Rome (25–30). Others sought "friendship" by sending embassies (29, 31, 32). "Many other peoples . . . have experienced the trust/faithfulness (*fides/pistis* [πίστις])[30] of the Roman people" (32). Augustus does not use the language of love highlighted by Cicero and later by Dio Cassius, but his account everywhere evidences his self-understanding as a "tender father" of the Roman people.

Sender of Agents

Augustus emphasizes his own active role in bringing about his accomplishments, but he also acknowledges the key contributions of those he commissions as agents of his power. Soldiers are prominent. He has "five hundred thousand soldiers . . . under a military oath of allegiance." Of these he settles "more than three hundred thousand . . . in colonies," as agents of Roman control and culture throughout the empire, and he returned others to their municipalities (*Res gestae* 3, also 16). He refers to "campaigns led successfully by me or my legates under my auspices on land or on sea" (4). His sons Gaius and Lucius Caesar were designated consuls (14). "All of Italy" and "the provinces of Gaul, Spain, Africa, Sicily, and Sardinia" swore an oath of allegiance to Augustus, thereby binding themselves to his purposes. More than 700 senators "served under my standards," 83 of whom were consuls and 170 priests (25). He "founded colonies for soldiers . . . in Africa, Sicily, Macedonia, both Spains, Achaia, Asia, Syria, Gallia Narbonensis, Pisidia. Italy also has 28 colonies founded by my authority" (28). Augustus's authority is enacted through the actions of these designated agents.

Recipient of Honors

Honors expressed the expected gratitude and submission of the ruled for the ruler's benefactions and efforts. Augustus is the constant recipient of honors that celebrate his glory and accomplishments, though some honors he "humbly" declines (e.g., *Res ges-*

tae 4, 5). He receives ovations and triumphs (4), vows and offerings "for my health" (9), annual sacrifices (11), the dedication of an altar of Augustan Peace (12), the threefold honor of having the doorway of Janus Quiranus closed in recognition of the worldwide peace he has established (13), and honors for his two sons (14). He receives the name "Augustus" and a golden shield that celebrates his virtue, clemency, justice, and piety (34). In this idealized relationship of ruler and ruled, there is no room for protest, dissent, or ungratefulness. Augustus's all-embracing crowning honor is receiving the name "Father of the Country" (35).

Augustus's work *Res gestae* thus narrates his accomplishments that elaborate his identity, roles, and relationship with his subjects as "Father of the Country." The work describes, constructs, and confirms the ruler–ruled relationship. He is giver of life and benefactions, ruler of the world, judge and lawgiver, creator of a people, sender of agents, and recipient of honors.[31] Though the official bestowal of the designation that sums up all these roles, "Father of the Country," came relatively late in his career—in 2 BCE, at which point the account of *Res gestae* ends—others used this designation of him much earlier, recognizing that his accomplishments expressed a ruler–ruled relationship that rendered him "Father of the Country."

The poet Horace attests this early recognition. He prays that after the great civil disorder, Octavian/Augustus's military skill and power might give life to the state by preserving and protecting it "while you are our leader, O Caesar." He prays, "May you love glorious triumphs, the name of 'Father' [*pater*] and 'Chief' [*princeps*]" (*Odes* 1.2.50)." Further, for Horace "Father" also denotes Augustus's task of creating a people or community in which the civic order is secure and morality renewed. "Whoe'er will banish impious slaughter and intestine fury, whoe'er shall seek to have inscribed upon his statues, 'Father (*pater*) of Cities,' let such have courage to curb our lawless license" (3.24.25). As "Father," the ruler is to preserve the state's life and secure it as a community with civic order and morality. Such a role is part of his divinely ordained task as ruler and judge of the world, as agent of the divine father Jupiter. Horace prays to Jupiter, "O Father and guardian of the human race, you son of Saturn, to you by fate has been entrusted the charge of mighty Caesar; may you be lord of all, with Caesar next in power! . . . Second to you alone shall he with justice rule the broad earth" (1.12.49–57). Horace honors Augustus with language that labels him as "mighty" and sees him becoming godlike in his exercise of power as military commander and rule. Augustus reflects Jupiter's power as his military agent: "We believe that Jove is king in heaven because we hear his thunders peal; Augustus shall be deemed a god on earth for adding to our empire the Britons and dread Parthians" (3.5.1–5).

Ando points out that Horace expresses this expectation that the emperor as father would keep the empire safe by using the term *tutela*, or guardian: Augustus is "present guardian [*tutela praesens*] of Italy and imperial Rome" (*Odes* 4.14.43–44).[32] Suetonius's biography of Augustus (*Aug.* 98) narrates the various omens that accompanied Augustus's birth (Apollo's generative intervention) and that marked him out in childhood as Jupiter's chosen (lightning, dreams, prophecies of a great rule). The omens include Quintus Catulus's dream and declaration that the young Augustus was to be "guardian [*tutelam*] of his country" (98.8).

Ovid constructs a similar relationship of ruler and ruled whereby Augustus as "Father of the Country" gives life, rules the world, judges and gives laws, creates a people, sends agents, and receives honor. Ovid addresses Augustus honorably as

Holy Father of thy Country [*sancte pater patriae*], . . . yet did you also receive, though late, your title true; long time had you been Father of the World [*pater orbis*]. You bear on earth the name which Jupiter bears in high heaven; of men [*sic*] you are the father [*pater*], he of the gods. . . . Caesar by his guardian care makes great your [Romulus's] city walls. (*Fasti* 2.127–134)

In his rule over the world, Augustus reflects and reveals Jupiter's power. "Jupiter controls the heights of heaven and the kingdoms of the triformed universe; but the earth is under Augustus's sway. Each is both father [*pater*] and ruler" (*Metam.* 15.858–860). Yet Ovid, though alienated from and banished from Rome by Augustus the judge, nevertheless honors him. Just as Jupiter exercises restraint in not punishing all humans for every wrong, Augustus does a similar thing: "Do you also, seeing you are called ruler and father of our native land [*patriae pater*] follow the way of the god who has the same title. And that you do; no one has ever been able to hold the reins of power with more restraint" (*Tristia* 2.39–42). He goes on to acknowledge that Augustus has not taken away his life ("Life was granted me," 2.127), but appeals to Augustus as creator of a secured people and as one who gently rules it, "by our native land which is safe and secure under your fatherly [*parente*] care. . . . Spare me, father of our country [*pater patriae*]" (2.157–158, 181). Subsequently, again in linking Jupiter's rule and Augustus's rule, he recognizes that Augustus as "the ruler of the world . . . does gaze about upon the world that depends upon you" (2.215–220).

Inscriptions from Asia Minor around 2 BCE, when Augustus accepted the title "Father of the Country," carefully specify the worldwide extent of these fatherly roles.[33] They specifically include the provinces in Augustus's dominion. Elite provincials make explicit their participation in the imperial rule by adding "and of the entire human race" to the title "Father of the Country" (πατὴρ τῆς πατρίδος καὶ τοῦ σύμπαντος τῶν ἀνθρώπων γένους, *patēr tēs patridos kai tou sympantos tōn anthrōpōn genous*).[34]

Emperors Tiberius,[35] Gaius Caligula,[36] and Claudius[37] employ or are associated with the title, and its use embraces similar themes in relation to them. Seneca addresses the young Nero in his work *On Mercy* and uses the father image to discuss the duty (*officium*) of the ruler (*princeps*).[38] Seneca elaborates familiar themes associated with the emperor's identity as father in terms of his roles as giver of life, ruler of the world, judge and lawgiver, creator of a people, sender of agents, and the recipient of honor. The work begins with a brief reference to virtuous deeds and the emperor's task of controlling "this vast throng—discordant, fractious, and unruly" (1.1). Seneca then gives Nero a soliloquy in which the emperor acknowledges his enormous power to give or take away life as ruler and judge of the world and claims just and merciful rule over it in remaining "innocent of wrong" (1.2–5). Seneca's concern is that in ruling, the emperor must judge fairly and wisely to create a community secure in his benevolent rule. Such mercy ensures that the emperor is honored (1.11.4). In commending gentleness and care (1.13.1, 4) over cruelty in a ruler, Seneca poses the question, "What, then, is his duty?" His answer evokes a father-child relationship marked by the father's just and loving care. "It is that of the good parent who is wont to reprove his children sometimes gently, sometimes with threats, who at times admonishes them even with stripes." Such a father does not disinherit his children at first offense but seeks their correction. This sort of ruler is appropriately honored: "No glory redounds to a ruler from cruel punishment" (1.17.3). But this is "the duty of a father, and it is also the duty of a prince, whom not in empty flattery we have been led to call 'the Father of the Country' [*patrem patriae*]." Seneca contrasts this genuinely given, prestigious title with others that express flattery because "to 'the Father of the Country' we have given the name in order that he may know that he has been entrusted with a father's power, which is most forbearing in its care for the interests of his children and subordinates his own to theirs" (1.14.1–3). To such literary material[39] can be added coins that frequently announce Nero's identity as *pater patriae* and present him in these same roles, as well as inscriptions.[40]

In the time of John's Gospel,[41] the same themes are evident in Statius's "poetics of empire", which both praise the emperor Domitian as "father" and express Statius's anxiety about negotiating imperial power.[42] In the imperially flattering poems of the *Silvae*, Statius has Janus address Domitian: "Hail, great Father of the world [*parens mundi*], who with me prepares to begin the ages anew" (4.1.17–18). This ruler of the world in this new age (on "life of the age," see chap. 8 above) ensures its order and the compliance of its people with "greater gentleness in arms" (1.1.25–27). As Jupiter's agent,[43] "[you fight and] win the wars of Jove and the battles of the Rhine, you do quell the strife of citizens" (1.1.79–80). The equestrian statue of Domitian "reining your steed" (1.1.5), whose building by loyal and skilled craftsmen is celebrated in the opening poem, witnesses to this military prowess (1.1). Domitian also accomplishes order and rule through his consulship and role as judge and lawgiver (4.1.5–15; 4.3.10, "with justice and courts of law"). By having his agents build the Via Domitiana, he enables the nations to flock to Rome, thus testifying to Rome and the emperor's attraction to and power over the world community. "Come then all you who beneath the sky of dawn owe fealty [*fidem*] to the Roman parent, flock hither all you races on this easy road, come more swiftly than before, you laurels of the East" (4.3.107–110). He ensures life for Italy's inhabitants by ordering the growing of wheat (not vines) in Italy (4.3.11–12), and he "forbids the strength of sex to be destroyed" in forbidding male castration (4.3.13–15; cf. Suetonius, *Dom.* 7). This father conducts public works not only for the people but also for the gods (*Silvae* 4.3.9–10, restoring fields to Ceres; 16, a temple for Jupiter; 17, the temple of Pax; 18–19, a temple dedicated to the deceased of the Flavian family). His world order reveals the will of the gods since Domitian is their agent (so 3.4). Statius experiences Domitian's greatness in being overcome with delight at being present at a banquet with Domitian. From afar, emphasizing the great social distance between himself and the exalted emperor, he addresses Domitian as "O ruler of the nations and mighty father [*magne parens*] of the conquered world. . . . O hope of men and care of the gods" (4.2.14–15). This is a distant father, so exalted that he must "temper his rays and gently veil the glory of his state" (4.2.42–43). He is an agent of the gods, one who is blessed by Jupiter (4.1.44–45) and "rules for him [Jupiter] the happy [blessed] world" (4.3.128–129). Domitian is agent of the gods, giver of life, ruler of the world (including conqueror of nature in 4.3),[44] judge and lawgiver, creator of a subdued and ordered people, sender of agents who accomplish his will, and worthy recipient of honor, including Statius's poems.

Other writers such as Martial and Suetonius,[45] as well as Domitian's coins on which *pater patriae* frequently appears,[46] and inscriptions[47] attest the same cluster of roles associated with being "Father of the Country": giver of benefactions and life, ruler of the world, judge and lawgiver, creator of a people, sender of agents, and recipient of honors. Later emperors such as Trajan are identified as "Father of the Fatherland" and continue these roles.[48] I am not suggesting that everyone in Ephesus was reading Statius and Martial each day. Their literary expressions, though, are consistent with the evidence of coins and inscriptions, and they attest a consistent and pervasive cluster of motifs defining the relationship of ruler and ruled, motifs widely associated with this title.

From the third century, the provincial Dio Cassius sums up some of the developments and emphases associated with "Father of the Fatherland." As givers of life, rulers of the world, judges and lawgivers, creators of a people, senders of agents, and recipients of honor, emperors nevertheless must exercise the relationship of ruler/father and ruled/children with love as Cicero and Julius Caesar (according to Dio) had maintained, and their subjects must reciprocate with due honor:

> The term "Father" perhaps gives them (emperors) a certain authority [ἐξουσίαν] over us all—the authority which fathers once had over their children; yet it did not signify this at first but betokened honor and served as an admonition both to them, that they should love their subjects as they would their children, and to their subjects, that they should revere them as they would their fathers. (53.18.3)

John's Gospel: God as Father

What happens in the intertextuality between this pervasive imperial framework and the frequent use of "Father" to designate God in John's Gospel?

With the same six categories in mind—giver of benefactions and life, ruler of the world, judge and lawgiver, creator of a people, sender of agents, and recipient of honor—I have examined John's 118 or so instances of identifying God as "Father," assigning each instance, if possible, to one of these six categories. Nearly all the references readily fit into at least one of these six categories. Some fit readily into several categories, indicating again that the categories overlap. A small percentage—about nine instances or about 7.5 percent—do not readily fit any category and thus constitute a separate category. I will return to this group below. By far the largest category concerns the Father as sender of agents, though in numerous instances the contexts are rich with multivalent meaning. Nevertheless, attention to the Father image alone does not constitute the whole of John's presentation of God.

Giver of Benefactions and Life

Explicitly John 5:21 declares that the Father raises the dead and gives life as part of God's continuing working (5:17). In 5:26 the Father has life in himself (the "living Father" in 6:57) and has granted life to the Son, presumably part of the "all things" that the Father has given to Jesus (13:3). Manifesting life to others is part of the works that the Father has granted to the Son (5:36; 12:50) since "the will of my Father" is for people to see the Son and believe and have eternal life (6:40). Jesus addresses God as Father before the raising of Lazarus (11:41). This emphasis coalesces with the Gospel's opening verses, which affirm God's cosmic life-giving and creative work (1:1–4).

This presentation of God as the patron of creation, whose benefits are encountered through Jesus, calls for appropriate responses of acknowledgement, gratitude, and commitment. So in 4:23–24 this response involves worship for the Father. In 5:19–30, where the use of Father is pervasive, it comprises "honor" for the Son and Father (5:23, τιμάω, *timaō*) and believing or entrusting oneself (πιστεύω, *pisteuō*) to "him who sent me," a common circumlocution for the Father (5:24; cf. 5:37).

Ruler of the World

The Father is greater than all (10:29) and has given all things into Jesus' hands (13:3). The Father's life-giving purposes for all creation from the beginning (1:1) have been recognized in the first category above, and control over Jesus' revelation will be identified in the discussion of agency below. The Father's sovereign rule (linked with all creation in 1:1–5) is also particularly associated with "giving" and "drawing" believers to Jesus (6:37, 44, 65), and "no one is able to snatch [them] out of the Father's hand" (10:29). The recognition of the Father as the "Ruler of the world" contrasts with the ironic use of this description for Pilate, the representative of Rome's power (12:31; 14:30; 16:11).[49] If Brian Bosworth is correct in arguing that Augustus in *Res gestae* emphasizes two actions, conquest of the world and his benefactions, in order to be recognized as a god, John's "Father" is clearly already God because he performs these tasks. Since antiquity is authority, John's "Father" would seem to be a greater God, who has done these things "in the beginning" (1:1–5).[50]

Judge and Lawgiver

This role is stated but receives relatively minimal attention. In 1:17 God or the Father, named in 1:18, is implied to be the giver of the law to Moses. In 5:22 the Father judges no one, but this is because he has given all judgment to the Son, who is the agent of God's will. In 5:45 Jesus assumes the Father's role as judge in saying that Moses, not he, "will accuse you to the Father." Both Jesus and "the Father that sent me" judge (8:16). This role is evidenced in 15:1, where the father is identified as the vinegrower who removes unfruitful branches (nonproductive disciples, 15:1–2).

Creator of a People

The Father's activity through Jesus creates a people or community of Jesus-believers. "Everyone who has heard and learned from the Father comes to me" (6:45 NRSV). The Father draws or gives these people to Jesus (6:44, 65; 10:29), and it is only through Jesus that people come to the Father (14:6). This people loves Jesus and has "one Father, even

God" (8:41–42 RSV, contrast 8:41–42). Loving Jesus means "keeping [his] word" (14:23) and knowing the Father's love (14:21, 23; 16:27). Prayer to the Father is one of this people's practices (14:16; 15:16; 16:23, 26; compare the prayers of Horace and Ovid above). It also means, according to Jesus' prayer to the Father, being one, staying in the Father's name or purposes, and being with Jesus (17:11, 24). Jesus' Father is also the Father of disciples (20:17), who are commissioned by Jesus to mission, just as the Father has sent Jesus (20:21).

Sender of Agents

This is by far the largest category in John's Gospel. Repeatedly the Gospel declares that Jesus comes from or is sent from/by the Father (1:14; 5:23, 43; 6:32, 57; 8:16; 16:28). The Father witnesses to, seals, consecrates, and charges Jesus for his life-giving mission (5:37; 6:27; 8:18; 10:18, 36). This sending expresses the Father's love for Jesus (3:35; 5:20; 10:17; 15:9). It expresses and is based in the intimate relationship of oneness (10:30) between Jesus and the Father (10:15, 38; 14:7, 9–11, 20; 16:32; 17:21). Accordingly, Jesus is the only one commissioned to reveal the Father (1:18; 6:46; 16:25). His revelation comprises "all things" (3:35; 13:3; 16:15), life (5:26), works (5:36; 10:25, 32, 37), and what he has learned from the Father based on what Jesus has seen the Father doing and heard from him (5:19–20; 8:28, 38; 12:49–50; 14:24; 15:15). Jesus is also commissioned to lay down his life (10:17–18), a commission that he lovingly obeys (14:31; 15:10) and does not shrink from (12:27; 18:11), for which the Father glorifies him (8:54). His commission requires a response either of belief (10:38), through which humans encounter the Father (14:7–9), or of nonunderstanding (5:43; 8:19, 27; 14:8–10) and hostility (15:23–24) because Jesus calls God his own Father (5:18). Hostility to Jesus and the Father means hostility to disciples (16:2–3).

Jesus, though, is not the only agent sent from the Father. The Father also sends the Holy Spirit to teach and remind believers of Jesus' teaching received from the Father (14:26; 15:26). And just as the Father has sent Jesus, so Jesus, as God's commissioned agent, sends disciples to continue his mission to reveal God's life-giving purposes (20:21).

Recipient of Honor

The Father receives worship (4:21, 23; 5:23; though not in the Father's house in Jerusalem: cf. 2:16). To honor the Son, the Father's agent, is to honor the Father (5:23); conversely, not to honor the Son is not to honor the Father (5:23; 8:42, 49; 15:23–24). Those who serve Jesus are honored by the Father (12:26). The Father is glorified in the Son (14:13; 17:1, 5) and in the "much fruit" borne in the lives of disciples (15:8; also 12:26).

The Father as Destiny

A group of nine texts using Father for God remains. These texts concern Jesus' destiny in departing to the Father through crucifixion, resurrection, and ascension (13:1; 14:12,

28; 16:10, 17, 28; 20:17), thereby returning to the one in whose presence he was "in the beginning" (1:1). As I will discuss in chapter 12 below, this motif of ascension and return creates interesting intertextuality with the ascension of deceased rulers such as Romulus, Julius Caesar, and Augustus to the gods, or in the case of Moses, "his pilgrimage from earth to heaven, . . . summoned hither by the Father" (Philo, *Mos.* 2.288–292).[51] Jesus' apotheosis or ascension has a significant impact also for disciples and their destiny: "In my Father's house are many rooms; if it were not so, would I have told you that I go to prepare a place for you?" (14:2 RSV).

It is possible to debate the assignment of some of these verses to particular categories. But in comparing John's texts about the Father with the cluster of ideas around *pater patriae*, significant similarities emerge. Although the texts on Jesus' departure to the Father, for example, are generally not paralleled by *pater patriae* traditions, other emphases clearly overlap. John emphasizes Jesus' agency, just as agency on behalf of the emperor is everywhere evident in the imperial world with allies, client kings, clients, soldiers, and other figures. The Gospel defines the nature of Jesus' agency in terms of giving life and exercising judgment, the same options that existed as far as the imperial elite were concerned for experiencing Rome's power manifested by the emperor's agents. Both the *pater patriae* tradition and John's Gospel emphasize the love of the respective Fathers for their subjects (cf. John 3:16). The *pater patriae* tradition locates the emperor in special relation to the gods, just as John's Gospel places Jesus in intimate relationship of love and unity with the Father, while elevating Jesus by recognizing this relationship existed "in the beginning" (1:1–3). John extends the love of the Father as sender and Jesus the agent to Jesus-believers (e.g., 10:17, 38; 14:10–11, 20–21, 23; 15:9; 17:23, 24, 26). Both texts emphasize claims to rule the world, though John's texts do not share the imperial tradition's emphasis on military conquest and negotiated alliance as a way of establishing and maintaining Rome's rule. Instead, as I argued in the previous chapter on "life of the age," John's Gospel imitates imperial ways in evoking eschatological traditions that crush enemies and forcibly establish God's purposes. Both present the Father's beneficence in terms of giving life, though as I argued in the previous chapter, these visions exhibit similarities and differences. Both also emphasize the creation of communities of followers.

What is very evident in this material, and what has not been explored in previous Johannine scholarship, is the fundamental similarity in the big-picture framework between notions of the emperor as "Father of the Fatherland" and John's presentation of God as "Father." While numerous details differ, the basic contours or frameworks of the respective presentations are quite similar. Both John's Father and Rome's emperor are presented as givers of life, rulers of the world, judges and lawgivers, creators of a people, senders of agents, and recipients of honor. Both are caught up in claims of cosmic benefaction and sovereignty.

Imitating, Paralleling, or Contesting Imperial Claims?

Thus far the discussion has established big-picture parallels between *pater patriae* traditions and John's Gospel in their respective uses of the image of Father. This is not to deny or minimize the important differences in details that I have observed. But in recognizing parallel data, we return to the questions I posed at the outset of this chapter concerning what happens in the intertextuality between John's presentation of God as Father and the presentation of the emperor as *pater patriae*. Is the intersection inconsequential and neutral, whereby John's texts may imitate and at a distance parallel big imperial claims but without interfering with them in any way? Or is the intersection much more contestive in questioning or undermining the imperial claims, exposing, invalidating, or relativizing them in offering an alternative understanding for an alternative community or antisociety? In posing the questions in this antithetical way, I do not mean to suggest that we must chose a monolithic answer. I pose the question antithetically only to highlight the issue. Given the hybridity that often marks imperial situations (discussed in chap. 2 above), it is much more likely that a mixture of these options exists whereby imitation coexists with contestive and/or relativizing functions as part of the Gospel's rhetoric of distance.

How, then, are we to determine the interaction and assess these possibilities? One approach could comparatively elaborate the content of each of the six claims. It could be argued that the Father's life, reign, justice, community, and agency differ greatly from those of the *pater patriae*. The discussion in previous and subsequent chapters in this book delineates some of these differences, along with similarities. It has to be observed that all imperial systems, though, claim that their rule is just, good, benevolent, beneficial, and of course universal.

A second approach, one that I will pursue here, involves locating John's presentation of God as Father within the Gospel's plot as part of the Gospel's rhetoric of distance. As I argued in chapter 6, the plot of

> John's story of Jesus narrates Jesus' identity to be God's chosen agent, authorized by God to make a definitive revelation of God's life-giving purposes and to take away the sin of the Roman-ruled world. In living out this claim in his words and works, Jesus conflicts with the Rome-allied Jerusalem elite and their Roman ally, the provincial governor Pilate, confronting and challenging their power over, and vision of, an unjust societal order, which is contrary to God's life-giving purposes. The Jerusalem elite reject Jesus' claim and revelation of God's purposes of life, preferring to defend the status quo by putting him to death. But surprisingly his death is not the end. God raises him, thereby revealing the limit of their power and the error of their societal order. Meanwhile some people discern Jesus' origin, identity, and mission, commit themselves to his revelation, and form a countercommunity or antisociety that, assisted by the Holy Spirit, continues Jesus' life-giving mission.

It is not difficult to see that the plot incorporates the six areas associated with the presentation of God the Father that I have just outlined. Throughout this story, Jesus functions as the revealer of the only God, the only true God the Father (5:44–45; 17:3), and his life-giving purposes. To crucify God's commissioned agent whom the Father has sent to embody and manifest the Father's life-giving purposes is to reject the Father. The Gospel regularly asserts this connection between Jesus and the Father:

- All may honor the Son as they honor the Father (5:23).
- Not to honor the Son is not to honor the Father (5:23).

- I have come in my Father's name, but you do not receive me (5:43).
- If you knew me, you would know the Father (8:19).
- "If God were your Father, you would love me" (8:42 NRSV).
- "I honor my Father, and you dishonor me" (8:49 NRSV).
- The Father will honor anyone who serves me (12:26).
- If you had known me, you would have known the Father also (14:7).
- Whoever loves me will be loved by my Father (14:21).
- "Whoever hates me hates my Father also" (15:23 NRSV).
- "But now they have seen and hated both me and my Father" (15:24 NRSV).
- "They will do this [kill disciples] because they have not known the Father or me" (16:3 NRSV).

To honor/love/know the Son is to honor/love/know the Father. Not to honor/know/ love Jesus is not to honor/know/love the Father. To hate Jesus is to hate the Father. The ruling elite's crucifixion of Jesus, the expression of their hate, is the definitive rejection of the Father. In crucifying Jesus whom the Father has sent, the elite announce a definitive "no" to the Father's purposes in order to maintain their commitment to and participation in the ways of the empire's *pater patriae*.

Their choice *for* the *pater patriae* and imperial ways rather than *for* the Father's ways manifested in Jesus the Father's agent is made quite explicit when Pilate asks the Jerusalem elite with reference to Jesus, "Shall I crucify your King?" The chief priests answer, "We have no king but Caesar" (19:15 RSV). The discussion in this chapter has shown the link between the language of kingship and Father in that both the *pater patriae* and the Father in John are presented as rulers of the world. In making their declaration of loyalty to the emperor as king, the chief priests as allies of Rome and agents of the emperor openly state their supreme allegiance to the emperor, the *pater patriae*. In doing so, they abandon Israel's age-old covenant with God as their King. God makes a covenant with the Davidic house, promising that "God will be a father" to the king who as God's son will represent God's reign (2 Sam 7:11–17). Psalms like 72 represent the king as agent of God's kingship.[52] In the light of kingly failures, the tradition also anticipates the time when God's reign will be established completely over the earth (Isa 24:23; 26:13).

But the Jerusalem elite have allied themselves with a king and father who does not represent God's life-giving purposes and reign (19:15). The Gospel's plot narrates their rejection of the Father who has sent Jesus (8:42). In crucifying Jesus, they have hated him and the Father and acted as agents of the emperor and the imperial structure. In doing so they express their origin from another father. In 8:40–44 their rejection of Jesus, expressed as their failure to "love" Jesus and desire to "kill" him (8:40, 42, 44), indicates their origin from "your father the devil." Opponents of Jesus and allies of the empire are presented as agents of the devil. If this is so for the Jerusalem elite, and for Judas who betrays Jesus at the devil's instigation (13:2, 27), it is certainly true for their ally Rome and its emperor, whose agent, Pilate the Roman governor, crucifies Jesus. As with Matthew (4:8–9) and Luke (4:5–6), John's Gospel sees the empire and its human agents as being of the devil.

The close alliance between Jesus and the Father, and the elite's crucifixion of Jesus as agents of the devil, indicate that the Gospel does not present the interaction of the Father with the *pater patriae* as neutral or without intertextual interference. As much as the presentation of the former resembles the big-picture framework of the presentation of the latter, the two figures collide in the plot through their agents' loyalties and actions. They have different purposes. Their life-giving reigns, though resembling each other in significant ways, also look different, as I elaborated in the previous chapter, and have vastly different consequences. They create different communities. Their agents embody and manifest different purposes. And the Gospel does not present the differences as neutral. There is no doubt that the Gospel consistently endorses the Father's purposes and will, manifested in Jesus, as that which brings life "in the beginning" (1:1). Again the Gospel's appeal to antiquity is very significant (so chap. 4 above). It identifies the Father as more ancient than the *pater patriae*, presents the latter as antithetical to the Father, and exposes his imperial agenda, claims, agents, and honor as false. Nor can we forget that the imperial Father serves as the agent of Father Jupiter/Zeus, while no one is superior to Jesus' Father.

In this contrapuntal reading of the interaction between elite imperial discourse and the Gospel's resistant discourse, the Gospel's "hidden transcript" or "little tradition" contests even while in some respects it imitates the dominant imperial elite's construction of reality (the great tradition or public transcript) and offers an alternative understanding of human society as an "antisociety" lived in relation to the life-giving Father God of Jesus. The Gospel's rhetoric of distance reveals the "true" nature of the imperial system so as to distance from it disciples who now are too accommodated to it. But the similarities in the presentation of the two Fathers significantly qualify this rhetoric of distance in which the Father's life-giving purposes manifested in Jesus are to redress the claims of the emperor, the *pater patriae*, as a benevolent ruler. Jesus' words and actions reveal that the imperial claim of benevolence masks oppressive, coercive, and exploitative rule and hides destructive consequences. Such rhetoric of distance is only possible, ironically, because it participates in that which it resists.

Notes

1. Matt 5:16, 45, 48; 6:1, 4, 6 (2x), 8, 9, 14, 15, 18 (2x), 26, 32; 7:11, 21; 10:20, 29, 32, 33; 11:25, 26, 27 (3x); 12:50; 13:43; 15:13; 16:17, 27; 18:10, 14, 19, 35; 20:23; 23:9; 24:36; 25:34; 26:29, 39, 42, 53; 28:19.

2. Mark 8:38; 11:25; 13:32; 14:36; excluding 11:26 on grounds of dubious manuscript attestation.

3. Luke 2:49; 6:36; 9:26; 10:21 (2x), 22 (3x); 11:2, 13; 12:30, 32; 22:29, 42; 23:34, 46; 24:49.

4. Mary Rose D'Angelo, "*Abba* and 'Father': Imperial Theology and the Jesus Traditions," *JBL* 111 (1992): 611–30; Gail R. O'Day, "'Show Us the Father and We Will Be Satisfied' (John 14:8)," *Semeia* 85 (1999): 11–18; G. Schrenk, "πατήρ," *TDNT* 5 (1967): 945–1022. W. K. Lacey, "Patria Potestas," in *The Family in Ancient Rome: New Perspectives*, ed. B. Rawson (Ithaca: Cornell University Press, 1986), 121–44, argues that "it was *patria potestas* which was the fundamental institution underlying Roman institutions" (123), and that "the Roman state was a family" (123, 125–30). T. R. Stevenson ("The Ideal Benefactor and the Father Analogy in Greek and Roman Thought," *Classical Quarterly* 42 [1992]: 421–436, esp. 429–31) is not convinced.

5. E.g., J. M. Soskice, "Can a Feminist Call God 'Father'?" in *Women's Voices: Essays in Contemporary Feminist Theology*, ed. T. Elwes (London: Marshall Pickering, 1992), 15–29; Dorothy Lee, "Beyond Suspicion? The Fatherhood of God in the Fourth Gospel," *Pacifica* 8 (1995): 140–54; Reinhartz, "'And the Word,'" 83–103.

6. C. K. Barrett, "'The Father Is Greater Than I' (John 14:28): Subordinationist Christology in the New Testament," *Essays on John* (Philadelphia: Westminster, 1982), 19–36.

7. Marianne M. Thompson, "The Living Father," *Semeia* 85 (1999): 19–31; Reinhartz, "'And the Word.'"

8. Meyer, "'The Father,'" 255–73; Paul N. Anderson, "The Having-Sent-Me Father: Aspects of Agency, Encounter, and Irony in the Johannine Father-Son Relationship," *Semeia* 85 (1999): 33–57.

9. Van Tilborg, *Reading John*, 27, mentions the prevalence of "Father" language in John, but in his chapter goes on only to explore "Son" language. Schrenk, "πατήρ," does not discuss *pater patriae*.

10. For the standard discussion, A. Alföldi, *Der Vater des Vaterlandes im römischen Denken* (Darmstadt: Wissenschaftliche Buchgesellschaft, 1971).

11. Kristeva, "Bounded Text," 36–63, esp. 36–37.

12. See chap. 2 above; Said, *Culture and Imperialism*, xxv.

13. See chap. 2 above.

14. Horace, *Odes* 1.2.2; 1.12.13–17: "the Father, who directs the destinies of men and gods, who rules the sea and lands and the sky with its shifting seasons? From whom is begotten nothing greater than himself'"; Ovid, *Tristia* 2.37, Jupiter is "the father [*genitor*] and ruler of the gods;" Pliny the Younger, *Pan.* 88.8, "He is the father [*parens*] of gods and men." On Zeus's evolution from a violent tyrant to loving figure, see Stevenson, "Ideal Benefactor," 432–33.

15. For Vespasian, see Harold Mattingly, *Coins of the Roman Empire in the British Museum*, vol. 2, *Vespasian to Domitian* (reprint, London: British Museum, 1966), pp. 95–103, nos. 451–452, 453 (with Ceres), 454 (with *Concordia*), 455–456, 457–458 (with Victory and dedicated to *Paci Augustae*, "to Augustan peace"), 459–461 (*Paci Orbis*, "for the peace of the world"); perhaps also 474–476, but the place of minting is uncertain. Cf. A. Burnett, M. Amandry, and I. Carradice, *Roman Provincial Coinage*, vol. 2, nos. 814–835, 850, 850A, 851–854. For Domitian, see Mattingly, *Coins*, vol. 2, pp. 352–54, no. 253 (with legionary eagle between standards, from Asia, probably Ephesus, dating to 95; also no. 259 (with trophy of armor and weapons).

16. Stefan Weinstock, *Divus Julius* (Oxford: Clarendon, 1971), 201.

17. Ibid., 201–2.

18. Ibid., 175–84.

19. Ibid., 180–84, 200–203; coins facing 208, plate 17, 1–2, *parens patriae*.

20. Ibid., 200. After Caesar's death, a cult was established in the forum along with a column bearing the inscription "Parenti patriae" (Suetonius, *Deified Julius* 85).

21. Weinstock, *Divus Julius*, 204–5, 217. Weinstock argues (206–17) that the redevelopment took place through the creation of a public cult of the Genius Caesaris involving Caesar's birthday, annual public vows for his welfare, oaths of allegiance, and the law rendering him *sacrosanctus* (inviolable). Gradel (*Emperor Worship*, 187) claims that the decisive shift from an honorary term to one defining a constitutional relationship of ruler and ruled does not occur until the reigns of Caligula and Claudius. Certainly the designation becomes more common through the century, but in the light of *Res gestae* 35 and Suetonius's account (below), along with the other Augustan material, it seems erroneous for Gradel to claim that "the title *pater patriae* had indeed seemed to disappear with Augustus."

22. Stevenson, "Ideal Benefactor."

23. In Asia, W. H. Buckler, "Auguste, Zeus Patroos," *Revue de philologie, de littérature et d'histoire anciennes* 9 (1935): 177–88.

24. Ando, *Imperial Ideology*, 146–47.

25. M. Charlesworth, "Providentia," 107–32, esp. 110, 113, 122.

26. Eck, *Age of Augustus*, 1.

27. Text with notes in ibid., 134–52.

28. Brian Bosworth ("Augustus, The *Res gestae* and Hellenistic Theories of Apotheosis," *JRS* 89 [1999]: 1–18) sees the work emphasizing euergetism or benefaction and world conquest as Augustus's "record of achievement which earned immortality" (18). See chap. 12 below.

29. Eck, *Age of Augustus*, 149.

30. See chap. 10 for further discussion.

31. R. K. Sherk, ed. and trans., *The Roman Empire: Augustus to Hadrian*, Translated Documents of Greece and Rome 6 (Cambridge: Cambridge University Press, 1988): Sherk presents several inscriptions identifying Augustus as "Father of the Country." An inscription from the people of Narbonese, Gaul, details celebrations of the imperial cult and dedicates an altar to Augustus in 11 CE. It twice identifies him as "Father of the Country" (lines A7 and B6). It recognizes that "an age of happiness produced him as the world's ruler," "his command over the whole world," and he "reconciled the judgments of the people with the decurions" (pp. 12–13). The designation appears three times (lines 8, 47, 50) in an inscription from Pisae in Etruria (4 CE; pp. 34–35).

32. Ando, *Imperial Ideology*, 401.

33. Ibid., 403.

34. Strabo (*Geogr.* 6.4.2) emphasizes similar themes of life-giving, ruling the world, creating community, sending agents, and honoring Augustus. He expresses the extension of Augustus's rule over the provinces by using only the title "Father," not "Father of the Country." After reporting dissension in Italy, he remarks, "But it were a difficult thing to administer so great a dominion otherwise than by turning it over to one man as to a father; at all events, never have the Romans and their allies thrived in such peace and plenty as that which was afforded them by Augustus Caesar," a state of affairs that continues under "his son and successor, Tiberius."

35. Valerius Maximus honors Tiberius in the preface to book 1 of his *Memorable Doings and Sayings* by describing Tiberius as "surest salvation of the fatherland [*salus patriae*]," as chosen by gods to rule ("in whose charge the unanimous will of gods and men has placed the governance of land and sea"), to create a people of virtue, and to judge or punish vice ("by whose celestial providence the virtues of which I shall tell are most kindly fostered and the vices most sternly punished"). Tiberius is "the best of leaders" (pref. 2), "our leader and savior" (pref. 2.9.6a; 8.13), "our leader and parent" (5.5.3), "our leader and father," who holds "the reins of the Roman Empire . . . in his saving hand" (9.11.4). Later in discussing piety, Valerius moves easily from that shown to parents and to brothers to that shown to one's country (5.4–6). Then follow two sections on fathers, with most of the examples drawn from elite figures who exercise political power, who love their children, and some who treat their children too harshly (5.7–8). Valerius's support for the former is clear. The offering of pardon after punishment is also recommended (5.9). Valerius uses Augustus as an example of a merciful and just ruler who intervenes on behalf of a son disinherited by his father. "The divine Augustus ordered him by his personal fiat to take possession of his father's goods, acting in the spirit of the Fatherland's father [*patris patriae*]" (7.7). Suetonius (*Tib.* 26) says Tiberius declined "the surname of Father of his Country [*patris patriae*]." A papyrus from Oxyrhynchus concerning the visit of Germanicus, Tiberius's son, to Alexandria, has Germanicus declare his identity as agent of Tiberius: "I have been sent by my father to set in order the overseas provinces" (Sherk, *Roman Empire*, 60–61, P.Oxy. 2435, lines 10–11).

36. For examples of coins so designating Gaius Caligula and their association with the emphases I have been developing, see Mattingly, *Coins*, vol. 1 (1965), p. 150, no. 29, plate 27.24 (with oak wreath); p. 150, no. 32, plate 27.26 (with oak wreath); p. 152, no. 38, plate 28.5 (with

oak wreath); p. 157, no. 67, and cf. plate 28.3 (with 5 soldiers, each bearing an aquila [eagle]); p. 157, no. 69, plate 29.14 (with seated Pietas, and sacrifice scene in front of the temple of Divus Augustus); p. 157, no. 70, plate 30.2 (with Nero and Drusus riding a horse); p. 158, no. 72, plate 30.1 (with Vesta on throne).

37. For examples of coins so designating Claudius, see ibid., p. 170, no. 42, plate 32.2 (with oak wreath); p. 172, no. 57, plate 32.12 (with female figure of *Constantiae Augustae*), also nos. 58–60, 199–201; p. 173, no. 61, plate 32.17 (with female figure Nemesis, and dedicated to *Paci Augustae*, also nos. 62–66, 68–71); p. 174, no. 72, plate 32.24 (with Agrippina, also nos. 73–76); p. 174, no. 79, plate 33.3 (with young Nero, also nos. 80–81); p. 190, no. 185, plate 36.1 (with oak wreath, also no. 186); p. 191, no. 188, plate 36.2 (with triumphal arch, soldier on horseback, trophies and spear, also nos. 189–91); p. 191, no. 192, plate 36.3 (with *Spes Augusta*, also nos. 193–96); p. 191, no. 197, plate 36.4 (with *Ceres* and corn ears, also no. 198); p. 192, no. 202, plate 36.6 (with *Libertas Augusta*, also nos. 203–5); p. 192, no. 207, plate 36.7 (with helmeted Minerva); pp. 192–93, nos. 208–23, plates 36.8–9; 37.1–2, 9 (with various imperial figures). Various elements appear on inscriptions: for example (Sherk, *Roman Empire*, 90–91), a document from the governor of Lycia-Pamphylia (43–48 CE) identifies himself as Claudius's agent, "legate of Tiberius Claudius Caesar Augustus." An inscription (45–46 CE; ibid., 94) declares the fulfilling of a vow taken for Claudius's victory in Britain and identifies Claudius as "Father of the Country" (line 7), as does an edict of Claudius that grants citizenship (46 CE; ibid., 95; line 6), a milestone acknowledging repair of the Via Claudia from northern Italy (47 CE; Sherk, *Roman Empire*, 96), as does an inscription acknowledging construction of the Aqua Claudia (aqueduct) at Rome's Porta Praenestina (52–53CE; ibid., 100); a letter to Miletus (ibid., 96); and a letter discharging a sailor at Misenum (52CE; ibid., 99).

38. For Seneca's concern in *De beneficiis* with ideal benefactors and the good father as a model for the good king, see Stevenson, "Ideal Benefactor," 425–27.

39. In reference to Nero, Petronius (d. 65 CE) has guests at Trimalchio's dinner party rise and shout, "Good fortune to the emperor, Father of the Fatherland [*patri patriae*]"; *Satyricon* 60.

40. For examples, see Mattingly, *Coins*, vol.1, pp. 200–284, nos. 9, 10, 12–51 (variously with Roma, Ceres, Virtus), 79–80 (with Jupiter), 113 (with temple of Janus), 114–21 (Roma), 122–30 (with soldiers), 130–224, 234, 240, 251–60; etc. Inscriptions confirm the same identity. A legate of Nero identifies him as Father of the Country (CE 60–66; Sherk, *Roman Empire*, 106), as does an inscription from Thrace (61–62 CE; ibid., 106–7), in which Nero "Father of the Country" "ordered inns and rest-houses built along the military highways." An inscription from Greece (ibid., 110–12) celebrated Nero's removal of taxation from Achaia and the Peloponnese. He is identified as "Lord of the Whole World," "Father of the Country, New Sun shining upon the Greeks, [who] has chosen to be a benefactor of Greece, requiting and reverencing our gods who stood by him at all times for care and deliverance." It dedicates an altar with an inscription, "To Zeus the Deliverer, Nero forever."

41. For inscriptions recognizing Vespasian and Titus as "Father of the Country," see ibid., 126–30, 134–35.

42. For a very informative discussion, see C. Newlands, *Statius' "Silvae" and the Poetics of Empire* (Cambridge: Cambridge University Press, 2002).

43. K. Scott, *Imperial Cult*, 133–40.

44. Newlands, *Statius' "Silvae,"* 292–309.

45. For example, Martial, *Epig.* 7.7, honors Domitian by assuring him of his prayers though he be absent in battle at the Rhine, addressing him as "the world's supreme ruler and earth's parent [*parens orbis*] and "supreme subjugator of the Rhine and Father of the World" (9.5.1). Suetonius (*Dom.* 3–9) presents Domitian initially attending to these roles through entertainments and benefactions of money (4), public works (5), military campaigns (6), changed customs including

bonuses for soldiers (7), administering justice, supervising officials and governors, guarding public morality and pietas (8–9), until "he turned the virtues into vices" (3) and abandoned "mercy or integrity" for cruelty and avarice (10).

46. See Mattingly, *Coins*, vol. 2, pp. 297–420, nos. 7–35, 37–50A, 70–129A, 139–40, 145–70, 176–98, 200–207, 214–26, 230–37, 248, 260–86, 323–67, 371–452, 458–80, 512–20. Domitian is depicted with a whole range of figures including Jupiter, Minerva, Virtus, Ceres/Annona, Fortuna, Fides, Victory, Mars, Felicitas, and with military symbols, eagles, and sacrifice scenes/altars/temples.

47. Sherk, *Roman Empire*, 137, line 5; 145, line 13; 150, line 23 (Pergamum).

48. Pliny the Younger (*Panegyricus*) continues the distinction that Trajan is a "fellow citizen, not a tyrant, one who is our father not our overlord" (2.3). Pliny praises Nerva: "His highest claim to be the Father of the Country [*publicus parens*] was his being father to you," thereby ensuring the well-being of the state in the gift of Trajan (10.6). Trajan, like Augustus, "refused the title of Father of the Country (*patris patriae*), and it was only after a prolonged struggle between us and your modesty that in the end you were persuaded. . . . Thus you alone have been Father of the Country [*pater patriae*] in fact before you were in name. . . . And now that you bear the name, how kind and considerate you show yourself, living with your subjects as a father with his children!" (21). From section 25 on, Pliny details Trajan's numerous and extensive beneficence and generosity to people as "our Father who in his wisdom and authority and devotion to his people has opened roads, built harbors, created routes overland, let the sea into the shore and moved the shore out to sea and linked far distant peoples by trade" (29). Everywhere Trajan encourages virtue and observance of law. Benign rule has restored social order so that "it is we who are the Emperor's friends, not our slaves, and the Father of the Country [*pater patriae*] puts his own subjects' affection above that of persons held in bondage to other men" (42.3). References to previous emperors show that "our father is amending and reforming the character of the principate, which had become debased by a long period of corruption." In such tasks, Trajan is "Father of the Country [*pater patriae*]" (57.5), "Father of us all [*parentis publici*]" (67.1), who secures the eternity of the empire (67.3).

49. Though often interpreted as the devil, four factors indicate that it is much more likely that this figure refers to Pilate, agent of Roman power: (1) Jesus first uses the term in 12:31 in reference to his "hour" (12:27) or time of crucifixion and departure to God. The crucifixion reference continues in 12:32, with Jesus' promise that in being lifted up he will draw everyone to himself. These events take place in the passion narrative of chapters 18–19 as the narrative resumes after Jesus' instructions to disciples in chapters 13–17. (2) The Gospel does not refer to Satan as a ruler. Rather, it uses the language of "ruler" (*archōn*, ἄρχων) to refer to human beings, and particularly members of the ruling alliance (3:1; 7:26, 48; 12:42), and not to supernatural beings. (3) The "world" is identified in 1:10 as that which rejects Jesus. The crucifixion is the ultimate rejection of Jesus. It expresses Roman power, whose primary representative in the narrative is Pilate, and it comes about on Pilate's instruction in alliance with the Jerusalem elite (19:16). (4) Jesus' words to Pilate that Pilate has no power over him (19:11) echoes Jesus' statement of 14:30 that "the ruler of this world . . . has no power over me." In part the claim of "no power" refers to Jesus giving himself to die (10:11, 17–18). But beyond this, Jesus overcomes Pilate in his resurrection.

50. Bosworth, "Augustus."

51. For Romulus's apotheosis to the gods, see Plutarch (*Lives: Rom.* 27.7) has Romulus caught up "to the gods [εἰς θεούς]." Subsequently (28.2) Romulus explains that it "was the pleasure of the gods . . . from whom I came, that I should be with humankind only a short time, and . . . I should dwell [οἰκεῖν] again in heaven [οὐρανόν]." Also Ovid, *Met.* 14.805–828; *Fasti* 2.487, "to the blue heavens"; Livy 1.16.7. For Julius Caesar's apotheosis, see Ovid, *Met.* 14.818, "to heaven [*caelo*]," 840–850. For Augustus's apotheosis, see Ovid, *Met.* 14.839, 870 "to heaven [*caelo*]"; Suetonius, *Aug.* 100.4, "to heaven [*in caelum*]"; Dio Cassius 54.42.3, "to heaven [εἰς τὸν οὐρανόν]."

For Moses' apotheosis, Philo, *Moses* 2.288–292. Seneca (*Apolocyntosis* [*Pumpkinification*] *of Claudius*) mocks the notion while attesting that both Augustus and Tiberius went up "to the gods [*ad deos*]" (1). The dead Claudius appears, unrecognized, before Jupiter (5); the deified Augustus has a motion passed that exiles Claudius from heaven (10–12), so he goes to the "lower regions," where he is sentenced to roll dice forever in a box with holes in it (14), though Caligula orders him to be the clerk of a freedman (15). For discussion of apotheosis, see chap. 12 below.

52. This is the solution to the problem of the relationship between an earthly ruler and God's kingship. Often the tradition presents the two in antithetical relationship. Gideon refuses the Israelite's request to "rule over us" by declaring, "The Lord will rule over you" (Judg 8:22–23 NRSV). In 1 Sam 8, God sees the people's demand for a king as rejection of God, though despite Samuel's warnings of the ways of kings, the people persist and God permits it (1 Sam 8:7–8, 10–11, 19, 22).

10

The Sacred Identity of John's Jesus-Believers

In this chapter I make explicit an aspect of the imperial negotiation implicit in the discussion of the previous chapters. John's rhetoric of distance seeks to create an alternative identity and way of life for the community of Jesus-believers in a city such as Roman Ephesus.[1] What does this alternative and more distanced way of life look like? The term "alternative" indicates a communal identity and lifestyle that do not primarily comprise accommodation with the empire (though some accommodation and imitation [mission, 17:18; 20:21] are present) but are constituted by a more contestive commitment to Jesus and distanced societal interaction. This chapter continues the emphasis on imperial negotiation by elaborating some features of this "antisociety."[2]

The Gospel does not spell out a comprehensive how-to-live program, but its rhetoric of distance does delineate some features of the distanced way of life the Gospel seeks for Jesus-believers in their imperial society. The focus of this chapter, selective rather than comprehensive in scope, will be predominantly on some aspects of John 13–17, the so-called Farewell Discourse. The premises of these chapters include Jesus' imminent departure to the Father, the end of his somatic presence with disciples (14:25), and the assurance that his presence nevertheless continues to "abide" or dwell with disciples.[3] That is, these chapters are especially concerned with the life of Jesus-believers in his (somatic) absence.[4]

The title of this chapter, "The Sacred Identity of John's Jesus-Believers," evokes the discussion of the Salutaris inscription from Ephesus in chapter 4 above and Guy Rogers's excellent study entitled *The Sacred Identity of Ephesus*. The wealthy landowning Ephesian Salutaris funded an annual distribution of money on the occasion of the celebration of the birth of Artemis, Ephesus's protector goddess. He also funded an event every two weeks in which a procession especially of youths of the city carried images of emperors (including Augustus and the current emperor) and of Artemis through the city along a carefully chosen route. The procession began and ended at the temple of Artemis. It entered the city near the Roman-built upper city, moved along the Embelos or Curetes Street, which especially recalled King Lysimachos, the city's Hellenistic heritage, and elite accomplishments; turned north past the Tetragonos Agora and through the city's economic and commercial center; and left the city at the Koression Gate, near the temple of Apollo, which commemorated the city's foundation myth in which Androklos followed Apollo's oracle to the site of the city, then returned to the temple of Artemis. Rogers argues that the procession provided a "privileged mental map" of the city that enculturated the youths into the city's history and civic structures. This turning to the past underlined the sacred identity of Ephesus and provided the context for negotiating new (Roman) citizens, founders, and gods by including them within Ephesus's history, society, and sacred cosmos, yet also by putting them in their place. Ephesus was above all "in the beginning" the city of Artemis.

This inscription and its attested imperial negotiation orchestrated by one of the city's very wealthy elites originated in Ephesus about the same time as (the final form of) John's Gospel. Rogers argues that Salutaris's act of imperial negotiation follows a century of increased Roman personnel and architectural presence in the city. In chapter 3 above, we noticed building activity stimulated by Augustus, continued through the century by other emperors and elites, and then again more actively by Domitian toward the end of the century. This increased Roman presence included the imperial cult temple dedicated to the Sebastoi, or exalted emperors and their families, in 89/90 CE. Rogers argues that Salutaris's plans, which received support from Ephesus's local and imperial ruling elites, negotiated this increased Roman presence through inclusion as well as assertion of local identity and distinctiveness.

In this chapter my argument is that at the same time and in the same imperial dynamics (though within the larger context of synagogue negotiation), John's rhetoric of distance asserts the "sacred identity" and lifestyle of Jesus-believers as an act of imperial negotiation. Distance and distinctiveness, much more than accommodation, mark this negotiation. Accordingly, I will discuss five aspects of this identity and lifestyle: the sacred household or temple of God, faithfulness (*fides*), loving service, greater works, and living as a community of friends.

A Sacred Household (or Temple)

In her study of "temple symbolism" in John's Gospel, Mary Coloe argues that the temple functions as both a christological and an ecclesiological symbol. As a christological symbol, "the Temple, as the dwelling place of God, points to the identity and role of Jesus." As an ecclesiological symbol, "the imagery of the Temple is transferred from Jesus to the Christian community, indicating its identity and role."[5] I have previously flagged the importance of John 2:21 in identifying the risen Jesus as the temple: "He spoke of the temple of his body" (RSV). Instead of a building, the temple is a person.[6] The transfer, or better, extension of the temple imagery from Jesus to the community of Jesus-believers takes place, according to Coloe, in chapter 14.[7] With Jesus' reference to "my Father's house" in 14:2 (cf. the christological use of "house" in 2:16), the "temple-as-community" is to the fore.

Coloe locates her analysis of temple symbolism in a context of a synagogue dispute and rejection of Jesus-believers after the destruction of the Jerusalem temple by Titus in 70 CE. In the post–70 chaotic context, Jewish groups were faced with the task of explaining the destruction of 70, she argues, and with finding a way ahead without the temple. While rabbi-led Judaism turned to Moses' Torah for atonement and the revelation of divine presence, the Christians understood Jesus as the temple.[8]

I have argued in chapter 2 above that the synagogue-separation scenario is not compelling and there is no need to repeat the arguments here. I have also argued that

post-70 many Jewish groups continued to negotiate imperial realities. Without denying
the likely use of Jewish temple traditions in 14:2, I do want to observe a limitation, at
least as far as a reading of John in an Ephesian context is concerned. Simply put, the
Jerusalem temple is not the only temple within the horizon of Ephesian Jesus-believers
engaging John's Gospel, and it is dubious as to whether it provides even the primary
intertextuality for the Gospel's temple material. By the time the Gospel is engaged in
Ephesus around the end of the first century, some three decades have passed since the
destruction of the Jerusalem temple. Previous to 70, as I argue in Appendix A, Jesus-
believers had already had explicit reason to engage the question of the relationship of
Jesus to the Jerusalem temple and imperial power on at least two previous occasions.
One occasion comprised Jesus' challenge to the temple before his crucifixion by Rome
(2:13–22). The second opportunity arose with Gaius Caligula's attempt to place a statue
in the Jerusalem temple in 40 CE. The fall of the temple in 70 CE was not, then, the first
opportunity for reflection concerning any relationship between Jesus and the Jerusalem
temple, though it no doubt highlighted the issue. Moreover, there were at least two
major temples in Ephesus (along with others, such as the temple of Apollo) that in all
likelihood provided a much more culturally prominent and immediate intertextuality
for Ephesian Jesus-believers than the destroyed Jerusalem temple: the temple of
Artemis and the temple of the Sebastoi, dedicated in 89/90 for the celebration of the
imperial cult. The sacred identity of Ephesus, asserted for instance by Salutaris and his
donation and his procession, drew these two temples together, even while elevating the
temple of Artemis as the foundation for Ephesus' sacred identity.

Further, for Jewish inhabitants of Ephesus, there was also the temple tax that focused
attention on another temple. Before 70, Ephesus was the collection point for the tax
from Jews in Asia for the temple in Jerusalem (so Josephus, *Ant.* 16.168; Philo, *Emb.*
315–316). But after 70, Rome co-opted the temple tax and collected it for another temple, that of Jupiter Capitolinus in Rome, the sanctioning god who had ensured victory
over the Jewish God in 70 and the destruction of the Jerusalem temple (Josephus, *J.W.*
7.218; Suetonius, *Dom.* 12.2; Dio Cassius 65.7.2).[9] Collected by Rome post-70 and used
by Vespasian to rebuild the temple of Jupiter Capitolinus, the tax had punitive and
propaganda value, defining Jews as "a defeated race punished for [their] nationality."[10]
This collection for the temple of Jupiter Capitolinus had been underway for nearly
thirty years when John's Gospel was written in its final form. These factors suggest that
negotiating these various temples in Roman Ephesus may provide the more immediate—though not exclusive—intertextuality for Ephesian Jesus-believers than the
Jerusalem temple, and it will be the focus in our discussion here.

Coloe discusses her "christological" temple texts (1:1–18; 2:13–25; 4:1–45; 7:1–8:59;
10:22–42) in relation to the post-70, post-Jerusalem temple scenario. If space permitted, it would be interesting to discuss all of these christological texts with the different
intertext of imperial negotiation concerning the temples of Artemis and the Sebastoi in
Ephesus. But given space restrictions, I will evoke this Ephesian cultural intertext here
primarily in relation to the "ecclesiological" text of John 14:2 ("my Father's house"),
which delineates Jesus-believers as a "temple-as-community."

With Coloe, I am arguing that John 14 evokes Jewish temple traditions to create a
"temple-as-community" identity for Jesus-believers. But moving beyond her analysis,
however, I am further arguing that this "temple-as-community-of-Jesus-believers," or

community with a sacred identity, interacts with and provides an alternative community to the imperially constituted and Artemis-blessed civic identity of Ephesus.

Jesus begins John 14 by encouraging the believers to have faith or loyalty (14:1; see below on *fides/pistis*). He assures them that he is preparing a place for them: "my Father's house" (14:2). This nomenclature evokes temple traditions from several cultural contexts. While the phrase itself does not appear in Jewish traditions, the term "house" or "house of the Lord" is commonplace for the Jerusalem temple.[11] "House" was also common language for temples in the Greek and Roman worlds.[12] That "Father's house" is also temple language for John's Gospel is immediately clear from Jesus' use of the same phrase in 2:16 in attacking the Jerusalem temple through citing Zechariah 14:21. Zechariah 14 speaks of Jerusalem under foreign control (14:1-2). God will defeat these nations (14:3-6, 12-15), transform the city into a place of light and life (14:7-8), become king (14:9), make Jerusalem secure (14:10-11), draw Jew and Gentile to Jerusalem to worship in purity at the temple; and there will be no traders in God's house (14:16-21). Zechariah's vision of the defeat of imperial powers and constituting of one people who worship God understands the temple as both a place and an international community of people.

John's Gospel also uses the same noun "house" in 14:2 (*oikia*, οἰκία) to refer explicitly to a household or the community of people that inhabits the space.[13] In 4:53 it designates the believing father along with other family members (presumably his wife and children) and servants (4:51). In 8:35 both a son and a slave are mentioned. The use of the noun "house" for people or household is common in the Ephesian inscriptions to refer to the "house of Augustus" or the "house of the Sebastoi."[14]

Also of interest is a tradition that encourages loyalty to the emperor, not by its expression in temple buildings (as pervasive as they were), but in human lives. The emperor Tiberius, in declining a request from Spain to erect a temple to Tiberius, declared famous words to the senate: "These are my temples in your breasts, these my fairest and abiding effigies" (Tacitus, *Ann.* 4.38). Dio Cassius (52.35) has Maecenas advise Augustus to decline temples but to encourage loyalty in his subjects' hearts: "By your benefactions fashion other images in the hearts of your people, images that will never tarnish nor perish; . . . within their thoughts you will ever be enshrined and glorified." The whole empire, the emperor's household, becomes in the loyalty and gratefulness of its subjects a living temple dedicated to the emperor.

The phrase "Father's house," then, has multiple levels of meaning, denoting a space, a temple, and a community. This combination suggests that in 14:2 it denotes John's Jesus-believers as a temple-community that encounters God's presence in Jesus. David Aune's suggestion, "It is probable that in John 14:2 (and also in 8:35) the term οἰκία τοῦ πατρός μου [my Father's house] reflects the self-designation of the Johannine community," is on target,[15] with the necessary modification that it at least reflects the designation that the writer/s of the Gospel use/s for the community of Jesus-believers. Whether it is a "self-designation" is a little more elusive.

This house or temple-community comprises "many rooms/dwellings" (μοναὶ πολλαί, *monai pollai*). There is debate over whether in this verse Jesus speaks of heaven or a heavenly dwelling place or temple,[16] or the community (the house) of Jesus' believers (many dwellings), as I am arguing. The matter is probably resolved by 14:23, where the same language of *monē* is used: "Those who love me will keep my word, and my Father will love them, and we will come to them and make our home [μονήν, *monēn*] with them." In this verse, the "we" comprises the Father and Son, who come to believers (plural language), who comprise the community with whom Father and Son dwell or abide while the community keeps or observes Jesus' word. Such dwelling/abiding is part of multiple "dwellings with" in this chapter: the Father with Jesus (14:10), the Paraclete or Spirit with and in believers (14:17), and Jesus with believers (14:25). All are linked together by the verb *menō*, meaning "dwell." This verb is a cognate of the noun *monē* in 14:2, 23, translated as "dwellings" or "home." Coloe rightly concludes that 14:2 depicts "a series of interpersonal relationships made possible because of the indwelling of the Father, Jesus, and Paraclete with the believers. The divine indwelling in the midst of a believing community makes it appropriate to speak of the community as a living Temple."[17]

Coloe goes on to discuss the language of Jesus' description of this "temple-as-community" as a "place prepared for you." In Jewish traditions both the language of "place" and "prepare" are associated with the temple.[18] "Prepare" is also associated with forming or founding a people.[19] Eschatological traditions anticipate a (renewed) temple-community comprising people of all nations centered on the Jerusalem temple (as with Zech 14 noted above as referenced by John 2:16).[20] John's Gospel sees these expectations already in large measure underway in the community of Jesus-believers. The presence of the Spirit or Paraclete with Jesus' disciples, understood to be a gift for the end of this age (Joel 2:28; Ezek 36:26–27), confirms that this eschatological temple-community is already being formed.[21] Jesus promises "the Spirit of truth" only to this community in contrast to the world that cannot receive this gift (John 14:16–17). The Spirit will teach and remind them of Jesus' words (14:26) until the time of Jesus' return.[22] The evoking of the international gathering in Zechariah 14, the belief of Samaritans (John 4:39–42), and approach of Gentiles to Jesus (12:20–22) suggest the eschatological inclusion of Gentiles in this temple-community in Ephesus.

The language of "Father's house," "many rooms/dwellings," "prepare," and "place" in 14:2–3 emphasizes the distinct identity of the community of Jesus-believers as a temple-community. After the destruction of the Jerusalem temple in 70 (2:19–22; 4:21; 11:48), Coloe argues, the Gospel claims that divine presence is encountered among this group. But while that might be so, reference to the Jerusalem temple does not exhaust the cultural intertexts associated with the temples in Ephesus that I noted above. How does this claim of divine presence abiding with a temple-community of Jesus-believers interface with the temples encountered in late first-century, everyday life in Ephesus, such as those of Artemis and the recently dedicated temple of the Sebastoi, and with the "sacred identity" of Ephesus as a city? How is this temple-community of Jesus-believers to live in the context of this sacred temple-city?

One implication from later in chapter 14 concerns the temple-community's obedience to Jesus' commandments (14:15). Exactly which commandments are in view is not specified, but the general point of obedience is repeated in verses 21 and 23, and through use of the negative in 14:24. The commands to serve one another (13:14–15) and love one another (13:34–35) were emphasized in the previous chapter. In chapter 14 doing the same works as and "greater" works than Jesus is also in view. Thus one implication for this temple community is not so much cultic activity (though prayer is important in 14:13–14) but lived acts of love, service, and transformation. I will return to these actions below.

A second implication indicates an important point of distinctiveness: this Johannine community-as-temple is one without images.²³ Both the temple of Artemis and the temple of the Sebastoi certainly contained images. The head and arm of the large statue of Domitian in the temple of the Sebastoi, reformulated as a statue of Vespasian after Domitian's murder in 96 CE, are in the Izmir museum.²⁴ And there were images of numerous other deities in the city, such as those of Dionysus.²⁵ In the exchange between Jesus and the Samaritan woman concerning worship, the verb (προσκυνέω, *proskyneō*) appears in 4:20–24 ten times. Jesus insists to the Samaritan woman that the place of worship is not important, but the object of the worship is very important. Four times "the Father" is literally the object (either dative or accusative case) of the verb "worship" (4:21, 23a, 23b, 24) and once, as the subject, the Father "seeks" worshippers (4:23b). Significantly, this God is spirit (4:24) and is not expressed by carved or stone images. Rather, the Son reveals the Father (1:18) in his words and works (14:7, 10–11). To see Jesus—as the Gentiles wish to do in 12:20–26—is to see the Father (14:9). The Gospel story conveys these words and works, providing the only "image" of Jesus or God necessary.

A third implication involves possible interfaces with temples in Ephesus. Van Tilborg observes that in the scene in which Jesus conflicts with the temple, John's narrative uses two significant words for the temple, ἱερόν (*hieron*, 2:14) and ναός (*naos*, 2:19, 20, 21). Both terms are prominent in first-century inscriptions from Ephesus with reference to the temple of Artemis; *naos* also refers to the temple of the Sebastoi.²⁶ These linguistic links also indicate a likely interface with these temples in Ephesus in engaging the scene in 2:13–22. More specifically, van Tilborg identifies "some interference in content"²⁷ between Jesus' actions in the temple in John 2 and the temple of Artemis in Ephesus. Jesus attacks the temple as a "marketplace" (2:16) or, as van Tilborg translates, a "trading center" (οἶκον ἐμπορίου, *oikon emporiou*), citing Zechariah 14:21. The intertext of Zechariah 14:21 evokes an eschatological scenario in which there will be no more "traders in the house of the Lord of hosts on that day" (NRSV). The emphasis on the commercial aspects of the temple is also present in Ephesian inscriptions. Van Tilborg reports limited inscriptions from Ephesus that reference the sacrificial activity of the temple of Artemis²⁸ but finds many more inscriptions referring to the temple functioning as a bank.²⁹ He also cites Dio Chrysostom's textual reference (*To the People of Rhodes* [*Or. 31*] 54) to the temple of Artemis functioning as a bank not only for wealthy Ephesians but also for "aliens and persons from all parts of the world and in some cases of commonwealths and kings," since no one would violate this sacred place. Also to be noticed is Strabo's reference to Ephesus as the "largest emporium" (ἐμπόριον, *emporion*), or "trading center" (using the same word as in John 2:16), "in Asia this side of Tarsus" (*Geogr.* 14.1.24). And Aristides describes Ephesus as "the common treasury of Asia" (Aristides, *Oration* 23.24). Van Tilborg suggests that the scene in the Jerusalem temple in John 2, with its focus on the buying and selling of sacrificial animals and exchanging money for sacrifices (2:14–15), resonates significantly with the commerce associated with the temple of Artemis in Ephesus, as does the reference in 8:20 to Jesus teaching in the temple's treasury storehouse (γαζοφυλάκιον, *gazophylakion*). Van Tilborg comments on the significant "interference" with the Ephesian context: "When Jesus, jealously proud of his God, is so enraged because of the commercial activity, which compared to the temple of Artemis is rather modest [?], how much more will that be when the commerce of the temple determines the social life of a city [as in Ephesus]."[30] Jesus' subsequent command, "Tear down this temple" (John 2:19a), and the reference to Jesus as the *naos* in whom God is known (2:21; 14:7, 9, 10) suggest a strong disqualification of the temple of Artemis and of the Sebastoi as places of legitimate encounter with the divine for Jesus-believers, distancing Jesus-believers from them.

But is it a case of only thinking such things? Are there any associated behaviors or actions by which the temple community of Jesus-believers might embody this more distanced societal participation? It is worth asking if the narration of Jesus' strong outrage against the Jerusalem temple commerce in John 2 suggests a total boycott of temples other than the Johannine "temple-as-community." Attacking its commerce implicates sacrificial observance since the two are closely related. Yet John's narrative does not show Jesus himself boycotting the temple. He returns there regularly (5:14; 7:14). But while his visits are often associated with festivals (5:1, 14; 7:2, 14; 10:22–23), the narrative does not describe him worshipping there. Rather, his activity is to teach there (5:14; 7:14, 28; 8:20, 59; 10:23; 18:20), revealing God's purposes and his own identity as agent and revealer of those purposes. Moreover, he does insist on honoring the only God (5:44), the only true God (17:3), whom he reveals (1:18).

These factors at least indicate that the Gospel's rhetoric seems to require distance from the temples of Artemis and of the Sebastoi. It would be reasonable to surmise that this distance excluded cultic and communal participation in activities such as the celebration of an emperor's or the goddess's birthday or in activities associated, for instance, with Salutaris's procession, or in any sacrifices or prayers offered to either emperors or Artemis. But since the activities of the temple of the Sebastoi and especially Artemis pervaded the city's life, not only cultically but also economically, politically, legally, and civically, as Richard Oster has shown,[31] nonparticipation in Sebastoi or Artemis-related activities could also mean significant distance or disassociation from a much greater range of activity in the city. For example, regular meetings of associations of trading and artisan groups, common in a city like Ephesus and an important form of social connection and economic networking, often included cultic activities such as prayers, oaths, and sacrifices in their regular meetings. Not attending such meetings would cut a person out of economic loops and threaten one's (often precarious) economic livelihood.[32] Borrowing money from the temple of Artemis as a bank would seem to be forbidden. So too presumably would be supplying either temple with materials as merchants or artisans, working on their maintenance (an inscription identifies Artemis-temple builders: IEph 2.295), consuming food or wine that had been sacrificed there or raised on the estates or in the lakes of Artemis (Strabo, *Geogr.* 14.1.26), distributing grain for or selling grain on feast days (named on inscriptions: IEph 2.274; 3.712B), trading with other suppliers or artisans with connections to the temples, being a client of an elite associated with the temples, claiming asylum at the temple of Artemis, or attending the theater or any civic gathering where an offering or prayer to the emperor or Artemis, the city's goddess, might be offered. These are possible behavioral implications from depicting the community of Jesus-believers as a distanced temple community in which God's purposes and presence are encountered.

Beyond these distancing practices, another possibility should be considered, though a lack of data underlines the considerable tentativeness of this suggestion. What is to be made of Jesus' strong condemnation of the temple as a "trading center" in John 2:16, which evokes the eschatological declaration in Zechariah 14:21? In the eschatological temple of Zech 14:21, there will be no traders. If John's community is the eschatological temple-community already that enacts Zechariah's vision (and John's Gospel consistently emphasizes the present realization of eschatological expectations[33]), does it mean that members of this eschatological community cannot be traders or have any involvement in any trading activity? The logic would presumably be that trade participates in and enmeshes one in imperial economic and political systems sanctioned by the gods, which are antithetical to God's purposes and condemned in the vision of Zechariah 14. Such a possibility—if it was to be the daily practice of Jesus-believers—would isolate Jesus-believers from involvement in much of the economic life of the city.[34] Harland notes associations of workers in Ephesus related to clothing, food, potters and smiths, building, banking and trade, physicians, and entertainers,[35] including bankers (IEph 2.454) and merchants and traders (IEph 3.800, 7.1.3079). The merchants (ἔμποροι, a cognate of the negative term "house of trade" used for the temple in John 2:16) "who are engaged in business in Ephesus" dedicate an inscription to "their savior and benefactor, the proconsul Gaius Pompeius Longinus Gallus, son of Publius" (IEph 3.800). Were some or all of these activities, clearly deeply embedded in the political-economic-social structures of the city and empire,[36] off-limits to Jesus-believers?

Such a view might get support from three factors. First, that civic economic distancing might be in view is consistent with Revelation 18, also addressed to the church in Ephesus, where the voice from heaven calls Jesus-believers, "Come out of her, my people, so that you do not take part in her sins" (Rev 18:4 NRSV). The chapter goes on to condemn "Rome's economic exploitation of her empire" in a sharply focused attack on the empire's trading practices, which are under God's judgment.[37] At least another Jesus-believer found it necessary to call for civic-economic distance.

Second, such an emphasis on socioeconomic civic distance raises the question of how community members would support themselves. If trade is not an option and artisans cannot be linked with the widespread economic activity associated with any temple in the city, do the scenes in the Gospel where Jesus' powerful intervention ensures that people have more than enough to drink (2:1–11) and to eat (6:1–14; 21:1–14) offer reassurance that Jesus will provide what they need? Is this one of the meanings of Jesus' declaration that he is the "bread of life" (6:35, 48, 51), the good shepherd (10:11, 14) who ensures the sheep have enough to eat, unlike the bad shepherds of Ezekiel 34 (Ezek 34:8–10, 27–29)? Is this a dimension of the disciples' "greater works" (14:12; see below)? Is the Gospel providing reassurance that distance from any civic socioeconomic trading activity is possible because Jesus can be trusted to supply his temple-community with what it needs? As outlined in chapter 8 (above), the scenes in John chapters 2; 6; and 14 evoke eschatological realities of abundant fertility, wine, bread, and fish, as does the good-shepherd image of John 10, appropriate for the eschatological temple-community among whom the eschatological Spirit is at work. And the scene of the supply of abundant bread (6:1–14) provides further reassurance since it evokes a story of liberation from political and economic hegemony, which involved a literal distancing or disassociation by "coming out from her" into the wilderness—yet God supplied the necessary food. Or perhaps instead of relying on dramatic divine intervention, Jesus-believers are to support one another in the exchanging of resources as an expression of love for one another (13:34–35).

Third, in the last chapter (21) of John's Gospel, some disciples go fishing in what seems to be a return to "normal" life after Jesus' crucifixion without being impacted by chapter 20's resurrection appearances. Fishing was a regulated and licensed industry, a participation in the imperial economic and political monopoly. It was predicated on the assumption that the emperor was "ruler of lands and seas and nations" (Juvenal, *Sat.* 4.83–84; Philostratus, *Life of Apollonius* 7.1–3), and that "every rare and beautiful thing in the wide ocean . . . belongs to the imperial treasury" (Juvenal, *Sat.* 4.51–55).[38] The well-known fishing-guild inscription marking the construction of a harbor tollhouse and its dedication to Nero in the 50s CE in Ephesus attests these realities also.[39] In John 21 Jesus' disciples return to imperial and economic involvement. But they cannot catch any fish (21:1–5) until Jesus commands it (21:6–14). Again, his power effects their supply of food for the breakfast cooking and eating scene (21:9–12), not their involvement in the imperial economy. Then follows a commission to Peter to "feed my lambs" and to "follow me" (21:15–19) and to the "disciple whom Jesus loved" to "follow me" (21:20–23). Both disciples are called away from fishing to following, from imperial-economic activity to ecclesial leadership. Fishing and its imperial economic involvement is not to be their way of life.[40]

The Gospel does not spell out the implications of civic distancing and does not provide us with any sure guide as to how far to push these implications. Mission activity seems to be expected in some form (John 17:18; 20:21). The possibility also exists that the Zechariah 14 prohibition on trading could apply only to specific involvement with or in a temple and not regarded as furthering God's purposes. This narrow reading, rather than the all-encompassing wider reading, would certainly make life in the city more sustainable by rendering it somewhat more accommodated. However the matter is to be resolved, and lack of data prevents any closer definition, these clues at least suggest that the identity of Jesus-believers as a "temple-community" has pragmatic and challenging implications in a daily life in Ephesus marked by considerable distance and differentiation, at least as far as the Gospel writer/s is/are concerned. Whether Jesus-believers were willing to replace their more-accommodated way of life with a lifestyle of civic distancing, with all its social and economic implications—whatever precisely they may have been—is another question.

Jesus-Believers: *Fides* and *Pistis*

In John 13–17 Jesus refers to "believing" some eleven times, including twice in 14:1: "Believe in God, believe also in me" (NRSV).[41] Throughout this book I have referred to those committed to Jesus as "Jesus-believers." The term "believer" or "believe" in English ("have faith," "be faithful") is hardly adequate for the numerous uses and various nuances of this verb in the Gospel. And the situation is not helped by our contemporary understandings of piety that often reduce this word to individualistic consent to doctrinal formulations. A brief survey of the verb's uses in the Gospel along with some imperial intertexts elaborate some of its rich meaning.

According to one count, John uses the verb *pisteuō* (πιστεύω) 98 times, three times as often as the three Synoptic Gospels combined, and nearly half of the 241 uses in the New Testament. John does not use the noun "faith" or "belief." The verb's uses fall into approximately four groups:[42]

- The Gospel frequently uses the adjectival or substantive participle form of the verb in both the singular and plural forms to denote "believer/s." This Greek construction is often hidden in English translations, which prefer the more fluid "everyone who believes" (3:16) or "those who believe" (3:18) to the more awkward "every believer" or "every believing one" (3:16) or "the believer in him" (3:18). The use of the participle to identify the believer indicates that faith is not "an internal disposition but [is] an active commitment."[43]

- In more than a third of the uses, the verb *pisteuō* is used with prepositions "into" (εἰς, *eis*) or "in/on" (*en*, ἐν). Sometimes God is the object (14:1), but mostly the object is either Jesus (3:15, 36) or his name (1:12). This use indicates "much more than trust in Jesus or confidence in him: it is an acceptance of Jesus and of what he claims to be and a dedication of one's life to him. The commitment is not emotional but involves a willingness to respond to God's demands as they are presented in and by Jesus."[44] This "believes in Jesus" construction also denotes doing certain actions (14:12). The verb also expresses commitment and loyalty by believing (or not believing) *in* Moses (5:46), the Scriptures (2:22), or Jesus' word (4:50; 5:47).

- The verb is used with another preposition "on account of" (*dia*, διά), which indicates the basis of the believing such as Jesus' words (4:41–42) and works (14:11).

- The verb is also used with the conjunction "that" (ὅτι, *hoti*) to introduce clauses containing affirmations about Jesus. Believe "that I am" (8:24); "that you are the Messiah [Christ], the Son of God" (11:27); "that I am in the Father and the Father is in me" (14:10–11); "that I came from God" (16:27); "that you have sent me" (17:21), "that Jesus is the Messiah, the Son of God" (20:31 NRSV in sentence). These are central Johannine understandings about Jesus and could easily be combined into a form of a creed; "I believe that Jesus. . . ." "Believing" here involves not only commitment to and relationship with Jesus, but also understanding of and consent to statements that accurately assert Jesus' origin, identity, authority, mission, and relationship with God. These statements express God's perspective on Jesus so that believing/entrusting oneself to him means allying oneself with God's verdict. Clearly these are affirmations with which nondisciples do not agree. What one believes functions, then, not only in establishing and maintaining relationship with God and Jesus but also socially to identify those who belong to John's distinctive community and to mark a division with outsiders.

It is impossible to find one English word that adequately expresses the range of meanings evidenced by these uses.[45] In English we often think of believing as a matter of thinking or accepting or agreeing with an understanding, and often in Christian traditions such "believing" has been presented as antithetical to actions or works. But for John the verb's usages clearly indicate a much greater range of meanings that span commitment or loyalty, entrusting oneself to, relationship with, lived fidelity to, actions (John 14:12!), understanding, alliance with God/Jesus, social division from nonbelievers, and belonging to the community of believers. For John, it is not just a matter of "beliefs" or individualistic thinking; it is also active and social. "Believing" denotes a lived communal way of life loyal to Jesus.

Throughout this book I have outlined some ways in which the presentation of this way of life committed to Jesus in John's Gospel contests significant aspects of Roman imperial power in Ephesus and ways of life accommodated to and participative in it. This same contestive reality is present, I am suggesting, in relation to this central Johannine notion of "believers." The concept of *fides* (Latin) or *pistis* (Greek for "faith/belief"; the verb is *pisteuō*)[46] was an integral part of Roman elite and imperial self-understanding and actions that centered on faithfulness or fidelity in honoring the commitments into which Rome and another people or community entered. Rome would loyally provide protection; the other people would be loyal to Rome. The larger framework for these understandings seems to be the pervasive structure and relational obligations involving patrons, clients, and benefaction.[47] Both patrons (Rome) and clients (the kings/peoples of the empire) were to show *fides* to each other in their actions; the *fides* of the patrons comprised constant protection and benefaction; the clients, confident of the patrons' loyalty, are obligated to reciprocate with displays of loyalty and honor that included, for instance, payment of taxes and tributes, supplying troops, and providing slaves.[48]

Josephus, for example, attests both dimensions.[49] Statements of Roman "faith" or loyalty are pervasive in contexts of treatment of allies and subject peoples. Herod's gift of eight hundred talents to Octavian (= Augustus) "caused Caesar to have even greater faith [πίστιν, *pistin*] in [Herod's] loyalty and devotion" (*Ant.* 15.200–201). Subsequently, Herod had, in making his will, "put his trust [πίστει, *pistei*] in Caesar" (Augustus). "Nor would the virtue and good faith of Caesar, which were unquestioned throughout the entire civilized world," allow him to question Herod's judgment and the performance of Archelaus (17.246–247). In an interesting example, the noun πίστις (*pistis*) and the verb πιστεύω (*pisteuō*) are used synonymously. Titus makes pledges of good faith (δεξιαῖς πίστεως, *dexiais pisteōs*) to the town of Gischala if it surrenders; the town "beheld in the secure enjoyment of their possessions all who had trusted the pledges [δεξιαῖς ἐπίστευσαν, *dexiais episteusan*] proffered by Roman hands" (*J.W.* 4.94–96). In response to displays of Roman faithfulness or loyalty, Josephus continually emphasizes the loyalty or faithfulness of Jewish people to Rome (*J.W.* 2.341; *Ant.* 14.192; 16.48; 19.289; *Ag. Ap.* 2.134).

In his recent study of conversion within the framework of patron-client and benefaction structures, Zeba Crook observes:

> There is a clear relationship between the language of kingship and the language of divinity and therefore of conversion. In other words, kings existed on a continuum that included the gods as holders of honour and power and as benefactors of humanity. Loyalty to the emperor and loyalty to one's divine patron were cut from the same cloth, and the political realm provided the ancients with many useful analogies for casting their relationship with the gods.[50]

In evoking the cultural intertexts surrounding *fides/pistis*, I am not primarily concerned with the origin of Johannine use; instead, I am exploring the interactions of John's language with imperial dimensions of late first-century Ephesus. Not surprisingly, given the neglect of any imperial or political dimensions of John's world, this imperial intertext of fidelity or loyalty from Rome and to Rome has commonly been ignored in Johannine scholarship.[51] Perhaps also the factor of lexical categorization accounts in part for this neglect. While John's term for believing or having faith or showing loyalty is the verb *pisteuō* (πιστεύω), the Latin term *fides* and its Greek equivalent *pistis* are both nouns. Johannine scholars have conventionally emphasized the significance of the verb in denoting a continuing, active reality ("believing") rather than a static quality, "faith" or "belief."[52] The following discussion will show—as do the examples from Josephus above—that any such argument based on the lexical distinction between a verb and a noun is irrelevant for this cultural intertextuality. *Fides* is not a static or internal quality, but one that is displayed in actions and lived out in relationships and through societal structures in the context of patron-client obligatory relationships. Whether verb or noun, it is dynamic and active.

Cicero exemplifies significant understandings of *fides/pistis*. In his work *On Duties/Obligations* (*De officiis*), he declares that faithfulness or loyalty holds the state together more powerfully than anything else (2.84). For example, he insists on the payment of debts because it honors commitments, ensures that the wealthy do not lose possessions, and protects the state. But the quality of "faithfulness" is much more foundational and pervasive: "The foundation of justice is good faith—that is, truth and fidelity to promises and agreements" (1.23).[53] *Fides* is lived in actions and relationships; it is not an internal quality. He presents Regulus as the ideal faithful Roman. In the First Punic War, Regulus was captured by the Carthaginians and sent to Rome to negotiate a return of prisoners, and he swore to return to Carthage afterward. In Rome, however, he proposed the opposite plan, that none be released. But rather than stay in Rome in freedom, "he chose to return [to Carthage] to a death by torture rather than prove false to his promise, though given to an enemy" (1.39). Cicero returns to Regulus in book 3 of this work. In Cicero's view, it is not worth losing the reputation of being a "good man" by failing to exhibit good faith or "honor and justice" in actions and relationships (3.82). So he strongly approves of Regulus keeping his oath because "an oath is an assurance backed by religious sanctity; and a solemn promise given, as before God as one's witness, to be sacredly kept. For the question [concerns] the obligations of justice and good faith. . . . Whoever, therefore, violates his oath violates Good Faith [whom] our forefathers chose that she should dwell upon the Capitol 'neighbor to Jupiter Supreme and Best'" (3.104).

Here Cicero refers to the common practice of the divinization, personification, and cult observance of an abstract value or quality.[54] *Fides* is not just a faithful human action, but also a divine power at work throughout society and guiding Rome in its dealings with other peoples.[55] Traditions linked this (goddess) Fides with Numa, who established annual sacrificial worship of Fides for the Roman people so that they would highly regard and observe "promises and oaths" not only among themselves but also with neighboring peoples (Livy 1.21; Dionysius of Halicarnassus, *Roman Antiquities* 2.75.1–4; Plutarch, *Numa* 16.1.). Such trust or faithfulness or commitment was crucial to dealings with other peoples (Livy 32.32.15). Polybius praises agents of Roman power, "magistrates and legates," who—unlike other peoples who "cannot keep their faith [πίστιν, *pistin*]"—rule with integrity because they have "pledged their faith [πίστεως, *pisteōs*] by oath" and so handle great sums of public money without being caught stealing it (Polybius, *Hist.* 6.56.6–15). Plutarch quotes from a celebratory hymn of the Chalcidians: "The Roman faith [πίστιν δὲ Ρωμαίων] we revere; . . . sing then . . . to great

Zeus, to Rome, to Titus, and to the Roman faith [Ῥωμαίων τε πίστιν]" (Plutarch, *Titus Flamininus* 16.4).

The temple of Fides Publica Populi Romani (Public Faith of the Roman people) had been set up in Rome in the mid-third century BCE. The cult continued to be honored at the end of the second century CE (Tertullian, *Apol.* 24.5). Either in the temple or on walls nearby and beside the temple of Jupiter, international treaties were displayed: Rome kept faith to agreements with subordinate allies and expected the same from them (Polybius, *Hist.* 3.25–28, esp. 26.1).[56] The placement of this temple next to that of Jupiter showed how intricately connected Fides was to Jupiter and to the imperial agenda. The same link is evident in Virgil. Addressing Venus, Jupiter declares Rome's imperial mission to be "lords of the world" and to be a city for which Jupiter has set "neither bounds nor periods of empire; dominion without end have I bestowed." Augustus will appear to "extend his empire to the ocean and his glory to the stars. . . . Wars shall cease and savage ages soften; hoary Faith [Fides] and Vesta . . . shall give laws" (Virgil, *Aen.* 1.254, 278–279, 282, 287, 291–293).[57] Horace also associates Fides with the emperor Augustus. The return of Fides (along with peace, honor, and modesty) occurs under Augustus's rule (*Carm.* 57; also *Odes* 4.5.20).

Later in the first century CE, Silius Italicus sets forth the virtue of Rome's honoring of Fides in its imperial ways by revisiting the story of the victory over Carthage after Carthage had broken its treaty (*Punica* 1.4–11). Silius Italicus wrote his epic poem *Punica* mostly during the reign of Domitian, and it is almost contemporary with John's Gospel. Liebeschuetz argues that Silius writes "not in a spirit of opposition but of support for the *status quo*. . . . Silius describes how the approach of Hannibal proves a challenge answered with a massive display of Roman virtues" (12.551–557, 587–594).[58] He sets the Flavian emperors—Vespasian, Titus, Domitian—in this context and has Jupiter address Domitian: "O son of gods and father of gods to be, rule the happy [blessed] earth with paternal sway" (3.593–630). Fides is a prominent value and power in this account of "Roman virtue in action" in the defeat of Hannibal. Rome is a people "famous for keeping *fides*" with its allies (1.634).

These virtuous displays of active loyalty are contextualized by Jupiter's faithful commitment to Rome and miraculous intervention on behalf of Rome. Hannibal cannot win because Jupiter repeatedly thwarts him (e.g., 12.605–645).[59] The presence of and concern with Fides ensures that "this supernatural government is concerned with moral behavior."[60] For Silius (as for Livy) the war with Hannibal was "a war of right against wrong, and . . . the Roman victory was a victory of right."[61] Carthage had broken the treaty that ended the First Punic War and so had broken *fides* while Rome had maintained it (1.5–6). Liebeschuetz points to two key episodes in which Fides figures prominently in Silius's epic: the siege of Saguntum in Spain (*Punica* 2.475–707), and the death of Regulus (in the First Punic War) by torture and crucifixion (2.344, 435) in keeping his oath sworn to the enemy (6.62–551).[62] Regulus was a man in whom Fides "had fixed her seat and remained the tenant of his heart" (6.132).

In the former episode, Silius presents Fides as the protective and energizing deity of Saguntum. With echoes of Israel's Wisdom and John's Jesus, she descends from heaven (2.542), to which she has withdrawn because the "human race was so fertile in wickedness" with evil kings and violent and greedy nations to punish the evil deeds of the breakers of treaties (2.484–514).[63] Fides has no home in such a context, except among the divinely chosen Romans and their allies. "Taking possession of their minds and pervading their breasts, . . . she instilled her divine power into their hearts. Then piercing even to their marrow, she filled them with a burning passion for herself" (2.515–517). Fides cannot save Saguntum, and Hannibal is victorious, but she does provide the city's residents eternal rest and fame in Elysium (2.696–707). The scene provides a warning to the nations: "Break not treaties of peace nor set power above loyalty" (*fidem*, 2.700–771). Throughout the poem, Rome is faithful in its actions and to its destiny. The supernatural governance of the world in which Rome participates and of which Rome is the agent is a moral power.[64]

Significantly, Silius Italicus was proconsul of Asia, based in the capital city Ephesus, during the reign of Vespasian in 77 CE. The presence of this emphasis on Fides in his poem *Punica* suggests that for this leading representative of Roman power in Asia Minor, *fides*, meaning loyalty or faithfulness to Roman commitments and destiny, had been a key value in framing Roman actions toward its provincial allies and cooperative subjects during his term in office. Whether there was any cultic celebration of Fides in Ephesus either before, during, or after his proconsulship is not known, though it certainly is possible. But there are other indications of the importance of Fides in the city.

While Silius Italicus certainly valued *fides*, he did not introduce the notion to Ephesus. Earlier in the first century, after Augustus's death in 14 CE, the Senate decreed that Augustus's work, the *Acts of Augustus* (*Res gestae*), an account of his accomplishments and gifts, should be made known throughout the empire. Copies were distributed to towns and cities such as Ephesus. There were readings in theaters, and copies in both Latin and Greek were carved in stone and displayed on temple walls, as in the surviving texts from Ancyra. In his *Acts* 26–33, Augustus catalogs numerous peoples who were subjugated to or who sought friendship with him and Rome. In section 32 he adds a generalizing sentence to the catalog: "During my principate, many other peoples, with whom no exchange of embassies and friendship existed before, have experienced the *trust* of the Roman people." The word "trust" is, in the Latin versions of his writing, *fidem*, and in the Greek texts *pisteōs* (πίστεως).[65] It denotes submission to and compliance with Rome, in exchange for which Rome kept faith with displays of goodwill.

A partial Latin inscription at Ephesus (IEph 1.19A) from a proconsul, whose name and titulary are missing, links "faith and constancy" (*fide et c[onstantia]*) in a context that might suggest a claim that he has exercised faithful Roman rule. The term *Fides Publica* also appears on coins from Asia Minor in the period of the Flavian emperors (69–96 CE). Vespasian,[66] Titus,[67] and Domitian[68] appear on the obverse; the reverse includes the words *FIDES PVBL* (*Fides Publica*), with some presentation of the clasped hands that signify Fides,[69] along with a caduceus, poppies, and ears of corn, signifying the prosperity and fecundity that accompany faithful Roman rule and the submissive loyalty of subject provinces. A coin from a loyal Roman client king, Antiochus IV of Commagene—appointed to rule that kingdom in Asia Minor in the mid-first century CE by the emperor Claudius, founded a city there named Caesarea Germanicia, and later supported Vespasian against the Jewish revolt in 69–70 CE—displays the Greek term *PISTIS*, with the standard clasped hands and caduceus.[70] The same term *PISTIS* and symbol of clasped hands appear on a coin from another of his kingdoms, Lycaonia in Galatia.[71] It is not clear whether *PISTIS* proclaims his loyalty to Rome, his faithfulness in ruling his subjects, the kingdoms' loyalty to Rome and their appointed king, or all of these options. Dio Chrysostom, born in Bithynia and active in Asia Minor, certainly understands the role of loyalty among elites in the exercise of power. He declares that a ruler maintains his power not so much through his wealth and military power as through the loyalty (τῇ πίστει) of his friends (*Kingship 3* [*Or. 3*] 86, 88; see below). But loyalty is not confined to a small group. In the second century, the Asian orator Aristides celebrates Rome's empire: "No one worthy of rule or trust [πίστεως, *pisteōs*] remains an alien, but a civil community of the World has been established as a free republic under one, the best, ruler and teacher, of order" (*Roman Oration* 60). Aristides later observes that in response to Rome's establishment of "universal order, . . . the altars of the gods received faith [πίστιν, *pistin*]" (*Roman Oration* 103).

The Fides coins recovered from Asia were part of various Fides coins across the empire. Per Gustav Hamberg observes "multiplicity" of representations including Fides as a divine being with human features (personification), appropriate symbols especially of the hand and of military power, symbolic actions that could be either quite specific, such as the Emperor Trajan joining hands with a soldier to represent mutual political-military loyalty, or more generalized depictions of loyalty, along with legends.[72] A group of Fides coins depicts military symbols and soldiers, indicating both loyalty to each other and loyalty to the duty of maintaining the empire. Some Fides coins also share features of presentations of *Concordia* (social harmony), suggesting the important sociopolitical expression of loyalty in relation to the imperial social order. This multiplicity of representation, Hamberg argues, shows "the central position of Concordia and Fides in the political thinking of the Empire."[73]

Such displays of Roman patronage and benefaction require reciprocal actions from clients. The Ephesian inscriptions attest the importance of Fides for (elite?) participation in the city's life as an expression of client loyalty. One inscription (IEph 1.216) comprising a partial edict of a proconsul concerning the rights of Sophists contains the phrase "faith/loyalty in/to the public works [πίστις εἰς τὰ δημόσια, *pistis eis ta demosia*]." Another inscription (IEph 3.683A) honors Herakleidos Didymus "because of his piety toward Artemis and because of the strength/ability in learning and loyalty/faithfulness [πίστιν, *pistin*] and because of benevolence toward the people/assembly [τὸν δῆμον, *ton dēmon*]." Although much of the first line is missing, the genitive case form of "Artemis" at the end of the line suggests that his piety toward her and his loyalty might have been expressed in some role in the Artemision. In another inscription (IEph 5.1587), the Ephesian M. Aurelius Agathopus gives thanks "to the god and to the lord savior," by whom he most likely means Artemis since τῇ κυρίᾳ is feminine, "because I have kept faith to the gerousia."[74] In these instances the term refers to human actions that consist of loyalty to the goddess or a civic body, as expressed in appropriate actions.

To such representations of civic loyalty could be added (if space permitted) numerous examples of other expressions of reciprocal loyalty to Rome.[75] These displays comprised such actions as the granting and exercise of political offices, oaths of allegiance, changes of name for persons and cities, construction of buildings, dedication of monuments, hosting imperial officials, royal wills, and other such actions. Patron-client relations, in which benefactions play a key role, display the pervasive importance of *fides* or loyalty in daily imperial life.

What interface might be created by these civic and imperial assertions of *fides/pistis* or loyalty with John's Gospel's repeated and emphatic use of the same language to denote faith in/loyalty to Jesus? Are these varying expression of *fides/pistis* readily compatible and easily accommodated assertions, or are they mutually exclusive? There are marked similarities in the uses of the terms in that both civic/imperial and Gospel uses denote understandings, commitment or loyalty, and faithful actions that express commitment.[76] It would be docetic and ahistorical to isolate the Gospel reality of "believing" from this cultural intertextuality. It would also be contrary to the pervasive postcolonial recognition of the importance of, albeit selective, imitation in imperial contexts.

Immediately the various objects of the commitment—Artemis, the emperor, the empire, the city council, one's word, Jesus, and so forth—raise the question of systems and objects of loyalties. But this question is not to be framed or addressed only in individual terms, as Bultmann for instance insisted (with many followers) in speaking of a new self-understanding and an individual crisis of decision in relation to John's usage.[77] The cultural intertextuality created by the use of the term points way beyond the individual to imperial systems, practices, and worldviews. When this context is made explicit, Bultmann's unelaborated insight that faith or loyalty to Jesus was "a smashing of all human standards and insights," a "decision against the world,"[78] might be demythologized to be understood helpfully as naming exclusive and excluding loyalties in an imperial context. What relationship exists between "believing in" Jesus and these other loyalties?

The Gospel's dualism concerning believing in Jesus is well known. To believe in Jesus is "the work of God" (John 6:29). To believe is to pass from death to life (5:24). Not to believe is to be condemned already (3:18) because some people do evil deeds and do not want their evil deeds exposed (3:19–20). Not to believe is to disobey Jesus and therefore to face the wrath of God (3:36). Believe or not believe, free from judgment or subject to condemnation, life or death: this dualistic framework creates antithetical relationships between believing in Jesus and any other "believing in" or "faithfulness to." Frequently neglected has been any such discussion of Roman imperial claims. Three examples will elaborate this antithesis.

The first example can be mentioned briefly because of the previous discussion in chapter 7 above. It comes from John 9, where Jesus has restored sight to the blind man. In 9:35 Jesus asks him, "Do you believe in [*pisteueis eis*] the Son of Man?" The man does not know who this figure is, Jesus declares himself to be the Son of Man, and the man confesses his belief, "I believe" (9:38). To what or to whom has he committed himself? He has pledged loyalty to one who, according to Daniel 7:13–14, ends all the empires of the earth, including Rome's, and to whom God has given everlasting "dominion and glory and kingship, that all peoples, nations, and languages should serve him" (NRSV). To believe in such a one involves his understanding, commitment, and consonant actions expressive of this loyalty. Such believing aligns itself against the empire in anticipation of its decline even while it significantly imitates an imperial mind-set and practice of worldwide domination.

Second, two chapters later, after Jesus has raised Lazarus, Caiaphas declares to the concerned chief priests and Pharisees, the Jerusalem power group in alliance with

Rome, "If we let him go on like this, everyone will believe in him, and the Romans will come and destroy both our holy place and our nation" (John 11:48 NRSV). Various elements of Caiaphas's statement could attract our attention, notably the scheming, the desire to protect elite interests and power against any disturbances,[79] the irony of the statement,[80] and the relation to the destructive events of 70 CE interpreted as the consequences for rejecting Jesus. But for our purposes, I want to stress the oft-missed antithesis between "believing in" Jesus and the putative response of the Romans. Caiaphas is concerned with loyalty to Jesus because it threatens loyalty to Rome and will provoke violent reassertion of Roman supremacy in destroying the temple and nation! To "believe in Jesus" threatens the imperial status quo. Just how Caiaphas perceives this threat is not at this point made clear: the only reason Caiaphas gives is the hypothetical declaration "Everyone will believe in him." We might guess that "everyone will believe"—in the Gospel's perspective—because loyalty to one who as God's agent has demonstrated life-giving practices and declared them to be sanctioned by God is more "attractive" or life-giving than the death-bringing, destructive ways of empire that Caiaphas, Rome's ally, names.

This is only a guess, but lest this suggestion be dismissed too quickly, we should recall that this scene follows Jesus' restoring of life to the dead Lazarus, which resulted in many of the *Ioudaioi*, predominantly the Jerusalem elite allied with Rome or their loyal followers, believing in him (11:45).[81] This loss of allegiance/loyalty ("believing") threatens their control because Jesus offers a different vision of life (see chap. 8 above). Caiaphas sees destruction as the consequences of their believing; conventional imperial death-bringing actions follow for those who appear not to "keep faith" with Rome but keep faith elsewhere. As I argued in chapter 8 above, Jesus' actions such as the raising of Lazarus successfully contest death, but Caiaphas is deathly determined to protect his imperial system. Believing thus concerns not only individual allegiances but also societal structures and priorities. "Believing in" Jesus is not only a private, individual, interior matter, but also one that has public, societal, and imperially contestive consequences. As with the titles used for Jesus that are also used of the emperors (discussed in chap. 7 above), this shared language of "believing/loyalty" suggests fundamentally incompatible loyalties and lived commitments.

Third, Jesus contributes to this antithesis between faith in or loyalty to Jesus and Roman *fides* in his talk of "driving out the ruler of the world" (12:31), who has no power over Jesus (14:30) and has been condemned (16:11). Though often interpreted as the devil (as noted earlier), in the narrative sequence this figure more likely refers to Pilate, agent of Roman power.[82] The Gospel does not refer to Satan as a ruler, and the world that rejects Jesus (1:10) is shown by the Gospel's crucifixion narrative to comprise Roman power represented by Pilate and its Jerusalem allies. The Gospel uses the language of "ruler" to refer to members of this alliance (3:1; 7:26) and not to supernatural beings. Moreover, Jesus declares to Pilate that Pilate has no ultimate power over him (19:11), echoing Jesus' statement of 14:30 that "the ruler of this world . . . has no power over me." Jesus' overcoming of Pilate takes place in his resurrection, in which Roman power is exposed to be no match for God's life-giving power. Jesus' resurrection signifies and anticipates the final demise of Rome's empire at the coming judgment, when "those who have done evil [will come out] to the resurrection of condemnation" (5:29 NRSV). Jesus-believers have made a choice (John 1:12; 6:47) that has systemic sociopolitical consequences. And since the future is to some degree already present in John's realized eschatology, loyalty to this condemned imperial order in Ephesus is incompatible with loyalty to or faith in Jesus. Attention to the cultural intertextuality of John's language highlights an important but neglected dimension of John's use of the term "believe."

We can conclude, then, that believing in Jesus in the sense of commitment, loyalty, and lived faithfulness to him is incompatible with any other commitment. In the Gospel's rhetoric of distance, one cannot be loyal to the empire and Artemis, as well as to Jesus. The identity of a Jesus-believer, as far as the Gospel is concerned, means a way of life distanced from loyalty to the imperial and civic order of Ephesus. The latter's claims of *fides* are disqualified because it fails to be loyal to or believe in God's life-giving purposes demonstrated in Jesus. The language of "believing," then, is part of the Gospel's rhetoric of distance, seeking to create a more differentiated and distanced way of life for Jesus-believers.

Loving Service (13:1–20)

A third feature of the lifestyle of John's temple-community or Jesus-believers comprises loving service. The episode of the footwashing has been much discussed, frequently with a christological emphasis on Jesus' death as the Suffering Servant. Since limited space is available here, I will highlight the passage's emphasis on Jesus' action as an example of the lifestyle of the community of Jesus-believers (13:12–15). Again imitation of as well as a contestive alternative to imperial practices are present.

The Setting

Jesus' footwashing action is set in the opening verses in the context of his divine origin, authority, destiny (13:1, 3), imminent crucifixion (Passover, "hour" 13:1), motivation (love, 13:1b), opposition (13:2), and agency (13:3a, "The Father had given all things into his hands" [NRSV]; also 3:35; 6:39). His agency concerns representing and revealing all of God's purposes among humans, including God's reign (3:3, 5), judgment, and giving life (5:21–22). All of this casts Rome in bad light, contests its claims of sovereignty, asserts God's claim on human affairs, and makes clear Jesus' inevitable collision with Rome, as I have established. It also provides the context for the footwashing action.

Slave Work

During the meal, Jesus washes the disciples' feet (13:4–5). Footwashing commonly comprised part of the hospitality, often associated with meals (Petronius, *Satyricon* 31) and performed by a servant (cf. Luke 7:44–46) or, as in the case of Mary in the preceding chapter, a woman (John 12:3; 1 Tim 5:9–10).[83] It was generally not an elite role. In John Thomas's view, it was "the most menial task" in a society in which honor and shame were principal values.[84] Meals could also function, as has been commonly recognized, to reflect and reinforce social honor with ranked seating or reclining order, different quantities and qualities of food, quality of tableware according to a person's social location, and roles of host, guest, and server.[85] Plutarch laughs at the guest who "saw no place left worthy of him," yet Plutarch also finds some value in recognizing places of honor (Plutarch, *Table Talk* 615D–6617E). Pliny the Younger disapproves of differentiated seating order and quality of food and wine (*Ep.* 2.6). Jesus, though the group leader, strangely takes the role of a low-status slave as well as host.

Soteriological Interpretation

Jesus' action receives two interpretations, the first of which comes in John 13:6–11 and is in relation to Jesus' intimate union with the Father, into which he invites disciples. Peter's refusal to have his feet washed by Jesus is a choice not to participate in this mutual union of love (cf. 5:20; 10:17a; 14:31; 15:9). Jesus insists on the necessity of Jesus' act of footwashing by telling him, "Unless I wash you, you have no share with me" (13:8 NRSV). The word "share" evokes traditions about a "share" or participation in God's purposes and promises comprising the promised land (Num 18:20; Deut 12:12),[86] and the language of "with me" anticipates the emphasis in John 14 of disciples abiding with Jesus (14:3, 20) and God (14:23). If Peter refuses Jesus' washing, he cannot participate in Jesus' gift of such life and relationship which, as the framing of the story indicates in 13:1–3, necessitates his death as the means of his return to the Father.

Ecclesiological Interpretation

A second interpretation, an ecclesiological one, follows this soteriological interpretation (13:12–20). Jesus identifies the central paradox of the scene in which he, their Teacher and Lord/Master, has in a Saturnalia-like gesture[87] functioned as their slave in order to provide them with an example of how they are to treat each other (13:16). He offers a blessing on the doing of such actions of loving service (13:17) and returns to a focus on his death by mentioning his betrayal by first Judas (13:17–20, 21–30) and then Peter (13:36–38).

Central to Jesus' action and example is the identity and actions of being a slave.[88] Slaves were a basic component of the imperial system, providing relatively cheap labor and numerous skills to maintain and service the way of life for the "free" elite (and some nonelite). They were political, economic, social, and religious functionaries whose purpose was to do the bidding of their master and to attend to their master's needs. In elite perspective, slavery was a domination system that upheld elite superiority (Seneca, *Ben.* 3.19.4, though some slaves can rise above it and save their master's life), in which the "more upright and more capable of good actions" rules over the inferior (3.28.1), who is bound to obey (3.19.1).[89] In John's Gospel, only elites own slaves, such as the host of the big wedding in 2:1–11 (2:5, 9), the royal official in 4:46–54 (4:51), and the Jerusalem elite. The high priest owns a slave Malchus, who loses his ear to Peter's sword

(18:10), as well as other slaves (18:18), including a relative of Malchus (18:26). Slaves appear in the narrative in this low status. No other slaves are mentioned in relation to serving meals, washing feet, or any other household or business tasks. Van Tilborg's data about slaves in the Ephesian inscriptions confirm their importance to the life of Ephesus as "slaves of private citizens," "city slaves" such as temple slaves of Artemis, freed slaves, and freedmen of the emperor.[90]

On one hand, Jesus' "example" of such slave behavior as the norm for the practices of Jesus-believers poses no challenge to this imperial structure and can be seen as not only its imitation but also its divinely sanctioned normalization and internalization.[91] In fact, several elite traditions had adopted aspects of the image of the slave such as seeking the best for the ruled in constituting the model for the ideal ruler (Plato, *Republic* 1.347D; 7.540B; Dio Chrysostom, *Kingship 1* (*Or. 1*) 1.12–36). Cynics described the philosopher-ruler performing a service as king (Seneca, *Ep.* 90.5) or as an individual who shares Zeus's reign over all humanity by ruling, serving, and giving one's life (Epictetus, *Discourse* 3.22.54–61, 77–85; 4.30–32).[92] Such ideal traditions borrowed the image of a slave, assumed its normative quality, and put it to use in sustaining the status quo. Van Tilborg rightly sees something of this happening in Jesus' example: "Slavery is natural and is not criticized. . . . Jesus and his disciples participate in the social ideology about slavery, but they do not profit from it."[93] This lack of questioning of the slave system indicates how deeply embedded is this text and its writer/s in the imperial system, even while it urges Jesus-believers to adopt greater distance from imperial involvement.

Yet as part of the Gospel's rhetoric of distance, some critique and alternative also seems to be present. As much as slavery is assumed and imitated, a somewhat different pattern of social interaction is created in that the whole community of Jesus-believers is designated as slaves. Unlike the Saturnalia, where master and slaves change roles for a short time before resuming normal roles, here none is a master. There is only one Master, and that is Jesus, and even he behaves as a slave in serving the disciples (13:14–16). In a social pattern of ubiquitous slavery, roles of honor and preeminence of rank are abolished. This is a significant alternative to imperial society, where rank and status were fundamental values and to be demonstrated at every opportunity through wealth, kinship, office, possessions, and so forth. Numerous inscriptions from Ephesus such as that of Salutaris attest this honorific society at work. Ramsay McMullen collects numerous examples of elite disdain for nonelites.[94] But this is not the way Jesus-believers are to interact with one another. Whether accommodated Jesus-believers in Ephesus found the requirement to adopt the model of the ideal slave compelling is impossible to tell.

Another elite category undergoes change in the example of being slaves. Honor or status was derived from various sources, including one's association with prestigious people. Ironically, and often ignored in studies of slavery, there was honor, wealth, and power for some slaves of important masters because the slaves were associated with and exercised power on behalf of a high-status master.[95] Philo, for instance, complains bitterly about the emperor Gaius Caligula's slave Helicon, "an abominable execrable slave," and "a piece of riffraff," who in exercising considerable power influences the emperor against the elite Jewish delegation from Alexandria (Philo, *Emb.* 166–178; 203–206). To have as Master the one whom God has sent (John 13:16b), albeit the one crucified by Rome yet raised by and ascended to God (cf. 13:1–3), is a great honor with great prestige, in the Gospel's worldview. It denotes the alliance of Jesus-believers with one who overpowered Roman power and thwarted Roman purposes.

In this interaction of imperial imitation, difference, and some reframing, Van Tilborg remarks, "Jesus himself uses the system to bring his message across 'propheti- cally': service is more important than power."[96] While the first part of van Tilborg's claim is correct, the second part poses a somewhat false alternative. While slaves cer- tainly do not have the power of their masters, and lacked rights and status, it is not accurate to say that all slaves were powerless. Slaves certainly lacked social and legal rights and were subject to numerous abuses. But some slaves, as extensions and instru- ments of their master's power, exercised considerable power on behalf of and for the benefit of their masters. Philo's frustrating struggle with the imperial slave Helicon illustrates the point.

John's Jesus' point seems not to be "service versus power" but "service as power." Slaves benefited their masters. Jesus calls Jesus-believers to benefit each other. This is not self-serving power to secure or enhance one's own status, wealth, honor, and power, but contrary to the elite imperial model, yet also imitative of an element of it, it is ser- vice that seeks the good of the other[97] and gives life to them. It thus is service that has a "part" or "share" in Jesus' life-revealing and life-giving work as agent of and in intimate relationship with the Father (13:8).[98] Again, knowledge of whether this model of daily existence appealed to accommodated Jesus-believers is not available to us.

Service as Mission

A further implication follows in 13:20. Jesus sends the disciples or Jesus-believers as his agents in mission, warning that they will face rejection just as he does (cf. 13:16), although some will receive them (13:20). He explains the significance of receiving or rejecting Jesus-believers in terms of their identity of being sent by Jesus, who in turn is sent by God. The same pattern is present in Jesus' postresurrection commission to the disciples: "As the Father has sent me, so I send you" (20:21b NRSV). The implication seems to be that while actions of loving service are to be performed for the benefit of other Jesus-believers, they are not restricted within the community but extend to out- siders also, even if the reception is not always positive (13:17, 20). Loving service com- prises a crucial aspect of this community's mission.

Again the irony is evident in that the Gospel's rhetoric of distance, intent on creat- ing a distanced community or antisociety, is imperially imitative in that Rome also saw its mission as the faithful bestowing of benefactions (e.g., laws, peace, justice: Virgil, *Aen.* 4.231; 6.851–853; Aristides, *Roman Oration* 103).

The "Greater Works" of Jesus-Believers

In 14:12 Jesus declares a further dimension of the temple-community of Jesus-believers committed to a life of loving service: "The one who believes in me will also do the works that I do and, in fact, will do greater works than these, because I am going to the Father"

(NRSV). In Jesus' somatic absence, Jesus-believers are to do "the works that [Jesus] does" as well as "greater works." What are these "works" (ἔργα, *erga*), and how are they greater?

Several times Jesus declares that his mission is to do the "work" of God (4:34; 17:4). These uses of the term "work" in the singular denote his fundamental commitment to God's purposes. This "work" is manifested in various "works" or actions in his ministry (7:3). These "works" reflect and reveal the "works" that the Father does and that have been revealed (5:20) and "given" to Jesus (5:36). "Judging" and "giving life" figure prominently in the intervening passage as examples of such works (5:21–30). In 7:21–23, the discussion of Sabbath observance and Jesus' making a man whole through physical healing suggests that Jesus' healing of the paralyzed man is the "one work" under discussion (5:1–9). In 9:3 and 4 the "works of God" are manifested in Jesus' healing and revealing actions described through the chapter and in the man's believing or faithfulness (cf. 6:29). In 10:32 Jesus claims to have worked "many good works from the Father" (NRSV; cf. 10:37), though his opponents prefer to label his work "blasphemy" and kill him because they do not recognize God at work through him (10:33). Thus Jesus' works reveal the world's sin and judgment (3:19–20; 15:24), God's powerful presence in and with Jesus (10:38; 14:10), and his identity as the one sent from God (5:36; 10:25). They provide people with a basis for believing Jesus (10:38; 14:11).

The term "work/works" refers, then, to the whole ministry of Jesus committed to God, as well as to specific actions that reveal God's life-giving purposes and powerful presence in the world. Given the broad reference of the term, any catalog of these works would have to embrace the whole of the Gospel story: calling disciples (1:35–51), turning water into wine (2:1–11), challenging the corrupt temple (2:13–22), revealing God's purposes in words (3:1–21; 4:4–42; 5:19–47; 6:25–71; chap. 7; 8:12–59; 9:35–10:39; 12:23–50; chaps. 13–16), baptizing (3:22; but 4:2?), converting Samaritans (4:4–42), healing (4:46–54; 5:1–18; 9:1–7), feeding hungry crowds (6:1–14), evading actions contrary to God's purposes (6:15; 8:59; 10:39; etc.), subduing the water (6:16–24), raising the dead (11:1–44), being anointed (12:1–8), entering Jerusalem in an antitriumphal entry (12:12–19), receiving Gentiles (12:20–22), washing feet in loving service (13:1–20), praying (chap. 17), dying (chaps. 18–19), and being raised (chaps. 20–21).

Jesus' statement in 14:12 that Jesus-believers "will do the works that I do and, in fact, will do greater works" locates their way of life in continuity with his own. Just as Jesus' work and works are located in the work and works of God, the works of Jesus-believers are rooted in the works of Jesus. Jesus-believers continue Jesus' ministry in his somatic absence, further manifesting God's life-giving and powerful purposes of God in the midst of Roman Ephesus. This mission of "greater works" opens the way to numerous actions that enact these purposes, including miracles,[99] but does not limit Jesus-believers to doing exactly what Jesus did. The emphasis is on continuity with his revelatory, life-giving work. Just as Jesus' healings and feedings rolled back imperial damage, so also do the healing actions of Jesus-believers (see chap. 8 on eternal life, above). Just as he called disciples, so do they (20:21). Just as he confronted the imperial status quo and revealed its evil works (7:7), so do Jesus-believers. Like Jesus, they are to perform miracles, speak words, gather community, and do acts of loving service. Their works are not restricted only to the temple-community of believers, but just as Jesus was sent into "the world," so also are they (20:21b) even if it means their death (13:8; 16:2). Their works are eschatological, just as Jesus' works were, because they manifest "life of the age." They are "greater" because there are many more Jesus-believers than Jesus alone.[100]

This is the job description that the Gospel presents for Jesus-believers. As part of the Gospel's rhetoric of distance, it constitutes a significantly differentiated and nonaccommodated way of life comprising works of transformation, not accommodation. Hence it would be a mistake to see these acts as "nice" or "helpful" things to do. In Ephesus, to heal the sick and feed the hungry—casualties of the imperial system that ensured the injustice of elite access to abundant resources at the expense of the rest, who paid the price of sickness and short life spans—was a huge task by all accounts of life in imperial cities for most residents.[101] To reveal God's purposes that, as we have seen, were so often at odds with imperial ways was difficult and dangerous. To roll back imperial damage, to bring life in the midst of death, means risking one's own life as the Gospel attests for Jesus' whole ministry, and especially when he raises Lazarus (11:45–53). Jesus' works get him crucified—they do not enable his societal accommodation. These "greater works" are not only eschatological but are also imperially contestive, repairing and transforming the status quo. Greater works result from believing in Jesus crucified by Rome but raised by God (14:12).

Community of Friends (15:12–15)

Space permits only a brief consideration of one more important dimension of the distinctive identity and distanced lifestyle of the community of Jesus-believers that the Gospel constructs. After exhorting disciples to love one another (15:12–13), Jesus declares, "You are my friends [φίλοι μού, *philoi mou*][102] if you do what I command you. I do not call you slaves [δούλους, *doulous*] any longer[103] because the slave does not know what the master is doing; but I have called you friends because I have made known to you everything that I have heard from my Father" (15:14–15 NRSV alt.).[104]

Friendship was a very important reality throughout the empire, with a long tradition of philosophical and popular reflection.[105] There is no space here to trace the continuities or variations of notions such as belonging to a group in contrast to outsiders; the importance of mutuality, reciprocity, amicability, and intimacy as defining marks of friendship; along with concord, frank and confidential speech, loyalty (πίστις, *pistis*);[106] the motivations and pragmatics of friendships; and the need for care in forming and reconciling friendships. Nor is there space to do anything but notice the important development from the Aristotelian emphasis on true friendship involving equals and free from the dynamics of domination and subordination, to the later more-Roman presumption of friendship among "unequals" involving people of different socioeconomic levels, where inequalities of wealth, power, and status were common in patron-client relations, with their attendant repertoire of duties and obligations. This increasingly politicized notion was, for instance, evident in Cicero, who emphasized the bonding power of common "pursuits," "moral habits," and "duties" among unequals. It was also evident in the courts and allies of Hellenistic kings (cf. 1 Macc 10:18–20) and Roman emperors, who gathered groups of advisers known as "friends" (Tacitus, *Ann.* 6.8) and who formed various patron-client relationships with others, including provinces or states (e.g., Strabo, *Geogr.* 8.5.5) and elite provincials as friends of the emperor (*amici-*

tia). This understanding is evident in the accusation of the Rome-allied Jerusalem elite that Pilate is "not Caesar's friend" if he releases Jesus (John 19:12). According to Plutarch, making friends with the governing Romans was a crucial duty for provincial urban elites so that they could gain benefits for themselves and their cities (*Precepts of Statecraft* 814C–E).

At least four interfaces with aspects of this diverse friendship tradition are significant for John's description of Jesus-believers as friends.[107] First, and underlined by the possessive pronoun "my" (*mou*, μου), are the related qualities of loyalty to and intimacy with Jesus. That Jesus abides with disciples and disciples with Jesus has been an emphasis not only in John 14 but also in the first part of chapter 15, with the image of the vine and branches (15:1–11; esp. 15:5, 7, 9, 10). Likewise in 15:14b, Jesus immediately justifies the description of Jesus-believers as friends by stipulating their loyalty demonstrated in their way of life: "if you do what I command you." To be a friend of Jesus is to belong to a community loyal to him and committed to living out his vision or teaching about human existence shaped by God's purposes. Does this loyalty permit other friends? The Gospel's rhetoric at least makes very clear which friendship is to be primary.

Second, in 15:15 Jesus asserts a second reason for no longer calling Jesus-believers slaves but calling them friends. While "the slave does not know what the master is doing; but I have called you friends, because I have made known to you everything that I have heard from my Father" (NRSV). The sharing of confidences, of "all your worries and reflections" (Seneca, *Moral Essays* 3.2–3), and in fact of everything one owns (possessions) with friends (in contrast to slaves, with whom one did not share confidences) was a commonplace in friendship discussions.[108] Jewish traditions also emphasized the sharing of confidences, including both Abraham (Gen 18:17–19) and Moses (Exod 33:11, a friend), who are recipients of God's revelation.[109] The image of "friend" continues to assert Jesus' identity as revealer, extends it to the community of "my friends" as the recipients of Jesus' revelation of God's loving purposes, and obligates them to be loyal to it in living or obeying it (15:14b).

Third, such a community of friends of Jesus has enemies with whom it lives in considerable tension. The enemies are so powerful that Jesus dies for his friends as a display of love for them (15:13). In ordering disciples to love each other, Jesus invites them to display the same sort of love for each other (15:12, 17). Traditions about friendship often employ antonymous experiences such as contrasts with false friends whose loyalty has not been tested, flatterers who are not to be trusted, or enemies (*echthroi*) who do harm.[110] Konstan cites Solon as the first to link friendship with civil dissension and to contrast "being sweet to one's friends and bitter to one's enemies."[111]

Not surprisingly, this section that exhorts loyalty to Jesus and love for other members of the community of friends is followed immediately by a section that speaks of the world's hate for this community (15:18–25). This hate directed to the community results from their not responding in the same way to Jesus as "the world" did, thereby revealing a fundamental difference between themselves and "the world" (15:19). Unlike "the world" that rejected Jesus, they received him (1:10–12). Or in other words, by being Jesus' friends, they experience the hate directed toward him as the revealer of God's purposes and directed toward God (15:18, 20–25). It has been common to "spiritualize" and "individualize" the notion of "the world," but the inappropriateness of such an interpretive move is highlighted first by the evoking of creation traditions in the opening Prologue, with their claims of God's sovereignty over all things (1:1–3, 10b); and second by locating Jesus "in the world" (1:10a) that is in the midst of the imperial structures of Judea-Galilee, part of the Roman province of Syria and thus subject to Roman sovereignty (highlighted by the juxtaposition to 1:10a of 10b: "The world was made through him" [RSV]), and third by describing "the world" as a rejecting place (1:10c), thereby anticipating his crucifixion by the Roman governor Pilate, "the ruler of the world" (12:31).[112] The Gospel story presents this hatred as the response of the empire, including its Jerusalem allies, whereby it protects its privileged power and guards the status quo against the "life of the age" that Jesus manifests (see chap. 8 above). Accommodation with such a world is impossible. This talk of enemies, hate, and death comprises the Gospel's rhetoric of distance, which seeks to create and norm a very differentiated community of disciples, even while it imitates common features of discussions about friendship.

Fourth, the antithetical relationship to the empire created by being friends of Jesus emerges clearly in the use of friendship language in the passion narrative. I will discuss this further in the next chapter, but for now it is sufficient to hear the cry of the Jerusalem elite, Pilate's allies, against Pilate in 19:12: "If you release this man, you are no friend [φίλος, *philos*] of the emperor" (NRSV). To be such a friend means being seen as loyal to and honoring of the emperor (as well as oneself!), as numerous inscriptions from Ephesus and various literary references attest.[113] As governor, Pilate's friendship or loyalty to the emperor Tiberius comprises furthering the emperor's interests, thereby recognizing his divinely sanctioned role as agent of the gods. Significantly, the Jerusalem elite's cry defines such friendship in antithetical terms to Jesus. To release Jesus is not to be a friend of Caesar. It is to give legitimacy to Jesus' claim to be sent from God as the Father's agent. To be a friend of Caesar is to kill Jesus because only the emperor recognizes legitimate kings and sanctions the use of power. To be a friend of Jesus is to recognize his identity and not to be a friend of, loyal to, committed to, obedient to Caesar. It is to be intimate with and loyal to Jesus, and obedient to his teaching, the revelation of God's life-giving purposes, which are at fundamental odds with imperial structures and agenda. Friendship with Caesar or with Jesus forms a stark antithesis to friendship with Jesus.

Van Tilborg's discussion of the use of the words *philosebastos* (φιλοσέβαστος, "friend of/loyal to the Emperor") and *philokaisar* (φιλοκαῖσαρ, "friend of/loyal to Caesar") in the Ephesian inscriptions sharply contextualizes this antithetical relationship.[114] Of the two terms, the latter is less common, though it is associated with emperors through the century and is used of people who promote the interests of the emperor. The former term, however, appears about 132 times, sometimes denoting an individual, sometimes a group such as the city council, council of elders, or the people of Ephesus. It is used in relation to Augustus and Claudius a few times, but its use explodes in the 80s and 90s in relation to Domitian, when the temple of the Sebastoi was built.

This use is significant for two reasons. It reflects the central role of the imperial temples and related imperial cult activity in expressing loyalty to the emperor in the city's life. And second, it defines the whole city as one whose identity is caught up in honoring the emperor. Where is the community of Jesus' friends in this scenario? The use of the term "friend of/loyal to Caesar" in 19:12 surely has special resonance for hearers of the Gospel in Ephesus, given the pervasiveness of this language. The sharp antithesis posed by the Jerusalem leaders in 19:12, put Jesus to death or not be a friend of Caesar, again emphasizes the incompatibility of the two. And in relation to the imperial temple and cult, the context of the particular focus on the terms may underline the distance between the friends of Jesus and loyalty to the emperor, showing the writer's/s' desire/s for this community of Jesus-believers, which is too accommodated and participative in honoring the emperor.

The Gospel does not, though, say precisely what this distance might mean, but reasonably, it would be consonant with the practices suggested above in discussing the other four identities as a temple-community, Jesus-believers, loving slaves, and doers of Jesus' works. For instance, it would be consistent to understand it to mean, among other things, not accepting the imperial propaganda or vision of society as the golden age or the way things are divinely sanctioned to be, not honoring the emperor in trade associations or in civic festivals, not participating in sacrifices or offerings, perhaps not being the emperor's friend in "holding all things in common" with the empire through trade practices. Does it suggest nonpayment of taxes? It does raise the possibility of martyrdom. Friends of Jesus are to invest themselves in each other in loving actions that constitute their alternative community or antisociety and reflect Jesus' self-giving and life-giving love. Sharon Ringe suggests that such actions might involve "accompaniment" (presence with another especially in the midst of hostility), shared meals (12:2–8; 13:1–30; 21:1–14), (transformative) caring in sickness and death (11:1–44), presence with friends and family especially in times of crisis (2:1–11; 19:26–27), and shepherding the community (10:1–18; 21:15–19).[115] On the basis of the mission command in 20:21, such actions would also extend beyond the community of friends to other residents in the city. Central to friendship with Jesus, though, is distance from imperial society.

Notes

1. As a sample of some recent discussions that weave Christology and community or ecclesiology together, see Marinus de Jonge, "Christology, Controversy, and Community in the Gospel of John," in *Christology, Controversy, and Community: New Testament Essays in Honour of David R. Catchpole*, ed. D. Horrell and C. Tuckett (Boston: Brill, 2000), 209–30; John Painter, "The Point of John's Christology: Christology, Conflict, and Community in John," in ibid., 231–52; and Stephen Barton, "Christian Community in the Light of the Gospel of John," in ibid., 279–301.

2. Halliday, "Antilanguages," 570–84. I do not claim that this discussion presents a comprehensive Johannine ecclesiology, even though it explores some important aspects. If space permitted, we should discuss further marks of the community such as peace, future suffering, and unity, all with imperially contestive dimensions.

3. The verb *menō* (μένω) that pervades John 14–15 carries this assurance of Jesus' continued abiding with disciples in his somatic absence (14:10, 17, 25; 15:4 [2x], 5, 6, 7, 9, 10 [2x], 16).

4. In addition to the commentaries, see, for example, Segovia, *Farewell*; Bruce Woll, *Johnnine Christianity in Conflict: Authority, Rank, and Succession in the First Farewell Discourse*, SBLDS 60 (Chico, CA: Scholars Press, 1981).

5. Mary Coloe, *God Dwells with Us: Temple Symbolism in the Fourth Gospel* (Collegeville: Liturgical Press, 2001), 3; see also A. J. Köstenberger, "Destruction," 68–108; A. R. Kerr, *The*

Temple of Jesus' Body: The Temple Theme in the Gospel of John, JSNTSup 220 (Sheffield: Sheffield Academic Press, 2002); James McCaffrey, *The House with Many Rooms: The Temple Theme of Jn. 14:2-3*, AnBib114 (Roma: Editrice Pontificio Istituto Biblico, 1988); Anthony T. Hanson, "The Theme of Christ as the True Temple in the Fourth Gospel," in *The New Testament of Scripture* (London: SPCK, 1980), 110–21; Christ is the place of God's presence, a newer and truer temple, where God is encountered, and Christ is "the locus of the Church, the community which is to be filled with the glory of the risen Lord" (121).

6. With reference to christological passages, Coloe (*God Dwells with Us*, 65–145) discusses 2:13–25; 4:1–45; 7:1–8:59; 10:22–42; 18:1–19:42.

7. Ibid., 7, 13, 157–78.

8. Ibid., 1–2, 61–63. On 63, she quotes Carter, "Prologue and John's Gospel," 47.

9. For discussion and bibliography, Warren Carter, "Paying the Tax to Rome as Subversive Praxis: Matthew 17:24–27," in Carter, *Matthew and Empire*, 130–44.

10. E. Mary Smallwood, *Jews under Roman Rule* (1981), 374.

11. E.g., 2 Chron 7:2, 7, 11; 20:5, 28; Pss 23:6; 42:4; 92:13; 135:2; Josephus, *J.W.* 4.281.

12. O. Michel, "οἶκος, οἰκία," *TDNT* 5:119–20.

13. Also a Hebrew Bible usage: Gen 24:38; 28:21; 46:31; and 2 Sam 7:11, 16, the house of David. John's Gospel, though, also uses the noun to refer to a place (11:31; 12:3).

14. For example, IEph 1.27, lines 345 and 385, "to the house of the Sebastoi/emperors"; 1.36a, a statue base dedicated "to Ephesian Artemis and the house of the emperors/Sebastoi"; 2.241 refers to Domitian and Domitia "and their house"; 2.431, 435, 438; in 4.1393 sacrifices are offered "on behalf of Augustus and the house of Augustus."

15. David Aune, *The Cultic Setting of Realized Eschatology in Early Christianity* (Leiden: Brill, 1972), 130.

16. Brown, *Gospel*, 2:625; Schnackenburg, *Gospel*, 3:60–61; McCaffrey, *House*, 54–64, 220.

17. Coloe, *God Dwells with Us*, 163.

18. Following ibid., 164–67: prepare a place for the ark, Exod 23:20; the temple, 2 Chron 3:1; 8:16; Wis 9:8; the temple as a (holy) place: 1 Kings 8:6, 8, 10; Ps 74:4–8; 76:2; 1 Macc 1:20–24. Note John 11:48, "destroy the place."

19. See 2 Sam 7:14; 2 Chron 29:35–36; Sir 49:12.

20. Isa 2:1–4; Mic 4:1–4.

21. For Qumran and Paul, see Coloe, *God Dwells with Us*, 168–71.

22. I do not understand the postresurrection appearances to be the referent for 14:3, 18, 28 (Bultmann, *Gospel*, 585–86; Dodd, *Interpretation*, 394–95). The chapter assumes a long period of absence. "The Paraclete, dwelling with the disciples, will mediate a continuing presence of Jesus in the time-gap before the parousia"; Coloe, *God Dwells with Us*, 175.

23. Kanagaraj ("Implied Ethics," 33–60) argues that the Gospel develops the Decalogue as its subtext. He sees (41–42) both 4:20–24 and 2:13–22 as echoes of the second commandment (Exod 20:4–6) against images. But he makes no connection to the Ephesian context, and he looks to the Jewishness of the Gospel author as the reason for this subtext (60), rather than its address to an Ephesian context (or any other locale).

24. Cornelius Vermeule, *Roman Imperial Art in Greece and Asia Minor* (Cambridge, MA: Harvard University Press, 1968), 232–33.

25. Van Tilborg, *Reading John*, 96.

26. For what follows, see ibid., 68–75, for data.

27. Ibid., 71.

28. The second-century *Ephesian Tale* by Xenophon begins with cultic activity directed to Artemis, a recurring theme through the book.

29. Van Tilborg, *Reading John*, 71–74.

30. Ibid., 75.

31. Richard Oster, "The Ephesian Artemis as an Opponent of Early Christianity," *Jahrbuch für Antike und Christentum* 19 (1976): 24–44, esp. 32–44.

32. Harland, *Associations*, 25–173.

33. For instance, "eternal" life or life of the age is encountered now, as is judgment (3:16; 5:25) and resurrection (11:25–26). The abundance of wine enacts the expected fertility of the coming age (2:1–11, evoking Isa 25:6–10); the healings enact the age's expected physical wholeness (4:46–54; 5:1–9).

34. J. Nelson Kraybill, *Imperial Cult and Commerce in John's Apocalypse*, JSNTSup 132 (Sheffield: Sheffield Academic Press, 1996), 57–141.

35. Harland, *Associations*, 39–40; *Clothing*: IEph 2.454, hemp workers, linen weavers, wool dealers; 3.727; 7.2.3803, wool dealers; 7.1.3063, clothing sellers. *Food*: 2.215, bakers; 3.728, wine tasters; 1.20, 5.1503, fish-sellers; 7.1.3216, measurers. *Potters and smiths*: 6.2402, potters; 2.425, 457, 585, 586; 6.2212; 2441, silversmiths. *Building*: 6.2213, bed-builders; 6.2115; 7.1.3075, carpenters, builders; 7.1.3216, workers. *Banking and trade*: 2.454, bankers; 3.800; 7.1.3079, merchants and traders. *Physicians*: 3.719, 4.1161–67; 6.2304, 4101a–b. *Entertainers*: 1.22, Dionysiac performers; 4.1084, 1087–89, 1098, 1122, athletes; 7.1.3055, 3070, gladiators.

36. As another example, the physicians in Ephesus "sacrifice to the ancestor Asklepios and to the *Sebastoi*" (IEph 3.719).

37. Richard Bauckham, "The Economic Critique of Rome in Revelation 18," in *The Climax of Prophecy: Studies on the Book of Revelation* (Edinburgh: T&T Clark, 1993), 338–83.

38. For the imperial fishing economy, see Hanson and Oakman, *Palestine*, 106–10; for an inscription of a fishing cartel in Ephesus, G. Horsley, "Fishing Cartel," 95–114.

39. Van Tilborg, *Reading John*, 92–93, IEph 1.20; G. Horsley, "Fishing Cartel."

40. A possible fourth factor might involve how Jesus and his disciples procure their daily needs. The Gospel says little about this. There is a common purse, but Judas steals "what was put into it" (12:6; 13:29). On several occasions the disciples go to buy food (4:8; 13:29), but each time the action is undercut: in 4:32 Jesus has other food; in 13:27 Judas is the betrayer. In 6:5–7 the question of buying enough for the crowd is entertained, but Jesus solves the problem with a display of power that makes a little go a long way (i.e., not ex nihilo; 6:9–13). Van Tilborg, *Reading John*, 75–76.

41. John 13:19; 14:1, 10, 11 (2x), 12, 29; 16:9, 27, 30, 31.

42. For discussion, see Ladd, *Theology*, 259–63; Brown, *John*, 1:501–3, 512–15; Bultmann, *Theology*, 2:70–92. I will not discuss here the topic of the relationship between "signs" and "faith."

43. Brown, *John*, 1:512.

44. Ibid., 1.513.

45. The term's richness is clarified by its synonyms and antonyms. "Believe" is used with terms such as see (1:50; 4:48; 6:30, 40; 11:40, 45; 12:44–45; 20:8, 25, 29), know (4:42; 6:69), hears my words (5:24; 12:44–47), comes to me (6:35), comes and eats/drinks (6:47–57; 7:37–38), abide in my word (8:31), worship and see (9:38–39), know and understand (10:38), loved me (16:27), received and know (17:8). These synonyms emphasize various dimension of "believing/entrusting." "Seeing" denotes not just physical sight but also insight into, perception of, and commitment to Jesus' identity, mission, and God's purposes (14:9). "Hearing" likewise indicates not just physical hearing, but also hearing that discerns the significance of Jesus. "Know" signifies both intellectual knowing as well as—also in the Hebrew Bible tradition—experiential, relational encounter with God. "Comes to" expresses not physical movement but a dynamic seeking after and commitment to Jesus. In 14:12 to believe is to do the life-giving works that Jesus does (and even greater), indicating that "believing" means a way of life in God's service. The verb "believe" is commonly negated (3:12, 18; 6:36; 10:37–38). In terms of antonyms, not to believe (in)

Jesus/God is to have other commitments (5:44), to value societal status and honor more than God's purposes (12:41-42), to love evil deeds (3:18-19), to disobey the Son and his revelation (3:36), to reject his claims (6:36; 8:45), not to belong to his community (10:26).

46. For the overlap of the two terms, see Zeba A. Crook, *Reconceptualising Conversion: Patronage, Loyalty, and Conversion in the Religions of the Ancient Mediterranean*, BZNW 130 (Berlin: W. de Gruyter, 2004), 209-14; for the wider discussion, 199-250.

47. Joseph Hellegouarc'h, *Le vocabulaire latin des relations et des parties politique sous la Républic* (Paris: Belles Lettres, 1963), 23.

48. Also Gérard Freyburger, *Fides: Étude sémantique et religieuse depuis les origins jusqu'à l'époque augustéenne* (Paris: Belles Lettres, 1986).

49. D. Lindsay, *Josephus and Faith: Πίστις and Πιστεύειν as Faith Terminology in the Writings of Flavius Josephus and in the New Testament* (Leiden: Brill, 1993), esp. 77-84, 113-21.

50. Crook, *Reconceptualising Conversion*, 200-201.

51. E.g., its absence from Rudolf Bultmann, "πιστεύω," *TDNT* 6 (1968): 174-228.

52. E.g., Brown, *John*, 1:512-13.

53. Dionysius of Halicarnassus (*Roman Antiquities* 2.75.1-4) also links *fides* and justice.

54. Cicero (*De Div.* 2.60-62) explains this practice: "For they believed that whatever brought great advantage to the human race could come about only through divine benevolence toward people." Harold Axtell, *The Deification of Abstract Ideas in Roman Literature and Inscriptions* (Chicago: University of Chicago Press, 1907), on Fides, 20-21.

55. For the following, see "Fides," *Brill's New Pauly: Encyclopaedia of the Ancient World*, 10 vols. (Boston: Brill, 2002-7), 5:414-18; Pierre Boyancé, *Études sur la religion romaine* (Rome: École française de Rome, 1972), 91-152; Marieluise Merten, *Fides romana bei Livius*, doctoral diss., Johann Wolfgang Goethe-Universität, Frankfurt, 1964 (Giessen: Schreib-Druck Chemoprint, 1965).

56. Boyancé, "Fides romana et la vie internationale," in *Études*, 105-19.

57. See Axtell, *Deification*, 20-21, for the close link to Jupiter.

58. J. H. W. G. Liebeschuetz, *Continuity and Change in Roman Religion* (Oxford: Clarendon, 1979), 167-82, esp. 168.

59. Ibid., 174.

60. Ibid., 175.

61. Ibid.

62. Fides is regularly mentioned or appealed to: e.g., Silius, *Punica* 6.64, 132, 468, 518, 548.

63. Cf. *1 En.* 42; John 1:10. Note also Petronius (*Satyricon* 124.249) who has peace, loyalty/faith (*fides*), justice, and concord abandon the earth and humankind as Pompey the Great flees from Rome in 49 BCE.

64. Liebeschuetz, *Continuity*, 178.

65. Greek and Latin texts of the *Res gestae divi Augusti* are in V. Ehrenberg and A. H. M. Jones, *Documents Illustrating the Reigns of Augustus and Tiberius*, 2nd ed. (Oxford: Clarendon, 1955), 2-31, esp. 28-29.

66. No. 1452 in Burnett et al., *Roman Provincial Coinage*, 2.1-2. K. Scott (*Imperial Cult*, 31) reports that elsewhere on Vespasian's coins Fides is linked to Augustus to show Vespasian as his successor.

67. No. 1459 in Burnett et al., *Roman Provincial Coinage*, 2.1-2. K. Scott (*Imperial Cult*, 43) sees Titus using Fides to establish another link with Vespasian.

68. Nos. 1461, 1467, in Burnett et al., *Roman Provincial Coinage*, 2.1-2. No. 1461 seems to read *FIDES IVBL* though the copy is not clear enough to ascertain whether an I or a P precedes VBL. I have included here in notes 66-68 only examples from Asia for Vespasian, Titus, and Domitian. There are many more instances from across the empire.

69. Boyancé, "La main de Fides," in *Études*, 121–33.

70. No. 3863 in Burnett et al., *Roman Provincial Coinage*, 1.1–2. This Antiochus IV (*not* Antiochus IV Epiphanes of Syria, d. 164 BCE) was in 38 CE first appointed to rule Commagene by Caligula (37–41), who also immediately deposed him, but he was reappointed by Claudius (41–54) and ruled till 72.

71. No. 3537 in Burnett et al., *Roman Provincial Coinage*, 1.1–2.

72. Hamberg, *Studies*, 18–32 and plate 1.

73. Ibid., 19–20.

74. εὐχαριστῶ τῷ θεῷ τῇ κυρίᾳ Σώτειρᾳ ὅτι τὴν πίστιν ἐτήρησα τῇ γερουσίᾳ; *eucharistō tō theō tē kyria Sōteira hoti tēn pistin etērēsa tē gerousia.*

75. See Crook, *Reconceptualising Conversion*, 217–26, for examples.

76. These shared dimensions of understandings, commitment, and actions minimize any significance that might be attached to John's use of a verb and the civic/imperial use of a noun.

77. Bultmann, *Theology*, 2:70–92.

78. Ibid., 2:76–77.

79. Josephus, *J. W.* 2:236–244; 2.336–341; Agrippa's speech against war, 2.345–404; emissaries sent to Florus after the cessation of sacrifices, 408–421, esp. 2.418.

80. Paul Duke, *Irony in the Fourth Gospel* (Atlanta: John Knox, 1985). They choose not to let Jesus "go on thus," but all three consequences come to pass.

81. See the discussion of *Ioudaioi* in chap. 6 above.

82. Callahan, *Love Supreme*, 81–82.

83. Thomas, *Footwashing*, 35–40, 46–56, 56–58.

84. Ibid., 115.

85. Dennis E. Smith and Hal Taussig, "The Greco-Roman Banquet: Defining a Common Meal Tradition," in *Many Tables: The Eucharist in the New Testament and Liturgy Today* (Philadelphia: Trinity Press International, 1990), 21–35; Jerome Neyrey, "Ceremonies in Luke-Acts: The Case of Meals and Table Fellowship," in *The Social World of Luke-Acts*, ed. Jerome Neyrey (Peabody, MA: Hendrickson, 1991), 361–87; Kathleen Corley, *Private Women, Public Meals: Social Conflict in the Synoptic Tradition* (Peabody, MA: Hendrickson, 1993), 24–75.

86. Brown, *John*, 2:565.

87. The Saturnalia (festivals) were observed for about five days in December, "the best of days" (Catullus 14.15; though Pliny the Younger did not agree, *Ep.* 2.17.23–24), involved much celebration, and included some brief reversal of societal roles including the master-slaves relationship. According to Macrobius, *Saturnalia* 1.24.22–23, a dinner is prepared as if for the master but is eaten by slaves before the table is set again for the master to eat. Lucian (*Saturnalia*) recognizes how lower orders "cheek your masters" (5); that there is no slavery (7–8; not in the time of Chronos, who exercises sovereignty for Saturnalia); all—slave and freeman, rich and poor—are to be treated equally (13); at banquets all drink the same wine, eat the same meat, and have same-size portions (17); a rich man will give a banquet to his servants, and his friends will help in waiting on them (17). Philo (*Emb.* 13) describes the beginning of Gaius's reign as an idyllic age of "life under Saturn," in which "the rich had no precedence over the poor, . . . nor masters above slaves." Though not at Saturnalia, Petronius (*Satyricon* 70) has slaves join the guests at the banquet. Mauro Pesce and Adriana Destro, "La lavanda dei peidi di Gv 13,1–20, il *Romanzo di Esopo*, e i *Saturnalia* di Macrobio," *Biblica* 80 (1999): 240–49.

88. The literature on slavery is enormous. E.g., T. Wiedemann, *Greek and Roman Slavery* (Baltimore: Johns Hopkins University Press, 1981); Orlando Patterson, *Slavery and Social Death: A Comparative Study* (Cambridge: Harvard University Press, 1982); Peter Garnsey, *Ideas of Slavery from Aristotle to Augustine* (Cambridge: Cambridge University Press, 1996); Moses I. Finley, *Ancient Slavery and Modern Ideology*, ed. Brent D. Shaw, expanded ed. (Princeton: Marcus

Wiener, 1998); Jennifer Glancy, *Slavery in Early Christianity* (Oxford: Oxford University Press, 2002); J. Albert Harrill, *Slaves in the New Testament: Literary, Social, and Moral Dimensions* (Minneapolis: Fortress, 2006).

89. Seneca recognizes that such domination can be cruel (*Ben.* 3.22.3) but justifies it in several ways, recognizing generous owners (3.21.1–2) and that domination cannot be complete since slavery does not "penetrate into the whole being" of a slave (3.20.1).

90. Van Tilborg, *Reading John*, 86–90.

91. There are few examples of critique of slavery. Garnsey (*Ideas of Slavery*) recognizes that "the abolition of slavery was not contemplated in antiquity" (64); yet he distinguishes criticisms about the effective operation of slavery and treatment of slaves (53–63), from "progressive utterances" that could perhaps in another time and set of circumstances have led to a campaign against it (e.g., Seneca [*Ep.* 47.1, 10] and Epictetus [*Discourses* 1.13] insist on the humanity of slaves, 64–74), and from "critical comments on slavery as an institution" (75–86). For example, Aristotle responds (*Pol.* 1.2.23) to the view, perhaps of Alcidamas, that does not recognize slavery as natural and therefore counts it as not moral. See also R. Schlaifer, "Greek Theories of Slavery from Homer to Aristotle," in *Slavery in Classical Antiquity*, ed. M. Finley (Cambridge: Heffer & Sons, 1960), 93–132, esp. 199–201. Philo (*Every Good Man Is Free* 79; *On the Contemplative Life* 70) says that Essenes oppose slavery and uphold the law of equality (inequality is the source of evil, imposing the power of the stronger over the weaker) and the law of nature (also Josephus, *Ant.* 18.21, "an injustice," ἀδικίαν, *adikian*). Yet CD 11.12 instructs that slaves and maidservants are not to be irritated on the Sabbath, and 12.10–11 instructs not to sell slaves to Gentiles. If Philo and Josephus are correct, diverse practices and views existed among Essenes. Philo himself seems to think slavery is necessary: *Spec. Laws* 2.123.

92. For discussion, see David Seeley, "Rulership and Service in Mark 10:41–45," *NovT* 35 (1993): 234–50.

93. Van Tilborg, *Reading John*, 81–82.

94. MacMullen, *Roman Social Relations.*

95. Dale Martin, *Slavery as Salvation: The Metaphor of Slavery in Pauline Christianity* (New Haven: Yale University Press, 1990), 1–50; esp. 47–49, "Ancient Slavery and Status"; 7–11 (money), 11–22 (jobs and managerial slaves), 22–30 (patron-client structure and honor), 30–42 (upward mobility).

96. Van Tilborg, *Reading John*, 81–82.

97. This is Aristotle's description of friendship in *Rhet.* 1.5.16. I will discuss Jesus' friends who are no longer servants (below).

98. Footwashing is thus understood in the passage as both a literal and metaphorical action. See Thomas, *Footwashing*, 60, 126–85.

99. On miracles, magic, and Artemis, see Clinton E. Arnold, *Ephesians: Power and Magic* (Cambridge: Cambridge University Press, 1989), 14–40; Van Tilborg, *Reading John*, 133–36.

100. It is tempting to see these works, especially the miraculous ones, as works of the Paraklete or Spirit. In one sense they are since the Paraklete is "another Paraklete," presumably like Jesus, who will be "with you" and "in you" (John 14:16–17) because Jesus goes away to the Father (14:12b). The second-person pronouns ("you") are plural, indicating a reference to all the Jesus-believers who do these works. In 1:32–33, at the beginning of Jesus' ministry, John testifies to the Spirit's descent on and remaining with Jesus, which sets the whole of Jesus' ministry in pneumatic context. Moreover, the Paraklete bears witness to Jesus just as Jesus' works do, suggesting a link between the two (15:26). And in 16:8–11 the Paraklete proves the world wrong about sin, justice, and judgment, just as Jesus' works have done (5:19–30; 10:32–33, 37). Yet it is only in these general terms of similar functions and of the notion of abiding or presence in chapters 14–15 that the link is made between these "greater works" and the Paraklete. John does not, as Paul does, employ the notion of *pneumatika* ("spiritual things," 1 Cor 12:1) or *charismata* (grace-gifts, 1 Cor 12:4) to suggest a particular link between actions and the Spirit (cf. 1 Cor 12:7–11).

101. For a helpful description of the difficult everyday realities for many nonelites in a city in the empire, see Stark, "Antioch," 189–210; Whittaker, "'The Poor," 272–99 (with bibliography); on these realities, see chap. 8 above.

102. Philo, *Sacrifices* 130, presents Moses as God's friend; Epictetus, *Discourse* 2.16.44; 2.17.29; in Hellenistic Jewish texts, Wis 7:14, 27.

103. 'There are various interpretations of this "no longer," all complicated by John 15:20, which repeats the servant (or slave, *doulos*) image for disciples from John 13:16. Some see a replacement of the servant image from 13:14–17; others appeal to the link between Jesus' love and his death in his approaching "hour." 'The key piece seems to be 15:15, which supplies the explanation: "because" (ὅτι, *hoti*) he has revealed to them everything from the Father. See below for sharing confidences and so forth as appropriate for friendship, but not for slavery. 'The change of image has nothing to do with obedience (15:17) but with the near-completion of Jesus revelatory mission. Philo, *Sobriety* 55, describes Wisdom as "God's friend [rather] than his servant."

104. Outside the three uses in 15:13, 14, 15, the noun φίλος (*philos*, friend) appears three times in John: 3:29; 11:11; 19:12, all referring to human friendships. On 19:12, see below. 'The noun is a cognate of the common verb φιλέω (*phileō*), which expresses, for example, the Father's love for the Son (5:20) and disciples (16:27), Jesus' love for the "other" disciple (20:2), Peter's love for Jesus (21:15, 16, 17), and the world's love for its own (15:19).

105. David Konstan, *Friendship in the Classical World* (Cambridge: Cambridge University Press, 1997); John T. Fitzgerald, ed., *Greco-Roman Perspectives on Friendship*, SBLRBS 34 (Atlanta: Scholars Press, 1997), includes essays on friendship in Aristotle, Cicero, Dionysius of Halicarnassus, Plutarch, and Lucian; for a helpful survey, see John T. Fitzgerald, "Paul and Friendship," in *Paul in the Greco-Roman World*, ed. Paul Sampley (Harrisburg: Trinity Press International/Continuum, 2003), 319–31. For John, see Ringe, *Wisdom's Friends*, 64–83; Dorothy Lee, "Friendship, Love, and Abiding in the Gospel of John," in *Transcending Boundaries: Contemporary Readings of the New Testament*, ed. R. M. Chennattu and M. L. Coloe (Roma: Libreria Ateneo Salesiano, 2005), 57–74; Gail O'Day, "Jesus as Friend in the Gospel of John," in Chennattu and Coloe, *Transcending Boundaries*, 75–92; and with a different use of the image, Reinhartz, *Befriending*.

106. See above. For examples of this vocabulary in relation to friendship, see Aristotle, *Eudemian Ethics* 7.2.40; in Jewish traditions, Sir 6:7–17; e.g., 6:7b, "Do not trust [μὴ ταχὺ ἐμπιστεύσῃς, *mē tachy empisteusēs*] them hastily" (NRSV); 6:14, "a faithful friend [φίλος πιστὸς, *philos pistos*]. Konstan, *Friendship*, 33, 51.

107. If space permitted, two more links with this philosophical tradition might be developed. One concerns laying down one's life for a friend as a display of love (15:13). Jesus lays down his life for his friends, but these friends are called to lay down their lives for Jesus and for each other if necessary (15:12–13, 17). Cf. 2 Macc 7; Josephus, *J.W.* 1.58, Hyrcanus's mother; Epictetus, *Discourse* 2.7.3. O'Day, "Jesus as Friend," 82–86, claims that Jesus' action of giving himself in death moves an "abstract philosophical maxim to an embodied promise and gift" (83) and not only models friendship but also "makes any subsequent acts of friendship by them possible" (86). Second, notice the connection between the love these friends are to show to each other (John 13:34–35; 15:12–13, 17) and the love that Jesus shows to the world and to the disciples. 'The vocabulary, ἀγαπάω (*agapaō*) and φιλέω (*phileō*), used for God's love (3:16, 35; 5:20; 10:17; 16:27) and Jesus' love (13:1; 14:21; 15:9), is used for the command to disciples to love one another (*agapaō*: 13:34–35; 15:12, 17) and for the cognate noun "friend" (*philos*: 15:14–15).

108. Aristotle, *Eudemian Ethics* 7.2.44; Cicero, *Amic.* 6.22; Martial, *Epig.* 2.43.1–16; 8.18.9–10; Plutarch, *Mor.* 65A–B; Josephus, *Ag. Ap.* 2.207. Philo, *Sobriety* 55–56, presents Abraham as God's friend, from whom God hides nothing, citing Gen 18:17.

109. See chap. 4 above for the Gospel's turn to the past, to "the beginning," to negotiate these claims.

110. Fitzgerald, "Paul and Friendship," 320–31.

111. Konstan, *Friendship*, 48–49; see also 5, 12.

112. For this identification as Pilate, see above; also chap. 11 and the appendix (below).

113. For discussion of the Ephesian inscriptions, see the next paragraph. Martial, *Epig.* 5.19.15–16; Pliny the Younger, *Pan.* 44.7; 85.8; Epictetus, *Discourse* 4.1.45–50; Dio Chrysostom, *Kingship 3* (*Or. 3*) 86–132, presents the king as friend of the people. Ernst Bammel, "Philos tou Kaisaros [John 19:12]," *Theologische Literaturzeitung* 77 (1952): 205–10.

114. Van Tilborg, *Reading John*, 197–216.

115. Ringe, *Wisdom's Friends*, 75–83.

11

The Governor and the King/Emperor

Pilate and Jesus (John 18:28–19:22)

The Pilate-Jesus scene (John 18:28–19:16) continues the Gospel's rhetoric of distance in the task of imperial negotiation. It presents direct and oppositional interaction between Jesus and the empire as Jesus and Pilate meet face-to-face before an alliance of the empire's ruling elite crucifies Jesus. Pilate, the Roman governor and representative of Roman elite interests, is the central figure in this alliance and is revealed by the Gospel's narrative to be opposed to Jesus and his role as agent of God's purposes.[1]

Yet discussions of the Pilate-Jesus scene have generally failed to recognize that the scene is political, involving issues of imperial negotiation. Since it involves Jesus and the Jerusalem elite—misleadingly identified as religious leaders—many interpreters treat it primarily as a religious scene, give minimal attention to Pilate, and often totally disregard the political and imperial dimensions. Several significant misunderstandings have often marked these discussions.

One major defect has been the long-standing willingness to "blame the Jews" for Jesus' death. This emphasis results from seeing the Gospel as primarily concerned with a religious dispute with a local synagogue rather than imperial negotiation in which as allies of Rome the Jerusalem leaders are the main protagonists against Jesus. The result has been that Pilate's role has been inappropriately minimized and the scene depoliticized.

A further problem has been the absence of informed considerations of the place of governors in the Roman imperial system. This lack has often misrepresented Pilate as weak, squeamish, and unwilling to execute Jesus. This presentation of the arm-twisted and bullied Pilate has further misled by stressing Jewish responsibility and the apolitical nature of Jesus' death by crucifixion.

A third issue has been the inadequate depiction of the Jerusalem leaders in this scene, taking them as religious figures carrying out a personal vendetta against Jesus, with Pilate unfortunately and reluctantly involved because of his office. This depiction mistakenly frames the interaction between Pilate and Jesus along ethnic lines, setting the Jews over against the Roman Pilate. It also fails to recognize the interconnectedness of the religious and the political in the first-century imperial world. Overlooked is the fact that the Jerusalem elite centered on the temple are societal leaders who exercise

289

power as allies with Rome yet as dependents on Rome and subordinates of Rome. They are another manifestation of the common Roman practice in the East of governing in alliances with and through local elites. The recognition that Pilate and the Jerusalem elite are allies is crucial for understanding the scene and the interactions between Pilate and the Jerusalem allies. In this alliance they must work together to exercise power and protect their mutual interests against the lowly but dangerous Jesus, who as "king of the Jews" (18:33, 39; 19:15, 19–22) is, like other royal pretenders,[2] a threat to their mutual interests. For this task they need each other. Yet in negotiating imperial power as allied yet subordinated provincials, the Jerusalem leaders also struggle with Pilate to secure influence and protect their interests. On the other hand, Pilate seeks to maintain the appearance of his superior and independent power while also recognizing the reality of his dependence on them. The neglect of these imperial dynamics has seriously misrepresented the scene. The following discussion will seek to rectify this neglect.

Pilate, the Ruler of the World

Pilate is named for the first time in John 18:29 (in Greek; NRSV added the name in 18:28). But this is not the first time the Gospel has indicated his presence. As I have mentioned, Jesus has talked previously of overcoming the "ruler of this world," who will be driven out (12:31), who has no power over Jesus (14:30), and has been condemned (16:11). Though often interpreted as the devil, four factors indicate that these references foreshadow the appearance of Pilate, agent of Roman power.[3]

1. Jesus first uses the term in 12:31 in reference to his "hour" (12:27), or time of crucifixion and departure to God.[4] The crucifixion reference continues in 12:32 with Jesus' promise that in being "lifted up"—crucified, resurrected, and ascended—he will draw everyone to himself. These events take place in the passion narrative of John 18–19, when the narrative resumes after Jesus' instructions to the disciples in chapters 13–17.

2. Further, the Gospel does not refer to Satan as a ruler. Rather, it uses the language of "ruler" to refer to human beings, and particularly members of the ruling alliance (3:1; 7:26, 48; 12:42), and not to supernatural beings. This use is reflected in inscriptions from Ephesus where the term ἄρχων (*archōn*, ruler) refers to various elite leadership functions.[5]

3. Moreover, the "world" over which this figure rules is identified in 1:10 as that which rejects Jesus. The crucifixion comprises the ultimate rejection of Jesus. It expresses Roman power, whose primary representative in the narrative is Pilate, and it comes about on Pilate's instruction in alliance with the Jerusalem elite (19:16).

4. And finally, Jesus' words to Pilate that Pilate has no power over him (19:11) echo Jesus' statement of 14:30 that "the ruler of this world . . . has no power over me" (NRSV). In part the claim of "no power" refers to Jesus giving himself to die (10:11, 17–18). But beyond this, Jesus overcomes Pilate in his resurrection: Roman power is exposed to be no match for God's life-giving power. Jesus' resurrection signifies and anticipates the final demise of Rome's empire at the coming judgment, when "those who have done evil [will come out] to the resurrection of condemnation" (5:29 NRSV).

The three references to Pilate as the "ruler of the world" anticipate Pilate's being driven out by the establishment of God's purposes (12:31), his inability to keep Jesus dead (14:30), and his condemnation as ruler of a societal order opposed to God's purposes and under God's judgment (16:11). They anticipate these narrative and cosmic events.

Pilate among Governors

While identifying Pilate as a "ruler," John does not explicitly identify Pilate as a "governor," unlike Matthew (27:2[6]) and Luke (3:1). Instead, John, as does Mark (15:16), identifies Pilate with a building. Pilate encounters Jesus at the praetorium, or "headquarters" (John 18:28–29). The Gospel assumes that the audience knows that this building is the headquarters for a provincial governor. The name "praetorium" derives in part from the title of a Roman official (praetor) who combined military and judicial functions, both of which comprised important aspects of a governor's role.

An inscription found at Caesarea in 1961 identifies Pilate as a *praefectus*, a prefect. This term and its Greek equivalent are often used interchangeably with "procurator" and its Greek equivalent to denote governors (so Tacitus, *Ann.* 15.44).[7] The term "prefect" has a military origin; "procurator" is a civilian term. The use of both terms is appropriate for the variety of administrative, fiscal, legal, and military duties entrusted to governors. These terms—governor, praetorium, prefect, procurator—attest Pilate's role as governor and representative of Rome's ruling elite and the social, political, and legal structures outlined in chapter 3 above.

The men whom emperors appointed as governors were often of the equestrian rank, the second aristocratic order below that of senators. Membership of this order required a certain level of wealth, usually based in land. Members of this rank were well connected with other elites, occupied civilian and military positions in the empire, and exerted considerable local power as magistrates and priests in the imperial cult. In all likelihood, Pilate, the fifth governor of Judea, from 26 CE to 36, came from a well-connected family of considerable status and wealth, part of the ruling elite. He most likely had some military and/or civilian experience before being appointed as governor.[8]

A Governor's Job Description

While a full discussion of the various roles of governors is not possible here, we can identify some of their tasks from references in Josephus and from the letters of Pliny the Younger, the governor of Pontus-Bithynia, northeast of the province of Asia. Governors were the public face of the empire in the provinces, representing Rome's interests in administrative, fiscal, military, and judicial matters.[9]

- Governors settle disputes and keep order, especially among different ethnic groups (Josephus, *J.W.* 2.487–493, in Alexandria; *Ant.* 19.301; 20.125).
- They collect taxes (Albinus in Josephus, *J.W.* 2.273) and have responsibility for fiscal administration (Philo, *Flaccus* 4), including intervening in municipal financial affairs as necessary (Pliny the Younger, *Ep.* 10.38, 44).

- They engage in public works and building projects. Pilate builds a controversial aqueduct after seizing money from the temple treasury (Josephus, *J.W.* 2.175; *Ant.* 18.60). Pliny, the governor of Pontus-Bithynia, consults the emperor Trajan about numerous building projects including aqueducts, theaters, gymnasiums, public baths (*Ep.* 10.37–44).

- Governors command troops (Pilate in Josephus, *Ant.* 18.55; Philo, *Flaccus* 5), take military action to quell troublesome subjects (Cestius against Galilee and Judea, Josephus, *J.W.* 2.499–565), and engage in military action against bandits (Varro in Josephus, *J.W.* 1.398).

- Governors administer justice. Some cases are brought to them (so Paul appears before Felix and Festus in Acts 23:24–26:32; cf. Philo, *Flaccus* 4). They hear other cases as they travel around their provinces.[10] It is possible that Pilate's presence at this praetorium results from a tour of designated prominent cities in his province, such as Jerusalem, to hear civic and criminal cases.[11] Pilate likely encounters Jesus as one case among others.

- Governors had the power to put people to death. In effect, this was the power to remove from society people who challenged the social order and interests of the elite. Josephus refers to governors (of senatorial provinces) who maintain control with the *fasces* (*J.W.* 2.365–66). The fasces, an axe and bundle of six rods, were often ceremonially paraded to represent the administration of Roman justice. They "constituted a portable kit for flogging and decapitation. Since they were so brutally functional, they not only served as ceremonial symbols of office but also carried the potential of violent repression and execution."[12] Hence, they secured the perception of the life-and-death power embodied in and executed by Rome's justice. The first governor of Judea, "Coponius, a Roman of the equestrian order, [was] entrusted by Augustus with full powers, including the infliction of capital punishment" (Josephus, *J.W.* 2.117). Philo reports Flaccus's power to crucify people (*Flaccus* 83–85). Clearly, Pilate is assumed to have such power when Jesus is brought to him, and he exercises it in condemning Jesus to death by crucifixion.

These tasks indicate the crucial and powerful roles of governors as local representatives of Roman power in provinces like Judea. The governor's central and encompassing task was to maintain Roman power and elite interests.

Roman Justice

The execution of effective justice is an aspect of the Roman world that is often celebrated as one of Rome's great gifts to the world. One aspect of Rome's self-understanding was, as we have seen, that it had been chosen by the gods to spread its wonderful laws throughout the world, as a precious gift to all people. In Virgil's *Aeneid*, Anchises tells Aeneas in the underworld that he and Rome are commissioned "to rule the nations with your power" and "to crown peace with law" (6.851–853).

But this administration of justice by governors was also colored by the political and social structure of the empire. Roman "justice" was administered with a profound bias in favor of the elite and against those of lower status. This extensive commitment to the elite's "legal privilege" is seen, for instance, in much more lenient penalties for higher-status offenders and far greater opportunity to appeal to the emperor.[13] The whipping and crucifixion of Jesus are typical penalties for low-status offenders. By contrast, Josephus is horrified when the governor Florus does "what none had ever done before," scourging and crucifying members *of the Jewish elite* (*J. W.* 2.308). Philo is similarly outraged when the Egyptian governor Flaccus ignores customs about different types of scourges for people of different social standing and treats all Alexandrian Jews as being "of the meanest rank" (*Flaccus* 78–80). Peter Garnsey comments:

> In general it can be said that judges and juries were suspicious of, if not resentful towards, low-status plaintiffs who attacked their 'betters' in court, and were prepared to believe the worst of low-status defendants, while the pleas of high-status plaintiffs or defendants . . . were given more credence.[14]

When Jesus is on trial before Pilate, these realities are at work. He is a socially low-status provincial on trial in Jerusalem, a local center of power, before the ruling elite that controls a system for its own benefit.

Pilate and His Allies

Governors, as representatives of the Roman elite's interests, had great power and responsibilities. But their task was not easy. With small staffs, limited (though feared and quite effective) military resources, a difficult role as the face of a governing power, and great distances from further resources and guidance in Rome—maintaining control and protecting Rome's interests was a challenge. Part of Rome's strategy for social control was to secure the cooperation of the local provincial elite through alliances that emphasized their common interest in maintaining the status quo.[15] The widespread use of alliances does not mean, though, that there were no conflicts between governors and local elites. Factions struggled with each other for the rewards of power, wealth, and status. Nor does it mean that Roman officials did not treat provincial elites with prejudice and disdain as when the governor Florus scourged and crucified Jewish men of equestrian rank (Josephus, *J. W.* 2.308). But it does indicate a common commitment to the status quo and to protecting their mutual interests.

Pilate's allies in Judea were the Jerusalem leaders based in the temple. Josephus identifies the high priests as the leaders of the nation (*Ant.* 20.251). One means of securing their loyalties to Rome involved Roman governors of Judea in appointing the chief priests (*Ant.* 20.249). The governors also kept control of the priestly garments, the symbol of their office and power, thereby "dressing" the chief priest for holy days (*Ant.* 15.403–408; 18.90–95). Josephus records that Pilate's predecessor, the governor Valerius Gratus, deposed and appointed at least five high priests throughout his eleven-year reign from 15–26 CE (*Ant.* 18.33–35). In contrast, Caiaphas remained high priest from 18–36, throughout the whole of Pilate's administration (26–36). This longevity suggests not only that Caiaphas enjoyed Pilate's favor but also that he was adroit at keeping the governor "happy," which meant furthering Pilate's interests.

Both the governors and the chief priests needed each other. Governors needed cooperative priests and local landowners to maintain the hierarchical social order and ensure compliance with Rome. Pleasing the governor was the main way that the chief priests had access to power, status, and wealth. The price for this position was to become agents of the Roman governors' interests. So later in the century, as war seems imminent in the 60s CE, the chief priests dutifully exhort the people in Jerusalem to submit to and not resist the corrupt and oppressive governor Florus (Josephus, *J.W.* 2.318–320). But as "brigands" seize power in Jerusalem, the usual hereditary ruling families who had cooperated with Rome lose their power. The "brigands" replace appointment by Rome to the high priesthood with election by lot, including, according to Josephus, the election of "lowborn" high priests (*J.W.* 4.147–157).

Hence, when the Jerusalem elite hands Jesus over to Pilate (John 18:28), it would be incorrect to imagine that the scene was playing off, on one hand, "religious" personnel with limited interests and power against, on the other, political personnel. Likewise it would be inaccurate to see this scene in terms of Jews against Romans. Categories of religion and ethnicity are not the primary categories operative in this scene. Rather, the scene takes place in the context of a hierarchical imperial system that allied a small governing elite—both Roman and local Jerusalem personnel—against the rest of the population. At work are the dynamics of aristocratic alliances, "legal privilege," and bias against those of lower status. This system had limited notions of checks and balances, burdens of proof, and a sense of public accountability.

Van Tilborg's discussion of the interference (intertext) between John's references to the high priests in the Pilate scene and the references to the high priests and priestesses of the imperial temple (dedicated in 88/89 CE) in the inscriptional record from Ephesus confirms this analysis. Van Tilborg argues that the Ephesian high priests

> belong to the rich upper class of the population. . . . Without doubt the high-priests took part in the exercise of power as it was exercised in Ephesus (including) the highest political and social functions. . . . [They] lean most closely to imperial power and government. . . . An intensive interference takes place between the Ephesian and the Johannine high priests; . . . they are rich and they have servants and slaves (in the plural) at their disposal; they exercise influence on what happens in the city in a special way; they assemble to take decisions on the lives of civilians; they are in contact with the Roman administration and influence its decisions. . . . It is clear from all this that the Johannine story about the relation between the high priests and Pilate is a political one, something which is not unknown in Ephesus.[16]

Accordingly Jesus is "handed over" to Pilate because the governor, the representative of Roman justice, is allied with the local urban elite and is the only one entrusted in the province by the emperor with the powers of life and death. Limiting the power to execute to the governor was another Roman means of controlling the local elite and making it dependent on the governor. The first governor of Judea, Coponius, had been entrusted with this power in the year 6 CE by the emperor Augustus (Josephus, *J.W.* 2.117). Now it is Pilate's responsibility.

Abusive, Exploitative Governors

Governors represent a system that sustains elite power, wealth, and status. They look out for the interests of the emperor, the empire, and the local elite in alliance with whom they exercise their rule. No doubt some governors did their best to fulfill a difficult role. Certainly elite writers like the orator Aristides extravagantly (and with obvious contradictions) praise governors for their devotion to the emperor and for their rule that "protects and cares for the governed":

> There is an abundant and beautiful equality of the humble with the great and of the obscure with the illustrious, and above all, of the poor man with the rich and of the commoner with the noble. (*Roman Oration* 31–39)

Unfortunately, wishing or saying that it is so does not make it so in reality.

Some have suggested that through the first century the quality of governors improved, with fewer abuses of power. But the first-century Egyptian Jew Philo did not think things had improved. He claims that the abuses of the governor prior to Flaccus in Egypt were serious but were initially repaired by the competent Flaccus (*Flaccus* 1– 5, 7). But Flaccus deteriorates quickly and surpasses his predecessor with many excesses, so that Philo can generalize:

> Some, indeed, of those who held governorships in the time of Tiberius and his father Caesar, had perverted their office of guardian and protector into domination and tyranny and had spread hopeless misery through their territories with their venality, robbery, unjust sentences, expulsion and banishment of quite innocent people, and execution of magnates without trial. (*Flaccus* 105)

Tacitus, no friend to Jews, does not present a picture of gradual improvement but seems to assume different intensities of abuse and progressively increasing levels of exploitation leading up to the outbreak of war in 66 CE. The governor Antonius Felix (52–60 CE), says Tacitus, "practiced every kind of cruelty and lust, wielding the power of king with all the instincts of a slave. . . . Still the Jews' patience lasted until Gessius Florus became procurator; in his time war began" (*Hist.* 5.9–10).

In presenting various governors attending to their tasks, Josephus distinguishes varying levels of competency but reserves his worst criticism for the two governors ruling in the 60s, Albinus and Florus, governors of Judea in 62–64 and 64–66 CE. "The administration of Albinus, who followed Festus, was of another order; there was no form of villainy which he omitted to practice" (*J. W.* 2.272). Josephus outlines those "villainies" as stealing property, imposing excessive taxation, freeing prisoners for a price, stimulating social disorder by permitting attacks on the (wealthy) "peaceable citizens" to go unchecked and unpunished (2.273–276). Clearly the governor personally benefited from stealing property, attacking wealthier citizens, and imposing extra taxes. Josephus continues, "Such was the character of Albinus, but his successor, Gessius Florus, made him appear by comparison a paragon of virtue" (2.277).

Governors as Bloodsucking Flies

In a significant passage about governors, Josephus employs a memorable image of governors as bloodsucking flies and attributes the figure to Tiberius, emperor during Pilate's governorship. The passage condemns all governors as unjust.

Josephus, an ally of the Flavian emperors Vespasian, Titus, and Domitian, is commenting on Tiberius's tendency to leave governors in office for lengthy tenures. He reports Tiberius's claim to do so "out of consideration for the feelings of the subject peoples. For it was in the law of nature that governors are prone to engage in extortion." He has Tiberius argue that short-term appointments provoked governors to engage in as much exploitation for personal profit as possible. If the governor was quickly replaced, a new governor would immediately continue the process of harsh exploitation, making things continually bad for the subject people, who would not get a break from such behavior! Instead, a long tenure meant that "those gorged by their robberies" would be sluggish to continue the exploitation, thereby giving the people some reprieve (*Ant.* 18.172–173).

Josephus has the emperor Tiberius illustrate his point with a fable in which a wounded man requests a kind but apparently misguided passerby not to shoo the flies away from his wounds because once the flies have had "their fill of blood," they do no more damage. But shooing them away and letting new flies near the wound with new appetites for blood would kill him.

> Once a man lay wounded, and a swarm of flies hovered about his wounds. A passerby took pity on his evil plight and, in the belief that he did not raise a hand because he could not, was about to step up and shoo them off. The wounded man, however, begged him to think no more of doing anything about it. At this the man spoke up and asked him why he was not interested in escaping from his wretched condition. "Why," said he, "you would put me in a worse position if you drove them off. For since these flies have already had their fill of blood, they no longer feel such a pressing need to annoy me but are in some measure slack. But if others were to come with a fresh appetite, they would take over my now weakened body, and that would indeed be the death of me." (18.175–176)

The fable is interpreted to show the demerits of short tenures for governors. Josephus goes on to explain that the emperor Tiberius

> for the same reason took the precaution of not dispatching governors continually to the subject-peoples who had been brought to ruin by so many thieves; for the governors would harry them utterly like flies. Their natural appetite for plunder would be reinforced by their expectation of being speedily deprived of that pleasure. (18.176)

The fable, whether actually spoken by Tiberius or not, is stunning for a number of reasons:

- It uses the image of flies sucking blood from an open wound to depict Roman provincial government administered by governors.
- It recognizes (in the mouth of an emperor!) that the relationship of governor and governed was one that sucked the lifeblood out of the provinces.
- It compares governors with pesky and potentially fatal flies.
- It compares governors with thieves.
- It identifies the provinces with a wounded and bleeding man who is close to death.
- It recognizes that such predatory and exploitative behavior is natural, inevitable, and uncontrollable.
- It has a wounded man (the provinces) request the passerby not to intervene lest things become worse.
- It demonstrates the wounded man's inability to request any other help.
- It shows the passerby's inability to imagine any other intervention except to shoo flies away, but not to heal the wounded man or change his situation.
- It attests to the elite's advocacy of structured exploitation.
- It exists in a work authored by a Jew of priestly descent and loyal ally of the Flavian emperors.

With this image of governors as bloodsucking flies, Josephus lays bare the dominant and corrupt role of governors in the imperial system. But their role is presented with a terrifying cynicism. In Josephus' narrative, the emperor Tiberius presents the image without any remorse for the damage that his system causes, without any proposal for curbing the exploitation, or without any thought for its abolition. This is simply the way things are. And his argument is that the alternative policy of shorter tenures would make things a whole lot worse! Provincials should be grateful for beneficent Roman rule.

But such analysis was not unique to Josephus's scene. Juvenal advises a new governor:

When you enter your long-expected province as its Governor, set a curb and limit to your passion, as also to your greed; have compassion on the impoverished provincials, whose very bones you see sucked dry of marrow. (*Sat.* 8.87–90)

Plutarch comments on "the procuratorships and governorships of provinces from which many talents may be gained" (*Mor.* 814d). He praises Brutus's good governorship in Gaul in contrast to "other provinces [that], owing to the insolence and frivolity of their governors, were plundered as though they had been conquered in war" (*Brut.* 6). The leader Civilis complains that "we are handed over to prefects and centurions; after one band is satisfied with murder and spoils, the troops are shifted, and new purses are looked for to be filled and various pretexts for plundering are sought" (Tacitus, *Hist.* 4.14). Suetonius criticizes Vespasian, emperor from 69–79, a decade or two before the time when John's Gospel was written, for using governors to further his "love of money":

He is even believed to have had the habit of designedly advancing the most rapa-
cious of his procurators to higher posts, that they might be the richer when he
later condemned them [and confiscated their wealth through fines]; in fact it was
common talk that he used these men as sponges because he, so to speak, soaked
them when they were dry and squeezed them when they were wet. (*Vesp.* 16)

Yet Rome had a vested interest in limiting the amount of plunder and keeping at least
some semblance of law and order so as not to alienate the local elite or aggravate the
local people into revolt.[17]

Legal Action against Governors

Although it might seem that governors like Pilate had unbridled or unaccountable
power, that was not the case, at least not in theory. Peter Brunt discusses the legal provision of *repetundae*, which prohibited various kinds of extortion by greedy and corrupt governors through force, intimidation, or fraud; undue extractions and illegal
enrichment from the governed; and other oppressive acts of misgovernment.[18] Provincials did have the right of appeal. Jews in Judea could appeal first to the governor of
Syria and then to Rome for redress.

But generally the odds were stacked in favor of the governors. Appeals against a governor who was sufficiently well-connected and enjoyed the emperor's and/or senate's
favor enough to be appointed in the first place often had little chance of success. Philo
cannot point to any governor removed from office in order to be tried for exploitative
actions, though he knows of some punished after leaving office (*Flaccus* 105–107). And
when the Jewish citizens in Alexandria try to appeal to Rome against the governor Flaccus, they need Flaccus's permission to do so! He, predictably, obstructs the process of
"justice" by omitting to pass the petition on to Rome (*Flaccus* 97–101)! Brunt catalogs
obstacles to such appeals: distance from Rome, the expense of travel and accommodation while awaiting a hearing, pressure from a governor's allies in the province not to
pursue action, the need even for the governor's consent for such a petition (Philo, *Flaccus* 97–101; Josephus *Ant.* 20.7, 193), the influence of a governor's supportive allies in
Rome, the risk of reprisal, divisions, and rivalries in the province.[19] Pilate is the subject
of such a complaint after attacking and killing a number of Samaritans. The Samaritans
appeal to Vitellius, the governor of Syria, who orders Pilate to "return to Rome to give
the emperor his account of the matters," but Tiberius dies before Pilate reaches Rome
(Josephus, *Ant.* 18.88–89). This action effectively ends Pilate's governorship, but Josephus does not indicate whether any punitive action is taken against Pilate.

Yet the province of Asia provides several examples of successful actions against corrupt governors. One proconsul, Volesus Messala, was indicted for misgoverning by the
emperor Augustus around 12 CE. Shortly afterward, around 20–21 CE, another proconsul, C. Iunius Silanus, was successfully accused of extortion before Tiberius and the
senate by "the most fluent advocates of all Asia," and by his legate and his quaestor.[20]
And the next year, the procurator Lucilius Capito was indicted and condemned for
inappropriate use of military force, in gratitude for which the province built a temple
for Tiberius in Smyrna.[21]

Summary

The Gospel references to Pilate as a Roman governor assume these sorts of imperial realities. These Roman provincial administrative practices and social order provide the assumed context for and the dynamics of the meeting between Pilate and Jesus. Pilate's role as governor is to protect and advance Rome's political and economic interests in alliance with the local elite. His role as governor in a trial assumes imperial dynamics of power, elite alliances, and legal privilege. Pilate represents and protects Rome's political, economic, military, and legal interests in an exploitative and oppressive relationship over those he governs, and with little accountability on his part. Presentations of a weak, disinterested, or apolitical governor fail to take account of these imperial realities.

Jesus and Pilate (John 18:28–19:16a)

Changes in the participants and in the location of the encounters mark the seven subsections of this long scene.[22] Pilate moves between the inside of the praetorium, or governor's headquarters, where he interacts with Jesus, and outside, where the Jerusalem elite gathers, especially the high priests and leading Pharisees (John 18:3). This alliance of the nation's leaders had in 7:32, 45–52 unsuccessfully acted against Jesus. In 11:47–53 they convene the council to consider, "What are we to do?" (11:47 NRSV). Their discussion there is framed as imperial negotiation and in terms of what is best for the nation. Faced with increasing elite and popular loyalty to Jesus (11:45, 48a; 12:42) and the possibility of Roman military intervention (11:48b), they agree with the chief priest Caiaphas that "it is better for you to have one man die for the people than have the whole nation destroyed" (11:50 NRSV). This position forms the basis for their strategy "to put him to death" (11:53). They invite intelligence from the populace so that they might arrest Jesus (11:55–57). In the scene with Pilate (18:28–19:16a), this leadership group is identified six times as "the *Ioudaioi*," or Judeans (18:31, 36, 38; 19:7, 12, 14) to underline their opposition to Jesus.

Scene	John	Locale	Participants	Movement
1	18:28–32	Outside	Pilate and "the *Ioudaioi*"	Pilate went out; 18:29
2	18:33–38a	Inside	Pilate and Jesus	Pilate entered the headquarters; 18:33
3	18:38b–40	Outside	Pilate and "the *Ioudaioi*"	Pilate went out; 18:38b
4	19:1–3	Inside	Jesus and the soldiers	Pilate took Jesus; 19:1
5	19:4–7	Outside	Pilate, Jesus, and "the *Ioudaioi*"	Pilate went out again; 19:4
6	19:8–12	Inside	Pilate and Jesus	Pilate entered the headquarters; 19:9
7	19:13–16	Outside	Pilate, Jesus, and "the *Ioudaioi*"	Pilate brought Jesus out; 19:13

Contrary to the claim that "John focuses on the responsibility of the Judean elite,"[23] the key figure in each scene is Pilate.[24] The narrative follows his movements. He initiates conversations with "the *Ioudaioi*" (18:29, 38b; 19:4, 12, 14) and with Jesus (18:33; 19:9). Even the whipping in scene 4 begins with ascribing that action to Pilate: "Pilate took Jesus and whipped him" (19:1). While commentators frequently claim that Pilate's soldiers probably did the task and the NRSV translates, "Pilate . . . had him flogged," the directness of the Greek statement maintains focus on Pilate's agency as Jesus' torturer.[25]

Scene 1: "The Ioudaioi" Hand Jesus Over (18:28–32)

John 18:28 carries the action forward from Jesus' brief appearance before the chief priest Caiaphas (18:19–24). Representatives of the Jerusalem elite, the chief priests and leading Pharisees (18:3), take Jesus to Pilate. In 18:31 they will openly declare their goal to have Jesus put to death, as stated in 11:53. The physical setting is Pilate's praetorium, the headquarters for Rome's occupation of this foreign nation, and a context that provides an intimidating display of power. The previous scene has shown Peter intimidated by the "world's" opposition into denying his loyalty to Jesus (18:25–27). But Jesus will not be intimidated. He will announce judgment on this misdirected power.

The scene's temporal setting locates Jesus' trial immediately before Passover (the day of Preparation, 19:14). This festival celebrates the deliverance of God's people from slavery in Egypt (Exod 13–16). Josephus links festivals and revolts, reporting that "it is on these festive occasions that sedition is most apt to break out" (*J.W.* 1.88). He also records Rome's awareness of and preparation for such occasions by stationing troops in the city and deploying them strategically in the temple area during festivals: "For a Roman cohort was permanently quartered there [the Antonia fortress], and at the festivals took up positions in arms around the porticoes to watch the people and repress any insurrectionary movements" (*J.W.* 5.244; also 2.224; *Ant.* 20.106).[26] Such a possibly explosive context poses challenges for the governing elite in moving against a populist king.

The repeated references to Passover (18:28, 39; 19:14) also underline an important irony. In one sense, nothing like another liberation from oppressive ruling power seems to be happening with Jesus. The elite, so it seems, are efficiently securing their control by removing a potential troublemaker. But the Passover intertext provides one of several strategies whereby the narrative presents the scenes as showing the elite's power being undermined, not secured. By association, Jesus' death is presented as an act of liberation from "the world" opposed to God's purposes (1:10; 16:33), a world shaped and ruled by the political, social, and religious elite. Jesus' resurrection will show how limited the elite's power is. They do not control the world even though they think they do. Their opposition cannot prevent God's purposes from being accomplished now and being completed at Jesus' return.

They bring Jesus to Pilate "early in the morning," the time when morning light overcomes night's darkness (18:28). Yet the language undermines elite power even as they express it: the image of light has depicted Jesus' revelation of God's salvation and life in the darkness of a sinful, rejecting, imperial world (1:5–9; 3:17–21; 8:12; 9:5). Jesus' death reveals God's salvation in and from a sinful world committed to rejecting God's purposes.

The Jerusalem elite do not enter the Gentile Pilate's headquarters so as to avoid becoming impure before the Passover. The verse does not explain how this defilement might happen. But they clearly take the Passover celebration very seriously. The irony is that the narrative does not present them as finding their involvement in the execution of an opponent, God's agent and revealer of God's salvation, to be impure!

Pilate respects the scruples of his allies and goes out from his headquarters to meet them (18:29). Outside his headquarters, Pilate takes charge by inquiring about the accusation against Jesus (18:29). The Jerusalem elite express surprise, even offense, at having to justify his arrest. With some animosity, they defend their action by asserting that if Jesus were not a "criminal" (literally, "one who does evil"; 18:30),[27] they would not have brought him. They do not specify his wrongdoing. They describe their transfer of Jesus to Pilate as "handing over." On each of its eight previous appearances, this verb has described Judas "betraying" Jesus (6:64, 71; 12:4; 13:2, 11, 21; 18:2, 5), an action that Jesus has predicted (6:64, 71; 13:11, 21). The choice of verb not only recalls Judas' action; it also shows that Jesus is not surprised or defeated by these actions. Despite appearances and claims to the contrary, Jesus is in control.

Their evasive and offended tone, and impatient animosity toward Pilate (that continues through the scene), may stem from their previous discussions with Pilate about Jesus. Jesus' arrest had involved both Roman soldiers and police from the Jerusalem temple (18:3, 12) in a display of "the world's" or the ruling elite's alliance and power against Jesus.[28] In a farcical scene that mocks Roman power in displaying its overkill, six hundred Roman soldiers, according to 18:3, overwhelm the garden where the nonviolent Jesus was, and then "retreat" and fall on their faces like dominoes when Jesus, voluntarily laying down his life (10:18), identifies himself with the revelatory "I am" (18:5–6). While divine power and presence overwhelm the apparently overwhelming imperial power and presence, revealing the latter to be by far inferior, the fact remains that these Roman troops could not have been deployed without Pilate's command. It seems, then, that the narrative assumes a previous meeting or meetings at which Pilate heard the Jerusalem elite's concern about Jesus as a major threat to the society over which he as governor and they as the Jerusalem elite rule (cf. 11:45–48). The presence of Roman troops at Jesus' arrest expresses Pilate's consent to remove Jesus. The outcome is a forgone conclusion. His inquiry about a charge against Jesus *after* Jesus' arrest seems out of place and surprises them.

But Pilate does not like their tone in reminding him that Jesus is an "evildoer." They might be allies, but he has the upper hand as the representative of the occupying power. So he puts them in their place by telling them to deal with Jesus themselves (18:31a). Of course, both groups know that they cannot do so because only the Roman governor has the power to execute. Pilate's comment signals his unwillingness to be their servant and do their will without appropriate deference on their part. It also makes clear their common and already-established commitment to execute Jesus.

In recalling their status as subjects of Rome, he humiliates them. They concede as much in admitting that they are powerless to remove Jesus without Pilate's assistance (18:31b). The exchange reestablishes his supremacy and their dependency within the alliance. It also confirms Jesus' previous predictions (3:14; 12:32) that he would die by crucifixion (a Roman form of execution), and not for example by stoning (18:32; cf. 8:59, 10:31–33; 11:8). The ruling elite think they are in control, but Jesus' prediction is another reminder that God's agenda controls the scene.

Two factors, then, establish that Jesus' death is certain at the outset of the scene. The involvement of Pilate's troops and temple police in Jesus' arrest attests their common commitment to remove Jesus. The elite's impatient response to Pilate's question about a charge assumes such an agreement. Pilate has already signed off on it, as his next question to Jesus also indicates.

Scene 2: Pilate Meets Jesus (18:33–38a)

Having put the Jerusalem leaders in their place, Pilate goes inside his headquarters and authoritatively summons Jesus. He asks Jesus, "Are you the King of the Jews?" (18:33), a question that presumably utilizes knowledge gained from his previous discussions with the Jerusalem elite before Jesus' arrest. In Rome's imperial world, this is a political charge of insurrection since only Rome legitimates local kings and makes alliances with them. As outlined above (chap. 7), Josephus mentions a series of Jewish figures who, claiming to be kings, led revolts that were harshly crushed. In essence Pilate's question is, "Are you leader of a revolt?" Given the Passover setting, the question is appropriate and necessary.

Previously Jesus has been addressed as king (1:49; 6:15; 12:13, 15), and the title recurs through the trial (18:33, 37, 39; 19:3, 12, 14, 15; also 19:19, 21). The issue concerns power and sovereignty, as well as *how* that sovereignty is expressed. The term "king" (βασιλεύς, *basileus*) was used for the Roman emperor (Josephus, *J.W.* 3.351; 4.596; 5.58; 5.563; 1 Pet 2: 13, 17), so it sets Jesus and the emperor in antithetical relationship (cf. John 19:15). While Jesus' kingship does not present a military threat to Rome, it is nevertheless a real political threat to the way that Rome and Jerusalem order the world. His kingship participates in the completion of God's purposes, the establishment of God's reign/empire (3:3, 5). That means the end of Rome's unjust order.

Jesus, the interrogated, becomes the interrogator (18:34). In response to Pilate's question, he asks Pilate about the source of his knowledge. Jesus' query draws attention to Pilate's alliance with the Jerusalem leaders. Pilate feigns ignorance of and tries to hide the alliance, but the narrative has already uncovered it (18:35). Pilate responds with a somewhat derisive question, "Am I a Jew/*Ioudaios*?" The question is formulated in Greek (introduced by μήτι, *mēti*) in a way that makes inevitable the answer "No, of course not!" But while Pilate uses the term to scorn his Jerusalem allies and to highlight an *ethnic* difference between himself and the Jerusalem elite, Pilate's actions show his commitment to his elite partners in Jerusalem against Jews.

Jesus responds to Pilate's questions about being King of the Jews (18:33) and about his actions (18:35) not with silence as in the Synoptic Gospels, but with a statement about the origin and nature of his reign (18:36). Twice Jesus asserts that his "kingdom/kingship/empire [βασιλεία, *basileia*] is not from this world." Again the term sets Jesus in antithetical relationship to Rome since the same term "kingdom/kingship/empire" (*basileia*) denotes Rome's empire.[29] A key part of the antithesis concerns the origin of Jesus' empire. It does not originate in what is hostile and hateful toward God, as does the reign of Pilate, "ruler of this world" (a world created and loved by God: 1:10; 3:16; 15:18–19; 14:30). Rather, Jesus' reign is from God (3:31; 8:23, 42; 16:28). It reveals God's claim on and sovereignty over human structures and lives. It is thus quite misleading to say that Jesus' kingship is not political. While it is not violent (18:36) or centered on one nation, it is very political in that it claims to establish God's rule over all things, including Pilate's empire. Pilate, though, cannot "see" or accept such an empire.[30]

The sign that Jesus' reign or kingdom is not "from the world" is the lack of armed resistance from his "followers" (18:36). Jesus identifies violence or military domination as the defining characteristic of worldly (hostile-to-God) empires like Pilate's. The absence of violence and force marks Jesus' reign. Jesus refers to his "followers" with exactly the same word that denotes the "police" sent from the chief priests to arrest Jesus (18:3, 12, 18, 22; 19:6). The same term contrasts Jesus' kingship as from God, from above, marked by love, service and faithfulness—with Pilate's empire, based on coercive power and domination. Such is the "world," dominated by Roman imperial power and its allies, that rejects Jesus.

Pilate asks again, "So you are a king?" (18:37). The question moves from the issue of the type of kingship and its origin (the exchange of 18:36) to the related issue of Jesus' identity. Jesus' response is vague. He sets about defining his kingship by rehearsing some important affirmations in the Gospel. The two clauses "For this I was born" and "For this I have come into the world" recall the extensive emphasis on Jesus being sent from the Father to do God's will (4:34; 8:42). The mission or purpose of his reign is "testify to the truth" in "the world."

The word "truth" is a key term in the Gospel and needs careful definition. Previously Jesus has described himself as "truth" (8:32; 14:6). While the term "truth" can mean "real" or "genuine," in the biblical tradition it often means "faithfulness" or "loyalty." It often denotes being faithful to one's commitments and obligations. So in Genesis 24:49 Abraham's servant, charged with procuring a wife for Isaac, appeals to Rebekah's father, Bethuel, and brother Laban to deal "loyally and truly" with Abraham in arranging the marriage. The opposite of such truthfulness or faithfulness is falseness, wickedness, and injustice, when humans do not carry out their commitments (see Isa 59:9–15). The same term "truth" or "true" (*ʾemet*), often translated "faithfulness" (so Gen 32:10; Exod 34:6), is applied to God. God acts "truthfully" or "in truth" or "truly" when God is faithful to God's covenant promises to show "loving-kindness" (*ḥesed*, "steadfast love" [NRSV]) and to save God's people. God's "truthfulness" means God acts powerfully and faithfully to save people from their enemies (see Pss 40:10–12; 108, esp. v. 4).

By declaring that his mission is to witness to "the truth," Jesus tells Pilate that he witnesses to God's faithfulness in saving the people. He witnesses to God acting faithfully to God's own commitments to save (3:33). When Jesus declares that he is "the truth" (14:6), he claims to reveal God's faithful saving action. When he declares that the truth shall set you free, he claims that God's saving actions, manifested in him, will free people from everything that resists and rejects God's purposes (8:32). Jesus comes from above (8:23), from heaven (3:13), where he has heard (8:26) and seen (5:19) the Father, so that he can reveal God's "truth" about God acting powerfully and faithfully to save the world (3:16–17; 8:14–18). This is not good news for Rome or its representative Pilate.

Jesus further explains to Pilate that the mark of "belonging to the truth," of participating in and trusting oneself to God's saving work and reign, is listening to Jesus' voice

(18:37b). To listen to Jesus is to accept and understand his truthful or faithful revelation of God's truthful or faithful saving purposes, to believe and do his commandments (10:3–5, 16). To listen to Jesus shows that one is "from God"; not to listen shows one is not from God (8:47), and that one is Jesus' opponent (10:20).

Pilate is not listening. Jesus' words about his empire and about "truth" (God's faithful saving action) give Pilate the opportunity to decide that Jesus speaks "truthfully" or faithfully about God's work. But Pilate cannot "see" any of it. Pilate has already decided against Jesus in allying with the Jerusalem elite to arrest and kill Jesus (18:3). He rejects the second chance that Jesus gives him. Though he asks Jesus, "What is truth?" he does not wait for an answer (18:38a).

Pilate's unwillingness to listen to Jesus' answer reveals Pilate's continued opposition, his blindness. He does not participate in God's saving work (18:37–38). He reveals that he does not "see" Jesus' identity, origin, and mission. Jesus' words place him in a "crisis of decision," and he condemns himself and the imperial system he represents by rejecting Jesus and God's saving purposes. He belongs to the unseeing world (12:40).

Scene 3: Pilate and "the Ioudaioi" (18:38b–40)

Pilate leaves Jesus and returns to his allies. His declaration that "I find no case against him" (NRSV) and his offer to release Jesus according to the Passover custom (18:39) seem quite strange after his previous consent to arrest Jesus, after Jesus talked about his empire (kingdom) and did not appear to dispute being a king!

These factors indicate that Pilate's comment cannot be taken at face value as an evaluation of Jesus' case but are part of his tensive struggle with his Jerusalem allies.[31] Pilate's comment has to be placed in the context of its audience, the Jerusalem elite, and Pilate's previous testy exchange with them in 18:29–31. Having heard the Jerusalem elite admit that they depend on him to remove Jesus (18:31), Pilate taunts them, provoking another expression of their subservience to, dependence on, and gratefulness toward him.

After declaring that he finds no fault in Jesus, he refers to their "custom that I release someone for you at the Passover" (18:39 NRSV). He offers Jesus, "King of the Jews." Indebted by his offer and so further subordinated to the governor, the Jerusalem elite nevertheless respond by (in effect) begging for Jesus' death and rejecting his release (18:40). They request instead the release of Barabbas the "bandit." The Jewish writer Josephus identifies "bandits" as political guerillas and insurrectionists, or "revolutionary fighters."[32] Such figures emerge from oppressive, agrarian socioeconomic circumstances to exploit lapses in control. They often employ violence in attacking members of the ruling elite and their property, and in establishing alternative realms of sovereignty.[33] In John 10:8 Jesus used the same word "bandits" to identify leaders who harm God's people (the sheep) by not heeding God's/Jesus' voice (see chap. 7 above).

There are several ironies in their choice. In preferring Barabbas (no reason is given), they reject Jesus as one who comes from God and reveals God's life and reign. In choosing Barabbas, they hold an impromptu referendum on preferred means of opposition to the Roman Empire: either violence against it now, or its demise at Jesus' return as Son of Man. They opt for violence, a form of resistance that Rome has shown it can contain.

But ironically, in 11:48, the Jerusalem leaders feared that Jesus' nonviolent but disruptive teaching and life-giving power would provoke Rome's action against them, yet now they call for the release of a violent revolutionary. Violence, though, is not God's way (18:36). The followers of Jesus are to live an alternative existence committed to service, not domination (13:12–20; see chap. 10 above) awaiting the completion of God's purposes and the end of all forces of sin and death, including Rome.

Scene 4: Pilate Whips Jesus (19:1–3)

Pilate responds to their appeal not to release Jesus by flogging Jesus. Such flogging or torture is degrading and usually preceded crucifixion. Some argue that this act is intended to placate the Jerusalem leaders, but it is hard to imagine that whipping Jesus and releasing him would satisfy people who want him dead! Rather, Pilate's action is consistent with his previous agreement to remove Jesus (18:3). He is preparing to put Jesus to death. Yet while Pilate honors his agreement with the Jerusalem elite, he continues to reinforce their subordination by means of his verbal games. The flogging also brutally demonstrates the futility of any aspirations for independence from Rome. The whipping asserts Pilate's control, their status as subjects, and his intolerance for any resistance to Rome. It is an act of imperial violence and intimidation.

Pilate's torture of Jesus is not only physical. Pilate's soldiers also mock Jesus with a fake coronation or investiture as king. "Crown" and "robe" are traditional symbols of ruling power, domination, and wealth (1 Macc 8:14; 10:20; 2 Macc 4:38), precisely the opposite of the servant community Jesus establishes (John 13:12–17). The crown and robe imitate the laurel wreath and purple robe worn by the emperor (and also identified as "king").[34] In this conflict between Rome's emperor and king/emperor Jesus, there is no doubt in their minds as to the winner. But amid this display of Roman power and intimidation, the narrative presents an irony. In calling Jesus "King," these Gentiles speak more truly than they know.

Scene 5: Pilate and "the Ioudaioi" (19:4–7)

Pilate parades Jesus outside before the Jerusalem elite (19:4–5). The repetition of the details of Jesus' kingly attire in 19:5 emphasizes the conflict over sovereignty and rule that pervades the scene. Jesus demonstrates what Rome does to Jews who claim kingship without Rome's consent.[35] Pilate's repeated comment that he finds no case against Jesus again can hardly be serious given his involvement in Jesus' arrest, previous humiliations of the elite, and the whipping of Jesus. Rather, Pilate continues to display his power (and his blindness about Jesus), mocking the subjugated political situation of the Jewish leaders by humiliating and bullying this kingly pretender, and reinforcing their dependence on him.

Pilate's dramatic announcement "Behold the man" is a disdainful taunt (this pathetic specimen is *your* king!). But ironically, the taunt is also a poor choice of words. The term "man" invokes the title "Son of Man" from earlier in the Gospel (see discussion in chap. 7 above). In 1:51 this title "Son of Man" identifies Jesus as the revealer of God's purposes. In 5:27–28 Jesus is the eschatological judge, in the tradition of Daniel 7, who exercises God's judgment over all (including the ruling powers now condemning him to death). "Son of Man" is also used in association with Jesus' "lifting up," a phrase the Gospel uses to describe his crucifixion, resurrection, and ascension to God. His death is the means of his return to God, of giving life to many, and anticipates his triumphant return to earth (3:14; 8:28; 12:23, 32–34). Pilate's parody thus is exposed in the very words he chooses. The one whom he mocks is none other than the eschatological judge, the revealer of God's saving purposes. Pilate cannot see it. With his own words he condemns himself and the imperial system he represents.

Pilate's taunt again forces the Jerusalem leaders, "the chief priests and the police," to recognize Pilate's superior power and their own dependence on him. Dutifully they shout (beg?) for Jesus' crucifixion (19:6). This is the first specific reference to the means of putting Jesus to death (18:31), and it comes from the Jerusalem elite. The narrative assumes that its audience knows about crucifixion. The Jewish writer Josephus described this death penalty as the "most pitiable of deaths" (*J.W.* 7.203).[36] Crucifixion was a distinctively Roman form of execution, reserved by Rome for noncitizens, foreigners, those of little status like slaves, those who posed a political or social threat, violent criminals, the nonelite. Roman citizens who committed treason (and so were not worthy to be citizens) could be crucified. Crucifixion thus removed those who were not welcome in Roman-controlled society. It divided the acceptable from the unacceptable, the vulnerable from the powerful, the noncooperative from the compliant. It was a symbol of shame, humiliation, pain, and social rejection. Crucifixion meant a painful death. Crucified people could take several days to die and sometimes died from being mauled by wild beasts and birds while on the cross. Crucifixions were used as a deterrent and social control. They were quite public and visible, often near scenes of crimes or busy roads and gathering places. The message for passersby was clear. Flogging and carrying one's crossbeam (*patibulum*) were part of the precrucifixion torture and social humiliation.

Pilate continues to mock the elite with his flip response, "Take him yourselves and crucify him" (19:6 NRSV). He knows that they have no such power (18:31), and the involvement of his troops in Jesus' arrest indicates his consent to so use this power (18:3, 12). He has the power of life and death; allies of Rome have only what Rome allows. Ironically, in calling for Jesus' crucifixion, the leaders demand that Jesus be lifted up, the very means by which he said he will draw all people to himself (12:32–34).

In the face of the governor's taunts and inaction, they now assertively and confrontationally get his attention. They remind Pilate, who already knows about Jesus' kingship, of Jesus' offensiveness. Jesus has claimed to be Son of God, God's agent (5:17–20; 10:30–39). If the term "Son of God" is understood in a restricted religious sense to denote equality with God (5:18), it would mean that according to Leviticus 24:16 he should die for such blasphemy or dishonoring of God. Evoking Leviticus, one could argue, might be a good tactic for several reasons.

Pilate has respected the religious commitments and practices of his governing allies. He has not forced them to enter his headquarters before Passover, but three times has gone outside to them (18:28, 29, 38b; 19:4). Their request expresses dependence on

Pilate. They have previously tried to stone Jesus without success (8:59; 10:31), so now they ask for Pilate's help to carry out the sentence. While Pilate has repeatedly reminded them of their dependence on him, their request, phrased in terms of their traditions, reminds Pilate that this is a partnership. He needs to act on their behalf and for their interests to ensure their cooperation. The narrative demonstrates a typical expedient, imperial, power-sharing arrangement among the elite!

Although there might be some truth in these factors, this "religious" interpretation of their identifying Jesus as "Son of God" misses the point. The language of "Son of God" gets *Pilate's* attention; in 19:8 he is "more afraid." This response suggests that "Son of God" was important language in his framework of meaning. As we saw in the discussion in chapter 7 (above), it was common imperial language. Various emperors were a "son of God," notably an emperor who was a *divus* or declared to be a god postmortem by the senate or so honored by a provincial civic declaration.[37] For Pilate, the use of the term indicates that they accuse Jesus, a kingly pretender ("King of the Jews"), of making himself emperor. Against such a hubristic practice, "we"—Pilate and his allies, the Jerusalem elite—have a law, a law about treason. In speaking to Pilate, choosing the language of "Son of God" underlines Jesus' threat as a "King of the Jews" not sanctioned by Rome (18:33, 37). For the Gospel audience it stresses the antithetical relationship between Jesus and Rome. Jesus' Father is not a dead emperor, but the Father is the God who was "in the beginning." Antiquity is authority.

Scene 6: Pilate and Jesus (19:8–12)

The change of tactic has certainly riveted Pilate's attention. Pilate becomes "very afraid." As a Roman, he knows that gods could be sons of other gods (Hermes was son of Zeus). Humans with exceptional abilities or actions were called divine. But primarily for him as Rome's representative, emperors were called sons of gods, and this is the claim they report Jesus to make. Their use of the title reminds Pilate of the seriousness of Jesus' challenge and the need for action.

Pilate returns to ask Jesus the Gospel's most important question: "Where are you from?" (19:9). The question makes sense given the use of the title "Son of God." Which god or ruler is Jesus descended from? The Gospel began by showing Jesus was with God "in the beginning" and comes from God (1:1–18). Throughout, various characters have wrestled with the issue of his origin (3:34; 6:33, 41–42; 7:25–29; 16:27–28). To know Jesus' origin is to know his authority and legitimacy as God's agent and as the one sent from God. To accept that Jesus is from God is to know one's own identity and allegiance (8:39–47). But Jesus does not answer. He had answered Pilate's question in 18:36–37 about the origin of his kingship from God, but Pilate wasn't listening. Like the suffering servant of Isaiah 53:7, Jesus adopts silence, a classic pose of the powerless (who accomplish God's redeeming purposes) before the "powerful."

Pilate interprets Jesus' silence as defiance (19:10). He will be answered. Impatiently he tries to intimidate Jesus by asserting complete power over Jesus, boasting that he has power to release or crucify Jesus (19:10). Basic to this claim again is the issue of sovereignty. Pilate thinks that his will is being done, that the interests of Roman power are being furthered. The matter is very political; death threats by the state are always political. Pilate, like the rest of the imperial rulers, uses the death sentence to coerce compliance in his society.

Pilate succeeds in getting Jesus to answer. His response, though, is probably not what Pilate wanted to hear. Jesus puts Pilate's claims and power into perspective by contextualizing them in God's purposes (19:11). Jesus recognizes that Pilate has power to kill him. But Jesus also claims that that power is given to Pilate "from above," from God to accomplish God's purpose (4:34). Jesus lays down his life (10:17–18). His crucifixion lies within God's purposes partly to expose Rome's fundamental rejection of God's purposes and partly—in Jesus' resurrection—to expose the limits of its power. It is not Pilate's or Rome's victory.

This theological perspective, specifically the claim that earthly rulers carry out God's will even without recognizing it, evokes various scriptural traditions. Babylon defeats Jerusalem without knowing that it thereby enacts God's punishment (2 Kings 24:1–7). Cyrus the Persian ruler defeats Babylon in 539 BCE and lets the Judean exiles return home, without knowing that he accomplishes God's purposes of salvation (Isa 44:28; 45:1). This traditional theological perspective undermines the claims of empires and rulers like Pilate to have absolute power by setting them in the context of God's greater, though often unseen, purposes. While Pilate can and will put Jesus to death, his goal of eliminating a threat to the empire's world will not be accomplished. Rather, God's purposes will be furthered, purposes that are not good news for Rome.

But this theological perspective does not exonerate Pilate from responsibility. Jesus identifies Pilate's action as "sin." In John's Gospel, sin consists primarily of not believing Jesus' revelation about God (8:24). Pilate does not recognize Jesus as God's agent. But as of this moment in the story, Pilate has not yet handed Jesus over for crucifixion. So Jesus' comment probably has multiple referents. Judas has handed Jesus over (6:64; 18:2, 5), as has the Jerusalem leadership (18:30, 35–36). As of this narrative moment, theirs is the "greater sin." But Pilate is about to join them (19:16).

Pilate responds to Jesus' words by trying to release him (19:12). Again his action has to be understood in relation to his previous commitment to arrest Jesus, and in whipping him, to crucify him. He has no intention of releasing Jesus but continues to taunt the Jerusalem leaders with reminders of their subservient and dependent status. And each time, his taunts bring forth expressions of dependency as they plead with the governor to act according to their wishes (see 18:31–32, 39–40; 19:4–6).

The same pattern is evident here. The Jerusalem leaders respond with another display of subservience and loyalty to Rome (19:12b), though not to the governor. They confront his subjugating taunts and in the process they gain some power over Pilate. They remind Pilate of his responsibilities and spell out Jesus' threat to Pilate in very personal terms. To release Jesus, one who claims to be a king and an emperor as the son of God, is to release one who sets himself against the emperor (19:12). Jesus is not a Rome-appointed client king (as was Herod; Josephus, *Ant.* 16.311). If Pilate does not crucify Jesus, Pilate would fail to do his job of upholding the "peace" of the empire and power of the emperor. He would betray Rome's interests. If Pilate releases someone who has committed treason in claiming kingship without Rome's consent, he would not be the emperor's friend or reliable servant, a trustworthy client deserving the emperor's patronage.[38] Their statement about Jesus as a king or emperor who sets himself against *the* emperor succinctly summarizes Jesus' threat: he asserts a sovereignty that challenges Rome's. The ruling alliance, both Rome and Jerusalem, cannot tolerate this assertion.

Pilate's Jerusalem allies have explained Jesus' claim to be Son of God (19:7) in political and personal terms. Jesus is a king who threatens Caesar's interests, which Pilate is obligated to uphold; Jesus threatens Pilate's status as a loyal client of the patron emperor. In expressing their view of Jesus in these terms, they not only remind Pilate of his job but also clearly confess their own loyalty to the emperor and to Roman interests. Being a friend of the emperor matters to them more than anything else. Being a friend of Jesus does not figure in the scene (cf. 15:15). In terms of the Gospel's rhetoric of distance, the exchange renders the alliances clear and the antithesis sharp: those accommodated to and supportive of the imperial order, those friends of Rome and its emperor, oppose Jesus, God's agent. Given this treatment of Jesus, the Jesus-believers can make no accommodation with the empire.

Scene 7: Pilate Pronounces Sentence (19:12–16a)

Pilate now acts as a friend of the emperor rather than a friend of Jesus. For the second time he brings Jesus out and sits on the judge's bench, the raised platform outside his headquarters. Verse 14 reports the time, emphasizing the Passover context first mentioned in the scene's opening verse (18:28). Pilate condemns Jesus, thinking that he asserts control but without "seeing" that he rejects and enables God's work of effecting another liberation from imperial control.

Pilate maintains the focus on the issue of sovereignty and allegiance by identifying Jesus as "your King" (19:14). Pilate continues to taunt the Jerusalem leaders by reminding them of their subjugation while also warning them of what happens to those who resist Roman control. The elite—unlike the other Gospels, John does not mention a crowd—distance themselves from Jesus by shouting again for Jesus' crucifixion (19:15; cf. 19:6). The shout rejects God's agent and embraces Rome's sovereignty. Pilate further secures their loyalty by asking again if he should crucify "your King." Again they reject any identification with Jesus by choosing Rome: "We have no king but the emperor" (19:15 NRSV).

Pilate has solicited another amazing confession. With these words, the Jerusalem leaders repudiate their centuries-old covenant with God as Israel's king (1 Sam 8:7; Ps 47:2; 93:1). God's kingship was manifested in the Davidic king (2 Sam 7:11–16), who as God's son, represented God's just and life-giving rule (Ps 2:7; 72). The Jerusalem leaders are supposed to represent and foster this covenant with God as king among the people. But with these words, they abandon their heritage and calling. They renounce the biblical traditions and aspirations that look for God's just and life-giving reign to be established over God's creation and over all empires (like Rome's) that resist God's purposes (Isa 2:1–4). Their cry is a complete vote of support for the way things are under their allies: Rome. In 8:33 they claimed never to have been slaves of anyone; yet here they further enslave themselves to Rome and recognize the emperor's rule, not God's. But in a sense, none of this is a surprise. The narrative of their cry simply reveals their "true" commitments that have been operative throughout the story as they reject Jesus, God's anointed agent.

After drawing from them this amazing statement of loyalty to Rome and renunciation of their heritage, Pilate hands Jesus over to be crucified (19:16). The use of the same verb ("hand over") to describe the actions of Judas (18:2, 5), the Jerusalem elite (18:30, 35), and now Pilate (19:16) allies them as "the world" in opposition to and rejection of God's purposes, and in support of the world over which this alliance presently claims to rule.

Pilate's Last Appearance (19:19–22)

Pilate appears once more, two verses later. Jesus is crucified according to Pilate's command (19:17–18). Pilate insists on a notice for Jesus' cross that reads, "Jesus of Nazareth, the King of the Jews" (19:21). The notice is written in three languages, Hebrew or Aramaic, Latin, and Greek, so that everyone can understand it (19:20). Jesus is Pilate's visual aid, a public poster boy for the futility of rebelling against Roman rule. Jesus' crucifixion comprises another aspect of Pilate's campaign to intimidate and silence Jewish aspirations for independence.

Pilate's allies, the Jerusalem elite, predictably resent the humiliation contained in Pilate's wording. Their success in having Jesus crucified has meant several confessions of absolute loyalty to Rome (19:12, 15). They now try to distance themselves from the notice's suggestion that Jesus was recognized by all as "King of the Jews," thereby continuing to assert their unwavering loyalty to Rome. They ask Pilate to qualify his notice by adding the words, "This man said, 'I am the king of the Jews'" (19:21). Pilate refuses. He remains the tough and efficient Roman governor who subjugates his Jewish allies, and who does not "see" God's purposes at work.

But again the narrative undermines his claims. While Pilate intends that his notice will intimidate and coerce compliance, ironically it proclaims Jesus' identity as the king who represents God's reign and identifies the cross as a place of coronation. Jesus had previously indicated that his "lifting up" would draw all people (12:32). In Jesus' resurrection, God's reign will be recognized as more powerful than Rome's empire, which is unable to keep Jesus dead. And in Jesus' return, God's reign will have the final word at Rome's expense. Pilate's notice anticipates such realities. At the very moment of Pilate's apparent triumph, the narrative ironically sets his actions in a larger context of God's purposes, which Pilate cannot see and in which he will not do well. The narrative underlines the antithetical relationship between God and empire.

But his Jerusalem allies fare no better. In fact, they share Pilate's dilemma. Their amendment to Pilate's proclamation, the addition of the words "This man said, 'I am . . . ,'" does the same thing. This change would highlight the words "I am," words that Jesus has used to announce his identity as God's revealer.[39] As much as Pilate wants to assert superiority over his Jerusalem allies, the narrative allies them even more, not just as friends of Rome but also as futile and unseeing opponents of God's purposes. Even in declaring their supposed triumph and Jesus' defeat, they end up together unknowingly proclaiming Jesus' identity and God-given mission. Unknowingly, they further God's purposes that will destroy their power and pretensions.

Conclusion

John's Pilate is an efficient and powerful governor who in crucifying Jesus protects Rome's interests against this threat. He walks a fine line between working with his Jerusalem allies to remove Jesus (even showing some respect for their religious customs), and repeatedly taunting them about their defeated status and keeping them in their subservient place as a people dependent on him. By the close of the scene, he has skillfully managed to draw from them two amazing declarations of their loyalty to Rome (19:12, 15). Pilate also clearly chooses loyalty to the emperor (who gave him this job) rather than openness to God's purposes, which he cannot see. But throughout, the scene employs considerable irony to offer glimpses into God's larger purposes, about which Pilate has no clue and which will eventually mean the demise of the very system that Pilate represents so efficiently.

For John's audience, the scene continues to employ the Gospel's rhetoric of distance in demonstrating that the Roman Empire is not committed to God's purposes but is their enemy. The empire is part of "the world" that opposes God's agent, Jesus. It cannot see what God is doing and resists God's work by defending its own interests violently and even to the death. Those allied with the empire and its governor crucify Jesus. For John's audience the scene draws a stark antithesis of loyalties, either to King Jesus or to Rome's emperor. That antithesis is not just an individual, private, and personal matter. It has profound sociopolitical implications. Believers in this crucified one cannot make friends with such a "world." They have a mission to it (17:18; 20:21). That mission does not mean violence against the empire (18:36), and it certainly does not mean peaceful coexistence with or accommodation to the empire. Rather, it means distance, a differentiated way of life, opposition, being in it but not of it (17:14–16), telling the "truth" and proclaiming God's saving purposes (18:37). The scene warns the Gospel's audience that often this mission will not be well received, that the empire will strike back. But conflict, even death, is not defeat. Even in the midst of displays of apparently untouchable and triumphant Roman power, God's purposes for a different order, one marked by God's just and abundant reign of life, are being worked out through and among Jesus-believers.

Notes

1. The analysis in this chapter is consonant with Carter, *Pontius Pilate*, 35–54, 127–52.

2. Other figures in Judea and Galilee claim to be kings in the first century as they seek sovereignty independent of Rome. Josephus names several (Judas son of Ezekias, Simon, Athronges; *Ant.* 17.271–285; *J.W.* 2.57–65) and generalizes about the rest: "Anyone might make himself a king (*Ant.* 17.285). Around 70 CE, Menachem (*J.W.* 2.433–448) and Simon bar Giora continue the tradition in rebelling against Rome (4.503–544, 556–584). These kings meet a common fate: Rome executes them (7.153–155, Simon's execution). Certainly Jesus did not employ the same means of opposition and did not make violent attacks on the elite and their property. But like them, Jesus had followers. And like them, Jesus claimed to exercise sovereignty that was not permitted by Rome or exercised on Rome's behalf or for Rome's benefit.

3. Callahan, *Love Supreme*, 81–82; contra Kovacs, "'Now Shall the Ruler,'" *JBL* 114 (1995): 227–47.

312 John and Empire

4. Brown, *John*, 1:517–18.

5. Van Tilborg, *Reading John*, 18–20.

6. The term is ἡγεμών, *hēgemōn*. Josephus, *Ant.* 18.170; 19.292. Josephus refers to governors of Syria such as Vitellius (*Ant.* 15.405), Titius (16.270), Saturninus and Volumnius (16.344), Petronius (19.301), Marsus (19.340), Varro (*J.W.* 1.398) and Ummidius Quadratus (*J.W.* 2.239), as well as governors of Judea such as Florus (*Ant.* 18.25) and Pilate (*Ant.* 18.55), and Tiberius Alexander, governor of Egypt (*J.W.* 2.492). Philo refers to the Egyptian governor Flaccus by this term (*Flaccus* 31, 163) as well as by ἐπίτροπος, *epitropos*, "steward" (*Flaccus* 43).

7. For details, see Carter, *Matthew and Empire*, chap. 9, note 2.

8. Peter A. Brunt, "The Administrators of Roman Egypt," in *Roman Imperial Themes* (Oxford: Clarendon, 1990), 215–54; "*Equites*," *Oxford Classical Dictionary*, 550–52.

9. Fergus Millar, ed., *The Roman Empire and Its Neighbours* (New York: Delacourte, 1966), 161–69; Brunt, "Administrators," 215; Brunt, "Procuratorial Jurisdiction," in *Roman Imperial Themes*, 163–87; Richard Alston, *Aspects of Roman History, AD 14–117* (New York: Routledge, 1998), 255–59. For the governor's exercise of justice as a delegated representative of, and in consultation with, the emperor, see Garnsey, *Social Status*, 72–85.

10. Cicero and Pliny the Younger describe their traveling assizes. See Anthony J. Marshall, "Governors on the Move," *Phoenix* 20 (1966): 231–46; Burton, "Proconsuls."

11. Brent Kinman, "Pilate's Assize and the Timing of Jesus' Trial," *TynBul* 42 (1991): 282–95. An additional factor that may contribute to Pilate's presence is the likelihood of outbreaks of revolt at the Passover festival (Josephus, *J.W.* 5.244).

12. Anthony J. Marshall, "Symbols and Showmanship in Roman Public Life: The Fasces," *Phoenix* 38 (1984): 120–41.

13. Garnsey, *Social Status*, 65–100, 103–52, 221–80; Klaus Wengst, *Pax Romana and the Peace of Jesus Christ* (Philadelphia: Fortress, 1987), 37–40.

14. Garnsey, *Social Status*, 100.

15. Brunt, "Romanization," 272; Garnsey, *Social Status*, 77–79.

16. Van Tilborg, *Reading John*, esp. 84–86, 101–9.

17. Wengst, *Pax Romana*, 35–37.

18. Peter A. Brunt, "Charges of Provincial Maladministration," in *Roman Imperial Themes*, 53–95, 487–506; for *repetundae* trials involving Pliny the Younger, see Garnsey, *Social Status*, 50–58.

19. Brunt, "Charges," 71–95; see Garnsey, *Social Status*, 65–85, 237–42, on the legal privileges of equestrians. Examples of these obstacles are readily available. Flaccus fails to pass on to Rome the petition against him. After the prosecution of Bassus, proconsul of Bithynia, the senate retaliates by trying to prosecute Theophanes, the leader of the provincial prosecutors. See Garnsey, *Social Status*, 55. Some Jews from Caesarea complain against the governor Festus. Josephus comments, "He would undoubtedly have paid the penalty for his misdeeds against the Jews had not Nero yielded to the urgent entreaty of Felix's brother Pallas, whom he held in the highest honor." And in retaliation for bringing the complaint, Syrian leaders successfully intervene and persuade Nero's tutor to urge the emperor to annul the grant of equal civic rights to the Jews in Caesarea (*Ant.* 20.182). When Jews in Jerusalem seek an embassy to Nero against the governor Florus in 66, Agrippa tells them that this action will only make matters worse: flattery rather than irritation is the best approach. Sending an embassy is an overreaction that "exaggerates minor errors"; it will lead to worse and open maltreatment; it will alienate the emperor, who after all "cannot see in the West their officers in the East." He advises them to survive as best they can, "for the same procurator will not remain for ever, and it is probable that the successors of this one will show greater moderation in taking office" (Josephus, *J.W.* 2.350–355). The Roman general Cerialis tells the Treviri and Lingones tribes in Gaul that they should endure "the extravagance or greed of

your rulers," knowing that better ones will come, just as they endure "barren years [and] excessive rains" (Tacitus, *Hist.* 4.74).

20. Tacitus, *Ann.* 3.66–69. He was allowed voluntary exile on the island of Cythnus.

21. Ibid., 4.15.

22. My reading has some affinity with Rensberger, *Johannine Faith*, 91–106; Helen K. Bond, *Pontius Pilate in History and Interpretation* (New York: Cambridge University Press, 1998), 175–93; Moore, *Empire and Apocalypse*, 50–63. In addition to the commentaries, see also Raymond E. Brown, *The Death of the Messiah* (New York: Doubleday, 1994), 1:743–877, selections.

23. E.g., Keener, *John*, 2:1103.

24. So also Moore, *Empire and Apocalypse*, 52–55.

25. Moore (*Empire and Apocalypse*, 56–63) urges attention to the directness of the statement that presents Pilate as "chief inquisitor and head torturer" (56), and labels the scene as one of "judicial torture" (60–61).

26. Examples of outbreaks of violent protest at festivals from Josephus include *J.W.* 2.10–13 (*Ant.* 17.213–218), Passover (4 BCE), against Archelaus; *J.W.* 2.42–75 (*Ant.* 17.254–298), Pentecost (4 BCE), against Rome, especially Sabinus, imperial finance officer for Syria; the action spreads through the efforts of figures such as Judas (2.56), Simon (2.57), and Athronges (2.60); *J.W.* 2.224–231 (*Ant.* 20.105–112), Passover (during Cumanus's governorship, 48–52 CE), after a lewd gesture by a soldier; widespread revolt follows. *J.W.* 2.232–244, an unnamed festival is abandoned for revenge after Samaritans murder some Galileans traveling to the festival. Further "robbery, raids, and insurrections" follow as Rome tries to establish order. *J.W.* 2.254–257, festivals during the 50s; the Sicarii assassinate key figures, beginning with the high priest Jonathan. *J.W.* 2.280–283, Passover (ca. 65 CE); verbal complaints are made to Cestius Gallus, governor of Syria, against the governor Florus (64–66). *J.W.* 2.425, festival of wood-carrying (66 CE); Sicarii and others take over the upper city and burn the Record Office containing money-lenders' bonds. *J.W.* 2.517–522, Festival of Tabernacles is abandoned (66 CE) as the Roman governor of Syria Cestius Gallus threatens Jerusalem with troops. *J.W.* 4.402–405, Sicarii based at Masada attack surrounding villages while villagers are in Jerusalem celebrating Passover. *J.W.* 6.300–309, Tabernacles (62 CE), Jesus son of Ananias begins seven years of announcing woes against Jerusalem and the temple. *J.W.* 6.420–429, Passover (66 CE), the beginning of war with Rome.

27. Ironically, the same image is used in 3:19–21 to describe the world of darkness and evil over which the elite rules and to which Jesus has a mission. That world resists the light and so judges itself. In charging Jesus they want to remove the one who judges them.

28. Several factors identify these soldiers as troops from the Roman army: (1) The term translated as "detachment of soldiers" in 18:3 denotes a cohort, a unit in the Roman army. Being one tenth of a legion, a cohort comprised about 600 soldiers. (2) Elsewhere in the New Testament, this term clearly denotes Roman soldiers (Matt 27:27; Acts 10:1). (3) Verse 12 identifies their commander or "officer" with a term that translates the Latin term *tribunus militum*, which designates the commander of a cohort. See BAGD, 761, 881. The use of 600 soldiers to arrest Jesus (whatever the historical likelihood) clearly indicates both a display of force and Roman involvement. The temple police had tried to arrest Jesus, unsuccessfully, in 7:32, 45. Their success on this occasion results from it being Jesus' "hour" to die (12:23, 27; 13:1). He is in control.

29. Josephus, *J.W.* 5.409; *Ant.* 18.120; Appian, *Bell. civ.* 2.86.

30. Andrew T. Lincoln, *Truth on Trial: The Lawsuit Motif in John's Gospel* (Peabody, MA: Hendrickson, 2000), 123–38, esp. 127.

31. Also ibid., 129; Rensberger, *Johannine Faith*, 93; Bond, *Pontius Pilate*, 181.

32. Ca. 4 BCE: Judah ben Hezekiah, Josephus, *J.W.* 2.56; *Ant.* 17.271–272; ca. 35–55: Eleazar ben Danai and Alexander, *J.W.* 2.235, *Ant.* 20.121; ca. 44–46 CE: Tholomaeus, *Ant.* 20.5; for summary statements, 48 CE: Josephus, *J.W.* 2.235, *Ant.* 20.121; 62–64 CE: *Ant.* 20.215; 64–66 CE: *Ant.*

314 John and Empire

20.255; 66 CE: *J.W.* 2.595–598; *Life* 126–131; 66 CE: *J.W.* 2.581–582; *Life* 77–79; 67–70 CE: *J.W.* 4.135–139, 160–161.

33. Horsley and Hanson, *Bandits, Prophets*, 48–87; Shaw, "Bandits in the Roman Empire," 3–52; idem, "Tyrants, Bandits," 176–204; Hanson and Oakman, *Palestine*, 86–90.

34. A leader of the Jewish revolt against Rome in 70 CE, Simon son of Gioras, surrendered to Rome in a purple cloak, then was executed in Vespasian's triumph in Rome (Josephus, *J.W.* 7.29–36, 153–155).

35. Herod has been appointed "king of the Jews" by Rome (Josephus, *Ant.* 16.311).

36. Hanson and Oakman, *Palestine*, 90–95; Martin Hengel, *Crucifixion in the Ancient World and the Folly of the Message of the Cross* (Philadelphia: Fortress, 1977).

37. See discussions in chap. 12 and the appendix below.

38. See the discussion of friendship in chap. 10 above.

39. E.g., John 6:35; 8:12; 10:9, 11; 11:25; 14:6; 15:1.

12

Where's Jesus?

Apotheosis and Ascension

John's Gospel ends with two chapters of resurrection appearance stories (chaps. 20–21). The risen Jesus appears first to Mary Magdalene (20:1–18), then to the disciples (20:19–23), to Thomas (20:26–29), and finally over breakfast to a small group of disciples (Simon Peter, Thomas, Nathanael, the sons of Zebedee (James and John), and two other disciples: 21:1–14). In this context Jesus has special conversations with Peter (21:15–19) and "the disciple whom Jesus loved" (21:20–23). He commissions these believers to ongoing mission, first Mary to proclaim the news of resurrection (20:17), then all disciples to continue Jesus' mission in the power of the Spirit (20:21–23), then Peter to leadership and death (21:15–19).

True to Jewish traditions of resurrection such as those in Daniel 12:1–2 and 2 Maccabees 7 that emerged in the second century BCE from the context of martyrdom and imperial aggression under the Seleucid tyrant Antiochus IV Epiphanes, John's two chapters present Jesus' resurrection as an act of divine faithfulness and power. With the ultimate display of its power, the empire has done its worst. It has taken the life of one who has challenged its authority. It has executed one who threatened its way of "life." But the resurrection of Jesus, God's agent, reveals the limits of the empire's power. The empire cannot keep him dead in the face of the justice-working, life-giving power of God.

But what happens to Jesus? Where does he go? And what role does his exit play in the Gospel's rhetoric of distance?

John's final two chapters do not include an ascension narrative as in Luke 24:50–52 and Acts 1:9–11. The absence of an ascension narrative, though, is not especially surprising because in various ways from its outset the narrative has emphasized that Jesus returns to the Father. This destiny is conveyed in numerous ways:

- The opening Prologue describes the Son who reveals God as the one "who is in the bosom of the Father," using a participle to denote his present location and role (1:18 RSV). Thus the Gospel opens with the assurance that Jesus is with God now.

- Three "lifted up" sayings in which the verb translated "lifted up" has a double meaning (3:14; 8:28; 12:32–34) also indicate Jesus' return to God. Not only does the verb mean "lifting up" on the cross; it also evokes royal traditions of exalting a king. In Psalm 89:19, for example, it refers to exalting the Davidic king. Jesus is exalted into heaven to be with God, who has sent him on his earthly mission (3:17, 34; 5:23; 6:29, 39; etc.). Jesus came down from heaven (6:38, 41, 51).

- The verb to "go up" or "ascend" is used four times for Jesus' translation into heaven. In 3:13 Jesus ascends "into heaven." In 6:62 he ascends "to where he was before," meaning to be with God, where he was "in the beginning" (1:1). Twice in 20:17, in the resurrection appearance to Mary Magdalene, he declares his ascent "to my Father" and "to my God" (20:17).

- Over twenty times, verbs of "coming,"[1] "going,"[2] and "departing"[3] stipulate his destination. They commonly take "God" or "the Father" or "the one who sent me" or "where I was before" as their object, to denote Jesus' return to the Father. He "goes" or "departs" to God.

- In close proximity to the crucifixion and resurrection narratives are chapters 13–17, the so-called "Farewell Discourse." These five chapters continually sound the theme that Jesus is going away and departing to God. The opening three verses of John 13, for instance, twice declare Jesus' knowledge that he is departing to the Father (13:1–3). This departure to God through crucifixion, resurrection, and ascension is Jesus' glorification (12:23, 27–28; 17:1–5). In these chapters the instruction to the disciples presumes this departure as Jesus addresses their continuing discipleship in his absence.

This language denoting Jesus' return to the Father is not to be confused or equated with resurrection. The verb "lifting up" can incorporate resurrection as the means of his exaltation into heaven. But otherwise resurrection and ascension, though linked, are not the same. The verb *anistēmi* (ἀνίστημι) denotes the raising up of the bodies at the last day (6:39, 40, 44, 54), the raising of Lazarus (11:23, 24), and the raising of Jesus from the dead to be alive on earth but not into heaven (20:9, in an editorial comment). The verb *egeirō* (ἐγείρω) introduces Jesus' resurrection in 2:19, 20, 22, at the beginning of the narrative in the temple-conflict scene, inviting readers/hearers to engage the Gospel in relation to this future event in the narrative. In 5:21 "raising the dead" is the Father's work, but it has been given to Jesus as part of his life-giving work. Accordingly, he "raises" Lazarus (12:1, 9, 17). In 20:17 the risen Jesus tells Mary that he has not yet ascended to my Father. In 21:14 another editorial comment identifies the third of his resurrection appearances to disciples. Resurrection is connected to ascension in that it precedes it, but the two are not the same.

This emphasis on Jesus' ascent into the heavens, though prominent in John's Gospel, was not unique to it. Interpreters have explored the issue in relation to the Synoptic Gospels and to Greek, Roman, and Jewish traditions of the apotheosis of significant figures.[4] The understanding that heroic or virtuous or ruling figures not only enjoyed special communication with the gods (Plutarch, *Lives: Numa* 4) but were also translated from earth to heaven, from the realm of humans to that of God or the gods both during their lifetime and postmortem to receive a higher status in the afterlife (Cicero, *Resp.* 6.13, 16, 18, 25), was widespread in the Greek and Roman worlds, and also known in Jewish traditions.[5] Greek traditions, for example, attest the apotheosis or deification of Alexander the Great (d. 323 BCE), and of Antiochus IV Epiphanes (d. 163 BCE).[6] The West developed the practice a little more slowly than the East, but in the first century BCE in Rome, for example, the families and allies of Scipio Africanus, Pompey, and Julius Caesar present these figures in godlike forms.[7] L'Orange sees the influence of the East on the West, but as Momigliano points out, this view needs nuancing by the recognition, among other things, of Rome's own challenge in the first century BCE to find a way in which to recognize the "legitimization of exceptional power."[8] The powerful influence of these figures is reflected, for example, in an inscription from Ephesus that identifies Julius Caesar as *Theos Epiphanes*, "God Made Manifest."[9] Extensive traditions also developed about the apotheosis of Romulus, Rome's legendary founder (see below). And Jewish traditions included the apotheosis of Moses, attested in Philo (see below).

Increasingly during the reign of Rome's emperors, their authority moves from that based in office and function to that based in divine election and sovereignty. Imperial authority is increasingly elevated from juridical power to theological legitimation, from the constitutional to the monarchical, from the functionary-emperor to the god-emperor.[10] The emperor's postmortem apotheosis looks back over his reign in part to recognize his special standing with the gods demonstrated in his achievements, and partly to begin and/or continue (depending on where one is located) a process of honoring him through temples, priesthood, ritual, statues, and coins,[11] thereby creating a new status for the emperor.[12]

Five of the first-century emperors received apotheosis from the senate (Augustus, Claudius, Vespasian, Titus, Nerva), signified by the term *divus*, while Tiberius, Gaius Caligula, Nero, and Domitian were not so recognized.[13] Gradel explains: "It was the Roman state who deified a *Divus* by ritual action, . . . senatorial decree,"[14] and granting the term *divus*.[15] "The actual ritual of apotheosis at the funeral of an emperor involved the sending off of an eagle from his pyre to take his worthy soul to heaven. . . . Eternal life awaited the emperor . . . in heaven [and] in the memory of those left on earth, who by deifying the late majesty and establishing a permanent cult in his honor promised eternal remembrance."[16] For Price, the apotheosis process was "deliberately ambivalent" in holding together worship of the emperor with dependence on the Senate in granting it by decree.[17] The pervasiveness of the practice and its special association with the emperors is attested by the second-century altar dedicated to the Antonine emperors in Ephesus, which depicts the apotheosis of Trajan and his wife, Plotina.[18]

From this context emerge the questions to be considered in this chapter. What happens in the intertextuality between claims of Jesus' translation into heaven to be with God and claims about numerous humans, especially Roman emperors, becoming gods postmortem? Is it a matter of imperial negotiation by imitation and assimilation to its context ("one more just like them"), or do claims about Jesus' apotheosis interact with claims of imperial apotheosis by contesting them and asserting Jesus to be "greater than" the emperors? Or are there several diverse interactions involving at least imitation and challenge? And what are the implications for the lives of Jesus-believers in late first-century Ephesus?[19]

Again, my interest is in the cultural intertextuality created by the interaction of the Gospel's accounts of Jesus' resurrection and return to the Father with this tradition of apotheosis, especially as it was connected with the Roman emperors. I am not arguing, for instance, that apotheosis traditions were the source of John's emphasis on Jesus' ascent to the Father. My argument is that when the Gospel's emphasis on Jesus' return to the Father interacts with this tradition of apotheosis, it ironically locates the one who was crucified by the empire as a provincial kingly/imperial pretender among the empire's great men—as being even greater. Yet the Gospel evokes apotheosis only, finally, to reject it, whether of emperors or Moses, thereby distancing Jesus from it by elevating him alone.

The Gospel seems to deny credibility to imperial apotheosis by its claim that only one has ascended (3:13), by its rejection of any attempts to make oneself a god or to let oneself be made a god (5:19; 10:33), and by its related presentation of Jesus' exclusive revelatory relationship with God "in the beginning" (1:1). His antiquity is his authority. Jesus returns to "the only true God" (5:44–45; 17:3), from whom he originated. Only one has descended from God to make God known (1:18; 3:13). Only one—Jesus—returns to the one from whom he came and by whom he was sent (13:1–3). Moreover, Jesus' "apotheosis" is framed by his resurrection. This tradition of God's justice-doing and transformative work among humans is not good news for empires.

This process of identification with, yet negation of, apotheosis traditions continues the Gospel's rhetoric of distance that endeavors to separate Jesus-believers from the imperial world (even while the Gospel imitates that world), disclosing it to be a world of false and self-made gods not worthy of honor, a world that is not Jesus' permanent home, that opposes him, from which Jesus is taken, and to which he will return only to take believers from it (14:2–3). If Jesus is in tension with this world and not accommodated to it, Jesus-believers must follow suit. The starting point will be to elaborate some examples of apotheosis, and then I will delineate some of John's interaction with it.

Greek and Roman Traditions

The Apotheosis of Romulus

Traditions about the apotheosis of Romulus, Rome's legendary founder, take various forms.[20] Plutarch's account is roughly contemporary with John's Gospel and gives some indication of Greek knowledge of these traditions in the East. Price argues that the apotheosis of Romulus is one of the models for imperial apotheosis.[21]

The setting for Plutarch's account of the apotheosis of Romulus involves some suspicion toward the elite because Romulus had given land to his soldiers, and the senate had felt insulted. "Unaccountably a short time after, he disappeared on the Nones of July," and suspicions arose that the elite had murdered him (Plutarch, *Lives: Romulus* 27.2, 5). The account of Romulus's apotheosis provided an alternative explanation for his absence. Plutarch presents the apotheosis as occurring during a gathering that involved king Romulus with the elite and crowds, outside Rome. Romulus disappears at a time when

> strange and unaccountable disorders with incredible changes filled the air; the light of the sun failed and night came down upon them, not with peace and quiet

but with the awful peals of thunder and furious blasts of driving rain from every quarter, during which the multitude dispersed and fled, but the nobles gathered closely together.... After the storm passed, the crowd reassembled and anxiously sought their king, [yet] the nobles would not suffer them to inquire into his disappearance ... but exhorted them all to honor and revere Romulus, since he had been caught up into heaven, and was to be a benevolent god for them instead of a good king. The multitude, accordingly, believing this and rejoicing in it, went away to worship him. (27.6–8)

Plutarch does not describe the mode of his being "caught up into heaven." Suspicions about a possible murder continued, and some alleged that the elite were "imposing a silly tale upon the people" to cover up their murder. Subsequently "a trusted and intimate friend also of Romulus himself" named Julius Proculus swears that

as he was traveling on the road, he had seen Romulus coming to meet him, fair and stately to the eye as never before, and arrayed in bright and shining armor. He himself, then, affrighted at the sight had said, "O king [Romulus], what possessed you, or what purpose had you, that you have left us patricians prey to unjust and wicked accusations, and the whole city without end at the loss of its father?" Whereupon Romulus had replied: "It was the pleasure of the gods, O Proculus, from whom I came, that I should be with [hu]mankind only a short time, and that after founding a city destined to be the greatest on earth for empire and glory, I should dwell again in heaven. So farewell, and tell the Romans that if they practice self-restraint and add to it valor, they will reach the utmost heights of human power. And I will be your propitious deity, Quirinus. (28.1–3)

Plutarch's Romulus attests the will of the gods in commissioning his time on earth, his mission, and his return ("dwell again") to the gods. Proculus's testimony allayed all fears that something untoward had happened, and everyone prayed to Romulus-Quirinus "as a god." Plutarch goes on to give some more examples of apotheosis in which people "improbably ascribe divinity to the mortal features in human nature." Rather, he argues, we should understand that bodies die but "an image of life ... comes from the gods and to them it returns" without a body. "Virtues and souls" ascend to the gods when they are "freed from mortality and sense" (28.6–8).

Five things should be noted here about Romulus's apotheosis or being "caught up" into heaven. First, the event has a cosmic setting attesting the involvement of the gods in enacting their "pleasure" that Romulus return to heaven from whence he had come. The will of the gods is emphasized by the storm and by Romulus's explanation to Julius Proculus.

Second, the people are instructed to honor him as a god, thereby interpreting his removal as an apotheosis and ensuring proper recognition of one who has been made a god. Absent from this account, but much more prominent in imperial apotheosis narratives, is any role for an elite decree authorizing Romulus's apotheosis. The instruction to worship him seems to fulfill something of this authorizing role, though in a less formalized way. Apotheosis is not only an event of heavenly elevation but also part of an ongoing process as mortals on earth render honor to the elevated figure.

Third, the scene explains Romulus's absence as the will of the gods. The role of Julius Proculus is crucial. He represents the people, both elite and nonelite, in asking the temporarily descended, recently apotheosized Romulus the question that all want answered about his absence. The now deified but descended Romulus explains that his physical absence does not mean his retreat from the people. He continues to be involved with them as a benevolent presence or a "propitious deity." But this blessing requires the people's virtue: their self-restraint and valor in continuing Romulus's divinely sanctioned mission. Julius Proculus fulfills a role that seems to be quite important in debates about the apotheosis of Julius Caesar and of Augustus, as a witness to Romulus's ascent into the heavens. Subsequently, this role of witness becomes choreographed in relation to the emperors. As their bodies are burned, an eagle is released to represent the ascending soul.

Fourth, having been summoned by the gods, Romulus offers exhortation and instruction to the people on how to live. They are to lead virtuous lives so that they can further Rome's power. Now that he is a god and among the gods, these words bear the authority of divine exhortation. Livy's account also has Romulus speak words of exhortation (1.16). He emphasizes Rome's world-dominant status but underlines prowess in war and Rome's unassailable power.

And fifth, in relation to John's Gospel, we see that Romulus appears to Julius Proculus after his apotheosis. He is presented as having come from the gods, to be on earth for a short time, and now to return to them.[22]

The Apotheosis of Julius Caesar

After Caesar's murder and funeral, in which his body was burned, his divinization was not certain even though decrees in 45 and 44 BCE "were intended to create a cult for Caesar."[23] His adopted son and heir Octavian/Augustus advocated it against its opponents such as Antony and organized games to honor Julius. Propitiously, a comet appeared for the seven days of the games. Octavian and others who had witnessed it interpreted the comet to be a sign of Caesar's soul in the heavens.

> [He] was numbered among the gods, not only by formal decree but also in the conviction of the common people. For at the first of the games which his heir Augustus gave in honor of his apotheosis, a comet shone for seven successive days, rising about the eleventh hour, and was believed to be the soul of Caesar, who had been taken to heaven; and this is why a star is set upon the crown of his head in his statue. (Suetonius, *Deified Julius* 88; also Dio Cassius 45.7.1)

Pliny the Elder also reports the understanding that

> the common people believed that this star signified the soul of Caesar received among the spirits of the immortal gods, and on this account the emblem of a star was added to the bust of Caesar that we shortly afterward dedicated in the forum. . . . [But Pliny also recognizes a different significance for the comet.] His late

Majesty Augustus had deemed this comet very propitious to himself; as it had appeared at the beginning of his rule; . . . privately he rejoiced because he interpreted the comet as having been born for his sake and as containing his own birth within it; and to confess the truth, it did have a health-giving influence over the world. (Pliny, *Nat.* 2.94)

Virgil also emphasized its beneficial properties in interpreting the comet to mean abundance in the fields of corn and grapes, the start of a new age or saeculum (*Ecl.* 9.47–49), which Horace and others linked to Augustus (on eternal life, see chap. 8 above).

Ovid's version is somewhat different. He links the apotheosis with the immediate circumstances of Caesar's death and explains the comet as the sign of Caesar's almost-immediate transformation to astral immortality. He recognizes Caesar's apotheosis as the will of Jupiter, who declares, "[It is time that] as a god he [Caesar] may enter heaven." Venus catches up Caesar's soul from his body as it lies in the senate house (*before* its cremation) and bears it "toward the stars of heaven. . . . Higher than the moon it mounted up and, leaving behind it a fiery train, gleamed as a star" (*Metam.* 15.818, 846–849). His soul thus leaves his dead body before cremation and undergoes further transformation as he ascends into the stars.

Ovid's account of Caesar's apotheosis also includes prophecies concerning his heir Augustus's reign. Augustus will rule earth as "sire and ruler" while Jupiter rules heaven. After he has established sway over land and sea, established peace, promoted the laws, and established his succession through Tiberius, then Augustus's own apotheosis will take place when he "shall mount to heaven, . . . attain the heavenly seats and his related stars, . . . and there, removed from our presence, listen to our prayers" (15.832–839, 858–870). Apotheosis honors the one elevated, but his successor is also honored as "son of a god." Caesar "must be made a god" so that Augustus is not "born of mortal seed" (15.760–761).

The Apotheosis of Augustus

When Augustus died in 14 CE, there was little hesitation about his divinization.[24] After eulogies by Tiberius and Drusus,

he was carried on the shoulders of senators to the Campus Martius and there cremated. There was even an ex-praetor who took oath that he had seen the form of the emperor, after he had been reduced to ashes, on its way to heaven. (Suetonius, *Deified Aug.* 100.4)

Augustus's widow, Livia, rewarded the ex-praetor Numerius Atticus for his testimony with a million sesterces (Dio Cassius 56.46.1–2). While Suetonius does not specify what form this vision took, Dio Cassius attests the release of an eagle "appearing to bear his spirit to heaven" (56.42.3).[25] A temple dedication in Campania recites the theme familiar in Augustan poets that Augustus will "return to your seat in heaven," implying that he has returned to the gods, from whence he came.[26] Tacitus does not seem so impressed. "His funeral ran the ordinary course; and a decree followed, endowing him with a temple and divine rites. Then all prayers were directed toward Tiberius" (*Ann.* 1.10–11). Tiberius the living emperor seems to have, for Tacitus at least, more power than Augustus the deified emperor! Gradel emphasizes the relative powerlessness of *divus* emperors. No particular area of influence was assigned to them, and there is little evidence of their interventions.[27] "At Augustus's death his power vanished; . . . dead men were not dangerous."[28] Gradel's claim receives some support from a comment that Dio Cassius attributes to the emperor Titus: "As for the emperors who are dead and gone, they will avenge themselves in case anyone does them a wrong, if in very truth they are demigods and possess any power" (67.19.2).

The Apotheosis of Titus

Shortly after the emperor Titus's death in 81 CE, his brother and successor, Domitian, deified Titus (Suetonius, *Dom.* 2.3; Dio Cassius 67.2.6). Domitian completed a temple dedicated to both his father, Vespasian (also deified[29]), and to Titus, and a temple dedicated to the Flavians (Statius, *Silvae* 4.3.18–19; 5.1.239–241; Martial, *Epig.* 9.1.6–10; 9.34).[30] He also dedicated an arch to Titus that commemorated his victory over Judea and the destruction of Jerusalem and its temple in 70 CE. Panels depicted scenes from his triumphal celebration in Rome in 71, including booty from the temple and Titus crowned by the goddess Victoria in a chariot led by the goddess Roma. Another panel depicts the apotheosis of Titus. In the center is Titus, or at least his head and shoulders, his most prominent features. In the foreground is a large eagle with wings spread, and Titus straddling it. Not only is the eagle a conventional symbol of Roman imperial power;[31] it also became the common means of transporting, or at least representing the transporting, of the emperor's soul into the heavens. Scott describes the eagle (often found on coins) as "one of the most common indications of apotheosis."[32] In this relief,[33] the eagle does not soar above the dead Titus to depict his ascending soul, but bears his whole body into the heavens. This act resembles the apotheosis of Romulus, who is removed bodily into the heavens. But it is not typical of the usual imperial scenarios, in which the soul ascends from the cremated body.

Criticisms of Apotheosis

While apotheosis had a long history and was by the end of the first century, the time of the writing of John's Gospel, increasingly accepted as an appropriate way of honoring an emperor, there was by no means universal consent for the practice. The above traditions carry indications of some skepticism. Some of the people think the elite have murdered Romulus; others think that claims of his apotheosis are "a silly tale" (so Plutarch). Julius Caesar's destiny is not clear until the comet appears. Tacitus thinks there is more point in praying to the living Tiberius rather than the apotheosized Augustus. Several brief examples from around the time of John's Gospel indicate further reserve about the practice, debate about an appropriate basis for it, and criticism of previous decisions to grant apotheosis.

First is the enigmatic comment that Suetonius attributes to Vespasian (Suetonius, *Deified Vesp.* 23). Suetonius observes that Vespasian often "resorted to witticisms" and offers four short examples. Suetonius comments that Vespasian "did not cease his jokes even when in apprehension of death" and gives three examples, one of which comprises a comment about apotheosis: "As death drew near, he said: 'Woe's me. Methinks I'm turning into a god.'" Whatever the veracity of the remark, it is not clear whether it reflects Vespasian's incredulity, serious rejection of the notion, embarrassment, innocuous levity, or fear of death (if people joke about that which matters), the criticism of opponents, or the particular association of *divus* status with death.[34]

Second, a comment by Pliny the Younger in his address to the emperor Trajan is less ambiguous in questioning the motives of emperors for ensuring the apotheosis of previous emperors.[35]

> Tiberius deified Augustus, but his purpose was to introduce the charge of high treason; Nero had done the same thing for Claudius in a spirit of mockery; Titus had similarly honored Vespasian, and Domitian [deified] Titus, but only for one to be thought the son and the other the brother of a god. (*Pan.* 11.1)

Pliny's examples involve four of the five emperors who received apotheosis in the first century! He certainly attests the value that apotheosis bestows on an heir and descendant: the following emperor becomes a son of a god.[36] But he also raises questions about the self-benefiting motives for each apotheosis on the part of successive emperors and the competency of the senate in approving them. Does Pliny thereby cynically disqualify the whole practice? Not quite. He goes on to approve of Trajan's action in deifying Nerva (emperor 96–98) and seems to anticipate the apotheosis of Trajan himself (89.2):

> You gave your father his place among the stars with no thought of terrorizing your subjects, of bringing the gods into disrepute, or of gaining reflected glory, but simply because you thought he was a god. (11.2)

Pliny commends Trajan for the genuineness of his belief in Nerva's worthiness, without saying how Trajan was led to it and without explicitly claiming that he was led to it by Nerva's wise and astute rule. It may seem, then, that Pliny repeats the mistake of those emperors that he criticizes. He makes apotheosis about the one or ones doing the act rather than about the quality of the one being apotheosized.

But subsequently, and not surprisingly, he recognizes the important role of virtue in apotheosis, at least as it involves Trajan. An emperor has to rule well to receive apotheosis at death.[37] According to Pliny, he has to pass the "virtue test." Pliny notices that "the divine Titus . . . had taken measures for our security and need for vengeance, and because of this was placed among the gods; but how much more will you [Trajan] one day deserve your seat in heaven, for all your additions to those measures for which we recognized his godhead" (35.4). And he commends Nerva for his wisdom in adopting Trajan as his successor, a virtuous act that by itself deserves apotheosis. Honoring Nerva was the right thing to do since Trajan "created and proved his [Nerva's] godhead still more by being the man you are. For there is no more certain proof of divinity in a ruler who has chosen his successor before he meets his end than the worthiness of his choice" (11.3). Just why Pliny does not apply this argument to Augustus or Vespasian, for instance, is not clear, though, of course, Pliny has vested interests in singing Trajan's merits.

Third, Seneca's attack on the apotheosis of Claudius elaborates this debate about the virtue "test." By contrast, Suetonius makes a brief reference to Claudius's apotheosis.

> He was buried with regal pomp and enrolled among the gods, an honor neglected and finally annulled by Nero, but later restored to him by Vespasian. (Suetonius, *Deified Claudius* 45)

Seneca, however, was neither so impressed nor so brief in his treatment of Claudius.[38] He begins his satirical account, the *Apocolocyntosis* [*Pumpkinification*] *of Claudius*, with a cynical discussion of the sources who might attest Claudius's apotheosis. Livius Geminius is the witness for the events of October 13, 54 CE, when Claudius died. He was an experienced apotheosis witness, having sworn previously that he saw Julia Drusilla, sister of emperor Gaius Caligula, ascend into the heavens when she died in 38 CE and was divinized at Caligula's insistence over fifteen years previously (*Apocol.* 1). The skeptical tone is also set in the opening sections with much abuse for Claudius as an "imperial dunce," who as he dies fears that he has messed himself just as he makes a mess of everything (4).

As Claudius gets to heaven and has to identify himself, he mumbles. Jupiter and Hercules do not recognize him, a comment that seriously undercuts any divine sanction for Claudius's rule. None of the gods knows if he is a Roman or a Greek. Seneca mocks his physical appearance and learning (5). Then in a scene whereby heaven parallels earth, the gods meet as a copy of the Roman senate to debate what to do with Claudius and whether to make him a god (8–11). Augustus, who has not said a word since he was made a god (*deus factus sum*; 10)—so much for the power of a divinized emperor—attacks Claudius as unworthy to be made a god (*deum facere*; 11). He proposes that because of Claudius's murders of various family members and unjust administration of "justice," Claudius should be banished from heaven and not made a god. Though there is division, the motion is approved. Mercury has the task of returning Claudius to earth. They descend to view Claudius's funeral, which is marked by "joy and rejoicing on every side, the Roman people walking about like free men" (12). Claudius is taken to the lower regions (13) and tried for killing 35 senators and 221 equestrians and "others as the sands and dust for multitude" (14). He is found guilty, though the judge hears only one side of the argument, as Claudius did in trials before him! He is sentenced to the futility of "rattling dice forever in a box with holes in the bottom," and Caligula makes him a slave.

Seneca's enigmatic and witty work has been variously understood as an attack on any granting of apotheosis, as an attack directed specifically against Claudius,[39] or in Gradel's view, a burlesque that positively recognizes and underlines the relative roles of humans and the gods in the process of apotheosis. Gradel argues that "the actual rites and rulings of the Roman state in making a god of Claudius are hardly touched on. . . . Humans can . . . elevate a man to heaven; only the gods, however, decide if he will actually be admitted." Seneca does not attack the rituals and decree of the senate because these matter the most in creating a god of the Roman state.[40] But whether the elevated one was actually admitted to heaven was the gods' concern. For Seneca, admission is a matter of the quality of the emperor's reign. Claudius is incompetent, unjust in administering justice, and a violent murderer of opponents. The gods cannot admit him because he did not show virtue in his reign. The model is Augustus, who delivers the speech that causes the gods to vote to reject Claudius, whereby he enters not heaven but the underworld and becomes not a god but a slave. This action, though, does not invalidate the senate's decision or the ritual, according to Gradel. Both Hercules, who supports his admission, and Augustus, who opposes it, call him *divus*, thereby recognizing the senate's decree and ritual (*Apocol.* 9.5; 10.4). Nevertheless, there is a clear message for Nero and subsequent emperors about the need for virtuous rule. Entry to the gods is earned by way of virtue.

These examples indicate some ambivalence about claiming apotheosis as well as some debate about granting it. It is quite difficult to ascertain how extensive such ambivalence and debate might have been among elites and nonelites, provincials and inhabitants of Rome.

The Apotheosis of Moses

Before engaging John's emphasis on Jesus' return or ascent to the Father, we need to recognize that apotheosis was not only a Greek and Roman phenomenon; a form of it—elevation to be with God a way of recognizing a hero's elevated status—is also attested in Jewish traditions.[41] According to the Septuagint, Enoch, being pleasing to God, does not experience death, but "he was not found because God had transported him" (Gen 5:24). Elijah is caught up into heaven in a chariot in a whirlwind (2 Kings 2:1–12). In his late first-century CE representations of these scenes, Josephus says that Enoch "returned to the divinity" (*Ant.* 1.85). He uses the same phrase for the virtuous Moses, who disappears in a cloud (4.326). When Moses is delayed on Sinai, some think he has been killed by wild beasts while others think it more likely that he has "returned to the deity" (same phrase) and been "translated by God to himself" (3.96–97). Josephus also links Enoch and Elijah, who "became invisible, and no one knows of their death" (9.28). In the sheep allegory of *1 Enoch* 89:52, written some time previous to Josephus, Enoch sees Elijah ascending to heaven to meet him.

Perhaps the most important text is Philo's account of the apotheosis of Moses: Moses, already named a partner with God and "god and king" during his lifetime (*Moses*, 1:155–58), comes to participate in and share divine attributes and nature.[42]

> Afterward the time came when he had to make his pilgrimage from earth to heaven, and leave this mortal life for immortality, summoned thither by the Father, who resolved his twofold nature of soul and body into a single unity, transforming his whole being into mind, pure as the sunlight. (Philo, *Mos.* 2.288)

Much of Philo's account is concerned with Moses' last-minute "very fitting" and "wonderful" prophecies "to each tribe" (2.288–289). But even better were his prophecies concerning his own death:

But most wonderful of all, . . . for when he was already being exalted [lit., "being taken up," ἀναλαμβανόμενος, *analambanomenos*) and stood at the very barrier, ready at the signal to direct his upward flight to heaven, the divine spirit fell upon him, and he prophesied with discernment while still alive the story of his own death. (2.290)

The story of his death included his burial "with none present, surely by no mortal hands but by immortal powers" in keeping with the biblical declaration that "no one knows his burial place to this day" (Deut 34:6). Instead of a known tomb, he has "a monument of special dignity" (*Mos.* 2.291).

As with the imperial traditions, Moses travels from earth to heaven, from mortality to immortality. Similarly, this translation is understood as the divine will. It involves a recognition of his special virtue in serving God. It includes the removal or at least transformation of the body as it is resolved into the unity of the "mind." And his life is marked by a large monument. Unlike a number of the accounts concerning Roman figures and emperors (Romulus, Julius Caesar), there are no witnesses and nor are there practices of worshipping Moses.

John's Jesus Going Up

In the previous section I have outlined some of the traditions surrounding apotheosis in Jewish, Greek, and Roman circles in the first century. Given the long history of apotheosis in the East, the eastern origin and Greek identity of some of the writers discussed, and the artwork on the Ephesian altar of the Antonines, constructed in the mid-second century and depicting the apotheosis of the emperor Trajan and his wife, Plotina—the phenomenon of apotheosis was well known in Ephesus in the late first century. How does the intertextuality between these apotheosis traditions and John's presentation of Jesus' ascent or return to the Father contribute to the imperial negotiation undertaken by John's Jesus-believers? There certainly are significant differences between Jesus' ascension (asserted but never described in the Gospel) and these accounts of imperial ascension. Jesus has no funeral pyre, no vote by the senate, no witnesses (to his ascension), no eaglelike ascent. He does experience a somatic resurrection, which the emperors do not. These are, though, differences of detail that do not undercut the fundamental similarity of a postmortem, honoring, vindicating ascent to be God/one of the gods and with God/with the gods that has implications not only for the emperor/Jesus but also for his subjects/believers. In this section I will explore the cultural intertextuality between these imperial apotheosis traditions and John's pervasive references to Jesus' return through crucifixion and resurrection to the Father. What happens in this interface of ascension stories? I will identify four dimensions of the imperial negotiation.

Ironic Glory by Association

One aspect of the intertextuality is to draw Jesus and the emperors together. The tradition of apotheosis honors the great. It recognizes those who have made immense contributions to the imperial cause. It elevates heroes like Romulus, the city's founder; Julius Caesar; Augustus, who restored the republic; and subsequent emperors Claudius, Vespasian, Titus, and Nerva. Seneca and Pliny the Younger want to debate the nature and extent of the emperors' contribution, emphasizing the need for virtuous rule and rejecting the notion that apotheosis should function only to serve the interests of those advocating its bestowal. But in advocating the "virtue" test, they do not question but rather emphasize the link between greatness and apotheosis. The same connection with greatness or virtue is evident in Philo's presentation of Moses' apotheosis. Apotheosis is not an honor for everyone. Unworthy emperors and nonelites do not ascend into the heavens.

The postmortem ascent of Jesus to God associates him with these great men. The Gospel conforms to this imperial pattern in elevating him to heaven. He is a king or emperor, as the term *basileus* can be translated (18:33; 19:19–22). He has an empire (18:36, βασιλεία, *basileia*). He has followers (18:36). He overcomes the ruler of the world (14:30) and claims ultimate power over Pilate as Rome's representative (19:11). He performs authenticating signs, just as emperors like Vespasian did, to confirm his divinely sanctioned status (2:11; 4:54; etc.) He exercises "ruling" functions of bestowing life and judging (5:21–22). He is the agent of God (5:19), doing the divine will and exercising sovereignty on God's behalf (4:34). He is "Savior of the world" (4:42). He prophecies future events after his death (16:2). As he is about to ascend, he gives his subjects/believers last minute instructions (17:18; 20:21; 21:15–23).

The irony concerns Jesus' route to heaven through crucifixion. Jesus is the one crucified by the empire, the one who experiences an ignominious death reserved for low-status provincials and criminals. His revelation of life (see chap. 8 above) collided with and challenged the structures and practices of these imperial agents. He announced judgment on the empire, and the empire always fights back. They remove him by crucifixion, employing a method that identifies him with the despised, the expedient, the powerless, the dishonored. His crucifixion, though, is ironically part of his ascent, the opportunity for a display of God's life-giving power that outpowers the empire. Yet in this ascent into heaven and return to the Father, he is elevated in the same way as the greats. He is honored in his ascent.

Apotheosis Democratized

There is a further ironic element. Whereas imperial apotheosis maintained and secured the division between the elite of the elite and the rest because it happens only to the select few and great, Jesus' apotheosis not only identifies him with the great but also democratizes apotheosis. John's Jesus declares that he departs to the Father to prepare a place for Jesus-believers (14:2), and that he will return (14:28) and take Jesus-believers to be with himself, so that where Jesus is, there Jesus-believers are also (14:3). This is not to suggest that Jesus-believers become God but it does mean they participate in the intimate relationship between God and Jesus (14:20). Apotheosis is no longer the preserve of only the great. It does not function to maintain the division of the great from the common, the elite from the nonelite. For John, the notion is modified in that it is not primarily about elevation above all others but the inclusion of others—Jesus-believers—by drawing them into the intimate loving relationship of life that Father and Son share. "Apotheosis" is democratized and ecclesiastical.

Apotheosis and Blessings

The Gospel also distances Jesus' elevation from the apotheosis of emperors in terms of differences in impact. The emperors die, the senate votes, their bodies are cremated, their souls are released, and they ascend from whence they are to bless the imperial world. Apotheosis not only honors the deceased emperor; it also ensures that the divinized emperor blesses the people. Romulus assures Proculus that he is a "propitious god." Augustus will listen to prayers.

The Gospel again imitates while it discounts. Jesus blesses disciples, but it is not with increase in empire. Jesus bestows peace—not Pax Romana, built on subjugation, compliance, and the transfer of resources to the elite—but the peace or wholeness of life in relation to God's just purposes (14:27). After his ascent, Jesus listens to prayers (14:13–14; 16:23–24) and he blesses believers by sending the Paraclete to be with disciples (14:16), to teach them and remind them of Jesus' teaching so as to sustain their alternative way of life and continue Jesus' ministry (15:26). All of this is framed in the context of the Prologue's declaration that God and Jesus, not the emperors, have made all things and bestow life (1:1–4; 5:21).

Transformation

Jesus is distanced from the emperors in another way. Apotheosis serves to maintain and sanction the imperial order. Deified emperors epitomize the hierarchical structure that pervades the empire, stretching the hierarchy from earth to heaven. Deified emperors sanction and bless the status quo. The temples, rituals, and priesthoods that accompany apotheosis ensure ongoing honor from their former subjects, thereby maintaining their deference to the ruling elite. The Gospel, though, presents Jesus as God's agent, who seeks its transformation through the offer of life. Jesus' ascension to the Father is placed in two contexts of transformation.

The first context of transformation is his ministry. As I have argued, his words and works reveal the life-giving purposes of God, which form an alternative community or antisociety (1:35–51; chaps. 13–17), bring fertility (2:1–11), feed the hungry (6:1–14; 21:1–15), heal the sick (4:46–54; 5:1–18; etc.), and raise the dead (11:38–44). As I outlined in chapter 10 (above), Jesus teaches the continuation of this ministry by Jesus-believers in their greater works (14:12) and through practices of self-giving love and seeking the good, not the goods, of the other (13:12–20, 34–35). His ministry offers a different understanding and experience of human society. In these transformative actions and teaching, he repairs and rolls back imperial damage. According to the Gospel's world, where the greatest good is to do the will of God (1:13; 4:34), Jesus passes the virtue test that Seneca and Pliny think so important, though in this case one person's virtue is another's treason. He also passes the power test that Tacitus thinks Augustus fails and about which Dio Cassius's Titus has grave (!) doubts.

And second, Jesus' ascension is placed in the context of somatic resurrection. The risen Jesus tells Mary that he is "ascending to my Father and your Father" (20:17). In chapter 8 (above) I discussed the cluster of eschatological motifs evident in the Gospel, to which its offer of "life of the age" belongs. From that discussion it is sufficient to recall the emergence of somatic resurrection expectations in contexts of imperial oppression as expressions of the assurance of God's justice-bringing work (2 Macc 7; John 20–21). Resurrection means restoration and transformation, not just of individuals but also of God's world and human communities. It signifies the end of imperial power and imperial damage and the establishment of God's life-giving and just purposes. The beginning of that end, says John, is underway in Jesus' ministry, including his somatic resurrection. He embodies the victory of "life of the age" over the death-dealing world of empire. In evoking apotheosis traditions and even in imitating them, the Gospel also challenges them with the claim that this is not an imperially blessed world. The ascent of Jesus belongs to a process, already under way, of rectifying that situation.

Apotheosis and Antiquity

Twice in John's Gospel, Jesus is accused of making himself God, equal to God or son of God (5:18; 10:33; 19:7). I have discussed this claim previously in chapter 4 (above) and will take it up further in the appendix in relation to Gaius Caligula's attempts to make himself god, so I will not repeat that material here. It is sufficient to note from that discussion that "making oneself (equal to) God" involves issues of power, honor, beneficial rule, imitation, and agency. These five aspects are clearly evident, for example, in Philo's and Josephus's attacks on Gaius Caligula's attempt to make himself a god.

- In relation to Gaius's power, both Philo and Josephus detail Gaius mocking the governor Petronius for not having learned to acknowledge the emperor's ultimate power by obeying his commands (Philo, *Emb.* 255–256; Josephus, *Ant.* 18.304). Josephus sees Gaius's aspirations emerge in relation to his imperial power: "But as time went on, he ceased to think of himself as a man and . . . imagined himself as a god because of the greatness of his empire" (*Ant.* 18.256).

- Gaius's desire to be worshipped as a god is about honor. He is honored in various cities and nations such as Alexandria, but not in Jerusalem or from Jews (Philo, *Emb.* 116, 338). "He wished to be considered a god and to be hailed as such" (Josephus, *J.W.* 184). To refuse statues and worship is to dishonor him, "amounting almost to rebellion, aggravated by insult" (*J.W.* 2.194).

- Third, his divine status is about beneficial rule. Philo describes Gaius at the beginning of his reign as a benefactor who oversees the "good of the empire" (*Emb.* 22). Gaius's approach to being emperor is "that whatever he wishes is beneficial and that what he has once decreed is as good as accomplished" (218).

- Fourth, becoming a god is about imitating the gods. Philo, though, mocks Gaius in this regard. In his parody of Gaius's ascent into the ranks of the divine through the demigods to the great gods (*Emb.* 74–114), Philo constantly complains that

Gaius does not imitate their virtues and so shows himself to be fake. Gaius's actions, in contrast to theirs, damage human well-being instead of benefiting it (e.g., 81–92, 98, 101–102, 114, etc.). People marvel "at the strange contradiction" that Gaius's actions "were the opposite of those whose honors he purposes to share as their equal" (ἰσότιμος, *isotimos*, 98). "Gaius has no right to be likened to any of the gods or demigods either, for his nature, his substance, his purpose in life, is different from theirs" (114). Gaius fails the virtue test.

- Fifth, becoming a god is about being agents of the gods. But Gaius, according to Josephus and Philo in the comments above, is self-made in seeking divine status. He is an agent of his own agenda.

Interestingly, these elements that make one a god—power, honor, beneficial rule, imitation, and agency—are present in John 5 and 10 as Jesus responds to the charges of making himself equal to God (5:18) and God (10:33). Jesus is the Father's agent (10:25). He has the power to bestow life (10:28). He shares in and manifests the Father's unassailable power (10:28–29, 32). The Father and the Son receive honor (5:23; 10:32, 38). Both God and the Son are benefactors in giving life (John 5:21, 24; 10:28, 32). Jesus imitates God in his works (5:19; 10:30, 32, 37). Jesus is sent from the Father (10:32, 36, consecrated and sent as God's Son or agent). He is one with the Father in receiving honor, exercising power, exerting benefaction, imitating the Father, and being the Father's agent (10:30, 38).

Jesus does not "make himself" the things that he is accused of being; he is these things by virtue of his origin with God and what God has entrusted to him. The language of "making himself" has particular force in relation to the apotheosis traditions in which the senate by decree and the people by consensual participation make a god. It is especially prevalent in Seneca's *Apocolocyntosis* when Augustus repeatedly speaks in these terms, as noted above. What is its force in the intertextuality of Jesus' ascension and these imperial apotheosis traditions?

One could argue that Jesus makes himself nothing and is not made anything by anyone. Contrary to the ritual for apotheosizing an emperor, there is no vote on Jesus' status, no witnesses to offer proof, no ritual to effect the transformation. The Gospel is adamant that Jesus *is* God from the beginning: "The Word was with God, and the Word was God (1:1). Likewise it presents Jesus as God *before* he ascends into the heavens. Thomas responds to the risen Jesus, "My Lord and my God" (20:28). His ascent does not transform him, does not make him into something he was not. This is true, but it would not be accurate to present this emphasis as an imperial counterdistinctive since emperors were commonly, though not ubiquitously or exclusively, recognized to be gods during their lifetime, especially in the East, and their apotheosis, as with Augustus, was understood as a return to the gods from whence they came. And Philo says the very virtuous and to be apotheosized Moses was named "god and king of the whole nation" during his lifetime (*Mos.* 1.158). In this dimension, imitation of or similarity to imperial claims seems to be more at work than a contesting of them.

Perhaps the force of the intertextuality concerns whether such claims are true, whether in fact humans are made gods. Is Jesus one more god among many? Especially important for John seems to be claims of exclusivity or monotheism. The Gospel identifies God as "the only God" (5:44) and the "only true God" (17:3), terms that evoke both the anti-idolatry and antipolytheistic traditions of Isaiah 37:14–20 and of the Decalogue in Exodus 20:3–4.[43] There are not two Gods since, as consistent with wisdom traditions, Jesus is the revelation of the will, words, and works of God (4:34; 5:30, 36; 14:10), and one with God (10:30), in whom God is encountered and known (14:7, 9). There is one God, and only one Son of God (1:18; 3:16), recalling from the discussion in chapter 7 (above) that "Son of God" interfaces with imperial claims for emperors as descendents of divinized emperors. And there is only one revealer of the one God. Only this Son has "made him known" (1:18), and only this one who descended from heaven "has ascended into heaven" (3:13); and certainly not Moses as Philo maintains. Such exclusive and excluding claims indicate no room for any other gods. The interface with the traditions of imperial apotheosis suggests that John disqualifies such claims. Jesus is not just "greater than" because there are no competitors, as far as the Gospel is concerned. Jesus is unique. Despite the imperial claims, emperors are not apotheosized; they do not become gods; not even the virtuous ones become gods.

Such a rejection can be contextualized by some of the above comments on the apotheosis traditions. Apotheosis is a "silly tale," say some in Plutarch's account of Romulus. Tacitus thinks the living emperor Tiberius has more power than the apotheosized Augustus. Titus, according to Dio Cassius, seems unsure if they are in the heavens and, if so, whether they have any power. Between them, Seneca and Pliny think four of the five apotheosized emperors in the first century were not worthy. And Seneca has Claudius excluded from heaven. These comments perhaps come close to a disqualification of the practice of imperial apotheosis, at least in specific instances if not in full.

Confirming John's evaluation are the instances that Wendy Cotter cites of scorn for and disqualification of the tradition of the apotheosis of Romulus among various Christian writers in the early centuries CE.[44] Tertullian in the mid-second century mocks the "glorious achievement" of the cowardly Aeneas, who fled the battle at Laurentum. He also disparages Romulus, "who became a god" as a murderer and a rapist and who left the empire with a legacy of violent warfare. "Therefore of course he becomes a god, and therefore a Quirinus ('god of the spear'), because then their fathers had to use the spear on his account" (Tertullian, *Ad nationes* 3.2.9).

In the third century Minucius Felix dismisses Romulus's apotheosis with a cryptic comment: "Unless perhaps you fancy that they were gods after death; as by the perjury of Proculus, Romulus became a god" (*Octavius* 4.23).

And Augustine dismisses both the credibility of the claim and scorns Rome's forcing of it upon conquered peoples. The tradition of Rome's ancestors was a "superstition" that Rome dictated "to all the nations over whom its sway extended." None of these nations believed it. "And these nations, though they might not believe that Romulus was a god, at least said so, that they might not give offense to their sovereign state by refusing to give its founder that title which was given him by Rome." At least twice more, Augustine repeats his point that the only reason states worshipped Romulus was their fear of offending powerful Rome (*City of God* 6). John's Gospel seems to anticipate such a tradition; there is only one valid apotheosis, that of Jesus.

But on what basis? Ultimately, in the Gospel's perspective, Jesus wins the virtue test (doing God's will) and the power test (Jesus gives life and judges, 5:21–22). But more important, he wins the antiquity test (see chap. 4 above). His ascent to the Father is a return to "where he was before" (6:62). This is not simply ascending to the Father (14:4–6) as Augustus returns to the gods and has his seat in heaven. Rather, the phrase takes us back to the beginning of the Gospel, to the beginning of creation, to the beginning itself. "In the beginning was the Word . . . with God, and . . . was God; . . . all things were made through him" (1:1–3). More than the virtue or the power test, the antiquity test is decisive. It provides authority and legitimacy, the means of testing other claims. There is one God "in the beginning," not an ongoing process of making new gods out of dead emperors. This antiquity test preempts the virtue test and the power test. The one who was in the beginning with God has seen the Father's works and so can do them (5:19). Virtue for John is not about furthering the empire but about doing the Father's will, which means life-giving works; this is the food that sustains creation (4:34). Herein is the power test also, the creation in which the Word participates (1:3), the life-giving works of repair in Jesus' ministry (cf. 4:48), and the greater works that disciples will do in continuing his mission (14:12). The Gospel's turn to the past, which is a turn to the beginning, is decisive in trumping claims about the emperors and about Moses.

What are the implications of this interface for John's Jesus-believers in Ephesus? The Gospel's work of negotiating the imperial order by seeking to distance overaccommodated Jesus-believers from it continues. The apotheosized emperors are revealed to be false and unworthy, illegitimate no-gods. They cannot give life. They have no power. They have no virtue because they do not do God's works. No honor is due them or their images. Honor or worship is due only to the Father (4:23–24) and to the Son as the Father's agent (5:23). Distance from the civic, trade association, and domestic observances of honoring the emperor is necessary. Perhaps some or many among Jesus-believers and in the synagogue engage in such practices as an act of social conformity or economic participation, based on a recognition that images of emperors or deities are nothing or that it is a harmless practice (cf. 1 Cor 8:4–6). Given the dualistic worldview in which the Gospel majors, and the recurrent rhetoric of distance, such participation in these rituals is not acceptable because it is too compromising.

Notes

1. The verb ἔρχομαι (*erchomai*): Jesus' opponents are not able to go where Jesus is going (7:34, 36; 8:21–22). In 13:1 the hour has come so that Jesus can depart from this world to the Father. In 13:33 he tells his disciples that he is going where they are not able to come. In the prayer of 17:11, 13, Jesus informs the "holy Father" that he is coming to him.

2. The verb πορεύομαι (*poreuomai*): Jesus' opponents are not able to go where Jesus is going (7:35–36). Jesus goes to the Father (14:28; 16:28).

3. The verb ὑπάγω (*hypagō*): Jesus goes to the one who sent him (7:33; 16:5); Jesus knows where he is going, but opponents do not (8:14, 21, 22); he departs to God (13:3); the disciples cannot go where Jesus is going (13:33, 36; 14:5); Jesus goes to the Father (14:28; 16:17).

4. For discussion of apotheosis traditions and the Synoptic Gospels, see Adela Yarbro Collins, "Apotheosis and Resurrection," in *The New Testament and Hellenistic Judaism*, ed. P. Borgen and S. Giversen (Peabody, MA: Hendrickson, 1997), 88–100 (on Mark); Carter, *Matthew and the Margins*, 553–54. Wendy Cotter, "Greco-Roman Apotheosis Traditions and the Resurrection Appearances in Matthew," in *The Gospel of Matthew in Current Study*, ed. David Aune (Grand Rapids: Eerdmans, 2001), 127–53.

5. A. Collins, "Apotheosis," 90–96, offers a brief sketch of this pervasive notion.

6. On Alexander, H. P. L'Orange, *Apotheosis in Ancient Portraiture* (New Rochelle, NY: Caratzas Brothers, 1947, 1982), 14–48; Michael Grant, *From Alexander to Cleopatra: The Hellenistic World* (New York: Charles Scribner's Sons, 1982), 95–100; for coins of Alexander and Antiochus, Larry Kreitzer, "Apotheosis of the Roman Emperor," *Biblical Archaeologist* 53 (1990): 210–17, esp. 212.

7. L'Orange, "The Hellenistic Savior-Type Invades Rome," in *Apotheosis*, 49–53, esp. 53.

8. Arnaldo Momigliano, "How the Roman Emperors Became Gods," in *On Pagans, Jews, and Christians* (Middleton, CT: Wesleyan University Press, 1987), 92–107, esp. 98.

9. Cited by Weinstock, *Divus Julius*, 296n9; Kreitzer, "Apotheosis," 212.

10. L'Orange, "The Imperial Savior-Type," in *Apotheosis*, 54–94, esp. 54. L'Orange traces the move in portraiture, artwork, and coins. See also Lily Ross Taylor, *The Divinity of the Roman Emperor* (Philadelphia: Porcupine, 1931, 1975), 243–46; Momigliano, "How the Roman Emperors," 92–107; Simon Price, "From Noble Funerals to Divine Cult: The Consecration of Roman Emperors," in *Rituals of Royalty: Power and Ceremonial in Traditional Societies*, ed. David Cannadine and Simon Price (Cambridge: Cambridge University Press, 1987), 56–105; Gradel, *Emperor Worship*, 261–371.

11. For coins, Kreitzer, "Apotheosis."

12. Gradel, *Emperor Worship*, 288–91.

13. Price ("Consecration," 57) counts apotheosis granted to 36 of the 60 emperors between Augustus and Constantine (14 CE–337 CE), and to 27 family members.

14. Gradel, *Emperor Worship*, 321.

15. Price, "Consecration," 77–87, on nomenclature, cult, and the role of the senate.

16. Gradel, *Emperor Worship*, 305.

17. Price, "Consecration," 57–58.

18. Vermeule, *Roman Imperial Art*, 109–10.

19. Gradel (*Emperor Worship*, passim) repeatedly warns against Christianizing the notion of apotheosis. My concern is with the interaction of the two traditions, not their blending, nor to explain the origins of one in terms of the other. Hence this discussion will be concerned with broad issues.

20. Livy 1.16; Cicero, *Resp.* 2.17–18; Dionysius of Halicarnassus, *Ant. rom.* 2.56, in darkness caught up by his father, Ares.

21. Price, "Consecration," 73.

22. Ovid (*Metam.* 14.804–851) elaborates some aspects. The storm is clearly Jupiter's work at Mars's request to bring his son Romulus back to heaven. The translation to heaven happens by chariot, and as Romulus ascends to heaven, his mortal part melts away.

23. For discussion, see Taylor, *Divinity*, 58–99; Weinstock, *Divus Julius*, 356–84; Price, "Consecration," 71–73.

24. Brian Bosworth, "Augustus, the *Res gestae* and Hellenistic Theories of Apotheosis," *JRS* 89 (1999): 1–18. Bosworth sees the work as Augustus's "record of achievement which earned immortality" by evoking Euhemerus's Zeus, and by emphasizing conquest and benefaction, "the traditional justification for admission to the pantheon" (18).

25. See Beard, North, and Price, *Religions of Rome*, 2:51–52, for an image of a relief depicting the apotheosis of the emperor Antoninus Pius and his wife, Faustina, in 161 CE, which includes an eagle; Dio Cassius 75.4.2–75.5.5 narrates the flight of an eagle as the emperor Pertinax is cremated in 193 CE. Gradel, *Emperor Worship*, 270, 291–95; also 312 for a "cameo cut in sardonyx" representing Claudius on an eagle and crowned by Victoria/Nike; see also the discussion of Titus below.

26. Cited by Gradel, *Emperor Worship*, 268–69.

27. Momigliano, "How the Roman Emperors," 105, mentions miracles by the deified Antinous, Hadrian's boyfriend, and Julian in the fourth century as competing with Christian saints.

28. Gradel, *Emperor Worship*, 264; also 333–36.

29. See Scott, *Imperial Cult*, 40–45, for coins and cult of *divus* Vespasian. For Titus, Brian W. Jones, *The Emperor Titus* (New York: St. Martin's Press, 1984), 154–57.

30. Scott, *Imperial Cult*, 61–82.

31. See Warren Carter, "Are There Imperial Texts in This Class? Intertextual Eagles and Matthean Eschatology as 'Lights Out' Time for Imperial Rome (Matthew 24:27–31)," *JBL* 122 (2003): 467–87.

32. Scott, *Imperial Cult*, 41.

33. For an image, see Kreitzer, "Apotheosis," 210.

34. Barbara Levick, *Vespasian* (London: Routledge, 1999), 74, 197–99, seems to suggest the mocking of critics as expressed in Seneca, *Apocolocyntosis* 4, where Claudius "messes himself."

35. I have only recently seen the discussion of Daniel Schowalter, *The Emperor and the Gods* (Minneapolis: Fortress, 1993), 61–67.

36. Gradel, *Emperor Worship*, 287.

37. Price, "Consecration," 87.

38. Ibid., 87–89; Gradel, *Emperor Worship*, 325–30.

39. Price, "Consecration," 87.

40. Gradel, *Emperor Worship*, 328–29.

41. For discussion, see A. Collins, "Apotheosis," 95–96; John J. Collins, "A Throne in the Heavens: Apotheosis in Pre-Christian Judaism," in *Death, Ecstasy, and Other Worldly Journeys*, ed. J. J. Collins and M. Fishbane (Albany: State University of New York Press, 1995), 43–58; Sievers, "Josephus and the Afterlife," 24–25.

42. Philo uses "deification" with different meanings: (1) making someone into a god (rejected with reference to Gaius Caligula in *Emb.* 118), (2) participation in divine nature, (3) sharing of divine attributes, (4) becoming like the divine. So Wendy Helleman, "Philo of Alexandria: On Deification and Assimilation to God," in *The Studia Philonic Annual*, vol. 2, ed. David Runia (Atlanta: Scholars Press, 1990), 51–71; also David Runia, "God and Man in Philo of Alexandria," *JTS* 39 (1988): 48–75.

43. Following but rewording Kanagaraj, "Implied Ethics," 39–40.

44. Cotter, "Greco-Roman Apotheosis Traditions," 136–38. Cotter's point is to show how widespread were apotheosis traditions. She also cites Arnobius, *Against the Heathen* 6.1.41, who uses the tradition of apotheosis as the basis for an appeal for tolerance of Christian claims about the ascended Christ.

Conclusion

In the preceding chapters I have addressed the question, How does John's Gospel negotiate Roman power? I have argued that this Gospel employs a rhetoric of distance to negotiate the empire, urging Jesus-believers to a more-distanced, less-accommodated engagement with imperial society and norming for them an alternative, antisociety, identity, and way of life. The Gospel employs this rhetoric of distance even while in key ways it imitates imperial practices and perspectives with its turning to the past (chap. 4), the use of the genre of biography (5), titles and images for Jesus (7), visions of agely life (8), Father language (9), ecclesial images (10), and apotheosis and resurrection patterns (12). Such ambivalence, comprising participation yet distance, critique yet mimicry, is typical of situations in which subordinated groups negotiate tyrannical imperial power, as postcolonial studies have shown. Or in terms of James Scott's work, the Gospel offers a little tradition, or hidden transcript, as a narrative means of nonviolently contesting the imperial great tradition.

I have also argued that in urging greater societal distance for Jesus-believers, the Gospel participates in a conversation with and is at variance with some (many?) Jesus-believers who, shaped by likely patterns of interaction that also dominated synagogue groups (chaps. 2–3), have embraced a much more participative and accommodated way of life. Thus I have suggested that among Jesus-believers in late first-century Asia there was no unanimity about strategies for engaging daily life in Rome's empire while remaining faithful to the one crucified by the empire but raised victorious over the empire. Rather, John's Gospel participates in and contributes to a debate among Jesus-believers and synagogue members concerning imperial negotiation.

The engagement with the question of how the Gospel negotiates the empire assumes a prior question identified in chapter 1 (above): Does John's Gospel have anything to do with the Roman order at all? Often, scholarly work on John's Gospel has rendered a negative answer, simply not asking the question. Concerned with individualistic or synagogal readings that falsely isolate the synagogue and Jesus-believers from all other contexts, the empire has not been on the radar of many Johannine studies. Some scholarly work offers an explicit rejection of the possibility of any interaction. There is no need to repeat the instances cited in chapter 1 (above) where scholars deny that even Jesus' sentencing to death by the distinctly Roman form of execution (crucifixion), by the Roman governor Pilate, and on charges of being an unsanctioned kingly wannabe that threatened Roman sovereignty and elite control—is somehow devoid of any political claim or challenge![1]

Other scholars seem equally dubious but a little more cautious in their expression. For instance, in commenting on a recent article on John's negotiation of the imperial cult in which Bill Salier points out nine areas of contestive interaction between the Gospel and the imperial cult involving John (chaps. 1; 2; 3; 4; 5; 9; 12; 13–17; 18–20), David Wenham comments:

> It is difficult to be sure how important the cult and the issues it raised may have been for the author of the Gospel, but, as Bill brings out, the choice between Jesus and the emperor is quite explicit in 19:12–15.[2]

Wenham devotes merely four sentences to Salier's article in a thirteen-page discussion of eleven articles on John's Gospel. Such minimal attention suggests that Wenham hardly attributes much importance to the topic. And in mentioning only the explicit reference to the emperor in 19:12–15, he avoids (ignores? dismisses?) all the other passages with less-explicit interactions that Salier highlights. Nor does Wenham express any interest in pursuing the undeniable dualism of 19:12–15 or in thinking about how it might be integrated with the rest of the Gospel's plot, Christology, theology, or ecclesiology, preferring to highlight our not knowing whether the author thought the imperial cult to be of any importance. Attention to the role of the temple in John's Gospel and intertextuality with numerous temples in a city of Ephesus is not even considered as a worthwhile avenue for exploration.

My twelve-chapter-plus-appendix argument has shown that the question as to whether John's Gospel negotiates Roman power must be answered in the affirmative. This discussion—involving aspects of the Gospel's engagement with Jewish traditions and Scriptures, its plot, genre, theology, Christology, soteriology, eschatology, and ecclesiology—has also shown that this negotiation is not a sporadic or peripheral matter, occasionally rearing its head in 11:47–53 or 18:28–19:22 (Pilate) or in the odd christological title; instead, it pervades the intertextuality between the Gospel and the empire. John's Gospel is a work of imperial negotiation.

The important issue concerns not *if* but *how* the Gospel interacts with imperial power. I have observed (above) that among the relatively few scholars who have engaged aspects of this question (whether the Pilate scene or a title for Jesus), scenarios of persecution have had particular appeal. I have offered significant reasons in chapters 2–3 (above) as to why this scenario is not convincing. There is no evidence for persecution, but we find much evidence suggesting that some (many?) synagogal groups and Jesus-believers actively accommodated to and participated in imperial society in all its possibilities. This situation of overaccommodation seems to be that which the book of Revelation engages in at least a number of the churches in Asia in Revelation 2–3, and it seems to be the situation that the writer of 1 Peter urges on Jesus-believers in several provinces including Asia. I have argued throughout that John's Gospel employs its rhetoric of distance to address and correct such a situation, urging more societal distance, without calling for complete withdrawal (as in Rev 18), yet while also, ironically, often imitating imperial practices and patterns.

In a number of ways the analysis offered here of the Gospel's ambivalent negotiation of the empire (and at odds with practices among some [many?] Jesus-believers) bears some affinity with Stephen Moore's emphasis on the Gospel's ambivalent imperial engagement.[3] On one hand, Moore argues that John's narrative "contains, embedded within it, the most trenchant critique of Roman imperialism of any of the canonical Gospels, not only in its implicit inclusion of Rome in a 'world' denounced in uncompromising terms," but also in its "searing critique" of Roman judicial power arising from its placement of Jesus' "judicial torture" by Pilate at the center of the trial narrative.[4] One could question Moore's claim that John's critique is the most trenchant of the canonical Gospels. I suggest that Matthew's analysis of the empire as the instrument of the devil (Matt 4:8) and subject to annihilation at God's hand (cf. 24:27–31) is equally trenchant, but nevertheless the point remains that John's Gospel does offer a trenchant critique.[5]

Yet on the other hand, Moore argues, John is "the Gospel of the imperial status quo."[6] Crucial to this claim is his observation that in contrast to both the book of Revelation and the Synoptic Gospels' eschatological scenarios, "the tyrannical empire," represented by Pilate the judicial torturer and his allies the elite *Ioudaioi*, "is never represented as the *object* of divine punishment, whether realized or merely anticipated."[7]

John lacks "an explicit parousia scenario" of the coming Son of Man (Mark 13:26; Matt 24:27–31[8]). There is no climactic divine irruption on the stage of human history. In fact, Rome's intervention in John 11:48, not God's, "assumes apocalyptic proportions."[9] There is no prophecy of the "end to Caesar's reign," no depiction of the "Roman empire as destined to be destroyed or replaced by the new Christian empire from without."[10] Moore concludes that "John is at once the most—and the least—political of the canonical Gospels."[11]

Moore is right to find ambivalence in the Gospel's negotiation of the empire, but some of the arguments offered are not convincing. For instance, while insisting that the Gospel does not anticipate the empire's downfall, Moore concedes "a veiled or implicit denunciation of the Roman empire" in the Gospel's depiction of the "world" as "plunged in darkness (8:12; 9:5; cf. 12:35; 1:5), given over to evil works (7:7), ignorant of the only true God (17:25; 14:17; 17:3)."[12] This is indeed a denunciation of the empire. And it is strengthened by an identification of "the ruler of the world" as Pilate, as I have argued above, and not as Satan, as Moore claims. This ruler Pilate has no power over Jesus (14:30; 19:10–11), as Jesus' resurrection demonstrates (chaps. 20–21).

But Moore does not press the consequences of these formulations and ignores the Gospel's muted, but nevertheless insistent, future eschatological orientation. Attention to the Pilate scene without sufficient engagement with the whole of the Gospel is too limited a basis for pronouncement about the whole Gospel. Such engagement indicates that the consequences of commitment to the realities of darkness and "the world" in John's "complex textualized universe," where the Gospel's "political management of reality" occurs,[13] are fatal and cosmic, present and future. The world is judged by Jesus' presence (3:17–18). The doing of "evil works" marks the darkness that rejects and hates (7:7; 15:18–19) the light, Jesus, as revealer of God's salvation (3:19). "For judgment I came into the world," announces Jesus (9:39). That judgment, entrusted to Jesus by the Father (5:22, 27), is certainly "now" (12:31) in John's well-known realized eschatology. But realized eschatology is not the sum of John's eschatology. However it got there— and the source theories have been numerous—the Gospel also embraces a cluster of features of a future eschatology, as I identified in chapter 8 (above).[14] Without repeating that whole analysis, it is sufficient to recognize that this cluster involves at least physical wholeness and fertility (2:1–11; 4:46–54; etc.), resurrection (6:39–40; etc.; chaps. 11; 20–21), Jesus' return (14:3, arguably; but not graphically depicted), and involvement of Gentiles (12:20–21[15]). All of the elements of this future eschatological cluster are, as I have argued, imperially contestive, and I will not repeat the material here. These features evoke larger traditions that point to imperial destruction. In 2 Maccabees 7, for example, the resurrection of the martyrs who faithfully resist the imperial power of Antiochus Epiphanes, which violates God's purposes, accompanies assurances that Antiochus and his empire will come to naught in God's judgment (2 Macc 7:14, 19, 35–36). John's Gospel employs these eschatological features that evoke divine realities of justice and life-giving power, not to sanction the empire's eternal existence, but to presage its transformation.

The cluster explicitly includes future judgment:

> Do not marvel at this: for the hour is coming when all who are in their graves will hear his voice and will come out—those who have done good, to the resurrection of life, and those who have done evil, to the resurrection of condemnation. (5:28–29)

The language of "having done evil" is unusual Johannine Greek vocabulary (οἱ δὲ τὰ φαῦλα πράξαντες, *hoi de ta phaula praxantes*) but not unique. It occurs previously in 3:20, in the context of John's Jesus' words about judgment in rejecting the light and in loving darkness. His judgment is directed to the world, both in the present and the future eschatological eruption of divine power and purpose. The language of judgment (κρίσεως, *kriseōs*) also takes us back to 3:19 in naming "the judgment" and to 5:22, 27 in terms of the judgment that the Father has given to the Son. That judgment of the world embraces both the present in response to Jesus, and the future in this eschatological scene. The scene in 5:29 is the Gospel's assurance of the future eschatological end of the Roman Empire and its condemnation.

A further reference to the eschatological consequences of rejecting God's agent Jesus comes in the summary of Jesus' revelation in 12:44–50. In 12:48, Jesus announces, "The one who rejects me and does not receive my word has a judge; on the last day the word that I have spoken will serve as judge" (NRSV). Although it is easy to read the verse in individualistic terms, we must remember that "the one who does not receive my word" includes generally the Jerusalem elite, who as allies with Rome—whose representative is the governor Pilate—are not interested in changing the societal status quo, from which they benefit so much at the expense of the rest. Their imperial order is condemned. "On that day" God's judgment will be effected.

Moore is right to see that there are no graphic descriptions of the parousia akin to Matthew's dramatic depiction of return, eschatological battle, and destroyed corpses and eagles (as in Matt 24:27–31). But he is wrong to conclude that John thereby lacks any anticipation or expectation of future reference to the empire's destruction. Its end is predicted and is already under way now. It is doomed to be destroyed. Its downfall is anticipated. Its present evil works, so contrary to God's life-giving purposes, constitute its darkness and anticipate its demise. The Gospel reveals its condemnation.

Moore neglects a second means that the Gospel employs to anticipate the empire's demise. Throughout, I have indicated numerous examples of a common technique in literature derived from oral cultures, what John Foley calls metonymic intertextuality. This strategy employs abbreviated references to larger well-known cultural codes, relying on the audience to supply and elaborate the assumed cultural tradition as the work is performed. John's Gospel employs this technique constantly in relation to Hebrew Bible traditions, as I have noted throughout, and especially traditions that concern the demise of empires. For example, the Gospel's references to the Son of Man evoke the Danielic vision of one to whom is given "dominion and glory and kingship, that all peoples, nations, and languages should serve him. His dominion is an everlasting dominion" (Dan 7:13–14 NRSV). The Son of Man ends all empires—including Rome's—and asserts God's sovereignty over all people. Further, the crucial temple scene in John 2:13–22 not only evokes eschatological traditions concerning resurrection and the temple, thereby underlining the establishment of God's life-giving justice (2:21–22); it also evokes the eschatological scenario of Zechariah 14, whereby all nations resisting God's purposes—including Rome—are defeated, and God's kingship over all the nations is established (14:9, 12–19). The constant references to festivals function the same way by evoking accounts of the assertion of God's sovereignty over previous empires such as those of Egypt and Babylon. This metonymic textuality continually anticipates the assertion of God's power against Rome, Rome's downfall, and the triumphant establishment of God's purposes. What is interesting is not the absence of anticipations of eschatological destruction (contra Moore) but rather their quite muted explicit statement in the Gospel. Compared with Matthew's constant and explicit recourse to eschatological scenes to bully compliance and assert imperial decline, or the book of Revelation's recurrent emphasis on the diabolical and evil empire's imminent demise as condemned by God, John's resort to explicit and open anticipations of eschatological demise is minimal. Why is this? We might look for some explanation by briefly speculating on three factors: the historical circumstances that the Gospel addresses, its rhetorical strategy, and the linguistic expression of its theologically shaped societal vision.

One factor concerns the historical circumstances that the Gospel addresses. As I have argued throughout, the Gospel employs a rhetoric of distance to urge Jesus-believers to greater differentiation from and less societal participation in imperial ways and structures *in the present*. The Gospel emphasizes the need for understanding the present nature of the empire as rejecting God's agent and light and preferring darkness, evil deeds, lies/falseness, and so forth. Herein lies the empire's present danger for Jesus-believers. There can be no accommodation with an empire that crucifies the one whom God sent. The Gospel's focus is the present; societal distancing is needed now for faithful/believing existence. It rejects any notion of "live as you like now and wait for future vindication"; such thinking may at least partly comprise that of (some?) Jesus-believers who enjoy greater accommodation. The Gospel rejects this way of thinking, emphasizes the present, and minimizes overt attention on the future.

A second factor might be located in the interplay between the situation that the Gospel addresses and the nature of its story as a hidden transcript. For an audience significantly accommodated societally, a telling of the Jesus story that openly attacks the empire with frequent announcements of its imminent eschatological demise may have been judged to be an unconvincing strategy internally, and perhaps a dangerous one externally. Clearly, for many living in a city such as Ephesus late in the first century, the empire did not seem dangerous or vulnerable, it did not seem too evil, and God's judgment on it did not seem likely. Such accommodation may provide some partial explanation for the Gospel's imperial mimicking. To gain a hearing and challenge such perceptions, the Gospel at times participates in, borrows from, and imitates familiar imperial practices and language: turning to the past and to antiquity, the use of the genre of biography, Father language, imperial titles for Jesus. I am not concerned with claiming that such was the author's intent in mimicking imperial ways. Intent is not available to us some two millennia later. But we can assess effect, and one of the effects of this imitation is to create a bridge between the Gospel and accommodated Jesus-believers that provides a means of communicating much more challenging material.

Moreover, the Gospel plot focuses the action on Jesus, constantly repeating his origin, authority, divine sanction, mission, identity as revealer, intimate relationship with God, rejection, and destiny. He comes from another world and departs to it. His origin and destiny thereby show this world to be not ultimate and not according to God's purposes. Depictions of conflict with and responses to him provide the basis for a dualistic representation of the world, a creation of a reality predicated on being either for or against Jesus, for or against God. Metonymic intertextuality provides a constant but somewhat disguised commentary on divine purposes at work in Jesus and the imperial world. In this scenario, the powerful elite defend their interests and status quo. They use their power to destroy Jesus, but God vindicates him in resurrection and ascension/apotheosis. Again the focus is on the present. The Christology functions to disturb accommodation with such a status quo, re-presenting what is taken for granted as rejecting of God's agent and purposes, and norming an alternative perspective, identity, and way of life for Jesus-believers. Direct denunciations and scenarios of destruction are muted perhaps self-protectively, though somewhat disguised intertextual references to imperial destinies along with explicit talk of judgment and confrontation are constant. Irony also plays a significant part in disguising some criticisms and engaging hearers as those who have insider's knowledge (cf. 11:46–53). Through these rhetorical strategies, these divine and imperial realities are continually presented as operative in the present, already, now, always confronting characters and audience alike. There is no waiting for the distant future judgment; that future is brought very near. It is present, up close and personal, as well as communal and societal, thus to emphasize that accommodation is not possible.

A third factor may also be at work. Matthew, for instance, constantly proclaims Jesus' manifestation of the kingdom or empire of God/heaven as the central metaphor for God's activity. John changes the language, significantly diminishing the frequency of the metaphor of "kingdom/empire" (only five times; 3:3, 5; 18:36 [3x]) and preferring to speak much more often of "life" or "life of the age." In chapter 8 (above) I have identified various dimensions of this life—communal, somatic, imperially contestive, and so forth—and there is no need to repeat the material here. But it is worth asking what role this relexification and preference for the language of "age-ly life" plays in the Gospel's relative muting of explicit future eschatological scenarios?

I have argued above that the language of "age" provides important and contestive intertextuality with imperial claims of an imperial golden age. Also relevant is John's employment of wisdom traditions. These traditions depict the important roles of Wisdom "at the beginning" (Prov 8:22) and depict Wisdom actively revealing God's life among and to humans in the present (8:35). The wisdom paradigm, with its embracing of life revealed and encountered in the present, also reduces focus on future eschatological dimensions. It is thus possible that the Gospel uses the language of "life" rather than "kingdom/empire" to conceive of God's activity and purposes in ways that significantly differ from imperial conceptions. One effect of such relexification is that the Gospel largely rejects Matthew's strategy of "out-empiring" the empire and making God's empire bigger, more menacing, more powerful, and more extensive in its reach than Rome's. Matthew presents God's empire as though it is Rome's empire writ large, at least in some ways but especially in relation to the future.[16] It attributes the things of Caesar to God. With the language of "life of the age" encountered now, John's Gospel seems to take another route. In a huge act of imagination shaped by parts of the tradition, it imagines a different form and way of human life. It imagines light coming into the world and enlightening everyone, not securing only the interests of the elite. It offers a daring alternative vision of human interaction and social structure—an antisociety marked by transforming works, love, and seeking the good of the other—rather than another empire marked by power over others, tyranny, and oppression.

But while the vision and language are bold and daring, that is not the whole story. There is a failure of imagination. And that failure is not surprising given our understandings of imperial contexts. As much as the Gospel offers a contestive alternative vision, it cannot help but mimic empire. At times, though infrequently (only five times), the language of "empire" or kingdom returns. So too does the concept of empire in some of the ways that it conceives this life of the age. While this life performs transformative acts in the present through Jesus and subsequently through his disciples (14:12), there are those who do not seem to be enlightened and who resist the revealer and his revelation of God's new age. And what happens to them? The Gospel does not choose the option of providing assurance that they will all be gradually or eventually enlightened or loved into becoming participants in what is just and life-giving for all. Rather, it resorts to dualistic language, drawing lines, making divisions, creating and mapping an either-or world where judgment is already experienced (3:18–20) and confirmed in the final divine intervention, the final retaliation, the final judgment or condemnation of those who do not cooperate with the ruling power of God (5:28–29). The Gospel's imaginings for an alternative antisociety are partial and unable to escape the grammar of empire. In the end the quest for another way of being human cannot escape paradigms of empire, thereby attesting their all-pervasive power. The Gospel finally mimics what it resists.

Stephen Moore argues that by not announcing destruction on Rome, the Gospel ensures the "Rome will eventually become Christianity and Christianity will eventually become Rome."[17] His conclusion that Christianity will eventually become Rome is correct, though his argument about the means whereby this transformation takes place is quite incorrect, as I have shown. "Becoming Rome" does not happen because of the Gospel's supposed failure to anticipate Rome's destruction. The Gospel does anticipate Rome's demise. It does intimate, though not describe, its condemnation in the judgment. Rather, "becoming Rome" happens not only because God's expected intervention does not take place and Rome continues until it joins forces with Christianity post-Constantine, but also because the Gospel does not follow through on its relexification and imagining of God's purposes as "life." Imagining the establishment of God's life-giving purposes after the destruction of all enemies, Christianity has become and continues to be imperial Rome, intolerant of, vindictive toward, and heaping destruction upon those who do not fall into line.

It will need further acts of imagination of God's life-giving and just action to find a way forward. Perhaps the Gospel offers a further hint. In 12:31 it speaks of drawing—not compelling nor crushing—all people to Godself. The means of doing so is, in part, the crucified and risen Jesus, a demonstration of the death-bringing work that empires can do, as well as an ironic revelation of the limits of their power, which is so often presented as absolute and final. Jesus' resurrection reveals the lie and points to new and different life. Perhaps such a scene "draws" people to the recognition that empires based on force, compulsion, and destruction are not consonant with God's life-giving purposes for all people. If God's commitment is to enlighten all people (1:9), then it will take many such "drawings" through the diversities of various traditions, practices, and actions to break out of the imperial paradigm that has so often shown itself to be extremely capable of resisting efforts to imagine and create human life and society in another key.

Notes

1. Brown, *John*, 2:885; Kvalbein, "Kingdom of God," 228; Hengel, "Reich Christi."
2. David Wenham, "Paradigms and Possibilities in the Study of John's Gospel," in Lierman, *Challenging Perspectives*, 1–13; Salier, "Jesus, the Emperor."
3. Moore, *Empire and Apocalypse*, 45–74.
4. Ibid., 74.
5. Carter, *Matthew and Empire*.
6. Moore, *Empire and Apocalypse*, 74.
7. Ibid., 64.
8. Carter, "Are There Imperial Texts?"
9. Moore, *Empire and Apocalypse*, 70–71.
10. Ibid., 73.
11. Ibid., 50, 74.
12. Ibid., 73.
13. Citing Jean Howard, "The New Historicism in Renaissance Studies," in *The New Historicism and Renaissance Drama*, ed. R. Wilson and R. Dutton (New York: Longman, 1992), 28, cited in an important article by Colleen Conway, "The Production of the Johannine Community: A New Historicist Perspective," *JBL* 121 (2002): 479–95, esp. 493.
14. To be completely fair, Moore (*Empire and Apocalypse*, 70n68) concedes in this note that 5:28–29; 6:39–40, 44, 54; 12:48 "might be read as implicit anticipations of an undramatized parousia," but this footnoted concession plays no role in his analysis.
15. See below for John's evoking of Hebrew Bible scenarios of God's purposes that embrace Gentiles.
16. Carter, *Matthew and Empire*, 169–79.
17. Moore, *Empire and Apocalypse*, 74.

Appendix

Is Gaius Caligula the Father of Johannine Christology?

Imperial Negotiation and Developing Johannine Traditions

Throughout, I have focused on the finished form of John's Gospel as Jesus-believers at Ephesus might have engaged it at the end of the first century. These Jesus-believers were probably still part of a synagogue community and also active participants in the daily life of imperial Ephesus. In this appendix I address an important question related particularly but not exclusively to the Gospel's Christology. Does the imperial negotiation that the previous discussion has highlighted occur only in the final form of the Gospel? Is this a new element introduced into Johannine traditions in the Ephesian context late in the first century? Or has imperial negotiation played an active role as the Johannine traditions developed, perhaps in Judea-Galilee, before the Gospel's final form—in the decades between 30 CE, the approximate date for Jesus' crucifixion, and 100 CE, the approximate date for the finished form of the Gospel?

My argument is that imperial negotiation occurs not only in engagement with John's finished text, but also throughout the whole development of the Johannine tradition. Two factors immediately suggest the likelihood of imperial negotiation throughout the developing traditions. At the outset of the tradition, one factor concerns the crucifixion of Jesus, a display of Roman power against a threatening provincial. The task of delineating the implications of following one whom Rome had crucified was constant through the first century. And second, the empire certainly did not suddenly come into existence in Ephesus late in the first century. Jesus-believers, wherever they lived in the empire, encountered it on a daily basis throughout the first century. Both of these factors indicate continual imperial negotiation in the decades before the Gospel's final form.

I do recognize that various factors contribute to a process of developing insights about Jesus throughout the first century. Yet more specifically, here I argue for significant and influential interface between developing Johannine traditions about Jesus and a major incident that occupied widespread attention in Judea-Galilee and beyond around 40 CE, ten years or so after Jesus' crucifixion. In that year, the emperor Gaius Caligula tried to install a statue of himself as Zeus/Jupiter in the Jerusalem temple. This event was a "focal point" in asserting central practices and ideas that comprised Roman imperial theology: showed that Rome was chosen by the gods as their agent to manifest or reveal their sovereignty, will, presence, and well-being among humans. There are significant similarities between Johannine affirmations about Jesus and claims associated with Gaius Caligula and evidenced in the accounts of this incident. I am not suggesting exclusive influence, but the presence of such similarities suggests that Johannine Jesus traditions are engaged in cultural intertextuality and that imperial negotiation is taking place in the pre-written-Gospel period. This negotiation comprises imitation of as well as competition with Roman claims, critique of them yet restatement of parts of them in relation to Jesus, who is greater than the emperor.

In exploring this period between Jesus and the late first-century final form of John's Gospel, scholars have proposed various factors of influence. I will momentarily review some of the theories as to how John's Gospel developed its distinctive understandings about Jesus. Here I recognize that, like these previous claims about John's Gospel and its developing traditions, the argument that some interface with Gaius's attempt to install a statue of himself in the temple plays some role in the developing Johannine traditions cannot finally be "proved." Yet the presence of some similarities suggests that it was one factor of some importance along with a number of others. My argument continues the critique of much Johannine scholarship for focusing on a narrow range of religious ideas and events and not recognizing the place of imperial negotiation—sociopolitical and socioeconomic—in the Gospel's story of Jesus. Such limited focus, I have argued throughout this book, has prevented us from seeing the Gospel as an act of imperial negotiation. In this appendix I suggest that imperial negotiation pervades not only the final form of negotiation with the Gospel but also the circumstances in which, and the processes by which, Johannine traditions and understandings developed.

The argument proceeds in three sections. First I briefly review previous discussions of how Johannine traditions and understandings of Jesus developed and justify the consideration of imperial negotiation. Then I describe three sources of information about the emperor Gaius Caligula's attempt to install a statue of himself in the Jerusalem temple. Finally, I discuss six points of cultural intertextuality between the Gaius incident and Johannine christological emphases.

Developing Johannine Traditions

Throughout I have referenced some of the elevated and distinctive claims about Jesus that John's Gospel makes:

- In the beginning was the Word, the Word was with God, and the Word was God. (1:1 RSV)
- The Word actively participates in the creation of the world. (1:3)
- The Word became flesh and dwelt among us. (1:14 RSV)

- No one has ever seen God; the only Son, who is in the bosom of the Father, he has made him known. (1:18 RSV)

- The Son can do nothing on his own accord, but only what he sees the Father doing. (5:19 RSV)

- I have come down from heaven, not to do my own will, but the will of him who sent me. (6:38 RSV)

- I and Father are one. (10:30 RSV)

- Jesus, knowing that the Father had given all things into his hands, and that he had come from God and was going to God, rose. (13:3 RSV)

His opponents dispute these and other claims.

- This is why the *Ioudaioi* sought all the more to kill him, because he not only broke the Sabbath but also called God his own Father, making himself equal with God. (5:18 RSV alt.)

- The *Ioudaioi* answered, "It is not for a good work that we stone you, but for blasphemy, because you being a man make yourself God." (10:33)

- We have a law, and according to that law he ought to die because he has claimed to be the Son of God. (19:7 NRSV)

These texts articulate central Johannine claims about Jesus. He participates in a relationship of oneness with God that seems to render him equal to God or even God. He is sent from God and by God as God's agent, to manifest or reveal God and God's life-giving purposes among humans. He facilitates encounter with God: to see, hear, or know Jesus is to see, hear, or know God. He descends from God and returns or ascends to God. Not surprisingly, scholars have investigated how these elevated and distinctive claims developed and have proposed numerous models.

Proposed Models of Developing Johannine Traditions

As I noted briefly in chapter 1 (above), some Johannine scholars have proposed that this Gospel developed through several stages and written versions before reaching its final form.[1] They argue that aporias (rough seams) in the final form of the Gospel attest these developing traditions. One form of aporias comprises narrative disjunctions. In John 5, for example, Jesus is in Jerusalem, but 6:1 has him on "the other side of the Sea of Galilee." In 14:31 he seems to end his talk to the disciples but then continues for two or three more chapters. The Gospel seems to end in 20:30–31, but then chapter 21 follows. A second form of aporias comprises inconsistent content. Does Jesus baptize (3:22) or not (4:2)? He says he is not going to Jerusalem (7:8) but then goes (7:10). A third form of aporias comprises theological claims. Do signs lead to faith (2:11), or is faith without signs better (20:29)? Are sacraments important (6:51–58), or by leaving out Jesus' baptism (1:31–33?) and institution of the Lord's Supper, are they irrelevant? Is John's eschatological interest focused on the present (5:24) or future (5:28–29)? Is Jesus the Messiah (low Christology) or Son of God and God (high Christology)? Is the Gospel about individuals believing or life in a community, the church?

Scholars have reconstructed various outlines of this development process involving changing theological insights, written versions of the Gospel, and crises in relation to a synagogue community. Perhaps the outlines proposed by J. Louis Martyn and by Raymond E. Brown have received most support. In general terms, the Martyn-Brown developmental hypothesis (to conflate them arbitrarily and override their differences) posits that oral traditions about the words and works of Jesus as the Messiah developed initially among Jesus-believers in Judea-Galilee. References to locations suggest local connections, such as Bethsaida (1:44), Cana (2:1; 4:46), and Capernaum (2:12; 6:24) in Galilee, and knowledge of Jerusalem such as the pool of Bethzatha in Jerusalem (5:2). These traditions undergo considerable revision and expansion as the result of the experiences of the community of believers first in Judea-Galilee, and later in a center like Ephesus in the 80s–90s. For instance, Brown argues that the story of the Samaritan woman and her city in 4:1–42 reflects the entry of Samaritans into the believing community. Their entry brought new understandings about Moses as one who had been with God, who had come from God as God's agent, and was the revealer of God's purposes. These understandings refigured the Davidic messianic understandings of John's Jesus-believers into a much higher Christology. The resultant "high" Christology emphasized Jesus as the one who had been with God in the beginning, who had been sent by God to earth, who had come down from God to reveal God, who enacted God's purposes in his words and works while remaining one with God, and who had returned to God through his crucifixion, resurrection, and ascension. Notions of preexistence, agency, revelation, intimate relationship, and ascension are important elements of this "high" Christology. Such claims, along with openness to Gentiles, resulted in inevitable conflict with other Jewish groups since they seemed to threaten Jewish affirmations concerning revelation and monotheism (5:18; 10:31–33). According to Brown, Jesus-believers are expelled from the synagogue and the first version of the Gospel is written. A subsequent editor or redactor adds further material to this version to create a second edition.

Basic to this approach of developing Johannine traditions is the interaction of three factors: crises in the relationship between Jesus-believers and a synagogue, developing theological and christological understandings, and multiple editions or versions and author/s and redactor/s of the Gospel. The disparate elements in the Gospel involving "high" and "low" Christology, present and future eschatology, individualistic and communal forms of discipleship, Jewish particularism and inclusion of Gentiles, and dualistic cosmic thinking reflect the intersection between developing insights, changing experiences, and multiple Gospel versions.

Scholars have posited that the Gospel developed through perhaps as many as three different written versions, which were edited and revised by different authors to reflect the changing understandings. In a thoughtful book much shaped by the Martyn-Brown hypotheses, Martin de Boer offers an example of developing christological understandings. He outlines a history of the Johannine tradition that has three editions:[2]

Edition	Crisis	*Sitz im Leben*, or Life-Setting	Christology
John 1	Expulsion for confessing Jesus to be the Messiah (9:22)	Mission to fellow Jews	The Messiah (Christ) is Jesus.
John 2	Execution for making Jesus God or the Son of God	Conversation and midrashic debate with Jewish authorities	Jesus is the Son of God.
John 3	Schism over Jesus "coming"	Jewish Christians on trial for their lives	Jesus is the Son of Man.

De Boer argues that three post-70 events are crucial for the developing christological reflection: expulsion from the synagogue, execution of believers, and schism among believers. These three events precipitate changing christological understandings centered first on Jesus as Messiah, then as Son of God, and then as Son of Man. In turn, circumstances and insights produce new versions of the Gospels. He argues that "it is probably not possible to reconstruct each edition in minute detail," that material in previous editions was probably not deleted from subsequent versions, that material such as christological titles already existing in an earlier version gained new emphases and meaning in subsequent editions, and that the three main titles that he discusses (Christ, Son of God, Son of Man) existed "from the earliest stages of the Johannine tradition and were already applied to Jesus in one way or another in the first edition."

Other Models

This approach (above) focuses on developing traditions, multiple Gospel versions, and changing social experiences; like all attempts to reconstruct the Gospel's pre-history, it is speculative and hypothetical. While it has received support, it has certainly not convinced all scholars. And not surprisingly, it is not the only way of understanding the origins of the Gospel.[3] Other ways of thinking about how the Gospel originated have been proposed. Some such as Robert Fortna and Urban van Wahlde have postulated the existence and use of written sources such as a collection of narratives concerning Jesus' signs—a Signs Gospel—and/or concerning his passion, which have been edited into the Gospel's final form.[4] Others have argued for the dependence of John's Gospel on the earlier Synoptic Gospels of Matthew, Mark, and Luke, though significant differences between the Synoptics and John limit the appeal of this argument.[5]

One of the strongest challenges to the developing traditions/multiple version approach perhaps comes from those who question models reliant on written sources. This challenge emphasizes the oral world in which traditions about Jesus developed; it finds assumptions related to literacy misleading and unhelpful.[6] Joanna Dewey, for example, identifies literacy as an elite skill irrelevant to the daily lives of 95 percent of the population. For most, oral storytelling was more important. Dewey acknowledges

the overlapping and interactive nature of oral and literate texts but argues that the latter are often written for the ear, being read out loud. Oral material is not fixed; it adapts
to and is shaped by different contexts including communal circumstances, cultural use-
fulness, time available for the performance, nonverbal features of the performance, an
audience's social levels and cultural contexts, polemical and argumentative functions,
and a participatory experiential quality. Yet while oral material adds and accumulates
episodes, it tends to solidify and coalesce fairly quickly (e.g., within a generation) into
a coherent narrative about a hero. In the case of John's Gospel, a comprehensive narrative about Jesus, with variants, would probably have emerged quite early in the 40s CE
among Jesus-believers in Judea-Galilee. Dewey suggests seven areas in which studies of
orality may well challenge the literary-oriented models that appeal to various versions
and sources to explain how John's Gospel may have been formed:

- Understandings of oral processes suggest that it is quite difficult to isolate material that originates with Jesus.

- Understandings of oral processes suggest that a comprehensive oral narrative
  about Jesus underlies the written Gospel.

- Theories that make written sources (such as a "signs Gospel") central to the
  Gospel's origin are unlikely in an oral milieu where aporias such as narrative disjunctions and theological tensions or inconsistencies (often used as "criteria" to
  identify and reconstruct such sources) are much more tolerable than in a literate
  society.

- For the same reasons, a pre-Gospel passion narrative is unlikely.

- Since there are only sporadic echoes of Mark in John's Gospel, the Gospel writer
  may well have heard the Synoptic Gospels but did not use them as sources.

- John's Gospel employs stylistic features that reflect oral performance: simple
  clauses, present tense, paratactic connectors ("and," "and then"), episodic construction, repeated scenes—miracles, "both/and" thinking (present and future
  eschatology? Jesus present and absent), polemic against the *Ioudaioi*; yet it also
  bears signs of written composition (20:30–31; 21:24; developed discourses).

- Initial work on oral reception suggests that the aporias, or so-called inconsistencies, are not regarded as being problematic as in a dominantly literate society, that
  polemic was expected, and identification with characters common.

Though not worked out in a detailed discussion of the Gospel, Dewey's discussion
of how the Gospel's oral milieu may have impacted the Gospel's formation—whether
with oral or written materials—provides an important alternative to the conventional
approaches based on written sources and multiple versions. In several ways it also use-
fully frames our discussion of possible imperial negotiation early in the development of
the Johannine tradition. First, an oral milieu provides for the development of coherent
material early in the Johannine tradition, even if we cannot reconstruct the forms of
these coalescing narratives. An oral milieu does not require a lengthy period of time for
literary traditions and texts to develop. The recognition that oral materials coalesce

fairly quickly into coherent narratives suggests the likely emergence of such coherence in the 40s CE. Second, it is not unreasonable to explore the possible interaction between a major event concerning Gaius Caligula from around 40 and coalescing oral traditions about Jesus. And third, if we can find signs of possible interaction between Johannine material and the actions of Gaius Caligula, it would indicate a significant role for imperial negotiation *early* in the Johannine tradition.

How Did John's Christology Develop?

The exploration of the role of imperial negotiation does not exclude other influences on developing Johannine Christology. Various theories have been offered to account for the development of John's "high" Christology.[7] I will briefly describe seven, recognizing that each approach merits much more discussion than is possible here, that there can be some overlapping of features from each approach, that one approach is unlikely to provide a total explanation, and that interactions among various factors probably provide the explanation.

Social setting. Evident in the summary above is the claim that certain social experiences—notably the presence of new converts, especially Samaritans, and conflict with other groups, especially a synagogue, over religious ideas—played a pivotal role in changing understandings about Jesus.[8] Earlier traditions change as they encounter new situations and ideas. This general framework is helpful but needs to be fleshed out in terms of particular experiences, traditions, and ideas to account for the particular forms that the "development" took. Scholars have thus sought to isolate particular clusters of ideas and experiences that have been at work.

Gnostic influences. Rudolf Bultmann argued that influences from Gnostic groups and thinking account for the Gospel's Christology.[9] Bultmann saw traditions about a descending and ascending revealer figure as central to this development. Bultmann's theory, though, has not proved to be compelling for several reasons, especially the recognition that the sources to which Bultmann appeals for his Gnostic traditions are post-first century.

Samaritan influences. Some scholars have suggested that an influx of Samaritan converts into the Johannine community at some point accounts for the christological developments. Raymond Brown finds evidence for this thesis in the narrative of the conversion of Samaritan believers in 4:4–42.[10] Various features—an anti-Jerusalem temple emphasis, a certain kind of Moses piety including Samaritan traditions about a revealer figure (the Taheb, sometimes seen as Moses returned from heaven)—play crucial roles, so the argument goes, in developing christological claims and creating conflict with other Jewish groups. Problematic for this theory are the late date of Samaritan sources, similarities between Samaritan traditions about Moses' ascension-enthronement traditions and Jewish Moses traditions (e.g., Philo) that make identification of the central role of the former problematic, and the arbitrary privileging of the narrative in John 4 to reconstruct the community's history. How do we know that John 4 reflects actual historical circumstances in the early years of the Johannine tradition and that it is responsible for the "high" Christology evident in 5:18? By parallel, should we conclude from 1:43–51 or from 5:1–18 that Galileans under fig trees and physically impaired Jerusalemites at the pool of Bethzatha/Bethsaida played similarly crucial roles?

Apocalyptic influences. Some scholars have detailed numerous Jewish traditions involving various Jewish revealer figures (Moses, Isaiah) that were well known in the first century.[11] Such figures gain insight into God's purposes, whether through visions or heavenly journeys, and make revelations to their followers. John, so the theory goes, reverses the familiar revelatory ascent-descent pattern to present Jesus as the definitive revealer who begins with God, descends to make the definitive revelation, and returns to God via ascension. This theory, coupled with changing social contexts (see on "social setting" above), is helpful. The remaining question concerns whether these Jewish traditions comprise the whole field of influence.

Wisdom influences. Wisdom traditions, not altogether removed from apocalyptic traditions, provide a good reason for questioning the adequacy of apocalyptic traditions alone to account for Johannine developments. Numerous recent studies (cf. chap. 4 above) have suggested that to interpret the significance of Jesus, John employs traditions concerning (personified) Wisdom, who was in the beginning with God and descended to dwell among humans and reveal God.[12] Like apocalyptic traditions, the question to be addressed concerns whether wisdom traditions alone can account for Johannine developments.

Organic development.[13] The five explanations above highlight the role of outside events and cultural traditions in the christological developments. This organic category does not deny outside influence but emphasizes more an internal development process, in which later affirmations do not introduce new claims from external sources but unfold what was already implicit in Jesus' own claims and impact. But such an approach does not explain why some three to four hundred years were needed until the councils of Nicaea (325) and Chalcedon (451) drew out these implications, nor does it account for the role of considerable debate and dispute through the process.

Authorial genius.[14] Whichever model we choose to explain how the Gospel came into being, there is no doubt that a key individual or individuals contributed creative insight to the process. Such a recognition does not negate the role of external circumstances, traditions, and communities in the process, but it does highlight an interactive role for key figures. Such a figure or figures are not removed from cultural interaction and communal participation. The issue under consideration concerns identifying the factors with which they might have engaged.

Summary evaluation. Of the above theories, two seem especially unconvincing: those relying on Gnostic and Samaritan traditions fail or must play a minor role because available sources largely postdate John's time. Nor can one deny the contribution of authorial genius and some organic development, but the recognition of their contribution to the process does not illumine how the process took place. The theories drawing on apocalyptic and wisdom traditions identify important religious influences, as shown in a number of studies. The social-setting theory identifies religious contexts and circumstances through which this influence might have taken effect. Yet is an emphasis on religious factors (social setting, apocalyptic, wisdom) adequate to account for the development of Johannine Christology?

Roman Imperial Negotiation

Significantly, these seven approaches (above) usually locate the christological development in largely religious traditions and social contexts, especially post-70. But as I have
argued (esp. in chaps. 1–3 above), it is arbitrary and anachronistic to attend only to the
so-called religious or spiritual or individualistic dimensions of the Johannine materials
as though they can be isolated from sociopolitical contexts. Apocalyptic traditions, for
example, including those asserted after 70 in response to Rome's destruction of
Jerusalem in *4 Ezra* (= 2 Esdras) and *2 Baruch*, engage a context of crisis that embraces
social, political, military, and religious dimensions. Synagogues, the likely location of
conflicts between John's group and nonfollowers of Jesus, were much engaged in negotiation with Roman power (as shown in chap. 2 above). Wisdom traditions, for example, show significant interactions with Hellenistic culture and often reflect Jewish
Diaspora attempts to acculturate to a dominant culture. Attention to these traditions
does not preclude influence from or engagement with other political forces.

Given that religious factors were interwoven with political and social contexts, it is
not unreasonable to explore an eighth area of interaction concerning John's Christology: Roman imperial theology and civic cultic observation. As I discussed in chapters
3 and 7 (section on Lord and God), on the few occasions when this possibility has been
considered, attention has usually focused on post-70 encounters with the imperial cult.
Lance Richey, for instance, argues that imperial cult observances in Ephesus—with
their claims of Roman sovereignty, revelation of divine purposes, and attribution of
divine being to the emperor—exercised a significant impact on Johannine Christology
by causing it to address questions of legitimate divinity.[15] Richard Cassidy sees situations of persecution as being instrumental, as noted in chapter 3 above. B. A. Mastin
thinks that claims that Domitian insisted on imperial cult observance and demanded
to be addressed as "Lord and God" account for Thomas's confession in 20:28 about the
risen Jesus.

As I have already indicated, for various reasons neither Cassidy nor Mastin is persuasive. Richey may be more on target, at least to some extent, in that there was active
and regular imperial cult observance in Ephesus, as we have seen, and some among the
Jesus-believers, including the Gospel author/s, saw fundamental incompatibilities
between claims about Jesus and those about the emperor. Nevertheless, the major problems with these approaches that highlight these areas of conflict are twofold. One is that
there is no evidence for major conflicts in Ephesus between Jesus-believers and the city
over imperial cult observance. The evidence discussed in chapters 2 and 3 above actually suggests considerable accommodation. Second, and perhaps more significant, the
need to negotiate Roman imperial power does not emerge afresh in the 80s or 90s CE.
Such negotiation is a constant from the 20s to the 80s. Jesus, after all, collides with and
suffers the consequences of Roman power in his crucifixion, and imperial cult celebrations pervaded the East. It is not unreasonable to suggest that some influence from such
negotiation is likely to be evident in the traditions developing about Jesus from the 30s
through the 70s. Ephesus was not the first time or place in which Johannine groups
encountered Roman imperial theology or cultic observances. It is more likely that the
dominant accommodated experience of imperial power in Ephesus—problematic for

the Gospel's author/s—caused a reassertion or more assertive statement of some affirmations that had already developed much earlier in Johannine traditions.

Thus I argue that coalescing Johannine traditions likely engaged and negotiated Roman claims much earlier in the first century. We cannot surely plot all the points of such negotiation. Nor am I suggesting that imperial negotiation accounts for every aspect of Johannine Christology, given the factors identified above. I am suggesting, though, that one likely point of negotiation that impacted the development and early coalescing of Johannine traditions in oral form involved Gaius Caligula's attempts to establish a statue of himself in the Jerusalem temple around 40 CE. This event comprised a vigorous assertion of Roman control, including its military and religious sanctions, as well as life-and-death Jewish opposition. It could be argued that other imperial events in the first century also provided focal points for negotiation, such as Jesus' crucifixion and the fall of the temple and Jerusalem in 70. I am not claiming an exclusive role for the Gaius incident. I am suggesting it is at least one focal point among others that have been neglected but are worthy of attention.

Why Bother with Gaius Caligula?

Two initial factors point to the Gaius incident's potential importance and suggest that it is worth investigating. These two factors concern its geographical and demographic reach, and the gravity of the threat that it posed. Both Philo and Josephus present the confrontation as no small matter for Jews in both Judea-Galilee and also across the empire. The narratives of both writers indicate widespread, firsthand involvement in the event by many residents.

The reach and gravity of the situation is reflected in Josephus's claim that in this incident "our own nation was brought to the very verge of destruction and would have been destroyed but for his [Gaius's] sudden death" (*Ant.* 19.15). Philo fears that "the overthrow of the temple" will lead to "the annihilation of our common name and nation" (*Embassy* 194). Its impact appears in the descriptions of both Philo and Josephus concerning the widespread involvement of many people. Though events unfold in Judea-Galilee, Philo himself hears of the news of the "very heavy calamity" that threatens "the whole body of the [Jewish] nation" in Puteoli, south of Rome, having followed the emperor Gaius there from Rome (184–188). The incident is sparked in part by events in "Jamneia [Jamnia/Jabneh], one of the most populous cities of Judea" (200). Gaius orders Petronius, "viceroy for the whole of Syria," to take the statue to Jerusalem, guarded by "half the army quartered on the Euphrates" (207). Such a procession with two legions[16] constitutes a very public parade of divinely sanctioned, militarily enforced, Roman power. Philo reports that Petronius fears that all Jews, within and outside the land, will resist (214–217).[17] He summons "the most clever craftsmen in Phoenicia" to construct the statue in Sidon (222) while he talks with Jewish leaders ("magnates, priests, magistrates," 222) hoping that they will instruct "all the rest of the population" not to resist (223). Instead, "the inhabitants of the holy city and the rest of the country" traveled to Phoenicia to protest to Petronius (225), taking "wives, our children, and our families" with them (231). The confrontation threatens the harvest, tribute payment, and social stability (*Emb.* 249; cf. Josephus, *J. W.* 2.200; *Ant.* 18.272–274, 283–284). Many in Judea-Galilee and beyond are caught up in this event.

Josephus locates the action in several areas of Galilee, in the coastal area around Ptolemais (Acco; *J. W.* 2.192); inland at Tiberias, on the western shore of the Sea of Galilee (*J. W.* 2.193; cf. *Ant.* 18.279, "many tens of thousands"); and subsequent private and public meetings at unspecified locations (*J. W.* 2.199). Petronius also encounters protestors from across the social strata, including women and children (2.192), elites and nonelites, and all in large numbers (2.192–193, 199). The "alarm soon became universal" (2.187), involved a "vast multitude" (2.192), and "crowded private conferences" (2.199). The face-off lasts a minimum of forty (*Ant.* 18.272) or fifty (*J. W.* 2.200) days.

These locations, time periods, and vast numbers, even allowing for hyperbole for dramatic effect, are significant. Johannine scholars, as noted above, have commonly suggested that the Johannine traditions were developing in Judea-Galilee in the decades of the 30s–50s. If Philo's account and Josephus's two accounts of the Gaius crisis have any historical credibility, they suggest a protracted and very public confrontation involving fundamental issues that shook elites and nonelites of the Jewish world in their engagement with Rome, within Judea-Galilee, and in the Diaspora. It does not seem unreasonable to suggest that those among whom the Johannine traditions were developing somewhere in Galilee-Judea were also caught up in this international incident involving many people, all social strata, extensive territory, and involving claims of divinity, sovereignty, divine agency, sacrifice, and the inviolability of the temple and the law—to name a few issues. Nor is it unreasonable to suggest that there might be some points of interaction with developing and coalescing Johannine traditions about Jesus since these matters of prominence in the incident are also prominent in John's Gospel.

At this historical distance, we cannot hope to trace such interaction with any precision, but we can at least do what Johannine scholarship has failed to do: identify some likely points of cultural intertextuality by way of recognizing that imperial negotiation played a prominent part in both the formation of Johannine traditions and of the Gospel. The next section will describe the three accounts of the Gaius incident.

Gaius Caligula and the Jerusalem Temple: Three Accounts

Three accounts provide the main sources for information about the emperor Gaius Caligula's action around 40 CE.[18] The longest and earliest is in Philo's *Embassy to Gaius* 184–367, written around 40. Two later accounts come from Josephus, a shorter account in *Jewish War* 2.178–203, written perhaps in the second half of the decade of the 70s; and a longer account in *Jewish Antiquities* 18.257–309, completed in the 90s, around the same time as the finished form of John's Gospel. The three accounts evidence significant similarities as well as differences, causing difficulties for reconstructing details of the incident with historical certainty.[19] To negotiate these differences, some approaches have taken the earliest account, Philo's, as the most historically reliable and used Josephus' accounts in a supplemental way.[20] Others have claimed Josephus as more historically reliable.[21] Others have sought not to privilege one account but to sort through the three accounts to discern the most historically viable details and thereby render a fourth account by way of historical reconstructions of the scene.[22]

My goal here is not primarily detailed historical reconstruction. Rather, my interest lies with interpretations of the event that pervade the accounts, especially the cluster of theological motifs, both Jewish and imperial. In historical reconstructions scholars have often dismissed or ignored these motifs. Though there is no doubt that redactional tendencies are quite evident in the accounts, it is arbitrary and anachronistic to view Gaius's action of trying to locate a statue of himself as Zeus in the Jerusalem temple as only political and divorced from any religious considerations. The event is both political and religious, an act of imperialism and of provincial negotiation in which religious commitments are very important to the political and ethnic interaction. I will briefly outline each source's account (in chronological order), identify the explicit and implicit theological claims evident in this multidimensional event, and then examine six theological issues that emerge in the Gaius incident and have some resonance with John's Gospel.

Philo, Embassy to Gaius *184–367*

- *Embassy to Gaius* 184–206. Philo, in Rome with an Alexandrian delegation seeking an audience with Gaius over treatment of Jews in Alexandria, hears news that "our temple is lost, Gaius has ordered a colossal statue to be set up within the inner sanctuary dedicated to himself under the name of Zeus" (188). Gaius's actions are fuelled by his desire "to be thought a god" by all, including dissenting Jews (198), and by an incident in Jamnia involving Jewish destruction of an altar, as reported to Gaius by Capito, the chief tax collector of Judea. Philo claims that Capito is well known for his hatred of Jews. Gaius, encouraged by further Jew-haters, plans retaliation by having a "colossal statue" set up in the Jerusalem temple.

- *Embassy* 207–224. Gaius orders Petronius, viceroy of Syria, to install the statue, using military force if necessary. Petronius struggles to obey the command from one who "already ranks himself as among the gods" (218), knowing that Jews throughout the empire value their laws as "vouchsafed by God" and are dedicated to their temple. As he begins work on the statue's construction, he meets with the Jewish leadership ("priests and magistrates/rulers") to explain Gaius's plan.

- *Embassy* 225–242. Jews from Jerusalem and throughout the country go to Phoenicia to protest nonviolently to Petronius. They declare a record of loyalty to Gaius, including "sacrifices in behalf of Gaius's reign" (232), a willingness to die in defense of the temple (233), a determination to balance "respectful fear of the emperor and loyalty to the consecrated laws" (236), and request for envoys to visit Gaius (239).

- *Embassy* 243–260. Petronius responds to the appeals by having those constructing the statue work slowly, by not opposing those who want to appeal to Gaius, by writing to Gaius, and by dismissing the crowds to harvest the crops in order to supply Gaius on a journey to Egypt. Gaius, angered by Petronius's failure to comply with his orders, responds to Petronius's letter, masking his anger but ordering the immediate installation of the statue.

- *Embassy* 261–329. Meanwhile back in Rome, King Agrippa, knowing nothing of the situation, pays respects to Gaius. Gaius complains that Agrippa's "fellow-citizens . . . alone of every race of men do not acknowledge Gaius as a god" and resist the installation of a statue of Zeus in the temple (265). Agrippa is so impacted by Gaius's plan that he falls into a coma for several days. On recovering, he writes to Gaius, detailing Jewish loyalty to the emperor, explaining the importance of the laws and temple, reminding Gaius of previous emperors who honored the temple (and of Pilate's dishonoring it, 299–305), and appealing for Gaius not to persevere in his action.

- *Embassy* 330–348. Apparently persuaded, Gaius orders the installation to stop. But he gives permission for others to set up imperial altars, temples, images, or statues in the land. Yet due to "the watchful care of God," no one takes advantage of this situation. However, the "untrustworthy" Gaius reorders another statue of himself to be constructed so it can be installed in Jerusalem on his journey to Egypt (337), and to have the temple bear Gaius's name, "the new Zeus made manifest" (346).

- *Embassy* 349–367. Philo describes his delegation's meeting with an angry but distracted Gaius over the treatment of Alexandrian Jews. Gaius greets the delegates as "god-haters who do not believe me to be a god" (353). They debate the Jewish practice of sacrificing *for* the emperor [ὑπὲρ ἐμοῦ, *hyper emou*, for me] but not *to* him [οὐ . . . ἐμοί, *ou . . . emoi*, to me][23], as well as not eating pork. But in response to the prayers of the anguished delegation, God compassionately intervenes, and Gaius mercifully dismisses the delegation, declaring them to be "unfortunate," not "wicked," to be "foolish in refusing to believe [μὴ πιστεύοντες, *mē pisteuontes*] that I do have the nature of a god."

Philo's account of Gaius's order that a colossal statue be set up within the inner sanctuary of the Jerusalem temple and be dedicated to himself under the name of Zeus (188, 265, 346) is the longest and most detailed. The vulnerability and frustration of the Alexandrian delegation in its attempts to meet with Gaius over the treatment of Jews in Alexandria shapes much of the account. Addressing these Alexandrian problems accounts for Philo's efforts to meet with Gaius in Rome. Philo (at least in his writings) does not hide his contempt for Gaius. His initial commentary on Gaius's order to place the statue in the temple is frank: It "is the work of a man whose thoughts are not those of a man" but of a reckless youth exercising "irresponsible dominion over all." Gaius has "unrestrainable impulses"; he is "a formidable power for evil" (190), "the destroyer of the all-holy place" (191). He is manipulative and confrontational. Philo concludes that Gaius callously and calculatingly repositions considerable military forces to "sacrifice" and "massacre" Jews, whom he foresaw "would take up arms to defend the laws and die for their national institutions" (208). Later, Philo describes Gaius as "a ruthless tyrant" with a "despotic brow" (350). His actions are fueled partly by his desire "to be thought a god" (198) and partly by a desire for revenge on Jews who dismantled an altar dedicated to Gaius in Jamnia (201–203). When Gaius does consent to Agrippa's written request to stop the installation, he nevertheless protects the right of others to set up altars, temples, and his images. He schemes to recommence the installation (334–338), an act that leads Philo to rehearse Gaius's untrustworthy actions (339–343) and violations of synagogues in Alexandria (346, also 148). With insistent regularity through the account, Philo disapprovingly reiterates Gaius's desire to be thought of and treated as a god (198, 201, 218, 265, 338, 347, 353, 357, 368, 372).

Philo underlines the magnitude of Gaius's evil (348) by constantly evoking its theological challenge. It violates land and temple, and threatens the people's existence. Gaius "insults that most notable and illustrious shrine" (191). Philo fears that "the overthrow of the temple" will lead to "the annihilation of our common name and nation" (194). Philo sees Gaius deliberately ruining "the sanctity of the temple" by appropriating "the most beautiful" of temples "for his own use" (198). Jews in Jamnia pulled down a statue and altar because it violated "the sanctity which truly belongs to the Holy Land" (202). Gaius's scheme is an affront to the laws for which Jews will die (192, 240). It threatens "the expulsion, enslavement, and wholesale spoliation of the Jews . . . everywhere" (330). It dishonors God and the laws (240). Gaius claims for himself the authority of total obedience (218, 255–256) and exceeds his legitimate sovereignty over heaven and earth by illegitimately challenging God's sovereignty in heaven and seeking to remove from earth any "trace or reminder . . . of the reverence and honor due to the truly existing veritable God" (347). Gaius's challenge comprises blasphemy against God (353, 368). Philo underlines Gaius's ill-used authority throughout by employing terms of address or reference such as "lord" (δεσπότης, *despotēs*[24]) and "lord and master" (ἡγέμονα καὶ δεσποτήν, *hēgemona kai despotēn*, 247; δεσποτὴν καὶ κύριον, *despotēn kai kyrion*, 286, 356).

Yet as powerful and evil as Gaius is, Philo, ironically, indicates the limits of his power. Not only can he not accomplish his will in Judea-Galilee; he also is vulnerable to his own fears. Philo highlights Gaius's fear of governorships like that of Petronius, who governs the large province Syria with considerable influence and military power. Gaius recognizes that "they had resources ready for an uprising" (259). So he must disguise his anger for the defiant Petronius and renew his orders with "ingratiating" speech (260).

But supremely, Gaius is powerless before God, who ensures that Gaius's plans come to naught. Perplexed about what to do in response to the initial news, Philo looks to the indestructible "hope in God our Savior, who has often saved the nation when in helpless straits" (196). The golden age that Philo and many others (elites?) had imagined dawning with the beginning of the reign of Gaius the savior (22) and lasting the first seven months was now an evil age (8–13).

Philo sees God's intervention in various ways. That Gaius does not send a ready-made statue from Rome but requires one to be made, thereby delaying its installation, occurred "through the providence of God, who unseen by us stretched out his hand to protect the wronged" (220). Various agents of God's purposes combine to thwart Gaius. Faithful Jews play a significant part. Petronius knows that Jews both within the land and beyond "would willingly endure to die not once but a thousand times" for their laws and temple (209–212). This knowledge causes him to delay the statue's construction (213–217), advise Jewish leaders of the project, warn against the military consequences of revolt (222), and sympathetically to receive supplications, declarations of loyalty, and commitments to die for the temple from a huge, distressed, but unarmed crowd (225–242). Philo gives God's intervention credit for Petronius's sympathetic response and subsequent actions of writing to Gaius: "But we find that to good men God whispers good decisions by which they will give and receive benefit, and this was true in his case"(245). Agrippa is also a "good man" to whom God whispers, as he intercedes with Gaius, reminding him in writing (276–329) of previous members of the imperial family—Marcus Agrippa, Augustus, Tiberius, but not Pilate (299–305)—who honored the temple (291–299) because "an instinct of reverence or fear" alerted them not to dishonor "the Maker and Father of all," for fear of "the irreparable calamities of divine visitations" (293). Gaius's subsequent schemes to permit altars in the land, provoke violence, and reinstall the statue are thwarted by "a dispensation of the providence and watchful care of God, who surveys and presides over all things with justice" as no violent confrontations occur (336). When Gaius finally dismisses Philo and the Alexandrian delegation as "unfortunate" but not "wicked" and does not execute them as they were expecting, it is because "God taking compassion on us turned his spirit to mercy" (367).

Josephus, Jewish War *2.178–203*

The shorter and earlier of Josephus's two accounts is written in the 70s, some three decades or so after Philo's account.

- *Jewish War* 2.178–180. Agrippa, son of Aristobulus, befriends Gaius, and after praying for the emperor Tiberius's death, is imprisoned.
- *War* 2.181–183. Gaius becomes emperor (37), frees Agrippa, gives him land (Philip's tetrarchy), and makes him king.
- *War* 2.184–187. Gaius in his "insolence" orders Petronius to install statues[25] of Gaius in the Jerusalem temple.
- *War* 2.188–198. At Ptolemais, on the coast of Galilee (2.188–191), and again in inland Galilee significantly at Tiberias, Petronius meets elite and nonelite Jews (with their wives and children) who resist Gaius's plan, appealing to "the laws of their fathers" against images. Petronius warns of the military consequences of defying the emperor, argues that all other conquered peoples honor the emperor with statues, and appeals to his own difficult situation of being "under orders." The Jews declare themselves ready to die rather than permit this sacrilege.
- *War* 2.199–203. After fifty days of further meetings with the elite and the people during seedtime, Petronius reports the impasse to Gaius. Gaius threatens Petronius's execution, but news of Gaius's death by assassination saves the day.

Theological claims abound in Josephus's account. The incident is introduced with Agrippa's prayers that "he might soon see Gaius master of the world through the decease of Tiberius" (2.179). This prayer frames Gaius's emperorship as the divine will and as an answer to prayer. As emperor and "master of the world," Gaius exercises sovereignty over the human realm with divine sanction. Yet, according to Josephus, Gaius is not satisfied with this realm and role. He is not content to be defined by what God has given to him in response to Agrippa's prayer. With hubris he overreaches, not satisfied with the role constituted by the daily sacrifices offered in the Jerusalem temple *for* "Caesar and the Roman people" but not *to* him (2.197). Doing the gods' will is one thing; being a god is another. Josephus openly ascribes ambition to Gaius in installing the statues. He wants to join the ranks of the gods: "He wished to be considered a god and to be hailed as such" (2.184). By installing the statues, Gaius thought he could force such worship of himself and significantly change temple practices, covenant identity, and Jewish monotheistic commitments. His new status as god would also redefine the relationship with Jewish provincials from ruler and ruled to god and worshippers.

Josephus delivers his judgment on Gaius's action by introducing the whole scene with the verb ἐξύβρισεν (exybrisen, 2.184). It is an act of hubris, of insolence, of stepping outside human boundaries. Petronius's verdict is different, at least here in *Jewish War*. His role is to be agent and military enforcer of Gaius's purposes (2.185–186, 195). In discussions with Judeans and Galileans, Petronius describes Gaius in very Johannine language as "the one who sent me" (ὁ πέμψας με, ho pempsas me, 2.195), a description that coheres with Josephus's previous narrative account that "Gaius sent Petronius to Jerusalem with an army" (2.185, ἔπεμψεν, epempsen).

But before employing the military option, Petronius appeals for Jewish compliance in a series of meetings with both elites and nonelites (2.192–194, 199). Petronius argues at length on behalf of Gaius (2.192–194). Though he respects Jewish resistance (2.198), repeatedly Josephus has him depict the Jews' refusal to submit to Gaius's order as "rebellion aggravated by insult" (2.194), as worthy of death and slavery (2.185), and as recklessness that would be met with Roman military power in war (2.193, 195–196, 199). Petronius's argument also sets Gaius's subjugating action in the context of conventional, imperial, civic-religious practice by arguing that "all the subject nations . . . had erected in each of their cities statues of Caesar along with those of their other gods" (2.194). Hence, the installation of the statue extends imperial cult observance to Jerusalem. The use of the phrase "other gods" (ἄλλοις, allois) reinforces Gaius's divine claims while also locating him with other (deified) emperors and with civic deities (such as Artemis in Ephesus) as those worthy of worship. The reference to civic imperial cult practices evokes the big themes of widely attested imperial theology, some of which we have previously noticed, and all of which are implicit in this scene: Rome's divinely chosen status; divine sanction for its empire and ruler; sovereignty over the world; representation through the emperor of the gods' will, presence, rule, and blessing; submission by subject peoples.[26] The civic practices of imperial cult observance reinforce the specific claims evident in Josephus's text of divine sanction for Gaius's rule, of his sovereignty as "master of the world," and his agency on behalf of the gods in manifesting their will and presence among humans who submit to Rome as expressive of the will of the gods.

Over against these imperial theological claims is set a Jewish theological framework that upholds monotheism, denies any role to images, and asserts the sovereignty of the God of Israel. Josephus's account indicates that immediately after Gaius sends Petronius to install the statue, Gaius's purposes will come to naught. "But these orders . . . were under God's care" (2.186). Israel's God thwarts Rome, triumphing over the Roman gods, as the people of God triumph over the Roman emperor in causing him eventually to stop the plan. In meetings with Petronius, the Jewish people consistently stand firm in their laws (2.192, 195), particularly the total prohibition on images, neither of God nor of humans, in the temple or beyond (2.195).

Their devotion is expressed, ironically, around shifting notions of sacrifice. They are willing to sacrifice *for* the emperor in the temple, but to place the emperor's statues in the temple would mean a reversal in roles. The emperor would have to become the sacrificer while they would be the sacrificed. "If [Gaius] wished to set up these statues, he must first sacrifice the entire Jewish nation; and that they presented themselves, their wives and their children, ready for the slaughter" (2.197). Yet to sacrifice the whole nation would destroy Gaius's purposes of being worshipped since there would be no one left to do so. Subsequently, Petronius seeks divine help (presumably Jupiter's) to stop Gaius. Perceiving the people's determination, he offers himself as a sacrifice for the good of the nation. He determines to report to Caesar, seeking divine aid (presumably Jupiter?). "Either God [Jupiter? the Jewish God?] aiding me, I shall prevail with Caesar and have the satisfaction of saving myself [σωθήσομαι, *sōthēsomai*] as well as you, or . . . I am ready on behalf of the lives of so many to surrender my own" (2.201). The crowd's blessing of Petronius, weather delays for those from Gaius bearing the sentence of death on Petronius, and Gaius's death do suggest intervention from Israel's God to thwart Gaius (2.202–203).

Josephus, Jewish Antiquities *18.257–309*

Josephus's longer account comes from the 90s, some fifty years after the incident.

- *Jewish Antiquities* 18.257–260. Strife in Alexandria results in a delegation of Jews (led by Philo) traveling to Rome, to defend before Gaius Caligula the Jewish refusal to honor him with statues and swear by his name.
- *Antiquities* 18.261–268. The indignant Gaius orders Petronius, legate of Syria, to set up an image of Gaius in the Jerusalem temple, using military force if necessary. "Tens of thousands" of Jews nonviolently resist at Ptolemais.
- *Antiquities* 18.269–272. Petronius travels to Tiberias in Galilee and encounters similar opposition.
- *Antiquities* 18.273–283. Jewish leaders prevail upon Petronius to write to Gaius informing him of Jewish resistance. Petronius agrees, recognizing that his defiance might mean sacrificing his own life.
- *Antiquities* 18.284–288. Petronius dismisses the crowds to plant the fields, God sends rain, and Petronius writes his letter to Gaius.
- *Antiquities* 18.289–301. Meantime in Rome, Gaius is impressed by the hospitality and loyalty of King Agrippa and offers to grant any request he makes. Agrippa asks him not to have the statue erected, which Gaius grants.
- *Antiquities* 18.302–309. Meantime Petronius's letter arrives. Gaius, suspecting revolt, is displeased with both the Jews and Petronius. Gaius's menacing reply to Petronius, though, arrives after Gaius's death.

Even more than the scene in *Jewish War*, explicit theological themes pervade this account from *Antiquities*. Josephus especially heightens the contrast between the God of Israel and Gaius's illegitimate quest to be recognized as a god. He frames the scene with a description of typical civic provincial honoring of the emperor through the imperial cult. In a brief discussion of civil strife in Alexandria (18.257–260), Apion, a member of the delegation from Alexandria opposed to the Jews, charges that "[Jews] neglected to pay the honors due to the emperor. For while all the subject peoples in the Roman Empire had dedicated altars and temples to Gaius and had given him the same attentions in all other respects as they did the gods, these people [Jews in Alexandria and elsewhere] alone scorned to honor him with statues and to swear by his name" (18.257–258). Provincial imperial cult observances honored the empire and emperor as agents of the gods, as exercising sovereignty over the world on behalf of the gods, and through pledging allegiance to the emperor. Gaius's attempt to install a statue of himself "in the temple of God" (18.261)—Josephus's descriptions heightens the Gaius-versus-God contest—seeks to extend these practices but to focus them in the act of worship of himself as a god. Josephus presents Gaius's attempt to introduce this worship as revenge. Gaius perceives that he was "slighted by the Jews alone" in their refusal to worship him. He promises to "visit some outrage upon them" (18.260–261). But his action is more than an outrage for Jews; in Josephus's view, it involves the more serious matter of offending God. By his action Gaius was "enlisting God against himself [Gaius]" (18.260). Gaius's action in trying to making himself a god violates the will of God and will "pollute the city" (18.271).

The opposition from Jewish people resembles closely that expressed in *Jewish War*. The statue, its required worship, and the claim that the emperor is god are contrary to the teaching of Moses and the tradition of "our lawgiver and our forefathers" (*Ant.* 18.264), requiring violation of "the law" (18.266). The people's "trust in the goodness of God" means faithfulness to the law and the willingness to die, if necessary, knowing that "God will stand by us." Such faithfulness is much preferable to experiencing God's wrath (18.266–268, 269–274). Josephus is clear that God will bless the resistance efforts.

Petronius's role here differs somewhat from that in *Jewish War*. He remains a key figure, but he is caught up in the heightening of the God-versus-Gaius emphasis. Instead of being an agent of Gaius's purposes, Petronius becomes an agent of God's in writing his letter to Gaius. In doing so, he disparages imperial authority and testifies to Israel's God as "sovereign of all." After hearing the Jewish protest, Petronius commends them for their loyalty to "the precepts of your law," bears witness (surprisingly for an imperial official!) to "the sovereign of all, almighty God," whose temple he does not wish to see subjected to "the insolence of imperial authority." He invokes God's blessing on the people, praying for God's assistance and enabling for them, and declares his willingness to suffer Gaius's displeasure (18.277–283)! "God, on his part, showed Petronius that he was with him and would lend his aid in all matters. . . . God straightaway sent a heavy shower" to assist in the seed planting. Petronius concludes that this is "unmistakable evidence that God's providence is over the Jews" and informs Gaius that this God's power is "unimpaired" (18.284–288).

Also an agent of God's purposes is King Agrippa. Having won Gaius's favor and been invited to ask for whatever he wants, Agrippa offers Gaius the opportunity for gaining reputation and lasting divine favor. Agrippa explains to Gaius that he is asking "for something that will bring you a reputation for piety [εὐσεβοῦς, *eusebous*] and will induce the Deity to help you in everything that you wish" (18.297). Thus he gives Gaius the opportunity to collapse the "God-versus-Gaius" divide and to become an agent of God's purposes. He requests that Gaius desist from his temple project. Gaius does so.

Gaius's death before his menacing reply reaches Petronius is further evidence of God's favor with Petronius. God was not unmindful of the risky favor or grace (χάριτι, *chariti*) Petronius had shown to the Jews in honoring God. God punishes Gaius and rewards Petronius's faithfulness with the emperor's death. "The removal of Gaius in displeasure at his rashness in promoting his own claim to worship was God's payment of the debt to Petronius" (18.306). Petronius marvels "at the providence of God, who swiftly and punctually had paid him his reward" (18.309). In honoring Petronius, God punishes Gaius for "rashness in promoting his own claim to worship." In his letter to Gaius, Petronius had warned him against holding the Jewish people "guilty for their reverence to God, and thus to spend the rest of his life in foreboding" (18.277). Throughout God protects these people and the Roman official Petronius from the powerful emperor, while thwarting the emperor, who seeks to become a god, to contravene God's purposes disclosed in the law, to violate the Jerusalem temple, and to turn subject Jews into idolatrous worshippers of a false god. Josephus, though, is careful not to condemn the whole imperial system; elsewhere he has made clear that it thrives because of God's election (*J. W.* 2.390–391). He presents Gaius's actions as an isolated aberration. "Rome and all the empire, and especially those of the senators who were outstanding in merit, favored Petronius" (*Ant.* 18.306).

Intertextuality: The Gaius Incident and Developing Johannine Christology

In this section, I identify six possible areas of cultural intertextuality between this incident and John's Gospel. My goal is not to claim the specific influence of particular paragraphs in Philo or Josephus on Johannine thinking, but at the risk of smoothing over important differences among the three accounts, to take a more general approach, identifying some central and recurring themes in the accounts of Gaius's action that suggest imperial negotiation in the Johannine traditions developing in Judea-Galilee in the 40s CE.

Sovereignty

Central in the accounts of this incident are the competing claims to exercise sovereignty over the world, as frequently asserted by Gaius, emperor of Rome, and countermanded by Jewish allegiance to the God of Israel. These quotes assert Gaius's sovereignty:

- Gaius succeeded to the sovereignty of the whole earth and sky, . . . with all parts east, west, south, north, harmoniously adjusted, the Greek in full agreement with the barbarian, the civil with the military to enjoy and participate in peace . . . and astonishment at his prodigious and indescribable prosperity . . . and dominion extending from the rising to the setting sun both within the ocean and beyond it. (Philo, *Emb.* 8–13)

- Agrippa finally raised his hands to heaven and openly prayed that he might see Gaius, master of the world. (Josephus, *J. W.* 2.179)

- You [Petronius] shall be cited by all men now and all that will come hereafter . . . that an emperor's commands are never to be flouted. (Josephus, *Ant.* 18.304) Petronius, you have not learned to hearken to an emperor. . . . You disregard the imperial commands of your sovereign. (Philo, *Emb.* 255–256)

Yet other quotes assert the sovereignty of Israel's God:

- [Jews] acknowledge one God who is the Father and Maker of the world, . . . [observing customs] in honor of the Maker and Father of all. (Philo, *Emb.* 115, 293)

- [God] even in your eyes must be accounted a higher power than Gaius. (Josephus, *Ant.* 18.268)

- [You are] serving the sovereign of all, almighty God. (Josephus, *Ant.* 18.280)

- [Petronius] said, moreover, that the Divinity who was in charge of them had shown his power to be unimpaired and was quite unambiguous in displaying this power. (Josephus, *Ant.* 18. 288)

- I have another particular motive in that the story [of Gaius's death] provides good evidence of God's power [πολλὴν πίστιν τοῦ θεοῦ τῆς δυνάμεως]. (Josephus, *Ant.* 19.16)

In this episode, in a context of existing Roman control of Judea-Galilee, Gaius tries afresh to assert his sovereignty and Rome's over Judean-Galilean territory, over Jewish temple worship and customs, over the wills of his appointees, over soldiers, over his opponents, over the produce of the land (Philo, *Emb.* 252–253), and over life and death.[27] He asserts common imperial claims made by every emperor that preceded him and followed him, claims that reinforce the huge divide between ruler and ruled, emperor and subjected, center and provinces. Whenever such power is asserted, it must be negotiated and—in this instance—contested as Philo and Josephus make clear. In these accounts, Gaius's failure is constantly portrayed as the victory of God's sovereignty.[28]

Not surprisingly in such a context, John's Gospel also engages the issue of sovereignty throughout. Space permits only a few illustrative examples. The Gospel opens with an astounding yet very traditional Jewish claim—repeated in the accounts of both Philo and Josephus—of God's sovereignty rooted in the act of creation. Evoking Gen 1:1 with its opening phrase "in the beginning [ἐν ἀρχῇ, *en archē*]," the Gospel attributes the creation of all things to God and executed "through him," the Word identified as Jesus (1:14; 17:24). The Gospel repeatedly asserts Jesus' origin in the beginning with God as the decisive legitimation for Jesus, which renders him superior to all other revealer figures, as I argued in chapter 4 above (8:42). Throughout his public activity, Jesus reveals and exercises the sovereignty in which he participated from his origin. In speaking God's words and doing God's will, including the central acts of judging (determining human destiny, 5:22) and giving life (sovereignty over death, 5:21; Lazarus, John 11), he asserts God's sovereignty over human allegiance and existence (1:35–51; 5:19–30). God has given him "authority over all people" (17:2). In healing the physically damaged, in feeding those without food and wine, and in walking on water (2:1–11; 4:45–5:9; 6:1–21), he asserts sovereignty over the created world in acts of re-creation. The acts of feeding and exercising power over water (6:1–21) not only recall God's sovereignty over Egyptian tyranny exercised through Moses, but are also imperially confrontational in exhibiting God's sovereignty anew. Gaius's (and Rome's) sovereignty extends over the seas, as both Philo (*Emb.* 8–13) and Josephus (*Ant.* 19.6, "lord of the sea") recognize. And as I have mentioned in chapters 6 and 8 above, disease and lack of food are two classic consequences of imperial power, whose damage Jesus begins to repair in his healings and feedings in accord with the biblical tradition (Isa 25:6–10; 35:5–6). Philo, as part of his parody of Gaius's rule (*Emb.* 74–114), charges Gaius with bringing "disease to the healthy, crippling to the sound of limb, and in general death to the living" (106–107), the exact reverse of Jesus' healing and life-giving actions in John's Gospel, and featured in a Signs collection—*if* the Johannine tradition began in this way (and the evidence is not especially compelling). Jesus' actions are part of a further assertion or revelation of God's sovereignty, which establishes another age with life marked by a different quality and quantity of life. This "life of the age" is available even now through Jesus' words and works (6:40; see chap. 8 above).

Throughout, various designations identify Jesus' role as revealing God's sovereignty. We can briefly recall three titles from the discussion in chapter 7 (above). Jesus is the heavenly Son of Man, the one who descends from heaven and returns there in ascension (1:51; 3:13). The designation "Son of Man" draws on Daniel 7:13–14, where it denotes a heavenly being "coming with the clouds of heaven," to whom God gives unending dominion, glory, and kingship over all people.[29] This figure, here identified with Jesus, enacts God's never-ending sovereignty over all empires and people. That certainly is not good news for Rome.

Just prior to this designation is another one that identifies Jesus as king of Israel (John 1:49). An extensive tradition identifies God as Israel's king (1 Sam 8:7; Ps 47:2; Zech 14:9, 16) and the king as representative and agent of God's rule not only in Israel but also among the nations (e.g., Ps 72). Jesus represents God's rule as king, but such a designation is quite threatening for Rome, and hence it is treasonous. Rome appointed kings for Israel (e.g., Herod, Josephus, *Ant.* 16.311) and killed other kingly claimants such as Judas, Simon, Athrongeus, and Simon bar Giora.[30] Jesus' kingship is the central issue in John's account of his crucifixion (where the term *basileus* is used 12 times[31]): his assertion of God's sovereignty collides with Rome's. "Every one who makes himself a king sets himself against Caesar" (John 19:12 RSV). Pilate asserts his power over Jesus by reminding him that Pilate can release or execute him, but Jesus counters by reminding Pilate that the only power he has comes from God (19:10–11). In 19:7 Rome's allies refer to Jesus as "Son of God," an imperial title and one that presents Jesus as a treasonous challenger of Rome's authority.

This relativizing of Rome's sovereignty is a constant element in the presentation of Jesus' death. The Gospel insists that Jesus dies not on Rome's terms and in Rome's timing, but on his own terms and timing. He gives himself to die; he is not put to death

(10:17–18). His death cannot happen until his "hour" comes (12:23–27). He predicts Judas' betrayal (13:21–27). Jesus controls his own arrest (18:1–14), and when he reveals himself with a formula of divine self-disclosure ("I am [he]," ἐγώ εἰμι, *ego eimi*, 18:5; cf. Exod 3:14), those who have come to arrest him ironically fall to the ground (John 18:6). He accepts the "cup" given by God (18:11). His resurrection reveals the limits of the devil's (13:2, 27) and the empire's power in alliance with the Jerusalem elite: they cannot keep him dead. And, ironically, his "lifting up" (crucifixion, resurrection, ascension) is the means by which "all people" encounter God's sovereignty (12:32). Jesus manifests a sovereignty greater than Rome's.

How much of these and other affirmations of God's sovereignty exercised in Jesus emerge directly in negotiating the Gaius incident cannot be determined. But two things are clear: The Gaius incident was a "focal point" for issues of sovereignty. And such issues pervade the Gospel. I am suggesting that the Gaius incident posed this issue of sovereignty in such a way that it could not be ignored. It is possible that Johannine traditions—emerging in circles of followers of Jesus, crucified by Rome—negotiated Rome's/Gaius's claims of sovereignty with what appear in the Gospel as defiant interpretations of his death and resurrection, of his public activity, and of his divine sanction. It is quite possible that the Gaius incident, like Jesus' crucifixion before it and the temple's destruction in 70 after it, along with other factors and traditions, provoked (further?) reflection on the relationship between Jesus and God's sovereign rule, on how loyalty to God's sovereignty enabled or restricted followers in negotiating Rome's sovereignty, and on understandings of Jesus as one who exercises a kingship and reveals a sovereignty much different from and greater than Rome's tyranny. The Gospel reflects the outcome of this and other experiences.

Dualism

A second aspect of Johannine thinking suggests possible interaction with the Gaius incident: the Gospel's well-known dualistic way of understanding the world. The three accounts of Gaius's actions are quite dualistic in their presentations. Gaius is set against the temple, against the law, against Jewish people, against the land, against God, as recounted above. People either comply or die. Gaius's military might opposes those who want to honor their customs peaceably (Josephus, *J.W.* 2.185–187; Philo, *Emb.* 229). His role as hostile master requires Jews to be slaves (119). His immature youthfulness is set against mature manhood (190), his "lunacy" against good judgment (Josephus, *Ant.* 18.177–178), unlawfulness against lawfulness (Philo, *Emb.* 348), "a formidable power for evil" against the good (191, also 118, 348). Ultimately Gaius is set against God (118). Philo asks Gaius, "Do you a mere man seek to annex also ether and heaven, not satisfied with the sum of so many mainlands, islands, nations, regions over which you assumed sovereignty, and do you deem God worthy of nothing here in our world below, no country, no city? (347). Josephus leads into the temple-statue incident by reporting on Gaius's disrespectful dismissal of Philo, "head of the [Alexandrian] delegation," without allowing him to answer accusations that Alexandrian Jews did not honor the emperor. He reports Philo as saying that "in fact he [Gaius] was now enlisting God against himself [Gaius]" (*Ant.* 18.260). It is Gaius as savior (Philo, *Emb.* 22) against God "our Savior" (196, σωτήρ, *sōtēr*).

The dualistic structuring of this scene is evident not only in the constant emphasis on the incompatibility between Gaius's plan and Jewish commitments to law (no images, Josephus, *J.W.* 2.195), temple (Philo, *Emb.* 290–291), land (202), and God. It is also evident in the constant attention (noted above) to God thwarting Gaius's attempts and punishing him in death. And it is further evidenced in that the situation is one that allows no compromise. The letters written to Gaius are not intended to negotiate a compromise (sacrifices are already offered *for* him; Josephus *J.W.* 2.197) but to persuade him "to relent and not adopt a cruel plan or have the heart to exterminate the nation (Josephus, *Ant.* 18.275). Similarly a proposed Jewish delegation is not going to negotiate a compromise but is "to persuade him" to desist (Philo, *Emb.* 240). Likewise Agrippa's letter is a "supplication" (290).

Significantly, Philo observes that this "either/or" situation is a change to previous "both/and" ways of negotiating Roman power. Agrippa appeals to Gaius by reminding him of previous emperors and leading Romans such as Marcus Agrippa, Augustus, and Tiberius, who did not demand an "either/or" interaction but allowed a "both/and" approach that respected Jewish customs along with appropriate recognition of Rome (299–305). Petronius is presented in his actions, Jewish sympathies, and alignment with God's purposes as being aware that Gaius's demand violates Jewish practices and convictions in ways not demanded by previous emperors (209–245; Josephus, *J.W.* 2.201; *Ant.* 18.284–288). The body of elders that addresses Petronius declares that its desire, blameless before God, is to maintain current practice motivated by "respectful fear of the emperor *and* loyalty to the consecrated law" (Philo, *Emb.* 236, emphasis added). Agrippa takes up the same theme in his appeal, stressing the consequences of Gaius continuing his demand: "Either I must seem a traitor to my people or no longer be counted your friend as I have been: there is no other alternative" (327). The existing negotiation of Roman power allows both fear of the emperor and fidelity to the law, loyalty to one's country and friendship with Caesar. Gaius's plan sets the two at odds and jeopardizes both.

John's dualistic framing of the world is well known. Life is set against death, light against darkness, God against the devil, truth against falsehood, that from above against that from below, love against hate.[32] Often the attempt to make sense of the post-70 CE experience of separation from the synagogue is suggested as one of the major influences on this structuring of reality, as are various other traditions such as wisdom or apocalyptic thinking. I do not deny likely influence from various sources, but neither should we look too quickly past the rigidly dualistic quality of the Gaius incident. It is a focal point for an "either/or" understanding of the Roman world, in which no compromise in negotiating Roman power seems possible. It is a focal point for seeing the opposition and incompatibility between the demands of empire and God. Though it does not cause Josephus, for instance, to revoke his view of Rome as chosen by God (*J.W.* 2.360, 390–391; 3.400–404; 4.622; 5.60, 363–419, esp. 378; 6.99–110), and though he presents the "either/or" confrontation as largely an aberration (*Ant.* 18.306), it does reveal some fundamental incompatibilities and lines that cannot be crossed when the empire claims ultimate sovereignty. The import of such a scene is caution and suspicion.

The Gospel attests a deep-seated suspicion of the world (as recognized in chaps. 6–7 above).[33] As much as God loves the world, and as much as the world is the arena of

God's saving activity (3:16–17), it is also a rejecting (1:10) and hostile place that rejects both Jesus and disciples (7:7; 15:18–19; 17:14). It is marked by evil deeds (3:19; 7:7). It is life contrary to God's purposes.

The ultimate display of such life and rejection of God's purposes is the crucifixion of Jesus. This death comes about through the work of the devil (13:2, 27) and through the Jerusalem elite allied with the Roman governor, who protect the status quo against Jesus' revelation of God's love and life (chaps. 18–19). They are "the world." As I have argued throughout, the ruler in the narrative is Pilate, the "ruler of the world," who has no power over Jesus and is cast out and judged by Jesus in his resurrection and ascension (12:31; 14:30; 16:11). John—like Matthew, Luke, and the writer of Revelation—sees the devil as the power behind the empire (Matt 4:8; Luke 4:5–6; Rev 12:7–17). The world has a false peace that contrasts with God's true peace (14:27), a likely reference in this context to the Pax Romana, Rome's peace comprising submission, chosen or enforced, to Rome's political, socioeconomic might and exploitative hierarchy. The call for distance from imperial society, which the author/s want/s for Jesus-believers in Ephesus, is rooted in the dualism of this developing tradition.

The question as to where this deep-seated suspicion of the imperial world was learned is worth pursuing even if ultimately it is answerable only by holding together a number of possibilities. The usual candidates are intrasynagogue conflict, and/or apocalyptic and/or wisdom and/or prophetic traditions. But one of the possibilities, previously neglected, should include confrontations with Roman imperial power throughout the first century as the Johannine Jesus traditions developed. Jesus' crucifixion is one such incident. The Gaius incident provides another "focal point" for learning a long-lasting lesson of suspicion. The destruction of the Jerusalem temple in 70 CE is a likely third incident. This profound suspicion is certainly not the only way in which the Johannine material negotiates the imperial world. It also affirms God's love for the world (3:16). Mission that continues and imitates Jesus' mission is a further aspect of imperial negotiation since Jesus is "the Savior of the world" (4:42); being sent to take away the sins of the world (1:29), Jesus in turn sends his disciples to continue that mission, whatever the consequences (15:18–25; 17:18, 23; 20:21). Also to be noticed are scenes in which people, having encountered Jesus, apparently continue to live their normal daily lives in this world without withdrawing from it (cf. 17:15). Examples include the married couple and wine steward of 2:1–11, the Samaritan woman who returns to her city (4:39–42), the Capernaum official whose son Jesus heals from his location in Cana (4:46–54), and Mary, Martha, and Lazarus (chap. 11). Although the Gospel reinforces the dualism between Jesus and the emperor, some participation in this world as well as mission to it coexist along with much suspicion: these form strategies for negotiating imperial power.

Making Oneself God

Repeatedly the three accounts depict Gaius wishing "to be considered a god" (Josephus, *J.W.* 2.184; Philo, *Emb.* 372). Postmortem deification had been accorded the emperor Augustus, but not his successor Tiberius. Yet it was clearly Gaius's desire, according to Philo, to be granted divine honors during his lifetime. "Gaius grew beside himself with vanity, not only saying but [also] thinking that he was God" (Philo, *Emb.* 162). Already Gaius "has soared above man's estate and already ranks himself as among the gods" (218). Philo parodies Gaius's ascent to godship by describing the emergence of Gaius's overstepping of the "bounds of human nature . . . in his eagerness to be thought a god" (75). Gaius identifies with various gods in dressing himself in their guise while failing to imitate them in manifesting any of their virtues and benefactions (75–118).[34] Philo's parody shows Gaius "soaring above" the human realm in "making himself a god," first by identifying with the superhuman and worshipped demigods (Dionysus: cf. John 2:1–11, water into wine; Heracles). Then "leaving the demigods below he proceeded to advance upwards" by identifying with the great gods Hermes, Apollo, and Ares (*Emb.* 93). He claimed to share "honors" with these gods "as their equals" (ἰσότιμος, *isotimos,* 98). This is the means of Gaius's self-made ascent into the realm of divinity.

The imposition of the statue of himself as Zeus/Jupiter in the Jerusalem temple extends his demand to be recognized as a god. Particularly he attempts to force Jews to worship him as a god, as do other cities, especially in the East, and "all subject nations [who] had erected in each of their cities statues of Caesar, along with those of their other gods" (Josephus, *J. W.* 2.194). Some Alexandrians had presented charges to Gaius against Alexandrian Jews for not paying "the honors due to the emperor. For while all the subject peoples in the Roman Empire had dedicated altars and temples to Gaius and had given him the same attentions in all other respects as they did the gods, these people had scorned to honor him with statues and swear by his name" (Josephus, *Ant.* 18.257–259; Philo, *Emb.* 355).

Philo's account addresses the charge with multiple refutations. The body of Jerusalem leaders declares, "Was our temple the first to accept sacrifices in behalf of Gaius's reign only that it should be the first or only to be robbed of its ancestral traditions of worship?" (*Emb.* 232). Agrippa protests that the Jewish nation "stood not a whit behind any other either in Asia or in Europe, in its prayers, its erection of votive offerings, its number of sacrifices" (280). And Philo's Alexandrian delegation responds to accusations that they have not honored the emperor by saying, "We are slandered. . . . We have done this thrice already, the first time at your accession to the sovereignty, the second when you escaped the severe sickness which all the habitable world suffered with you, the third as a prayer of hope for victory in Germany" (356). Yet Gaius encourages the construction of altars, temples, images, and statues dedicated to himself throughout Judea-Galilee (334–337), ignores forcible impositions of images in Jewish meeting houses (134–137), and had himself forcibly installed images and statues in the synagogues of Alexandria (346). By way of contrast, Philo observes that the emperor Augustus did not do these things (148).

Such observances constituted celebrations of the imperial cult. Honoring the emperor took diverse forms: not contesting Roman power, compliance with its laws and social order, paying taxes, and in Gaius's case prostration (*proskynēsis*) in his presence and to his image (116; cf. 352, actions of the Alexandrian Jewish delegation; Dio Cassius 59.24.4). Imperial cult observances provided an arena for especially focused expressions of asserting and acknowledging Roman power.[35] Elites often took the lead in sponsoring celebrations and providing leadership through priesthoods. Celebrations marked significant imperial events and involved a range of locations and activities: civic festivals, parades, games, street parties; offering sacrifices of wine, cakes, and animals; locating statues and images in various temples, gymnasia, baths, council houses, theaters; singing hymns (Philo, *Emb.* 96–97), celebrating in trade guilds or associations; making oaths; distributing free food in cities. These events and practices proclaimed an imperial theology that sanctioned the empire and emperor as chosen by the gods, especially Jupiter,[36] as their agent in manifesting their sovereignty, will, presence, and blessings.[37] This theology, expressed in the various rituals, presented the hierarchical, military-enforced, elite-benefiting, imperial society (as in chap. 3 above) as the divine will requiring submission and compliance. Participation in imperial cult celebrations, mostly chosen and not coerced, provided a means to demonstrate socially compliant behavior.

Gaius, though, seems persuaded by the charges of Jewish failure to honor him since he himself complains about a lack of Jewish expressions of honor. He ranks the Jewish nation "my worst enemy" (256, also 201), the ones he hates (133), the only ones "of every race of men [who] do not acknowledge Gaius as a god" (265, also 198). Gaius confronts the Alexandrian Jewish delegation: "Are you the god-haters who do not believe me to be a god, a god acknowledged among all the other nations but not to be named by you?" (353). He concedes that Jews have sacrificed *for* him, but that is not as honoring as sacrificing *to* him (357). God's verdict on Gaius's aspirations for divine honors is clear. Gaius's death is God's response "in displeasure at his rashness in promoting his own claim to worship" (Josephus, *Ant.* 18.306).[38] The incident raises significant questions about what is at stake in being acknowledged as a god.

Interestingly, John's Jesus is accused of quite similar things three times.[39] He is charged with making himself "equal to God" (ἴσον . . . τῷ θεῷ, *ison . . . tō theō*, 5:18). Blasphemously, "You, being a man, make yourself God" (10:33 RSV). "He ought to die, because he has made himself the Son of God" (19:7). The three charges, worded with different objects (equal to God; God; Son of God), emphasize the illegitimacy of "making oneself" something more than human. Though the objects differ, the charges bear the same weight. All three are so serious that his opponents declare that Jesus should die (5:18, kill; 10:31, stone; 19:7, ought to die). In all three instances, the accusers are "the *Ioudaioi*," consistent opponents of Jesus, and a narrative indication that their charge that Jesus "makes himself" equal to God or God is false. Yet the Gospel recognizes that Jesus is God in 1:1 (from the beginning) and 20:28 ('Thomas' confession after touching the risen Jesus, "My Lord and my God"). The paradox of accusation and confession raises intriguing questions. On one hand, what do the opponents find so offensive? On the other, how is it possible for this Gospel that is so at home in its Jewish monotheistic tradition to make the confession that Jesus is in some sense God?[40] In what sense and how did this affirmation come into being?

This double-sided problem evident in the finished form of the Gospel results, in one view, from decades of theological reflection by which, as Wayne Meeks says, "a new religious movement interpreted Scripture, interpreted Jesus, interpreted its own history, and interpreted the world in one complex dialectic."[41] Following J. Louis Martyn, Meeks argues, "It was precisely in arguments with other Jews that this circle of Jesus followers had to work out the sense in which Jesus was for them 'equal to God.'"[42] Particularly important for Meeks are the exegetical debates about visions or prophetic theophanies that John claims cannot be visions of God (1:18; 6:46) but are visions of the heavenly, enthroned Son of Man—identified now as Jesus—to whom Moses, Abraham, and Isaiah bear witness (5:46; 8:56; 12:41). Meeks particularly links these debates and affirmations to the pain of the Johannine group's separation post-70 from Jewish communities to which they had previously belonged.

As always, Meeks's discussion is wonderfully insightful. But for our purposes here, several modifications are necessary. Meeks focuses on the end of the interpretive process and centers on post-70 separation from the synagogue. Setting aside the dubious claim that there has been a separation (see chap. 1–2 above), he does not explore what might have happened to launch the Johannine community toward these affirmations between 30 and 70. Do we know enough about the development of the Johannine tradition to be sure that claims about Jesus' identity and function as "equal to God/being God" emerge only late in the process? Meeks's own data show that there was a long, widespread, and diverse debate about divine status across the ancient world well before 70 CE. Badian, for example, explores the meaning of *isotheos* (ἰσόθεος, "equal to God"?) in Homer and Aeschylus, as well as Persian uses in relation to Alexander of Macedonia (often called "the Great").[43] Can we be sure that Johannine tradition developed in its earlier stages untouched by any of this centuries-old discussion, and by events such as the Gaius incident, especially when the issue of divine status is central to it?

Moreover, Meeks's conception of the emergence of these claims centers on a very narrowly defined sectarian context and in finally irreconcilable, intellectual disputes among Jewish groups involved in an exegetical process, a process that Meeks helpfully sketches. Meeks immediately distances John's controversies from Philo and Gaius by arguing: "The scale of the struggle which we can glimpse behind the apologetic sections of the Fourth Gospel is much smaller. While in Philo's writings we see the Moses traditions being used in a broad *Kulturkampf* here in John they are employed in a sectarian controversy."[44] Yet such a claim is only true if scholars restrict discussion of John's Gospel to a context of "sectarian controversy"! But it is precisely this claim that I have questioned throughout this book in positing John's Gospel—in both finished form and in its developing traditions—as a work of imperial negotiation. Our discussion of the themes of sovereignty and dualism in the sections on John's traditions and the Gaius crisis (above), plus the discussion in chapters 1–12 above, are more than enough to cast major doubts on such a narrow formulation. Meeks's construction of the debate over "equal to God" suggests that studious sectarian groups myopically focused only on religious issues, emerging from their bunkers to fire the next exegetical weapon at their opponents, being counterattacked, and retreating to find further textual ammunition, all the time oblivious to the rest of the world and daily life. Meeks's own data, which he strangely ignores in his conclusions, along with Badian's study mentioned above, cast doubts on this scenario. Both studies clearly show that questions of divine status were not exclusively—or even primarily—religious questions since they were very much involved in legitimizing philosophical and political claims.[45]

The Gaius scene provides ample evidence of both the public context and the political content of debate about divine status. It is certainly not sectarian in location, as the accounts of Philo and Josephus amply demonstrate. Nor is it an isolated religious or theological issue, as their accounts also make clear. And nor are the weapons of the debate primarily exegetical.

Noting cultural hesitations about the position of the emperor in relation to the gods, Simon Price discusses a phrase reminiscent of the language in John 5:18 ("equal to

God") used in relation to the imperial cult that identifies *isotheoi timai*, "honors equivalent to those paid to the gods."[46] The phrase designated cult observances that were "modeled on the cult of the traditional gods but were distinguished from them," the premise being that divinized emperors, whether pre- or postmortem, were not the equal of the gods[47] since "the Greek gods are powers, not persons."[48] Gaius's complaints that Jews do not honor him adequately in offering, for instance, sacrifices *for* but not *to* him reflect this argument as to what "equivalent" honors might be and express Gaius's protest against what he understands to be a demoted status. Price quotes a further maxim that reflects something of the same differentiation: "What is a god? The exercise of power. What is a king? Godlike" or "equal to a god" in exercising power (ἰσόθεος, *isotheos*).[49] The latter phrase is precisely the terminology used of Jesus in 5:18 after he has exhibited Godlike power in healing the paralyzed man on a Sabbath (e.g., Exod 15:11, 26; 2 Kings 5; Ps 103:3). The important point that both Gaius's protest and Price's discussion make that is relevant to our discussion here is that questions about or charges concerning divine status are not primarily theological or sectarian but chiefly imperial and societal. These are arguments from the political and civic spheres. Despite positing a process of multifaceted interpretation of Scripture, Jesus, community history, and world, Meeks's final discussion focuses only on the first three, understands them in religious terms, and ignores the last one.

I suggest that interpreting the world, especially the Roman imperial world, plays an important role early in the Johannine traditions in formulating claims about Jesus. I am not denying important contributions from the other factors that Meeks helpfully identifies in the issue's final and full expression. But it seems strange to ignore the possible role of interaction with the high-profile Gaius event in 40, which involved many people over a wide area of Judea-Galilee and beyond, and in which claims about making oneself god are central and contentious. Jewish scruples about Gaius's claims are expressed elsewhere, as Meeks notes (2 Macc 9:12; Philo, *Alleg. Interp.* 1.49), and Greek and Roman ambivalences about imperial quests for divine status (see chap. 12 above) are evident in other writings (e.g., Seneca's satire on Claudius's divinization, *Apocalyntosis* [*Pumpkinification*] *of Claudius*; the presentations of Gaius, Nero, and Domitian in subsequent writing[50]). Such reservations attest that there was public debate about the notion and the validity of attributing divine status to living and/or dead mortals.

Through this debate, however, a repertoire of meanings from Greek and Roman discussion of being "equal to (a god or) God" emerges. Being "equal to (a god or) God" is a matter of honor, of power, of benefaction, of imitating God, of being sent as an agent of the gods.[51] We can compare this repertoire of factors to hints in Philo and Josephus about Gaius's aspirations for and understandings of divine status. According to Philo and Josephus, Gaius's aspirations seem to comprise similar dynamics of power, honor, benefaction, imitation, and agency.

Josephus sees claims of divine status as the natural corollary of Gaius's constant assertions of his vast and "godlike" imperial power and expectation of instant obedience.[52] Josephus explains the emergence of Gaius's aspirations thus: "But as time went on, he ceased to think of himself as a man, and . . . he imagined himself as a god because of the greatness of his empire" (*Ant.* 18.256). In both Josephus and Philo we saw how Gaius mocks Petronius for not having learned to acknowledge the emperor's power by obeying his commands (Philo, *Emb.* 255–256; Josephus, *Ant.* 18.304). Great power attests divine status and requires instant compliance.

Second, Gaius's desire to be worshipped as a god is about honor. He is so honored, as we noted above, in other cities and nations (e.g., Philo, *Emb.* 116), but not in Jerusalem or from Jews. Philo attributes Gaius's "extraordinary and passionate love for Alexandria" to its fostering "the idea of godship, which occupied his dreams," and as a "pattern to other cities of the worship due to him" (338). Philo's Gaius dismisses Jewish sacrifices made *for* him but not *to* him as inadequate, as not honoring enough: "What good is it then?" (357). "He wished to be considered a god and to be hailed as such" (Josephus, *J.W.* 2.184). Petronius speaks on Gaius's behalf, warning that failing to allow the statue and practices of its worship would dishonor the emperor. To resist "this prac- tice [of erecting statues of Gaius and worshipping him as other cities have done] amounted almost to rebellion, aggravated by insult" (2.194).

Third, his divine status is about beneficial rule. Philo describes Gaius at the begin- ning of his reign as a benefactor (Philo, *Emb.* 22). As such, Gaius, like other emperors and gods, oversees "the good" of the empire (cf. Philo's praise for Augustus as benefac- tor, 143–150). Gaius has the power to effect the "good things" that he decides. Philo has Petronius argue that Gaius's approach to being emperor is "that whatever he wishes is beneficial and that what he has once decreed is as good as accomplished" (218).

Philo highlights a fourth factor concerning imitation of the gods, or more accurately Gaius's failure to imitate them. In his parody of Gaius's ascent into the ranks of the divine through the demigods to the great gods (74–114), Philo constantly complains that Gaius does not imitate their virtues and so shows himself to be fake. Gaius's actions, in contrast to theirs, damage human well-being instead of benefiting it (e.g., 81–92, 98, 101–102, 114, etc.). People marvel "at the strange contradiction" that Gaius's actions "were the opposite of those whose honors he purposes to share as their equal [ἰσότιμος, *isotimos*]" (98). "Gaius has no right to be likened to any of the gods or demigods either, for his nature, his substance, his purpose in life, is different from theirs" (114). Philo thus applies a criterion of imitation to Gaius's claims for divine sta- tus to deny them. Gaius fails the virtue test.

A fifth aspect, agency, can be listed briefly here since I will return to it below. Gener- ically Gaius is the agent of the gods as emperor, but Philo and Josephus emphasize in their accounts that he is self-made in seeking divine status. Philo's parody (74–114) mocks his attempted ascent and lack of virtue. He is an agent of his own agenda.

In the accounts of Philo and Josephus, Gaius is presented as matching the features of divine status that Meeks identifies well: honor, power, benefaction, imitation, agency. But such qualities are not neutral: they need content. They are encountered and evalu- ated only in being exercised. Is Gaius honorable? Does his power benefit? Does he imi- tate God? Philo's own verdict is negative (e.g., 74–114; e.g., 90, 114). Gaius's offense "included the supremely evil vices of infidelity and ingratitude to the Benefactor of the whole world who through his power bestows blessings poured in unstinted abundance on every part of the All" (118). Numerous others in the accounts also offer negative ver- dicts. Petronius (209, 213), Jewish leaders (222–224), the inhabitants of the holy city Jerusalem (225), and the elders (229–242) do not see Gaius's action concerning the Jerusalem temple as beneficial. It is misused power, it dishonors, it does not imitate

God's requirements, it brings death (237–238). Jews in Josephus's account declare, "We have put our trust in the goodness of God and in the labors of our forefathers" (*Ant.* 18.266), both of which Gaius's power and benefaction threaten, thereby precluding any honor for him. Philo's elders indicate their different commitments in concluding their appeal to Petronius by asking, "For what more profitable gain can men have than holiness?" (*Emb.* 242).

In both accounts the Gaius incident presses the question publicly and politically of what it means to claim to be a god, just as John's Gospel does. Is there a direct link between the two? It would not be surprising if the public debate and evaluation of Gaius's claims and actions impacted the traditions developing about Jesus among Jesus-followers in Judea-Galilee in the 40s–50s in some way, whether through participation in the societal debate or reflection internal to the community. It is impossible to know how or if this circle of followers of Jesus actively participated in the conflict. Did they actively side with those opposed to Gaius's demands, or did the conflict have some other effect? In such a heated political context, however, it is not difficult to imagine followers of Jesus wrestling with questions raised by Gaius's demand: What did it mean for followers of Jesus to honor Jesus? What was the significance of Jesus' numerous powerful benefactions and their relation to God's purposes and presence? What do such actions say about his identity? And how do they differ from Gaius's claims and actions? Can one honor Gaius and Jesus? How are the two similar and/or different? All of these are issues of imperial negotiation, and as a "focal point" the Gaius incident forces intertextual engagement with them. One need not imagine that this is the first or last time such issues emerge, but the "either/or" nature of the dispute poses them sharply around 40 CE.

Significantly for contemplating the possible impact of such engagement, we should observe that the repertoire of five characteristics of divine status discussed above resembles claims made in John 5 and 10 in response to the accusation of Jesus making himself God or equal to God. Jesus' responses do not address the charge of "making himself" God/equal to God/Son of God with a simple "yes" or "no," but he does provide content for these terms of divine status. Not surprisingly, the content in both chapters 5 and 10 centers on honor, power, benefaction, imitation, agency. The Father and the Son receive honor (5:23; 10:32, 38). Both God and the Son are benefactors in giving life (5:21, 24; 10:28, 32). Jesus imitates God in his works (5:19; 10:30, 32, 37). Jesus is sent from the Father (10:32, 36, consecrated and sent as God's son or agent). He is the Father's agent (10:25). He bestows life (10:28). He shares in and manifests the Father's unassailable power (10:28–29, 32). He is one with the Father in receiving honor, exercising power, exerting benefaction, imitating the Father, and being the Father's agent (10:30, 38). It is not unreasonable to posit that these insights may well comprise part of the legacy of negotiating the Gaius incident.

One other dimension is to be considered. At the beginning of this section, I referred to Philo's parody of Gaius's ascent into heaven. According to Philo, Gaius lifts himself up through the demigods to the great gods. For Philo, Gaius's claim is laughably illegitimate. John's Gospel certainly makes much of Jesus' ascent into the heavens (see chap. 12 above). He will be lifted up (3:14; 8:28; 12:32). He departs to the Father (13:1; 14:1–4). But there are several huge differences between Jesus' ascent and Gaius's attempted ascent. One is that while Gaius tries to elevate himself into the heavens, Jesus is lifted up by God. Moreover, Jesus is lifted up through his crucifixion. Ironically, this display of Rome's power provokes a greater display of God's life-giving power. What is meant to destroy Jesus facilitates his enthronement, the revelation of his kingship to the world (12:32; 19:19–22), and his return to God (13:1–3; apotheosis). And further, in relation to Gaius, Jesus' ascent is a return to his origin. He comes down from God/heaven before he goes back up (3:13–14; 6:33). His ascent is legitimate since he returns to God, from whence he comes "in the beginning" (13:3). The possibility exists that this descending-ascending pattern, so crucial for John's Gospel's claims about Jesus as the definitive revealer, was shaped as a contrastive response in part to Gaius's illegitimate ascent—at least as one possible factor among others.[53] While Gaius illegitimately forces his way into the divine realm and fails to imitate the gods, Jesus does the will of God (4:34), imitates the acts of God (5:19), speaks the words of God (14:10), and returns to what he has known "in the beginning" (1:1). These distinctive Johannine formulations may well have something of their beginnings or shaping in negotiating the Gaius incident.

The Temple

That the temple is the object of Gaius's assault is clear from the above discussion, and there is no need to rehearse the data. Johannine scholars have noted, especially in more recent work, the centrality of the temple theme in the Gospel; they have seen the prominence of the depiction of Jesus himself as the temple (e.g., 2:17–22) in response to the destruction of the temple in 70 by Rome. This focus, though, only on 70 is somewhat myopic. The narrowness of such focus is immediately clear, for instance, from the discussion in the previous chapters that has highlighted the prominence of the imperial cult in Ephesus throughout the century, including the dedication of the temple of the Sebastoi in 89/90 CE. Moreover, the temple of Artemis played a central role in the city's life and was linked to the imperial cult. And as the above discussion has made clear, the destruction of the temple in 70 was not the only temple crisis in Jerusalem in the first century. Here I simply suggest that the Gaius incident was a "focal point" or catalyst, among others, for developing reflection on the relationship between Jesus and the temple.

I say "among others" because it seems that the issue of Jesus' relationship with the temple is already present in the life of the historical Jesus. That Jesus engaged in some sort of symbolic action against the temple—whatever its motive, significance, and detail—is widely accepted as a historically reliable datum.[54] Its inclusion in both the Synoptics (Mark 11:15–19 par.) and John (2:13–22) satisfies the criterion of multiple attestation. The references to destroying and rebuilding it in both his trial (Mark 14:58; Matt 26:61) and his crucifixion (Mark 15:29; Matt 27:40) satisfy the criterion of coherence, as does the conflict with the Jerusalem temple-based, Roman-allied elite that pervades the Gospels. In addition, numerous scholars have traced out various expressions of dissatisfaction with the temple and diverse expectations for its overthrow and replacement, historically contextualizing the conflict.[55] Jesus' conflictual relationship with the temple, it seems, is already on the radar by around 30, ten years before the Gaius incident.

At some point before 80–90, John's key affirmations emerge: "Zeal for your house will consume me" (2:17, quoting Ps 69:9 [68:10 LXX]) and "but he spoke of the temple of his body" (2:21).[56] The text makes it explicit that these insights emerge from Jesus' followers, not from Jesus. The link with Psalm 69 occurs because "his disciples remembered that it was written" (2:17a), not that Jesus had said so. The claim that his statement about raising up the destroyed temple in three days refers to his body is also not attributed to Jesus but is an editorial comment in verse 21, "But he spoke of the temple of his body." And it is followed by another statement attributing insight to the disciples and specifically indicating that it is postresurrection: "When therefore he was raised from the dead, his disciples remembered that he had said this" (2:22 RSV); the "this" refers to Jesus' statement about raising up the temple up in three days. The Scripture (presumably Ps 69), however, proves decisive for their understanding: "They believed the scripture and the word that Jesus had spoken" (2:22 NRSV).

Just how soon after the resurrection all of this occurs is unknown. We could speculate, as is often done, that the temple's destruction in 70 provokes these links, and that is quite possible. But the temple did not go away between 30 and 70, and the Gaius incident in 40 threatened its very existence.

Pervading Philo's and Josephus's accounts is the notion of zeal for God's house, a zeal that destroys. Most obviously Gaius's zeal to be worshipped as a god that he does not see Jews honoring—that zeal drives him to threaten temple worship. Philo stresses Gaius's misplaced zeal in not imitating the virtues of gods like Heracles and Dionysus (*Emb.* 81, ζηλοῦν, *zēloun*; 90, ἐζήλωσας, *ezēlōsas*); instead, he "zealously practiced lawlessness" (119, ἐζηλωκότος, *ezēlōkotos*). Particularly he greatly valued Alexandria's attentiveness to worshipping him as a god because it made other cities zealous to imitate the practice (338, ζηλοῦν, *zēloun*). Repeatedly Jewish people declare that they will not fight Gaius but that they will die rather than witness his action of defiling the temple, law, land, nation, and blaspheming against God (192, 209–210, 233; Josephus, *J.W.* 2.196–198; *Ant.* 18.264, 266, 271, 274). In his letter to Gaius, Agrippa specifically addresses the challenge to the temple and cites previous Roman respect for it (Philo, *Emb.* 290–329). He asks Gaius to consider: "How many deaths, think you, would those who have been trained in holiness in these matters willingly endure if they should see the statue imported thither? I believe that they would slaughter their whole families, women and children alike, and finally immolate themselves upon the corpses of their children" (308). Petronius responds to the resolute defiance of the Jewish crowd by declaring that he will try to persuade Gaius to change his mind: "Either God [Jupiter? the Jewish God?] aiding me I shall prevail with Caesar and have the satisfaction of saving myself as well as you, or if his indignation is aroused, I am ready on behalf of the lives of so many to surrender my own" (Josephus, *J.W.* 2.201). Despite the willingness of Petronius and Jewish people to die for the temple, finally and ironically, Gaius's "zeal for the temple" to be a place of worship for himself leads to his own death "in the providence of God" (Josephus, *Ant.* 18.308–309).

Several dimensions of the "zeal for the temple" exhibited in this Gaius scene provide interesting intertextuality with emerging Johannine traditions. Quoting Psalm 69, Jesus is zealous (ζῆλος, *zēlos*) for the temple in challenging its abuses (however they be understood). Psalm 69 describes the desperate person who needs God's intervention and waits impatiently for it: "Save me, O God, for the waters have come up to my neck" (69:1–3 NRSV). Opposed by numerous enemies "who hate me without cause," the psalmist admits, "It is zeal for your house that has consumed me," but yet he cries, "Let me be delivered from my enemies" (69:4, 9, 14 NRSV). From the references to Jesus' threats to the temple in the Synoptic trial accounts, it is clear that this challenge was understood by some followers at least to be a major factor in his death (Mark 14:58; Matt 26:61). There are some significant links in vocabulary and content between these Synoptic references and John 2:19.[57] In chapter 6 above I observed the importance of the temple scene's placement at the beginning of John's plot, so that this conflict stands over all subsequent action.

Also to be recognized are Hebrew traditions concerning God as a zealous God (ζηλωτής, *zelōtēs*). Frequently this zealousness is asserted in the contexts of idolatry and forbidding of other gods. So in the Decalogue of Exodus 20:5b, God's zealousness is the reason for forbidding other gods (Exod 20:3, "jealous"), the making of images (20:4), and bowing down to them (20:5a). In Deuteronomy 4:24 Moses urges the people not to make any graven images, "for the Lord your God is a consuming fire, a zealous [jealous] God." This zeal protects Israel's identity as a people committed to God, and it maintains Israel's distinctive quality of aniconic and monotheistic worship.

In the context of Jesus' confrontation with the temple and its leadership, how did John's Jesus-believers engage the Gaius incident? Did they understand it as an expression of God's judgment on the temple establishment for rejecting Jesus and thus a confirmation for the justness of his challenge? Or having seen the passion with which the temple was defended against Gaius's threat, did they understand afresh that Jesus' attack on the temple was truly the death of him? Did they support the passionate zeal demonstrated in defense of the temple in any way? Or did it distance them from the temple as not worthy of such commitment, reinforcing their sense of its vulnerability and their own awareness of being a minority community increasingly alienated from their fellow Judean-Galileans? If this latter process was at work, it is not unrealistic to suggest that they gained, or strengthened, insight into Jesus as the locus of God's presence and purposes and so fostered an awareness of him as an alternative temple in which God is encountered. Yet like most of the claims about developing Johannine traditions, we do not know any of this for certain, but these suggestions have some historical plausibility.

Also important for imperial negotiation is another dimension of the Gaius scene: its lack of violence. The zeal that destroys does not come by enjoining military struggle against Rome even though Gaius orders Petronius to take legions with him to enforce the statue's installation, and Petronius warns that refusal to comply means war with Rome (Josephus, *J.W.* 185–87, 195–196; Philo, *Emb.* 233). Philo places this military intimidation in a larger context of Gaius's "vast and truceless war . . . against the nation" because of Jewish unwillingness to sacrifice to Gaius (119). The Jewish participants, though, deny any interest in waging war. There is no appeal to the holy war traditions of 1 Maccabees or of Phinehas in *Num* 25:1–13 . Rather, the zeal that destroys comes in nonviolently refusing to comply with the imperial edict, even to death, as with the martyrs of 2 Maccabees 7.

Jesus' crucifixion belongs in the latter category as the consequence of nonviolently confronting the Jerusalem ruling elite. The refusal of violence in his arrest belongs with the same zeal (John 18:10–11). So too does Jesus' comment to Pilate about his kingship not being from this world but from God. If it were from this world, Jesus says, it would be marked by violence: "My followers would fight" (18:36). Violent empire is set against nonviolent resistance and loyalty to God's purposes. Twenty-five years before the 66–70 war showed that violent revolt against Rome was futile, the Gaius incident evidences the power of nonviolent resistance as a way of negotiating Roman power, a strategy that John's Gospel shows Jesus embracing. This is another point of interaction between the two, perhaps suggesting the Johannine tradition's negotiation of imperial power.

Sacrifice

The accounts of the Gaius episode are rich in multivalent uses of the notion of sacrifice. Gaius orders sacrifices offered *to* his statue in the Jerusalem temple, where sacrifices are currently offered *for* him (Josephus, *J.W.* 2.197; cf. Dio Cassius 59.4.4). But the temple offers sacrifices to God alone and will not tolerate any others. The Jews inform Gaius that he will have to sacrifice (προθύσασθαι, *prothysasthai*) the nation first in order to accomplish his will (Josephus, *J.W.* 2.197). Jewish men, "their wives, and their children" present themselves willingly as sacrifices to be slaughtered by Gaius's troops (2.197). Philo accuses Gaius of planning the whole confrontation while knowing that Jews would not permit his image to be placed in the temple: "You ordered the army to be brought in so that the first sacrifices [θυσίαις, *thysiais*] with which the image was consecrated might be polluted with the massacre of unhappy men and women alike" (208). Philo's body of elders dramatically declares, "But what need of an army! We ourselves will conduct the sacrifices [θυμάτων, *thymatōn*], priests of a noble order: wives will be brought to the altar by wife-slayers, brothers and sisters by fratricides, boys and girls in the innocence of their years by child-murderers" (*Emb.* 234).

Most dramatic, though, is Josephus's presentation in *Jewish War* of the self-sacrifice of Petronius, Gaius's legate, or governor, of the province of Syria.[58] Convinced by the Jewish leaders and people not to proceed with Gaius's scheme, he writes to Gaius and urges him to desist. But he does so knowing that his refusal to execute Gaius's order means his own execution, as shown in these quotes:[59]

- Petronius: If I transgress [Gaius's order] and spare you, I shall be put to death with justice. (2.195)

- Petronius: Either God [Jupiter? the Jewish God?] aiding me, I shall prevail with Caesar and have the satisfaction of saving myself [σωθήσομαι, *sōthēsomai*] as well as you, or if his indignation is roused, I am ready on behalf of [ὑπέρ, *hyper*] the lives of so many to surrender my own. (2.201).

- Josephus: But if, after all, Gaius should turn some of his wrath against him (Petronius], a man who made virtue his goal might well die on behalf of [ὑπέρ, *hyper*] such a multitude of people. (18.278)

- Petronius: I do not, however, . . . deem it right not to hazard my own safety and position in order to save you, who are so numerous, from perishing. (18.280)

- Josephus: Hazardous as he considered this petition—for if Gaius did not regard it with favor, it would bring him certain death—yet . . . he chose to make the gamble on this occasion. (18.298)

Whatever the historical actuality of Petronius's role, and Philo is less admiring than Josephus, the three accounts agree in presenting him as putting himself in danger by delaying action on Gaius's order and questioning it. If the people sacrifice themselves, there will not be a nation. If Petronius sacrifices himself, there is at least a possibility of their survival.

The willingness to sacrifice one person for the good of the nation echoes a passage in John 11:47–53. Following the raising of Lazarus, the Jerusalem leaders, Pharisees and chief priests, are concerned about Jesus' popularity and effectiveness: "If we let him go on thus, every one will believe in him, and the Romans will come and destroy both our holy place and our nation" (RSV). The high priest, Caiaphas, responds, "You do not understand that it is expedient for you that one man should die for [ὑπέρ, *hyper*] the people, and that the whole nation should not perish" (RSV). In 18:14, as Jesus' death approaches, Caiaphas is reintroduced to the story, being described with a repetition of this declaration: "It was Caiaphas who had given counsel to the Jews that it was expedient that one man should die for the people" (RSV). John's scene in 11:47–53 drips with dramatic irony. They do not "let him go on thus" in crucifying Jesus, yet in 70 Rome still comes and destroys the "holy place and nation." They think that they put Jesus to death, but he lays down his life voluntarily (10:16–18). After 70, Caiaphas turns out to know less than those he describes as not understanding, yet he speaks unintentional truth. Jesus' death does and does not "save" the nation.

In the Gaius episode, Petronius emerges as the man willing to die for the people. Agrippa, significant in both Philo and Josephus's accounts, does not contemplate self-sacrifice as the price of his intervention. But Petronius risks it all.

The notion of a sacrificial victim offered in the place of and for the benefit of others is certainly integral to Hebrew traditions and well known in Greek traditions, as numerous commentaries point out. And the notion of a person sacrificing himself for the greater good of the nation is by no means restricted to the Gaius scene. As but one example (involving punishment and multiple deaths), the martyr scene of 2 Maccabees 7 makes the same claim: seven sons, encouraged by their mother, refuse to abandon faithfulness to the ancestral laws and thereby disobey Antiochus Epiphanes. It recognizes that their suffering is because of their nation's sins (7:18, 32), but their faithful deaths are an appeal to God "to show mercy soon to our nation" and "through me and my brothers to bring to an end the wrath of the Almighty that has justly fallen on our whole nation" (7:37–38 NRSV; cf. 4 Macc 17:17–22).

Whether Caiaphas's expedient suggestion is historical cannot be verified with certainty. But it is plausible. The removal of a troublemaker to protect the elite's beneficial status quo and defend its interests is basic to the workings of any empire. And the Gospels, both Synoptic and John, agree in claiming popularity for Jesus at the expense of the ruling elite. The concern shown by Caiaphas for Roman retaliation against social unrest, especially if it is perceived to be threatening elite interests, is commonplace, since Rome exercised rule through tensive alliances with provincial elites. Perhaps there are also echoes in Caiaphas's politically expedient claim of Jesus' statement of giving his life for many (Mark 10:45 par.). Others point out the well-attested association of prophecy and priesthood. At least an appearance of historical verisimilitude appropriate to about 30 is evident.

The scene, though, bears signs of what is often identified as post-70 theological interpretation of Rome's coming and destroying the holy place (temple) and city (Jerusalem) as punishment of the city and its elite for its rejection of Jesus. This may well be so, but again we should not rush too quickly from 30 to 70 without pausing on major events such as the Gaius incident. In this scene the possibility that Rome will come and destroy the city is very high if Gaius does not get his way. Did the Johannine followers in about 40 entertain the possibility in this context that Jerusalem was about to be justifiably punished for its action against Jesus just ten or so years previously? Did such a possibility foster understandings of Jesus' identity as a temple? And we have testimony that many were willing to sacrifice themselves to prevent the destruction. The perception is also evident that one man in particular, Petronius, in sacrificing himself by resisting Gaius, might save the people. Hence, the Gaius incident is a "focal point" for this cluster of ideas that bear remarkable similarity to John 11:47–53, though in relation to Jesus, not Petronius. I am not suggesting an uninterrupted line between the two and certainly not excluding the influence of 70. But it is not unreasonable to posit the impact of the Gaius scene on the Johannine traditions' developing imperial negotiation expressed in reflection on the nature of Jesus' death, on the fate of Jerusalem and its temple as objects of God's punishment, and on the identity of Jesus as a new temple.

Agency

A sixth dominant feature of the Gaius scene concerns agency. This motif is implicit in most of the categories discussed above, and I isolate it here only to examine it more explicitly. Gaius presents himself as agent of the gods. His identification through clothing and symbols with various gods has been observed (Philo, *Emb.* 74–114). His identification with Zeus/Jupiter is evident in that the statue of himself (Josephus, *Ant.* 18.261) is to be "dedicated to himself under the name of Zeus" (Philo, *Emb.* 188, 265), with the temple "to bear the name of Gaius 'the new Zeus/Jupiter made manifest'" (346). Gaius thus presents himself in typical imperial theological terms as the one commissioned to re-present and reveal Zeus/Jupiter among his subjects. To see Gaius is to see Zeus/Jupiter. To hear and obey Gaius's words is to hear and obey Zeus/Jupiter since Gaius reveals the god's presence and will. He is the agent of Zeus/Jupiter's will. The narratives evaluate this agency negatively, as we have recognized above. Philo's verdict is that he is an agent of evil, "a formidable power for evil" (191, 348).

Agrippa, in response to Gaius's offer to do anything for him, holds out to him a different sort of agency in Josephus's account (*Ant.* 18.292–296), proposing that Gaius be the agent of the Jewish God, or perhaps on a more accurate reading, that the Jewish God will be Gaius's agent: "But I shall ask for something that will bring you a reputation for piety and will induce the Deity to help you in everything that you wish" (18.297). Certainly the three accounts see the pleas of Jewish people and Agrippa (e.g., Philo, *Emb.* 278–279) for Gaius to rescind his command as a request to act according to God's will.

Petronius's agency is ambiguously presented and conflicted. Gaius delegates agency to him by appointing him as governor of Syria, thereby obligating him as agent of Gaius's interests and will (Josephus, *Ant.* 18.261). Gaius "orders" his agent (κελεύων, *keleuōn*, 18.261) and "sent" him (ἔπεμψεν, *epempsen*, Josephus, *J.W.* 2.185–186) with troops to set up Gaius's image in the Jerusalem temple. When Jews protest, Petronius appeals to his identity as Gaius's agent: "I too must obey the law of my master, for I too like you am under orders" (2.195). His agency involves military enforcement. He warns them that their defiance will mean war made by "the one who sent me, not by me [ὁ πέμψας με καὶ οὐκ ἐγώ, *ho pempsas me kai ouk egō*]." According to Josephus, Petronius "angrily [ὀργήν, *orgēn*]" responds to the Jewish challenge to his and Gaius's authority: "As it is, I am Caesar's emissary," or more literally, "since Caesar has sent me [Καίσαρος ἐπεσταλκότος, *Kaisaros epestalkotos*], I am bound to carry out the decision he has already made" (*Ant.* 18.265). Later Petronius declares the obligation and gratefulness that marks such agency: "It is only right that one upon whom such high position had been conferred by grant of the emperor should thwart him in nothing" (18.279). He is Gaius's agent, sent by Gaius to carry out Gaius's will.

Yet as the scene unfolds, especially in Josephus's accounts and especially in *Antiquities*, Petronius becomes God's agent, accomplishing God's purposes of thwarting Gaius's will! In *Jewish War* Petronius's appeal to Gaius to revoke the order cites God's prohibition of images (2.195, 202). In *Antiquities* he appeals to Gaius because he does not think it right to punish Jews for "reverence to God" (18.277). To the Jews he explains his dispatch to Gaius and prays, "May God assist you, since his might is above any human ingenuity and strength; may he enable you to maintain and preserve your ancestral laws" (18.281). God acknowledges Petronius's agency with a literal shower of blessing, which Petronius interprets as a sign of God's favor. "God, on his part, showed Petronius that he was with him and would lend his aid in all matters. . . . Petronius, on his part, was struck with amazement when he saw unmistakable evidence that God's providence was over the Jews and that he had shown his presence so abundantly" (18.284–286). And Josephus interprets Gaius's timely death as God's vindication of Petronius: "God could never have been unmindful of the risks that Petronius had taken in showing favor to the Jews and honoring God. No, the removal of Gaius . . . was God's payment of the debt to Petronius" (18.306, 308). Philo also acknowledges Petronius's agency on God's behalf (*Emb.* 213) and Petronius's sympathetic listening when "God whispers good decisions by which [good men] will give and receive benefits" (245). Through Petronius, God is more powerful than Gaius, and it is God's will, not Gaius's or Zeus's, that is accomplished.

Scholars have long recognized the importance of agency in John's presentation of Jesus.[60] As I indicated in chapter 9 above, more than forty times the Gospel uses verbs of "sending" to define God as "the one who sent" Jesus and Jesus as the agent of God's life-giving purposes. Jesus does God's works (5:19–24, 36). He speaks God's words (12:49). He does God's will (4:34; 5:30; 6:38). To see Jesus is to see God, who sent him (12:45). To hear Jesus is to hear God (14:10).

From whence does this understanding of Jesus as God's agent develop? Numerous possibilities have been suggested. Scholars have appealed to God sending prophets (2 Sam 12:1; 2 Kings 17:13), Moses (Exod 3:10, 14–15), wisdom (Wis 9:10) or angels (Gen 24:7; Exod 23:20; 1 Chron 21:15), to people sending other people (Moses sends Joshua, Josh 14:7), to the notion of the *shaliach* (*šālîaḥ*, agent) in Jewish society, to the son's role in households, to the institution of slavery. The post-70 disputes are often posited as the context in which claims about Jesus are asserted over other Jewish revealer figures and insist that no one but Jesus can see God.[61] One conclusion to be drawn from this list is that trying to identify one exclusive source for the notion of Jesus' agency is futile. It was a pervasive notion.

Hence, in drawing attention to the importance of the notion of agency in imperial society in general and in the Gaius incident in particular, I am recognizing and adding to the complexity of its use. The scene is a focal point for a multilayered notion of agency embracing claims of divine and imperial agency. Divine election underlies Gaius's action. Gaius rules because of Rome's divine chosenness. Emperors and empires rule as the agents of the gods. Not only is Gaius their representative; he also incarnates and reveals their will and presence. He belongs among them. As such he sends his own agents such as Petronius to carry out his will to be worshipped. To send an agent is to delegate and authorize. To be an agent is to obey and reveal or manifest the sender's will. To see Petronius is to see Gaius is to see Jupiter/Zeus. Petronius's works are Gaius's works are the gods' works. In turn, for Jews to honor Petronius with compliance is to honor Gaius is to honor the gods.

Josephus's account shares the same language as John in using the same verbs of "sending" and having the one sent define the superior as "the one who sent me [ὁ πέμψας με, *ho pempsas me*]" (*J.W.* 2.195); "since Caesar has sent me [Καίσαρος ἐπεσταλκότος, *Kaisaros epestalkotos*, *Ant.* 18.279). As John the Baptist bears witness, he uses the identical phrase to describe God as "the one who sent me to baptize" (John 1:33). Jesus uses the same phrase in 5:37 to describe his Father as "the one who sent me" (6:44; 8:26, 29). Just as the language is the same, so also is the concept, with the same embracing delegation, revelation, obedience. The one who is sent does the will of the sender. Jesus obeys and reveals God (5:19). To honor Jesus is to honor God (5:23). In turn, Jesus is the one sent by God to reveal God's will and purposes in his words and works; he delegates an ongoing task to disciples, sending them to manifest his will, which is God's will (20:21).

I am not claiming the Gaius incident as the exclusive or direct source of this Johannine christological category. But I am identifying striking similarities between John's dominant christological framework and a very public event in 40 CE that was experienced by many in Judea-Galilee. The incident publicly and starkly displayed imperial agency at work, with its presuppositions and claims. And it provoked a contesting of that agency by those with different cultural and theological commitments. What role, if any, did negotiating this assertion of imperial agency play for Johannine followers of Jesus around 40? Did it facilitate the adoption of this imperial framework of agency as a way of asserting Jesus' superiority by framing his sending as God's work and thereby shaping the community's existence and mission also? There were plenty of cultural models in place, as I have just noted. Perhaps negotiating the Gaius incident was a catalyst in this development. Ultimately, of course, we do not know, but this suggestion, while recognizing other forces at work also, has the merit of proposing the likelihood that imperial negotiation played some significant part in the emerging Johannine traditions.[62]

Conclusion

Is the emperor Gaius Caligula the father of Johannine Christology? No one event or source of influence can account for the development of every aspect of Johannine Christology. But using the concept of cultural intertextuality, I have demonstrated in this appendix that interface with Gaius's attempt to install a statue of himself in the

Jerusalem temple is both likely and important in the development of Johannine traditions.

This argument significantly modifies aspects of conventional explanations for the development of Johannine traditions between the time of Jesus and the writing of the Gospel. As I have observed from the outset, a major shortcoming in this approach is that it commonly concerns itself only with religious issues and communities, isolating them—docetically and ahistorically—from all other human experience, including negotiation of Rome's pervasive empire. I have also identified a tendency in Johannine studies to jump from the time of Jesus to the post-70 world and to synagogal separation, ignoring pre-70 and imperial events such as Gaius's action in 40. I have argued that imperial negotiation, evident in the final form of the Gospel, may also actually play a significant part in the development of the Johannine traditions after Jesus' death on a Roman cross. I have pointed to the incident in which the emperor Gaius Caligula sought to establish a statue of himself as Zeus/Jupiter in the Jerusalem temple in 40 as a possible focal point for such negotiation. I have identified six possible points of negotiation that may have been significant for the developing Johannine traditions: claims of sovereignty, dualism, claiming to be a god or equal to God, Jesus as the temple, sacrifice, and agency. To be clear, I have not argued that the Gaius incident is the direct cause of all these developments, but I have suggested that it is a likely or possible factor along with others in the pre-Gospel development of these Johannine claims.

If these interactions, imperial negotiations, and insights are in motion around and after 40, why, then, is the creation of (the final form of) the Gospel as an act of imperial negotiation necessary in Ephesus around 100? The most likely answer is that the author or authors of the Gospel are dissatisfied with the imperial negotiation undertaken by some (many?) Jesus-believers in late first-century Ephesus. The author/s perceives that some (many?) Jesus-believers are overaccommodated and without appropriate societal distance, no longer viewing active participation in imperial society as a troublesome act. Whether because of pragmatism or familiarity or "ease of daily life" or lack of apparent threat or theological understandings of Abraham and Moses as culture-embracing figures or synagogal example—a more accommodated stance has become normative for some (many?). But for the writer/s of the Gospel, the imperial world of Ephesus around 100 CE is dangerous and evil, requiring more cultural distance and a distinctive antistructure way of life. Hence, the oppositional story of Jesus, crucified by the empire but raised by God, is told again: its rhetoric of distance seeks to shape their imperial negotiation by much greater differentiation and distance from daily imperial society.

Notes

1. Richter, "Präsentische und futurische Eschatologie," 346–82; for discussion, see Mattill, "Johannine Communities: Georg Richter's Analysis," *TS* 38 (1977): 294–315; Martyn, *History and Theology*; idem, "Source Criticism," 99–121; idem, "Glimpses," 90–121; Brown, *Community*, passim; for summary chart, 167–68; Painter, *Quest*, 61–135.
2. Martin de Boer, *Johannine Perspectives on the Death of Jesus* (Kampen: Kok Pharos, 1996), 77, for modified version of diagram (excluding a fourth version focusing on the Epistles); 19–82.

3. See the summary provided by Tom Thatcher, "Introduction," in Fortna and Thatcher, *Jesus in Johannine Tradition*, 1–9; also Carter, *John: Storyteller*, chaps. 7–8.

4. De Boer, *Johannine Perspectives*, 76; Robert Fortna, *The Gospel of Signs: A Reconstruction of the Narrative Underlying the Fourth Gospel* (Cambridge: Cambridge University Press, 1970); idem, *Fourth Gospel and Its Predecessor*; Urban C. von Wahlde, *The Earliest Version of John's Gospel: Recovering the Gospel of Signs* (Wilmington, DE: Michael Glazier, 1989).

5. For two different approaches, Benjamin W. Bacon, *The Fourth Gospel in Research and Debate* (New York: Moffat, 1910); Thomas Brodie, *The Quest for the Origin of John's Gospel: A Source-Oriented Approach* (New York: Oxford University Press, 1993).

6. Dewey, "Gospel of John," 239–52. Dewey's discussion on 248–51 identifies seven issues related to oral literature that raise significant questions about the customary developmental approach.

7. For one summary, McGrath, *John's Apologetic Christology*, 1–47.

8. This approach is favored by McGrath, *John's Apologetic Christology*, 28–47.

9. Bultmann, *John*, e.g., 280.

10. Brown, *Community*, 36–47; Meeks, *Prophet-King*, 216–57; McGrath, *John's Apologetic Christology*, 17–19.

11. Dunn, "Let John Be John," 293–322; Carter, "Prologue," 35–58.

12. Ringe, *Wisdom's Friends*; Ben Witherington III, *John's Wisdom: A Commentary on the Fourth Gospel* (Louisville: Westminster John Knox, 1995); M. Scott, *Sophia*.

13. McGrath, *John's Apologetic Christology*, 21–27.

14. Ibid., 27–28.

15. Richey, "'Truly This Is the Savior of the World.'" Roman imperial negotiation in general and the Gaius incident in particular receive little consideration in relation to New Testament and Johannine material. Several exceptions: Gerd Theissen, *The Gospels in Context: Social and Political History in the Synoptic Tradition* (Minneapolis: Fortress, 1991), explores discussions between the Gaius incident and the developing tradition of the eschatological discourse in Mark 13 (125–65) and the Sayings Source, especially the temptation story (203–34). Adela Yarbro Collins ("The Worship of Jesus and the Imperial Cult," in *The Jewish Roots of Christological Monotheism*, ed. C. Newman, J. Davila, and G. Lewis [Leiden: Brill, 1999], 234–57, draws some connections between the imperial cult and Mark's Gospel. Borgen ("Emperor Worship," 493–509) draws links between Gaius and Rev 13. Most significantly for John, Meeks ("Divine Agent," 43–67) focuses on the divine king as "the image of the ideal emissary of God," in contrast to Philo's parody of divine kingship represented by Gaius (45), and the presentation of Jesus as God's emissary, though Meeks suggests considerable distance and differences (e.g., 54).

16. Josephus identifies two legions in *Ant.* 18.262 but three in *J.W.* 2.187.

17. The sixth-century chronicler Malalas claims to report riots in Antioch in 39–40 CE in which a Jewish synagogue is burned. If the report is accurate, and that is debatable, it may also reflect the impact of events in Judea-Galilee.

18. Also Tacitus, *Hist.* 5.9, briefly notes that in response to Caligula's order, "the Jews chose rather to resort to arms, but the emperor's death put an end to their uprising." There is a brief reference in *Megillat Ta'anit* (*Scroll of Fasting*) 11b, and possibly Mark 13:14–20, Acts 5:34–39, and 2 Thess 2:4. Suetonius's biography of Gaius Caligula does not mention the episode. For text and discussion of *Megillat Ta' anit*, S. Zeitlin, "Megillat Taanit as a Source for Jewish Chronology and History in the Hellenistic and Roman Times," *Jewish Quarterly Review* 9 (1918–19): 71–102; 10 (1919–20): 49–80, 237–290, esp. 237–42, 260–61.

19. For attempts at historical reconstruction, as well as bibliography, see E. Mary Smallwood, "The Chronology of Gaius' Attempt to Desecrate the Temple," *Latomus* 16 (1957): 3–17; Per Bilde, "The Roman Emperor Gaius (Caligula)'s Attempt to Erect His Statue in the Temple of Jerusalem," *Studia theologica* 32 (1978): 67–93; Anthony A. Barrett, *Caligula: The Corruption of*

Power (New Haven: Yale University Press, 1990), 187–91; James MacLaren, *Power and Politics in Palestine: The Jews and the Governing of Their Land 100 BC–AD 70*, JSNTSup 63 (Sheffield: Sheffield Academic Press, 1991), 114–26.

20. E.g., Smallwood, "Chronology"; Barrett, *Caligula*.

21. E. g., Bilde, "Roman Emperor," 92–93.

22. E.g., MacLaren, *Power*, 123.

23. Cf. 1 Tim 2:1–2.

24. *Embassy* 119, 168, 178, 183, 208, 218, 222, 233, 237, 239, 271, 276, 290, 301, 314, 321, 326, 355.

25. Josephus uses a plural term in *J.W.* 2.185, 192 (and a plural but different term in 197) and a singular of the same word in *Ant.* 18.261, as does Philo, *Emb.* 203, 207.

26. J. Rufus Fears, "The Cult of Jupiter and Roman Imperial Ideology," *ANRW* II.17.1 (1981): 3–141; Price, *Rituals and Power*; Carter, *Matthew and Empire*, 9–34.

27. Christopher J. Simpson ("Caligula's Cult: Immolation, Immortality, Intent," in A. Small, *Subject and Ruler*, 63–71) argues that Gaius's active promotion of excess in his cult demonstrated "publicly his exceptional authority, his power over his subjects." Simpson includes the Jerusalem temple incident as a further "demonstration of his ultimate supremacy" (70n54).

28. I will discuss Philo's parody of Gaius's kingship below.

29. Nor should *1 En.* 37–71 be overlooked, esp. 46–48. There the son of man is a heavenly judge who destroys the oppressive and wealthy "kings and mighty ones . . . and the strong ones" (46:3–5, 7) and "the kings and the mighty landowners" (48:8) while establishing God's purposes.

30. See Josephus, *Ant.* 17.271–272, 273–276, 278–285; *J.W.* 4.507–513.

31. *Basileus*, "king": John 18:33, 37 (2x), 39; 19:3, 12, 14, 15 (2x), 19, 21 (2x); *basileia*, "kingship/kingdom" (RSV/NRSV): 18:36 (2x).

32. Carter, *John: Storyteller*, 86–106.

33. Ibid., 91–92.

34. Meeks, "Divine Agent," 49–51.

35. Price, *Roman Imperial Cult*; for a summary, Carter, "Going All the Way?" 14–33, esp. 16–23.

36. For Gaius's association with and identification with Jupiter/Zeus (in addition to Philo's references): Gaius talks with Jupiter as a brother (Josephus, *Ant.* 19.4), alternately shouting at and whispering to Jupiter (Suetonius, *Cal.* 22). While the latter suggests some rivalry, Suetonius continues with reference to Gaius wanting to replace Jupiter's head on statues with his own, and being greeted as Jupiter Latiaris. Josephus (*Ant.* 19.11) and Dio Cassius (59.28.7) say that Gaius placed his daughter on the knees of Jupiter/Zeus, suggesting that she was Jupiter's child, before entrusting her to Minerva for upbringing. Suetonius (*Cal.* 25) indicates that he placed her on Minerva's knees.

37. Carter, *Matthew and Empire*, 9–34.

38. Cf. Antiochus Epiphanes, who thought he was "greater than any god" (Dan. 11:36) but ironically manifests God to all in his death (2 Macc. 9).

39. So Meeks, "Divine Agent," 54–55.

40. On Jewish monotheism and the debate about the applicability and content of the term, see Larry Hurtado, *Lord Jesus Christ: Devotion to Jesus in Earliest Christianity* (Grand Rapids: Eerdmans, 2003), 27–64.

41. Wayne Meeks, "Equal to God," in *The Conversation Continues: Studies in Paul and John*, ed. R. Fortna and B. Gaventa (Nashville: Abingdon, 1990), 309–21, esp. 311.

42. Meeks, "Equal to God," 312, 316; see also idem, "Divine Agent," 54–60.

43. Badian, "Alexander the Great," 11–26, esp. 15–22.

44. Meeks, "Divine Agent," 54.

45. Meeks, "Equal to God," 312–14; also evident in idem, "Divine Agent," 45–49; Badian, "Alexander the Great."

46. Price, "Gods and Emperors," 79–95, esp. 88.

47. Ibid., 88.

48. Ibid., 94.

49. Ibid., 95.

50. On Domitian, see the discussion and bibliography in chapter 3.

51. Meeks, "Equal to God," 312–16; see also Meeks's discussion of Philo's divine king Moses ("Divine Agent"), who displays virtue, enters the divine realm, returns to "manifest the divine to his subjects," and occupies "an intermediary status between the human and the divine" (46–47).

52. Price, "Gods and Emperors."

53. For example, Moses' ascent, Philo, *Mos.* 1.158; Meeks, "Divine Agent"; Peder Borgen, "Moses, Jesus, and the Roman Emperor: Observations in Philo's Writings and the Revelation of John," *NovT* 38 (1996): 145–59. Strangely, Borgen (146) seems to minimize Meeks's attempt to discuss Philo's Moses, Gaius, and John's Gospel, suggesting that the discussion is more appropriate for Revelation.

54. Edward P. Sanders, *Jesus and Judaism* (Philadelphia: Fortress, 1985), 61–90; John Dominic Crossan and Jonathan L. Reed, *Excavating Jesus* (HarperSanFrancisco, 2001), 220–22; James D. G. Dunn, *Jesus Remembered*, vol. 1 (Grand Rapids: Eerdmans, 2003), 636–40.

55. Craig Evans, "Jesus' Actions in the Temple and Evidence of Corruption in the First Century Temple," in *SBL 1989 Seminar Papers* (Atlanta: Scholars, 1989), 522–39.

56. See the discussions of 2:13–22 in chapters 6 and 10 above.

57. These include destroy ([κατα]λύω), this temple (τὸν ναὸν τοῦτον), three days. Differences include John's use of the second-person plural imperative "destroy" rather than the first-person singular "I will destroy" (as in Mark); and John not referring to "not made with hands" and "I will build" (both in Mark).

58. Philo presents Petronius as being less self-sacrificing and more self-protective. His letter to Gaius is more a justification for delays in the statue's installation than an appeal for Gaius to desist. He hopes that Gaius will find the delays reasonable (*Emb.* 246–253).

59. For another example, Josephus narrates the refusal of Memmius Regulus to ship the fragile statue of Olympian Zeus to Rome as ordered by Gaius. Memmius sends Gaius a letter "explaining his refusal to carry out his orders. In consequence he risked being executed, but was saved by the death of Gaius which intervened" (*Ant.* 19.9–10).

60. E.g., Meeks, "Divine Agent," 54–60.

61. Dunn, "Let John be John"; Carter, "The Prologue."

62. A final note: If space permitted, there is at least one further dimension in the accounts of Gaius Caligula that could be explored. In these accounts I am struck by the focus on the clash of cultural traditions and appeals to those traditions to justify current practices (another turn to the past; see chap. 4 above).

Bibliography

Ahl, Frederick. 1984. "The Art of Safe Criticism in Greece and Rome." *The American Journal of Philology* 105:174–208.

Alcock, Susan E. 2001. "The Reconfiguration of Memory in the Eastern Roman Empire." In *Empires: Perspectives from Archaeology and History*, 323–50. Edited by S. Alcock, T. D'Altroy, K. Morrison, and C. Sinopoli. Cambridge: Cambridge University Press.

Aldrete, Greg S., and David J. Mattingly. 1999. "Feeding the City: The Organization, Operation, and Scale of the Supply System for Rome." In *Life, Death, and Entertainment in the Roman Empire*, 171–204. Edited by D. S. Potter and D. J. Mattingly. Ann Arbor: University of Michigan Press.

Alexander, Philip. 1992. "'The Parting of the Ways' from the Perspective of Rabbinic Judaism." In *Jews and Christians: The Parting of the Ways A.D. 70 to 135*, 1–26. Edited by J. D. G. Dunn. WUNT 66. Tübingen: Mohr-Siebeck.

Alföldi, Andreas. 1971. *Der Vater des Vaterlandes im römischen Denken*. Darmstadt: Wissenschaftliche Buchgesellschaft.

Alföldy, Géza. 1985. *The Social History of Rome*. Totowa, NJ: Barnes & Noble Books.

Alston, Richard. 1998. *Aspects of Roman History, AD 14–117*. New York: Routledge.

Anderson, Benedict. 1991. *Imagined Communities: Reflections on the Origin and Spread of Nationalism*. London: Verso.

Anderson, Paul N. 1996. *The Christology of the Fourth Gospel: Its Unity and Disunity in the Light of John 6*. Valley Forge, PA: Trinity Press International.

———. 1999. "The Having-Sent-Me Father: Aspects of Agency, Encounter, and Irony in the Johannine Father-Son Relationship." *Semeia* 85:33–57.

———. 2006. *The Fourth Gospel and the Quest for Jesus: Modern Foundations Reconsidered*. Library of New Testament Studies. London: T&T Clark.

Ando, Clifford. 2000. *Imperial Ideology and Provincial Loyalty in the Roman Empire*. Berkeley: University of California Press.

Arnold, Clinton E. 1989. *Ephesians: Power and Magic*. Cambridge: Cambridge University Press.

Ashcroft, Bill, Gareth Griffiths, and Helen Tiffin, eds. 1995. *The Post-colonial Studies Reader*. London; New York: Routledge.

Ashton, John A. 1991. *Understanding the Fourth Gospel*. Oxford: Clarendon.

Attridge, Harold W. 2002. "Genre Bending in the Fourth Gospel." *Journal of Biblical Literature* 121:3–21.

Aune, David E. 1972. *The Cultic Setting of Realized Eschatology in Early Christianity*. Leiden: Brill.

———. 1987. *The New Testament in Its Literary Environment*. Philadelphia: Westminster.

———. 2003. "Biography." In *The Westminster Dictionary of New Testament and Early Christian Literature and Rhetoric*, 78–81. Louisville: Westminster John Knox.

———. 2003. "Gospels, Literary Genre of." In *The Westminster Dictionary of New Testament and Early Christian Literature and Rhetoric*, 204–6. Louisville: Westminster John Knox.

Axtell, Harold. 1907. *The Deification of Abstract Ideas in Roman Literature and Inscriptions*. Chicago: University of Chicago Press.

Bacon, Benjamin W. 1910. *The Fourth Gospel in Research and Debate*. New York: Moffat.

Badian, Ernst. 1996. "Alexander the Great between Two Thrones and Heaven: Variations on an Old Theme." In *Subject and Ruler: The Cult of the Ruling Power in Classical Antiquity; Papers Presented at a Conference Held in the University of Alberta on April 13-15, 1994, to Celebrate the Sixty-fifth Anniversary of Duncan Fishwick*, 11–26. Edited by Alastair Small. Journal of Roman Archaeology: Supplementary Series 17. Ann Arbor, MI: JRA.

Bammel, Ernst. 1952. "Philos tou Kaisaros John 19:12," *Theologische Literaturzeitung* 77 (1952): 205–10.

Barbalet, Jack M. 1985. "Power and Resistance." *British Journal of Sociology* 36:521–48.

Barclay, John M. G. 1996. *Jews in the Mediterranean Diaspora from Alexander to Trajan (323 BCE-117 CE)*. Edinburgh: T&T Clark.

———. 2004. "Poverty in Pauline Studies: A Response to Steven Friesen." *Journal for the Study of the New Testament* 26:363–66.

Barnes, Andrew E. 2001. "Church and Society." In *Encyclopedia of European Social History from 1350 to 2000*, 263–73. Edited by P. N. Stearns. New York: Charles Scribner's Sons.

Barnes, Timothy D. 1968. "Legislation against the Christians." *Journal of Roman Studies* 58:32–50.

Barrett, Anthony A. 1990. *Caligula: The Corruption of Power*. New Haven: Yale University Press.

Barrett, Charles Kingsley. 1955. *The Gospel according to St. John*. London: Society for Promoting Christian Knowledge.

———. 1982. "Christocentric or Theocentric? Observations on the Theological Method of the Fourth Gospel." In *Essays on John*, 1–18. Edited by C. K. Barrett. Philadelphia: Westminster.

———. 1982. "'The Father Is Greater Than I' (John 14:28): Subordinationist Christology in the New Testament." In *Essays on John*, 19–36. Philadelphia: Westminster.

Barton, Stephen C. 2000. "Christian Community in the Light of the Gospel of John." In *Christology, Controversy and Community: New Testament Essays in Honour of David R. Catchpole*, 279–301. Edited by D. Horrell and C. Tuckett. Leiden; Boston: Brill.

Bauckham, Richard. 1993. "The Economic Critique of Rome in Revelation 18." In *The Climax of Prophecy: Studies on the Book of Revelation*, 338–83. Edinburgh: T&T Clark.

———. 1997. "Qumran and the Fourth Gospel: Is There a Connection?" In *The Scrolls and the Scriptures: Qumran Fifty Years After*, 267–79. Edited by S. Porter and C. Evans. Journal for the Study of the Pseudepigrapha: Supplement Series 26. Sheffield: Sheffield Academic Press.

———. 1998. "Life, Death, and the Afterlife in Second Temple Judaism." In *Life in the Face of Death: The Resurrection Message of the New Testament*, 80–95. Edited by R. N. Longenecker. Grand Rapids: Eerdmans.

———. 2006. "Messianism according to the Gospel of John." In *Challenging Perspectives on the Gospel of John*, 34–68. Edited by John Lierman. Wissenschaftliche Untersuchungen zum Neuen Testament 2.219. Tübingen: Mohr Siebeck.

Beard, Mary, John North, and Simon Price. 1998. *Religions of Rome*. 2 vols. Cambridge: Cambridge University Press.

Beasley-Murray, George. 1986. *John*. Word Biblical Commentary 36. Waco: Word.

Beutler, Johannes. 1991. "Der alttestamentlich-jüdische Hintergrund der Hirtenrede in Johannes 10." In *The Shepherd Discourse of John 10 and Its Context*, 18–32. Edited by J. Beutler and R. Fortna. Cambridge: Cambridge University Press.

Bhabha, Homi K. 1994. *Location of Culture*. London: Routledge.

Bilde, Per. 1978. "The Roman Emperor Gaius (Caligula)'s Attempt to Erect His Statue in the Temple of Jerusalem." *Studia theologica* 32:67–93.

Binder, Donald. 1999. *"Into the Temple Courts": The Place of the Synagogues in the Second Temple Period*. Society of Biblical Literature Dissertation Series 169. Atlanta: Society of Biblical Literature.

Boismard, Marie-Émile. 1993. *Moses or Jesus: An Essay in Johannine Christology*. Minneapolis: Fortress.

Bolt, Peter G. 1998. "Life, Death, and the Afterlife in the Greco-Roman World." In *Life in the Face of Death: The Resurrection Message of the New Testament*, 51–79. Edited by R. N. Longenecker. Grand Rapids: Eerdmans.

Bond, Helen K. 1998. *Pontius Pilate in History and Interpretation*. New York: Cambridge University Press

Bonino, José Miguez. 2005. "The Economic Dimensions of Biblical Hermeneutics." In *God's Economy: Biblical Studies from Latin America*, 34–42. Edited by R. Kinsler and J. Kinsler. Maryknoll, NY: Orbis Books.

Borgen, Peder. 1965. *Bread from Heaven: An Exegetical Study of the Concept of Manna in the Gospel of John and the Writings of Philo*. Leiden: Brill.

———. 1996. "Emperor Worship and Persecution in Philo's *In Flaccum* and *De Legatione ad Gaium* and the Revelation of John." In *Geschichte—Tradition—Reflexion*, 3:493–509. Edited by H. Cancik, H. Lichtenberger, and P. Schäfer. Tübingen: Mohr Siebeck.

———. 1996. "Moses, Jesus, and the Roman Emperor: Observations in Philo's Writings and the Revelation of John." *Novum Testamentum* 38:145–59.

———. 1996. "'Yes,' 'No,' 'How Far?' The Participation of Jews and Christians in Pagan Cults." In *Early Christianity and Hellenistic Judaism*, 15–43. Edinburgh: T&T Clark.

Bosworth, Brian. 1999. "Augustus, the *Res gestae* and Hellenistic Theories of Apotheosis." *Journal of Roman Studies* 89:1–18.

Bowie, Ewen L. 1974. "Greeks and Their Past in the Second Sophistic." In *Studies in Ancient Society*, 166–209. Edited by M. Finley. London: Routledge & Kegan Paul.

Boyancé, Pierre. 1972. *Études sur la religion romaine*. Rome: École française de Rome.

Boyarin, Daniel. 2002. "The *Ioudaioi* in John and the Prehistory of 'Judaism.'" In *Pauline Conversations in Context: Essays in Honor of Calvin J. Roetzel*, 216–39. Edited by J. C. Anderson, P. Sellew, and C. Setzer. Journal for the Study of the New Testament: Supplement Series 221. London: Sheffield Academic Press.

Brodie, Thomas. 1993. *The Quest for the Origin of John's Gospel: A Source-Oriented Approach*. New York: Oxford University Press.

Brothwell, Don R., and Patricia Brothwell. 1969. *Food in Antiquity: A Survey of the Diet of Early Peoples*. New York: Praeger.

Brown, Raymond E. 1966–70. *The Gospel according to John*. 2 vols. Anchor Bible 29–29A. New York: Doubleday. 2nd ed., 1979.

———. 1979. *The Community of the Beloved Disciple*. New York: Paulist Press.

———. 1994. *The Death of the Messiah*. New York: Doubleday.

———. 2003. *An Introduction to the Gospel of John*. Edited by F. J. Moloney. New York: Doubleday.

Brunt, Peter A. 1990. "The Administrators of Roman Egypt." In *Roman Imperial Themes*, 215–54. Oxford: Clarendon.

———. 1990. "Charges of Provincial Maladministration." In *Roman Imperial Themes*, 53–95, 487–506. Oxford: Clarendon.

———. 1990. "Procuratorial Jurisdiction." In *Roman Imperial Themes*, 163–87. Oxford: Clarendon.

———. 1990. "The Romanization of the Local Ruling Classes in the Roman Empire." In *Roman Imperial Themes*, 267–81. Oxford: Clarendon.

———. 1997. "Laus Imperii." In *Paul and Empire: Religion and Power in Roman Imperial Society*, 25–35. Edited by Richard A. Horsley. Harrisburg, PA: Trinity Press International.

Buckler, William Hepburn. 1935. "Auguste, Zeus Patroos." *Revue de philologie, de littérature et d'histoire anciennes* 9:177–88.

Bultmann, Rudolf. 1952–55. *Theology of the New Testament*. 2 vols. London: SCM.

———. 1969. "The Gospels (Form)." In *Twentieth Century Theology in the Making*, 1:86–92. Edited by J. Pelikan. London: Collins/Fontana.

———. 1971. *The Gospel of John*. Philadelphia: Westminster.

———. 1986. "The History of Religions Background of the Prologue to the Gospel of John." In *The Interpretation of John*, 18–35. Edited by J. A. Ashton. Philadelphia: Fortress.

Bureth, Paul. 1964. *Les titulatures impériales dans les papyrus, les ostraca, et les inscriptions d'Égypte (30 a.C.–284 p.C.)*. Brussels: Fondation égyptologique Reine Élisabeth.

Burke, Peter. 1989. "History as Social Memory." In *Memory: History, Culture, and the Mind*, 97–113. Edited by T. Butler. Oxford: Blackwell.

Burkett, Delbert. 1991. *The Son of Man in the Gospel of John*. Sheffield: JSOT Press.

Burnett, Andrew M., Michel Amandry, and Ian Carradice. 1999. *Roman Provincial Coinage.* Vol. 2.1–2. *From Vespasian to Domitian (AD 69–96).* London: British Museum Press.

Burnett, Andrew M., Michel Amandry, and Pere Pau Ripollès. 1992. *Roman Provincial Coinage.* Vol. 1.1–2, *From the Death of Caesar to the Death of Vitellius,* 363–81, 431–38. London: British Museum Press.

Burridge, Richard A. 1992. *What Are the Gospels? A Comparison with Graeco-Roman Biography.* Cambridge: Cambridge University Press.

Burton, G. P. 1975. "Proconsuls, Assizes, and the Administration of Justice under the Empire." *Journal of Roman Studies* 65:92–106.

Callahan, Allen D. 2005. *A Love Supreme: A History of Johannine Tradition.* Minneapolis: Fortress.

Carey, George L. 1981. "The Lamb of God and Atonement Theories." *Tyndale Bulletin* 32:97–122.

Carter, Warren. 1990. "The Prologue and John's Gospel: Function, Symbol and the Definitive Word." *Journal for the Study of the New Testament* 39:35–58.

———. 2000. *Matthew and the Margins: A Sociopolitical and Religious Reading.* Maryknoll, NY: Orbis Books.

———. 2001. *Matthew and Empire: Initial Explorations.* Harrisburg: Trinity Press International.

———. 2002. "Vulnerable Power: The Roman Empire Challenged by the Early Christians." In *Handbook of Early Christianity,* 453–88. Edited by A. J. Blasi, J. Duhaime, and P.-A. Turcotte. Walnut Creek: AltaMira.

———. 2003. "Are There Imperial Texts in This Class? Intertextual Eagles and Matthean Eschatology as 'Lights Out' Time for Imperial Rome (Matthew 24:27–31)." *Journal of Biblical Literature* 122:467–87.

———. 2003. *Pontius Pilate: Portraits of a Roman Governor.* Collegeville, MN: Liturgical Press.

———. 2004. "Going All the Way? Honoring the Emperor and Sacrificing Wives and Slaves in 1 Peter 2:13–3:6." In *A Feminist Companion to the Catholic Epistles and Hebrews,* 14–33. Edited by A.-J. Levine and M. M. Robbins. London: T&T Clark.

———. 2004. *Matthew: Storyteller, Interpreter, Evangelist.* Rev. ed. First ed., 1996. Peabody, MA: Hendrickson.

———. 2006. *John: Storyteller, Interpreter, Evangelist.* Peabody, MA: Hendrickson.

———. 2006. *The Roman Empire and the New Testament: An Essential Guide.* Nashville: Abingdon.

Cassidy, Richard J. 1992. *John's Gospel in New Perspective: Christology and the Realities of Roman Power.* Maryknoll, NY: Orbis Books.

Castle, Gregory, ed. 2001. *Postcolonial Discourses: An Anthology.* Oxford: Blackwell.

Castriota, David. 1995. *The Ara Pacis and the Imagery of Abundance in Later Greek and Early Imperial Art.* Princeton: Princeton University Press.

Cavallin, Hans C. C. 1974. *Life after Death,* part 1, *An Inquiry into the Jewish Background.* Lund: Gleerup.

Charles, Robert H. 1899, 1963. *Eschatology: The Doctrine of a Future Life in Israel, Judaism and Christianity: A Critical History.* New York: Schocken Books.

Charlesworth, James H. 1996. "The Dead Sea Scrolls and the Gospel according to John." In *Exploring the Gospel of John: In Honor of D. Moody Smith*, 65–97. Edited by R. A. Culpepper and C. C. Black. Louisville: Westminster John Knox.

———, ed. 1983–85. *The Old Testament Pseudepigrapha*. 2 vols. Garden City, NY: Doubleday.

Charlesworth, James H., with C. D. Elledge, James. L Crenshaw, Hendrikus Boers, and W. Waite Willis Jr. 2006. *Resurrection: The Origin and Future of a Biblical Doctrine*. New York: T&T Clark.

Charlesworth, Martin. 1936. "Providentia and Aeternitas." *Harvard Theological Review* 29:107–32.

Chatman, Seymour B. 1978. *Story and Discourse: Narrative Structure in Fiction and Film*. Ithaca, NY: Cornell University Press.

Chestnut, G. F. 1978. "The Ruler and the Logos in Neopythagorean, Middle Platonic, and Late Stoic Political Philosophy." In *Aufstieg und Niedergang der römischen Welt*. Part 2, *Principat,* 16.2:1310–32. Edited by H. Temporini and W. Haase. New York: de Gruyter.

Clark-Soles, Jaime. 2003. *Scripture Cannot Be Broken: The Social Function of the Use of Scripture in the Fourth Gospel*. Boston: Brill Academic Publishers.

Collins, Adela Yarbro. 1997. "Apotheosis and Resurrection." In *The New Testament and Hellenistic Judaism*, 88–100. Edited by P. Borgen and S. Giversen. Peabody, MA: Hendrickson.

———. 1999. "The Worship of Jesus and the Imperial Cult." In *The Jewish Roots of Christological Monotheism*, 234–57. Edited by C. Newman, J. Davila, and G. Lewis. Leiden: Brill.

Collins, John J. 1974. "Apocalyptic Eschatology as the Transcendence of Death." *Catholic Biblical Quarterly* 36:21–43.

———. 1984. *The Apocalyptic Imagination: An Introduction to the Jewish Matrix of Christianity*. New York: Crossroad.

———. 1986. *Between Athens and Jerusalem: Jewish Identity in the Hellenistic Diaspora*. New York: Crossroad.

———. 1995. "A Throne in the Heavens: Apotheosis in Pre-Christian Judaism." In *Death, Ecstasy, and Other Worldly Journeys*, 43–58. Edited by J. J. Collins and M. Fishbane. Albany: State University of New York Press.

Coloe, Mary. 2001. *God Dwells with Us: Temple Symbolism in the Fourth Gospel*. Collegeville, MN: Liturgical Press.

Conway, Colleen. 2002. "The Production of the Johannine Community: A New Historicist Perspective." *Journal of Biblical Literature* 121:479–95.

Corbier, Mireille. 1989. "The Ambiguous Status of Meat in Ancient Rome." *Food and Foodways* 3:223–64.

Corell, Alf. 1958. *Consummatum Est: Eschatology and Church in the Gospel of St. John*. London: Society for Promoting Christian Knowledge.

Corley, Kathleen. 1993. *Private Women, Public Meals: Social Conflict in the Synoptic Tradition*. Peabody, MA: Hendrickson.

Cotter, Wendy. 2001. "Greco-Roman Apotheosis Traditions and the Resurrection Appearances in Matthew." In *The Gospel of Matthew in Current Study*, 127–53. Edited by D. Aune. Grand Rapids: Eerdmans.

Crane, Ronald S. 1966. "The Concept of Plot and the Plot of Tom Jones." In *Approaches to the Novel: Materials for a Poetics*, 233–43. Edited by R. Scholes. Rev. ed. San Francisco: Chandler.

Crook, Zeba A. 2004. *Reconceptualising Conversion: Patronage, Loyalty and Conversion in the Religions of the Ancient Mediterranean*. Beihefte zur Zeitschrift für die neutestamentliche Wissenschaft und die Kunde der älteren Kirche: Beiheft 130. New York: W. de Gruyter.

Crossan, John Dominic, and Jonathan L. Reed. 2001. *Excavating Jesus*. San Francisco: HarperSanFrancisco.

————. 2004. *In Search of Paul: How Jesus's Apostle Opposed Rome's Empire with God's Kingdom*. San Francisco: HarperSanFrancisco.

Culpepper, R. Alan. 1987. *Anatomy of the Fourth Gospel: A Study in Literary Design*. Philadelphia: Fortress.

————. 1998. *The Gospel and Letters of John*. Interpreting Biblical Texts. Nashville: Abingdon.

————, ed. 1997. *Critical Readings of John 6*. Leiden: Brill.

Culpepper, R. Alan, and C. Clifton Black, eds. 1996. *Exploring the Gospel of John: In Honor of D. Moody Smith*. Louisville: Westminster John Knox.

Cumont, Franz. 1922. *After Life in Roman Paganism*. New Haven: Yale University Press.

Cuss, Dominique. 1974. *Imperial Cult and Honorary Terms in the New Testament*. Fribourg: University Press.

D'Angelo, Mary Rose. 1992. "*Abba* and 'Father': Imperial Theology and the Jesus Traditions." *Journal of Biblical Literature* 111:611–30.

Davies, Margaret. 1992. *Rhetoric and Reference in the Fourth Gospel*. Journal for the Study of the New Testament: Supplement Series 69. Sheffield: JSOT Press.

De Boer, Martinus. 1996. *Johannine Perspectives on the Death of Jesus*. Kampen: Kok Pharos.

Deissmann, Adolf. 1909. *Light from the Ancient East*. New York: Hodder & Stoughton.

————. 2000. "Christology, Controversy, and Community in the Gospel of John." In *Christology, Controversy and Community: New Testament Essays in Honour of David R. Catchpole*, 209–30. Edited by D. Horrell and C. Tuckett. Leiden; Boston: Brill.

De Ligt, L. 1990. "Demand, Supply, Distribution: The Roman Peasantry between Town and Countryside; Rural Monetization and Peasant Demand." *Münstersche Beiträge zur antiken Handelsgeschichte* 9:24–56.

Dewey, Joanna. 2001. "The Gospel of John in Its Oral-Written Media World." In *Jesus in Johannine Tradition*, 239–52. Edited by R. Fortna and T. Thatcher. Louisville: Westminster John Knox.

Dodd, Charles H. 1953. *The Interpretation of the Fourth Gospel*. Cambridge: Cambridge University Press. Reprint, 1968.

Donaldson, Laura, ed. 1996. *Postcolonialism and Scriptural Reading*. Semeia 75. Atlanta: Scholars Press.

Dorey, Thomas A. 1960. "Agricola and Domitian." *Greece and Rome* 7:66–71.

————. 1969. "Agricola." In *Tacitus*, 1–11. New York: Basic Books.

Downey, Glanville. 1951. "The Water Supply of Antioch on the Orontes in Antiquity." *Annales archéolgiques de Syrie* 2:171–87.

Dube, Musa W. 1998. "Savior of the World, but Not of This World: A Postcolonial Reading of Spatial Construction in John." In *The Postcolonial Bible,* 118–35. Edited by R. S. Sugirtharajah. Sheffield: Sheffield Academic Press.

———. 2002. "Reading for Decolonization (John 4:1–42)." In *John and Postcolonialism: Travel, Space, and Power,* 51–75. Edited by M. W. Dube and J. Staley. London: Continuum.

Dube, Musa W., and Jeffrey Staley, eds. 2002. *John and Postcolonialism: Travel, Space, and Power.* Bible and Postcolonialism 7. London: Continuum.

Duke, Paul. 1985. *Irony in the Fourth Gospel.* Atlanta: Westminster John Knox.

Duling, Dennis C. 2005. "Empire: Theories, Methods, Models." In *The Gospel of Matthew in Its Roman Imperial Context,* 49–74. Edited by J. Riches and D. C. Sim. London: T&T Clark International.

Dunn, James D. G. 1990. "Let John Be John: A Gospel for Its Time." In *The Gospel and the Gospels,* 293–322. Edited by P. Stuhlmacher. Grand Rapids: Eerdmans.

———. 2003. *Jesus Remembered.* Vol. 1. Grand Rapids: Eerdmans.

Dyson, Stephen. 1971. "Native Revolts in the Roman Empire." *Historia* 20:239–74.

———. 1975. "Native Revolt Patterns in the Roman Empire." *Aufstieg und Niedergang der römischen Welt.* Part 2, *Principat,* 2.3:138–75. Edited by H. Temporini and W. Haase. New York: de Gruyter.

Eck, Werner. 2003. *The Age of Augustus.* Translated by D. L. Schneider. Malden, MA: Blackwell.

Egan, Kieran. 1978. "What Is a Plot?" *New Literary History* 9:455–73.

Ehrenberg, Victor, and Arnold Hugh Martin Jones. 1955. *Documents Illustrating the Reigns of Augustus and Tiberius.* 2nd ed. Oxford: Clarendon.

Elliott, John H. 1986. "Social-Scientific Criticism of the New Testament: More on Methods and Models." In *Social-Scientific Criticism of the New Testament and Its Social World,* 1–33. Edited by J. H. Elliott. Semeia 35. Decatur, GA: Scholars Press.

Engels, Donald W. 1980. "The Problem of Female Infanticide in the Greco-Roman World." *Classical Philology* 75:112–20.

Erim, Kenan. 1986. *Aphrodisias: City of Venus Aphrodite.* New York: Facts on File.

Esler, Philip. 2005. "Rome in Apocalyptic and Rabbinic Literature." In *The Gospel of Matthew in Its Roman Imperial Context,* 9–33. Edited by J. Riches and D. C. Sim. London: T&T Clark International.

Evans, Craig. 1989. "Jesus' Action in the Temple and Evidence of Corruption in the First-Century Temple." *Society of Biblical Literature 1989 Seminar Papers,* 522–39. Society of Biblical Literature Seminar Papers. Atlanta: Scholars Press.

Evans, John K. 1980. "Plebs Rustica: The Peasantry of Classical Italy." *American Journal of Ancient History* 5:19–47, 134–73.

Fanon, Frantz. 1968. *The Wretched of the Earth.* New York: Grove.

Fears, J. Rufus. 1981. "The Cult of Jupiter and Roman Imperial Ideology." *Aufstieg und Niedergang der römischen Welt.* Part 2, *Principat,* 17.1:3–141. Edited by H. Temporini and W. Haase. New York: de Gruyter.

Feldman, Louis H. 1987. "Hellenizations in Josephus' *Jewish Antiquities*: The Portrait of Abraham." In *Josephus, Judaism, and Christianity,* 133–53. Edited by L. H. Feldman and G. Hata. Detroit: Wayne State University Press.

———. 1993. "Josephus' Portrait of Moses: Part Three." *Jewish Quarterly Review* 83:301–30.

Finley, Moses I. 1998. *Ancient Slavery and Modern Ideology.* Edited by Brent D. Shaw. Expanded ed. Princeton: Marcus Wiener.

Fitzgerald, John T., ed. 1997. *Greco-Roman Perspectives on Friendship.* Society of Biblical Literature Resources for Biblical Studies 34. Atlanta: Scholars Press.

———. 2003. "Paul and Friendship." In *Paul in the Greco-Roman World,* 319–31. Edited by P. Sampley. Harrisburg: Trinity Press International/Continuum.

Fitzpatrick-McKinley, Anne. 2002. "Synagogue Communities in the Graeco-Roman Cities." In *Jews in the Hellenistic and Roman Cities,* 55–87. Edited by J. R. Bartlett. London: Routledge.

Foerster, Werner. 1971. "εὐσεβής, εὐσέβεια, εὐσεβέω." *Theological Dictionary of the New Testament* 7:175–85. Grand Rapids: Eerdmans.

Foerster, Werner, and Gottfried Quell. 1963. "κύριος." *Theological Dictionary of the New Testament* 3:1039–98. Grand Rapids: Eerdmans.

Foley, John M. 1991. *Immanent Art: From Structure to Meaning in Traditional Oral Epic.* Bloomington: Indiana University Press.

Forestell, J. Terence. 1974. *The Word of the Cross: Salvation as Revelation in the Fourth Gospel.* Rome: Pontifical Biblical Institute.

Fortna, Robert T. 1970. *The Gospel of Signs: A Reconstruction of the Narrative Underlying the Fourth Gospel.* Cambridge: Cambridge University Press.

———. 1988. *The Fourth Gospel and Its Predecessor.* Philadelphia: Fortress.

Fortna, Robert T., and Tom Thatcher, eds. 2001. *Jesus in Johannine Tradition.* Louisville: Westminster John Knox.

Foster, Edward Morgan. 1962. *Aspects of the Novel.* New York: Penguin Books.

Fox, Sherry C. 2005. "Health in Hellenistic and Roman Times: The Case Studies of Paphos, Cyprus, and Corinth, Greece." In *Health in Antiquity,* 59–82. Edited by H. King. London: Routledge.

Foxhall, Lin, and Hamish A. Forbes. 1982. "*Sitometreia*: The Role of Grain as a Staple Food in Classical Antiquity." *Chiron* 12:41–90.

Frenschkowski, Marco. 2002. "Kyrios in Context: Q 6:46, the Emperor as 'Lord,' and the Political Implications of Christology in Q." In *Zwischen den Reichen: Neues Testament und römische Herrschaft,* 95–118. Edited by M. Labahn and J. Zangenberg. Tübingen: Francke.

Freyburger, Gérard. 1986. *Fides: Étude sémantique et religieuse depuis les origins jusqu'à l'époque augustéene.* Paris: Belles Lettres.

Frier, Bruce W. 1999. "Roman Demography." In *Life, Death, and Entertainment in the Roman Empire,* 85–109. Edited by D. S. Potter and D. J. Mattingly. Ann Arbor: University of Michigan Press.

Friesen, Steven. 1993. *Twice Neokoros: Ephesus, Asia, and the Cult of the Flavian Imperial Family.* Leiden: Brill.

———. 2001. *Imperial Cults and the Apocalypse of John: Reading Revelation in the Ruins.* Oxford: Oxford University Press.

———. 2004. "Poverty in Pauline Studies: Beyond the So-called New Consensus." *Journal for the Study of the New Testament* 26:323–61.

Frye, Northrop. 1971. *Anatomy of Criticism: Four Essays*. Princeton: Princeton University Press.

Fuglseth, Kåre Sigvald. 2005. *Johannine Sectarianism in Perspective: A Sociological, Historical, and Comparative Analysis of the Temple and Social Relationships in the Gospel of John, Philo, and Qumran*. Leiden: Brill.

Gager, John G. 1972. *Moses in Greco-Roman Paganism*. Nashville: Abingdon.

Gapp, Kenneth S. 1935. "The Universal Famine under Claudius." *Harvard Theological Review* 28:258–65.

Garland, Robert. 1995. *The Eye of the Beholder: Deformity and Disability in the Graeco-Roman World*. Ithaca, NY: Cornell University Press.

Garlinsky, Karl. 1996. *Augustan Culture: An Interpretive Introduction*. Princeton: Princeton University Press.

Garnsey, Peter. 1970. *Social Status and Legal Privilege in the Roman Empire*. Oxford: Clarendon.

———. 1983. "Grain for Rome." In *Trade in the Ancient Economy*, 118–30. Edited by P. Garnsey, K. Hopkins, and C. R. Whittaker. London: Hogarth.

———. 1988. *Cities, Peasants and Food in Classical Antiquity*. Cambridge: Cambridge University Press.

———. 1988. *Famine and Food Supply in the Graeco-Roman World*. Cambridge: Cambridge University Press.

———. 1990. "Responses to Food Crisis in the Ancient Mediterranean World." In *Hunger in History: Food Shortage, Poverty and Deprivation*, 126–46. Edited by L. F. Newman. Oxford: Blackwell.

———. 1996. *Ideas of Slavery from Aristotle to Augustine*. Cambridge: Cambridge University Press.

———. 1999. *Food and Society in Classical Antiquity*. Cambridge: Cambridge University Press.

Garnsey, Peter, and Richard Saller. 1987. *The Roman Empire: Economy, Society, and Culture*. Berkeley: University of California Press.

Georgi, Dieter. 1986. "Who Is the True Prophet?" In *Christians among Jews and Gentiles: Essays in Honor of Krister Stendahl*, 100–126. Edited by G. MacRae, G. Nickelsburg, and A. Sundberg. Philadelphia: Fortress.

Gilbert, Gary. 1992. "Pagans in a Jewish World: Pagan Involvement in Jewish Religious and Social Life in the First Four Centuries CE." PhD diss., Columbia University.

Gill, Christopher. 1990. "Character-Personality Distinction." In *Characterization and Individuality in Greek Literature*, 1–31. Edited by C. Pelling. New York: Oxford University Press.

Glancy, Jennifer. 2002. *Slavery in Early Christianity*. Oxford: Oxford University Press.

Glasson, T. Francis. 1963. *Moses in the Fourth Gospel*. Naperville, IL: Allenson.

Goodenough, Erwin R. 1928. "The Political Philosophy of Hellenistic Kingship." In *Yale Classical Review* 1:55–102. Edited by A. Harmon. New Haven: Yale University Press.

———. 1967. *The Politics of Philo Judaeus: Practice and Theory*. Hildesheim: G. Olms.

Goodman, Martin. 1991. "Opponents of Rome: Jews and Others." In *Images of Empire*, 222–38. Edited by L. Alexander. Journal for the Study of the Old Testament: Supplement Series 122. Sheffield: JSOT Press.

————. 1999. "Diaspora Reactions to the Destruction of the Temple." In *Jews and Christians: The Parting of the Ways, A.D. 70 to 135*, 27–38. Grand Rapids: Eerdmans.

Goodyear, Francis R. D. 1970. *Tacitus*. Oxford: Clarendon.

Gordon, Pamela. 1997. "Review." *Bryn Mawr Classical Review* 8:482–86.

Gradel, Ittai. 2002. *Emperor Worship and Roman Religion*. Oxford: Clarendon.

Grant, Michael. 1982. *From Alexander to Cleopatra: The Hellenistic World*. New York: Charles Scribner's Sons.

Greimas, Algirdas Julien. 1976. *Sémantique structurale: Recherche de méthode*. Rev. ed. Paris: Larousse.

Grigsby, Bruce. 1982. "The Cross as an Expiatory Sacrifice in the Fourth Gospel." *Journal for the Study of the New Testament* 15:51–80.

Gruen, Erich S. 1992. *Culture and National Identity in Republican Rome*. Ithaca, NY: Cornell University Press.

————. 1998. *Heritage and Hellenism: The Reinvention of Jewish Tradition*. Berkeley: University of California Press.

————. 2002. *Diaspora: Jews amidst Greeks and Romans*. Cambridge: Harvard University Press.

Habicht, Christian. 1975. "New Evidence on the Province of Asia." *Journal of Roman Studies* 65:64–91.

Hafemann, Scott J. 1990. "Moses in the Apocrypha and Pseudepigrapha: A Survey." *Journal for the Study of the Pseudepigrapha* 7:79–104.

Hägerland, Tobias. 2003. "John's Gospel: A Two-Level Drama?" *Journal for the Study of the New Testament* 25:309–22.

Hägg, Tomas. 1983. *The Novel in Antiquity*. Berkeley: University of California Press.

Halliday, Michael A. K. 1976. "Antilanguages." *American Anthropologist* 78:570–84.

Hamberg, Per Gustaf. 1945. *Studies in Roman Imperial Art*. Uppsala: Almqvist & Wiksell.

Hanson, Anthony T. 1980. "John 1:14–18 and Exodus 34." In *The New Testament Interpretation of Scripture*, 97–109. London: Society for Promoting Christian Knowledge.

————. 1980. "The Theme of Christ as the True Temple in the Fourth Gospel." In *The New Testament of Scripture*, 110–21. London: Society for Promoting Christian Knowledge.

Hanson, Kenneth C., and Douglas E. Oakman. 1998. *Palestine in the Time of Jesus: Social Structures and Social Conflicts*. Minneapolis: Fortress.

Harland, Philip A. 2000. "Honouring the Emperor or Assailing the Beast: Participation in Civic Life among Associations (Jewish, Christian and Other) in Asia Minor and the Apocalypse of John." *Journal for the Study of the Old Testament* 22, no. 77:99–121.

————. 2003. *Associations, Synagogues, and Congregations*. Minneapolis: Fortress.

Harrill, J. Albert. 2006. *Slaves in the New Testament: Literary, Social, and Moral Dimensions*. Minneapolis: Fortress.

Harrington, Wilfrid. 1993. *Revelation*. Sacra pagina 16. Collegeville, MN: Liturgical Press.

Harrison, Nicholas. 2003. *Postcolonial Criticism: History, Theory and the Work of Fiction*. Oxford: Polity/Blackwell.

Hedrick, Charles. 2002. "The Four/Thirty-Four Gospels: Diversity and Division among the Earliest Christians." *Bible Review* 18:20–31, 46–47.

Hellegouarc'h, Joseph. 1963. *Le Vocabulaire latin des relations et des parties politique sous la Républic*. Paris: Belles Lettres.

Helleman, Wendy. 1990. "Philo of Alexandria: On Deification and Assimilation to God." In *The Studia Philonic Annual*. Vol. 2:51–71. Edited by D. Runia. Atlanta: Scholars Press.

Hengel, Martin. 1974. *Judaism and Hellenism: Studies in Their Encounter in Palestine during the Early Hellenistic Period*. Philadelphia: Fortress.

———. 1977. *Crucifixion in the Ancient World and the Folly of the Message of the Cross*. Philadelphia: Fortress.

———. 1991. "Reich Christi, Reich Gottes und Weltreich in Johannesevangelium." In *Königsherrschaft Gottes und himmlischer Kult im Judentum, Urchristentum und in der hellenistischen Welt*, 163–84. Edited by M. Hengel and A. M. Schwemer. Tübingen: Mohr Siebeck.

Hill, David. 1967. *Greek Words and Hebrew Meanings: Studies in the Semantics of Soteriological Terms*. Cambridge: Cambridge University Press.

Horn, Friedrich Wilhelm. 1994. "Zwischen der Synagogue des Satans und dem neuen Jerusalem: Die christlich-jüdische Standortbestimmung in der Apokalypse des Johannes." *Zeitschrift für Religions- und Geistesgeschichte* 46:143–62.

Hornblower, Simon, and Andrew Spawforth, eds. 1999. *The Oxford Classical Dictionary* 3rd edition. Oxford: Oxford University Press.

Horsley, G. H. R. 1989. "A Fishing Cartel in First-Century Ephesos." In *New Documents Illustrating Early Christianity: Linguistic Essays*, 5:95–114. North Ryde, NSW, Australia: The Ancient History Documentary Research Centre, Macquarrie University.

———. 1992. "The Inscriptions of Ephesos and the New Testament." *Novum Testamentum* 34:105–68.

Horsley, Richard A. 1987. *Jesus and the Spiral of Violence: Popular Jewish Resistance in Roman Palestine*. San Francisco: Harper & Row.

———. 1992. "Messianic Movements in Judaism." *Anchor Bible Dictionary* 4:791–97. New York: Doubleday.

———. 2001. *Hearing the Whole Gospel: The Politics of Plot in Mark's Gospel*. Louisville: Westminster John Knox.

———. 2003. *Jesus and Empire: The Kingdom of God and the New World Disorder*. Minneapolis: Fortress.

———, ed. 2000. *Paul and Politics*. Harrisburg: Trinity Press International.

———, ed. 2004. *Hidden Transcripts and the Arts of Resistance: Applying the Work of James C. Scott to Jesus and Paul*. Semeia Studies 48. Atlanta: Society of Biblical Literature.

———, ed. 2004. *Paul and the Roman Imperial Order*. Harrisburg: Trinity Press International/Continuum.

Horsley, Richard A., and John S. Hanson. 1985. *Bandits, Prophets, and Messiahs: Popular Movements at the Time of Jesus*. San Francisco: Harper & Row.

Howard, Jean. 1992. "The New Historicism in Renaissance Studies." In *New Historicism and Renaissance Drama*, 19–32. Edited by R. Wilson and R. Dutton. London: Longman.

Hurtado, Larry. 2003. *Lord Jesus Christ: Devotion to Jesus in Earliest Christianity*. Grand Rapids: Eerdmans.

Jaeger, Werner. 1965. "The Greek Ideas of Immortality." In *Immortality and Resurrection*, 97–114. Edited by K. Stendahl. New York: Macmillan.

James, Paula. 2000. "Essay Ten: The Language of Dissent." In *Experiencing Rome: Culture, Identity, and Power in the Roman Empire*, 277–303. Edited by J. Huskinson. London: Routledge.

Johnson, Luke T. 1989. "The New Testament's Anti-Jewish Slander and the Conventions of Ancient Polemic." *Journal of Biblical Literature* 108:419–41.

Jones, Brian W. 1973. "Domitian's Attitude to the Senate." *American Journal of Philology* 94:79–91.

———. 1984. *The Emperor Titus*. New York: St. Martin's Press.

———. 1992. *The Emperor Domitian*. London: Routledge.

Jonge, Marinus de. 1992. "Messiah." *Anchor Bible Dictionary* 4:777–88. New York: Doubleday.

———. 2000. "Christology, Controversy, and Community in the Gospel of John." In *Christology, Controversy, and Community: New Testament Essays in Honour of David R. Catchpole*, 209–30. Edited by D. Horrell and C. Tuckett. Boston: Brill.

Kanagaraj, Jey J. 2001. "The Implied Ethics of the Fourth Gospel: A Reinterpretation of the Decalogue." *Tyndale Bulletin* 52:33–60.

Karris, Robert J. 1990. *Jesus and the Marginalized in John's Gospel*. Collegeville, MN: Liturgical Press.

Käsemann, Ernst. 1966. *The Testament of Jesus*. Philadelphia: Fortress.

———. 1969. "On the Subject of Primitive Christian Apocalyptic." In *New Testament Questions of Today*, 108–37. Philadelphia: Fortress.

Katz, Stephen. 1984. "Issues in the Separation of Judaism and Christianity after 70 C.E.: A Reconsideration." *Journal of Biblical Literature* 103:43–76.

Kautsky, John. 1982. *The Politics of Aristocratic Empires*. Chapel Hill: University of North Carolina Press.

Keck, Leander E. 1986. "Toward the Renewal of New Testament Christology." *New Testament Studies* 32:362–77.

———. 1996. "Derivation as Destiny: 'Of-ness' in Johannine Christology, Anthropology, and Soteriology." In *Exploring the Gospel of John: In Honor of D. Moody Smith*, 274–88. Edited by R. A. Culpepper and C. C. Black. Louisville: Westminster John Knox.

Kee, Howard Clark. 2005. *The Beginnings of Christianity: An Introduction to the New Testament*. New York: T&T Clark.

Keener, Craig. 2003. *The Gospel of John: A Commentary*. 2 vols. Peabody, MA: Hendrickson.

Kerr, Alan R. 2002. *The Temple of Jesus' Body: The Temple Theme in the Gospel of John*. Journal for the Study of the New Testament: Supplement Series 220. Sheffield: Sheffield Academic Press.

Kim, Seon-Jeong. 2001. "The Johannine Jesus and Its Socio-political Context." *Yonsei Review of Theology and Culture* 6:209–21.

Kimelman, Reuven. 1981. "Birkat Ha-Minim and the Lack of Evidence for an Anti-Christian Jewish Prayer in Late Antiquity." In *Jewish and Christian Self-Definition*, 2:226–44. Edited by E. P. Sanders, A. I. Baumgarten, and A. Mendelson. Philadelphia: Fortress.

King, Helen, ed. 2005. *Health in Antiquity*. London: Routledge.

King, Winston L. 1987. "Religion." In *Encyclopedia of Religion*, 12:282–93. Edited by M. Eliade. New York: Macmillan.

Kinman, Brent. 1991. "Pilate's Assize and the Timing of Jesus' Trial." *Tyndale Bulletin* 42:282–95.

———. 1995. *Jesus' Entry into Jerusalem*. Leiden: Brill.

Kinsler, Ross, and Gloria Kinsler, eds. 2005. *God's Economy: Biblical Studies from Latin America*. Maryknoll, NY: Orbis Books.

Klijn, Albertus F. J. 1983. "2 (Syriac Apocalypse of) Baruch." In *Old Testament Pseudepigrapha*, 1:615–52. Edited by J. H. Charlesworth. Garden City, NY: Doubleday.

Koester, Craig R. 1990. "'The Savior of the World' (John 4:42)." *Journal of Biblical Literature* 109:665–80.

———. 1995. *Symbolism in the Fourth Gospel*. Minneapolis: Fortress.

———. 2002. "Comedy, Humor, and the Gospel of John." In *Word, Theology, and Community in John*, 123–41. Edited by J. Painter, R. A. Culpepper, and F. F. Segovia. St. Louis: Chalice.

Koester, Helmut. 1992. "Jesus the Victim." *Journal of Biblical Literature* 111:3–15.

———, ed. 2005. "Ephesos." In *Cities of Paul: Images and Interpretations from the Harvard New Testament Archaeology Project*. Minneapolis: Fortress. Compact Disk.

Konstan, David. 1997. *Friendship in the Classical World*. Cambridge: Cambridge University Press.

Köstenberger, Andreas, J. 2006. "The Destruction of the Second Temple and the Composition of the Fourth Gospel." In *Challenging Perspectives on the Gospel of John*, 68–108. Edited by J. Lierman. Wissenschaftliche Untersuchungen zum Neuen Testament 2.219. Tübingen: Mohr Siebeck.

Kovacs, Judith. 1995. "'Now Shall the Ruler of This World Be Driven Out': Jesus' Death as Cosmic Battle in John 12:20–36." *Journal of Biblical Literature* 114:227–47.

Kraft, Robert A. 1991. "Philo and the Sabbath Crisis: Alexandrian Jewish Politics and the Dating of Philo's Works." In *The Future of Christianity: Essays in Honor of Helmut Koester*, 131–41. Edited by B. Pearson. Minneapolis: Fortress.

Kraybill, J. Nelson. 1996. *Imperial Cult and Commerce in John's Apocalypse*. Journal for the Study of the New Testament: Supplement Series 132. Sheffield: Sheffield Academic Press.

Kreitzer, Larry. 1987. "A Numismatic Clue to Acts 19:23–41: The Ephesian Cistophori of Claudius and Agrippina." *Journal for the Study of the New Testament* 30:59–70.

———. 1990. "Apotheosis of the Roman Emperor." *Biblical Archaeologist* 53:210–17.

Kristeva, Julia. 1980. "The Bounded Text." In *Desire in Language: A Semiotic Approach to Literature and Art*, 36–63. Edited by L. S. Rondiez. New York: Columbia University Press.

Kuhn, Heinz-Wolfgang. 1966. *Enderwartung und gegenwärtiges Heil: Untersuchungen zu den Gemeindeliedern von Qumran mit einem Anhang über Eschatologie und Gegenwart in der Verkündigung Jesu.* Studien zur Umwelt des Neuen Testaments 4. Göttingen: Vandenhoeck & Ruprecht.

Kümmel, Werner. 1972. *The New Testament: The History of the Investigation of Its Problems.* Nashville: Abingdon.

Kuschel, Karl-Josef. 1995. *Abraham: Sign of Hope for Jews, Christians, and Muslims.* New York: Continuum.

Kvalbein, Hans. 2003. "The Kingdom of God and the Kingdom of Christ in the Fourth Gospel." In *Neotestamentica et Philonica: Studies in Honor of Peder Borgen,* 215–32. Edited by D. Aune, T. Seland, and J. Ulrichsen. Leiden: Brill.

Kysar, Robert. 1975. *The Fourth Evangelist and His Gospel: An Examination of Contemporary Scholarship.* Minneapolis: Augsburg Fortress.

———. 1986. *John.* Minneapolis: Augsburg Fortress.

———. 1993. *John: The Maverick Gospel.* Rev. ed. Louisville: Westminster John Knox.

———. 2005. *Voyages with John: Charting the Fourth Gospel.* Waco: Baylor University Press.

Labahn, Michael. 2002. "'Heiland der Welt': Der gesandte Gottessohn und der römische Kaiser—ein Thema johanneischer Christologie?" In *Zwischen den Reichen: Neues Testament und römische Herrschaft,* 147–73. Edited by M. Labahn and J. Zangenberg. Tübingen: A. Franke.

Lacey, Walter K. 1986. "Patria Potestas." In *The Family in Ancient Rome: New Perspectives,* 121–44. Edited by B. Rawson. Ithaca, NY: Cornell University Press.

Ladd, George E. 1974. *A Theology of the New Testament.* Grand Rapids: Eerdmans.

Laurence, Ray. 2005. "Health and Life Course at Herculaneum and Pompeii." In *Health in Antiquity,* 83–96. Edited by H. King. London: Routledge.

Lee, Dorothy A. 1994. *The Symbolic Narratives of the Fourth Gospel.* Journal for the Study of the New Testament: Supplement Series 95. Sheffield: Sheffield Academic Press.

———. 1995. "Beyond Suspicion? The Fatherhood of God in the Fourth Gospel." *Pacifica* 8:140–54.

———. 2005. "Friendship, Love, and Abiding in the Gospel of John." In *Transcending Boundaries: Contemporary Readings of the New Testament,* 57–74. Edited by R. M. Chennattu and M. L. Coloe. Roma: Libreria Ateneo Salesiano.

Lenski, Gerhard. 1984. *Power and Privilege: A Theory of Social Stratification.* Chapel Hill: University of North Carolina Press.

Levick, Barbara. 1999. *Vespasian.* London: Routledge.

Levine, Lee. 1996. "The Nature and Origin of the Palestinian Synagogue Reconsidered." *Journal of Biblical Literature* 115:425–48.

———. 1998. "Synagogue Leadership: The Case of the *Archisynagōgoi.*" In *Jews in a Graeco-Roman World,* 195–213. Edited by M. Goodman. Oxford: Clarendon.

Levinskaya, Irina. 1996. *The Book of Acts in Its Diaspora Setting.* Grand Rapids: Eerdmans.

Liebeschuetz, John Hugo Wolfgang Gideon. 1979. *Continuity and Change in Roman Religion.* Oxford: Clarendon.

Lierman, John, ed. 2006. *Challenging Perspectives on the Gospel of John.* Wissenschaftliche Untersuchungen zum Neuen Testament 2.219. Tübingen: Mohr Siebeck.

Lieu, Judith. 1999. "Temple and Synagogue in John." *New Testament Studies* 45:51–69.

Liew, Tat-Siong Benny. 2002. "Ambiguous Admittance: Consent and Descent in John's Community of 'Upward' Mobility." In *John and Postcolonialism: Travel, Space, and Power,* 193–224. Edited by M. W. Dube and J. Staley. London: Continuum.

Lincoln, Andrew T. 1998. "'I Am the Resurrection and the Life': The Resurrection Message of the Fourth Gospel." In *Life in the Face of Death: The Resurrection Message of the New Testament,* 122–44. Edited by R. N. Longenecker. Grand Rapids: Eerdmans.

———. 2000. *Truth on Trial: The Lawsuit Motif in John's Gospel.* Peabody, MA: Hendrickson.

Lindars, Barnabas. 1972. *The Gospel of John.* New Century Bible Commentary. Grand Rapids: Eerdmans.

Lindsay, Dennis R. 1993. *Josephus and Faith: Πίστις and Πιστεύειν as Faith Terminology in the Writings of Flavius Josephus and in the New Testament.* Leiden: Brill.

L'Orange, Hans Peter. 1947, 1982. *Apotheosis in Ancient Portraiture.* New Rochelle, NY: Caratzas Brothers.

———. 1985. "The Floral Zone of the Ara Pacis." In *Art Forms and Civic Life,* 211–30. Edited by H. P. L'Orange. New York: Rizzoli.

Lowe, Martin. 1976. "Who Were the *Ioudaioi?*" *Novum Testamentum* 18:102–7.

MacCormack, Sabine. 1972. "Continuity and Change in Late Antiquity: The Ceremony of *Adventus.*" *Historia* 21:721–52.

MacLaren, James. 1991. *Power and Politics in Palestine: The Jews and the Governing of Their Land 100 BC–AD 70.* Journal for the Study of the New Testament: Supplement Series 63. Sheffield: Sheffield Academic Press.

MacMullen, Ramsay. 1974. *Roman Social Relations 50 B.C. to A.D. 284.* New Haven: Yale University Press.

———. 1990. "How to Revolt in the Roman Empire." In *Changes in the Roman Empire: Essays in the Ordinary,* 198–203. Princeton: Princeton University Press.

———. 1990. "Notes on Romanization." In *Changes in the Roman Empire: Essays on the Ordinary,* 56–66. Princeton: Princeton University Press.

Macro, Anthony D. 1980. "The Cities of Asia Minor under the Roman Imperium." *Aufstieg und Niedergang der römischen Welt.* Part 2, *Principat,* 7.2:658–97. Edited by H. Temporini and W. Haase. New York: de Gruyter.

Magie, David. 1950. "Centralization and Prosperity under the Flavians." In *Roman Rule in Asia Minor to the End of the Third Century after Christ,* 1:566–92. Princeton: Princeton University Press.

Malina, Bruce J. 1987. "Wealth and Property in the New Testament and Its World." *Interpretation* 41:354–67.

Malina, Bruce J., and Richard L. Rohrbaugh. 1998. *Social Science Commentary on the Gospel of John.* Minneapolis: Fortress.

Mann, Michael. 1986. *The Sources of Social Power.* Vol. 1, *A History of Power from the Beginning to A.D. 1760.* Cambridge: Cambridge University Press.

Marshall, Anthony J. 1966. "Governors on the Move." *Phoenix* 20:231–46.

———. 1984. "Symbols and Showmanship in Roman Public Life: The Fasces." *Phoenix* 38:120–41.

Martin, Dale. 1990. *Slavery as Salvation: The Metaphor of Slavery in Pauline Christianity*. New Haven: Yale University Press.

Martin-Achard, Robert. 1960. *From Death to Life: A Study of the Development of the Doctrine of the Resurrection in the Old Testament*. Edinburgh: Oliver & Boyd.

Martyn, J. Louis. 1968. *History and Theology in the Fourth Gospel*. Nashville: Abingdon. 3rd ed., 2003.

———. 1968. "Source Criticism and Religionsgeschichte in the Fourth Gospel." In *The Interpretation of John*, 99–121. Edited by J. A. Ashton. Philadelphia: Fortress.

———. 1978. *The Gospel of John in Christian History*. New York: Paulist Press.

———. 1979. "Glimpses into the History of the Johannine Community." In *The Gospel of John in Christian History*, 90–121. New York: Paulist Press.

———. 2003. *History and Theology in the Fourth Gospel*. 3rd ed. Louisville: Westminster John Knox.

Mastin, B. A. 1973. "The Imperial Cult and the Ascription of the Title θεός to Jesus (John XX.28)." *Studia evangelica* 6:352–65.

———. 1975–76. "A Neglected Feature of the Christology of the Fourth Gospel." *New Testament Studies* 22:32–51.

Matson, Mark. 2001. "The Temple Incident." In *Jesus and Johannine Tradition*, 145–53. Edited by R. T. Fortna and T. Thatcher. Louisville: Westminster John Knox.

Mattill, A. J. 1977. "Johannine Communities behind the Fourth Gospel: Georg Richter's Analysis." *Theological Studies* 38:294–315.

Mattingly, David J. 1996. "First Fruit? The Olive in the Roman World." In *Human Landscapes in Classical Antiquity: Environment and Culture*, 213–53. Edited by G. Shipley and J. Salmon. New York: Routledge.

———, ed. 1997. *Dialogues in Roman Imperialism: Power, Discourse, and Discrepant Experience in the Roman Empire*. Journal of Roman Archaeology: Supplementary Series 23. Portsmouth, RI: JRA.

Mattingly, Harold. 1934. "Virgil's Golden Age: Sixth Aeneid and Fourth Eclogue." *Classical Review* 48:161–65.

———. 1965–66. *Coins of the Roman Empire in the British Museum*. Vol. 1, *Augustus to Vitellius*. Vol. 2, *Vespasian to Domitian*. Reprints. London: British Museum.

Mayo, Philip. 2006. *"Those Who Call Themselves Jews": The Church and Judaism in the Apocalypse of John*. Princeton Theological Monograph Series 60. Oregon: Pickwick Publications.

McCaffrey, James. 1988. *The House with Many Rooms: The Temple Theme of Jn. 14:2–3*. Analecta biblica 114. Rome: Editrice Pontificio Istituto Biblico.

McCready, Wayne. 1990. "Johannine Self-Understanding and the Synagogue Episode in John 9." In *Self-Definition and Self-Discovery in Early Christianity: A Study in Changing Horizons; Essays in Appreciation of Ben F. Meyer from Former Students*, 149–66. Edited by D. Hawkin and T. Robinson. Lewiston: Edwin Mellen.

McGrane, Bernard. 1989. *Beyond Anthropology: Society and the Other*. New York: Columbia University Press.

McGrath, James F. 2001. *John's Apologetic Christology: Legitimation and Development in Johannine Christology*. Society for New Testament Studies Monograph Series 111. Cambridge: Cambridge University Press.

McLaren, James. 2005. "A Reluctant Provincial: Josephus and the Roman Empire in *Jewish War.*" In *The Gospel of Matthew in Its Roman Imperial Context*, 34–48. Edited by J. Riches and D. C. Sim. Journal for the Study of the New Testament: Supplement Series 276. London: T&T Clark.

Mead, A. Hugh. 1985. "The *Basilikos* in John 4:46–54." *Journal for the Study of the New Testament* 23:69–72.

Meeks, Wayne. 1967. *The Prophet-King: Moses Traditions and the Johannine Christology*. Leiden: Brill.

———. 1972. "The Man from Heaven in Johannine Sectarianism." *Journal of Biblical Literature* 91:44–72.

———. 1976. "The Divine Agent and His Counterfeit in Philo and the Fourth Gospel." In *Aspects of Religious Propaganda in Judaism and Early Christianity*, 43–67. Edited by E. S. Fiorenza. Notre Dame, IN: University of Notre Dame Press.

———. 1990. "Equal to God." In *The Conversation Continues: Studies in Paul and John in Honor of J. Louis Martyn*, 309–21. Edited by R. Fortna and B. Gaventa. Nashville: Abingdon.

Merten, Marieluise. 1965. *Fides romana bei Livius*. Doctoral diss., Johann Wolfgang Goethe-Universität, Frankfurt, 1964. Giessen: Schreib-Druck Chemoprint.

Metzger, Bruce M. 1971. *A Textual Commentary on the Greek New Testament*. London: United Bible Societies.

———. 1983. "Fourth Ezra." In *Old Testament Pseudepigrapha*, 1:516–59. Edited by J. H. Charlesworth. Garden City, NY: Doubleday.

Meyer, Paul W. 1996. "'The Father': The Presentation of God in the Fourth Gospel." In *Exploring the Gospel of John: In Honor of D. Moody Smith*, 255–73. Edited by R. A. Culpepper and C. C. Black. Louisville: Westminster John Knox.

Michel, Otto. 1967. "οἶκος, οἰκία." *Theological Dictionary of the New Testament* 5:119–20. Grand Rapids: Eerdmans.

Migne, Jacques-Paul, ed. 1857–66. *Patrologiae cursus completus: Series graeca*. Paris. Reprint, Athens: Kentron Paterikon Ekdoseon.

Millar, Fergus, ed. 1967. *The Roman Empire and Its Neighbours*. New York: Delacorte.

Mitchell, Stephen. 1993. *Anatolia: Land, Men, and Gods in Asia Minor*. Vol. 1. Oxford: Clarendon.

Moles, John. 1983. "The Date and Purpose of the Fourth Kingship Oration of Dio Chrysostom." *Classical Antiquity* 2:251–78.

Moloney, Francis J. 1978. *The Johannine Son of Man*. Rome: Libreria Ateneo Salesiano.

———. 1998. *The Gospel of John*. Edited by D. J. Harrington. Sacra pagina 4. Collegeville, MN: Liturgical Press.

Momigliano, Arnaldo. 1987. "How the Roman Emperors Became Gods." In *On Pagans, Jews, and Christians*, 92–107. Middleton, CT: Wesleyan University Press.

Mongia, Padmini, ed. 1996. *Contemporary Postcolonial Theory: A Reader*. London: Arnold.

Moore, Stephen. 2006. *Empire and Apocalypse: Postcolonialism and the New Testament*. Sheffield: Sheffield Phoenix Press.

Moore-Gilbert, Bart. 1997. *Postcolonial Theory: Contexts, Practices, Politics*. London: Verso.

Moralee, Jason. 2004. *"For Salvation's Sake": Provincial Loyalty, Personal Religion, and Epigraphic Production in the Roman and Late Antique Near East*. London: Routledge.

Moritz, Ludwig Alfred. 1958. *Grain-Mills and Flour in Classical Antiquity*. Oxford: Clarendon.

Morley, Neville. 2005. "The Salubriousness of the Roman City." In *Health in Antiquity*, 192–204. Edited by H. King. London: Routledge.

Morrow, Stanley B. 2002. "Κόσμος in John." *Catholic Biblical Quarterly* 64:90–102.

Mowery, Robert L. 1999. Review of Bernd Wander, *Gottesfürchtige und Sympathisanten: Studien zum heidnischen Umfeld von Diasporasynagogen*. Wissenschaftliche Untersuchungen zum Neuen Testament 104. Tübingen: Mohr Siebeck, 1998. *Catholic Biblical Quarterly* 61:607–9.

Mowvley, Henry. 1983–84. "John 1:14–18 in the Light of Exod. 33:7–34:35." *Expository Times* 95:135–37.

Neill, Stephen, and Tom Wright. 1988. *The Interpretation of the New Testament, 1861–1986*. 2nd ed. New York: Oxford University Press.

Neverov, Oleg. 1986. "Nero-Helios." In *Pagan Gods and Shrines of the Roman Empire*, 189–94. Edited by M. Henig and A. King. Oxford University Committee for Archaeology Monograph 8. Oxford: Oxford University Committee for Archaeology.

Newlands, Carole E. 2002. *Statius' "Silvae" and the Poetics of Empire*. Cambridge: Cambridge University Press.

Neyrey, Jerome H. 1988. *An Ideology of Revolt: John's Christology in Social-Science Perspective*. Philadelphia: Fortress.

———. 1991. "Ceremonies in Luke-Acts: The Case of Meals and Table Fellowship." In *The Social World of Luke-Acts*, 361–87. Edited by J. Neyrey. Peabody, MA: Hendrickson.

———. 2001. "The 'Noble Shepherd' in John 10: Cultural and Rhetorical Background." *Journal of Biblical Literature* 120:267–91.

Nicholson, Godfrey C. 1983. *Death as Departure: The Johannine Descent-Ascent Schema*. Chico, CA: Scholars Press.

Nickelsburg, George W. E. 1972. *Resurrection, Immortality, and Eternal Life in Intertestamental Judaism*. Harvard Theological Studies 26. Cambridge: Harvard University Press.

———. 1992. "Early Judaism and Resurrection." *Anchor Bible Dictionary* 5:684–91. New York: Doubleday.

———. 1992. "Eschatology (Early Jewish)." *Anchor Bible Dictionary* 2:579–94. New York: Doubleday.

———. 2003. *Ancient Judaism and Christian Origins: Diversity, Continuity, and Transformation*. Minneapolis: Fortress.

Nutton, Vivian. 1978. "The Beneficial Ideology." In *Imperialism in the Ancient World*, 209–21. Edited by P. Garnsey and C. R. Whittaker. Cambridge: Cambridge University Press.

———. 1995. "Galen and the Traveler's Fare." In *Food in Antiquity*, 359–70. Edited by J. Wilkins, D. Harvey, and M. Dobson. Exeter, UK: University of Exeter Press.

Oakes, Peter. 2004. "Constructing Poverty Scales for Graeco-Roman Studies: A Response to Steven Friesen's 'Poverty in Pauline Studies.'" *Journal for the Study of the New Testament* 26:367–71.

O'Day, Gail R. 1986. *Revelation in the Fourth Gospel: Narrative Mode and Theological Claim.* Philadelphia: Fortress.

———. 1995. "The Gospel of John." In *The New Interpreter's Bible,* 9:491–865. Edited by L. E. Keck. Nashville: Abingdon.

———. 1998. "John." In *The Women's Bible Commentary,* 381–93. Expanded ed. Edited by C. A. Newsom and S. H. Ringe. Louisville: Westminster John Knox.

———. 1999. "'Show Us the Father and We Will Be Satisfied' (John 14:8)." *Semeia* 85:11–18.

———. 2002. "'I have said these things to you . . .': The Unsettled Place of Jesus' Discourses in Literary Approaches to the Fourth Gospel." In *Word, Theology, and Community in John,* 143–54. Edited by J. Painter, R. A. Culpepper, and F. F. Segovia. St. Louis: Chalice Press.

———. 2005. "Jesus as Friend in the Gospel of John." In *Transcending Boundaries: Contemporary Readings of the New Testament,* 75–92. Edited by R. M. Chennattu and M. L. Coloe. Rome: Libreria Ateneo Salesiano.

Oliver, James H. 1953. *The Ruling Power: A Study of the Roman Empire in the Second Century after Christ through the Roman Oration of Aelius Aristides.* Transactions of the American Philosophical Society: New Series 43.4. Philadelphia: APS.

Olsson, Birger. 2005. "'All My Teaching Was Done in Synagogues . . .' (John 18,20)." In *Theology and Christology in the Fourth Gospel,* 203–24. Edited by G. van Belle, J. van der Watt, and P. Maritz. Bibliotheca ephemeridum theologicarum lovaniensium 184. Louvain: Leuven University Press.

O'Neill, John Cochrane. 1991. "The Word Did Not 'Become' Flesh." *Zeitschrift für die neutestamentliche Wissenschaft* 82:125–27.

Oster, Richard. 1976. "The Ephesian Artemis as an Opponent of Early Christianity." *Jahrbuch für Antike und Christentum* 19:24–44.

Painter, John. 1993. *The Quest for the Messiah: The History, Literature, and Theology of the Johannine Community.* Nashville: Abingdon.

———. 2000. "The Point of John's Christology: Christology, Conflict, and Community in John." In *Christology, Controversy, and Community: New Testament Essays in Honour of David R. Catchpole,* 231–52. Edited by D. Horrell and C. Tuckett. Boston: Brill.

Parkins, Helen, ed. 1997. *Roman Urbanism: Beyond the Consumer City.* London: Routledge.

Patterson, Orlando. 1982. *Slavery and Social Death: A Comparative Study.* Cambridge: Harvard University Press.

Pelling, Christopher, ed. 1990. *Characterization and Individuality in Greek Literature.* New York: Oxford University Press.

Perkins, Phil, and Lisa Nevett. 2000. "Urbanism and Urbanization in the Roman World." In *Experiencing Rome: Culture, Identity, and Power in the Roman Empire,* 213–45. Edited by J. Huskinson. London: Routledge.

Pesce, Mauro, and Adriana Destro. 1999. "La lavanda dei piedi di Gv 13,1–20, il *Romanzo di Esopo,* e i *Saturnalia* di Macrobio." *Biblica* 80:240–49.

Petersen, Norman R. 1993. *The Gospel of John and the Sociology of Light: Language and Characterization in the Fourth Gospel*. Valley Forge, PA: Trinity Press.

Pixley, Jorge. 2005. "The Political Dimension of Biblical Hermeneutics." In *God's Economy: Biblical Studies from Latin America*, 18–33. Edited by R. Kinsler and J. Kinsler. Maryknoll, NY: Orbis Books.

Pleket, Harry W. 1961. "Domitian, the Senate, and the Provinces." *Mnemosyne* 14:298–315.

Potter, David S. 1990. *Prophecy and History in the Crisis of the Roman Empire: A Historical Commentary on the Thirteenth Sibylline Oracle*. Oxford: Clarendon.

Price, Simon. 1984. "Gods and Emperors: The Greek Language of the Roman Imperial Cult." *Journal of Hellenic Studies* 104:79–95.

———. 1984. *Rituals and Power: The Roman Imperial Cult in Asia Minor*. Cambridge: Cambridge University Press.

———. 1987. "From Noble Funerals to Divine Cult: The Consecration of Roman Emperors." In *Rituals of Royalty: Power and Ceremonial in Traditional Societies*, 56–105. Edited by D. Cannadine and S. Price. Cambridge: Cambridge University Press.

Purcell, Nicholas. 1985. "Wine and Wealth in Ancient Italy." *Journal of Roman Studies* 75:1–19.

———. 1996. "Rome and the Management of Water: Environment, Culture, and Power." In *Human Landscapes in Classical Antiquity: Environment and Culture*, 180–212. Edited by G. Shipley and J. Salmon. London; New York: Routledge.

Rajak, Tessa, ed. 2001. *The Jewish Dialogue with Greece and Rome: Studies in Cultural and Social Interaction*. Leiden: Brill.

Rajak, Tessa, and David Noy. 2001. "*Archisynagōgoi*: Office, Title, and Social Status in the Greco-Jewish Synagogue." In *The Jewish Dialogue with Greece and Rome: Studies in Cultural and Social Interaction*, 393–429. Edited by T. Rajak. Leiden: Brill.

Ramage, Edwin S. 1983. "Denigration of Predecessor under Claudius, Galba, and Vespasian." *Historia* 32:201–14.

———. 1989. "Juvenal and the Establishment: Denigration of Predecessor in the Satires." *Aufstieg und Niedergang der römischen Welt*. Part 2, *Principat*, 33.1:640–707. Edited by H. Temporini and W. Haase. New York: de Gruyter.

Reinhartz, Adele. 1999. "'And the Word Was Begotten': Divine Epigenesis in the Gospel of John." *Semeia* 85:83–103.

———. 2001. *Befriending the Beloved Disciple: A Jewish Reading of the Gospel of John*. New York: Continuum.

———. 2002. "The Colonizer as Colonized: Intertextual Dialogue between the Gospel of John and Canadian Identity." In *John and Postcolonialism: Travel, Space and Power*, 170–92. Edited by M. W. Dube and J. L. Staley. London: Continuum.

Rensberger, David. 1988. *Johannine Faith and Liberating Community*. Philadelphia: Westminster.

Reynolds, Joyce, and Robert Tannenbaum. 1987. *Jews and God-Fearers at Aphrodisias*. Proceedings of the Cambridge Philological Society 12. Cambridge: CPS.

Rhea, Robert. 1990. *The Johannine Son of Man*. Abhandlungen zur Theologie des Alten und Neuen Testaments 76. Zurich: Theologischer Verlag.

Richey, Lance. 2004. "'Truly This Is the Savior of the World': Christ and Caesar in the Gospel of John." PhD diss., Marquette University.

Richter, Georg. 1977. "Präsentische und futurische Eschatologie im 4. Evangelium." In *Studien zum Johannesevangelium*, 346–82. Edited by J. Hainz. Biblische Untersuchungen 13. Regensburg: Pustet.

Rickman, Geoffrey. 1980. *The Corn Supply of Ancient Rome*. Oxford: Clarendon.

Riley, Gregory J. 1995. *Resurrection Reconsidered: Thomas and John in Controversy*. Minneapolis: Fortress.

Ringe, Sharon H. 1999. *Wisdom's Friends: Community and Christology in the Fourth Gospel*. Louisville: Westminster John Knox.

Rives, James. 2000. "Religion in the Roman Empire." In *Experiencing Rome: Culture, Identity and Power in the Roman Empire*, 245–75. Edited by J. Huskinson. London: Routledge.

Rogers, Guy M. 1991. *The Sacred Identity of Ephesos: Foundation Myths of a Roman City*. London: Routledge.

Rubinkiewicz, Ryszard. 1983. "Apocalypse of Abraham." In *Old Testament Pseudepigrapha*, 1:681–705. Edited by J. H. Charlesworth. Garden City, NY: Doubleday.

Runia, David. 1988. "God and Man in Philo of Alexandria." *Journal of Theological Studies* 39:48–75.

Said, Edward. 1993. *Culture and Imperialism*. New York: Alfred Knopf.

Saldarini, Anthony J. 1988. *Pharisees, Scribes, and Sadducees*. Wilmington, DE: Michael Glazier.

Salier, Bill. 2006. "Jesus, the Emperor, and the Gospel according to John." In *Challenging Perspectives on the Gospel of John*, 284–301. Edited by John Lierman. Wissenschaftliche Untersuchungen zum Neuen Testament 2.219. Tübingen: Mohr Siebeck.

Saller, Richard. 1982. *Personal Patronage under the Early Empire*. Cambridge: Cambridge University Press.

Sanders, Edward P. 1983. "Testament of Abraham." In *The Old Testament Pseudepigrapha*, 1:871–902. Edited by J. H. Charlesworth. Garden City, NY: Doubleday.

———. 1985. *Jesus and Judaism*. Philadelphia: Fortress.

Sandmel, Samuel. 1971. *Philo's Place in Judaism: A Study of Conceptions of Abraham in Jewish Literature*. New York: Ktav.

Sasse, Hermann. 1964. "αἰών, αἰώνιος." *Theological Dictionary of the New Testament* 1:197–209. Grand Rapids: Eerdmans.

Schäfer, Peter. 1975. "Die sogenannte Synode von Jabne: Zur Trennung von Juden und Christen im ersten/zweiten Jahrhundert n. Chr." *Judaica* 31:54–64, 116–24.

Scherrer, Peter. 1995. "The City of Ephesos: From the Roman Period to Late Antiquity." In *Ephesos Metropolis of Asia: An Interdisciplinary Approach to Its Archaeology, Religion, and Culture*, 1–26. Edited by H. Koester. Valley Forge, PA: Trinity Press International.

Schiffman, Lawrence. 1981. "At the Crossroads: Tannaitic Perspectives on the Jewish-Christian Schism." In *Jewish and Christian Self-Definition*, 2:115–56. Edited by E. P. Sanders, A. I. Baumgarten, and A. Mendelson. Philadelphia: Fortress.

———. 1992. "Messianic Figures and Ideas in the Qumran Scrolls." In *The Messiah: Developments in Earliest Judaism and Christianity*, 116–29. Edited by J. H. Charlesworth. Minneapolis: Fortress.

Schlaifer, Robert. 1960. "Greek Theories of Slavery from Homer to Aristotle." In *Slavery in Classical Antiquity*, 93–132. Edited by M. Finley. Cambridge: Heffer & Sons.

Schnackenburg, Rudolf. 1980–82. *The Gospel according to St. John*. 3 vols. New York: Seabury.

Schneiders, Sandra. 1987. "Death in the Community of Eternal Life: History, Theology, and Spirituality in John 11." *Interpretation* 41:44–56.

Schowalter, Daniel. 1993. *The Emperor and the Gods*. Minneapolis: Fortress.

Schrenk, Gottlob. 1967. "πατήρ." *Theological Dictionary of the New Testament* 5:945–1022. Grand Rapids: Eerdmans.

Schwarz, Henry, and Sangeeta Ray, eds. 2000. *A Companion to Postcolonial Studies*. Oxford: Blackwell.

Schweizer, Eduard. 1939. *Ego eimi: Die religionsgeschichtliche Herkunft und theologische Bedeutung der johanneischen Bildreden, zugleich ein Beitrag zur Quellenfrage des vierten Evangeliums*. Forschungen zur Religion und Literatur des Alten und Neuen Testaments 38. Göttingen: Vandenhoeck & Ruprecht.

Scobie, Alexander. 1986. "Slums, Sanitation, and Mortality in the Roman World." *Klio* 68:399–433.

Scott, James C. 1985. *Weapons of the Weak: Everyday Forms of Peasant Resistance*. New Haven: Yale University Press.

———. 1990. *Domination and the Arts of Resistance*. New Haven: Yale University Press.

Scott, Kenneth. 1936. *The Imperial Cult under the Flavians*. Stuttgart: W. Kohlhammer.

Scott, Martin. 1992. *Sophia and the Johannine Jesus*. Journal for the Study of the New Testament: Supplement Series 71. Sheffield: JSOT Press.

Seeley, David. 1993. "Rulership and Service in Mark 10:41–45." *Novum Testamentum* 35:234–50.

Segal, Alan. 2004. *Life After Death: A History of the Afterlife in Western Religion*. New York: Doubleday.

Segovia, Fernando F. 1991. *The Farewell of the Word: The Johannine Call to Abide*. Minneapolis: Fortress.

———. 1991. "The Journey(s) of the Word of God: A Reading of the Plot of the Fourth Gospel." In *The Fourth Gospel from a Literary Perspective*, 23–54. Edited by R. A. Culpepper and F. F. Segovia. Semeia 53. Atlanta: Scholars Press.

———. 2000. *Decolonizing Biblical Studies: A View from the Margins*. Maryknoll, NY: Orbis Books.

———. 2002. "John 1:1–18 as Entrée into Johannine Reality: Representation and Ramifications." In *Word, Theology, and Community in John*, 33–64. Edited by J. Painter, R. A. Culpepper, and F. F. Segovia. St. Louis: Chalice.

Seland, Torrey. 1996. "Philo and the Clubs and Associations of Alexandria." In *Voluntary Associations in the Graeco-Roman World*, 110–27. Edited by J. S. Kloppenborg and S. G. Wilson. London: Routledge.

Shaw, Brent D. 1984. "Bandits in the Roman Empire." *Past and Present* 102:3–52.

———. 1988. "Roman Taxation." In *Civilization of the Ancient Mediterranean*, 2:809–27. Edited by M. Grant and R. Kitzinger. New York: Charles Scribner's Sons.

———. 1993. "Tyrants, Bandits, and Kings: Personal Power in Josephus." *Journal of Jewish Studies* 44:176–204.

Shepherd, A. R. R. 1979. "Jews, Christians and Heretics in Acmonia and Eumeneia." *Anatolian Studies* 29:169–80.

Sheppard, Beth. 2003. "The Rise of Rome: The Emergence of a New Mode for Exploring the Fourth Gospel." *Summary of Proceedings: Fifty-Seventh Annual Conference of the American Theological Library Association*, 175–87. June 26–28, 2003. Portland, OR: ATLA.

Sherk, Robert K., ed. and trans. 1988. *The Roman Empire: Augustus to Hadrian*. Translated Documents of Greece and Rome 6. Cambridge: Cambridge University Press.

Sievers, Joseph. 1998. "Josephus and the Afterlife." In *Understanding Josephus: Seven Perspectives*, 20–34. Journal for the Study of the Pseudepigrapha: Supplement Series 32. Sheffield: Sheffield Academic Press.

Siker, Jeffery S. 1991. *Disinheriting the Jews: Abraham in Early Christian Controversies*. Louisville: Westminster John Knox.

Simpson, Christopher J. 1996. "Caligula's Cult: Immolation, Immortality, Intent." In *Subject and Ruler: The Cult of the Ruling Power in Classical Antiquity; Papers Presented at a Conference Held in the University of Alberta on April 13–15, 1994, to Celebrate the Sixty-fifth Anniversary of Duncan Fishwick*, 63–71. Edited by Alastair Small. Journal of Roman Archaeology: Supplementary Series 17. Ann Arbor, MI: JRA.

Sippel, Donald V. 1987. "Dietary Deficiency among the Lower Classes of Late Republican and Early Imperial Rome." *Ancient World* 16:47–54.

———. 1987. "Some Observations on the Means and Cost of the Transport of Bulk Commodities in the Late Republic and Early Empire." *Ancient World* 16:35–45.

Sloyan, Gerard. 1988. *John*. Atlanta: Westminster John Knox.

Smallwood, E. Mary. 1957. "The Chronology of Gaius' Attempt to Desecrate the Temple." *Latomus* 16:3–17.

———. 1976. *The Jews under Roman Rule from Pompey to Diocletian*. Leiden: Brill.

Smith, D. Moody. 1995. *The Theology of the Gospel of John*. Cambridge: Cambridge University Press.

———. 1996. "John." In *Early Christian Thought in Its Jewish Context*, 96–111. Edited by J. Barclay and J. Sweet. Cambridge: Cambridge University Press.

———. 1999. *John*. Abingdon New Testament Commentaries. Nashville: Abingdon.

Smith, Dennis E., and Hal Taussig. 1990. "The Greco-Roman Banquet: Defining a Common Meal Tradition." In *Many Tables: The Eucharist in the New Testament and Liturgy Today*, 21–35. Philadelphia: Trinity Press International.

Smith, Roland R. R. 1987. "The Imperial Reliefs from the Sebasteion at Aphrodisias." *Journal of Roman Studies* 77:88–138.

———. 1988. "*Simulacra Gentium*: The *Ethnē* from the Sebasteion at Aphrodisias." *Journal of Roman Studies* 78:50–77.

Soskice, Janet Martin. 1992. "Can a Feminist Call God 'Father'?" In *Women's Voices: Essays in Contemporary Feminist Theology*, 15–29. Edited by T. Elwes. London: Marshall Pickering.

Southern, Pat. 1997. *Domitian: Tragic Tyrant*. London: Routledge.

Spaeth, Barbette. 1996. *The Roman Goddess Ceres*. Austin: University of Texas Press.

Stambaugh, John. 1988. *The Ancient Roman City*. Baltimore: Johns Hopkins University Press.

Stark, Rodney. 1991. "Antioch as the Social Situation for Matthew's Community." In *Social History of the Matthean Community*, 189–210. Edited by D. Balch. Minneapolis: Fortress.

———. 1996. "Urban Chaos and Crisis: The Case of Antioch." In *The Rise of Christianity: A Sociologist Reconsiders History*, 147–62. Princeton: Princeton University Press.

Stern, Menachem. 1987. "Josephus and the Roman Empire as Reflected in *The Jewish War*." In *Josephus, Judaism, and Christianity*, 71–81. Edited by L. Feldman and G. Hata. Detroit: Wayne State University Press.

Stevenson, Tom R. 1992. "The Ideal Benefactor and the Father Analogy in Greek and Roman Thought." *Classical Quarterly* 42:421–36.

Stibbe, Mark W. G. 1994. *John's Gospel*. New York: Routledge.

Stoop, Robert. 1989. "Riot and Assembly: The Social Context of Acts 19:23." *Journal of Biblical Literature* 108:73–91.

Sugirtharajah, Rasiah S. 2002. *Postcolonial Criticism and Biblical Interpretation*. Oxford: Oxford University Press.

———. 2005. *The Bible as Empire: Postcolonial Explorations*. Cambridge: Cambridge University Press.

———, ed. 1998. *The Postcolonial Bible*. Sheffield: Sheffield Academic Press.

Sutherland, Carol H. V. 1959. "The Intelligibility of Roman Imperial Coin Types." *Journal of Roman Studies* 49:46–55.

Swain, Simon. 1996. *Hellenism and Empire: Language, Classicism, and Power in the Greek World AD 50–250*. Oxford: Clarendon.

Tacitus, Cornelius. 1967. *De vita Agricolae*. Edited by Robert M. Ogilvie and Ian Richmond. Oxford: Oxford University Press.

Talbert, Charles H. 1992. *Reading John*. New York: Crossroad.

Taylor, Lily Ross. 1931, 1975. *The Divinity of the Roman Emperor*. Philadelphia: Porcupine.

Tcherikover, Victor. 1961. *Hellenistic Civilization and the Jews*. Philadelphia: Jewish Publication Society of America.

Thatcher, Tom. 2000. *The Riddles of Jesus in John: A Study in Tradition and Folklore*. Society of Biblical Literature Monograph Series 53. Atlanta: Society of Biblical Literature.

———. 2001. "Introduction." In *Jesus in Johannine Tradition*, 1–9. Edited by R. Fortna and T. Thatcher. Louisville: Westminster John Knox.

Theissen, Gerd. 1991. *The Gospels in Context: Social and Political History in the Synoptic Tradition*. Minneapolis: Fortress.

Thomas, Christine. 1995. "At Home in the City of Artemis: Religion in Ephesos in the Literary Imagination of the Roman Period." In *Ephesos Metropolis of Asia: An Interdisciplinary Approach to Its Archaeology, Religion, and Culture*, 81–117. Edited by H. Koester. Valley Forge, PA: Trinity Press International.

Thomas, John Christopher. 1991. *Footwashing in John 13 and the Johannine Community*. Journal for the Study of the New Testament: Supplement Series 61. Sheffield: JSOT Press.

Thompson, Leonard. 1990. *The Book of Revelation: Apocalypse and Empire*. New York: Oxford University Press.

Thompson, Marianne M. 1989. "Eternal Life in the Gospel of John." *Ex auditu* 5:35–55.

———. 1997. "Thinking about God: Wisdom and Theology in John 6." In *Critical Readings of John 6*, 221–46. Edited by R. A. Culpepper. Leiden: Brill.

———. 1999. "The Living Father." *Semeia* 85:19–31.

———. 2001. *The God of the Gospel of John.* Grand Rapids: Eerdmans.

Tilborg, Sjef van. 1996. *Reading John in Ephesus.* Supplements to Novum Testamentum 83. New York: Brill.

Tobin, Thomas H. 1990. "The Prologue of John and the Hellenistic Jewish Speculation." *Catholic Biblical Quarterly* 52:253–69.

Trebilco, Paul. 1991. *Jewish Communities in Asia Minor.* Society for New Testament Studies Monograph Series 69. Cambridge: Cambridge University Press.

———. 1994. "Asia." In *The Book of Acts in Its First Century Setting*, 2:291–362. Edited by D. Gill and C. Gempf. Grand Rapids: Eerdmans.

———. 2004. *The Early Christians in Ephesus from Paul to Ignatius.* Tübingen: Mohr Siebeck.

Turner, John D. 1991. "The History of Religions Background of John 10." In *The Shepherd Discourse of John 10 and Its Context: Studies*, 33–52. Edited by J. Beutler and R. T. Fortna. Society for New Testament Studies Monograph Series 67. New York: Cambridge University Press.

Unwin, Tim. 1991. *Wine and the Vine: An Historical Geography of Viticulture and the Wine Trade.* London: Routledge.

Van den Heever, Gerhard A. 1999. "Finding Data in Unexpected Places (or: From Text Linguistics to Socio-rhetoric). Towards a Socio-Rhetorical Reading of John's Gospel." *Neotestamentica* 32:343–64.

Van der Horst, Pieter. 1994. "The Birkat Ha-Minim in Recent Research." *Expository Times* 105:363–68.

Vermeule, Cornelius C. 1968. *Roman Imperial Art in Greece and Asia Minor.* Cambridge, MA: Harvard University Press.

Von Martitz, Peter Wülfing. 1972. "υἱός." *Theological Dictionary of the New Testament* 8:335–40. Grand Rapids: Eerdmans.

Von Rad, Gerhard, Georg Bertram, and Rudolf Bultmann. 1965. "ζάω, ζωή." *Theological Dictionary of the New Testament* 2:832–72. Grand Rapids: Eerdmans.

Von Wahlde, Urban C. 1989. *The Earliest Version of John's Gospel: Recovering the Gospel of Signs.* Wilmington, DE: Michael Glazier.

Vouga, François. 1977. *Le cadre historique et l'intention théologique de Jean.* Paris: Beauchesne.

Wallace-Hadrill, Andrew. 1982. "The Golden Age and Sin in Augustan Ideology." *Past and Present* 95:19–36.

———, ed. 1989. *Patronage in Ancient Society.* London: Routledge.

Wander, Bernd. 1998. *Gottesfürchtige und Sympathisanten: Studien zum heidnischen Umfeld von Diasporasynagogen.* Wissenschaftliche Untersuchungen zum Neuen Testament 104. Tübingen: Mohr Siebeck.

Wankel, Hermann, ed. 1979–84. *Die Inschriften von Ephesos.* Vols. *1A–8.2.* Bonn: Habelt.

Waters, Kenneth H. 1964. "The Character of Domitian." *Phoenix* 18:49–77.

Webster, J., and N. J. Cooper, eds. 1996. *Roman Imperialism: Post-Colonial Perspectives.* Leicester Archaeology Monographs 3. Leicester: University of Leicester, School of Archaeological Studies.

Weinstock, Stefan. 1971. *Divus Julius*. Oxford: Clarendon.

Wengst, Klaus. 1987. *Pax Romana and the Peace of Jesus Christ*. Philadelphia: Fortress.

White, K. D. 1976. "Food Requirements and Food Supplies in Classical Times in Relation to the Diet of the Various Classes." *Progress in Food and Nutrition Science* 2:143–91.

———. 1984. *Greek and Roman Technology*. London: Thames & Hudson.

White, L. Michael. 1995. "Urban Development and Social Change in Imperial Ephesos." In *Ephesos Metropolis of Asia: An Interdisciplinary Approach to Its Archaeology, Religion, and Culture*, 27–79. Edited by H. Koester. Valley Forge, PA: Trinity Press International.

Whittaker, Charles R. 1993. *Land, City and Trade in the Roman Empire*. Collected Studies 408. Aldershot: Variorum.

———. 1993. "The Poor." In *The Romans*, 272–99. Edited by A. Giardina. Chicago: University of Chicago Press.

Wiedemann, Thomas E. J., ed. 1981. *Greek and Roman Slavery*. Baltimore: Johns Hopkins University Press.

Wilken, Robert. 1983. *John Chrysostom and the Jews: Rhetoric and Reality in the Late Fourth Century*. Berkeley: University of California Press.

Williams, Margaret. 2000. "Jews and Jewish Communities in the Roman Empire." In *Experiencing Rome: Culture, Identity, and Power in the Roman Empire*, 305–33. Edited by J. Huskinson. London: Routledge.

Williams, Patrick, and Laura Chrisman, eds. 1994. *Colonial Discourse and Post-Colonial Theory*. New York: Columbia University Press.

Wilson, Bryan R. 1973. *Magic and the Millennium: A Sociological Study of Religious Movements of Protest among Tribal and Third-World Peoples*. New York: Harper & Row.

Wilson, J. Christian. 1993. "The Problem of the Domitianic Date of Revelation." *New Testament Studies* 39:587–605.

Wilson, Marcus. 2003. "After the Silence: Tacitus, Suetonius, Juvenal." In *Flavian Rome: Culture, Image, Text*, 523–42. Edited by A. J. Boyle and W. Dominik. Leiden: Brill.

Winter, Bruce W. 1995. "Acts and Food Shortages." In *The Book of Acts in Its Graeco-Roman Setting*, 59–78. Edited by D. W. Gill and C. Gempf. Grand Rapids: Eerdmans.

Wiplinger, Gilbert, and Gudrun Wlach. 1996. *Ephesus: 100 Years of Austrian Research*. Österreichisches Archäologisches Institut. Vienna: Böhlau.

Wiseman, Timothy Peter. 1996. "Domitian and the Dynamics of Terror in Classical Rome." *History Today* 46:19–24.

Witherington, Ben, III. 1995. *John's Wisdom: A Commentary on the Fourth Gospel*. Louisville: Westminster John Knox.

Woll, Bruce. 1981. *Johannine Christianity in Conflict: Authority, Rank, and Succession in the First Farewell Discourse*. Society of Biblical Literature Dissertation Series 60. Chico, CA: Scholars Press.

Woodman, Tony, and David West, eds. 1984. *Poetry and Politics in the Age of Augustus*. Cambridge: Cambridge University Press.

Wright, Robert B. 1985. "*Psalms of Solomon*: Theological Importance." In *The Old Testament Pseudepigrapha*, 2:639–70. Edited by J. H. Charlesworth. Garden City, NY: Doubleday.

Zanker, Paul. 1988. *The Power of Images in the Age of Augustus.* Ann Arbor: University of Michigan Press.

Zeitlin, Solomon. 1918–1920. "Megillat Taanit as a Source for Jewish Chronology and History in the Hellenistic and Roman Times." *Jewish Quarterly Review* 9:71–102; 10:49–80, 237–90.

Index

146, 153, 165, 180, 190, 193, 204, 221, 237, 260, 267, 303, 304, 307, 311, 321, 322, 365, 377

Valerius Gratus, 293
Valerius Maximus, 56
Van Tilborg, Sjef, 10, 36, 52, 56-57, 63, 182, 193-194, 197, 225, 261, 275-276, 280, 294
Van Wahlde, 347
Vespasian, 37, 62, 64, 70, 86, 153, 189, 192, 194, 207, 219, 236, 258, 261, 268-269, 296-297, 317, 322-324, 327
Vesta, 207, 268
Vitellius, 85, 203, 298, 312
Virgil, 79, 151, 153, 169, 199, 204, 207, 223, 268, 276, 321
Virtue, 332

Weinstock, Stefan, 236-237
Wenham, David, 336

Whittaker, Charles R., 54, 221
Wilson, Bryan, 8-9
Wisdom, 15, 93, 110, 144, 196, 197, 220, 230, 268, 331, 340-341, 350-351, 365, 379; Jesus as, 115-117; personified, 116; and John's Prologue, 136, 149-53
Wholeness (healing), 80, 81, 129, 138, 161, 162, 165, 186, 212, 220, 223, 225, 227, 283, 328, 338
Works, 277-278

Xenophon of Ephesus, 150

Zealots, 12
Zechariah, **14**, 159, 164, 259-261, 263-264, 339
Zephaniah, **3:15-16**, 167
Zeus, 64, 136, 151, 166, 188, 236, 250, 268, 275, 307, 344, 354, 355, 367, 378-381
Zōē, 212; see *Eternal Life.*